NAVAL LAW

Second Edition

Department of Leadership, Ethics and Law
United States Naval Academy
Annapolis, Maryland

Brent G. Filbert

Alan G. Kaufman

KENDALL/HUNT PUBLISHING COMPANY
4050 Westmark Drive   Dubuque, Iowa 52002

CONTENTS

CHAPTER I
THE HISTORY AND BACKGROUND OF MILITARY JUSTICE

CHAPTER II
FUNDAMENTALS OF MILITARY JUSTICE

CHAPTER III
COURTS-MARTIAL

CHAPTER IV
NONJUDICIAL PROCEDURES

CHAPTER V
MILITARY CRIMES

CHAPTER VI
GOVERNMENT ETHICS

CHAPTER VII
SEARCH AND SEIZURE

CHAPTER VIII
SELF-INCRIMINATION

CHAPTER IX
MILITARY INVESTIGATIONS

CHAPTER X
APPREHENSION AND RESTRAINT

CHAPTER XI
INTERNATIONAL LAW

CHAPTER XII
WAR CRIMES

APPENDIXES

TABLE OF CASES

PREFACE

This book is designed as an introduction to military naval law. While it is a helpful resource for law students and practicing lawyers, it is geared toward midshipmen, cadets, and other college level students. The primary focus of the text is the law as it relates to military naval matters. Thus, it is most beneficial as a tool to understanding Navy and Marine Corps law. Because of the nature of military law, there is, however, a significant amount of carry over to the other branches of the service, as well.

Chapter I is an overview of the history of military justice. It traces the development of criminal law for both naval and land forces. This introduction is appropriate because the book focuses on the historical development of military law. Against this background, Chapter II introduces some of the basic principles of military criminal law that are essential to a comprehension of military justice. Chapters III and IV examine the forums and procedures for disposing of crimes in the military. These chapters focus on the jurisdiction and authority of courts-martial, nonjudicial punishment and administrative separations. The rules and concepts related to these forums are introduced via statutes, regulations and instructions. Cases that address the legality of the military justice system are used to explain its nature and to help the student understand the development of current military law.

Chapter V explores certain offenses that are unique to the military. It introduces the elements and basic tenets of these crimes, and provides military cases that question and apply these principles. Chapter VI addresses the expanding area of government ethics. The chapter traces the history and growth of ethics law, and examines why there has been such an increased emphasis on ethics regulations. It includes some of the most common ethics rules and provides explanations of how these regulations are interpreted.

Chapters VII and VIII examine the relationship between the military and the Constitution. Chapter VII deals with the complex nature of search and seizure. It introduces the basic concepts of the Fourth Amendment and provides cases that consider how the amendment applies in the military setting. Self-incrimination is addressed in Chapter VIII. The chapter discusses the constitutional and statutory bases for the privilege, and like Chapter VI, it contains cases that examine the relationship between the military and self-incrimination protections.

Chapter IX explores the numerous types of investigations conducted by the military. It considers both criminal and administrative inquiries and compares the different varieties of probes utilized in the armed forces. Chapter X deals with the law of apprehension and restraint. It provides the basic rules concerning restraint, confinement and custody. It also addresses offenses that relate to these concepts. Finally, Chapter XI introduces the law relating to war crimes. The chapter provides a brief overview of the history of war crimes law, including the development of customary and conventional law. It considers the fundamental concepts in this area of the law through cases, articles and international agreements and conventions.

The first two appendices to the text relate to the military justice topics addressed in Chapters I through X. The remaining appendices focus on international law. Appendix 3, *The Commander's Handbook on the Law of Naval Operations* (NWP 9), thoroughly discusses international law, law of the sea and the law of war. Appendix 4 is a summary of Geneva Law and Appendix 5 is the full text of *Hague Convention IV*. The final two appendices deal with rules of engagement. Appendix 6 contains the United States Standing Rules of Engagement and Appendix 7 consists of the rules of engagement for ground forces in Desert Shield/Desert Storm.

Portions of some of the cases in this text have been omitted due to length and relevancy considerations. Also, the footnotes contained in the cases have been modified so that the numbers are sequential within each case.

Each chapter contains frequent questions and issues, and at the end of each chapter are study questions. These problems and questions are designed to focus the student's attention on the fundamental aspects of naval law, and to challenge the student's understanding of these concepts.

We would like to thank Legalman First Class (AW) Cynthia P. Campise, whose dedicated efforts and unending patience were crucial to the completion of this book. We would also like to acknowledge the research assistance of Captain Daniel J. Lecce, USMC.

Brent G. Filbert

Alan G. Kaufman

June 1995

CHAPTER I

THE HISTORY AND BACKGROUND OF MILITARY JUSTICE

There are limits on the extent to which the essentially autocratic armed forces are able to adopt notions regarded as precious by a democratic society. And there are limits on the extent to which civilian society will accept whatever such adaptations the services attempt, however much in good faith they may be acting. The tension between **discipline**—*regarded as indispensable in a military force—and* **justice**—*similarly respected in the civilian community—may help to determine where those boundaries lie.*

William T. Generous, *Swords and Scales*, Kennikat Press, London, 4 (1973)

INTRODUCTION

The stated purpose of military justice in today's United States' armed services is "to promote justice, to assist in maintaining good order and discipline, to promote efficiency and effectiveness in the military establishment, and thereby strengthen the national security of the United States." This statement contains two goals for the military legal system: justice and discipline. The development of military justice as we know it today is really a story of the competition of these two principles: a competition in which neither principle can yet claim victory. As you read this chapter, consider which of these concepts is the driving force behind the developments in military justice.

The development of military justice did not occur in a vacuum. Hence, developments in military justice in many instances directly relate to significant events. Although many of these events involve war or combat operations, many do not. In recent years, the effect of particular events on the military legal scheme has increased. In tracing the progression of military justice, question why certain incidents result in changes in the military legal system and others do not. Also, consider why it seems that particular events impact the law more frequently today than in the past.

1

DEVELOPMENT OF MILITARY JUSTICE

Military justice as we know it today developed from two distinct bodies of law: that of the sea and that of land armies. Brigadier General James Snedeker, U.S. Marine Corps (Ret.), in his book, *A Brief History of Courts-Martial*, describes the reasons for this bifurcated development.

> On land, proceedings leading to punishment were based upon theories of vengeance and prevention by example; at sea, upon a theory of protection of the ships and cargoes in maritime commerce. On land, in an era when war was a normal state of existence among tribes and kingdoms, the rules were established and abolished with the rise and fall of dynasties on shore; at sea, there was a continuous and growing body of rules recognized as international in character, independent of dynastic changes. On land, justice was administered for the most part by the same individuals in peace and war, the civil judges being military commanders; at sea, special courts set up by the world traders retained jurisdiction over maritime matters and had no authority over non-maritime affairs.

As you study military justice, consider whether differences still exist between the law for naval and land forces. Also question if the reasons for different treatment of soldiers and sailors exist today. *See The Uniform Code of Military Justice* below for a discussion of this issue.

MILITARY JUSTICE FOR LAND FORCES

Military tribunals began almost simultaneously with the establishment of organized armies. For instance, the armies of the Roman Empire instituted military tribunals to hear cases involving military offenders. In early German armies, the duke or military chief heard cases involving members of the army in time of war. The Germans later developed courts of regiments presided over by either the military commander or his delegate. These early Roman and German tribunals tried offenses which still exist under the Uniform Code of Military Justice (UCMJ): desertion; mutiny; cowardice under fire; and assaulting a superior officer. Although these crimes still exist, the severe punishment prescribed for these offenses may not seem so familiar: decimation; denial of burial after execution; maiming; exposure to the elements; and civil disqualification.

During the Middle Ages, military commanders were also civil judges, making the distinction between civil and military jurisdiction in some cases nonexistent. Beginning in the fifth century, authentic military codes emerged, and by the ninth century, military codes existed in many nation-states in Europe. From these early codes emerged articles of war. In 1621, The King of Sweden, Gustavus Adolphus, issued a comprehensive set of articles regulating the conduct of his soldiers and establishing a system to try offenders. The articles set up a regimental court-martial, presided over by the regimental commander, and a general court-martial, presided over by the royal marshal of Sweden, with senior officers sitting as members (jurors). The regimental court-martial tried cases such as theft, insubordination, cowardice and other minor offenses, while the general court-martial heard cases of treason and other serious crimes. General Snedeker describes the Articles of War of Sweden:

> These Articles of War were the best that had been issued anywhere. The Swedish soldier was exemplary, but he did, of course, occasionally disobey. . . . In one notable aspect, the military law of Gustavus differed widely from that of the Norman court of chivalry. Whereas, the latter sanctioned the trial by single combat, Gustavus forbade promotion of duelling under pain of death. His code of articles was comprehensive, containing 167 articles, and was carefully drafted. When it was translated and published in London in 1639, it greatly influenced the later English codes.

English Military Justice for Land Forces

Following the fall of the Roman Empire, the feudal system and age of chivalry emerged. Feudal knights sat on courts of chivalry established during this time. William the Conqueror introduced this system into England at the time of his conquest in 1066. His senior military officers became members of the court of chivalry, which acquired jurisdiction over military cases. When the power of the court of chivalry essentially disappeared in the sixteenth century, in its place emerged courts roughly equivalent to today's court-martial. General Snedeker described these early courts-martial as follows:

> In the early British courts-martial, the general or governor convening the court ordinarily sat as the president. The power of the court was plenary, and its sentences were executed without confirmation by any higher authority. Such a court was legally convened, however, only in time of war.

As the power of Britain expanded, the English Army began issuing specific military ordinances during wartime or prior to expeditions. In 1385, it issued 26 articles of war effective during time of war. During the next several centuries, the British Army continued to issue various articles of war. However, the authority to conduct courts-martial during peacetime remained unclear. By 1640, the king and Parliament were at war, with each side maintaining its own armed force. The Parliament enacted a military code to govern its army. This was the first set of military justice regulations enacted by a legislature. General Snedeker describes this statute:

> This legislation, the first directly authorizing courts-martial, named the commanding general and 56 others as commissioner for executing military law, 12 or more of whom constituted a quorum for the trial of military cases. The court

was empowered to sit, to appoint a judge advocate, a provost marshal, and other necessary officers, and to punish, according to the ordinance, the convicted offenders.

In 1660, England established a standing army, resulting in a need to maintain discipline during times of peace. Partly because of the limited ability to punish offenders during peacetime, discipline in the British Army became increasingly lax. In 1689, 800 English and Scotch dragoons mutinied, causing the British Parliament to pass the First Mutiny Act. This statute empowered courts-martial to prescribe the death penalty, or lesser punishment, for mutiny or desertion, even during peacetime. By 1803, Parliament had enacted the Articles of War previously issued by the King and assumed complete control over laws relating to military justice. To this day, Parliament retains cognizance over all military justice laws.

Until the twentieth century, discipline of the troops was the overriding purpose of the British military justice system. Thus, punishments were severe and procedural rights of service members were few. Why was this the case? The Duke of Wellington offered some insight on this issue in 1811 when he described the armed services of Britain: "None but the worst description of men enter the regular service. The scum of the earth who have all enlisted for drink."

United States Military Justice for Land Forces

Given that the United States legal system developed from English jurisprudence, it not surprising that American military law initially paralleled the British scheme. Massachusetts passed the first Articles of War in the United States on April 5, 1775. The Provisional Congress of Massachusetts Bay modeled these articles almost entirely on the British Articles of War of 1765. This was the first written code of military law in America. In June 1775, the Continental Congress appointed a committee to prepare rules and regulations for the government of the Continental Army. George Washington sat as a member of this committee which adopted a set of 69 articles known as the American Articles of War. Another committee of the Continental Congress revised this code in 1776 to more closely match the British Articles of War of 1774. John Adams, Thomas Jefferson and John Rutledge were members of this panel. These articles remained in effect until 1806, with one major revision in 1786.

Punishments in the United States Army during this period were severe to say the least. For instance, the Continental Congress reduced the number of lashes that could be given under the British system from 1,000 to 100. George Washington, however, wanted at least 500, and unsuccessfully petitioned the Continental Congress to increase the number above the 100 initially authorized. This harsh approach to punishments continued following the adoption of the Constitution in 1789. The Legion Army, assembled to defeat the Indian tribes along the Northwestern frontier of the United States, illustrates this point. The following is a statistical breakdown of three of the most common offenses and the punishments awarded in the Legion Army between July 1792 and August 1793:

	Desertion	Sleeping	Drunkenness
Number tried	112	18	13
Convictions	93	16	13
Acquittals	19	2	0
Death	19	5	NA
Average Lashes	91	87.5	95
Conviction Rate	83%	88%	100%

See 1 American State Papers Military Affairs 67 (1832).

The early American Articles of War provided for three types of courts-martial—general, regimental and detachment or garrison. A general court-martial required a jury of 13 members, while the other two types required only five jurors. The large number of members necessary for a general court-martial caused an incident at Fort McIntosh in 1786 that had significant implications for the existing Articles of War. Desertions were rampant at the fort and the major in command decided to make examples of captured deserters. Desertion was a capital offense only triable at general court-martial. The major, however, did not have a sufficient number of officers to sit on the panel. Not to be deterred, he convened a general court-martial with only five members. This court sentenced two offenders to death. The major then requested that the Secretary of War confirm the sentences. He refused to do so and instead overturned the convictions as illegal, stating that "[t]o supersede the laws in this respect is to assume the sovereignty and annul the compact, which the public have made with the troops, that they shall be governed by the rules and articles of war." Congress responded by repealing the existing rules relating to Army courts-marital, and specifically provided that a general court-martial could consist of only five members.

Consider whether Congress has passed legislation in other situations where the law was nonexistent or inadequate. Also consider the reaction to the *Somers* mutiny discussed in *United States Military Justice At Sea* below. Did perceived inadequacies in military justice prompt Congress to enact the UCMJ? Certain laws exist today which some would argue are outmoded and need to be stricken. Contemplate the following UCMJ articles: Article 114 (dueling); Article 134 (abusing a public animal); Article 134 (adultery); and Article 125 (consensual heterosexual sodomy). Do these provisions still serve a purpose in the military? If not, why has Congress not repealed these articles?

In 1806, Congress enacted a new set of Articles of War. These articles added a fourth type of court-martial, the field officer's court, authorized only in time of war. The 1806 articles also abolished flogging as a lawful punishment. Congress did not enact a new collection of articles until 1874. This long hiatus in congressional action was largely due to the belief that the civilian and military legal systems were, of necessity, completely different animals. General William Tecumseh Sherman, a practicing lawyer before returning to military duties during the Civil War, had this to say about military justice:

> [I]t will be a grave error if by negligence we permit the military law to become emasculated by allowing lawyers to inject into it the principles derived from their practice in the civil courts, which belong to a totally different system of jurisprudence. The object of the civil law is to secure to every human being in a community all the liberty, security, and happiness possible, consistent with safety of all. The object of military law is to govern armies composed of strong men, so as to be capable of exercising the largest measure of force at the will of the nation.

> These objects are as wide apart as the poles, and each requires its own separate system of laws, statute and common. An army is a collection of armed men obliged to obey one man. Every enactment, every change of rules which impairs the principle weakens the army, impairs its value, and defeats the very objects of its existence.

The 1874 code did add maximum punishments for all offenses in time of peace and established the one-officer summary court-martial. In 1916, Congress issued a revised version of the Articles of War. At the same time, the Army published its first Manual for Courts-Martial (MCM)) to explain and amplify the Articles of War of 1916.

World War I significantly impacted the Army's military justice system. During the war, the Army commissioned over 200,000 new officers and enlisted nearly 400,000 soldiers. Given this huge influx of personnel, it is not surprising that the Army's procedures underwent acute examination that resulted in profound changes to its system. During the war, a particular incident also raised questions about the fairness of the Army's procedures. A mutiny of black troops occurred at Fort Sam Houston in 1917. The black soldiers revolted because of their treatment at the hands of the Army and the local Texas community. Courts-martial convicted thirteen of the alleged mutineers and sentenced each of the soldiers to death. Article of War 48 provided that in time of war, the local commander could execute sentences without approval of higher authority. Although neither the troops nor the command were engaged in combat operations, the commander carried out the executions almost immediately following the verdicts, without apprising any higher authority of the results of the trials. The Fort Sam Houston mutinies caused the Army to provide thereafter mandatory reviews by the Army Judge Advocate General (JAG) of cases involving death sentences or dismissal of officers. This incident and other troubling episodes, coupled with the overall experiences of soldiers in World War I, caused the Army to push for overhaul of the Articles of War of 1916.

The Articles of War of 1920 provided significantly broader protections to the accused than any of the previous codes. For example, the articles made defense counsel mandatory in all but summary courts-martial. A "thorough and impartial" pretrial investigation also became a prerequisite prior to a general court-martial. The articles further banned the upward revision of sentences and reconsideration of findings by commanders following trial. Although the Articles of War of 1920 afforded soldiers significantly more rights than ever before, the rules still contained many provisions that purposely limited the protections of the accused and retained power in the hands of the commanders. For instance, enlisted members were not eligible to sit on courts-martial, and trial judges did not have to be attorneys. Also, the recommendations of the pretrial investigator were not in any way binding on the commanding officer. This was the set of articles that governed the Army through World War II.

The 1920 Articles of War resulted from significant events affecting the Army (World War I and the Fort Sam Houston mutinies). Do you see a trend in this regard? Consider the Fort McIntosh cases and the Articles of War of 1874. Does it surprise you that the move to change the Articles of War of 1916 came from within the Army? From the above discussion, do you think that the Articles of War of 1920 stressed discipline over fairness? Are some of the provisions contained in the Articles of War of 1920 still in place today? *See* Article 20, UCMJ (no right to defense counsel at summary court-martial) and Article 32, UCMJ (commanding officer may ignore the findings of the pretrial investigating officer).

MILITARY JUSTICE AT SEA

General Snedeker describes the origins of military justice at sea:

> A body of sea-law began to take shape under the Phoenicians [circa 500 B.C.]. It was a unique system, independent and unchallenged, because its jurisdiction was in a region owned by no king or local chieftain. The mariners who lived aboard the galleys shared a common life and experience. Their dangers, trials, and tribulations were similar, regardless of their origin, race, or creed. Although the empires ashore rose and fell, one after another, the growing body of sea-law continued to mature, independent of dynastic changes.

Rhodes emerged as a prominent sea power about 300 B.C., and developed a set of maritime laws that endured for more than 1,000 years. Unlike military law on land, which emanated from a particular king or tribal leader, custom and practice formed the basis for this code. This explains in large measure why the maritime laws of the Rhodians survived for such an extended period.

In the thirteenth century, Barcelona produced an extensive set of maritime laws known as the *Consulado del Mar*, or the Book of the Jurisdiction of the Sea. As with the earlier laws of Rhodes, the code of Barcelona also derived from custom and practice. Barcelona printed the *Consulado del Mar* in 1494, and by that time, it contained some 250 chapters. Meanwhile, the island of Oleron, an English possession off New Rochelle in the Bay of Biscay, had produced its own code of the sea. Based on the Rhodes model, the laws of Oleron served as the maritime code of Northwestern Europe for several centuries. Other areas also developed sets of laws regulating life at sea. For example, the city of Wisby on the Baltic Sea developed a code of maritime laws that gained widespread acceptance in the Baltic area during this period.

All of the codes discussed above evolved from custom, i.e., a deed practiced over a long period of time that becomes law. These customs developed from several sources, including local maritime courts, local regulations, treatises and legislation by guilds of sea traders. Each of these sets of sea law addressed many areas of maritime law, such as contracts, ship's liability, wages and dismissal of crew members. Not surprisingly, these laws also dealt with discipline on board vessels. The dominating feature of early disciplinary rules on board vessels was their extreme severity. General Snedeker provides an illustration:

> The Hansa Ordinance of 1482 provided that desertion of a mariner be punished thus: For the first offense, by the town authorities or judge; for the second offense, public flogging; for the third offense, the death penalty. For mutiny, as a first offense, the mariner was publicly beaten with rods in the pillory; as a second offense, he was condemned to death. Deserting the shipmaster or plotting against him to his damage or loss, while at sea, was punished capitally [by death].

Compare the prescribed punishments discussed above with the events in the *Somers* mutiny below. Is it surprising that the commanding officer considered the death penalty an appropriate measure? Also look at Chapter V regarding authorized punishments for desertion under the UCMJ. Are the punishment considerations different today than in the fifteenth and sixteenth centuries? Do custom and practice still form the basis for naval law? Consider the sources of international law and law of the sea discussed in Chapters XI and Appendix 3.

English Military Justice at Sea

As England emerged as the dominant maritime nation, it developed naval laws and customs that naturally influenced other nations, in particular the United States. At first, the maritime courts of the English seacoast towns determined the law on board the king's ships. As the British Navy grew in strength, it sought to retain jurisdiction over its own vessels. As a result, a publication entitled the *Black Book of the Admiralty* was compiled during the first half of the fourteenth century. It stated that the administration of justice "according to the law and ancient customs of the sea" was among an admiral's duties. Eventually, admirals began to issue regulations upon assuming command of a fleet. In 1652, the British Parliament issued rules for the governing of the fleet applicable to all British naval forces. The code had universal and continuous authority over the Royal Navy. These rules provided the groundwork for the early regulations governing the United States Navy.

Punishments in the British Navy during this period were notoriously cruel. General Snedeker describes typical punishments:

> Punishments of this period were . . . barbarous. A thief was tied up to the capstan, and every man in the ship gave him five lashes on his bared back with a three-thronged whip. The habitual thief, after flogging, was dragged ashore astern of a boat, and there ignominiously dismissed. For sleeping on watch the offender had three buckets of water poured over his head and into his sleeves; but for a fourth such offense he was placed in a basket hung from the bowsprit, with a can of beer, a loaf of bread, and a knife, and left to starve or drown at his own election.

Another common punishment was keelhauling—the process of drawing a man by rope under the ship from one side to the other, usually resulting in death.

United States Military Justice at Sea

In the fall of 1775, the Second Continental Congress adopted the first American naval articles, entitled the Rules for the Regulation of the Navy of the United Colonies. These articles set forth only a few specific offenses, but provided that all other "faults, disorders, and misdemeanors committed on board ship should be punished 'according to the laws and customs in such cases at sea.'" Thus, Congress recognized that naval justice evolved from long-standing practice and authorized commanding officers to punish sailors based upon this body of law.

When the Federal Convention met in 1787, there was much heated debate concerning whether the Constitution should provide for a standing military. The framers feared a strong military. Consequently, the Convention gave Congress, not the President, the power to raise and maintain a military, and in Article I, § 8, clause 14, the authority to "make rules for the government and regulation of the land and naval forces." Although the colonies ratified the Constitution in 1788, the President did not appoint a Secretary of the Navy until 1798, and Congress did not enact the Rules and Regulations for the Government of the Navy until 1800. General Snedeker describes the naval justice system following passage of this first set of regulations:

> During the ensuing half century, the administration of naval justice was lamely and imperfectly conducted. There was no corps of trained judge advocates, such as the Army possessed, and there was a scarcity of legal materials relating to naval

law. Books of foreign origin, generally British, were used in the Navy, and the practices of naval courts-martial became inconsistent and contradictory. There was no settled and uniform interpretation in either substantive or procedural matters.

Consider the above statement in connection with the *Somers* mutiny as described by Edward M. Byrne in *Military Justice*.

United States v. Midshipman Philip Spencer
On Board USS SOMERS
November 29, 1842

Acting Midshipman Philip Spencer, U.S. Navy, 18 years of age, must have regarded the USS SOMERS with awe when he first beheld her on 13 August 1842. The SOMERS was a beautiful new brig-of-war that had just been released from the shipyards some months ago. Although displacing 266 tons, she was so sharply built that she only carried a crew of 120. Designed for swiftness, the brig was very top-heavy and carried only ten cannons.

Anyone observing this young midshipman would hardly envision him as the principal participant in the first recorded mutiny on board a United States vessel since the founding of our country.

An indolent, dull-witted boy in many ways, Spencer attended Hobart College from 1838 to 1841, when he was withdrawn for academic failure. He next attended Union College, where he was one of the founders of Chi Psi fraternity. He especially enjoyed and originated some of the secret rituals for his fraternity. Shortly thereafter, he obtained an appointment as an acting midshipman in the United States Navy.

His father was perhaps instrumental in his appointment, as he was then Secretary of War in President Tyler's cabinet. What the elder Spencer did not know, or chose to ignore, was that his son's highest dream was to become a famous and renowned pirate.

During short tours on two previous U.S. vessels before he arrived on board the SOMERS, Spencer retained his dream—and often discussed it. However, the reasons given for Spencer's transfer from his previous ship were "drunkenness and scandalous conduct."

When Philip Spencer reported to the USS SOMERS, there was no United States Naval Academy. The Navy had begun to realize, however, that there was a need for training future officers and had chosen to do so by setting up small schools in some of the principal cities of the east and utilizing vessels as "floating academies." The USS SOMERS was the first of such training ships.

As captain of the SOMERS, the Navy had selected Commander Alexander Slidell Mackenzie, a well-known naval officer-author of his day and a man with wealth, power and influence in his own family. For example, his sister, Jane Slidell, was the wife of Commodore Matthew Calbraith Perry.

The SOMERS left on 13 September 1842 for a cruise to Africa, thence to travel to the West Indies, and finally home to New York. Spencer, for whatever reasons, was never accepted by his fellow officers and sought the comfort of the crew—many of whom he generously furnished with rum and cigars. For example, by 26 November

1842, Spencer had purchased ten pounds of tobacco and 700 cigars. Spencer had two intimate enlisted friends—Samuel Cromwell and Elisha Small.

During the voyage, it was apparent that Spencer's obsession with piracy had not ended. Outside his intimate circle, he discussed pirates and what a pirate ship the SOMERS would make. He discussed a pirate flag and what it would look like. After the captain criticized him for another matter, he stated he would like to throw the captain overboard. Whether these were just the rantings of an insubordinate dolt whose father happened to be in a position of importance, we shall never know.

However, Spencer did more than talk. He put his aspirations in writing.

A list, written in Greek, indicated whom he considered would join him, whom he considered doubtful, and who would not join in an apparent takeover of the ship. Only four names were listed as "certain" and those included Spencer himself. One man was never involved, and James W. Wales, who was listed as "certain," first reported Spencer to the captain. An "E. Andrews" was listed. No such man was aboard the ship, but Spencer insisted the name was an alias for Small.

On 25 November 1842, Midshipman Spencer approached Purser Steward Wales, listed as "certain" on his Greek list, and asked him to join in a mutiny. Spencer reportedly told Wales that he had 20 men in his group and that he planned to take over the SOMERS and turn her into a pirate ship. All the officers were to be killed. He then threatened Wales not to divulge his plan and asked him to join the mutiny. Small was in the vicinity and appeared to be involved with Spencer in the plan, according to Wales.

Wales related the story to the captain, who at first dismissed it as a joke, but as a precaution, asked Lieutenant Gansevoort to investigate the matter. The lieutenant did develop that Spencer had asked another officer if he was familiar with the Isle of Pines, a well-known pirate haunt. That was the only corroborative evidence prior to the ordering of Spencer's arrest on 27 November 1842. It is worthwhile relating what occurred prior to Spencer's apprehension. At evening quarters the following transpired:

MACKENZIE: I learn, Mr. Spencer, that you aspire to the command of the SOMERS.

SPENCER: Oh, no, sir!

MACKENZIE: Did you not tell Mr. Wales, sir, that you had a plan to kill the commander, the officers, and a considerable portion of the crew of this vessel and convert her into a pirate?

SPENCER: I may have told him so, sir, but in joke.

Spencer was then searched and placed in irons.

Small and Cromwell were arrested one day later. Later, the lieutenant interviewed Spencer, who admitted he had this plot on every ship he had been attached to, but had never gone as far with it as he had aboard the SOMERS. Spencer thought it was a "mania" with him. He also stated that "E. Andrews," the name on the list, stood for Small and not Cromwell.

The captain and his officers became convinced that a mutiny was possible at any moment and that the only way to avoid it was to hang the ringleaders. In truth, the evidence to this effect was, at its best, slim. Apparently Lieutenant Gansevoort had discussed the possibility of hanging the three captives with most of the officers and had majority approval. However, they felt they needed a reason for hanging the men at this time. They told the captain that if more prisoners were taken this would obstruct navigation (the prisoners were in irons on the quarterdeck) and increase the possibility of rescue of the prisoners. Commander Mackenzie then arrested four more men for mutiny (none of whom were ever convicted of any crime regarding the mutiny). Upon this basis, the captain then asked his officers "to take into deliberate and dispassionate consideration the present condition of the vessel and the contingencies of every nature that the future may embrace, throughout the remainder of our cruise, and enlighten me with your opinion as to the best course to be pursued."

The officers heard thirteen witnesses, all of whom were sworn and their testimony written down. They then signed these statements. Lieutenant Gansevoort, who had already expressed his opinion of the guilt of the accused on several occasions and had garnered most of the evidence, was the senior man present. The prisoners were not brought before the officers, nor did they know they were being tried. The captain had already begun to prepare a watch bill for the executions; however, the council still continued to hear evidence. The inquiry did not arrive at a decision and resumed the next day. By midmorning they had reached a decision. They recommended the three accused should be put to death based upon the fact that "it would be impossible to carry them to the United States" due to the possibility of further mutinous acts. Even before they were led away, both Cromwell and Spencer asserted Cromwell's innocence. The three were then hanged with the roll of drums and the thunder of cannon, as prescribed in the commander's watch bill.

When the SOMERS arrived in New York and the story was released, Commander Mackenzie was considered a hero. However, Secretary of War Spencer and Cromwell's widow began to raise questions about the nature of the proceedings. A court of inquiry was held and found Mackenzie blameless. Mackenzie was later tried for murder of the three men by a court-martial and acquitted.

Even in 1842, an accused was entitled to appear before the tribunal, make objections, plead, confront the witnesses against him and examine them and present a defense as outlined in Regulations for the Navy and Marine Corps, 19 February 1841. Did Commander Mackenzie make an appropriate decision in denying these procedural protections to the accused? What does his decision tell us about the condition of naval justice in 1842? Can you think of recent instances in the military where procedural rights of accused and suspects may have been inappropriately disregarded?

The *Somers* incident resulted in significant changes in the both the Navy and its justice system. The incident emphasized the need for developing a truly professional academy for naval officers; this result led to the formation of the United States Naval Academy. Frederic F. Van de Water in his book *The Captain Called It Mutiny* expressed it thus: "George Bancroft was the father of the professional school at Annapolis, but Alexander Slidell Mackenzie, in association with Philip Spencer, were among the academy's remoter forebears." The *Somers* court of inquiry and the subsequent court-martial also brought to light that flogging was the main instrument for enforcing discipline on board Navy vessels. In 1850, the Navy abolished flogging as a punishment. The summary hangings, without the intervention of a court-martial or formal investigation, affected the

Navy's policy as regards the death sentence for over a hundred years. While the Army and Air Force have executed 159 persons since 1930, the Navy has not carried out a single execution since 1849.

The *Somers* case received intense public interest because Midshipman Spencer was the son of the Secretary of the War. *Compare* the *Somers* situation with the case of *United States v. Kelly*, which involved the Secretary of the Navy's son.

United States v. Yeoman Seaman Apprentice Chad E. Kelly
Navy and Marine Corps Court of Military Review
40 M.J. 558, June 13, 1994

PER CURIAM:

. . . .

Consistent with his pleas, the appellant was found guilty of numerous offenses involving the theft and wrongful use of other service members' credit cards, including conspiracy to commit larceny, larceny, forgery, and stealing mail matter, in violation of Articles 81, 121, 123, and 134, Uniform Code of Military Justice (UCMJ), 10 U.S.C. Section 881, 921, 923, 934. He was sentenced by the military judge to a dishonorable discharge, confinement for 2 years, forfeiture of all pay and allowances, and reduction to pay grade E-1. The convening authority approved the sentence; however, pursuant to a pretrial agreement, he mitigated the dishonorable discharge to a bad-conduct discharge. The case is now before us upon mandatory review pursuant to Article 66(c), UCMJ, 10 U.S.C. Section 866(c).

The first issue presented is whether unlawful command influence was exercised in the appellant's case to his prejudice. The second issue is whether the appellant's case is closely related to that of Yeoman Seaman [YNSN] H. Lawrence Garrett, IV, U.S. Navy, the son of the then-Secretary of the Navy, whose offenses were disposed of at nonjudicial proceedings under Article 15, UCMJ, 10 U.S.C. Section 815, and, if so, whether the disparate treatment between the two cases resulted from impermissible considerations and inappropriate actions rather than good and cogent reasons. We conclude that the record contains no evidence of unlawful command influence regarding the appellant's case. We further conclude that the appellant's and YNSN Garrett's cases are closely related and that the widely disparate treatment between the two cases resulted from favoritism towards YNSN Garrett due to his status as the son of the then-Secretary. Therefore, exercising our broad authority pursuant to Article 66(c) to affirm only findings and a sentence that we conclude should be affirmed, we will substantially reduce the appellant's sentence.

At trial, the appellant did not raise an issue of unlawful command influence concerning this case. He pled guilty to the conspiracy specification by adding the name of Yeoman Third Class (Frocked) Garrett[1] as a co-conspirator. The appellant was found guilty in accordance with this guilty plea. During the sentencing portion of the trial, in an unsworn statement, the appellant said

---

[1]During the investigation of the two cases, YNSN Garrett was frocked to Yeoman Third Class. For the sake of simplicity, we refer to him throughout this decision as a yeoman seaman, YNSN.

that YNSN Garrett and another person talked him into the theft of the credit cards, and that YNSN Garrett and the other individual were active participants in the use of the stolen cards. [citation omitted]. A defense exhibit was introduced that showed that YNSN Garrett's offenses had been disposed of at an Article 15, UCMJ, nonjudicial proceeding, referred to as "Captain's Mast" in the Navy [footnote omitted].

. . . .

II. EVIDENCE SUBMITTED

a. NIS Investigation

The following information is taken from NIS investigative reports submitted as a result of our limited grant of discovery as set out above. We summarize only the relevant information from the extensive investigation.

During the late spring of 1991, Sailors at Naval Air Station, North Island, located near San Diego, California, failed to receive credit cards issued to them, yet they received credit card bills with charges on the cards. They reported this to the local NIS office, and it opened an investigation. All of the cards had been sent through the Shore Intermediate Maintenance Activity [SIMA] post office at North Island.

On 11 October 1991, a petty officer provided a statement to an NIS agent that the appellant had used credit cards in an especially generous fashion. He said that YNSN Garrett and the appellant were friends. He also said that a female Sailor [C.R.], who was a friend of his, said that she had heard that the appellant was taking other persons' credit cards and using them. The same day, an NIS agent interviewed C.R., who was a roommate of YNSN Garrett and another person [A.M.]. She said

that YNSN Garrett had told her that the appellant had occasionally stolen credit cards from the mail room in which the appellant worked, but she opined that Garrett was not involved. That same day, the appellant confessed to an NIS agent to having stolen credit cards from the SIMA mail room and to using them.

On 21 October 1991, the Bureau of Naval Personnel [BUPERS] issued permanent orders transferring YNSN Garrett to the Chief of Naval Personnel Support Division, Washington, D.C., a division of BUPERS. The orders stated that YNSN Garrett was to be transferred in November 1991 and was to report no later than 6 January 1992.

On 22 October 1991, an NIS interim report was submitted that did not mention YNSN Garrett as a lead or a suspect. On 15 November 1991, however, an NIS Investigative Summary Report was submitted, with distribution copies to Naval Investigative Command Headquarters and the NIS Regional Office for the 11th Naval District that did mention YNSN Garrett by name. That report contained a summary of the statements of YNSN Garrett's roommate, C.R., and the appellant's admissions regarding the stolen credit cards.

On 30 January 1992, the appellant stated under oath to an NIS agent that YNSN Garrett was involved in the theft of the cards. He said that on one occasion YNSN Garrett encouraged him to steal a card, so they went together to the SIMA mail room where the appellant stole one in YNSN Garrett's presence. The appellant said he gave the card to YNSN Garrett, who made all the fraudulent purchases with that card. The appellant alleged a cover-up because YNSN Garrett was the son of the Secretary of the Navy. The appellant questioned why no one had interviewed YNSN Garrett to which the agent replied that YNSN Garrett's involvement was unknown.

On 11 February 1992, another one of YNSN Garrett's roommates, A.M., was interviewed and denied any involvement in or knowledge of the theft or use of the credit cards. The same date, another female roommate of YNSN Garrett said that in the summer months of 1991, she knew that the appellant used stolen credit cards; however, she did not implicate YNSN Garrett.

On 24 February 1992, YNSN Garrett was interviewed in Washington, D.C., by NIS agents. After receiving an appropriate rights advisement, he gave a sworn statement in which he denied any criminal involvement in the stolen credit cards. The next day he provided handwriting exemplars and submitted to a polygraph examination. After the polygraph examiner evaluated the charts, he opined that YNSN Garrett was not truthful in denying involvement in or knowledge of the thefts. YNSN Garrett then admitted that his earlier sworn statement was false and that he had received property obtained through the use of the cards. The interview was terminated by YNSN Garrett after he received a telephone call from his mother.

On 26 February, YNSN Garrett was re-interviewed. This time he admitted driving the appellant to the appellant's office in the mail room, knowing that the appellant was going to steal a credit card there. Afterwards, he accompanied the appellant to a restaurant where the appellant paid for meals for Garrett and others with the card that Garrett knew had just been stolen. On the way home from the restaurant, the appellant also used the card to pay for gasoline for both his and Garrett's cars. YNSN Garrett also admitted being present in a hotel room where food and beverages were ordered from room service. He assumed that the appellant had paid for the room and these other items with a stolen card. On one occasion, he and another roommate, [T.C.], went to a shopping mall. On

the way, the two put gas in Garrett's car, and T.C. paid for the gasoline with a card that Garrett knew had been stolen by the appellant and given to T.C. to use. At the mall, Garrett selected a pair of shorts and gave them to T.C. for purchase with a credit card that Garrett knew was stolen. Later, T.C. gave him the shorts and a T-shirt that also had been purchased using the card. On another occasion, Garrett and T.C. asked the appellant to purchase an expensive vacuum cleaner with a stolen card, but the appellant refused. Garrett denied ever asking the appellant to get a stolen card for him or possessing or using a stolen credit card. He admitted again that his sworn statement of 24 February was false. He stated again under oath that this statement was the complete truth and was as much as he knew about the entire affair.

The next day, 27 February, Garrett provided additional information. This time he said there "might" have been an occasion when T.C. gave him a stolen credit card that Garrett, himself, used to pay for gasoline. After the interrogation into the theft and use of the credit cards, he also admitted smoking marijuana on two occasions at hotels rented through the use of stolen credit cards. He explained how he drank substantial quantities of water and used physical exercise in an effort to preclude a positive result on a urinalysis test. Again, he was administered a polygraph examination; his denial of having stolen any credit cards was inconclusive. After the examination, he admitted that he "might" have used a stolen card on two occasions to purchase gasoline.

Subsequently, during an NIS interview on 16 March 1992, T.C. provided a sworn statement that he was present: (1) when Garrett picked out merchandise for purchase with stolen credit cards, (2) when stolen credit cards were used at the restaurant to pay for meals, and (3) when he and Garrett solicited the appellant to purchase the expensive vacuum cleaner. He said he was also in the hotels where on two occasions, the rooms, food, and beverages were paid for using stolen credit cards and marijuana was used by the occupants, including Garrett. He said that while he was Garrett's roommate, they frequently used marijuana.

On 17 March 1992, another roommate, A.M., provided a sworn statement to an NIS agent in which he admitted using marijuana with Garrett "almost nightly." He said he knew that Garrett went with T.C. to buy merchandise using stolen credit cards. He knew that on at least two occasions, stolen cards were used to put gasoline in Garrett's car because Garrett talked openly about it. He knew that Garrett had received two or three pairs of shorts purchased with stolen credit cards. He said that just prior to Garrett's punishment at captain's mast, Garrett telephoned him and said that a shirt he had traded to A.M. for a sweatshirt was purchased with a stolen credit card.

On 2 April 1992, Captain [CAPT] Carlson M. LeGrand, Judge Advocate General's Corps, U.S. Navy, the Director of Legal Counsel to the Bureau of Naval Personnel, was briefed on the status of the investigation and was provided documentation regarding it.

b. First Declarations

On 19 November 1992, Rear Admiral Luther F. Schriefer, U.S. Navy, the convening authority in this case, executed a sworn affidavit. In it, he states that he was not influenced in his decisions in appellant Kelly's case by the then-Secretary of the Navy or any other superior authority.

On 23 November 1993, Commander [CDR] Michael J. Landers, U.S. Navy, Commanding Officer, Staff Enlisted Personnel, BUPERS, executed a sworn affidavit. He conducted the Article 15, UCMJ, nonjudicial punishment proceeding in the case of YNSN Garrett. In determining a proper disposition of the case, he considered the NIS Report of Investigation, YNSN Garrett's statements, and other information. He also relied on the recommendation from CAPT LeGrand.[2] CDR Landers said that he awarded punishment pursuant to Article 15 because he believed such action to be appropriate. He also said he was not subjected to any external influence and "treated YNSN Garrett as [he] would have treated any other sailor under similar circumstances."

On 23 November 1993, CAPT LeGrand executed a sworn affidavit. The affidavit states that YNSN Garrett reported to BUPERS on 16 December 1991, having detached from his command in San Diego on 30 November 1991. CAPT LeGrand asserts that neither he, nor, to his knowledge, anyone at the Bureau of Naval Personnel, was aware of YNSN Garrett's suspected implication in the investigation into the theft of credit cards at the time of Garrett's transfer. He first heard about Garrett's involvement in late February 1992, after which he followed the investigation closely, to include receiving an NIS Report of Investigation and briefings by involved agents. During the investigation, he kept the Chief of Naval Personnel, VADM R.J. Zlatoper, U.S. Navy, apprised of its status.[3] They agreed

---

[2]Then-Captain LeGrand has since been promoted to the rank of rear admiral. He now serves as the Deputy Judge Advocate General of the Navy and the Commander, Naval Legal Service Command. Because he held the rank of captain at the time of his actions in this case, we will refer to him in that grade in this decision.

that VADM Zlatoper should not discuss the case with any subordinates at the Bureau, especially CDR Landers. Captain LeGrand discussed the case with CDR Peter Fagan, Judge Advocate General's Corps, U.S. Navy, the Special Assistant to the Secretary of the Navy for Legal and Legislative Affairs, and, in effect, Secretary Garrett's military legal advisor. Both recognized the sensitivity of the case and the need to ensure that no improper influence occurred.

Ultimately, after reviewing the NIS reports, Captain LeGrand recommended that the charges against YNSN Garrett be disposed of at an Article 15 proceeding. He based his recommendation on the following factors:

(1) the relatively low monetary value of the property and services Garrett obtained with the stolen credit cards;

(2) the drug offenses were for use instead of distribution;

(3) the extent of Garrett's prior cooperation with NIS; and

(4) Garrett's prior exemplary evaluations and his lack of any previous disciplinary actions.

CAPT LeGrand was aware that, due to the appellant's more extensive criminality and the monetary value of the property with which he was involved (over $10,000), his charges would probably be referred for trial by general court-martial. At this time, YNSN Garrett was considered to be a potential witness for the prosecution. CAPT LeGrand further considered what would occur if Garrett's charges were referred to a special court-martial. This included the requirement to corroborate Garrett's admissions regarding marijuana use and the possible location and sequence of any prosecutions. He believed he knew the full extent of Garrett's involvement based in part on the results of the polygraph examination taken after his confession.

On 24 November 1993, CDR Fagan executed a sworn affidavit which is supplemented by answers to specific questions asked by this Court. In pertinent part, the affidavit states his opinion that he did nothing that could be construed to be unlawful command influence in the appellant's case. When he became aware of the investigation concerning YNSN Garrett in late February 1992, he informed Under Secretary of the Navy Howard and Secretary Garrett. They all agreed that the Secretary should have no involvement in the case.

On 4 February 1994, VADM Boorda executed a declaration in which he states that he was Chief of Naval Personnel and Deputy Chief of Naval Operations for Manpower, Personnel, and Training when YNSN Garrett's transfer from San Diego to Washington, D.C., was ordered. He states that "sometime during the summer of 1991, [he] phoned YNSN Garrett to see how he was doing." They discussed YNSN Garrett's work and future plans such as going to college. YNSN Garrett said that he would like a transfer because he was unhappy in San Diego. VADM Boorda states that he believes that he discussed the matter with his Executive Assistant, Captain Lugo. At the time of this conversation, VADM Boorda indicates he was unaware of any criminal involvement by Garrett and did not learn of his alleged misconduct until later. He concludes the declaration as follows: "I did not receive any request or

---

[3]VADM Zlatoper replaced VADM Boorda as the Chief of Naval Personnel when VADM Boorda was promoted to admiral and transferred to Europe.

direction from Secretary Garrett to transfer his son to Washington."

c. Second Declarations

On 23 March 1994, NIS Special Agent [SA] Kathleen Bray, who was the case agent in San Diego investigating appellant's crimes, executed a sworn affidavit. In it, she states that when on 11 October 1991 C.R. said that Garrett told C.R. that appellant had stolen a credit card from his command's mail room, the focus of the investigation was identifying victims and obtaining evidence. It was after the appellant implicated Garrett on 30 January 1992 that Garrett became a suspect. She asserts no one interfered with her actions in the case and she felt no pressure to treat Garrett any differently than any other suspect.

Also on 23 March 1994, NIS SA T.A. Miller executed a witnessed, unsworn statement. He states that prior to YNSN Garrett's first polygraph examination, CDR Fagan called NIS and "indicated that he needed the telephone number of where the polygraph was taking place so that he could provide it to Garrett's mother who wanted to talk to her son." SA Miller told CDR Fagan to call back. SA Miller believes that he then spoke with NIS Deputy Commander Charles Lannom who told him to give CDR Fagan the telephone number. SA Miller subsequently called NIS Deputy Regional Director Victor McPherson to tell him to put any call from Mrs. Garrett through to her son. YNSN Garrett was then called by his mother while being interviewed regarding the polygraph examination, and Garrett thereafter terminated the interview. SA Miller opined that the investigating agents were upset that YNSN Garrett was allowed to talk with his mother during the course of the interrogation.

On 24 March 1994, the special agent in charge of the San Diego office of NIS provided a sworn statement. He could not remember when the case agent mentioned YNSN Garrett's name during the investigation. He also said he received no special guidance or pressure in investigating the case.

On 24 March 1994, NIS SA Kimberly Phillips-Rizzo executed a sworn statement. In it, she relates the events following YNSN Garrett's polygraph examinations on 25 February 1992. Following the tests, Deputy Regional Director McPherson called to say that YNSN Garrett's mother would be calling and that the agents "were directed to interrupt the interrogation and allow [YNSN] Garrett to talk to her." Shortly thereafter, Mrs. Garrett called, YNSN Garrett spoke with her, and he subsequently terminated the interview.

SA Phillips-Rizzo also relates events on the next day when YNSN Garrett returned. Garrett opened the session by saying that the previous evening he had spoken with "a high ranking Navy lawyer who 'knew NIS very well' and was advised that 'NIS agents were professionals and would act like his friend and they would play upon his manhood.'" YNSN Garrett refused to identify the lawyer but told the agents they "would know who he was." He then made incriminating admissions. On the same day or the day thereafter, YNSN Garrett said that he had asked his father to use his influence to obtain YNSN Garrett's transfer from San Diego to Washington, D.C. YNSN Garrett said he did not like the San Diego area because "military personnel were treated like second-class citizens" and "he could not get a date." He said that his father "told him to deal with it for approximately one year before he intervened and arranged for him to be transferred." Thereafter, he admitted marijuana use and provided a pair of shorts and a T-shirt that he had received from the use of a stolen credit card.

The same day, 24 March 1994, SA Philip-Rizzo's co-agent, NIS SA Robert Iorio, executed a sworn statement. He states that on 25 February 1992, after a polygraph examiner indicated YNSN Garrett was deceptive, SA Iorio received a telephone call from Deputy Regional Director McPherson, who said that Garrett's "mother would be calling." McPherson said that they were to interrupt the interrogation to allow Garrett to speak to his mother. Garrett terminated the interrogation "within minutes" after receiving his mother's call.

SA Iorio also related that the next day, Garrett returned for reinterrogation. Garrett told him he had spoken with "a high ranking Navy lawyer" who Garrett said worked with the NIS on a regular basis and knew NIS "very well." Garrett said that this officer said NIS agents were "professionals" who wold "play on [his] manhood" to coax him into making incriminating statements. Garrett refused to identify this officer, but he said that the agents would know who he was. Garrett then made incriminating statements. The next day, Garrett returned again to expand on his admitted culpability. This statement included admissions of repeated use of marijuana as well as other incriminating statements. He also said that he had been depressed in San Diego due to his inability to find a date. He said he had called his father frequently, requesting a transfer from San Diego, and that his father "finally intervened on his behalf and 'pulled some strings' to obtain a transfer for him to BUPERS that would allow him to live at home with his parents.

On 24 March 1994, NIS SA Blaine Thomas sent an unsworn electronic mail statement to NIS headquarters. In it, he recounts a meeting after the interrogation of Garrett in which Rear Admiral [RADM] Duvall M. Williams, Judge Advocate General's Corps, U.S. Navy, then the commander of the Naval Investigative Service Command, apologized "for his interference in [the] investigation into former SECNAV's son." RADM Williams said he was "sorry for copious phone calls from either himself . . . and/or Miller during Garrett's investigation." RADM Williams "also stated it appeared he was interfering; however, he was only concerned because of his friendship with the then-SECNAV." SA Thomas recalled one phone call in which he and others had to allow YNSN Garrett to talk to his mother. This agent recounts that at the meeting NIS SA Frank Kauffman openly expressed his disgust with interruptions during an official investigation and asserted "that the ADM was on the borderline of obstructing justice." He stated that SA Kauffman told RADM Williams that he (Kauffman) would not be a party to such conduct and that he and SA Kauffman wondered whether they would have a job when it was all over. He said that SA Kauffman spoke the truth because RADM Williams' response to Kauffman's statement was "nothing more than a stare."

In a similar electronic mail message the same date, SA Kauffman generally supported this account. SA Kauffman stated:

> Following the interrogations, searches, etc. re Garrett's son, ADM Williams called a meeting to explain or attempt to explain why he thought it necessary to allow the interruption of the polygraph of Garrett's son by a phone call from Garrett's mother. Though I'm not able to quote verbatim what he said, I specifically asked him if he was responsible for allowing that phone call to get through to the son. He said it was his decision and, right or wrong, he felt he owed it to SECNAV because he was a close friend. He acknowledged that his decision might not be viewed as a popular one but it was his nonetheless.

Also on 24 March 1994, NIS SA Michael Vogel executed a sworn statement. SA Vogel administered a polygraph examination to YNSN Garrett. During one session, YNSN Garrett showed deception during a test. Prior to a subsequent interrogation, NIS SA Ray Reese received a telephone call from the Deputy Regional Director for the NIS Capital Region [SA McPherson] who said the agents should expect a call from either YNSN Garrett's mother or the lawyer for the Secretary. SA Reese was directed to interrupt the interrogation to allow YNSN Garrett to take the call. He states that YNSN Garrett terminated the interrogation following a polygraph examination, which resulted in deceptive results when another Special Agent indicated YNSN Garrett had a telephone call which he should answer. The agents were extremely displeased with this order. Later, SA Vogel attended a meeting with RADM Williams during which agents noted that it was not normal procedure to interrupt an interrogation with a telephone call.

Also on 24 March 1994, SA Reese executed a sworn statement. He was present at the polygraph examinations and the subsequent interrogation that led to YNSN Garrett's termination of the interview after receiving a call from his mother. He states that he interrupted the interrogation because he had been ordered to do so by the Deputy Assistant Director of the NIS National Capital Region, SA McPherson, who earlier indicated that Mrs. Garrett or the Secretary's lawyer, CDR Fagan, might call and that he was to interrupt the interrogation and allow Garrett to talk to her in this case. SA Reese expressed his displeasure with this direction, and McPherson empathized, indicating that he had received this direction from Miller.

Also on 24 March 1994, SA McPherson executed a sworn statement. When YNSN Garrett was interrogated, SA McPherson was Deputy Regional Director of the NIS Regional Office of the National Capital Region. He received a telephone call from SA Miller, who was acting Deputy Commander of NIS headquarters at the time. SA Miller specifically reminded SA McPherson that he (SA Miller) was acting Deputy Commander. SA Miller said that he was about to give SA McPherson "an order he suspected [SA McPherson] might not be in complete agreement with, but that he wanted carried out as stated." SA Miller asked for the telephone number for the NIS office where Garrett was to be interrogated. SA McPherson provided the number. SA McPherson states that "SA Miller then informed me either YNSN Garrett's mother or the Secretary of the Navy's lawyer, CDR Peter Fagan, USN, would call the NIS office to speak to YNSN Garrett and [SA McPherson] was to ensure that NIS Agents placed the call through to him promptly." SA Miller said that the order came from either COMNISCOM, then RADM Williams, or SA Lannom, then Deputy Commander, NISCOM, and SA Miller was "to make certain either CDR Fagan or Mrs. Garrett were allowed to speak to [YNSN] Garrett." SA McPherson also indicates that the agent who received this order openly disagreed with it.

On 29 March 1994, RADM Williams executed a declaration under penalty of perjury. In it, he states that he has known the Secretary since 1978 and considered him a close personal friend. He learned of YNSN Garrett's criminal involvement when Garrett was in Washington, D.C. He did not brief higher authorities because of the sensitive nature of Garrett's case and to prevent any hint of illegal command influence. About 24 February 1992, he informed the Secretary that his son was in custody and was being interrogated. After this, on the same date, he informed the Vice Chief of Naval Operations and the Under Secretary of the Navy, both of whom appeared to have prior knowledge of the case. The following day, the Secretary asked for an update. RADM Williams told the Secretary that he had passed on all that the Secretary needed to know. That same day, NIS headquarters received a call from CDR Fagan, requesting the telephone number where Garrett was being interrogated. RADM Williams states that authorities at NIS, including himself, agreed that the number should be revealed.

RADM Williams disputes whether he directed that Mrs. Garrett's call go through immediately. In the meeting after Garrett's interrogation was completed, RADM Williams said that he "did not give the order to let the phone call go through." He also says that, after reviewing the electronic mail messages from Special Agents Kauffman and Thomas, their allegations that RADM Williams made the decision to let the phone call from Garrett's mother to go through during the interrogation are untrue. He further states that SA Thomas' perception is also inaccurate.

On 30 March 1994, CDR Fagan provided a second declaration under penalty of perjury. In it, he states that he did not know why YNSN Garrett received his transfer from San Diego and learned of the transfer only after Garrett arrived in Washington, D.C. CDR Fagan learned of Garrett's alleged misconduct the day that NIS agents searched the Secretary's house.[4] On a day when Garrett was being interrogated by NIS agents, the Secretary's wife called him and said she was concerned for her son's well-being. CDR Fagan suggested that she call her son. CDR Fagan called the NIS office to obtain the number which he passed to Mrs. Garrett. He says he did not request that NIS agents put through the call.

CDR Fagan also states that one evening the Secretary called him at home and expressed concern that his son had not been fully advised of his rights. CDR Fagan said that he could advise him, although he could not represent his son or discuss the allegations of misconduct with him. The Secretary then put his son on the phone. CDR Fagan then conducted a "one-way conversation" with YNSN Garrett in which he advised him of his right to remain silent and to request counsel. He also said that NIS agents were trained to get him to talk. CDR Fagan does not remember telling YNSN Garrett that the NIS agents would play on his manhood.

On 31 March 1994, SA Kathleen Bray executed a second sworn affidavit. In it, she states that on 11 October 1991, when C.R. mentioned the name of H. Lawrence Garrett, IV, she knew he was the Secretary's son. She also confirms that the Investigative Summary Report of 15 November 1991, which mentioned YNSN Garrett's name, was distributed to NIS headquarters. She states that she did not interview Garrett because higher priority work, such as obtaining physical evidence, had to be done. She concludes by stating that had the appellant's case been prepared for trial, she would have interviewed YNSN Garrett but for the appellant's implication of Garrett in January 1992.

Also on 31 March 1994, H. Lawrence Garrett, III, the former Secretary of the Navy, executed a declaration under penalty of perjury. In it, he recounts the background of his son's decision to join the Navy and his (the Secretary's) solely professional relationship with VADM Boorda. He states that before his son enlisted in the Navy, VADM Boorda spoke to YNSN Garrett about the decision. In a four page statement, the Secretary indicates that his son was harassed while he was on active duty because he was the son of the Secretary. In the summer of 1991, young Garrett expressed his displeasure with San Diego, in part because he wanted to attend college.

---

[4]YNSN Garrett was living at home with his parents and consented to a search of his room on 24 February 1992.

The Secretary advised him to go to school at night. The Secretary recommended that he request sea duty but refused to intervene in his son's behalf. Sometime thereafter, VADM Boorda asked the Secretary how his son was doing, to which the Secretary replied that his son was unhappy and that the Secretary had advised him to request sea duty. In the fall of 1991, Garrett phoned his father to say that he had orders to Washington, D.C. The Secretary denies pulling strings to get the transfer. He further says that his son denied ever having made an allegation to NIS that the Secretary pulled strings to get the transfer.

The Secretary mentions his long personal relationship with RADM Williams. Before the search of portions of his house by NIS, he spoke to RADM Williams about his son being taken into custody. After the search, his son denied major involvement in the credit card thefts, however, the Secretary informed his son of the extent of his son's potential criminal liability as a thief in the eyes of the law.

Prior to his son taking a polygraph examination, the Secretary advised his son of his rights and told him that he should exercise his right to have a lawyer assist him. The Secretary also states that he clearly indicated to his son and his wife that he would do nothing to affect the situation. The Secretary does not remember a telephone conversation between himself, his son, and CDR Fagan, although he does not dispute that it may have occurred.

On 25 February 1992, the Secretary says he called RADM Williams to find out information about his son, but RADM Williams declined further comment. The Secretary thinks that his wife called CDR Fagan to get the number of the NIS office where his son's polygraph exam was being conducted. She later admitted calling that office. The Secretary then advised the Secretary of Defense of the developments. He asserts that while that he did nothing to influence the disposition of the offenses of which his son was suspected, he did ask CDR Fagan about the forum the offenses might warrant.

d. Other Evidence

The record shows that YNSN Garrett's offenses were disposed of at an Article 15, UCMJ, nonjudicial proceeding on 28 April 1992, about 5 months prior to the appellant's trial. The charges upon which he was punished include one specification of use of marijuana on two occasions, one specification of larceny of food and gasoline, one specification of receipt of stolen property, including beverages, gasoline, a pair of men's shorts, and a T-shirt, and one specification of soliciting another to steal a vacuum cleaner. His punishment included restriction and extra duties for 30 days, forfeiture of $880 pay, and reduction to pay grade E-2. [citation omitted]. Although pertinent regulations permitted appropriate authorities to initiate procedures for administrative separation from the Navy based on the offenses for which he was punished under this Article 15 proceeding, YNSN Garrett was not processed for administrative discharge.

III. ANALYSIS

. . . .

b. Case Disposition and Punishment Comparison Under Article 66, UCMJ

. . . .

We conclude, first, that the appellant's and YNSN Garrett's cases are closely related. The appellant's crimes involved the theft of mail matter and use of stolen credit cards to steal goods and services. YNSN Garrett admitted driving the appellant to the SIMA mail room where the appellant was to steal or retrieve a stolen credit card that came from the mail. YNSN Garrett later was a principal to several thefts through use of the stolen credit cards. Undoubtedly, under the law of principals, YNSN Garrett was the actual thief of at least one of the cards and was active in their subsequent unlawful use. These acts were generally similar in nature and seriousness to the appellant's offenses.

In addition, the two cases arose from a common scheme. Even assuming that the appellant began stealing the cards on his own initiative in order to steal goods and services, YNSN Garrett and others certainly joined the scheme at some point. As noted previously, YNSN Garrett apparently aided the theft of one card, and he frequently benefitted from the theft and use of the cards. He ultimately became sufficiently involved in the criminal enterprise for us to find that this and the appellant's offenses arose from a common scheme in which both took part.

There is no reasonable question that the disposition and sentence in the two cases are widely disparate. The appellant received a federal criminal conviction, a punitive discharge, substantial confinement, and the loss of over $14,000 in pay. YNSN Garrett received an administrative punishment not considered a conviction, no punitive discharge, no confinement (only extra duties and restriction to a base for 30 days), and the loss of $880 in pay.

A central issue is whether this disparity in disposition and sentence is for good and cogent reasons. We conclude that such reasons are wholly absent in the record before us.

The Government emphasizes the number and seriousness of the appellant's offenses and stresses that his punishment is appropriate. We agree entirely. The Government's suggestion, however, that YNSN Garrett's offenses were minor and of a nature and seriousness that warranted disposition by an Article 15, UCMJ, proceeding is without any basis in experience or reason.[5] The evidence before us indicates that YNSN Garrett was a principal to the theft of at least one credit card from the mails. He stole gasoline and clothing on several occasions, received stolen food and beverages on several occasions, and solicited the theft of an expensive vacuum cleaner. These offenses alone warrant trial by a special court-martial with authority to adjudge a punitive discharge and confinement of up to 6 months. Yet these offenses do not stand alone. He also confessed to multiple uses of marijuana, and the evidence indicates regular and steady use. Lastly, he lied under oath more than once to NIS agents, crimes that are also punishable under the UCMJ.[6] Had YNSN Garrett been tried by a general court-martial for these crimes, the maximum sentence he could have received would have included a dishonorable discharge and confinement for 23 years. We conclude that nothing in this record justifies the disparity in disposition and sentence between these two cases.

The most difficult issue is whether the unreasonable disparity between the cases results from an unfortunate but relatively benign factor, such as poor judgment or inexperience in military justice matters on the part of the officers who directed the disposition of YNSN Garrett's case, or

---

[5]Such an argument is totally inconsistent with the position the Government takes in other cases which involve a single drug offense or a single theft, where it argues that such offenses are serious and warrant punitive separation.

[6]It appears that all of the charges against YNSN Garrett were derived from his own admissions rather than from a complete and thorough investigation. Thus we are unsure of his full complicity in the criminal activity that took place in San Diego.

worse, from an impermissible factor. Unfortunately, we conclude that just such an impermissible factor infects the processing of YNSN Garrett's case.

We turn first to YNSN Garrett's transfer from San Diego to Washington, D.C. At the time of this transfer, he was a single Sailor who had been assigned to shore duty on a major staff in California immediately after receiving his initial military training—certainly a desirable assignment for most naval personnel in similar circumstances. After reports of the loss of credit cards at SIMA and the opening of an NIS investigation, YNSN Garrett contacted his father to complain that his petty officers were harassing him, he wanted to attend college, and his romantic interests were unsatisfied. Complaints by young Sailors in the Navy concerning their superior petty officers are hardly uncommon. As the Secretary's own statement makes clear, higher educational opportunities were available in San Diego. YNSN Garrett's romantic prospects were a frivolous concern. From all of the circumstances, there is a reasonable inference that YNSN Garrett's true motive for wanting to leave San Diego was other than the reasons he related to his father. He certainly did not want to be caught by the growing investigation into the theft and wrongful use of the credit cards, and he probably thought that duty in Washington would provide him a safe haven. Therefore, he sought his father's assistance.

The Secretary informed VADM Boorda that YNSN Garrett was not happy in San Diego. While we do not doubt the statements that the Secretary did not solicit VADM Boorda's phone call, we conclude, nevertheless, that VADM Boorda called YNSN Garrett in response to the Secretary's comment some time during the summer of 1991. VADM Boorda then told his Executive Assistant that the Secretary's son was unhappy in San Diego and to discuss the matter with YNSN Garrett. We believe that YNSN Garrett's transfer was the anticipated and predictable result of the Secretary mentioning this situation to the Chief of Naval Personnel, the senior officer in the Navy having cognizance over personnel transfers.

We conclude that YNSN Garrett's transfer resulted solely from his status as the son of the secretary of the Navy. His shore assignment was terminated well before the normal rotation date for reasons that are uncompelling. The only conclusion left to us is that he was transferred cross-country because the Secretary mentioned his son's unhappiness to VADM Boorda, and not because the needs of the Naval Service were furthered by the move. There is no evidence, however, that either VADM Boorda or any of the officers who effected the transfer were aware of YNSN Garrett's suspected criminal involvement at the time of the transfer.

When the appellant disclosed YNSN Garrett's offenses, YNSN Garrett had been removed from the place where most of his crimes had been committed. While NIS was certainly able to continue the investigation of YNSN Garrett in Washington, we are convinced that, once he left San Diego, the eventual disposition of the charges against him was affected because those who had the responsibility to handle his case in Washington were more likely to be influenced by his status than others in a different location. The investigation in Washington, D.C., is replete with actions by naval and NIS personnel that demonstrate that YNSN Garrett's case was not handled in the normal course of military justice.

First, YNSN Garrett conversed with the Secretary's military legal advisor, a member of the Judge Advocate General's Corps and an officer who represents the Naval Service rather than any particular officer or service member. This officer elected to obtain the telephone number of the NIS office where YNSN Garrett was being interrogated so that his mother could interrupt that interrogation. The evidence shows that the night before an NIS interrogation, that officer chose to provide a rights advisement to a military accused, to include advice regarding NIS interrogation techniques. Predictably, the following day, YNSN Garrett explained his close relationship with this lawyer to NIS special agents for whatever effect he thought that relationship might have on them.

Additionally, the Commander, Naval Investigative Service Command, intervened in the investigation to further the perceived interests of the Secretary. We find that, contrary to his assertions, RADM Williams did direct that Mrs. Garrett's or CDR Fagan's telephone call be put through during YNSN Garrett's interrogation. We also find that his actions in the case of YNSN Garrett were motivated by loyalty to a close personal friend, a desire to spare the Secretary personal anguish and public embarrassment, and a desire to dispose of an awkward situation in the most expeditious manner possible instead of fulfilling his duty as the head of NIS to ensure that a complete and accurate investigation of YNSN Garrett's case was completed. This fact became obvious to the NIS agents who investigated YNSN Garrett's alleged offenses.

The NIS investigation ultimately went before CAPT LeGrand, the senior military lawyer in BUPERS. His explanation for recommending that YNSN Garrett's case be disposed of at an Article 15, UCMJ, nonjudicial proceeding is unconvincing. First, he spoke of the low monetary value of the property and services YNSN Garrett obtained. The evidence before us does not indicate what that overall value was because no investigator was called upon to tally the total, however, it certainly was at

least several hundred dollars. He next considered that the drug offenses were for use as opposed to distribution. Convincing evidence of record suggests numerous if not frequent and prolonged use of marijuana by YNSN Garrett. We note that in our experience, cases of multiple drug use, standing alone, are commonly referred to trial by special court-martial where, upon conviction, the accused often receives a punitive discharge and months of confinement. We are perplexed by the reference to YNSN Garrett's cooperation with NIS as a reason for leniency in light of his evasion and showings of deception or inconclusiveness in his polygraph examinations results. In fact, by his own admission, YNSN Garrett lied under oath to NIS agents, an offense unmentioned by CAPT LeGrand in his declaration. Finally, while YNSN Garrett's prior clean record was a legitimate factor to consider in the disposition of the charges against him, this factor pales substantially given the gravity of the offenses he faced. We also note that the appellant also had a good record prior to his general court-martial with no prior disciplinary actions.

CAPT LeGrand added that YNSN Garrett was a potential witness against the appellant. However, YNSN Garrett had lied under oath to NIS agents, and the appellant had already confessed. Consequently, both the usefulness and necessity for YNSN Garrett's testimony as a prosecution witness were in considerable doubt. Next, CAPT LeGrand referred to the requirement to corroborate YNSN Garrett's admissions. Considering the seized charge card receipts, the potential testimony of YNSN Garrett's roommates, and the other incriminating admissions in the case, this requirement was one that any prosecutor could easily meet. Finally, he referred to the situs of any prosecution, a problem arising solely from YNSN Garrett's early transfer, and one which was easily remedied by transferring him back to San Diego for disciplinary action. In short, the reasons for recommending disposition of YNSN Garrett's offenses at an Article 15 UCMJ nonjudicial proceeding are unconvincing, and, in light of other evidence in this case, the only rational explanation for the extremely lenient treatment YNSN Garrett received was his status as the son of the Secretary.[7]

Anyone familiar with the NIS investigation in this case when YNSN Garrett's offenses were referred to an Article 15 nonjudicial proceeding in April 1992 must have been aware that when YNSN Garrett was transferred from San Diego, he had committed serious offenses and that the transfer took him away from the location of the witnesses and other evidence. Further, they must have known that YNSN Garrett was aware of his own misconduct when he pressed his father for a transfer. In the Navy, it is common practice to transfer an accused for disciplinary action from a current location back to a previous command where the alleged offenses occurred. When senior naval officers recognized the effect of YNSN Garrett's transfer from San Diego, the expected result would have been his transfer back to San Diego, where his alleged offenses could have been fully pursued in the same course as though he had not obtained his transfer. The failure of responsible officers to follow this common practice is further evidence that YNSN Garrett received preferential treatment.

Finally, we note that YNSN Garrett was charged at the Article 15 proceeding with but one charge for two separate uses of marijuana. The evidence, however, indicated numerous uses. Only one larceny specification embraced his multiple larcenies. Only one specification of receipt of stolen property was drafted in spite of the evidence of several receipts. The charges did include one specification for soliciting the theft of an expensive vacuum cleaner, but no specification mentioned his false swearing to the NIS agents during his interrogation.

Although YNSN Garrett was punished for his offenses, he was not processed for administrative discharge following the Article 15 proceeding. Not only is it uncommon, but it is extraordinary that a Sailor could be found to have used marijuana repeatedly, to have stolen property using stolen credit cards taken from a Navy mail room, to have received stolen property stolen by using these cards, to have asked another Sailor to steal a vacuum cleaner by using another Sailor's stolen credit card, and to have lied to NIS agents under oath and then be retained on active duty without being processed for discharge. In this case, that result is not inexplicable. Based on our experience, we state with confidence that, absent extraordinary circumstances, any other Sailor in the U.S. Navy who faced such charges would have been tried by court-martial.

In summary, we find that YNSN Garrett's transfer was based solely on his status as the son of the Secretary. The decision that his offenses should be disposed of at an Article 15 proceeding and that he would not be processed for administrative discharge thereafter was based on the same status. We find that in YNSN Garrett's case the military justice process was infected throughout by senior naval officer who considered who the accused was rather than what he had done.

---

[7]In his statement, RADM Williams acknowledges that he conversed with CAPT LeGrand regarding factual information in the case prior to nonjudicial punishment being imposed on YNSN Garrett. RADM Williams did not further disclose the details of the conversation, and CAPT LeGrand did not mention this conversation in his affidavit.

IV. CONCLUSIONS

We find that neither Secretary of the Navy Garrett, Under Secretary of the Navy Howard, VADM Boorda, VADM Zlatoper, nor CDR Fagan exerted any unlawful or undue influence in the disposition of the appellant's case, nor was RADM Schriefer, the convening authority, subjected to any such influence.

We do find that RADM Williams, due to his close personal friendship with the Secretary, engaged in actions of favoritism toward YNSN Garrett to such an extent that NIS agents believed he might have been obstructing justice. He impeded the investigation of YNSN Garrett's involvement in the credit card scheme and later spoke with CAPT LeGrand, the legal advisor to the office that would make the final decision concerning the disposition of the charges against YNSN Garrett.

We conclude that the appellant's and YNSN Garrett's cases are closely related and that their punishments are widely disparate. We further conclude not only that the disparity is not supported by good and cogent reasons, but also that it occurred as the result of an impermissible factor.

In deciding what action to take in light of our conclusions, we state the obvious: we are reviewing the appellant's conviction and sentence and not those of YNSN Garrett. We have no authority under the UCMJ to take any action regarding YNSN Garrett.[8] Therefore, we can attempt to balance the scales only by reducing the appellant's otherwise totally appropriate sentence. The Government has argued that the appellant's sentence should be affirmed in spite of what has taken place. We cannot accept such a result. More importantly, the integrity and fairness of the military justice system cannot accept such a result. Preferential treatment of a suspect based on his family relationship to a high-ranking officer or civilian has no place in any reputable justice system. Therefore, we have decided to reduce the appellant's sentence substantially.

V. DISPOSITION

Accordingly, as discussed in the beginning of this decision, the erroneous findings of guilty entered by the military judge as to specifications 14 and 15 of Charge V are set aside and those specifications are dismissed. The remaining findings of guilty are affirmed. Upon reassessment, and considering the disparate treatment and the reasons therefor, and considering the unique circumstances for this case, we affirm only so much of the sentence as includes confinement for 15 months, forfeiture of $420.00 pay per month for 15 months and reduction to pay garde E-1.

In assessing the *Somers* and *Kelly* cases, consider Article 98, UCMJ:

> Any person subject to this chapter who . . . knowingly and intentionally fails to enforce or comply with any provision of this chapter regulating the proceedings before, during, or after trial of an accused: shall be punished as a court-martial may direct.

Did Commander MacKenzie violate the spirit of this provision? What about Secretary Garrett? Rear Admiral Williams?

---

[8]YNSN Garrett has been administratively discharged from the Navy.

In 1862, Congress recognized the need to formally update existing naval justice laws and enacted the Articles for the Government of the Navy. These articles, traditionally known as the "Rocks and Shoals," remained in effect for over eighty years and survived four major wars. Like its predecessors, Rocks and Shoals emphasized discipline over fairness and imposed harsh punishments for violations of its articles.

Unlike the Army's system, which underwent a major overhaul after World War I, the Navy was not the target of legal reform until following World War II. What do you think is the explanation for this difference? William T. Generous, Jr. in his book *Swords and Scales*, provides the following reason:

> [T]he Navy did much less to rearrange the social patterns and customs of its population than the Army did. During peacetime, both services made officers out gentlemen and enlisted men out of lower class recruits. During the mobilization, the Navy continued that practice by commissioning mostly college graduates. But the Army selected its officers on the basis of merit. The result . . . was that in the Navy those who were likely victims of perceived court-martial abuse were the same who had been abused in civilian life. In the Army, on the other hand, the scions of high society who were forced by circumstances to serve in the enlisted ranks complained at every real or fancied maltreatment. The overall consequence was great agitation for changes in military law, but much less, almost none, in the sea service.

THE UNIFORM CODE OF MILITARY JUSTICE

WORLD WAR II

During World War II, the United States expanded its armed forces to a maximum strength of over 12 million men and women. As a consequence, the number of court-martials during the period of hostilities was staggering: approximately two million court-martial convictions, with 80,000 of those handed down by general court-martials. This activity placed the military justice system under scrutiny by a great number of Americans who had no previous contact with its workings. The experience of many of these service members was not positive. Former President Gerald R. Ford, Jr., at the time a member of the House of Representatives, had this to say about Navy justice:

> In general, while I was in the service, I always rebelled, and I still think it is true, as far as the manner in which military justice was meted out by the various people in charge of it in the Navy, and otherwise. It seems to me that a general statement

U.S. Navy court-martial prior to passage of the UCMJ in 1950. Judge Advocates now sit as Military Judges at all special and general courts-martial. Photo courtesy of U.S. Naval Institute.

can be made, with all honesty, that in the Navy, at least, justice is sometimes forgotten in order to impose on people in the service punishment of some kind or other. I am particularly concerned about the fact that in courts-martial, too often a court-martial board does not determine the guilt or innocence of the accused; but rather seeks to award punishment of one sort or another. I can recall hearing conversations between members of boards along this line: "What does the Old Man want us to do?"

Several studies conducted by the services after World War II confirmed the sentiments expressed above. As a result, calls for reform and unification of the systems into a single scheme increased. Congress responded by significantly revising the Army's Articles of War under the Elston Act of 1948, but did not modify the Navy's Rocks and Shoals. However, the move to reform military justice gained momentum, and by 1949 it was clear that Congress would enact a uniform code. The unanswered question was what would such a code contain?

ADOPTION OF A UNIFORM CODE OF MILITARY JUSTICE

In 1949, the newly established Secretary of Defense appointed a committee to draft a code applicable to all the services. This draft provided the basis for the Uniform Code ultimately adopted by Congress in 1950.

Unlawful influence by commanders in the trial process was the major issue debated by Congress in considering passage of the UCMJ. Those who feared such influence argued that commanders should be totally removed from the courts-martial process. Proponents of this view emphasized justice as the most important aspect of the new code. Others, like Army Colonel Frederick Bernays Wiener, argued to Congress that "if you trust [the line officer] to command, if you trust him with only the lives and destinies of these millions of citizens under his command . . . you can certainly trust him with the appointment of a court." Thus, opponents of removing commanders from the process believed that discipline was the primary purpose of military justice. In the end, Congress resolved the controversy by reaching a compromise on this issue. The commander retained power to appoint counsel, the law officer [judge] and court members [jurors]. However, the UCMJ provided that a neutral officer would conduct the pretrial investigation, qualified defense counsel would represent the accused and the all-civilian Court of Military Appeals (now the Court of Appeals for the Armed Forces) would provide appellate review of court-martial decisions.

As you will see in later chapters, the tension between the concepts of justice and discipline continues to this day. Which principle dominates the UCMJ? Which of the above arguments is most appealing? Has the basis for the above arguments changed since enactment of the UCMJ in 1950?

Although the UCMJ contains many uniquely military provisions, it clearly moved military justice much closer to civilian criminal law. Some would argue that this trend has continued and is today damaging the authority of commanding officers and hurting the morale of service members. Do you agree with this assessment?

A second area of debate that arose in enacting the UCMJ focused on just how uniform the UCMJ would be. The Army's Articles of War influenced Congress to a much greater degree than the Articles for the Government of the Navy; however, the Navy and Marine Corps pushed hard to retain unique aspects of the existing naval justice system. Colonel Melvin Maas, National President of the Marine Corps Reserve Association, argued this point before Congress:

> And we want to point out to you that while this bill is a compromise of the naval justice system and the Articles of War, that there is a definite difference in disciplinary control that is required at sea and the disciplinary control required on land. Therefore, the types of punishments may be quite different, of necessity. A

relatively minor infraction at sea may become a very major thing from a disciplinary standpoint. A minor infraction may endanger the lives of all those on the ship, and it may involve a whole flotilla of ships. It is very rare that such a situation could exist in any other type of organization . . . Therefore, it is necessary for discipline at sea to be very much more rigid and very much more drastic than is necessary on shore. That is recognized, gentleman, through the ages in maritime law as well as in naval law.

Congress enacted several provisions which distinguished between personnel attached to or embarked in a vessel and members at shore commands. Consider Article 15, UCMJ:

> [E]xcept in the case of a member attached to or embarked in a vessel, punishment may not be imposed upon any member of the armed forces under this article if the member has, before the imposition of such punishment, demanded trial by court-martial in lieu of such punishment.

> [A]ny commanding officer may . . . impose . . . upon a person attached to or embarked in a vessel, confinement on bread and water or diminished rations for not more than three consecutive days.

Do you agree that the disciplinary concerns are different for ships than for shore commands? If yes, do increased punishments and fewer procedural rights help commanders at sea instill discipline? Take a look at the punishments awardable at courts-martial and at nonjudicial punishment in Chapters III and IV.

From 1951 to 1968, Congress enacted only relatively minor changes to the UCMJ. However, in 1968 Congress significantly modified the code. These changes came about because of the continuing tension between military discipline and civilian concepts of fairness and due process. For example, the 1968 act did away with law officers and replaced them with military judges and required that all defense counsel meet certain qualifications in order to represent military accused. Also in 1968 the Navy created a separate and distinct corps of lawyers entitled the Judge Advocate General's Corps (JAG Corps).

SUMMARY

The struggle between fairness and discipline continues in the military. Important world and societal events also continue to shape the military justice system. Increased access to information in today's society will likely cause the impact of these types of occurrences to persist. The Tailhook investigation and the military's policy on homosexuality provide ample evidence of this phenomena. One can, therefore, expect that military justice will change at an even more rapid pace in the future.

STUDY QUESTIONS

1. How did military justice for naval forces develop? How was its evolution different from the development of military law for land forces?

2. What impact did the British have on the United States military legal system? Is the influence of the English still present today?

3. How did the United States Army develop its legal system? How did its development differ from the Navy's?

4. What effect have significant events, i.e., wars, disasters, scandals, etc., had on military law in the United States? Do such incidents still result in changes in military jurisprudence?

5. Is there a trend in United States military law towards "civilianization." If yes, what are the positive and negative aspects of such an inclination?

6. What caused Congress to enact the UCMJ? Has the code been significantly modified since it was adopted?

7. Does either principle, justice or discipline, dominate American military justice today? Does the UCMJ properly balance the two concepts?

CHAPTER II

FUNDAMENTALS OF MILITARY JUSTICE

Military law is a vital element in maintaining a high state of morale and discipline. Members of the armed forces must have a clear understanding of the standards of conduct to which they must conform, and they must also have confidence that the system of justice will operate in a fair and just manner.

Senator Sam Nunn, *The Fundamental Principles of the Supreme Court's Jurisprudence in Military Cases*, 29 Wake Forest Law Review 557 (1994)

INTRODUCTION

Military justice continues to move towards civilian criminal law. Given this trend, it is not surprising that many of the fundamental legal principles of civilian criminal jurisprudence apply to the military justice system as well. Thus, to understand criminal law in the military, it is necessary to grasp certain basic legal concepts. Some of these concepts are discussed below. It is also important to understand the sources that make up military laws, rules and regulations. These sources are for the most part unique to the military. They are discussed below as well. To facilitate the reader's understanding of the military justice system, commonly used military legal terms and phrases and their abbreviations and acronyms are contained in Figure 2-A at the end of this chapter.

Unlike their civilian counterparts, military personnel, particularly officers, are an integral part of the justice system. For instance, officers and enlisted personnel routinely serve in a police function as members of security forces and as investigators of minor criminal offenses. Officers also act as legal advisors, making them responsible for all aspects of military law, including consulting with the commanding officer on legal matters affecting the command. Both enlisted members and officers sit as members of courts-martial as well.

SOURCES OF MILITARY LAW

As discussed in Chapter I, military justice for naval forces originated from custom and practice. Today the sources of military law are firmly established, and are modified not by practice, but by changes to the sources themselves. That is not to say, however, that developments in the military and in society do not eventually cause changes in military justice practice. To the contrary, the military legal system is continually modified in response to developments in both areas. Also, note that international law is still made and altered by accepted customs and practice. *See* Appendix 3, *The Commander's Handbook on the Law of Naval Operations* (NWP 9).

UNITED STATES CONSTITUTION

Article I, Section 8, of the United States Constitution states: "Congress shall have the power . . . to make rules for the government and regulation of the land and naval forces." Article II, Section 2, appoints the President as the "Commander-in-Chief of the Army and Navy of the United States." Thus, Congress enacts the laws governing the military, while the executive branch promulgates administrative regulations pertaining to the armed forces. The Supreme Court in *Ex Parte Milligan*, 71 U.S. 2 (1866) explained this relationship.

> The power to make the necessary laws is in Congress; the power to execute in the President. Both powers imply many subordinate and auxiliary powers. Each includes all authorities essential to its due exercise. But neither can the President, in war more than in peace, intrude upon the proper authority of Congress, nor Congress upon the proper authority of the President. Both are servants of the people, whose will is expressed in the fundamental law. Congress cannot direct the conduct of campaigns, nor can the President, or any commander under him, without the sanction of Congress, institute tribunals for the trial and punishment of offenses. . . .

Chief Justice of the Supreme Court John Marshall, himself once an officer on General Washington's staff, declared in *Marbury v. Madison*, 1 Cranch 137 (1803), that the judiciary has the authority to strike down laws that are repugnant to the Constitution. Thus, all laws and regulations affecting the military must be in line with the Constitution. Federal and military courts continually construe the military's laws and regulations to assess the constitutionality of such provisions. *See* Appendix 1 for the full text of the Constitution.

THE UNIFORM CODE OF MILITARY JUSTICE (UCMJ)

As discussed in Chapter I, the UCMJ is applicable to all service personnel "in all places." Also known as the "code," the UCMJ is divided into twelve subchapters, addressing every aspect of military justice, including: jurisdiction; investigations; apprehension and restraint; courts-martial; nonjudicial punishment; sentences; and appeals. The UCMJ also sets forth all military crimes in what are known as the punitive articles.

MANUAL FOR COURTS-MARTIAL (MCM)

Congress in enacting the UCMJ recognized that it could not write a rule for every aspect of military justice. Consequently, it delegated to the President the following authority:

> Article 36. President May Prescribe Rules. (a) The procedure including modes of proof, in cases before courts-martial, courts of inquiry, military commissions, and other military tribunals may be prescribed by the President by regulations which shall, so far as he considers practicable, apply the principles of law and the rules of evidence generally recognized in the trial of criminal cases in the United States district courts, but which may not be contrary to or inconsistent with the chapter.

Thus, in delegating significant authority to the executive branch to establish the rules and the procedures before courts-martial, Congress required that the President follow the federal rules of evidence and procedure except where inconsistent with the UCMJ.

The President responded to the authority vested in him by Congress by the promulgating Manual for Courts-Martial (MCM). The MCM is the basic directive implementing the UCMJ, and it is available on all ships and stations in the naval service. Every officer has a responsibility to have a working knowledge of the MCM because it provides regulations which explain, amplify and implement the UCMJ. For example, the MCM explains the elements to military offenses and contains the Military Rules of Evidence (MRE), the Rules for Courts-Martial (RCM), and provides the maximum punishments for each offense under the UCMJ. *See* Appendix 2 for the MCM Maximum Punishment Chart. The MCM is an executive order signed by the President and is applicable to all military branches. The most recent version of the MCM became effective in 1995.

MANUAL OF THE JUDGE ADVOCATE GENERAL

There are certain matters peculiar to the individual services that the MCM cannot adequately address. Consequently, the UCMJ and MCM permit the "Secretary concerned" to prescribe regulations in certain areas. For example, the

Secretary of the Navy, under Article 23 of the UCMJ, has the authority to designate other commanding officers or officers in charge who may convene a special court-martial, in addition to those discussed in Article 23 of the UCMJ. Another example of this delegated authority is the Manual of the Judge Advocate General (the JAG Manual), a directive of the Department of the Navy, signed by the Judge Advocate General of the Navy and approved by the Secretary of the Navy. The JAG Manual, applicable only to the Navy and Marine Corps, contains many of the regulations peculiar to naval military justice, and is, therefore, a significant source of military law in the naval services. It contains important regulations concerning administrative matters, such as claims, legal assistance, and nonjudicial punishment. This resource is particularly important for officers because it provides the rules and guidelines for conducting administrative investigations (known as JAG Manual investigations).

SERVICE REGULATIONS

Numerous other regulations and orders are promulgated by commanders, ranging from the Secretary of the Navy to commanding officers of Navy and Marine Corps units. Chapter V spends considerable time addressing the legal status of these regulations.

COURT DECISIONS

Opinions from courts that hear cases involving members of the armed forces also provide a source of military law. The military has criminal courts (trial and appellate) which strictly deal with military justice matters. A court-martial is the military equivalent of a civilian criminal trial court. A Court of Criminal Appeals for each branch of the service is the first level of appeal from special and general courts-martial (these courts were known as Courts of Military Review until 1994). Thus, the Navy and Marine Corps has the Navy-Marine Corps Court of Criminal Appeals. Above the Court of Criminal Appeals for each service is the Court of Appeals for the Armed Forces which hears cases from all branches (until 1994, the Court of Military Appeals). An appeal from this forum is to the highest appellate court in the land, the United States Supreme Court. Other federal courts also consider military law issues. Federal courts consider and rule, for example, on such issues as the military's policy on homosexuality, treatment of refugees, women in combat and separation of personnel. Because they continually interpret and change military law, decisions by these courts provide an important source of military law. *See* Chapter III for a full discussion of military courts.

Throughout the book, the reader will note that cases are described as follows: *United States v. Cotten*, 10 M.J. 260 (C.M.A. 1981). This means that the case of United States versus Cotten may be found on page 260 of Volume 10 of the *Military Justice Reporter*. The parenthetical information tells us that the Court of

Military Appeals (now the Court of Appeals for the Armed Forces) decided the case in 1981.

FUNDAMENTALS OF CRIMINAL LAW

MENS REA

United States v. Thomas O. Bastian, Junior, Private U.S. Marine Corps
United States Navy Court of Military Review
47 C.M.R. 203
March 26, 1973

EVANS, Judge

Appellant, contrary to his pleas, was convicted inter alia of wrongful appropriation of a truck belonging to his friend, Lance Corporal Haney [among other things], in violation of Article 121, UCMJ.

Appellant asserts the evidence is insufficient to establish his criminal intent with respect to the wrongfulness of the taking. Lance Corporal Haney testified that on the night in question, he went on liberty with appellant using Haney's truck for transportation. After visiting several bars, Haney decided to stay ashore for some time and gave appellant 200 yen for transportation back to the base. Since he knew appellant did not have a driver's license, he never had authorized him to drive the truck on a public street. Appellant was a friend of the owner and had on prior occasions assisted in repairing the vehicle. At those times, appellant was permitted to drive the truck only in a parking lot. Appellant testified that after visiting several bars with Haney, he decided to return to the base alone, since Haney intended to visit another bar. After they had separated, appellant became concerned about Haney's welfare and com-

menced to look for him on foot. Later he came to the area where the truck was parked. He started the vehicle and drove it for about an hour along the street, trying to locate the owner. Subsequently he hit a pole while avoiding another vehicle. Appellant maintains since he took the vehicle for the purpose of assisting its owner, the taking was not wrongful within the meaning of Article 121, UCMJ. As we view appellant's testimony, his alleged pure motive, does not obviate the fact the taking was wrongful, i.e., his self-justification, a matter of motive constitutes no defense to wrongful appropriation. . . . As previously noted, the evidence of record shows beyond a reasonable doubt the relationship between appellant and Haney did not extend to appellant's use of the vehicle. While we are unable to give any specific definition of mens rea as it applies to wrongful appropriation . . . it is a tincture of moral turpitude and a violation of the existing social relationship between the putative borrower and property owner. We do not delve into the philosophic basis of the crime of wrongful appropriation, suffice to say that the evil sought to be avoided is the nonconsensual, socially aberrant, temporary loss of one's property.

Typically, for a time the victim does not know what happened to his property. If the appropriator's unsolicited acts are such that they result in increasing the probability the owner cannot timely find his property, such acts establish circumstantial evidence of the necessary mens rea. [footnote omitted]. In this case, appellant's motive was pure only to the extent he desired to help the owner as opposed to protecting the truck. Since he was not a licensed driver, the probability of the owner recovering the property was reduced. Indeed, there was evidence one week expired before the owner finally found his damaged property in a Navy salvage yard. This is the result Article 121, UCMJ aims to avoid. Additionally, appellant does not assert he was laboring under the mistaken belief he was authorized to drive the vehicle; or he took it with an innocent purpose to protect it for the benefit of the owner. [citation omitted]. In short, appellant's possession of the truck was wrong. We consider the evidence clearly shows appellant had at the time of the wrongful taking the necessary mens rea or criminal state of mind to commit the offense of wrongful appropriation.

Accordingly, the findings of guilty and the sentence as approved below are affirmed.

Black's Law Dictionary 1136 (5th ed. 1979) describes *mens rea* as "[a] guilty mind; a guilty or wrongful purpose; a criminal intent." Does the court's analysis of *mens rea* comport with the description in *Black's Law Dictionary*? Based upon *Bastian*, is there any difference between the definition of *mens rea* in the civilian and military criminal courts? Is evidence of *mens rea* on the part of the accused necessary at nonjudicial punishment? At administrative separation hearings?

SPECIFIC INTENT

United States, Appellee, v. James J. Greene, Aviation Structural Mechanic (Hydraulic) Third Class, U.S. Navy, United States Court of Military Appeals
20 U.S.C.M.A. 297; 43 C.M.R. 137
January 29, 1971

FERGUSON, Judge

The accused was convicted by general court-martial, convened at Luzon, Republic of the Philippines, of one specification each of willful damage to military property of the United States by burning and simple arson, in violation of Articles 108 and 126, Uniform Code of Military Justice. . . . [citation omitted]. The res of the two specifications was the same—an SP-2H aircraft, located at the Naval Air Station, Whidbey Island, Washington. . . . The accused's sentence, as his petition reaches this Court, extends to a bad conduct discharge, confinement at hard labor for two years, forfeiture of $109.00 per month for a like period, and reduction to the grade of E-1. We granted review on the following questions:

1. Whether the law officer erred to the prejudice of the accused by failing to instruct the court-martial on the effect of intoxication upon the element of willfulness

and maliciousness involved in simple arson.

. . . .

Government counsel concede that voluntary intoxication not amounting to legal insanity may constitute a defense to a crime requiring a specific intent. . . . If raised by the evidence, the issue of voluntary intoxication on the specific intent element of the offense would be one to be decided by the trier of fact. *United States v. Lewis*, 14 U.S.C.M.A. 79, 33 C.M.R. 291 (1963). As stated in their brief, "the sole issue before this Honorable Court in this case is whether simple arson, as defined by the Code, is a specific intent offense by virtue of the requirement that the burning be 'willful and malicious.'" Since simple arson requires only a general criminal intent, they argue, there was no need for the law officer to instruct on the effect thereon of the accused's intoxication.

Defense counsel assert, in their brief, that "'willfully and maliciously' as used in Article 126(b) means intentionally setting a fire or burning with the specific purpose or premeditation to burn the property of another, without just cause or excuse. . . . Thus it is contended that simple arson requires the specific intent to burn."

Article 126(b), Code, *supra*, defines simple arson as follows:

"(b) Any person subject to this chapter who willfully and maliciously burns or sets fire to the property of another, except as provided in subsection (a) [aggravated arson], is guilty of simple arson and shall be punished as a court-martial may direct."

. . . .

In *United States v. Krosky*, 418 F.2d 65, 67 (CA 6th Cir.) (1969), the court defined "willfully" as follows:

"An act is done 'willfully' if done voluntarily and purposely with the specific intent to do that which the law forbids; that is to say, with bad purpose either to disobey or to disregard the law. Willfulness includes an evil motive. *James v. United States*, 366 U.S. 213, 81 S. Ct. 1052, 6 L. Ed. 2d 246 (1961)."

Of particular importance to the question before us is our holding in *United States v. Groves*, 2 U.S.C.M.A. 541, 10 C.M.R. 39 (1953). Groves was charged, among other offenses, with "willfully damaging military property" under Article 108, Code, *supra*. The record was replete with evidence that Groves was deeply intoxicated at the time of the commission of the charged offense. Finding that specific intent was an element of the offense of willful damage to military property, we reversed his conviction for that offense because the law officer gave no instruction to the court as to the possible legal effect of intoxication upon Groves' ability to entertain a specific intent.

This accused, too, was charged with "willfully damaging, by setting fire to, an SP-2H aircraft . . . military property of the United States," in violation of Article 108, Code, *supra*. . . .

We hold, therefore, that intoxication having been raised by the evidence, it was error, prejudicial to the substantial rights of the accused, for the law officer to fail to instruct on the affirmative defense of intoxication. *United States v. Groves, supra*; *United States v. Meador,* 18 U.S.C.M.A. 91, 39 C.M.R. 91 (1969).

. . . .

The decision of the Court of Military Review is reversed.

Black's Law Dictionary defines specific intent as the "purpose to use particular means to effect certain results." In addition to possessing *mens rea*, an accused must have a specific intent for certain offenses. What was the specific intent element in *Greene*? Why was the court concerned with the issue of whether arson is a specific intent offense?

STANDARD OF PROOF

United States, Appellee, v. Russell Owen Cotten, Electrician's Mate Fireman, U.S. Navy, Appellant
United States Court of Military Appeals
10 M.J. 260
February 9, 1981

FLETCHER, Judge

The appellant was tried before a special court-martial convened by Commanding Officer, U.S. Naval Station, Norfolk, Virginia, on 13 specifications of sale, transfer and possession of both marihuana and lysergic acid diethylamide, in contravention of Article 92, Uniform Code of Military Justice, 10 U.S.C. @ 892. Appellant was tried by a court consisting of members and, contrary to his pleas, on May 31, 1979, was convicted of the Charge and all specifications. Appellant was sentenced to be reduced to pay grade E-1, confined at hard labor for 3 months, and discharged from the service with a bad-conduct discharge. On July 18, 1979, the convening authority approved the sentence subject to a suspension of all confinement in excess of 85 days. The supervisory authority, on August 15, 1979, also approved the sentence with the same modification regarding confinement. The United States Navy Court of Military Review affirmed the findings and sentence, and this Court, on June 11, 1980, granted the petition for review. (9 M.J. 139).

As part of his general instructions to the court-martial members trying appellant [footnote omitted], the military judge quoted [footnote omitted] the following language:

> [B]y reasonable doubt, it is intended not a fanciful and ingenious doubt or conjecture but substantial, honest, conscientious doubt suggested by the material evidence, or lack of it, in the case. It is an honest, substantial misgiving generated by insufficiency of proof of guilt.

This followed a prior reference in the military judge's preliminary instructions that reasonable doubt was defined as "substantial" doubt. [footnote omitted]. After the general instructions, the defense counsel entered a strong objection to this equation of "reasonable doubt" with so-called "substantial doubt." As an alternative, the defense counsel proffered an instruction [citation omitted] which had no reference to "substantial doubt." The defense counsel's objection was overruled and his offered instruction rejected. We conclude this equation was improper and prejudicial to the appellant.

Very early in the history of this Court, we ruled that absent a request, a law officer had no duty to define "reasonable doubt." [citation omitted]. [footnote omitted] All that the Code and Manual required was that he inform the court members that the guilt of the accused must be "established . . . beyond reasonable doubt" and that any "reasonable doubt . . . must be resolved in favor of the accused." "[B]eyond reasonable doubt" is the constitutionally required standard. As such, a proper instruction on this issue "is indispensable, for it 'impresses on the trier of fact the necessity of reaching a subjective state of certitude of the facts in issue,'" [citations omitted], and is thus "a prime instrument for reducing the risk of convictions resting on factual error." [citation omitted]. [footnote omitted]. We do not imply that "some definition of 'reasonable doubt' is [not] desirable" or required in certain cases. [citation omitted]. Failure to explain reasonable doubt may constitute error where the request is appropriately made at trial. *United States v. Crumb*, 10 M.J. 520 (A.C.M.R. 1980). This instructional responsibility, however, calls for the finest exercise of the trial judge's craft and mere recourse to a thesaurus may result in unnecessary error.

We have recently made clear in *United States v. Salley*, 9 M.J. 189 (C.M.A. 1980), that the equation of "reasonable doubt" with "substantial doubt" is in disfavor with appellate courts generally [footnote omitted] and that any such reference to this equation should be avoided in military tribunals.

. . . .

This was a highly contested drug case with controverted testimony from two government witnesses, and the appellant completely denied the charge on which he was ultimately convicted. In this case, a proper jury understanding of "reasonable doubt" was essential. Here, however, the military judge made an absolute equation of "substantial doubt" with "reasonable doubt." This required the jury to make its decision based on a lesser evidentiary standard. *United States v. Atkins*, 487 F.2d 257, 260 (8th Cir. 1973). Furthermore, the trial counsel urged the members to believe that the evidence in contest was "clear and convincing." Evaluating such in the factual light of this case, we do not believe these errors are harmless.

. . . .

In light of the foregoing as well as our examination of the instructions issued in this case and the evidence in the entire record, we do not believe the error was harmless. The decision of the United States Navy Court of Military Review is reversed. The findings and sentence are set aside. The record of trial is returned to the Judge Advocate General of the Navy. A rehearing may be ordered.

This text discusses standards of proof throughout. The "proof beyond a reasonable doubt" standard is not required in all proceedings in the military. What is the standard of proof at nonjudicial punishment? At administrative separation hearings? *See* Chapter IV concerning the standard of proof in administrative proceedings.

DIRECT AND CIRCUMSTANTIAL EVIDENCE

United States, Appellee, v. Daniel Kirby, Private, U.S. Army, Appellant
United States Court of Military Appeals
16 U.S.C.M.A. 517; 37 C.M.R. 137
February 17, 1967

OPINION: Kilday, Judge

Appellant was arraigned before a general court-martial convened at Fort Campbell, Kentucky, charged with desertion, in violation of Uniform Code of Military Justice, Article 85, 10 USC @ 885. He pleaded not guilty but was found guilty as charged. He was sentenced to a dishonorable discharge, total forfeitures, confinement at hard labor for three years, and reduction to the lowest enlisted grade. The convening authority approved the sentence. A board of review in the office of the Judge Advocate General of the Army affirmed both the finding of guilty and the sentence.

. . . .

The evidence of record shows petitioner was absent without authority from Fort Jackson, South Carolina, for the period June 14 to December 3, 1965. On this latter date, he was apprehended by a Tennessee Highway Patrol comprised of a State officer and the deputy sheriff of Morgan County, Tennessee. When asked for identification, Kirby turned over Social Security and Selective Service registration cards, both bearing the name of Allen Ray Diamond. He carried no other identification. Later, at trial, these documents were admitted into evidence on the issue of specific intent.

It further appears that on September 20, 1965, during the unauthorized absence, accused had registered for the draft in Casper, Wyoming, using the name of Diamond. In so doing, he listed his next of kin as Mrs. Marvin Watson, a sister, of Thomaston, Georgia. In keeping with Selective Service practices, a draft card was mailed to appellant's Casper, Wyoming, address. It was returned marked "Moved, left no address." Thereafter, the draft board received a change of address, ostensibly from the accused, giving his address as care of Gary D. Masters, General Delivery, Greensburg, Kansas. The draft registration card mailed to this second address was never returned.

The evidence further reflects that while still in Casper, accused was given dental treatment on September 27, 1965, by a local oral surgeon. Here again, he used the name of Allen Ray Diamond.

In a voluntary statement given to the Commander of the Casual Detachment, Fort Campbell, accused acknowledged using the name of Diamond, explaining that he had secured a wallet containing this identification and had used it to obtain employment, being without any other means of identification. In Greensburg, Kansas, he had worked for a construction firm using this alias and then for a rancher under his true name. Accused further stated that he gave the name of Diamond to the apprehending officers so he could get home to see his family.

In testifying in his own behalf, accused admitted using the Social Security and draft registration cards but denied forwarding a change of address notice to the draft board. According to the accused, these items were given him by his traveling companions. He had not signed any of these cards. On the other hand, he did acknowledge having a sister in Thomaston, Georgia, whose married name was Watson. Finally, Kirby asserted he was just "goofing off" with the apprehending officers when he used the false name. According to him, his true identity was known to these officers.

. . . .

The single issue remaining is: Whether it was sufficient to instruct that: "A reasonable doubt may arise from the insufficiency of circumstantial evidence. . . ."

. . . .

[D]efense errs in saying that a stronger standard of proof is required in a circumstantial evidence case as compared with a direct evidence case. We rejected this contention in *United States v. Mason*, 8 U.S.C.M.A. 329, 24 C.M.R. 139, relying upon *Holland v. United States*, 348 U.S. 121, 99 L ed 150, 75 S Ct 127 (1954), rehearing denied January 31, 1955. Under the circumstances of this case, where the instruction as a whole correctly conveys the concept of "reasonable doubt to the jury," as it does here, we can ask for nothing more. Accordingly, we find no error.

Kirby is a case involving proof of desertion. What other types of circumstantial evidence might assist in proving the intent to desert? What direct evidence would be helpful? As you might guess, direct evidence of an intent to remain away permanently is rare. *See* Chapter V for a discussion of desertion as a military crime.

Direct evidence is commonly defined as "that means of proof which tends to show the existence of a fact in question, without the intervention of the proof of any other fact. . . ." Circumstantial evidence is described as facts that "gives rise to inferences" of other facts. According to the above cases, which type of evidence is more reliable? Which type of evidence are the following: urinalysis results; an eyewitness account; DNA test results; a bloody knife; and a paternity test result? Based on *Kirby,* does categorizing direct and circumstantial evidence make any difference?

STUDY QUESTIONS

1. What are the primary sources of military law?

2. Which of the following sources of military law is **ONLY** applicable to Navy and Marine Corps personnel?

    a. The Manual for Courts-Martial

    b. The JAG Manual

    c. The Uniform Code of Military Justice

    d. The Military Rules of Evidence

    e. Decisions by the Court of Military Appeals

3. Who is the UCMJ applicable to and where? Which government body enacted the UCMJ?

4. Who promulgates the MCM? What does it contain? Who signs and who approves the JAG Manual? What does it contain?

5. Define *mens rea*. What is the difference between *mens rea* and specific intent?

6. What is a standard of proof? What does "proof beyond a reasonable doubt" mean? Where is this standard applicable?

7. Explain the difference between direct and circumstantial evidence. Which type, if either, is a better type of evidence?

FIGURE 2-A

MILITARY JUSTICE TERMS

ACC	Accused
ACMR	Army Court of Military Review
AFCMR	Air Force Court of Military Review
BCD	Bad Conduct Discharge
B&W	Bread and Water
CA	Convening Authority
CAAF	Court of Appeals for the Armed Forces
CCA	Court of Criminal Appeals
CC or CCU	Correctional Custody Unit
CGCMR	Coast Guard Court of Military Review
CHL	Confinement at Hard Labor
CHNAVPERS	Chief of Naval Personnel
CMC	Commandant, USMC
CMO	Court-Martial Order
CMR	Court of Military Review
CNO	Chief of Naval Operations
CO	Commanding Officer or Convening Order
CMA or COMA	Court of Military Appeals
CPO	Chief Petty Officer
C-M	Court-Martial
CWO	Chief Warrant Officer
DC	Defense Counsel
DD	Dishonorable Discharge
DIMRATS	Diminished Rations
DO	Division Officer
ED	Extra Duty
EMI	Extra Military Instruction
E&M	Extenuation and Mitigation
FORF,FF	Forfeiture of Pay
GCM	General Court-Martial
G	Guilty
HL w/o C	Hard Labor without Confinement
INST	Instruction
IMC	Individual Military Counsel
JAG	Judge Advocate General of the Navy
JAGC	Judge Advocate General's Corps
JAGMAN	Manual of the Judge Advocate General
LIO	Lesser Included Offense

LN	Legalman
LOD	Line of Duty
MAA	Master-At-Arms
MCM	Manual for Courts-Martial
MJ	Military Judge
MJR	Military Justice Reports
MAST	Captain's Mast
N/A	Not Applicable
MILPERSMAN	Naval Military Personnel Manual
NAVREGS	Navy Regulations
NMCMR	Navy-Marine Corps Court of Military Review
NCO	Non-Commissioned Officer
NG	Not Guilty
NCIS	Naval Criminal Investigative Service
NLSO	Naval Legal Service Office
NLSO DET	Naval Legal Service Office Detachment
NJP	Nonjudicial Punishment
OINC, OIC	Officer-in-Charge
OTH	Other than Honorable Discharge
PIO	Preliminary Inquiry Officer
PO	Petty Officer
PTA	Pretrial Agreement
RIR	Reduction in Rate
REST	Restriction
RO	Reviewing Officer
PTIO	UCMJ, Pre-trial Investigating Officer
SA	Supervisory Authority
SCM	Summary Court-Martial
SECNAV	Secretary of the Navy
SJA	Staff Judge Advocate
SOL	Statue of Limitations
SOFA	Status of Forces Agreement
SP	Shore Patrol
SPCM	Special Court-Martial
SPEC	Specification
SR/SRB	Service Record Book
TAD	Temporary Additional Duty
TC	Trial Counsel
UA	Unauthorized Absence
UCMJ	Uniform Code of Military Justice
UPB	Unit Punishment Book
US	United States Code
USCA	United States Code Annotated
VA	Veteran's Administration
XO	Executive Officer

CHAPTER III

COURTS-MARTIAL

[I]t is the primary business of armies and navies to fight or be ready to fight wars should the occasion arise. But trial of soldiers to maintain discipline is merely incidental to an army's primary fighting function. To the extent that those responsible for performance of this primary function are diverted from it by the necessity of trying cases, the basic fighting purpose of armies is not served. . . . [M]ilitary tribunals have not been and probably never can be constituted in such way that they can have the same kind of qualifications that the Constitution has deemed essential to fair trials of civilians in federal courts.

Toth v. Quarles, 350 U.S. 11, 17 (1955)

INTRODUCTION

The above quotation from the United States Supreme Court highlights the underlying tension in the military courts-martial system between the mission of the military and due process protections of service members. Unquestionably, the military's war fighting purpose affects the nature of courts-martial, resulting in trial and appellate courts that are very different than their civilian counterparts. Competing with the fundamental mission of the military is the requirement that courts-martial provide service members with rights and protections in line with the Constitution. The result of this dichotomy is a judicial system that must juggle the oftentimes divergent interests of military readiness and procedural fairness to service members.

NATURE AND TYPES OF COURTS-MARTIAL

The following case describes the organization of trial and appellate courts in the military. It also considers the constitutionality of the military's court system.

Eric J. Weiss, Petitioner, v. United States
Supreme Court of the United States
114 S. Ct. 752
January 19, 1994

* Together with *Hernandez v. United States*,
also on certiorari to the same court.

OPINION: Chief Justice Rehnquist

We must decide in these cases whether the current method of appointing military judges violates the Appointments Clause of the Constitution, and whether the lack of a fixed term of office for military judges violates the Fifth Amendment's Due Process Clause. We conclude that neither constitutional provision is violated.

Petitioner Weiss, a United States Marine, pleaded guilty at a special court-martial to one count of larceny, in violation of Article 121 of the Uniform Code of Military Justice (UCMJ or Code), 10 U.S.C. @ 921. He was sentenced to three months of confinement, partial forfeiture of pay, and a bad-conduct discharge. Petitioner Hernandez, also a Marine, pleaded guilty to the possession, importation, and distribution of cocaine, in violation of Article 112a, UCMJ, 10 U.S.C. @ 912a, and conspiracy, in violation of Article 81, UCMJ, 10 U.S.C. @ 881. He was sentenced to 25 years of confinement, forfeiture of all pay, a reduction in rank, and a dishonorable discharge. The convening officer reduced Hernandez's sentence to 20 years of confinement.

The Navy-Marine Corps Court of Military Review, in separate appeals, affirmed petitioners' convictions. The Court of Military Appeals granted plenary review in petitioner Weiss' case to address his contention that the judges in his case had no authority to convict him because their appointments violated the Appointments Clause, and their lack of a fixed term of office violated the Due Process Clause. Relying on its recent decision in *United States v. Graf*, in which the Court unanimously held that due process does not require military judges to have a fixed term of office, the Court rejected Weiss' due process argument. In a splintered decision, the Court also rejected petitioner's Appointments Clause challenge.

Two of the five judges concluded that the initial appointment of military trial and appellate judges as commissioned officers is sufficient to satisfy the Appointments Clause (plurality opinion). A separate appointment before taking on the duties of a military judge is unnecessary, according to the plurality, in part because the duties of a judge in the military justice system are germane to the duties that military officers already discharge. *Ibid.* One judge concurred in the result only, concluding that the Appointments Clause does not apply to the military. The other two judges dissented separately. Both stressed the significant changes brought about by the Military Justice Act of 1968, particularly the duties added to the newly created office of military judge, and both concluded that the duties of a military judge are sufficiently distinct from the other duties performed by military officers to require a second appointment. [citations omitted].

The Court of Military Appeals accordingly affirmed petitioner Weiss' conviction. Based on its decision in *Weiss*, the Court, in an unpublished opinion, also affirmed petitioner Hernandez's conviction. Weiss and Hernandez then jointly petitioned for our review, and we granted certiorari. [citation omitted].

It will help in understanding the issues involved to review briefly the contours of the military justice system and the role of military judges within that system. Pursuant to Article I of the Constitution, Congress has established three tiers of military courts. At the trial level are the courts-martial, of which there are three types: summary, special, and general. The summary court-martial adjudicates only minor offenses, has jurisdiction only over service members, and can be conducted only with their consent. It is presided over by a single commissioned officer who can impose up to one month of confinement and other relatively modest punishments. Arts. 16(3), 20, UCMJ, 10 U.S.C. @@ 816(3), 820. The special court-martial usually consists of a military judge and three court-martial members,[1] although the Code allows the members to sit without a judge,

or the accused to elect to be tried by the judge alone. Art. 16(2), UCMJ, 10 U.S.C. @ 816(2). A special court-martial has jurisdiction over most offenses under the UCMJ, but it may impose punishment no greater than six months of confinement, three months of hard labor without confinement, a bad conduct discharge, partial and temporary forfeiture of pay, and a reduction in rank. Art. 19, UCMJ, 10 U.S.C. @ 819. The general court-martial consists of either a military judge and at least five members, or the judge alone if the defendant so requests. Art. 16(1), UCMJ, 10 U.S.C. @ 816(1). A general court-martial has jurisdiction over all offenses under the UCMJ and may impose any lawful sentence, including death. Art. 18, UCMJ, 10 U.S.C. @ 818.

The military judge, a position that has officially existed only since passage of the Military Justice Act of 1968, acts as presiding officer at a special or general court-martial. The judge rules on all legal questions, and instructs court-martial members regarding the law and procedures to be followed. Art. 51, UCMJ, 10 U.S.C. @ 851. The members decide guilt or innocence and impose sentence unless, of course, the trial is before the judge alone. *Ibid.* No sentence imposed becomes final until it is approved by the officer who convened the court-martial. Art. 60, UCMJ, 10 U.S.C. @ 860.

Military trial judges must be commissioned officers of the armed forces[2] and members of the bar of a federal court or a State's highest court. Art. 26, UCMJ, 10 U.S.C. @ 826. The judges are selected and certified as qualified by the Judge Advocate General of their branch of the armed

---

[1]Court-martial members may be officers or enlisted personnel, depending on the military status of the defendant; the members' responsibilities are analogous to, but somewhat greater than, those of civilian jurors. *See* Art. 25, UCMJ, 10 U.S.C. @ 825.

[2]All commissioned officers are appointed by the President, with the advice and consent of the Senate.

forces.[3] They do not serve for fixed terms and may perform judicial duties only when assigned to do so by the appropriate Judge Advocate General. While serving as judges, officers may also, with the approval of the Judge Advocate General, perform other tasks unrelated to their judicial duties. *Ibid*. There are approximately 74 judges currently certified to preside at general and special courts-martial. An additional 25 are certified to preside only over special courts-martial. [citation omitted].

At the next tier are the four Courts of Military Review, one each for the Army, Air Force, Coast Guard, and Navy-Marine Corps. These courts, which usually sit in three-judge panels, review all cases in which the sentence imposed exceeds one year of confinement, involves the dismissal of a commissioned officer, or involves the punitive discharge of an enlisted service member. Art. 66, UCMJ, 10 U.S.C. @ 866. The courts may review de novo both factual and legal findings, and they may overturn convictions and sentences. *Ibid*.

Appellate judges may be commissioned officers or civilians, but each must be a member of a bar of a Federal court or of a State's highest court. *Ibid*. The judges are selected and assigned to serve by the appropriate Judge Advocate General. *Ibid*. Like military trial judges, appellate judges do not serve for a fixed term. There are presently 31 appellate military judges.

I

The Appointments Clause of Article II of the Constitution reads as follows:

"[The President] shall nominate, and by and with the Advice and Consent of the Senate, shall appoint Ambassadors, other public Minsters and Consuls, Judges of the supreme Court, and all other Officers of the United States, whose Appointments are not herein otherwise provided for, and which shall be established by Law: but the Congress may by Law vest the Appointment of such inferior Officers, as they think proper, in the President alone, in the Courts of Law, or in the Heads of Departments."

We begin our analysis on common ground. The parties do not dispute that military judges, because of the authority and responsibilities they possess, act as "officers" of the United States. *See Freytag v. Commissioner*, 501 U.S. (1991) (concluding special trial judges of Tax Court are officers); *Buckley v. Valeo*, 424 U.S. 1, 126 (1976) ("Any appointee exercising significant authority pursuant to the laws of the United States is an 'Officer of the United States,' and must, therefore, be appointed in the manner prescribed by [the Appointments Clause]"). The parties are also in agreement, and rightly so, that the Appointments Clause applies to military officers. As we said in Buckley, "all officers of the United States are to be appointed in accordance with the Clause. . . . No class or type of officer is excluded because of its special functions." *Id*., at 132.

It follows that those serving as military judges must be appointed pursuant to the Appointments Clause. All of the military judges involved in these cases, however, were already commissioned officers when they were assigned to serve as judges, [footnote omitted] and thus they had already been appointed by the President with the advice and consent of the Senate. [footnote omitted]. The question we must answer, therefore, is whether these officers needed another appointment pursuant to the Appointments Clause before assuming

---

[3]The Judge Advocate General for each service is the principal legal officer for that service. [citations omitted].

their judicial duties. Petitioners contend that the position of military judge is so different from other positions to which an officer may be assigned that either Congress has, by implication, required a second appointment, or the Appointments Clause, by constitutional command, requires one. We reject both of these arguments.

Petitioners' argument that Congress by implication has required a separate appointment is based in part on the fact that military judges must possess certain qualifications, including membership in a state or federal bar. But such special qualifications in themselves do not, we believe, indicate a congressional intent to create a separate office. Special qualifications are needed to perform a host of military duties; yet no one could seriously contend that the positions of military lawyer or pilot, for example, are distinct offices because officers performing those duties must possess additional qualifications.

. . . .

Congress' treatment of military judges is thus quite different from its treatment of those offices, such as Chairman of the Joint Chiefs of Staff, for which it wished to require a second appointment before already-commissioned officers could occupy them. This difference negates any permissible inference that Congress intended that military judges should receive a second appointment, but in a fit of absentmindedness forgot to say so.

Petitioners' alternative contention is that even if Congress did not intend to require a separate appointment for a military judge, the Appointments Clause requires such an appointment by its own force. They urge upon us in support of this contention our decisions in *Buckley, supra, Freytag, supra,* and *Morrison v. Olson,* 487 U.S. 654 (1988). These decisions undoubtedly establish the analytical frame-

work upon which to base the conclusion that a military judge is an "officer of the United States"—a proposition to which both parties agree. But the decisions simply do not speak to the issue of whether, and when, the Appointments Clause may require a second appointment.

. . . .

By enacting the Uniform Code of Military Justice in 1950, and through subsequent statutory changes, Congress has gradually changed the system of military justice so that it has come to more closely resemble the civilian system. But the military in important respects remains a "specialized society separate from civilian society," *Parker v. Levy,* 417 U.S. 733, 743 (1974). Although military judges obviously perform certain unique and important functions, all military officers, consistent with a long tradition, play a role in the operation of the military justice system.

Commissioned officers, for example, have the power and duty to "quell quarrels, frays, and disorders among persons subject to [the UCMJ] and to apprehend persons subject to [the UCMJ] who take part therein." Art. 7(c), UCMJ, 10 U.S.C. @ 807(c). Commanding officers are authorized to impose "non-judicial punishment" which includes restricting a service member's movement for up to 30 days, suspending the member from duty, forfeiting a week's pay, and imposing extra duties for up to two consecutive weeks. Art. 15, UCMJ, 10 U.S.C. @ 815. A commissioned officer also may serve as a court-martial member. When the court-martial is held without a judge, as it can be in both summary and special courts-martial, the members conducting the proceeding resolve all issues that would otherwise be handled by the military trial judge. Art. 51, UCMJ, 10 U.S.C. @ 851. Convening officers, finally, have the authority to review and modify the sentence imposed by courts-martial.

Art. 60, UCMJ, 10 U.S.C. @ 860. Thus, by contrast to civilian society, non-judicial military officers play a significant part in the administration of military justice.

By the same token, the position of military judge is less distinct from other military positions than the office of full-time civilian judge is from other offices in civilian society. As the lead opinion in the Court of Military Appeals noted, military judges do not have any "inherent judicial authority separate from a court-martial to which they have been detailed. When they act, they do so as a court-martial, not as a military judge. Until detailed to a specific court-martial, they have no more authority than any other military officer of the same grade and rank." 36 M.J., at 228. Military appellate judges similarly exercise judicial functions only when they are "assigned" to a Court of Military Review. Neither military trial nor appellate judges, moreover, have a fixed term of office. Commissioned officers are assigned or detailed to the position of military judge by a Judge Advocate General for a period of time he deems necessary or appropriate, and then they may be reassigned to perform other duties. Even while serving as military trial judges, officers may perform, with the permission of the Judge Advocate General, duties unrelated to their judicial responsibilities. Art. 26(c), UCMJ, 10 U.S.C. @ 826(c). Whatever might be the case in civilian society, we think that the role of military judge is "germane" to that of military officer.

In sum, we believe that the current scheme satisfies the Appointments Clause. It is quite clear that Congress has not required a separate appointment to the position of military judge, and we believe it equally clear that the Appointments Clause by its own force does not require a second appointment before military officers may discharge the duties of such a judge.

II

Petitioners next contend that the Due Process Clause requires that military judges must have a fixed term of office. Petitioners recognize, as they must, that the Constitution does not require life tenure for Article I judges, including military judges. *See United States ex rel. Toth v. Quarles*, 350 U.S. 11, 17 (1955). Nor does the trial by an Article I judge lacking life tenure violate a defendant's due process rights. *See Palmore v. United States*, 411 U.S. 389, 410 (1973). Petitioners thus confine their argument to the assertion that due process requires military judges to serve for some fixed length of time—however short.

Congress, of course, is subject to the requirements of the Due Process Clause when legislating in the area of military affairs, and that Clause provides some measure of protection to defendants in military proceedings. *See Rostker v. Goldberg*, 453 U.S. 57, 67 (1981); *Middendorf v. Henry*, 425 U.S. 25, 43 (1976). But in determining what process is due, courts "must give particular deference to the determination of Congress, made under its authority to regulate the land and naval forces, U.S. Const., Art. I, @ 8."

. . . .

We therefore believe that the appropriate standard to apply in these cases is found in *Middendorf, supra*, where we also faced a due process challenge to a facet of the military justice system. In determining whether the Due Process Clause requires that service members appearing before a summary court-martial be assisted by counsel, we asked "whether the factors militating in favor of counsel at summary courts-martial are so extraordinarily weighty as to overcome the balance struck by Congress." *Middendorf*, 425 U.S., at 44. We ask the same question here with respect to fixed terms of office for military judges.

It is elementary that "a fair trial in a fair tribunal is a basic requirement of due process." In re *Murchison*, 349 U.S. 133, 136 (1955). A necessary component of a fair trial is an impartial judge. *See ibid.; Tumey v. Ohio*, 273 U.S. 510, 532 (1927). Petitioners, however, do not allege that the judges in their cases were or appeared to be biased. Instead, they ask us to assume that a military judge who does not have a fixed term of office lacks the independence necessary to ensure impartiality. Neither history nor current practice, however, supports such an assumption.

A

Although a fixed term of office is a traditional component of the Anglo-American civilian judicial system, it has never been a part of the military justice tradition. The early English military tribunals, which served as the model for our own military justice system, were historically convened and presided over by a military general. No tenured military judge presided. *See* Schlueter, The Court-Martial: An Historical Survey, 87 Mil. L. Rev. 129, 135, 136-144 (1980).

In the United States, although Congress has on numerous occasions during our history revised the procedures governing courts-martial, it has never required tenured judges to preside over courts-martial or to hear immediate appeals therefrom.[4] *See* W. Winthrop, Military Law and Precedents, 21-24, 953-1000 (2d ed. 1920) (de-

scribing and reprinting the Articles of War, which governed court-martial proceedings during the 17th and 18th centuries); F. Gilligan & F. Lederer, 1 Court-Martial Procedure 11-24 (1991) (describing 20th century revisions to Articles of War, and enactment of and amendments to UCMJ). Indeed, as already mentioned, Congress did not even create the position of military judge until 1968. Courts-martial thus have been conducted in this country for over 200 years without the presence of a tenured judge, and for over 150 years without the presence of any judge at all.

B

As the Court of Military Appeals observed in *Graf*, the historical maintenance of the military justice system without tenured judges "suggests the absence of a fundamental fairness problem." Petitioners in effect urge us to disregard this history, but we are unwilling to do so. We do not mean to say that any practice in military courts which might have been accepted at some time in history automatically satisfies due process of law today. But as Congress has taken affirmative steps to make the system of military justice more like the American system of civilian justice, it has nonetheless chosen not to give tenure to military judges. The question under the Due Process Clause is whether the existence of such tenure is such an extraordinarily weighty factor as to overcome the balance struck by Congress. And the historical fact that military judges have never had tenure is a factor that must be weighed in this calculation.

---

[4]Congress did create a nine-member commission in 1983 to examine, interalia, the possibility of providing tenure for military judges. Military Justice Act of 1983, Pub. L. 98-209, @ 9(b), 97 Stat. 1393, 1404-1405 (1983). The commission published its report a year later, in which it recommended against providing a guaranteed term of office for military trial and appellate judges. *See* D. Schlueter, Military Criminal Justice: Practice and Procedure 33-34, and nn. 86, 87 (3d ed. 1992) (listing members of commission and describing report). Congress has taken no further action on the subject.

A fixed term of office, as petitioners recognize, is not an end in itself. It is a means of promoting judicial independence, which in turn helps to ensure judicial impartiality. We believe the applicable provisions of the UCMJ, and corresponding regulations, by insulating military judges from the effects of command influence, sufficiently preserve judicial impartiality so as to satisfy the Due Process Clause.

Article 26 places military judges under the authority of the appropriate Judge Advocate General rather than under the authority of the convening officer. 10 U.S.C. @ 826. Rather than exacerbating the alleged problems relating to judicial independence, as petitioners suggest, we believe this structure helps protect that independence. Like all military officers, Congress made military judges accountable to a superior officer for the performance of their duties. By placing judges under the control of Judge Advocates General, who have no interest in the outcome of a particular court-martial, we believe Congress has achieved an acceptable balance between independence and accountability.

Article 26 also protects against command influence by precluding a convening officer or any commanding officer from preparing or reviewing any report concerning the effectiveness, fitness, or efficiency of a military judge relating to his judicial duties. *Ibid.* Article 37 prohibits convening officers from censuring, reprimanding, or admonishing a military judge "with respect to the findings or sentence adjudged by the court, or with respect to any other exercise of its or his functions in the conduct of the proceeding." 10 U.S.C. @ 837. Any officer who "knowingly and intentionally fails to enforce or comply" with Article 37 "shall be punished as a court-martial may direct."

Art. 98, UCMJ, 10 U.S.C. @ 898. The Code also provides that a military judge, either trial or appellate, must refrain from adjudicating a case in which he has previously participated, Arts. 26(c), 66(h), UCMJ, 10 U.S.C. @@ 826(c), 866(h), and the Code allows a defendant to challenge both a court-martial member and a court-martial judge for cause, Art. 41, UCMJ, 10 U.S.C. @ 841. The Code also allows a defendant to learn the identity of the military judge before choosing whether to be tried by the judge alone, or by the judge and court-martial members. Art. 16, UCMJ, 10 U.S.C. @ 816.

The entire system, finally, is overseen by the Court of Military Appeals, which is composed entirely of civilian judges who serve for fixed terms of 15 years. That Court has demonstrated its vigilance in checking any attempts to exert improper influence over military judges. In *United States v. Mabe*, 33 M. J. 200 (1991), for example, the Court considered whether the Judge Advocate General of the Navy, or his designee, could rate a military judge based on the appropriateness of the judge's sentences at courts-martial. As the Court later described: "We held [in *Mabe*] that the existence of such a power in these military officers was inconsistent with Congress' establishment of the military 'judge' in Article 26 and its exercise violated Article 37 of the Code." *Graf*, 35 M. J., at 465. And in *Graf*, the Court held that it would also violate Articles 26 and 37 if a Judge Advocate General decertified or transferred a military judge based on the General's opinion of the appropriateness of the judge's findings and sentences. *Ibid.*[5]

---

[5]This added limitation on the power of the Judge Advocates General to remove military judges refutes petitioners' contention that Judge Advocates General have unfettered discretion both to appoint and remove military judges.

The absence of tenure as a historical matter in the system of military justice, and the number of safeguards in place to ensure impartiality, lead us to reject petitioners' due process challenge. Petitioners have fallen far short of demonstrating that the factors favoring fixed terms of office are so extraordinarily weighty as to overcome the balance achieved by Congress. *See Middendorf,* 425 U.S., at 44.

For the reasons stated, we reject the petitioners' Appointments Clause and Due Process Clause attacks on the judges who convicted them and those who heard their appeals. The judgments of the Court of Military Appeals are accordingly affirmed.

The Supreme Court in *Weiss* describes the military's court-martial system. What was the accused's basis to attack the constitutionality of the system? Do you think the current procedures for appointing military judges affect their fairness and neutrality? Can the military take action against a judge based upon his or her decisions? *See* Articles 26 and 37, UCMJ.

The Rules for Courts-Martial (RCM) describe special and general courts-martial.

RCM 201(f) Types of courts-martial.

(1) General courts-martial.

    (A) Cases under the code.

        (i) Except as otherwise expressly provided, general courts-martial may try any person subject to the code for any offense made punishable under the code. . . .

        (ii) Upon a finding of guilty of an offense made punishable by the code, general courts-martial may, within limits prescribed by this Manual, adjudge any punishment authorized. . . .

(2) Special courts-martial.

    (A) In general. Except as otherwise expressly provided, special courts-martial may try any person subject to the code for any noncapital offense made punishable by the code and, as provided in this rule, for capital offenses.

    (B) Punishments.

        (i) Upon a finding of guilty, special courts-martial may adjudge, under limitations prescribed by this Manual, any punishment authorized . . . except death, dishonorable discharge, dismissal, confinement for more than 6 months, hard labor without confinement for more than 3 months, forfeiture of pay exceeding two-thirds pay per month, or any forfeiture of pay for more than 6 months.

The *Weiss* case focused on general and special courts-martial and appeals from those courts. The above sections from the RCM describe special and general courts-martial as well. The following case discusses a forum, the summary court-martial, that is entirely unique to the military, and considers the constitutionality of procedures used at that forum.

Middendorf, Secretary of the Navy, et al., v. Henry et al.
Supreme Court of the United States
425 U.S. 25
March 24, 1976

OPINION: Mr. Justice Rehnquist

In February 1973 plaintiffs [footnote omitted]—then enlisted members of the United States Marine Corps—brought this class action in the United States District Court for the Central District of California challenging the authority of the military to try them at summary courts-martial without providing them with counsel. Five plaintiffs [footnote omitted] had been charged with "unauthorized absences" [footnote omitted] in violation of Art. 86, UCMJ, 10 U.S.C. @ 886, convicted at summary courts-martial, and sentenced, inter alia, to periods of confinement ranging from 20 to 30 days at hard labor. The other three plaintiffs, two of whom were charged, inter alia, with unauthorized absence and one with assault, Art. 128, UCMJ, 10 U.S.C. @ 928, had been ordered to stand trial at summary courts-martial which had not been convened. Those who were convicted had not been provided counsel—those who were awaiting trial had been informed that counsel would not be provided. All convicted plaintiffs were informed prior to trial that they would not be afforded counsel and that they

could refuse trial by summary court-martial if they so desired. In the event of such refusal, their cases would be referred to special courts-martial at which counsel would be provided. All plaintiffs consented in writing to proceed to trial by summary court-martial, without counsel. [footnote omitted]. Plaintiffs' court-martial records were reviewed and approved[1] by the Staff Judge Advocate pursuant to Art. 65 (c), UCMJ, 10 U.S.C. @ 865 (c). Plaintiffs did not file a petition for review with the Judge Advocate General of the Navy pursuant to Art. 69, UCMJ, 10 U.S.C. @ 869. [footnote omitted].

. . . .

I

The UCMJ provides four methods for disposing of cases involving offenses committed by servicemen: the general, special, and summary courts-martial, and disciplinary punishment administered by the commanding officer pursuant to Art. 15, UCMJ, 10 U.S.C. @ 815. General and special courts-martial resemble judicial proceedings, nearly always presided over by lawyer judges with lawyer counsel for

---

[1] At least one plaintiff, McLean, was found not guilty as to certain charges at the summary court-martial. Upon review at the supervisory authority level, guilty findings on certain other charges upon which he had been convicted were reversed.

both the prosecution and the defense.[2] General courts-martial are authorized to award any lawful sentence, including death. Art. 18, UCMJ, 10 U.S.C. @ 818. Special courts-martial may award a bad-conduct discharge, up to six months' confinement at hard labor, forfeiture of two-thirds pay per month for six months, and in the case of an enlisted member, reduction to the lowest pay grade, Art. 19, UCMJ, 10 U.S.C. @ 819. Article 15 punishment, conducted personally by the accused's commanding officer, is an administrative method of dealing with the most minor offenses. *Parker v. Levy*, 417 U.S. 733, 750 (1974).[3]

The summary court-martial occupies a position between informal nonjudicial disposition under Art. 15 and the courtroom-type procedure of the general and special courts-martial. Its purpose "is to exercise justice promptly for relatively minor offenses under a simple form of procedure." Manual for Courts-Martial 79a (1969) (MCM). It is an informal proceeding conducted by a single commissioned officer with jurisdiction only over non-commissioned officers and other enlisted personnel. Art. 20, UCMJ, 10 U.S.C.@ 820. The presiding officer acts as judge, fact finder, prosecutor, and defense counsel. The presiding officer must inform the accused of the charges and the name of the accuser and call all witnesses whom he or the accused desires to call.[4] MCM 79d (1). The accused must consent to trial by summary court-martial; if he does not do so, trial may be ordered by special or general court-martial.

The record of the trial is then reviewed by the convening officer, Art. 60, UCMJ, 10 U.S.C. @ 860, and thereafter by a judge advocate. Art. 65 (c), UCMJ, 10 U.S.C. @ 865 (c).

The maximum sentence elements which may be imposed by summary courts-martial are: one month's confinement at hard labor; 45 days' hard labor without confinement; two months' restriction to specified limits; reduction to the lowest enlisted pay grade; and forfeiture of two-thirds pay for

---

[2]These features are mandatory for general courts-martial. Special courts-martial may be, but seldom are, convened without a military judge; in such cases, the senior member of the court presides. Appointed defense counsel at a special court-martial is required to be an attorney, unless an attorney cannot be obtained because of physical conditions or military exigencies. In addition to the appointed counsel at a general or special court-martial, the accused may retain civilian counsel at his own expense, or he may be represented by a military lawyer of his own selection, if such lawyer is "reasonably available." Arts. 16, 25, 27 (b), 27 (c), 38 (b), UCMJ, 10 U.S.C. @@ 816, 825, 827 (b), 827 (c), 838 (b).

[3]The maximum punishments which may be imposed under Art. 15 are: 30 days' correctional custody; 60 days' restriction to specified limits; 45 days' extra duties; forfeiture of one-half of one month's pay per month for two months; detention of one-half of one month's pay per month for three months; reduction in grade. Enlisted members attached to or embarked on a vessel may be sentenced to three days' confinement on bread and water or diminished rations. Correctional custody is not necessarily the same as confinement. It is intended to be served in a way which allows normal performance of duty, together with intensive counseling. Persons serving correctional custody, however, may be confined. Art. 15 (b). *See* Department of the Navy, SECNAV Inst. 1640.9, Corrections Manual, c. 7, June 1972; Department of the Army, Pamphlet No. 27-4, Correctional Custody, 1 June 1972; Department of the Air Force, Reg. 125-35, Correctional Custody, 7 Oct. 1970.

[4]Additionally, the officer must inform the accused of his right to remain silent and allow him to cross-examine witnesses or have the summary court officer cross-examine them for him. The accused may testify and present evidence in his own behalf. If the accused is found guilty, he may make a statement, sworn or unsworn, in extenuation or mitigation. MCM 79d.

one month. Art. 20, UCMJ, 10 U.S.C. @ 820.[5]

II

The question of whether an accused in a court-martial has a constitutional right to counsel has been much debated and never squarely resolved.

. . . .

We find it unnecessary in this case to finally resolve the broader aspects of this question, since we conclude that even were the Sixth Amendment to be held applicable to court-martial proceedings, the summary court-martial provided for in these cases was not a "criminal prosecution" within the meaning of that Amendment. [footnote omitted].

. . . .

We have only recently noted the difference between the diverse civilian community and the much more tightly regimented military community in *Parker v. Levy*, 417 U.S. 733, 749 (1974). We said there that the UCMJ "cannot be equated to a civilian criminal code. It, and the various versions of the Articles of War which have preceded it, regulate aspects of the conduct of members of the military which in the civilian sphere are left unregulated. While a civilian criminal code carves out a relatively small segment of potential conduct and declares it criminal, the Uniform Code of Military Justice essays more varied regulation of a much larger segment of the activities of the more tightly knit military community." *Ibid*. Much of the conduct proscribed by the military is not "criminal" conduct in the civilian sense of the word. *Id*., at 749-751. Here, for example,

most of the plaintiffs were charged solely with "unauthorized absence," an offense which has no common-law counterpart and which carries little popular opprobrium. Conviction of such an offense would likely have no consequences for the accused beyond the immediate punishment meted out by the military, unlike conviction for such civilian misdemeanors as vagrancy or larceny which could carry a stamp of "bad character" with conviction. [footnote omitted].

. . . .

[A] summary court-martial is procedurally quite different from a criminal trial. In the first place, it is not an adversary proceeding. Yet the adversary nature of civilian criminal proceedings is one of the touchstones of the Sixth Amendment's right to counsel [footnote omitted] which we extended to petty offenses in *Argersinger v. Hamlin*, 407 U.S. 25 (1972).

. . . .

The function of the presiding officer is quite different from that of any participant in a civilian trial. He is guided by the admonition in 79a of the MCM: "The function of a summary court-martial is to exercise justice promptly for relatively minor offenses under a simple form of procedure. The summary court will thoroughly and impartially inquire into both sides of the matter and will assure that the interests of both the Government and the accused are safeguarded." The presiding officer is more specifically enjoined to attend to the interests of the accused by these provisions of the same paragraph:

"The accused will be extended the right to cross-examine these witnesses. The

---

[5]Not all these sentence elements may be imposed in one sentence, and enlisted persons above the fourth enlisted pay grade may not be sentenced to confinement or hard labor by summary courts-martial, or reduced except to the next inferior grade.

summary court will aid the accused in the cross-examination, and, if the accused desires, will ask questions suggested by the accused. On behalf of the accused, the court will obtain the attendance of witnesses, administer the oath and examine them, and obtain such other evidence as may tend to disprove or negative guilt of the charges, explain the acts or omissions charged, show extenuating circumstances, or establish grounds for mitigation. Before determining the findings, he will explain to the accused his right to testify on the merits or to remain silent and will give the accused full opportunity to exercise his election." MCM 79d (3).

We believe there are significant parallels between the Court's description of probation and parole revocation proceedings in *Gagnon* and the summary court-martial, which parallels tend to distinguish both of these proceedings from the civilian misdemeanor prosecution upon which Argersinger focused. When we consider in addition that the court-martial proceeding takes place not in civilian society, as does the parole revocation proceeding, but in the military community with all of its distinctive qualities, we conclude that a summary court-martial is not a "criminal prosecution" for purposes of the Sixth Amendment.[6]

III

The Court of Appeals likewise concluded that there was no Sixth Amendment right to counsel in summary court-martial proceedings such as this, but applying the due process standards of the Fifth Amendment adopted a standard from *Gagnon v. Scar-*

pelli, 411 U.S. 778 (1973), which would have made the right to counsel depend upon the nature of the serviceman's defense. We are unable to agree that the Court of Appeals properly applied *Gagnon* in this military context.

We recognize that plaintiffs, who have either been convicted or are due to appear before a summary court-martial, may be subjected to loss of liberty or property, and consequently are entitled to the due process of law guaranteed by the Fifth Amendment.

However, whether this process embodies a right to counsel depends upon an analysis of the interests of the individual and those of the regime to which he is subject. *Wolff v. McDonnell,* 418 U.S. 539, 556 (1974).

In making such an analysis we must give particular deference to the determination of Congress, made under its authority to regulate the land and naval forces, U.S. Const., Art. I, @ 8, that counsel should not be provided in summary courts-martial. As we held in *Burns v. Wilson,* 346 U.S. 137, 140 (1953): "[T]he rights of men in the armed forces must perforce be conditioned to meet certain overriding demands of discipline and duty, and the civil courts are not the agencies which must determine the precise balance to be struck in this adjustment. The Framers especially entrusted that task to Congress." [footnote omitted].

We thus need only decide whether the factors militating in favor of counsel at summary courts-martial are so extraordinarily

---

[6]No one of the factors discussed above—the nature of the proceedings, of the offenses, and of the punishments—is necessarily dispositive. Rather, all three combine with the distinctive nature of military life and discipline to lead to our conclusion. The dissent, by discussing these factors independently and attempting to demonstrate that each factor cannot stand by its own force does not come to grips with this analysis.

weighty as to overcome the balance struck by Congress.[7]

We first consider the effect of providing counsel at summary courts-martial. As we observed in *Gagnon v. Scarpelli, supra*, at 787: "The introduction of counsel into a . . . proceeding will alter significantly the nature of the proceeding. If counsel is provided for the [accused], the State in turn will normally provide its own counsel; lawyers, by training and disposition, are advocates and bound by professional duty to present all available evidence and arguments in support of their clients' positions and to contest with vigor all adverse evidence and views."

In short, presence of counsel will turn a brief, informal hearing which may be quickly convened and rapidly concluded into an attenuated proceeding which consumes the resources of the military to a degree which Congress could properly have felt to be beyond what is warranted by the relative insignificance of the offenses being tried. Such a lengthy proceeding is a particular burden to the Armed Forces because virtually all the participants, including the defendant and his counsel, are members of the military whose time may be better spent than in possibly protracted disputes over the imposition of discipline. [footnote omitted].

As we observed in U.S. ex rel. *Toth v. Quarles*, 350 U.S. 11, 17 (1955):

"[I]t is the primary business of armies and navies to fight or be ready to fight wars should the occasion arise. But trial of soldiers to maintain discipline is merely incidental to an army's primary fighting function. To the extent that those responsible for performance of this primary function are diverted from it by the necessity of trying cases, the basic fighting purpose of armies is not served. . . . [M]ilitary tribunals have not been and probably never can be constituted in such way that they can have the same kind of qualifications that the Constitution has deemed essential to fair trials of civilians in federal courts."

. . . .

But if the accused has such a claim, if he feels that in order to properly air his views and vindicate his rights, a formal, counseled proceeding is necessary, he may simply refuse trial by summary court-martial and proceed to trial by special or general court-martial at which he may have counsel.[8] Thus, he stands in a considerably more favorable position than the probationer in *Gagnon* who, though subject to the possibility of longer periods of incarceration, had no such absolute right to counsel. [footnote omitted].

---

[7]Prior to the enactment of the UCMJ into positive law in 1956, it was suggested that summary courts-martial be abolished. Congress rejected this suggestion and instead provided that no person could be tried by summary court-martial if he objected thereto (unless he had previously refused Art. 15 punishment). 70A Stat. 43. Prior to the 1968 amendments to the Code, the elimination of summary courts-martial was again proposed and rejected. *E.g.,* Subcommittee on Constitutional Rights of Senate Committee on the Judiciary, 88th Cong., 1st Sess., Summary—Report of Hearings on Constitutional Rights of Military Personnel, 34-36 (1963). Instead, the Art. 15 exception to the right to refuse was eliminated as a compromise between those favoring retention of summary courts-martial and those who would abolish them. S. Rep. No. 1601, 90th Cong., 2d Sess., 6 (1968). It is thus apparent that Congress has considered the matter in some depth.

[8]Article 20 UCMJ, 10 U.S.C. @ 820, provides in pertinent part that "[n]o person with respect to whom summary courts-martial have jurisdiction may be brought to trial before a summary court-martial if he objects thereto. . . ."

Article 38(b) UCMJ, 10 U.S.C. @ 838(b), provides: "The accused has the right to be represented in his defense before a general or special court-martial by civilian counsel if provided by him, or by military counsel of his own selection if reasonably available, or by the defense counsel detailed under section 827 of this title."

It is true that by exercising this option, the accused subjects himself to greater possible penalties imposed in the special court-martial proceeding. However, we do not find that possible detriment to be constitutionally decisive. We have frequently approved the much more difficult decision, daily faced by civilian criminal defendants, to plead guilty to a lesser included offense. *E.g., Brady v. United States*, 397 U.S. 742, 749-750 (1970). In such a case the defendant gives up not only his right to counsel but his right to any trial at all. Furthermore, if he elects to exercise his right to trial, he stands to be convicted of a more serious offense which will likely bear increased penalties. [footnote omitted].

Such choices are a necessary part of the criminal justice system:

> "The criminal process, like the rest of the legal system, is replete with situations requiring 'the making of difficult judgments' as to which course to follow. *McMann v. Richardson*, 397 U.S., at 769. Although a defendant may have a right, even of constitutional dimensions, to follow whichever course he chooses, the Constitution does not by that token always forbid requiring him to choose." *McGautha v. California*, 402 U.S. 183, 213 (1971).

We therefore agree with the defendants that neither the Sixth nor the Fifth Amendment to the United States Constitution empowers us to overturn the congressional determination that counsel is not required in summary courts-martial. The judgment of the Court of Appeals is therefore Reversed.

Do you concur with the court's decision regarding defense counsel at summary courts-martial? What is the military's justification for not providing an attorney at such a proceeding? Generally, junior line officers sit as summary courts-martial. Would you have a difficult time wearing all the "hats" required of a summary courts officer (prosecutor, defense counsel, judge)?

In *United States v. Booker*, 5 M.J. 238 (C.M.A. 1977), a divided Court of Military Appeals held that before a record of a summary court-martial could be admitted to escalate or aggravate the sentence at a special or general court-martial, the prosecution must show that the accused had been advised of the right to consult with independent counsel before opting for summary court-martial. The prosecution also had to show that the accused affirmatively and personally waived in writing his or her right to object to summary court-martial. The *Booker* decision thus established the practice of making counsel available to provide advice on whether to accept or refuse summary court-martial. However, the Navy-Marine Corps Court of Criminal Appeals ruled that *Booker* restrictions on admitting records of prior summary courts-martial during the presentencing procedure of a subsequent court-martial should not continue in light of *Nichols v. United States*, 114 S. Ct. 1921 (1994). In *United States v. Kelly*, 40 M.J. 558 (1995), evidence of a prior summary court-martial, not accompanied by evidence of compliance with

Booker, was admitted during a presentencing hearing, over defense counsel's objection. The *Kelly* opinion found that the Supreme Court's decision in *Nichols* clarifies that an uncounseled but constitutionally valid conviction (which under *Middendorf v. Henry* includes summary courts-martial) may be used to enhance (aggravate or escalate) the sentence in a subsequent trial without any further advisement respecting counsel. The Supreme Court found that the same applies to nonjudicial punishment. Although the Court of Appeals for the Armed Forces has yet to consider the issue, it appears that *Kelly* signals the end of *Booker*. For the application of *Booker* to nonjudicial punishment, *see United States v. Mathews* in Chapter IV.

Weiss and *Middendorf* describe the military's court-martial system. Figure 3-A compares the three types of courts-martial.

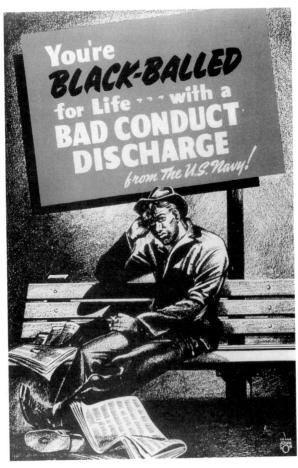

A poster used during World War II. Punitive discharges, only authorized at special and general courts-martial, still carry serious consequences for former service members. Photo courtesy of Naval Historical Society.

FIGURE 3-A

COURTS-MARTIAL COMPARISON

	SCM	SPCM	GCM
Jurisdiction	Minor offenses; enlisted only; voluntary	Non-capital or capital crimes if mandatory sentence does not exceed punishment limitations	Non-capital or capital crimes
Composition	Summary court officer (commissioned officer, 0-3 or above, same armed force)	MJ; TC; DC; at least three members NOTE: The accused may request trial by MJ alone rather than members	MJ; TC; DC; at least 5 members NOTE: In non-capital cases, the accused may request trial by MJ alone rather than members
Standard of Proof	Beyond reasonable doubt	Beyond reasonable doubt; 2/3 majority	Beyond reasonable doubt; 2/3 majority (3/4 majority for confinement greater than 10 years; unanimous for death penalty)
Counsel Rights	No representation by military counsel	Representation by detailed military lawyer *or* requested military lawyer *and* civilian lawyer at your own expense	Representation by detailed military lawyer *or* requested military lawyer *and* civilian lawyer at own expense
Maximum permissible punishment; Enlisted	Confinement x 30 days (E-4 and below) Reduction in Rate to E-1 (E-5 and above only one paygrade) Forfeitures of 2/3 pay per month for 1 month	Lesser of maximum permissible for offense or: BCD; CHL x 6 months; Forfeiture of 2/3 pay per month for 6 months; Reduction in rate to E-1	Maximum permissible for the offense. This may include: Death penalty; DD; confinement for life; Total Forfeitures; Reduction to E-1
Maximum permissible punishment; officer	NOT APPLICABLE	Restriction x 60 days; Forfeiture of 2/3 pay per month for 6 months; Loss of lineal numbers	Maximum permissible for the offense. This may include: Death penalty; Dismissal; confinement for life; Total forfeitures; Loss of lineal numbers

CONVENING COURTS-MARTIAL

AUTHORITY TO CONVENE COURTS-MARTIAL

Who has authority to convene courts-martial in the Navy and Marine Corps? The JAG Manual provides specific guidance on this matter.

JAG Manual 0120

a. General courts-martial. The Secretary of the Navy, acting under Article 22(a)(8), UCMJ, has authorized the following officers . . . to convene general courts-martial . . .:

    (1) All flag or general officers [and those superior to such officers] in command of units or activities of the Navy or Marine Corps.

b. Special courts-martial. The Secretary of the Navy, acting under Article 23(a)(7), UCMJ, has authorized the following officers . . . to convene general courts-martial. This list is in addition to those officers authorized to convene special courts-martial by Article 23(a)(5) and (6), UCMJ:

    (1) Commanding officers of all battalions and squadrons.

    (2) Any commander whose subordinates in the operational or administrative chain of command have authority to convene special courts-martial.

    (3) All commanders and commanding officers of units and activities of the Navy.

    [Article 23(a)(5), UCMJ, provides that "[s]pecial courts-martial may be convened by the commanding officer of any naval . . . vessel, shipyard, base, or station; the commanding officer of any Marine brigade, regiment, detached battalion, or corresponding unit. . . .]

c. Summary courts-martial. Those officers who are empowered to convene general and special courts-martial may convene summary courts-martial. In addition, the Secretary of the Navy has empowered all commanders, commanding officers, and officers in charge . . . to convene summary courts-martial.

May the authority to convene courts-martial be delegated? The RCM answers this question:

RCM Rule 504(b)(4): Delegation prohibited. The power to convene courts-martial may not be delegated.

PROCEDURES FOR CONVENING COURTS-MARTIAL

Convening Orders

RCM 504(d) Convening orders.

(1) General and special courts-martial. A convening order for a general or special court-martial shall designate the type of court-martial and detail the members and may designate where the court-martial will meet. . . .

(2) Summary courts-martial. A convening order for a summary court-martial shall designate that it is a summary court-martial and detail the summary court-martial, and may designate where the court-martial will meet. . . .

The following is an example of a convening order for a general court-martial.

FIGURE 3-B

20 October 1994

COMMANDER, NAVAL SURFACE FORCE ATLANTIC

NORFOLK, VIRGINIA 23511

GENERAL COURT-MARTIAL CONVENING ORDER 51-94

A general court-martial is hereby convened. It may proceed at Naval Legal Service Office, Norfolk, Virginia, to try such persons as may properly be brought before it. The court will be constituted as follows:

MEMBERS

Captain Mark E. PERRAULT, U.S. Navy
Commander Robert J. DOONAN, U.S. Navy
Lieutenant Commander Joseph W. KINSEY, U.S. Navy
Lieutenant Commander Michael F. HAGEN, U.S. Navy
Lieutenant Richard H. ENDERLY, U.S. Navy
Ensign Kenneth G. TUEBNER, U.S. Naval Reserve
Chief Warrant Officer (CWO-2) Stanley C. S BOLLINGER, U.S. Navy

/S/
R. E. NICHOLSON
Vice Admiral, U.S. Navy
Commander, Naval Surface
Force Atlantic

Convening General Courts-Martial

There are unique procedures for convening a general court-martial. The military does not have a grand jury process. Instead, a pretrial investigative procedure is utilized under Article 32, UCMJ.

Art. 32, UCMJ. Investigation

(a) No charge or specification may be referred to a general court-martial for trial until a thorough and impartial investigation of all the matters set forth therein has been made. . . .

(b) The accused has the right to be represented at that investigation [by counsel. . . . At that investigation full opportunity shall be given to the accused to cross-examine witnesses against him if they are available and to present anything he may desire in his own behalf, either in defense or mitigation, and the investigation officer shall examine available witnesses requested by the accused. . . .]

RCM 405. Pretrial Investigation

(c) Who may direct investigation. [A]n investigation may be directed under this rule by any court-martial convening authority.

(i) Military Rules of Evidence. The Military Rules of Evidence—other than Mil. R. Evid. 301, 302, 303, 305, and Section V [rules relating to self-incrimination and privileges]—shall not apply in pretrial investigations under this rule.

. . . .

(j) Report of Investigation

(1) In general. The investigating officer shall make a timely written report of the investigation to the commander who directed the investigation.

(2) Contents. The report of investigation shall include:

. . . .

(I) The recommendations of the investigating officer, including disposition.

RCM 407. Action by commander exercising general court-martial jurisdiction

(a) Disposition. When in receipt of charges, a commander exercising general court-martial jurisdiction may:

(1) Dismiss any charges;

(2) Forward charges (or, after dismissing charges, the matter) to a subordinate commander for disposition;

. . . .

(4) Refer charges to a summary court-martial or a special court-martial for trial;

. . . .

(5) [R]efer charges to a general court-martial.

Based on the above rules, a commanding officer who is not a general court-martial convening authority cannot convene a general court-marital. How may such a commander have a case tried at general court-martial? Note that the general court-martial convening authority is not bound by the recommendation of the pretrial investigating officer. As noted above, the Article 32 pretrial investigation is essentially the equivalent to the grand jury system used in civilian criminal law. Which procedure is most fair to the accused?

JURISDICTION

GENERALLY

Ex Parte Milligan
Supreme Court of the United States
71 U.S. 2
December, 1866 Term

PRIOR HISTORY:

. . . .

Lamdin P. Milligan, a citizen of the United States, and a resident and citizen of the State of Indiana, was arrested on the 5th day of October, 1864, at his home in the said State, by the order of Brevet Major-General Hovey, military commandant of the District of Indiana, and by the same authority confined in a military prison, at or near Indianapolis, the capital of the State. On the 21st day of the same month, he was placed on trial before a "military commission," convened at Indianapolis, by order of the said General, upon the following charges; preferred by Major Burnett, Judge Advocate of the Northwestern Mili-

tary Department, namely:

1. "Conspiracy against the Government of the United States;"

2. "Affording aid and comfort to rebels against the authority of the United States;"

3. "Inciting insurrection;"

4. "Disloyal practices;" and

5. "Violation of the laws of war."

Under each of these charges there were various specifications. The substance of them was, joining and aiding, at different times, between October, 1863, and August,

1864, a secret society known as the Order of American Knights or Sons of Liberty, for the purpose of overthrowing the Government and duly constituted authorities of the United States; holding communication with the enemy; conspiring to seize munitions of war stored in the arsenals; to liberate prisoners of war; resisting the draft . . . "at a period of war and armed rebellion against the authority of the United States, at or near Indianapolis, [and various other places specified] in Indiana, a State within the military lines of the army of the United States, and the theater of military operations, and which had been and was constantly threatened to be invaded by the enemy." These were amplified and stated with various circumstances.

Mr. Justice DAVIS delivered the opinion of the court.

The controlling question in the case is this: Upon the facts stated in Milligan's petition, and the exhibits filed, had the military commission mentioned in it jurisdiction, legally, to try and sentence him? Milligan, not a resident of one of the rebellious states, or a prisoner of war, but a citizen of Indiana for twenty years past, and never in the military or naval service, is, while at his home, arrested by the military power of the United States, imprisoned, and, on certain criminal charges preferred against him, tried, convicted, and sentenced to be hanged by a military commission, organized under the direction of the military commander of the military district of Indiana. Had this tribunal the legal power and authority to try and punish this man?

No graver question was ever considered by this court, nor one which more nearly concerns the rights of the whole people; for it is the birthright of every American citizen when charged with crime, to be tried and punished according to law. The power of punishment is, alone through the means

which the laws have provided for that purpose, and if they are ineffectual, there is an immunity from punishment, no matter how great an offender the individual may be, or how much his crimes may have shocked the sense of justice of the country, or endangered its safety. By the protection of the law human rights are secured; withdraw that protection, and they are at the mercy of wicked rulers, or the clamor of an excited people. If there was law to justify this military trial, it is not our province to interfere; if there was not, it is our duty to declare the nullity of the whole proceedings. The decision of this question does not depend on argument or judicial precedents, numerous and highly illustrative as they are. These precedents inform us of the extent of the struggle to preserve liberty and to relieve those in civil life from military trials.

. . . .

It is claimed that martial law covers with its broad mantle the proceedings of this military commission. The proposition is this: that in a time of war the commander of an armed force (if in his opinion the exigencies of the country demand it, and of which he is to judge), has the power, within the lines of his military district, to suspend all civil rights and their remedies, and subject citizens as well as soldiers to the rule of his will; and in the exercise of his lawful authority cannot be restrained, except by his superior officer or the President of the United States.

If this position is sound to the extent claimed, then when war exists, foreign or domestic, and the country is subdivided into military departments for mere convenience, the commander of one of them can, if he chooses, within his limits, on the plea of necessity, with the approval of the Executive, substitute military force for and to the exclusion of the laws, and punish all persons, as he thinks right and proper, without fixed or certain rules.

The statement of this proposition shows its importance; for, if true, republican government is a failure, and there is an end of liberty regulated by law. Martial law, established on such a basis, destroys every guarantee of the Constitution, and effectually renders the "military independent of and superior to the civil power"—the attempt to do which by the King of Great Britain was deemed by our fathers such an offense, that they assigned it to the world as one of the causes which impelled them to declare their independence. Civil liberty and this kind of martial law cannot endure together; the antagonism is irreconcilable; and, in the conflict, one or the other must perish.

This nation, as experience has proved, cannot always remain at peace, and has no right to expect that it will always have wise and humane rulers, sincerely attached to the principles of the Constitution. Wicked men, ambitious of power, with hatred of liberty and contempt of law, may fill the place once occupied by Washington and Lincoln; and if this right is conceded, and the calamities of war again befall us, the dangers to human liberty are frightful to contemplate. If our fathers had failed to provide for just such a contingency, they would have been false to the trust reposed in them. They knew—the history of the world told them—the nation they were founding, be its existence short or long, would be involved in war; how often or how long continued, human foresight could not tell; and that unlimited power, wherever lodged at such a time, was especially hazardous to freemen. For this, and other equally weighty reasons, they secured the inheritance they had fought to maintain, by incorporating in a written constitution the safeguards which time had proved were essential to its preservation. Not one of these safeguards can the President, or Congress, or the Judiciary disturb, except the one concerning the writ of habeas corpus.

It is essential to the safety of every government that, in a great crisis, like the one we have just passed through, there should be a power somewhere of suspending the writ of habeas corpus. In every war, there are men of previously good character, wicked enough to counsel their fellow-citizens to resist the measures deemed necessary by a good government to sustain its just authority and overthrow its enemies; and their influence may lead to dangerous combinations. In the emergency of the times, an immediate public investigation according to law may not be possible; and yet, the peril to the country may be too imminent to suffer such persons to go at large. Unquestionably, there is then an exigency which demands that the government, if it should see fit in the exercise of a proper discretion to make arrests, should not be required to produce the persons arrested in answer to a writ of habeas corpus. The Constitution goes no further. It does not say after a writ of habeas corpus is denied a citizen, that he shall be tried otherwise than by the course of the common law; if it had intended this result, it was easy by the use of direct words to have accomplished it. The illustrious men who framed that instrument were guarding the foundations of civil liberty against the abuses of unlimited power; they were full of wisdom, and the lessons of history informed them that a trial by an established court, assisted by an impartial jury, was the only sure way of protecting the citizen against oppression and wrong. Knowing this, they limited the suspension to one great right, and left the rest to remain forever inviolable. But, it is insisted that the safety of the country in time of war demands that this broad claim for martial law shall be sustained. If this were true, it could be well said that a country, preserved at the sacrifice of all the cardinal principles of liberty, is not worth the cost of preservation. Happily, it is not so.

It will be borne in mind that this is not a question of the power to proclaim martial law, when war exists in a community and the courts and civil authorities are overthrown. Nor is it a question what rule a military commander, at the head of his army, can impose on states in rebellion to cripple their resources and quell the insurrection. The jurisdiction claimed is much more extensive. The necessities of the service, during the late Rebellion, required that the loyal states should be placed within the limits of certain military districts and commanders appointed in them; and, it is urged, that this, in a military sense, constituted them the theater of military operations; and, as in this case, Indiana had been and was again threatened with invasion by the enemy, the occasion was furnished to establish martial law. The conclusion does not follow from the premises. If armies were collected in Indiana, they were to be employed in another locality, where the laws were obstructed and the national authority disputed. On her soil there was no hostile foot; if once invaded, that invasion was at an end, and with it all pretext for martial law. Martial law cannot arise from a threatened invasion. The necessity must be actual and present; the invasion real, such as effectually closes the courts and deposes the civil administration.

It is proper to say, although Milligan's trial and conviction by a military commission was illegal, yet, if guilty of the crimes imputed to him, and his guilt had been ascertained by an established court and impartial jury, he deserved severe punishment. Open resistance to the measures deemed necessary to subdue a great rebellion, by those who enjoy the protection of government, and have not the excuse even of prejudice of section to plead in their favor, is wicked; but that resistance becomes an enormous crime when it assumes the form of a secret political organization, armed to oppose the laws, and seeks by stealthy means to introduce the enemies of the country into peaceful communities, there to light the torch of civil war, and thus overthrow the power of the United States. Conspiracies like these, at such a juncture, are extremely perilous; and those concerned in them are dangerous enemies to their country, and should receive the heaviest penalties of the law, as an example to deter others from similar criminal conduct. It is said the severity of the laws caused them; but Congress was obliged to enact severe laws to meet the crisis; and as our highest civil duty is to serve our country when in danger, the late war has proved that rigorous laws, when necessary, will be cheerfully obeyed by a patriotic people, struggling to preserve the rich blessings of a free government.

If the military trial of Milligan was contrary to law, then he was entitled, on the facts stated in his petition, to be discharged from custody by the terms of the act of Congress of March 3d, 1863. The provisions of this law having been considered in a previous part of this opinion, we will not restate the views there presented. Milligan avers he was a citizen of Indiana, not in the military or naval service, and was detained in close confinement, by order of the President, from the 5th day of October, 1864, until the 2d day of January, 1865, when the Circuit Court for the District of Indiana, with a grand jury, convened in session at Indianapolis; and afterwards, on the 27th day of the same month, adjourned without finding an indictment or presentment against him. If these averments were true (and their truth is conceded for the purposes of this case), the court was required to liberate him on taking certain oaths prescribed by the law, and entering into recognizance for his good behavior.

Why did the military tribunal not have jurisdiction over Milligan? The discussion in *Milligan* discloses the limited nature of courts-martial jurisdiction under the law of the United States. The following section from the MCM sets forth the general requirements for jurisdiction of courts-martial today.

RCM 201. Jurisdiction in general

(a) Nature of courts-martial jurisdiction.

   (1) The jurisdiction of courts-martial is entirely penal or disciplinary.

   (2) The code applies in all places.

   (3) The jurisdiction of a court-martial with respect to offenses under the code is not affected by the place where the court-martial sits. The jurisdiction of a court-martial with respect to military government or the law of war is not affected by the place where the court-martial sits except as otherwise expressly required by this Manual or applicable rule of international law.

(b) Requisites of court-martial jurisdiction. A court-martial always has jurisdiction to determine whether it has jurisdiction. Otherwise for a court-martial to have jurisdiction:

   (1) The court-martial must be convened by an official empowered to convene it;

   (2) The court-martial must be composed in accordance with these rules with respect to number and qualifications of its personnel. As used here "personnel" includes only the military judge, the members, and the summary court-martial;

   (3) Each charge before the court-martial must be referred to it by competent authority;

   (4) The accused must be a person subject to court-martial jurisdiction; and

   (5) The offense must be subject to court-martial jurisdiction.

RCM 201(b) sets forth the five prerequisites for a court-martial to have jurisdiction over a case. How courts-martial are convened is discussed in the preceding section. The proper composition of courts-martial is discussed below. Referral of charges to a particular court-martial rests with commanders who have authority to convene the type of court-martial where the charged is to be tried. The final two conditions, jurisdiction over the person and offense, are discussed in the next two subsections.

JURISDICTION OVER THE ACCUSED

Status of Accused

The following UCMJ provision describes those individuals subject to jurisdiction of courts-martial.

Article 2, UCMJ. Persons subject to this chapter

(a) The following persons are subject to this chapter;

(1) Members of a regular component of the armed forces. . . .

(2) Cadets, aviation cadets, and midshipmen.

(3) Members of a reserve component while on inactive-duty training.

(4) Retired members of a regular component who are entitled to pay.

. . . .

(7) Persons in custody of the armed forces serving a sentence imposed by a court-martial.

. . . .

(9) Prisoners of war in custody of the armed forces.

The jurisdiction of the military begins when a service member comes on active duty. Hence, reserve personnel are subject to court-martial for offenses committed while on active duty. When does court-martial jurisdiction terminate? The discussion to RCM 202 explains:

(B) Termination of jurisdiction over active duty personnel. As indicated above, the delivery of a valid discharge certificate or its equivalent ordinarily serves to terminate court-martial jurisdiction.

Does the military still have jurisdiction over a service member who commits an offense during a prior enlistment? The following Supreme Court case addresses this issue.

United States ex rel. Hirshberg v. Cooke, Commanding Officer
United States Supreme Court
336 U.S. 210
February 28, 1949

OPINION: Mr. Justice Black

This case raises important questions concerning the statutory jurisdiction of general courts-martial of the Navy.

In 1942 the petitioner was serving a second enlistment in the Navy. Upon the surrender of the United States forces on Corregidor, petitioner became a war prisoner of Japan. After liberation in September, 1945, petitioner was brought back to the United States and hospitalized. He was restored to duty in January, 1946. March 26, 1946, he was granted an honorable discharge because of expiration of his prior enlistment. The next day he re-enlisted, obligating himself to serve four years "subject to such laws, regulations, and articles for the government of the Navy as are or shall be established by the Congress . . . or other competent authority. . . ."

About a year later, petitioner was served with charges directing his trial by a general court-martial of the Navy. The specifications included charges that during his prior enlistment, the petitioner had maltreated two other naval enlisted men who were also Japanese prisoners of war and who were members of groups of prisoners working under petitioner's charge. Petitioner filed a plea in bar of the trial, one ground being that the court-martial was without jurisdiction to try him for alleged offenses committed during a prior enlistment, at the end of which he had received an honorable discharge. His plea was overruled. He was acquitted on some specifications but was convicted on others that charged maltreatment. His sentence was ten months confinement, reduction from chief signalman to apprentice seaman, and dishonorable discharge from the Navy.

Petitioner then brought this habeas corpus proceeding in a federal district court, charging that the court-martial judgment was void because of want of statutory power to convict him for an offense committed if at all during his prior enlistment. [footnote omitted]. That court sustained petitioner's contention and ordered his release from custody. 73 F. Supp. 990. The Court of Appeals reversed, one judge dissenting. 168 F.2d 503. The importance of the statutory construction, which appeared to affect the court-martial powers of the Army as well as the Navy, caused us to grant certiorari. 335 U.S. 842.

. . . .

Aside from naval regulations to which reference will later be made, court-martial authority to try and to punish petitioner for his prior enlistment conduct primarily depends on the language in Article 8 (Second) of the Articles for the Government of the Navy (34 U. S. C. @ 1200, Art. 8), which particularly provides that "such punishment as a court-martial may adjudge may be inflicted on any person in the Navy . . . guilty of . . . maltreatment of, any person subject to his orders. . . ." The Government contends that this language, given its literal meaning, authorized the court-martial to try and to punish petitioner for conduct during a prior enlistment. It is pointed out that petitioner was "in the Navy" when the offense was committed and when he was tried; this language, it is argued, brings his case under the Article. In aid of this interpretation the Government emphasizes that during the whole period of time involved, petitioner was continuously "in the Navy" except for an interval of a few hours between his honorable discharge and his re-enlistment.

. . . .

Obviously Article 8 (Second), which subjects to court-martial jurisdiction persons "in the Navy," supports an argument that petitioner was subject to trial by this court-martial. It is equally obvious that the language of Article 8 (Second), particularly in view of Article 14 (Eleventh), supports an argument that this court-martial could not try petitioner for an offense committed prior to his honorable discharge. Under these circumstances the manner in which court-martial jurisdiction has long been exercised by the Army and Navy is entitled to great weight in interpreting the Articles.

The question of the jurisdiction of a naval court-martial over discharged personnel was submitted by the Secretary of the Navy to the Attorney General in 1919. The precise question of whether re-enlistment could revive jurisdiction of a military court was not considered, but as to the power of military courts over discharged personnel in general, the Attorney General reached the conclusion that a person discharged from the Navy before proceedings were instituted against him "for violations of the Articles Governing the Navy, excepting article 14" could not "thereafter be brought to trial . . . for such violations, though committed while he was in the service." 31 Op. Atty. Gen. 521, 529. This conclusion of the Attorney General relied on statements of the Judge Advocate Generals of the Army and Navy that their offices had "from the beginning and

uniformly held that a person separated from the service ceases to be amenable" to military and naval jurisdiction. Previous to the Attorney General's 1919 opinion neither the Navy nor Army had ever claimed court-martial power to try their personnel for offenses committed prior to an honorable discharge where proceedings had not been instituted before discharge. *See* Winthrop Military Law and Precedents 93 (2d ed. 1920). The Government concedes that the Army has always so construed its court-martial jurisdiction whenever the question arose. And the Government concedes that the Navy also followed this view of its jurisdiction until 1932.[1]

. . . .

This revised naval interpretation was given in 1932. Before that time, both Army and Navy had for more than half a century acted on the implicit assumption that discharged servicemen, whether re-enlisted or not, were no longer subject to court-martial power. The Attorney General of the United States had proceeded on the same assumption. And *see United States v. Kelly*, 15 Wall. 34, 36. Under these circumstances, little weight can be given to the 1932 separate effort of the Navy to change the long-accepted understanding of its statutory court-martial power. For should this belated naval interpretation be accepted as correct, there would be left outstanding an Army interpretation of its statutory court-martial powers directly opposed to that of the Navy. Since the Army and Navy court-martial powers depend on substantially the same statutory foundations, the opposing interpretations cannot both be right, unless it be assumed that Congress has left each free to determine its own court-martial boundaries. We cannot

---

[1]Since 1932 the Navy has consistently adhered to its revised interpretation of Art. 8 (Second). In 1934 the Navy Department incorporated this revised interpretation in an official Navy publication, Naval Courts and Boards, and this interpretation became @ 334 (a) of Naval Courts and Boards (1937 ed.).

assume that Congress intended a delegation of such broad power in an area which
so vitally affects the rights and liberties of
those who are now, have been, or may be
associated with the Nation's armed forces.

Reversed.

Does is seem equitable that Chief Hirshberg was not subject to court-martial
jurisdiction even though he was still on active duty? The case was a focal point of
the legislative hearings on enactment of the UCMJ. The following discussion
regarding *Hirshberg* took place during the House of Representatives hearings:

> Mr. Elston. I would like to ask you this question. I think it was since you
> completed your hearings that a case has been decided by the Supreme Court of the
> United States.
>
> Dr. Morgan. The Hirschberg [sic] case?
>
> Mr. Elston. Yes. To the effect that a person who has left the service, that is, who
> has been separated from the service, cannot be tried subsequently by a military
> court for an offense committed prior to such separation.
>
> Mr. Kilday. Even though he has reenlisted?
>
> Mr. Elston. Even though he has reenlisted?
>
> Dr. Morgan. That is right.
>
> Mr. Elston. Now, you have not anything in your bill covering that?
>
> . . . .
>
> Mr. Elston. Yes. He may have even committed a murder within 3 days of his
> separation from the service.
>
> Dr. Morgan. That is right. We have not covered that.
>
> Mr. Elston. He reenlists and cannot be tried for it.
>
> Dr. Morgan. That is right.
>
> Mr. Elston. I think this committee can write something into the law that will take
> care of that ridiculous situation.

In light of *Hirshberg*, Congress enacted the following UCMJ provision.

> Art. 3. Jurisdiction to try certain personnel

(a) [N]o person charged with having committed, while in a status in which he was subject to this chapter, an offense against this chapter, punishable by confinement for five years or more and for which the person cannot be tried in the courts of the United States or of a State, a Territory, or the District of Columbia, may be relieved from amenability to trial by court-martial by reason of the termination of that status.

The above provision is limited in scope in that it only applies to serious offenses and in situations where the other federal or state courts do not have jurisdiction to try the case (the *Hirshberg* scenario). *United States v. Clardy*, 13 M.J. 308 (C.M.A. 1982) finally resolved the issue of whether a service member could be tried for offenses committed during a prior enlistment where there was no break in active service. *Clardy* held that court-martial jurisdiction exists over a service member who is discharged solely for the purpose of reenlistment and if his military status in the active service did not change. The court in *Clardy* also held, however, that a break in service as in *Hirshberg* (one day) precludes jurisdiction by the military—unless the case falls under Article 3(a).

Former Jeopardy

"Former jeopardy" (also commonly termed "double jeopardy") prohibits the retrial of an accused for the same offense by the same authority. Consider the application of the former jeopardy rule in the following case.

United States, Appellee, v. David P. Schneider, Major U.S. Army, Appellant
United States Court of Military Appeals
38 M.J. 387
September 30, 1993

OPINION: Ryan, Circuit Judge

A general court-martial sitting at Fort Leavenworth, Kansas, convicted appellant, Major David P. Schneider, contrary to his pleas, of attempted premeditated murder, conduct unbecoming an officer by committing adultery, and conduct unbecoming an officer by committing perjury in a state court, in violation of Articles 80 and 133, Uniform Code of Military Justice, 10 USC @@ 880 and 933, respectively. He now appeals the decision of the Court of Military Review affirming his conviction and sentence. 34 M.J. 639 (1992). He argues that there was insufficient evidence to convict him of these specifications and also that there were several procedural errors during and after trial. 37 M.J. 191 (1993). For the reasons discussed below, we affirm.

I

In 1987, appellant moved to California with his wife and two children, pursuant to his assignment to the Lawrence Livermore National Laboratory. At the Laboratory, he worked with a woman named Paula, and by April 1989, their relationship had become sexual.

In 1989 appellant was assigned to attend the U.S. Army Command and General Staff College at Fort Leavenworth, Kansas, and moved with his family into government quarters there. In August 1989, he met with an insurance agent and purchased an additional $150,000 in life insurance coverage on his wife. He was the beneficiary of this policy, which had an effective date of October 1, 1989. That same summer, appellant sold the former family home in California and used the proceeds to purchase a home in Tracy, California; he convinced his wife that her name should not be on the deed. He then spent Labor Day weekend with Paula in California.

The incident out of which the specification of attempted murder arose occurred on October 20, 1989. That night, appellant's wife awoke with intense pain in her head and was pulled to a sitting position in her bed. She saw appellant, visibly shaken, standing next to the bed. The toilet tank lid from the bathroom lay broken on the floor near his feet. She felt a baseball-sized lump on her head, which was "oozing." She brushed small pieces of porcelain from her hair. He then assisted her to the bathroom, and she sat on the toilet. When she began shaking, he helped her to the bathroom floor and covered her with a quilt. Appellant told his wife, repeatedly, "You must have hit your head." Although appellant suggested taking her to a doctor, his wife wanted only to go back to bed. The next morning, he took her to the medical

facility and there told medical personnel that Debbie was sleepwalking, picked up the toilet tank lid, tripped, and hit her head. Other evidence at trial, however, indicated that his wife had never walked in her sleep.[1]

Two weeks later, on November 4, appellant and his wife were to attend the Armor Ball. Appellant made arrangements for a "romantic" night at Embassy Suites Hotel. At appellant's insistence, he and his wife left prior to the end of the ball in order to go to the hotel. Upon arriving, appellant learned that, although he had asked for an eighth-floor room when making reservations, he was given a room on the seventh floor instead.

They nonetheless took the elevator to the eighth floor, where they were observed by two 16-year-old girls. The girls saw appellant and his wife walk side by side down the hallway. One girl then saw appellant make vigorous hand movements in front of his wife as she faced him with her back to a rail overlooking an interior courtyard. The girl observed appellant put his left arm around his wife at the point where the rail met her back, put his right hand on her chest, and flip her over the rail. The wife fell some 70 or 80 feet, and hit a table on the atrium floor. The girl watched appellant look over the railing, say ("he didn't yell") "for someone to call an ambulance," then walk to the elevator, and walk back to the railing. He then walked back to the elevator and proceeded down. When he reached the atrium floor, appellant was cool and collected. His wife's pelvis was fractured in thirteen places; both left and right femurs were broken in several places;

---

[1] Appellant testified in state trial proceedings that after his wife had gone to bed, he stayed up to work. He noticed the toilet was running and fixed it, but did not replace the tank lid. He then went to bed, but was awakened by a motion on the bed or noise. His wife was sitting on the bed, moaning, with her hand to her head. When he got up to help her, he discovered the shards of the toilet tank lid. She told him she didn't know what had happened. He also testified that he did not "believe" he had told the medical personnel that she had been sleepwalking, because he knew she never walked in her sleep.

a bone penetrated her abdominal cavity, damaging her colon; and an ankle and several ribs were fractured.

On December 4, one month after the ball and two days after his wife returned home from the hospital, appellant told his wife that he did not love her any more and was getting a divorce. On December 5, he admitted to police that he had had an affair with Paula and that he loved her and hoped to marry her when his divorce was final.[2]

Appellant was charged by state authorities with first-degree assault, in violation of @ 565.050, Revised Statutes of Missouri, for the incident at the Embassy Suites Hotel. At the state trial, appellant testified that the incident at the Embassy Suites Hotel occurred when he attempted to carry his wife across the threshold. He picked her up and was carrying her at high port when she told him that they were on the wrong floor. He then turned and tripped; his wife slipped from his grasp, causing her to fall over the balcony railing to the atrium floor. He testified that he did not intend to injure his wife.[3] He was acquitted.

Shortly after the state case was concluded, military authorities charged appellant with specifications of attempted premeditated murder, conduct unbecoming an officer by committing adultery, and conduct unbecoming an officer by committing perjury. A court consisting of officer members found appellant guilty and sentenced him to dismissal, confinement for 23 years, and total forfeitures. The convening authority approved the sentence, except that he suspended forfeitures in excess of $400 pay

per month until execution of the dismissal, provided that the suspended forfeitures be paid to appellant's now ex-wife.

II

. . . .

B

The next issue we consider is appellant's contention that his prosecution for conduct unbecoming an officer ("by wrongfully . . . testifying falsely" under "lawful oath" before a jury sitting in the Platte County, Missouri, District Court) "was an abuse of discretion and a violation of double jeopardy." [citation omitted].

Appellant complains that in prosecuting him for falsely testifying, the military is merely attempting to do indirectly what it cannot do directly. We disagree. Plainly, the Fifth Amendment would have permitted the military to reprosecute appellant directly for first-degree assault or an equivalent offense under the Uniform Code of Military Justice. The Double Jeopardy Clause does not bar one sovereign from proceeding on a charge of which an accused has been acquitted by another sovereign. [citations omitted]. Furthermore, the doctrine of collateral estoppel is inapplicable to prosecutions by a separate sovereign. *United States v. Cuellar*, 27 M.J. 50, 54-55 (C.M.A. 1988), *cert. denied*, 493 U.S. 811 (1989). Since appellant could have been reprosecuted by the military for first-degree assault or its equivalent, he clearly could be prosecuted for the entirely separate offense of conduct unbecoming an officer, which was committed at a wholly

---

[2]A week prior to this occasion, appellant had taken his wife for yet another "romantic" overnight stay on the top floor of a local downtown hotel. That night he had tried to get her to drink more champagne than she normally consumed, and then, after dinner, tried to get her out on the balcony of their room. She refused, however, because it was too cold and because she was afraid of heights.

[3]This testimony led to the specification in his general court-martial charging him with conduct unbecoming an officer by committing perjury.

Military can always ~~follow~~ try someone they "own" even after local authorities try ($ convict) EXCEPT federal trials (because military is federal)

distinct place and time.[4] Appellant's subordinate contention that his prosecution for falsely testifying was barred by Army policy also fails. Para. 4-2, Army Regulation 27-10, "Military Justice," provides the general rule:

> A person subject to the UCMJ who has been tried in a civilian court may, but ordinarily will not, be tried by court-martial or punished under Article 15, UCMJ, for the same act over which the civilian court has exercised jurisdiction.

Paragraph 4-3 of the same regulation provides, however, that an officer exercising GCM [general court-martial] jurisdiction may authorize disposition of a case under the UCMJ and the MCM [Manual for Courts-Martial, United States, 1984] despite a previous trial. The general court-martial convening authority here personally authorized appellant's trial on the falsely-testifying specification, after the requisite findings were made. Art. 34(a), UCMJ, 10 USC @ 834(a)(1983). And, as already pointed out, appellant was not, in any event, prosecuted for "the same act" for which he was tried by the State of Missouri. Thus, the military was in full compliance with its policy. There was no bar to appellant's prosecution for falsely testifying at his civilian trial, so the issue is without merit.

The decision of the United States Army Court of Military Review is affirmed.

The following provision of the RCM specifically addresses jurisdiction over uniquely military crimes and discusses the former jeopardy principle.

RCM 201:

(d) Exclusive and nonexclusive jurisdiction.

(1) Courts-martial have exclusive jurisdiction of purely military offenses.

(2) An act or omission which violates both the code and local criminal law, foreign or domestic, may be tried by a court-martial, or by a proper civilian tribunal, foreign or domestic, or, subject to . . . regulations of the Secretary concerned, by both.

(3) Where an act or omission is subject to trial by court-martial and by one or more civil tribunals, foreign or domestic, the determination which nation, state, or agency will exercise jurisdiction is a matter for the nations, states, and agencies concerned, and is not a right of the suspect or accused.

For former jeopardy to apply, the accused must be tried by the same authority. Courts-martial are under the authority of the United States and, therefore, may not retry members previously tried in other United States federal courts (military or

---

[4]Appellant misperceives the charge of conduct unbecoming an officer by falsely testifying under oath as amounting to a mere inappropriate overreaching by the military into internal state matters, namely "ensuring the truthfulness of testimony in state courts." Final Brief at 27. The military's own interest, however, in not having its officers testify falsely anywhere is a thoroughly legitimate basis of concern for military authorities. Art. 133, UCMJ, 10 USC @ 933; *see Solorio v. United States*, 483 U.S. 435 (1987).

civilian). Trials by the courts of a state or foreign country, however, are not under federal authority and will not bar subsequent trial by courts-martial. Nonetheless, the services have a policy to limit trial by courts-martial of members previously tried by state or foreign courts for the same offense to those unusual cases where punishment imposed by the military is considered essential in the interests of justice, discipline and proper administration within the military. Consider whether *Schneider* is the type of case contemplated by such a policy.

JURISDICTION OVER THE OFFENSE

United States, Appellee, v. Private John W. Mauck, U. S. Army, Appellant
United States Army Court of Military Review
17 M.J. 1033
April 16, 1984

OPINION: Yawn, Judge

Appellant is before this Court convicted of larceny, maiming, forcible sodomy and attempted murder, violations of Articles 121, 124, 125 and 80, Uniform Code of Military Justice, 10 U.S.C. 921, 924, 925 and 880, respectively. His approved sentence provides for a dishonorable discharge, confinement at hard labor for fifteen years, and total forfeitures. He argues that the court-martial lacked jurisdiction over the subject matter of the charged offenses since they occurred off-post. For the purposes of adjudicating the question of jurisdiction at trial, the following facts were agreed upon:

On or about 4 January 1982 Billy Ray Hutcherson and John W. Mauck reported to Redstone Arsenal, Alabama. Hutcherson and Mauck were assigned to the 8th Student Company. Several days after reporting to Redstone Arsenal, Mauck and Hutcherson became acquainted with each other. Prior to 22 January 1982, their acquaintance had grown into a friendship. Not long after coming to Redstone Arsenal, Hutcher-son met Julie [F.], the dependent daughter of a military retiree. Julie's family lives only a short distance from the Redstone Arsenal boundary line, near gate 5. Julie had many friends who were service members. Moreover, Julie frequented and socialized at the Enlisted Man's Club and at other locations on Redstone Arsenal. On various occasions Julie talked with Hutcherson at the Enlisted Man's Club. Their acquaintance soon blossomed into an intimate friendship. Their resulting sexual acts all occurred at Redstone Arsenal. On the night of 21 January 1982, Hutcherson and Julie engaged in sexual intercourse in the 8th Student Company billets. On the morning of 22 January, Hutcherson may have told Mauck about the sexual affair that had occurred the previous evening with Julie. On the afternoon of 22 January, Mauck met Julie through his friend Hutcherson. Plans were made to go out on the town in Huntsville, Alabama, the evening of 22 January 1982. Since Mauck did not have a date, and since he was [a] good friend of Hutcherson, Julie agreed to arrange a blind date for Mauck. On the same afternoon of 22 January 1982, Mauck drove Julie to her home while Hutcherson showered and changed into civilian clothes. Upon returning to post, the three of them, all dressed in civilian clothing, went to dinner at the unit mess hall where they met service members Buck, a friend of Mauck and Hutcherson, and Linda [G.], a friend of Julie's. After dinner the five of them went to the Enlisted Man's Club where they consumed beer and danced. Some time later, all five left the Enlisted Man's Club and went to a local beverage store off post and purchased two quarts of Jack Daniels which they passed around inside the car. The party then went to the Sunshine Lounge, Huntsville, Alabama, where they continued to drink Jack Daniels. About midnight, Mauck learned that his blind date was not going to show up and he became very enraged. Consequently, Mauck and Hutcherson decided to drive Julie [F.] home. While en route Mauck and Hutcherson continued to argue with and execrate Julie for the failure of his blind date to show up. The argument became so intensified that Julie got out of the car twice. Finally, Mauck drove to an abandoned road approximately 15 feet outside the boundary line of Redstone Arsenal, at secured Gate 5. All parties exited the car, leaving the lights on. It was here that Julie was sodomized and brutally and violently beaten. Mauck and Hutcherson left Julie's naked, beaten, maimed, and bloody body in the freezing rain. They believed Julie was dead. After everything occurred at Gate 5, Mauck and Hutcherson returned to Redstone Arsenal. On 3 February 1982, Mauck and Hutcherson were arrested by the Huntsville Police Department. On 19 February 1982, Mauck and Hutcherson were indicted by the Madison County Grand Jury for assault and sodomy of Julie [F.]. On 5 May 1982, Hutcherson was tried in the circuit court of Madison County and found guilty of

assault in the second degree and sexual abuse in the second degree. Hutcherson was sentenced to serve fifteen years at hard labor in the Alabama penitentiary. In early July 1982, the District Attorney's Office of Madison County nol-prossed Mauck's case. We hold there was jurisdiction and affirm.

The basic law on this issue is found in *Relford v. Commandant*, 401 U.S. 355, 91 S. Ct. 649, 28 L. Ed. 2d 102 (1971), and *O'Callahan v. Parker*, 395 U.S. 258, 89 S. Ct. 1683, 23 L. Ed. 2d 291 (1969). In *O'Callahan,* the Supreme Court held that courts-martial lack jurisdiction over the subject matter of an offense unless it is "service connected." *Id.* at 279, 89 S. Ct. at 1694. Such jurisdiction was found lacking in *O'Callahan* because *O'Callahan's* offenses, attempted rape and related crimes, were committed offpost while he was on pass and within the Territory of Hawaii; there was no connection between the offenses and his military duties; he was not in uniform; and his victim had no ties to the military. *Relford*, on the other hand, raped both a military dependent and an employee of the post-exchange on the post where he was stationed. A unanimous Court found the offenses service connected, and clarified *O'Callahan* by holding "that when a serviceman is charged with an offense committed within or at the geographical boundary of a military post and violative of the security of a person or of property there, that offense may be tried by a court-martial." *Relford v. Commandant*, 401 U.S. at 369, 91 S. Ct. at 657. The Court recognized, however, that some offenses perpetrated offpost could be service connected, and, in particular, quoted Winthrop for the proposition that they even included offenses committed upon or against civilians near a military post. [citations omitted].

Recognizing that the question of jurisdiction will turn on the unique facts surrounding the commission of an offense, the Court said,

[A]ny ad hoc approach leaves outer boundaries undetermined. *O'Callahan* marks an area, perhaps not the limit, for the concern of the civil courts and where the military may not enter. The case today marks an area, perhaps not the limit, where the court-martial is appropriate and permissible. What lies between is for decision at another time. [citations omitted].

As might be imagined, the issue of jurisdiction over the subject matter of an offense remained an unsettled area of military law for some time after *O'Callahan* and *Relford*. *See generally United States v. Trottier*, 9 M.J. 337, 340-45 (C.M.A.1980); *Cooper, O'Callahan* Revisited: Severing the Service Connection 76 Mil.L.Rev. 165 (1977). However, recent pronouncements by the Court of Military Appeals somewhat settled the muddied waters. For example, the Court concluded "that almost every involvement of service personnel with the commerce of drugs is 'service-connected.'" *United States v. Trottier*, 9 M.J. at 350 (footnote omitted). *See* also *Murray v. Haldeman*, 16 M.J. 74, 80 (C.M.A.1983) (serviceman's wrongful use of drugs while on extended leave far away from any military installation is service connected if he later enters a military installation while subject to any physiological or psychological effects of the drug). Moreover, the Court recently held that a serviceman's status of unauthorized absence when he commits an offense is a factor tending to establish the service connection of that offense, even if committed off-post. *United States v. Johnson*, 17 M.J. 73 (C.M.A.1983). Most importantly, though, the Court articulated the guiding principle that "the conduct of service members which takes place outside a military enclave is service connected and subject to trial by court-martial if it has a significant effect within that enclave." *United States v. Lockwood*, 15 M.J. 1, 6 (C.M.A.1983). The effect of an offense is measured by its impact upon the persons assigned to the post

and the morale, reputation and integrity of the post itself. *Id.* at 10.

The border of a military post is not a demarcation line where court-martial jurisdiction ends. The fact that the appellant's crimes were not committed within the borders of Redstone Arsenal does not, when considered in the totality of the circumstances, exempt him from trial by court-martial. The appellant and his victim became acquainted as a result of his military status. Victim, a dependent daughter of a military retiree living just off the post, was a member of the military community. On the evening in question, they met and socialized on the post where the appellant was stationed, then left with other military personnel for additional socializing. Finally, after the offenses were committed, the appellant and his confederate returned to the post, leaving what they thought was a dead body "approximately 15 feet outside the boundary line" of the post. *See United States v. Mitchell*, 2 M.J. 1020 (A.C.M.R.1976), pet. denied, 3 M.J. 105 (C.M.A.1977).

We find that these offenses were committed "at the geographical boundary" of a military post and were violative of the security of persons therein, and that the appellant's conduct had a significant effect upon that enclave. We also note that 10 U.S.C. 1071 et seq., authorizes medical care at military treatment facilities for dependents of retired personnel, and the record reflects that a portion of the victim's medical care was performed in the medical facility at Redstone Arsenal. *See United States v. Dimas*, 12 Mil.L.Rev. (Pub.L.Educ.Inst.) 2053 (N.M.C.M.R. Nov. 18, 1983). The role played by the State of Alabama in this case had no effect on our decision. We presume this sovereign state had good and sufficient reason to prosecute Hutcherson but not Mauck, just as we presume the convening authority in this case had good and sufficient reason to prosecute Mauck but not Hutcherson.

The findings of guilty and the sentence are affirmed.

In *United States v. Solario,* 483 U.S. 435 (1987) the Supreme Court held that "jurisdiction of a court-martial depends solely upon the accused's status as a member of the armed forces, and not on the service-connection of the offense charged." Hence, the location of the offense is no longer a factor in deciding whether the military has jurisdiction. *Solario* significantly increased the number of cases that the military may try at courts-martial. Given this expanded jurisdiction, it is not surprising that the number of courts-martial cases grew rapidly following the *Solario* decision. However, the military drawdown caused by the end of the Cold War has since caused a downward spiral in the number court-martial cases. Figure 3-C demonstrates this trend.

FIGURE 3-C

DEPARTMENT OF THE NAVY CONVICTIONS AND NONJUDICIAL PUNISHMENTS

NAVY AND MARINE

	FY-91 (10/01/90 TO 09/30/91)	FY-94 (10/01/93 TO 09/30/94)
GCM:	1765	380
SPCM:	7289	1454
SCM:	5244	1564
TOTAL C/Ms:	14298	3398
NJPs:	102474	31747

MARINE

	FY-91 (10/01/90 TO 09/30/91)	FY-94 (10/01/93 TO 09/30/94)
GCM:	370	48
SPCM:	1569	276
SCM:	936	263
TOTAL C/Ms:	2875	587
NJPs:	15050	4113

NAVY

	FY-91 (10/01/90 TO 09/30/91)	FY-94 (10/01/93 TO 09/30/94)
GCM:	1395	332
SPCM:	5720	1178
SCM:	4308	1301
TOTAL C/Ms:	11423	2811
NJPs:	87424	27634

TRIAL PROCEDURES

PARTICIPANTS AT COURTS-MARTIAL

The RCM sets forth the personnel who make up a court-martial and their required qualifications.

Rule 502. Qualifications and duties of personnel of courts-martial

(a) Members.

  (1) Qualifications. The members detailed to a court-martial shall be those persons who in the opinion of the convening authority are best qualified for the duty by reason of their age, education, training, experience, length of service, and judicial temperament. Each member shall be on active duty with the armed forces and shall be:

  (A) A commissioned officer;

  (B) A warrant officer, except when the accused is a commissioned officer; or

  (C) An enlisted person if the accused is an enlisted person and has made a timely request under R.C.M. 503(a)(2).

  (2) Duties. The members of a court-martial shall determine whether the accused is proved guilty and, if necessary, adjudge a proper sentence, based on the evidence and in accordance with the instructions of the military judge. Each member has an equal voice and vote with other members in deliberating upon and deciding all matters submitted to them, except as otherwise specifically provided in these rules. No member may use rank or position to influence another member. No member of a court-martial may have access to or use in any open or closed session this Manual, reports of decided cases, or any other reference material, except the president of a special courts-martial without a military judge may use such materials in open session.

(b) President.

  (1) Qualifications. The president of a court-martial shall be the detailed member senior in rank then serving.

  (2) Duties. The president shall have the same duties as the other members and shall also:

  (A) Preside over closed sessions of the members of the court-martial during their deliberations;

  (B) Speak for the members of the court-martial when announcing the decision of the members or requesting instructions from the military judge; and

(C) In a special courts-martial without a military judge, perform the duties assigned by this Manual to the military judge except as otherwise expressly provided.

(c) *Qualifications of military judge.* A military judge shall be a commissioned officer on active duty in the armed forces who is a member of the bar of a Federal court or a member of the bar of the highest court of a State and who is certified to be qualified for duty as a military judge by the Judge Advocate General of the armed force of which the military judge is a member. In addition, the military judge of a general court-martial shall be designated for such duties by the Judge Advocate General or the Judge Advocate General's designee, certified to be qualified for duty as a military judge of a general court-martial, and assigned and directly responsible to the Judge Advocate General or the Judge Advocate General's designee. . . .

(d) Counsel.

(1) *Certified counsel required.* Only persons certified under Article 27(b) as competent to perform duties as counsel in courts-martial by the Judge Advocate General of the armed force of which the counsel is a member may be detailed as defense counsel or associate defense counsel in general or special courts-martial or as trial counsel in general courts-martial.

(2) *Other military counsel.* Any commissioned officer may be detailed as trial counsel in special courts-martial, or as assistant trial counsel or assistant defense counsel in general or special courts-martial. The Secretary concerned may establish additional qualifications for such counsel.

(3) *Qualifications of individual military and civilian defense counsel.* Individual military or civilian defense counsel who represents an accused in a court-martial shall be:

(A) A member of the bar of a Federal court or of the bar of the highest court of a State; or

(B) If not a member of such a bar, a lawyer who is authorized by a recognized licensing authority to practice law and is found by the military judge to be qualified to represent the accused upon a showing to the satisfaction of the military judge that the counsel has appropriate training and familiarity with the general principles of criminal law which apply in a court-martial.

The above rules apply only to general and special court-martial. Summary courts are composed of one active duty commissioned officer of the same armed force as the accused. *See Types of Courts-Martial* and the *Middendorf* case above for discussions of the procedures at summary courts-martial. Members (jurors) at general and special courts-martial are active duty officers who are senior to the accused. Enlisted accused may elect to have one-third of the members be enlisted. Unlike most civilian jurisdictions, which require unanimous verdicts, only two-thirds of the panel have to agree on guilt or innocence. Note, however, that where confinement may exceed ten years a three-fourths majority is necessary, and, in capital cases, the verdict must be unanimous. *See* Figure 3-A for a comparison of the composition of members at special and general courts-martial.

RCM 502 above discusses the role and qualifications of defense counsel. The following case addresses the ethical responsibilities of defense counsel.

United States, Appellee, v. Private Angela H. Bryant, U.S. Army, Appellant
United States Army Court of Military Review
35 M.J. 739
September 23, 1992

OPINION: Gravelle, Judge

Contrary to her pleas, the appellant was convicted by a military judge sitting as a special court-martial of two specifications of failing to go to her appointed place of duty, two specifications of disobeying the orders of a noncommissioned officer, and one specification of disrespect toward a noncommissioned officer, in violation of Articles 86 and 91, Uniform Code of Military Justice, 10 U.S.C. @@ 886 and 891 (1982). The convening authority approved the adjudged sentence of a bad-conduct discharge, confinement for three months, forfeiture of $490 pay per month for three months, and reduction to Private E1.

In this case, we must decide whether the defense counsel's conduct in providing advice to his client regarding choice of forum, advice with which the counsel did not personally agree, amounted to ineffective assistance of counsel. We hold that the defense counsel's conduct amounted to ineffective assistance of counsel.

I.

The appellant's court-martial occurred in Saudi Arabia. On appeal, she initially asserted that her defense counsel, MAJ D [then CPT D], was ineffective during the sentencing proceedings at trial and during the post trial processing of this case. She has filed an affidavit with this court detailing her reasons for believing that her de-

fense counsel was ineffMAJective. The defense counsel has also filed an affidavit in reply. Based on these affidavits, the government has conceded that MAJ D was ineffective in his representation of the appellant during and after sentencing. In light of our holding, we need not examine the correctness of the government's concession regarding ineffectiveness in the sentencing and posttrial phases of the court-martial process.

The defense counsel's affidavit also raised a troubling issue regarding his effectiveness during the pretrial phase involving a decision made by the appellant at trial. [footnote omitted]. In his affidavit, the trial defense counsel asserted, inter alia:

4. Prior to trial, I made two trips out to the desert [in Saudi Arabia] where the 1st Armor [sic] Division was encamped to interview my client and prepare the case. I had no means of transportation nor communication and was forced to rely upon transportation provided by the 1st Armor [sic] Division. During these two visits, I focused my investigation on the guilt/innocence portion of the trial and expended a lot of energy attempting to convince the command to dispose of the charges either administratively or through nonjudicial punishment.

. . . .

8. Despite my attempts to make the charges go away, I was notified several days prior to February 23, 1991 that we would be going to trial. I did not arrive at Log Base Echo until the late afternoon of February 22, 1991. The 1st Armor [sic] Division had just moved forward and it was well known that the ground war would be starting in the immediate future. Although I was well prepared for the guilt/innocence phase of the trial, I knew that I had done nothing to put together an extenuation and mitigation case.

9. Moreover I was faced with a dilemma that I had never faced before—being torn between my loyalties as an officer and my loyalties as a defense counsel. I knew that the case against PV2 Bryant was full of problems and that there was a chance for acquittal before a panel. I also knew that the ground war was to about start and that the 1st Armor [sic] Division needed each and every officer and noncommissioned officer to do their part. I am sorry to admit that CPT [D] the officer won over CPT [D] the defense counsel and I convinced PV2 Bryant that she should choose to go judge alone. I knew that this was a classic case which warranted a panel. In fact, after trial the judge questioned me about why I did not go with a panel and indicated that he thought I would have done better with a panel. I gave my client advice which was in the best interest of the war effort and not in her best interest.

Because of these statements, we specified the following issue:

WHETHER THE APPELLANT'S TRIAL DEFENSE COUNSEL WAS IN-EFFECTIVE AS TO THE MERITS PORTION OF APPELLANT'S TRIAL, BASED UPON ADMISSIONS CONTAINED WITHIN [THE DEFENSE COUNSEL'S] SWORN AFFIDAVIT.

In response to the specified issue, appellate defense counsel, not surprisingly, assert that the trial defense counsel's actions amount to ineffective assistance of counsel under the standards of *Strickland v. Washington*, 466 U.S. 668, 80 L. Ed. 2d 674, 104 S. Ct. 2052 (1984), and because the actions involve a conflict of interest, citing *United States v. Cronic*, 466 U.S. 648, 80 L. Ed. 2d 657, 104 S. Ct. 2039 (1984). In addition, the appellant has submitted a new affidavit in which she asserts that MAJ D failed to call a number of witnesses to testify on the merits of the case on her behalf.[1]

The government responds that we should not find ineffective assistance of counsel because it is human nature for a defense counsel to second-guess his own decisions and trial tactics after an unfavorable trial result, that "speculation based on hindsight is not the proper standard" for determining whether MAJ D was ineffective, and that the advice was "not unreasonable under the circumstances and was well within professional norms." Assuming, arguendo, that the advice was erroneous, the government further argues that "the appellant was not prejudiced as a result of the counsel's actions because the decision regarding forum was ultimately appellant's to make." Appellate government counsel argues that the record shows that the appellant knowingly, intelligently, freely, and unequivocally elected trial by military judge alone.

---

[1]The government has presented a countervailing affidavit from MAJD explaining his reasons for not calling the witnesses. Because of our holding in this case, we need not determine the merits of this particular aspect of the appellant's allegation of ineffectiveness.

II.

The Sixth Amendment right to counsel includes the right to effective representation of counsel. *Strickland*, 466 U.S. at 690. The appellant is entitled to effective representation of counsel before, during, and after trial. *United States v. Holt*, 33 M.J. 400 (C.M.A. 1991). A counsel's performance is judged under standards set out in Strickland which are applicable in the military justice system. *United States v. Scott*, 24 M.J. 186 (C.M.A. 1987). Under *Strickland*, a counsel's performance is presumed to be competent. To overcome this presumption, an appellant must point out specific errors made by his defense counsel that were unreasonable under prevailing professional norms. *Cronic*, 466 U.S. 648, 80 L. Ed. 2d 657, 104 S. Ct. 2039. Under Strickland, there is a two-part test for showing ineffectiveness of counsel. First, the appellant must show that the counsel's performance was deficient. Second, the appellant must show that the deficient performance prejudiced the defense. *Id*. at 687. However, prejudice may be presumed when the defense counsel is burdened by an actual conflict of interest, or when an accused has been denied the effective assistance of counsel at a critical stage of trial. [citations omitted]. "Only when the surrounding circumstances justify a presumption of ineffectiveness can a Sixth Amendment claim be sufficient without inquiry into counsel's actual performance at trial." *Cronic*, 466 U.S. 648 at 662, 80 L. Ed. 2d 657, 104 S. Ct. 2039.

A defense counsel must "guard the interests of the accused zealously within the bounds of the law" and must "represent the accused with undivided fidelity." R.C.M. 502(d)(6), discussion (B).

III.

We reject the government's arguments summarized in Part I above. We cannot agree that the defense counsel's advice to the appellant before trial was "not unreasonable under the circumstances and was well within professional norms." Nor can we agree that we should treat the contents of the defense counsel's affidavit as merely the product of human nature to second-guess his own performance and as "speculation based on hindsight." Finally, while the record of proceedings may ostensibly show that the appellant's choice of forum was knowingly, intelligently, and freely made, the defense counsel's affidavit shows the contrary. A component of a client's knowing and intelligent decisions prior to and at trial is the counsel's best advice, unencumbered by divided loyalties.

In our system of military justice, it is clear that the interests of the Army are best served when the interests of the defense counsel's client are paramount in that counsel's mind. In the case before us, the defense counsel failed to understand, or lost sight of the fact, that a defense counsel's duty to the Army is to provide his or her client with representation unclouded by the government's operational considerations.

We judicially note that the ground war against Iraq began during Operation Desert Storm on 24 February 1991, and that the First Armored Division was an active participant throughout. We also note that the trial of this case occurred on 23 February 1991. We find that the defense counsel's affidavit is believable, credible, and forthright, and we accept it as accurate. By the defense counsel's own admission, he placed what he perceived to be the Army's interests over those of his client. Utilizing the standards for measuring the effectiveness of counsel set out in *Strickland v. Washington*, we hold that the defense counsel provided ineffective assistance of counsel when he gave advice regarding the critical decision of choice of forum, advice that he himself did not agree with and which he was convinced was not in his client's best interest. Under the unique circumstances of this case, we find the defense counsel was laboring under an actual conflict of interest and will presume prejudice.

The findings of guilty and the sentence are set aside. A rehearing may be ordered by the same or a different convening authority.

Do you agree that a military defense counsel's first obligation is to his or her client? Should operational commitments ever be taken into account by a defense counsel? Note that military defense counsel are members of various state and federal bars. Ethical violations on their part subjects them not only to decertification as military attorneys but also to disciplinary action by their respective bars.

SENTENCING

Following conviction of an accused at court-martial, a second phase of the trial occurs, referred to as the "sentencing hearing." During this hearing, the court must decide on an appropriate sentence. The government and defense will usually introduce evidence during the sentencing phase that bears on the appropriate type and amount of punishment that the court should award. The following case considers the role of the convening authority in this process.

United States, Appellee, v. Private First Class Gene A. Hill, U.S. Army, Appellant
United States Army Court of Military Review
18 M.J. 75
August 13, 1984

OPINION: McKay, Senior Judge

In accordance with his pleas, the appellant, Private Hill, was convicted by a military judge sitting as a special court-martial of two specifications of distribution of marijuana in the hashish form, a violation of Article 134, Uniform Code of Military Justice (UCMJ), 10 U.S.C. @ 934 (1982). He was sentenced to a bad-conduct discharge, confinement at hard labor for three months, forfeiture of $382.00 pay per month for six months, and reduction to the lowest enlisted grade. The convening authority approved the sentence.

Before this Court, the appellant has alleged several errors regarding the presence and impact of unlawful command influence within the 3d Armored Division. Two of these errors allege, in substance, that the convening authority, Major General Anderson, was disqualified from referring the appellant's case to trial and from reviewing and taking action on the case. We resolve these issues adversely to Private

Hill. [citations omitted]. The appellant also argues that the military judge improperly prohibited Private Hill's defense counsel from developing facts relevant to the issue of the effect of illegal command influence upon the presentation of evidence favorable to Private Hill during the sentencing portion of his trial and, in a related vein, that Private Hill was denied a fair sentencing proceeding due to the presence of unlawful command influence. We agree and will take corrective action.[1]

We believe Private Hill's decision to plead guilty was not affected by the existence of illegal command influence within the 3d Armored Division, but was based instead on his evaluation of the evidence against him and on his desire to limit the punishment he might receive.

During the sentencing portion of the appellant's trial, First Lieutenant David Sanders was called as a defense witness. Lieutenant Sanders, who was a member of Private Hill's battalion, testified that he was aware of the letter written and distributed by the Division Command Sergeant Major (hereinafter referred to as the Haga letter) and containing his thoughts on what a good noncommissioned officer should and should not do regarding testimony at courts-martial. Lieutenant Sanders further testified that his battalion commander, at an officer's professional development class, read and "interpreted" a policy letter from General Anderson indicating that although a witness called before a court-martial should testify truthfully, he should "not paint so rosy a picture that all of the effort and time expended in creating the . . . court-martial packet would be just

wasted, by recommending that the soldier remain on active duty." Lieutenant Sanders averred that his battalion commander's "guidance" had not influenced his testimony. He testified that Private Hill could be rehabilitated and be of benefit to the Army.

On redirect examination, Private Hill's defense counsel asked Lieutenant Sanders whether he knew what effect the Haga letter may have had on any of the other witnesses in the appellant's case. The trial counsel objected to the question and his objection was sustained. Although Lieutenant Sanders was examined further regarding the Haga letter and his battalion commander's statements, he was not permitted to answer the question regarding the effect of these matters on other witnesses. When the appellant's defense counsel attempted to delve deeper into Lieutenant Sanders' knowledge of the effect of command influence on the appellant's case, the military judge abruptly curtailed questioning, demanding that the defense counsel demonstrate the relevance to the appellant's trial of testimony regarding command influence. When the defense counsel's response—that, although Lieutenant Sanders had not been affected, others might have been—did not satisfy the military judge, he refused to allow further questioning regarding command influence.

Article 37, UCMJ, prohibits coercion or unauthorized influence on actual or prospective witnesses with respect to the content of their testimony. *United States v. Treakle*, CM 443599 (A.C.M.R. 29 June 1984). A finding that unlawful pressure has been brought to bear in violation of

---

[1]Although not raised by counsel, we have considered the issue of whether the providency of Private Hill's pleas was affected by unlawful command influence. We find the pleas to be provident. Private Hill sold hashish to an undercover military police investigator on two separate occasions. He later rendered a sworn statement admitting the sale. He negotiated a pretrial agreement with the convening authority in exchange for his promise to plead guilty. Private Hill's pleas of guilty were accepted after a thorough and searching providency inquiry.

Article 37 triggers a rebuttable presumption that the recipient of the unlawful pressure was in fact influenced. *Id.* Accordingly, if any prospective character witness for Private Hill heard, either directly or indirectly, General Anderson's message, the battalion commander's interpretation of the message, or the Division Command Sergeant Major's message, and reasonably understood them to be discouraging favorable character testimony, such discouragement would amount to unlawful pressure under Article 37, UCMJ, and would raise the presumption.

In this case, the military judge denied the defense counsel the opportunity to present evidence that potential witnesses were influenced not to testify on Private Hill's behalf. In a situation where the evidence of unlawful command influence within the 3d Armored Division was so squarely raised, the military judge's refusal to allow defense counsel to pose a question so fundamental to his case was error.

We turn now to the question of prejudice. Lieutenant Sanders testified that he was not influenced by his commander's statements. He was not allowed to answer the question as to whether any other witnesses might have been influenced. This Court has previously found that unlawful command influence was present in the 3d Armored Division as a result of conduct by that unit's commander. [citations omitted]. On these facts alone, we believe a rehearing would be justified to enable Lieutenant Sanders to answer the fundamental question. In this case, however, we have determined a different disposition to be more appropriate.

We can gain some insight into the information Lieutenant Sanders's might have provided by examining Defense Appellate Exhibit M, an affidavit executed by Lieutenant Sanders a little more than two weeks after Private Hill's trial. This information exposes another serious problem in this case resulting from the conduct of General Anderson.

Referencing Private Hill's court-martial, Lieutenant Sanders stated that after the Haga letter had been disseminated throughout his battalion, it was discussed during a meeting of the battery commanders and the battalion staff. A point of the discussion was that a witness could refuse to answer the question of whether a convicted soldier should be retained in the Army. The battalion command sergeant major, who attended the meeting, presented the letter the following day to the battalion first sergeants, who, in turn, distributed the letter to the section chiefs. The letter was again discussed at an S-2 and S-3 Section meeting among officers, noncommissioned officers, and enlisted members. The impression of the letter among those present was that no senior noncommissioned officer or officer should testify favorably before an administrative board or a court. The battalion commander's advice not to "embarrass the command by making a recommendation, in testimony, that the board or court should allow the individual to remain on active duty" was reiterated. Although members of the battalion were also made aware of a later letter from General Anderson, it was not perceived as a retraction of the Haga letter.

In light of the information contained in Lieutenant Sanders' post-trial affidavit, we believe it is clear that at least one witness who testified in Private Hill's behalf was adversely influenced by what was perceived as General Anderson's message. Staff Sergeant Noris Bodley, Private Hill's section chief, when asked whether Private Hill could be rehabilitated and retrained and still benefit the Army, replied:

> Sir, in my opinion, and I hope it goes good on the record, I feel that PFC Hill

can be rehabilitated due to the fact of my prior knowledge of PFC Hill. If he was a problem within the unit, within the personnel that works around him, myself, his platoon sergeant, platoon leader, then I can see where he would not benefit the Army, but there's one thing the Army doesn't tolerate, and that's drugs, so I wouldn't care to answer that as far as the Army keeping him, but he can be rehabilitated. (Emphasis added).

We believe that Sergeant Bodley's concern for how he would sound "on the record" and his reluctance to opine whether Private Hill should be retained in the service can be attributed directly to the unlawful influence visited upon him by General Anderson, the Division Command Sergeant Major, and his battalion commander.

Finding that Sergeant Bodley's testimony was in fact negatively influenced by the presence of command influence, we need no longer concern ourselves with the operation of a presumption of prejudice and whether such presumption has been rebutted. The only question is the nature of the relief to be provided the appellant.

Since the unlawful command influence brought to bear upon members of the 3d Armored Division was directed primarily toward the discouragement of testimony which might encourage a military judge or court-members to retain a convicted soldier within the Army, we believe that the prejudice suffered by Private Hill can best be remedied by reassessing his sentence not to include a punitive discharge.

The findings of guilty are affirmed. Only so much of the sentence is approved as provides for confinement at hard labor for three months, forfeiture of $382.00 pay per month for six months, and reduction to the lowest enlisted grade.

In *Hill* the court concluded that there was sufficient evidence of unlawful influence. How did the actions of the Major General Anderson constitute illegal command influence? The UCMJ was designed to limit unlawful command influence, however, as *Hill* demonstrates, improper persuasion of witnesses and proceedings still occurs. *See* Chapter I and, in particular, *United States v. Kelly*. Because commanders convene and review courts-martial, will it ever be possible to totally eradicate command influence?

STUDY QUESTIONS

1. What are the three types of courts-martial? What is the maximum permissible punishment that may be awarded at each?

2. What are the appellate courts in the military? How are trial and appellate judges appointed? Is the current system of appointing judges constitutional?

3. Which of the following is *TRUE* regarding general courts-martial?

    a. An Article 32, UCMJ, pretrial investigation is required before charges may be referred to a general court-martial.

    b. A general court-martial may be convened by any commanding officer.

    c. The minimum number of members needed to sit on a general court-martial is three.

    d. The maximum punishment at a general court-martial is six months confinement, forfeiture of 2/3 pay per month for six months, reduction in rate to paygrade E-1 and a bad conduct discharge.

    e. All of the above are true.

4. What rights does a service member have at a special court-martial? At a general court-martial? At a summary court-martial? At which proceedings is military defense counsel detailed to an accused?

5. Which of the following is *FALSE* regarding summary courts-martial?

    a. A summary court-martial is composed of one commissioned officer in the paygrade 0-3 or above from the same armed force as the accused.

    b. An accused has the right to refuse trial by summary court-martial.

    c. An accused does not have the right to be represented by counsel at a summary court-martial.

    d. All of the above are true.

6. Who has authority to convene the three types of courts-marital? May a commander delegate the authority to convene courts-martial?

7. When does jurisdiction over service members begin and terminate? May a member be tried for offenses committed during a prior enlistment?

8. When does the principle of former jeopardy preclude prosecution of a service member? Does former jeopardy apply to cases where the court does not reach a verdict, i.e., a finding of guilty or innocent?

9. Who are the participants at each of the three types of courts-martial? What is the minimum number of members (jurors) at a general court-martial? At a special court-martial?

10. Explain the concept of command influence. Can unlawful influence occur during the sentencing phase of a court-martial?

CHAPTER IV

NONJUDICIAL PROCEDURES

... There is a strong implication that discipline is something the Captain does to men when they appear at mast. On the contrary, discipline is not something one man does to another. Discipline is a personal quality that each person has or does not have. Therefore, the purpose of "disciplinary action" at Captain's Mast is to convince men without discipline, or those who have a temporary lapse of discipline, that it is better to have it or develop it ...

USS ENTERPRISE (CVN 65) Leadership Manual, 1985

INTRODUCTION

There are multiple factors that influence disposition of possible military crimes. Discipline, order, morale, deterrence, expediency, operational readiness and force planning all impact determinations about potential offenses. Balanced against these factors is the need to provide accused with sufficient procedural safeguards. Because of the multitude and nature of these interests, commanders require sufficient flexibility and discretion in selecting the best method to handle a possible offense. This explains to some degree why the military justice system contains such a unique mixture of administrative, disciplinary and criminal measures. A judge on the Court of Military Appeals (now the Court of Appeals for the Armed Forces) compared the flexibility of the military justice system to civilian criminal procedure:

> While the volume of serious crime is ever-increasing, the great bulk of offenses dealt with in the criminal justice system, civilian and criminal, are of a routine and minor nature, such as disorders of various kinds. The civilian prosecutor who believes that some kind of punishment is essential for rehabilitation of the accused has no choice but to submit the offense to trial. A significantly different choice is open to the military commander. He can resort to . . . disciplinary punishment as a substitute for the criminal proceedings of courts-martial.

RCM 306(a) provides that a commander "has discretion to dispose of offenses by members of that command." A commander may elect to dispose of a suspected offense under RCM 306(c) by:

(2) Administrative action. A commander may take or initiate administrative action, in addition to or instead of other action taken under this rule. . . .

(3) Nonjudicial punishment. A commander may consider the matter pursuant to Article 15, nonjudicial punishment.

This chapter will focus on nonjudicial procedures as a means of disposing of offenses, including nonpunitive measures, nonjudicial punishment and administrative separations.

NONPUNITIVE MEASURES

Military criminal law monitors the behavior of service members to a much greater degree than civilian criminal law. For example, the UCMJ proscribes being late for work, making unkind remarks about your employer, disobeying the direction of a superior, performing your job in a poor fashion and acting inappropriately outside of work. All of these violations of the UCMJ can result in the imposition of nonjudicial punishment or trial by court-martial. In many instances, however, such actions do not satisfy the commander's desires concerning discipline, morale or operational readiness (i.e., a commander may want to use other measures to address these offenses); nonpunitive measures provide an alternative to more formal and harsh disciplinary action. These "administrative corrective measures" are not punishment, and may be used for acts or omissions that are not criminal in nature, as well as for violations of the UCMJ.

RELATIONSHIP TO NONJUDICIAL PUNISHMENTS

Paragraph 1, Part V, MCM, explains the relationship between nonpunitive measures and nonjudicial punishments:

g. Relationship of nonjudicial punishment to administrative corrective measures. [The regulations regarding nonjudicial punishment] do not apply to include, or limit use of, administrative corrective measures that promote efficiency and good order and discipline such as counseling, admonitions, reprimands, exhortations, disapprovals, criticisms, censures, reproofs, rebukes, extra military instruction, and administrative withholding of privileges.

Based on the above, a commander can assign nonpunitive measures in lieu of, or in addition to, nonjudicial punishments under Article 15, UCMJ. *See Authority to Impose Nonjudicial Punishment* discussed below.

TYPES OF NONPUNITIVE MEASURES

Nonpunitive measures encompass a wide range of actions aimed at correcting the performance of service members. These measures range from oral counseling (i.e., a "chewing out," verbally encouraging or praising, etc.) to infringing on the liberty of a service member through after-hours instruction. The JAG Manual regulates the use of certain types of administrative corrective actions for Navy and Marine Corps personnel. These regulations are discussed below.

Extra Military Instruction

JAG Manual 0103 defines extra military instruction.

Definition. Extra military instruction (EMI) is defined as instruction in a phase of military duty in which an individual is deficient, and is intended for and directed towards the correction of that deficiency. It is a bona fide training technique to be used for improving the efficiency of an individual within a command or unit through the correction of some deficiency in that individual's performance of duty. It may be assigned only if genuinely intended to accomplish that result. It is not to be used as a substitute for judicial (court-martial) action or nonjudicial punishment (NJP), and must be logically related to the deficiency in performance for which it was assigned.

JAG Manual 0103 also sets specific limits on the assignment of extra military instruction.

Limitations. EMI shall be conducted within the following limitations:

(1) EMI normally will not be conducted for more than 2 hours per day.

(2) EMI may be conducted at a reasonable time outside normal working hours. . . .

(3) EMI will not be conducted over a period that is longer than necessary to correct the performance deficiency for which it was assigned.

(4) EMI should not be conducted on the member's Sabbath.

(5) EMI will not be used for the purpose of depriving the member of normal liberty to which the member is otherwise entitled. A member who is otherwise entitled thereto may commence normal liberty upon completion of EMI.

(6) Authority to assign EMI that is to be performed during normal working hours is not limited to any particular grade or rate, but is an inherent part of that authority over their subordinates which is vested in officers and noncommissioned/petty officers in connection with duties and responsibilities assigned to them. This authority to assign EMI that is to be performed during normal working hours may be withdrawn by any superior if warranted.

(7) Authority to assign EMI to be performed after normal working hours is vested in the commanding officer or officer in charge. Such authority may be delegated, as appropriate, to officers and noncommissioned/petty officers, in connection with duties and responsibilities assigned to them, only if authorized by regulations of the Chief of Naval Operations or the Commandant of the Marine Corps, as appropriate.

JAG Manual 0103 forbids the use of extra military instruction as a form of punishment or to deprive liberty. The regulation also attempts to ensure that extra military instruction is used to improve performance in a phase of military duty, and that assigned tasks logically relate to a deficiency. However, outside of supervision by members of the chain of command, there are no formal means to ensure that abuses do not occur. This means that the Navy and Marine Corps must rely on their personnel to act appropriately in assigning nonpunitive measures. Is this a positive or negative aspect of the broad delegation of authority to impose corrective measures?

Under JAG Manual 0103(5), liberty is essentially deemed a right of naval personnel. Who has authority to restrict this right? *See Nonjudicial Punishment* below. Extra military instruction cannot be assigned at unreasonable times outside of working hours. What times are considered unreasonable? Does it depend on the operational schedule of the ship or unit? JAG Manual 0103b(6) discusses assigning extra military instruction during working hours. Ask: Is assigning tasks designed to improve performance during working hours really extra military instruction subject to the above limitations?

Administrative Withholding of Privileges

As in other parts of society, the military designates particular benefits as rights or privileges. The distinction between the two is significant because withholding a right triggers more process for the service member. *See Nonjudicial Punishment* below. Consider the definition of a "privilege" and the rules regarding the withholding of liberty contained in JAG Manual 0104.

Privilege. A privilege is a benefit, advantage, or favor provided for the convenience or enjoyment of an individual. Examples of privileges that may be temporarily withheld as administrative corrective measures are: special liberty; exchange of duty; special command programs; access to base or ship libraries, base or ship movies, or enlisted or officers' clubs; base parking; and base or ship special services events. It may also encompass the withholding of special pay as well as commissary and exchange privileges, provided such withholding complies with applicable rules and regulations, and is otherwise in accordance with law. In all instances, unless properly delegated, final authority to withhold a privilege, however temporary, must ultimately rest with the level of authority empowered to grant that privilege.

Deprivation of liberty. Deprivation of normal liberty as a punishment, except as specifically authorized under the UCMJ, is illegal. Therefore, except as the specific result of punishment imposed under Article 15, UCMJ, or as the result of the sentence of a court-martial, it is illegal for any officer or noncommissioned/petty officer to deny to any subordinate normal liberty, or privileges incident thereto, as punishment for any offense. Lawful deprivation of normal liberty, however, may result from other lawful actions such as authorized pretrial restraint, or deprivation of normal liberty in a foreign country or in foreign territorial waters, when such action is deemed essential for the protection of the foreign relations of the United States. . . . Moreover, it is necessary to the efficiency of the naval service that official functions be performed and that certain work be accomplished in a timely manner. It is, therefore, not a punishment when persons in the naval service are required to remain on board and be physically present outside of normal working hours for work assignments that should have been completed during normal working hours, for the accomplishment of additional essential work, or for the achievement of the currently required level of operational readiness.

As a general rule, denial of liberty is a punishment that can be imposed only at nonjudicial punishment or courts-martial. However, JAG Manual 0104 refers to withholding liberty in foreign countries. This is known as placing a member in a "liberty risk" status, and is for the purpose of avoiding embarrassment to the United States. Liberty risk is a lawful deprivation of liberty. *See United States v. Wilkes* in Chapter X, which considers whether liberty risk is equivalent to restriction for purposes of speedy trial.

Nonpunitive Censure

JAG Manual 0105 explains the difference between punitive and nonpunitive censure:

General. "Censure" is a statement of adverse opinion or criticism of an individual's conduct or performance of duty expressed by a superior in the member's chain of command. Censure may be punitive or nonpunitive.

Nonpunitive censure. . . . Nonpunitive censure may be issued by any superior in the member's chain of command, and may be either oral or in writing. . . .

A nonpunitive letter is not considered punishment; rather, the letter is issued to remedy a noted deficiency in conduct or performance of duty. The contents of a nonpunitive letter are not limited to but may include the following: identification of conduct or performance of duty deficiencies, direction for improvement, language of admonishment, identification of sources of assistance, outline of corrective action, and the consequences of failing to correct the deficiencies.

A nonpunitive letter will be kept a personal matter between the member and the superior issuing the nonpunitive letter. Other than Secretarial letters of censure (see section 0114b), the letter may not be forwarded to the Chief of Naval Personnel or the Commandant of the Marine Corps, quoted in or appended to fitness reports, included as enclosures to investigations pursuant to the Manual of the Judge Advocate General or to other investigations, or otherwise included in official departmental records of the recipient.

Nonpunitive censure is issued to remedy identified deficiencies in conduct or performance. Compare nonpunitive censure with a punitive letter of reprimand discussed below under *Nonjudicial Punishment*. Consider when it is wise to use nonpunitive censure. When should it be in writing? Figure 4-A below summarizes the nonpunitive measures available.

FIGURE 4-A

ADMINISTRATIVE/NONPUNITIVE MEASURES

Counseling

Extra military instruction

Administrative admonition/reprimand (not part of permanent service record)

Adverse conduct rating

Adverse efficiency rating

Transfer to another work section

Withholding of privileges

NONJUDICIAL PUNISHMENT

Article 15, UCMJ, authorizes nonjudicial punishment (also referred to as "Captain's Mast" in the Navy and "Officer Hours" in the Marines Corps). Part V, MCM, augments Article 15, as does Chapter 1 of the JAG Manual with respect to the Navy and Marine Corps. In contrast to nonpunitive measures, nonjudicial punishment is disciplinary in nature. This feature results in greater oversight of nonjudicial proceedings by the military and in broader procedural protections for accused.

AUTHORITY TO IMPOSE NONJUDICIAL PUNISHMENT

Article 15 permits the Secretaries of each service to determine which officers should have nonjudicial punishment authority. JAG Manual 0106 sets forth the officers in the Navy and Marine Corps who possess Article 15 authority.

Commander. Any commander or commanding officer, including a commanding officer as designated pursuant to subsection d, may impose nonjudicial punishment upon officers and enlisted persons of the command.

Officer in charge. Any commissioned officer who is designated as officer in charge . . . may impose upon enlisted persons assigned to the unit admonition or reprimand and one or more of the punishments listed in paragraph 5b(2)(A)(i) to (vi) of Part V, MCM.

Paragraph 1d, Part V, MCM, provides guidance on when it is appropriate to impose nonjudicial punishment.

(1) Commander's responsibility. Commanders are responsible for good order and discipline in their commands. Generally, discipline can be maintained through effective leadership including, when necessary, administrative corrective measures. Nonjudicial punishment is ordinarily appropriate when administrative corrective measures are inadequate due to the nature of the minor offense or the record of the service member, unless it is clear that only trial by court-martial will meet the needs of justice and discipline. Nonjudicial punishment shall be considered on an individual basis. Commanders considering nonjudicial punishment should consider the nature of the offense, the record of the service member, the needs for good order and discipline, and the effect of nonjudicial punishment on the service member and the service member's record.

(2) Commander's discretion. A commander who is considering a case for disposition under Article 15 will exercise personal discretion in evaluating each case, both as to whether nonjudicial punishment is appropriate, and, if so, as to the nature and amount of punishment appropriate. No superior may direct that a subordinate authority impose nonjudicial punishment in a particular case. No superior may issue regulations, orders, or "guides" which suggest to subordinate authorities that certain categories of minor offenses be disposed of by nonjudicial punishment instead of by court-martial or administrative corrective measures, or that predetermined kinds or amounts of punishments be imposed for certain classifications of offenses that the subordinate considers appropriate for disposition by nonjudicial punishment.

A commander may not delegate his or her authority under Article 15. However, the officer who is second in command, normally the executive officer, may award nonjudicial punishment if he or she succeeds to command as acting commanding officer during an official absence of the commander. How should this assumption of command be done? In writing? The above language indicates that a commander should exercise "personal discretion" in adjudicating each case. The executive officer in many cases will conduct his or her own inquiry prior to nonjudicial punishment. May the executive officer award punishment at such a proceeding? What about nonpunitive measures? Note, finally, that in a recent change to the JAG Manual, multiservice commanders are now authorized to impose nonjudicial punishment on naval members assigned to their units or staffs. Prior to this modification, a multiservice commander only had Article 15 authority over

Captain's mast on board USS _Greer_. Enactment of the UCMJ in 1950 did not alter the fundamental aspects of captain's mast on board Navy vessels. Photo courtesy of U.S. Naval Historical Society.

members of his or her own service. Such authority will surely assist multiservice commanders in light of the increased emphasis on joint warfare and operations.

The process for handling nonjudicial punishment cases is generally standardized in each of the services. Figures 4-B and 4-C are examples of the forms used to report and dispose of cases in the Navy.

FIGURE 4-B

REPORT AND DISPOSITION OF OFFENSE(S)
NAVPERS 1626/7 (REV 8-81) S/N 0104-LF-016-2624

To: Commanding Officer, (Name of Unit)   Date of Report _____

1. I hereby report the following named person for the offense(s) noted:

NAME OF ACCUSED	SERIAL NO.	SOCIAL SECURITY NO.	RATE/GRADE	BR. & CLASS	DIV/DEPT

PLACE OF OFFENSE(S)	DATE OF OFFENSE(S)
For EACH offense (Be Specific)	For EACH offense (Be Specific)

DETAILS OF OFFENSE(S) (Refer by article of UCMJ, if known. If unauthorized absence, give following info: time and date of commencement, whether over leave or liberty, time and date of apprehension or surrender and arrival on board, loss of ID card and/or liberty card, etc.)

List offenses separately, by Charge and Specification. Use sample specifications (PART IV, MCM) for correct format and content. Include as much information as necessary for clarity. See attachment 5-B for example.

NAME OF WITNESS	RATE/GRADE	DIV/DEPT	NAME OF WITNESS	RATE/GRADE	DIV/DEPT
List ALL known witnesses, even if currently unavailable.					

_____   _____
(Rate/Grade/Title of person submitting report)   (Signature of person submitting report)

I have been informed of the nature of the accusation(s) against me. I understand I do not have to answer any questions or make any statement regarding the offense(s) of which I am accused or suspected. However, I understand any statement made or questions answered by me may be used as evidence against me in event of trial by court-martial (Article 31, UCMJ).

Witness: _____   Acknowledged: _____
(Signature)   (Signature of Accused)

PRE-MAST RESTRAINT

☐ PRETRIAL CONFINEMENT   RESTRICTED: You are restricted to the limits of _____
                                 _____ in lieu of arrest
☐ NO RESTRICTIONS   by order of the CO. Until your status as a restricted person is terminated by the CO, you may not leave the restricted limits except with the express permission of the CO or XO. You have been informed of the times and places which you are required to muster.

_____   _____
(Signature and title of person imposing restraint)   (Signature of Accused)

INFORMATION CONCERNING ACCUSED

CURRENT ENL. DATE	EXPIRATION CURRENT ENL. DATE	TOTAL ACTIVE NAVAL SERVICE	TOTAL SERVICE ON BOARD	EDUCATION	GCT	AGE

* * * * * * *INFORMATION FROM THE SERVICE RECORD OF THE ACCUSED* * * * *

MARITAL STATUS	NO. DEPENDENTS	CONTRIBUTION TO FAMILY OR QTRS ALLOWANCE (Amount required by law)	PAY PER MONTH (including sea or foreign duty pay, if any)

* *NOT APPLICABLE* *

RECORD OF PREVIOUS OFFENSE(S) (Date, type, action taken, etc. Nonjudicial punishment incidents are to be included.)

List all prior court-martial convictions and non-judicial punishments. Include type of action (NJP, SCM, etc.), nature of offense(s) including UCMJ article violated and description of violation (eg. Violation of Article 86, UA from 5-8 JAN 95), date of offense, date of action, and punishment or sentence imposed.

PRELIMINARY INQUIRY REPORT

From: Commanding Officer   Date _____

To: (Name of Preliminary Inquiry Officer)

1. Transmitted herewith for preliminary inquiry and report by you, including, if appropriate in the interest of justice and discipline, the preferring of such charges as appear to you to be sustained by expected evidence.

Remarks of Division Officer (Performance of duty, etc.)

Remarks of the division officer may be summarized by the PIO, or this section may be completed by the division officer, personally. Remarks should include past performance of the accused, potential for further service, and disciplinary record.

NAME OF WITNESS	RATE/GRADE	DIV/DEPT	NAME OF WITNESS	RATE/GRADE	DIV/DEPT

RECOMMENDATION AS TO DISPOSITION:

☐ REFER TO COURT MARTIAL FOR TRIAL OF ATTACHED CHARGES
(Complete Charge Sheet (DD Form 458) through Page 2)

☐ DISPOSE OF CASE AT MAST   ☐ NO PUNITIVE ACTION NECESSARY OR DESIRABLE   ☐ OTHER

Comment (Include data regarding availability of witnesses, summary of expected evidence, conflicts in evidence, if expected. Attach statements of witnesses, documentary evidence such as service record entries in UA cases, items of real evidence, etc.)

Should include specific discussion of the offense, including evidence available, and any anticipated conflicts in evidence. Sworn statements should be attached, if obtained. Anticipated absence of any material witness should be noted. A recommendation for disposition should be included if desired by the CO.

_____
(Signature of Investigation Officer)

ACTION OF EXECUTIVE OFFICER

SIGNATURE OF EXECUTIVE OFFICER

☐ DISMISSED   ☐ REFERRED TO CAPTAIN'S MAST

RIGHT TO DEMAND TRIAL BY COURT-MARTIAL
(Not applicable to persons attached to or embarked in a vessel)

I understand that nonjudicial punishment may not be imposed on me if, before the imposition of such punishment, I demand in lieu thereof trial by court-martial. I therefore (do) (do not) demand trial by court-martial.

WITNESS   SIGNATURE OF ACCUSED

INAPPLICABLE IF ACCUSED IS ATTACHED TO OR EMBARKED IN A VESSEL

ACTION OF COMMANDING OFFICER

☐ DISMISSED
☐ DISMISSED WITH WARNING (Not considered NJP)
☐ ADMONITION: ORAL/IN WRITING
☐ REPRIMAND: ORAL/IN WRITING
☐ REST. TO _____ FOR ___ DAYS
☐ REST. TO _____ FOR ___ DAYS WITH SUSP. FROM DUTY
☐ FORFEITURE: TO FORFEIT $ _____ PAY PER MO. FOR ___ MO(S)

☐ DETENTION: TO HAVE $ _____ PAY PER MO.
FOR (1, 2, 3) MO(S) DETAINED FOR ___ MO(S)

☐ CONF. ON _____ 1, 2, OR 3 DAYS
☐ CORRECTIONAL CUSTODY FOR ___ DAYS
☐ REDUCTION TO NEXT INFERIOR PAY GRADE
☐ REDUCTION TO PAY GRADE OF _____
☐ EXTRA DUTIES FOR ___ DAYS
☐ PUNISHMENT SUSPENDED FOR _____
☐ ART. 32 INVESTIGATION
☐ RECOMMENDED FOR TRIAL BY GCM
☐ AWARDED SPCM   ☐ AWARDED SCM

DATE OF MAST	DATE ACCUSED INFORMED OF ABOVE ACTION	SIGNATURE OF COMMANDING OFFICER

It has been explained to me and I understand that if I feel this imposition of nonjudicial punishment to be unjust or disproportionate to the offenses charged against me, I have the right to immediately appeal my conviction to the next higher authority within 5 days.

SIGNATURE OF ACCUSED	DATE	I have explained the above rights of appeal to the accused.
		SIGNATURE OF WITNESS DATE

FINAL ADMINISTRATIVE ACTION

APPEAL SUBMITTED BY ACCUSED   FINAL RESULT OF APPEAL

DATED _____

FORWARDED FOR DECISION ON _____

APPROPRIATE ENTRIES MADE IN SERVICE RECORD AND PAY ACCOUNT ADJUSTED WHERE REQUIRED   FILED IN UNIT PUNISHMENT BOOK

DATE _____ INITIALS _____   DATE _____ INITIALS _____

FIGURE 4-C

REPORT AND DISPOSITION OF OFFENSE(S)
NAVPERS 1626/7 (REV 8-81) S/N 0104-LF-016-2624

To: Commanding Officer, USS BENSON (DD-895)   Date of Report 15 June 199X

1. I hereby report the following named person for the offense(s) noted:

NAME OF ACCUSED	SERIAL NO.	SOCIAL SECURITY NO.	RATE/GRADE	BR. & CLASS	DIV/DEPT
WILLIAMS, John P.	NA	888-88-8888	RDSN/E-3	USN	OPS

PLACE OF OFFENSE(S)	DATE OF OFFENSE(S)
Quarterdeck, USS BENSON (DD-895)	15 June 199X

DETAILS OF OFFENSE(S) *(Refer by article of UCMJ, if known. If unauthorized absence, give following info: time and date of commencement, whether over leave or liberty, time and date of apprehension or surrender and arrival on board, loss of ID card and/or liberty card, etc.)*

Charge: Violation of the Uniform Code of Military Justice, Article 134.

Specification: In that RDSN John P. WILLIAMS, USN, USS BENSON (DD-895), on active duty, did, onboard USS BENSON (DD-895), on or about 15 June 199X, unlawfully carry on or about his person a concealed weapon, to wit: a switch-blade knife.

NAME OF WITNESS	RATE/GRADE	DIV/DEPT	NAME OF WITNESS	RATE/GRADE	DIV/DEPT
Harold B. Johnson	YNC	X			
Robert A. Hudson	CWO2	ENG			

_____YNC, USN_____   ____/s/ Harold B. Johnson____
(Rate/Grade/Title of person submitting report)   *(Signature of person submitting report)*

I have been informed of the nature of the accusation(s) against me. I understand I do not have to answer any questions or make any statement regarding the offense(s) of which I am accused or suspected. However, I understand any statement made or questions answered by me may be used as evidence against me in event of trial by court-martial (Article 31, UCMJ).

Witness: _/s/ H. O. Kay, ENS., USN_   Acknowledged: _/s/ John P. Williams_
(Signature)   *(Signature of Accused)*

PRE-MAST RESTRAINT

☐ PRETRIAL CONFINEMENT

☒ NO RESTRICTIONS

RESTRICTED: You are restricted to the limits of _____
_____ in lieu of arrest
by order of the CO. Until your status as a restricted person is terminated by the CO, you may not leave the restricted limits except with the express permission of the CO or XO. You have been informed of the times and places which you are required to muster.

_____   _____
(Signature and title of person imposing restraint)   *(Signature of Accused)*

INFORMATION CONCERNING ACCUSED

CURRENT ENL. DATE	EXPIRATION CURRENT ENL. DATE	TOTAL ACTIVE NAVAL SERVICE	TOTAL SERVICE ON BOARD	EDUCATION	GCT	AGE
24 May 93	23 May 97	1 yr 1 mo	10 mos	HS	57	19

MARITAL STATUS	NO. DEPENDENTS	CONTRIBUTION TO FAMILY OR QTRS ALLOWANCE *(Amount required by law)*	PAY PER MONTH *(including sea or foreign duty pay, if any)*
Single	0	NA	$XXX.XX

RECORD OF PREVIOUS OFFENSE(S) *(Date, type, action taken, etc. Nonjudicial punishment incidents are to be included.)*

NONE

PRELIMINARY INQUIRY REPORT

From: Commanding Officer

Date 20 June 199X

To: ENS David W. Willis, USNR

1. Transmitted herewith for preliminary inquiry and report by you, including, if appropriate in the interest of justice and discipline, the preferring of such charges as appear to you to be sustained by expected evidence.

Remarks of Division Officer (Performance of duty, etc.)

Seaman Williams is a good worker who is learning his rate through on-the-job training. He needs occasional supervision, but works willingly when assigned a job. I consider him petty officer material, and this is his first offense.   /s/ LT Garry V. Brown

NAME OF WITNESS	RATE/GRADE	DIV/DEPT	NAME OF WITNESS	RATE/GRADE	DIV/DEPT

RECOMMENDATION AS TO DISPOSITION:

☐ REFER TO COURT MARTIAL FOR TRIAL OF ATTACHED CHARGES (Complete Charge Sheet (DD Form 458) through Page 2)

☒ DISPOSE OF CASE AT MAST   ☐ NO PUNITIVE ACTION NECESSARY OR DESIRABLE   ☐ OTHER

Comment (Include data regarding availability of witnesses, summary of expected evidence, conflicts in evidence, if expected. Attach statements of witnesses, documentary evidence such as service record entries in UA cases, items of real evidence, etc.)

SN Williams was discovered to be carrying a switchblade knife with a 5" blade by YNC H. B. Johnson when he was the JOOD on 15 June. SN Williams was about to depart the ship on liberty at approx. 1630, when Johnson noticed a bulge in his front pocket. The knife was discovered when Johnson had Williams empty his pocket. YNC Johnson reported the incident to the OOD, CWO2 R. A. Hughes, who directed that Williams be put on report (Continued on attached sheet)

/s/ David S. Willis
(Signature of Investigation Officer)

ACTION OF EXECUTIVE OFFICER

SIGNATURE OF EXECUTIVE OFFICER

☐ DISMISSED   ☒ REFERRED TO CAPTAIN'S MAST   /s/ R. D. Line, LCDR, USN

RIGHT TO DEMAND TRIAL BY COURT-MARTIAL
(Not applicable to persons attached to or embarked in a vessel)

I understand that nonjudicial punishment may not be imposed on me if, before the imposition of such punishment, I demand in lieu thereof trial by court-martial. I therefore (do) (do not) demand trial by court-martial.

WITNESS	SIGNATURE OF ACCUSED

ACTION OF COMMANDING OFFICER

☐ DISMISSED
☐ DISMISSED WITH WARNING (Not considered NJP)
☐ ADMONITION: ORAL/IN WRITING
☐ REPRIMAND: ORAL/IN WRITING
☐ REST. TO _____ FOR ___ DAYS
☐ REST. TO _____ FOR ___ DAYS WITH SUSP. FROM DUTY
☒ FORFEITURE: TO FORFEIT $ 50.00 PAY PER MO. FOR 1 MO(S)

☐ DETENTION: TO HAVE $ _____ PAY PER MO. FOR (1, 2, 3) MO(S) DETAINED FOR ___ MO(S)

☐ CONF. ON _____ 1, 2, or 3 DAYS
☐ CORRECTIONAL CUSTODY FOR ___ DAYS
☐ REDUCTION TO NEXT INFERIOR PAY GRADE
☐ REDUCTION TO PAY GRADE OF _____
☐ EXTRA DUTIES FOR ___ DAYS
☐ PUNISHMENT SUSPENDED FOR _____
☐ ART. 32 INVESTIGATION
☐ RECOMMENDED FOR TRIAL BY GCM
☐ AWARDED SPCM   ☐ AWARDED SCM

DATE OF MAST	DATE ACCUSED INFORMED OF ABOVE ACTION	SIGNATURE OF COMMANDING OFFICER
25 June 199X	25 June 199X	/s/ S. D. Dunn, CDR, USN

It has been explained to me and I understand that if I feel this imposition of nonjudicial punishment to be unjust or disproportionate to the offenses charged against me, I have the right to immediately appeal my conviction to the next higher authority within 5 days.

SIGNATURE OF ACCUSED   DATE

/s/ John P. Williams   25 June 9X

I have explained the above rights of appeal to the accused.

/s/ H. O. Kay   25 June 9X
SIGNATURE OF WITNESS   DATE

FINAL ADMINISTRATIVE ACTION

APPEAL SUBMITTED BY ACCUSED

DATED 28 June 199X

FORWARDED FOR DECISION ON 3 July 199X

FINAL RESULT OF APPEAL

Appeal denied by Commander, CRUDESGRU 8, 7 July 199X

APPROPRIATE ENTRIES MADE IN SERVICE RECORD AND PAY ACCOUNT ADJUSTED WHERE REQUIRED

DATE 25 June 199X   INITIALS HOK

FILED IN UNIT PUNISHMENT BOOK

DATE 25 June 199X   INITIALS HOK

NAVPERS 1626/7 (REV 8/81)(BACK)

US GPO 1982.539 003 2045 Region 3

JURISDICTION

"Jurisdiction" is the authority to adjudicate a particular offense. The officer conducting nonjudicial punishment must have authority over both the service member and the offense. JAG Manual 0107 describes the persons subject to nonjudicial punishment jurisdiction of Navy and Marine Corps officers.

> General rule. When nonjudicial punishment is imposed, the accused must be a member of the command, or of the unit, of the officer imposing the punishment. A member is "of the command," or "of the unit," if assigned or attached thereto. A member may be "of the command," or "of the unit," of more than one command or unit at the same time and, consequently, be subject to the nonjudicial punishment authority of both commanders. For example, members assigned to or attached to commands or units for the purpose of performing temporary duty (TDY) are subject to the nonjudicial punishment authority of the commanders of both the parent and TDY commands. Similarly, members assigned or attached to a detachment under the operational control of another command or unit by virtue of operational orders, or other authorized means, are subject to the nonjudicial punishment authority of the commanders of both the parent and supported units.

Although a commander of a unit attached to a ship retains nonjudicial punishment authority, as a matter of policy, the commander refrains from exercising nonjudicial punishment power while embarked. Why does this rule exist? JAG Manual 0108 explains that the policy is a "necessary corollary to the latter's [commanding officer of the ship] overall responsibility for the safety, well being, and efficiency of the ship." The commanding officer of a ship may, nevertheless, permit a commander of a unit attached to that ship to exercise nonjudicial punishment authority. When would this happen? Does it depend on the type of case? JAG Manual 0108 states that "[c]ertain types of offenses, or offenses committed by certain categories of personnel, may nonetheless be required to be referred to the commanding officer of the ship for disposition." What types of cases do you think would best be handled by the commander of the ship?

Paragraph 1e, Part V, MCM, discusses "minor offenses." Consider the following case, which addresses the ramifications of a determination that a crime is a "minor offense."

> Minor offenses. Nonjudicial punishment may be imposed for acts or omissions that are minor offenses under the punitive articles (see Part IV). Whether an offense is minor depends on several factors: the nature of the offense and the circumstances surrounding its commission; the offender's age, rank, duty assignment, record, and experience; and the maximum sentence imposable for the offense if tried by general court-martial. Ordinarily, a minor offense is an offense for which the maximum sentence imposable would not include a dishonorable discharge or

confinement for longer than 1 year if tried by general court-martial. The decision whether an offense is "minor" is a matter of discretion for the commander imposing nonjudicial punishment, but nonjudicial punishment for an offense other than a minor offense (even though thought by the commander to be minor) is not a bar to trial by court-martial for the same offense. [citation omitted]. However, the accused may show at trial that nonjudicial punishment was imposed, and if the accused does so, this fact must be considered in determining an appropriate sentence. [citation omitted].

United States, Appellee, v. Jack M. Fretwell, Lieutenant, U.S. Navy, Appellant United States Court of Military Appeals
11 U.S.C.M.A. 377; 29 C.M.R. 193
April 8, 1960

OPINION: George W. Latimer, Judge

Upon his plea of guilty, a general court-martial [footnote omitted] convicted accused of violations of Articles 112 and 133, Uniform Code of Military Justice, 10 USC @@ 912 and 933, respectively. The convening authority approved, except that he reduced the adjudged punishment to forfeiture of $100.00 per month for five months and a reprimand, and the record was then referred to a board of review pursuant to Article 69 of the Code, 10 USC @ 869. The board affirmed, and thereafter The Judge Advocate General of the Navy certified the case to this Court under the provisions of Article 67 (b)(2), Uniform Code of Military Justice, 10 USC @ 867, requesting our action on the following issue:

"Was trial of the accused barred by punishment imposed by his commanding officer under Article 15?"

The charges for which accused was tried grow out of events that occurred January 16, 1959. On that date accused was assigned as officer-of-the-deck for the midwatch aboard the aircraft carrier U.S.S. HANCOCK. He judicially confessed and there is no dispute that after having assumed and while on such duty he was found drunk in uniform, lying unconscious in a passageway of the ship. However, before accused entered his plea admitting his guilt, the defense moved to dismiss the charges on the ground of former punishment. It was stipulated that on January 23, 1959, the commanding officer of the U.S.S. HANCOCK imposed nonjudicial punishment upon accused under Article 15, Uniform Code of Military Justice, 10 USC @ 815, for the same acts of misconduct that were the basis of the charges being tried, whereby he restricted accused to his stateroom for ten days and recommended that the Commander, Fleet Air Alameda, issue accused a letter of reprimand. Accused served the imposed restriction, but the Commander, Fleet Air Alameda, when the matter was referred to him for the recommended letter of reprimand, stated his belief that the nature of the alleged violations by accused more appropriately warranted trial by court-martial, for he considered the actions did not constitute minor offenses. Subsequently, charges were preferred against accused and forwarded, together with the recommendations of the commanding officer, U.S.S. HANCOCK, and the Commander, Fleet Air Alameda, to the Commandant of the Twelfth Naval District, who acted as convening authority and referred them for trial to the instant general court-martial. After the Government and the defense had presented their respective arguments, the law officer denied the motion to dismiss. At the outset, we deem it worthwhile to point out that we are not here concerned with a situation where true former jeopardy is asserted as the basis for relief. A plea in bar so predicated is available in the civilian and the military communities alike, for that fundamental protection to an accused is spelled out in the Fifth Amendment to the United States Constitution and Article 44, Uniform Code of Military Justice, 10 USC @ 844. It is to be borne in mind, however, that the right thereby extended to an accused concerns itself solely with prior judicial proceedings, as is clear from the terms of the last-mentioned Article. And there can be no doubt that the prior punishment visited upon accused in the case at bar is not of that nature. True it is that he was previously punished, but not judicially. To the contrary, the commanding officer of his ship undertook to discipline him under Article 15 of the Code, *supra*. Congress, in its wisdom recognizing the inherent necessity of administrative sanctions in the military, enacted that statute in order to permit summary disciplinary action by a commander for minor offenses committed by members of his command. The Congressional intent involved is obvious from even a casual perusal of the legislative history, the wording of the Article, and its entitlement: "Commanding officer's non-judicial punishment."

It is clear, then, that the prior punishment in the case at bar does not bring Article 44, Uniform Code of Military Justice, *supra*, into play. That is not to say, however, that our problem does not sound in jeopardy. Indeed, quite the contrary is true, as may be gleaned from our language in *United States v. Vaughan*, 3 U.S.C.M.A. 121, 11 C.M.R. 121. There, in discussing a somewhat similar situation involving disciplinary punishment, this Court alluded to the "double jeopardy provisions express and implied" in Article 15(e) of the Code, *supra*, and paragraphs 68g and 128b, Manual for Courts-Martial, United States, 1951. Perhaps it would be more technically correct to denote the basis for such a plea in bar as "former punishment"—to use the language of the Manual—instead of "double jeopardy." But regardless of the label we place upon it, there can be no question, and the parties are agreed, that the three last cited sections of the Code and the Manual govern the certified issue.

In Article 15(e), Uniform Code of Military Justice, *supra*, Congress provided:

"The imposition and enforcement of disciplinary punishment under this article for any act or omission is not a bar to trial by court-martial for a serious crime or offense growing out of the same act or omission, and not properly punishable under this article; but the fact that a disciplinary punishment has been enforced may be shown by the accused upon trial, and when so shown shall be considered in determining the measure of punishment to be adjudged in the event of a finding of guilty."

Paragraph 68g of the Manual, *supra*, restates the codal provision as follows:

"Non-judicial punishment previously imposed under Article 15 for a minor offense may be interposed in bar of trial for the same offense."

Our problem, then, narrows to whether the delicts charged against the accused were minor offenses, and paragraph 128b of the Manual, *supra*, affords us some assistance in that regard. That paragraph undertakes to set forth a yardstick to measure the gravity of offenses in these terms:

"Whether an offense may be considered 'minor' depends upon its nature, the time and place of its commission, and the person committing it. Generally speaking the term includes misconduct not involving moral turpitude or any greater degree of criminality than is involved in the average offense tried by summary court-martial. An offense for which the punitive article authorizes the death penalty or for which confinement for one year or more is authorized is not a minor offense. Offenses such as larceny, forgery, maiming, and the like involve moral turpitude and are not to be treated as minor. Escape from confinement, willful disobedience of a noncommissioned officer or petty officer, and protracted absence without leave are offenses which are more serious than the average offense tried by summary courts-martial and should not ordinarily be treated as minor."

Likewise this Court, in fixing the seriousness of offenses for another purpose, has spelled out tests that are helpful. In *United States v. Moore*, 5 U.S.C.M.A. 687, 18 C.M.R. 311, we held, inter alia, that an offense carrying a penalty of more than one year's confinement or which permits imposition of a dishonorable discharge could be equated to a felony. *See also United States v. Fisher*, 22 C.M.R. 676; *cf. United States v. Yray*, 10 C.M.R. 618; and *United States v. Mahoney*, 27 C.M.R. 898.

Applying the above principles to the facts of the instant case, we are constrained to the conclusion that accused's acts of misconduct were not merely minor offenses. In two fairly recent decisions, this Court has indicated misgivings about rules which depend upon whether the accused is an officer or an enlisted man. *See United States v. Smith*, 10 U.S.C.M.A. 153, 27 C.M.R. 227; *United States v. Claypool*, 10 U.S.C.M.A. 302, 27 C.M.R. 376. In this instance, however, it is of no moment that any act charged against an officer as a violation of Article 133, Uniform Code of

Military Justice, *supra*, would permit his punitive separation from the service by dismissal. Here we have a more precise measuring rod, for accused's misconduct is punishable by dishonorable separation from the service aside and apart from the Article proscribing conduct unbecoming an officer. Drunk and disorderly conduct, whether by an officer or by enlisted personnel, is a much more serious offense if committed aboard ship than otherwise and will permit imposition of six months' confinement and punitive separation from the service. And drunkenness on duty is one step further up the ladder of aggravated offenses, for it may be punished by punitive discharge and nine months' incarceration. *See* Table of Maximum Punishments, paragraph 127c, Manual for Courts-Martial, United States, 1951, pages 223 and 225. Without doubt accused's actions here constitute an even more flagrant breach of the law. Not only was he both drunk aboard ship and while on duty but, as the board of review pointed out, his duty was as officer-of-the-deck and, as such, he was the direct representative of the commanding officer of the ship, which position carries great responsibility. Thus, even apart from the punishment that could be permissibly adjudged, there can be no doubt that the accused's misconduct in so incapacitating himself and thus endangering the ship and its crew was attended with grave consequences and shows a "greater degree of criminality than is involved in the average offense tried by summary court-martial." It would be downgrading and belittling to the responsibility placed upon an officer-of-the-deck—whether on a ship at sea or, as here, in drydock—to conclude otherwise.

Accordingly, we hold that the law officer properly overruled the defense motion to dismiss, and the certified question is, therefore, answered in the negative. Affirmed.

RIGHTS OF ACCUSED

Paragraph 3, Part V, MCM, discusses the right to demand trial by court-martial.

Except in the case of a person attached to or embarked in a vessel, punishment may not be imposed under Article 15 upon any member of the armed forces who has, before the imposition of nonjudicial punishment, demanded trial by court-martial in lieu of nonjudicial punishment. This right may also be granted to a person attached to or embarked in a vessel if so authorized by regulations of the Secretary concerned. A person is "attached to" or "embarked in" a vessel if, at the time nonjudicial punishment is imposed, that person is assigned or attached to the vessel, is on board for passage, or is assigned or attached to an embarked staff, unit, detachment, squadron, team, air group, or other regularly organized body.

The above paragraph raises the issue of what is a "vessel" for purposes of the right to demand trial? The following case addresses this question.

United States v. Michael H. Forester, Seaman, U.S. Navy
United States Navy Court of Military Review
8 M.J. 560
October 19, 1979

OPINION: Michel, Judge

The issue raised by appellant presents this Court with a case of first impression.

During the presentencing stage of his special court-martial, the prosecution was permitted, over defense objection, to introduce into evidence a document purporting to reflect that appellant had previously been punished by his commanding officer at a proceeding conducted in accordance with Article 15, Uniform Code of Military Justice (UCMJ), 10 U.S.C. @ 815, for the wrongful use of marijuana in violation of Article 92, UCMJ, 10 U.S.C. @ 892, as being violative of Article 1151, U.S. Navy Regulations, 1973. Appellant at trial, as he does here, challenged the admissibility of this document, averring that, because at the time that this prior nonjudicial punishment was imposed appellant was a member of the precommissioning unit of the USS MEMPHIS (SSN—691),

appellant should have been advised of his right to refuse punishment under Article 15, and that his punishment should not have been considered by the military judge in this case as a matter bearing on the appropriate punishment for appellant's present offenses. *See United States v. Booker,* 5 M.J. 238, 243-244 (C.M.A. 1977). The linchpin for appellant's argument in support of his position is that since, at the time the non-judicial punishment at issue here was administered, appellant was not "attached to or embarked in a vessel," within the contemplation of Article 15, UCMJ, *see* paragraph 132, Manual for Courts-Martial, 1969 (Rev.), the exception to a service member's right of removal to a judicial forum left intact by our judicial superiors, *see Booker, supra,* does not apply to him and thus his sentence should be set aside. *See* also *United States v. Booker,* 5 M.J. 246 (C.M.A. 1978). Succinctly, appellant avers that, at the time his prior non-judicial punishment was imposed, the precommissioning unit of the USS MEMPHIS (SSN-691) was not "a vessel" as that term was contemplated by Congress when it enacted the statute.

The pertinent facts are not in dispute. Appellant's prior punishment was meted out by the commanding officer of the precommissioning unit[1] on 7 November 1977. On that date appellant's "unit," *see* Article 86, UCMJ, 10 U.S.C. @ 886, was located at Newport News, Virginia; appellant had been assigned for duty there since 8 May 1977. As of 31 July 1977, appellant's duties consisted inter alia of practical training at sea to support his watchstander qualifications and of standing shipboard security watches with the responsibility for the water-tight integrity of the ship forward of its engineering spaces. As of the period immediately prior to 7 November 1977, appellant's duties were expanded to include standing watches as Petty Officer of the Deck in port and watchstanding as a sonar operator at sea during builder's trials. Also worthy of note is 3 April 1976, the date that the USS MEMPHIS (SSN-691) was launched, and 17 December 1977, the date that the ship was commissioned. The issue thus narrows to encompass the inquiry of whether or not a waterborne conveyance, intended for use by the U.S. Navy, which is launched but yet not commissioned, is a "vessel" within the ambit of Article 15, for if it is then appellant's contention must fail. [citations omitted].

Sixty years ago, Mr. Justice Pitney, writing for an undivided Court in a case dealing with asserted admiralty jurisdiction over a contract dispute wherein the basic claim was for recovery of a balance claimed to be due for work, labor, material, and related services furnished to repair the steamship Yucatan, paused to note that:

'[A] ship is born when she is launched, and lives so long as her identity is preserved. Prior to her launching she is a mere congeries of wood and iron—an ordinary piece of personal property—as distinctly a land structure as a house, and subject to mechanics' liens created by state law enforceable in the state courts. In the baptism of launching she receives her name, and from the moment her keel touches the water she is transformed, and becomes a subject of admiralty jurisdiction.' *Tucker v. Alexandroff*, 183 U.S. 424, 438, 22 S. Ct. 195, 46 L. Ed. 264, 270.

North Pacific Steamship Company v. Hall Brothers Marine Railway & Shipbuilding Company, 249 U.S. 119, 127, 39 S. Ct. 221, 63 L. Ed. 510 (1919). Later, Mr. Justice Butler addressed the question of whether a wharf boat which had sunk in a river causing damage to the merchandise which had been placed thereon was, as respects admiralty jurisdiction, a "vessel" at the time it sank. Answering that question in the negative, that jurist noted several dispositive factors, among which were that the wharf boat was not capable of being used as a means of transportation; that the various water, power, and telephone systems linked between the boat and the adjacent city evidenced a permanent location; and that the boat performed no function that could not have been also suitably performed by an appropriate structure on land. *Evansville & Bowling Green Packet Company v. Chero Cola Bottling Company*, et al., 271 U.S. 19, 22, 46 S. Ct. 379, 70 L. Ed. 805 (1926). Other federal courts have, on occasion, conducted exhaustive inquiries into the same matter, in the main seeking to define the ebb and flow of admiralty jurisdiction for the ultimate resolution of civil law disputes. Most noteworthy

---

[1] Upon commissioning of the USS MEMPHIS (SSN-691), this officer acceded to the status of the submarine's commanding officer with all duties, responsibilities, and privileges pertaining to that office.

is *Charles Barnes Company v. One Dredge Boat*, et al., 169 F. 895 (E.D. Ky. 1909) (collecting cases), wherein it was held that a vessel is a navigable structure used or intended for transportation. *Id.* at 896-897. Unfortunately, these definitions are applicable to statutes and issues other than 10 U.S.C. @ 815.

. . . .

From the foregoing, it would be difficult, if not impossible, to conclude other than that a ship commissioned into the service of the U.S. Navy is, at all times, a "vessel" for Article 15 purposes. Similarly, such other fully operational ships as may come under the jurisdiction of the Department of the Navy in time of war should be considered "vessels" for Article 15 purposes. [footnote omitted]. Further examination is required, however, because the maritime entity at the focus of this discussion was not yet commissioned on the peacetime date that the Article 15 punishment complained of here was administered. Keeping in mind the purpose sought to be achieved by the exemption clause in Article 15, *see United States v. LeColst, supra* at 802, and *United States v. Penn, supra* at 883, ascertaining the precise state of readiness for sea of the USS MEMPHIS (SSN-691) is prerequisite to the resolution of the issue at bar.

Current practice indicates that a new conventionally powered surface ship or submarine is commissioned at or shortly after the date of delivery to the Navy; nuclear powered surface ships and submarines, such as the USS MEMPHIS (SSN-691), are normally placed "in commission" concurrent with delivery by the builder to the Navy. This status signals approximate readiness for the performance of all mission requirements. *See* OPNAVINST 9080.3E of 7 August 1972. Further, nuclear powered surface ships and submarines in construction normally are assigned to an active status of "in service"[2] when they are ready for sea. This usually occurs prior to underway builder's trials[3] and during the period beginning approximately two weeks before commencement of the first sea trials and ending with delivery of the ship. *See id.* At this time the prospective commanding officer, who is also commanding officer of the precommissioning unit, becomes officer-in-charge of the ship. *Id.* Another similar category, "in commission, special," applies to all other new ships, except non-nuclear submarines, at the point at which the ship, although not yet commissioned, is capable of underway operation. *See* OPNAVINST 4700.8F of 24 June 1972. About two months prior to delivery and prior to the first underway builder's trial, a non-nuclear submarine undergoing construction is placed "in commission"/"in service," depending upon whether construction takes place in a private or naval shipyard. *See id.*

The purpose to be served by the exception clause of Article 15 is justified by a number of factual conditions relating to the state of operational readiness of an expectant commissioned surface ship or submarine of the U.S. Navy. These factors are best marshalled by consideration of the status category assigned by the Chief of Naval Operations or his designee and obtaining at the time of the imposition of

---

[2]This is the same category into which naval ships and ships of the Military Sealift Command (MSC) are placed which are being utilized in an active fleet supporting role. *See* OPNAVINST 4700.8F of 24 June 1972.

[3]Builder's trials are evaluation trials and inspection conducted underway by the builder for the purpose of assuring the builder and the Navy that the ship is, or will be, ready for acceptance trials, and should be a comprehensive test of all ship's equipment, and which should approximate the scope of the acceptance trials. *See id.*

summary punishment under the auspices of Article 15. Perforce, an ad hoc approach must be utilized to determine the overall state of affairs which, although it does not facially delineate individual criteria, *see Relford v. Commandant*, 401 U.S. 355, 91 S. Ct. 649, 28 L. Ed. 2d 102 (1971), nonetheless embraces an analytical balancing of these criteria. *See United States v. Moore*, 1 M.J. 448 (C.M.A. 1976). Thus, when, as here, a question arises as to the applicability of the exception clause of Article 15 to a member of a precommissioning unit, the touchstone for resolution shall be whether the Chief of Naval Operations or his designee has assigned the ship or submarine one of the following status categories:[4]

1. "In service," as respects nuclear surface ships and submarines.

2. "In commission, special," as respects non-nuclear surface ships.

3. "In commission"/"in service," as respects non-nuclear submarines, as appropriate.

If such a category has been assigned, then the service member attached to or embarked in that surface ship or submarine, *see* par. 132, Manual for Courts-Martial, 1969 (Rev.), has neither the right to refuse punishment under Article 15, nor standing to complain that documentary evidence memorializing that proceeding is unlawfully admitted as sentence aggravating matter at a subsequent judicial proceeding in violation of *United States v. Booker, supra.*

In the case at bar, no direct evidence appears of record indicating whether, on 7 November 1977, the Chief of Naval Operations or his designee assigned the status category of "in service" to the nuclear submarine USS MEMPHIS (SSN-691). However, there is clear evidence that, prior to imposition of Article 15 punishment on that date, appellant had functioned aboard as a sonar operator during builder's trials. Additionally, and of equal import, other specific evidence establishes that on or before 7 November 1977 the commanding officer of the precommissioning unit had assumed the additional duties and responsibilities of officer-in-charge of the submarine. In sum, this circumstantial evidence[5] convinces us that the status category of "in service" had in fact been assigned to appellant's ship prior to the imposition of his non-judicial punishment and thus that ship was a "vessel" for Article 15 purposes on 7 November 1977.

To reiterate, commissioned ships of the U.S. Navy are clearly "vessels" for Article 15 purposes, as are newly constructed ships which have been duly designated "in commission, special," and "in service." What other watercraft as may be found within the definitional ambit of "vessel" under the statute must await an ad hoc determination appropriate to a future case or controversy.

Accordingly, the assignment of error is rejected. The findings of guilty and the sentence, as approved below, are affirmed.

Forester focuses on when an accused has the right to demand trial by court-martial. If an accused does have such a right, should he or she have access to

---

[4]These categories are not intended to be all-inclusive in that some other existing equivalent category may have escaped the notice of this Court or may be created and duly assigned in the future by the Chief of Naval Operations or his designee.

[5]*See* Prosecution Exhibit 1 and Defense Exhibit A, Record.

counsel to assist in this decision? The following case addresses this question: Does an accused have a right to consult a lawyer before deciding whether or not to accept Captain's Mast?

United States, Appellee, v. Jerry L. Mathews, Private First Class, U.S. Army, Appellant.
United States Court of Military Appeals
6 M.J. 357
April 9, 1979

OPINION: Fletcher, Chief Judge

The issue presented in this case examines whether or not the military judge erred in questioning the appellant concerning his waiver of both counsel and right to trial in relation to a prior Article 15, 10 U.S.C. @ 815 punishment.

The pertinent facts are clear. The appellant entered his plea of guilty, and the tendered plea was accepted by the trial judge. Prior to the presentation of any evidence at the hearing regarding extenuation and mitigation, the Government offered for admission DA Form 2627, Record of Proceedings under Article 15, UCMJ, relating to the appellant. Upon inquiry by the trial judge, the defense counsel stated that he had no objection to its admission. The appellant then called two witnesses, one of which testified concerning the Article 15. Subsequent to hearing this witness, the trial judge had a bench colloquy with the appellant concerning his understanding of Article 15 procedures and rights exercisable under the law by the appellant. The trial judge on the record satisfied himself that the appellant had waived his right to consult with an attorney prior to his acceptance of an Article 15 proceeding.

Resolution of this issue requires evaluation of our language in *United States v. Booker*, 5 M.J. 238, 244 (C.M.A. 1977), as follows:

We believe that the Supreme Court's and this Court's longstanding position of requiring that every reasonable presumption against waiver of the assistance of counsel be indulged, *Glasser v. United States*, 315 U.S. 60, 62 S. Ct. 457, 86 L. Ed. 680 (1942), mandates that the record affirmatively demonstrate a valid personal waiver by the individual of his right to trial in a criminal proceeding rather than having us infer or assume one solely on the basis of a single check in a box on a prepared form. If the exhibit does not affirmatively establish a valid waiver, the trial judge must conduct an inquiry on the record to establish the necessary information. (Footnotes omitted.)

Under the facts of *Booker*, this language refers to the introduction of summary court-martial convictions during the hearing on extenuation and mitigation. As dicta, this language could be read to embrace within its concepts the admission of a record of a prior Article 15 punishment. We believe, and hereby hold, that the requirements set forth in Booker are likewise applicable to the introduction of a record of an Article 15 hearing in extenuation and mitigation at a court-martial.

Booker considered the right to consult with counsel prior to accepting or declining summary court-martial. The court in *Mathews* relied on that case in addressing the issue of the right to consult with counsel prior to deciding whether to accept or decline nonjudicial punishment. According to the *Mathews* court, what is the effect of not making counsel available prior to nonjudicial punishment? Does it make the conviction null and void? JAG Manual 0109a explains the consequences.

> There is no right for an accused to consult with counsel prior to nonjudicial punishment; however, commanding officers are encouraged to permit an accused to so consult subject to the immediate availability of counsel, the delay involved, or operational commitments or military exigencies. Failure to provide the opportunity for an accused to consult with counsel prior to nonjudicial punishment does not preclude the imposition of nonjudicial punishment; it merely precludes the admissibility of the record of nonjudicial punishment in aggravation at a later court-martial (unless the accused was attached to or embarked in a vessel at the time of the imposition of nonjudicial punishment).

Note that *United States v. Kelly* and *United States v. Nichols*, discussed in Chapter III, appear to overrule the *Booker* requirement to consult with counsel. Thus, the statement in JAG Manual 0109a regarding the effect of failing to make counsel available for consultation may no longer be true. However, the Court of Appeals for the Armed Forces has yet to directly rule on the issue.

LIMITATIONS ON IMPOSITION OF NONJUDICIAL PUNISHMENT

Paragraph 1f, Part V, MCM, spells out specific restrictions on nonjudicial punishment.

f.   Limitations on nonjudicial punishment.

  (1) Double punishment prohibited. When nonjudicial punishment has been imposed for an offense, punishment may not again be imposed for the same offense under Article 15. But *see* paragraph 1e concerning trial by court-martial.

  (2) Increase in punishment prohibited. Once nonjudicial punishment has been imposed, it may not be increased, upon appeal or otherwise.

  (3) Multiple punishment prohibited. When a commander determines that nonjudicial punishment is appropriate for a particular service member, all known offenses determined to be appropriate for disposition by nonjudicial punishment and ready to be considered at that time, including all such offenses arising from a single incident or course of conduct, shall ordinarily be considered together, and not made the basis for multiple punishments.

  (4) Statute of limitations . . . nonjudicial punishment may not be imposed for offenses which were committed more than 2 years before the date of imposition.

NONJUDICIAL PUNISHMENT PROCEDURES

Paragraph 4a, Part V, MCM, describes the procedures that occur prior to a nonjudicial punishment hearing.

Notice. If, after a preliminary inquiry . . . the nonjudicial punishment authority determines that disposition by nonjudicial punishment proceedings is appropriate . . . the nonjudicial punishment authority shall cause the service member to be notified. The notice shall include:

(1) A statement that the nonjudicial punishment authority is considering the imposition of nonjudicial punishment;

(2) A statement describing the alleged offenses—including the article of the code—which the member is alleged to have committed;

(3) A brief summary of the information upon which the allegations are based or a statement that the member may, upon request, examine available statements and evidence;

(4) A statement of the rights that will be accorded to the service member . . .;

(5) Unless the right to demand trial is not applicable . . . a statement that the member may demand trial by court-martial in lieu of nonjudicial punishment, a statement of the maximum punishment which the nonjudicial punishment authority may impose by nonjudicial punishment; a statement that, if trial by court-martial is demanded, charges could be referred for trial by summary, special, or general court-martial; that the member may not be tried by summary court-martial over the member's objection and that at a special or general court-martial the member has the right to be represented by counsel.

Paragraph 4b, Part V, MCM, details the hearing procedures, including the determinations that the nonjudicial punishment authority must make.

(1) If the service member demands trial by court-martial (when this right is applicable), the nonjudicial proceedings shall be terminated. It is within the discretion of the nonjudicial punishment authority whether to forward or refer charges for trial by court-martial. . . .

c. Nonjudicial punishment accepted.

(1) Before nonjudicial punishment may be imposed, the service member shall be entitled to appear personally before the nonjudicial punishment authority who offered nonjudicial punishment, except when appearance is prevented by the unavailability of the nonjudicial punishment authority or by extraordinary circumstances, in which case the service member shall be entitled to appear before a person designated by the nonjudicial punishment authority who shall prepare a written summary of any proceedings before that person and forward it and any written matter submitted by the service member to the nonjudicial

punishment authority. If the service member requests personal appearance, the service member shall be entitled to:

(A) Be informed in accordance with Article 31(b)[UCMJ];

(B) Be accompanied by a spokesperson. . . .

(C) Be informed orally or in writing of the information against the service member and relating to the offenses alleged;

(D) Be allowed to examine documents or physical objects against the member which the nonjudicial punishment authority has examined in connection with the case and on which the nonjudicial punishment authority intends to rely in deciding whether and how much nonjudicial punishment to impose;

(E) Present matters in defense, extenuation, and mitigation orally, or in writing, or both;

(F) Have present witnesses, including those adverse to the service member, upon request if their statements will be relevant and they are reasonably available. For purposes of this subparagraph, a witness is not reasonably available if the witness requires reimbursement by the United States for any cost incurred in appearing, cannot appear without unduly delaying the proceedings, or, if a military witness, cannot be excused from other important duties;

(G) Have the proceeding open to the public unless the nonjudicial punishment authority determines that the proceeding should be closed for good cause, such as military exigencies or security interests. . . .

. . . .

(3) Evidence. The Military Rules of Evidence, . . . other than with respect to privileges, do not apply at nonjudicial punishment proceedings. Any relevant matter may be considered. . . .

(4) Decision. After considering all relevant matters presented, if the nonjudicial punishment authority—

(A) Does not conclude that the service member committed the offenses alleged, the nonjudicial punishment authority shall so inform the member and terminate the proceedings;

(B) Concludes that the service member committed one or more of the offenses alleged, the nonjudicial punishment authority shall:

(i) So inform the service member;

(ii) Inform the service member of the punishment imposed; and

(iii) Inform the service member of the right to appeal. . . .

The commander must decide on the guilt or innocence of the accused. The government must prove an accused's guilt at court-martial beyond a reasonable doubt. *See* Chapter III. JAG Manual 0110b describes the standard used to decide nonjudicial punishment cases in the Navy and Marine Corps.

Standard of proof. Captain's mast or office hours that result in nonjudicial punishment is not a criminal trial; it is a disciplinary proceeding. Its purpose is to determine whether an offense was committed by the member and, if appropriate, to provide punishment therefor. Such punishment is designed for minor misconduct in a nonjudicial forum, without the permanent stigma of a record of "Federal conviction." As such, the standard of proof by which facts must be established at mast or office hours is a "preponderance of the evidence," rather than "beyond a reasonable doubt," as it is at courts-martial.

Compare this standard with procedures used at administrative separation boards. *See Administrative Separation Procedures* below. Note that an accused at nonjudicial punishment must be warned of the right to remain silent under Article 31(b), UCMJ. *See* Chapter VIII concerning the right against self-incrimination. Is an admission of guilt at nonjudicial punishment admissible at a subsequent court-martial? The following case addresses that issue.

United States, Appellee, v. Cecil D. Jordan, Lance Corporal, U.S. Marine Corps, Appellant
United States Court of Military Appeals
20 U.S.C.M.A. 614; 44 C.M.R. 44
June 22, 1971

OPINION: Darden, Judge

A special court-martial consisting of a military judge alone convicted the appellant of assault with force likely to produce grievous bodily harm, burglary, and assault with intent to commit rape. Earlier appellate review affirmed only convictions of assault and battery and unlawful entry.

At the trial, the prosecution used the appellant's pretrial statement to impeach him while he was testifying before findings. He had made the pretrial statement after having been warned in compliance with Article 31, Uniform Code of Military Justice, 10 USC @ 831, but without his having been notified of his right to counsel promulgated by this Court in *United States v. Tempia*, 16 U.S.C.M.A. 629, 37 C.M.R. 249 (1967).

. . . .

After completion of the Government's case, Jordan was called to the witness stand by his own counsel. When asked on direct examination whether he had been at the victim's home at 227-Banchi Aza-Kin, Kin-Son, Okinawa, on October 29, 1969, Jordan replied, "No I wasn't." He was asked during cross examination if he had had "Battalion Office Hours for this offense"; whether Lieutenant Colonel Harris, the battalion commander, had warned him of his rights under Article 31; and if he had voluntarily given a statement after the warning. In each instance, Jordan answered in the affirmative. When questioned about what he had told his battalion commander, Jordan replied, "I told him that I was there." He admitted having lied earlier on direct examination "Because I got shook up." Jordan went on to explain that on the night in question he was "out getting drunk" and mistook the victim's residence for a house of prostitution.

His counsel now maintain that Jordan was improperly cross-examined regarding his prior out-of-court statement, since the Government did not demonstrate in compliance with *Miranda v. Arizona*, 384 U.S. 436, 16 L Ed 2d 694, 86 S Ct 1602 (1966), and *United States v. Tempia*, *supra*, that the appellant was also first warned of his right to counsel before Lieutenant Colonel Harris questioned him.

Miranda and *Tempia* are apposite only if Jordan made a statement during a custodial interrogation. Such a determination depends not on whether he technically was in custody but on whether he was "otherwise deprived of his freedom of action in any significant way." *Miranda*, *supra*, at page 444.

In *Tempia*, the accused was summoned to the Office of Special Investigations for interrogation. Noting that if he had not obeyed he would have been liable for prosecution, this Court concluded that he had been significantly deprived of his freedom of action within the meaning of those words in *Miranda*.

At the time Jordan gave the statement . . . he was the prime suspect, if not the only one. Other indications that the interrogation was custodial include the battalion commander's having read to him the charges on which he was later tried and the commander's having given him an Article 31 warning. Like Tempia, Jordan could not have disregarded the call to battalion office hours without hazarding himself, and he hardly could have left the commander's office with impunity until he was dismissed. The Court of Military Review conceded that Jordan's appearance at office hours "could be termed custodial in the sense that he had little practical choice but to be there." They reasoned, however, that "there is not only no evidence of an interrogation but every reason to believe, from the accused's testimony, that he was not interrogated." On this basis the court of Military Review concluded that Jordan had not been subject to a custodial interrogation. . . .

. . . .

If circumstances exist that make *Miranda* and *Tempia* requirements inapplicable, the Government has the responsibility of establishing these circumstances just as it also has the burden of showing compliance with *Miranda* and *Tempia* when the requirements of those cases are applicable. For this reason we hold that Jordan was in a coercive situation for *Miranda* and *Tempia* purposes and that he should have been informed of his right to counsel.

We do not hold that a member of the armed forces who is questioned by a superior in rank is subjected to custodial interrogation solely because the questioning is conducted by a superior. And a member of the armed forces is not in custody solely as a result of his status. Each case must be examined for indicia of a more significant deprivation of freedom than status as a member of the armed forces or questioning by a superior in rank. But questioning by a commanding officer or military police or investigators at which the accused is given an Article 31 warning strongly suggests that an accused is also entitled to a right to counsel warning under *Miranda* and *Tempia*.

. . . .

Accordingly, we reverse the decision of the Court of Military Review and return the record of trial to the Judge Advocate General of the Navy. A rehearing may be ordered.

Based on *Jordan*, would it be wise to provide both Article 31 and *Miranda* warnings to an accused at nonjudicial punishment? *See United States v. Tempia* in Chapter VIII.

PUNISHMENTS

There are several types of punishments awardable at nonjudicial punishment. Paragraph 5c, Part IV, MCM, describes the nature of each of these punishments.

(1) Admonition and reprimand. Admonition and reprimand are two forms of censure intended to express adverse reflection upon or criticism of a person's conduct. A reprimand is a more severe form of censure than an admonition. When imposed as nonjudicial punishment, the admonition or reprimand is considered to be punitive, unlike the nonpunitive admonition and reprimand provided for in paragraph 1(F) of this Part. In the case of commissioned officers and warrant officers, admonitions and reprimands given as nonjudicial punishment must be administered in writing. In other cases, unless otherwise prescribed by the Secretary concerned, they may be administered either orally or in writing.

(2) Restriction. Restriction is the least severe form of deprivation of liberty. Restriction involves moral rather than physical restraint. The severity of this type of restraint depends on its duration and the geographical limits specified when the punishment is imposed. A person undergoing restriction may be required to report to a designated place at specified times if reasonably necessary to ensure that the punishment is being properly executed. Unless otherwise specified by the nonjudicial punishment authority, a person in restriction may be required to perform any military duty.

(3) Arrest in quarters. As in the case of restriction, the restraint involved in arrest in quarters is enforced by a moral obligation rather than by physical means. This punishment may be imposed only on officers. An officer undergoing this punishment may be required to perform those duties prescribed by the Secretary concerned. However, an officer so punished is required to remain within that officer's quarters during the period of punishment unless the limits of arrest are otherwise extended by appropriate authority. The quarters of an officer may consist of a military residence, whether a tent, stateroom, or other quarters assigned, or a private residence when government quarters have not been provided.

(4) Correctional custody. Correctional custody is the physical restraint of a person during duty or nonduty hours, or both, imposed as a punishment under Article 15, and may include extra duties, fatigue duties, or hard labor as an incident of correctional custody. A person may be required to serve correctional custody in a confinement facility, but, if practicable, not in immediate association with persons awaiting trial or held in confinement pursuant to trial by court-martial. A person undergoing correctional custody may be required to perform those regular military duties, extra duties, fatigue duties, and hard labor which may be assigned by the authority charged with the administration of the punishment.

(5) Confinement on bread and water or diminished rations. Confinement on bread and water or diminished rations involves confinement in places where the person so confined may communicate only with authorized personnel. The ration to be furnished a person undergoing a punishment of confinement on bread and water or diminished rations is that specified by the authority charged with the administration of the punishment, but the ration may not consist solely of bread and water unless this punishment has been specifically imposed.

(6) Extra duties. Extra duties involve the performance of duties in addition to those normally assigned to the person undergoing the punishment. Extra duties may include fatigue duties. Military duties of any kind may be assigned as extra duty.

(7) Reduction in grade. Reduction in grade is one of the most severe forms of nonjudicial punishment and it should be used with discretion. As used in Article 15, the phrase "if the grade from which demoted is within the promotion authority of the officer imposing the reduction or any officer subordinate to the one who imposes the reduction" does not refer to the authority to promote the person concerned but to the general authority to promote to the grade held by the person to be punished.

(8) Forfeiture of pay. Forfeiture means a permanent loss of entitlement to the pay forfeited. "Pay," as used with respect to forfeiture of pay under Article 15, refers to the basic pay of the person or, in the case of reserve component personnel on inactive-duty, compensation for periods of inactive-duty training, plus any sea or foreign duty pay. "Basic pay" includes no element of pay other than the basic pay fixed by statute for the grade and length of service of the person concerned and does not include special pay for a special qualification, incentive pay for the performance of hazardous duties, proficiency pay, subsistence and quarters allowances, and similar types of compensation. If the punishment includes both reduction, whether or not suspended, and forfeiture of pay, the forfeiture must be based on the grade to which reduced.

Maximum punishments depend upon the rank/rate of both the accused and the nonjudicial punishment authority. Figure 4-D on the next page sets forth the maximum punishments in the Navy and Marine Corps.

Note that Paragraph 5d, Part V, MCM, limits the way certain deprivations of liberty may be combined.

(1) Arrest in quarters may not be imposed in combination with restriction;

(2) Confinement on bread and water or diminished rations may not be imposed in combination with correctional custody, extra duties, or restriction;

(3) Correctional custody may not be imposed in combination with restriction or extra duties;

(4) Restriction and extra duties may be combined to run concurrently, but the combination may not exceed the maximum imposable for extra duties;

(5) Subject to the limits [in the subparagraphs above] all authorized punishments may be imposed in a single case in the maximum amounts.

FIGURE 4-D

NJP PUNISHMENT CHART

PUNISHMENT	ON OFFICERS BY				ON ENLISTED PERSONNEL BY	
	CO who is 0-3 or below	CO who is 0-4 or above	CO who is GCM CA	Officer who is Flag Rank	CO who is 0-3 or below (or any OINC)	CO who is 0-4 or above
Admonition or Reprimand *plus* one or more of the following	Written	Written	Written	Written	Oral or Written	Oral or Written
Confinement on B&W *if* attached to or embarked in a vessel (1)					3 days	3 days
Correctional custody (1)					7 days	30 days
Restriction to limits with or w/o suspension of duty	15 days	30 days	30 days	60 days	14 days	60 days
Arrest in Quarters			30 days	30 days		
Extra duties (2)					14 days	45 days
Forfeiture				$\frac{1}{2}$ pay for 2 months	7 days pay	$\frac{1}{2}$ pay for 2 months
Reduction in rate (3)					One grade	One grade

(1) May be imposed only on E-3 and below.

(2) Normally limited to 2 hours per day.

(3) No reduction from pay grade E-7 or above in Navy. No reduction from pay grade E-6 or above in the Marine Corps.

Based on the above, may a commander combine bread and water with restriction? With correctional custody? Can restriction be combined with extra duties? If yes, what are the maximum number of days of restriction permissible?

POST NONJUDICIAL PUNISHMENT ACTIONS

One of the primary purposes of nonjudicial punishment is to maintain discipline. To that end, the Navy and Marine Corps authorize publication of the results of Article 15 proceedings. JAG Manual 0115 describes the rules for dissemination of nonjudicial punishment information.

Publication. Publication of nonjudicial punishment results is rooted in the reasonable belief that it serves to deter other members of the organization from committing similar offenses and that it has salutary effects upon the morale of the organization. Accordingly, commanding officers may, if the interests of the rehabilitation of the offender, good order, high morale, and perceptions of fairness so warrant, establish a policy whereby the disposition of nonjudicial punishment cases should be announced. Announcement may be, for example, by any or all of the methods below.

Plan of the Day publication. The name, rate, offense(s), and disposition of the offender may be published in the plan of the day within 1 month of the imposition of nonjudicial punishment or, if the punishment is appealed, within 1 month of the date the appeal is denied, provided that the plan of the day is disseminated to military personnel only. If the plan of the day is disseminated to other than military personnel, nonjudicial punishment results may be published without the name of the accused.

Bulletin boards. The name, rate, offense(s), and disposition of the individual case may be posted within 1 month of the imposition of nonjudicial punishment or, if the punishment is appealed, within 1 month of the date the appeal is denied, on command bulletin boards for military personnel only. If command bulletin boards are accessible to other than military personnel, nonjudicial punishment results may be published without the name of the accused.

Daily formation (Marine Corps) or morning quarters (Navy). The name, rate, offense(s), and disposition of nonjudicial punishment cases may be announced at daily formations or morning quarters within 1 month of the imposition of nonjudicial punishment or, if the punishment is appealed, within 1 month of the date the appeal is denied.

Do you think the above actions deter misconduct on the part of other service members? Does publication of information violate the accused's privacy rights? For that matter, does a person ever have a right of privacy in his or her own misconduct?

Following nonjudicial punishment, the nonjudicial punishment authority may take certain actions with respect to the punishment imposed. Paragraph 6, Part V, MCM, describes those actions.

    a. Suspension. The nonjudicial punishment authority who imposes nonjudicial punishment . . . may, at any time, suspend any part or amount of the unexecuted punishment imposed and may suspend a reduction in grade or a forfeiture, whether or not executed, subject to the following rules:

        (1) An executed punishment of reduction or forfeiture of pay may be suspended only within a period of 4 months after the date of execution.

        (2) Suspension of a punishment may not be for a period longer than 6 months from the date of the suspension, and the expiration of the current enlistment or term of service of the service member involved automatically terminates the period of suspension.

        (3) Unless the suspension is sooner vacated, suspended portions of the punishment are remitted, without further action, upon the termination of the period of suspension.

        (4) Unless otherwise stated, an action suspending a punishment includes a condition that the service member not violate any punitive article of the code. The nonjudicial punishment authority may specify in writing additional conditions of the suspension.

    b. Mitigation. Mitigation is a reduction in either the quantity or quality of a punishment, its general nature remaining the same.

    c. Remission. Remission is an action whereby any portion of the unexecuted punishment is cancelled. Remission is appropriate under the same circumstances as mitigation.

    d. Setting aside. Setting aside is an action whereby the punishment or any part or amount thereof, whether executed or unexecuted, is set aside and any property, privileges, or rights affected by the portion of the punishment set aside are restored. . . . The power to set aside punishments and restore rights, privileges, and property affected by the executed portion of a punishment should ordinarily be exercised only when the authority considering the case believes that, under all the circumstances of the case, the punishment has resulted in a clear injustice. Also, the power to set aside an executed punishment should ordinarily be exercised only within a reasonable time after the punishment has been executed. In this connection, 4 months is a reasonable time in the absence of unusual circumstances.

Following imposition of nonjudicial punishment, a service member has the right to appeal. Paragraph 7, Part V, MCM, describes the appeal process.

    a. In general. Any service member punished under Article 15 who considers the punishment to be unjust or disproportionate to the offense may appeal through the proper channels to the next superior authority.

      . . . .

c. Format of appeal. Appeals shall be in writing and may include the appellant's reasons for regarding the punishment as unjust or disproportionate.

d. Time limit. An appeal shall be submitted within 5 days of imposition of punishment, or the right to appeal shall be waived in the absence of good shown. A service member who has appealed may be required to undergo any punishment imposed while the appeal is pending except that if action is not taken on the appeal within 5 days after the appeal was submitted, and if the service member so requests, any unexecuted punishment involving restraint or extra duty shall be stayed until action on the appeal is taken.

. . . .

f. Action by superior authority.

(1) In general. In acting on an appeal, the superior authority may exercise the same power with respect to the punishment imposed as may be exercised . . . by the officer who imposed the punishment. The superior authority may take such action even if no appeal has been filed.

An appeal may be filed if the service member believes the nonjudicial punishment was "unjust or disproportionate." The chances of success on appeal from nonjudicial punishment are less than those of an appeal of a court-martial conviction. The relatively low standard of proof at nonjudicial punishment (preponderance of the evidence) partially accounts for the low success rate on appeal. The absence of formal rules of evidence at nonjudicial punishment also plays a part. What other factors may influence the decision of an appeal authority?

ADMINISTRATIVE SEPARATION PROCEDURES

RELATIONSHIP TO NONJUDICIAL PUNISHMENT AND COURTS-MARTIAL

In addition to courts-martial and nonjudicial punishment, the military has the option of administratively separating service members. In many instances, administrative separations involve commission of military crimes; however, unlike disciplinary proceedings, administrative separations relate solely to a service member's fitness for future useful service and do not focus on punishment or rehabilitation. Because an administrative separation can usually occur before or after, or even in the absence of, nonjudicial punishment or court-martial, it provides a commander another method with which to dispose of suspected offenses. This section will center on administrative separations involving wrongdoing on the part of service members.

ADMINISTRATIVE SEPARATION PROCEDURES

The military employs two types of procedures to administratively separate service members: (1) the administrative board procedure and (2) the notification procedure. *See* Figure 4-E for a summary of these procedures. The selection of the separation procedure depends on the nature of the discharge. Thus, a separation that results in an adverse characterization of discharge (other than honorable) or carries a negative stigma (homosexuality), or involves a service member with significant time in the military (six years of service), will entail more process. A hearing will be afforded service members in these categories (i.e., an administrative board). Naval Military Personnel Manual 3640350 describes the procedural rights of service members (referred to as "respondents") appearing before such boards.

> The board functions as an administrative rather than a judicial body. Strict rules of evidence need not be observed; however, reasonable restrictions shall be observed concerning relevancy and competency of evidence. . . .

> While board proceedings . . . are not a judicial trial, they should be formalized to the extent of assuring a full opportunity for presentation of the respondent's case. . . .

> Witnesses. No authority exists for the issuance of subpoenas in connection with these hearings. . . . Attention is directed to the fact that military personnel on active duty may not be compelled to testify or produce evidence that will incriminate them. . . .

Rights of the Respondent. A respondent who has elected an administrative board and whose case is presented to such board has the following rights:

> Respondents may appear in person, with or without counsel, or in their absence be represented by counsel, at all open proceedings of the Board.

> Respondents may challenge a voting member of the board or the legal advisor, if any, for cause only.

> Respondents may request the attendance of witnesses in their behalf at the administrative board.

. . . .

> The respondent or respondent's counsel may question any witness who appears before the board.

> The respondent or respondent's counsel may present argument prior to the board's closing for deliberation on findings and recommendations.

. . . .

> The respondent or respondent's counsel may present argument prior to the board's closing for deliberation on findings and recommendations.

> The respondent may testify in his or her own behalf, subject to the provisions of Article 31, UCMJ. If the respondent elects to remain silent, that fact shall not be considered by the board for any purpose on any issue before it.

. . . .

Findings and Recommendations

. . . .

> The board shall determine shall determine whether each allegation . . . is supported by a preponderance of the evidence.

. . . .

> The board shall make recommendation as to the following:

> The board shall recommend retention or separation. . . .

> If separation . . . is recommended, the board shall recommend characterization of service or description of service. . . .

Compare the rights of a service member at a discharge board with the rights at nonjudicial punishment and courts-martial. In particular, compare summary courts-martial with discharge boards. A respondent at a discharge board is afforded counsel, while an accused at summary court-martial is not. *See* Chapter III. Does this protection relate to the discharge board's authority to recommend an other than honorable discharge? Also note the standard of proof at an administrative separation board—preponderance of the evidence. This is the same standard as in nonjudicial punishment proceedings, but lower than the measure of proof at courts-martial (beyond a reasonable doubt).

An administrative separation board provides a respondent with several procedural rights, including the right to counsel, to call witnesses, to cross examine witnesses, make argument and challenge board members for cause. The next case addresses the adequacy of these procedures.

Luis Perez, Plaintiff, v. The United States of America, Defendant.
United States District Court for the
Northern District of Illinois, Eastern Division
850 F. Supp. 1354
April 14, 1994

OPINION: Ann Claire Williams

Plaintiff Luis Armando Perez ("Perez" or "PN2 Perez") has brought suit against the United States. Perez seeks a declaratory judgment pursuant to the Declaratory Judgment Act, 28 U.S.C. @@ 2201, 2202, finding that his administrative discharge from the U.S. Navy is void and that he has never been legally separated from the armed services. He also seeks an order compelling the Secretary of the Navy to formally vacate his administrative discharge and restore plaintiff to his pre-discharge status as a Petty Officer, Second Class in the United States Navy.

BACKGROUND

In August 1992, Perez, was administratively discharged from the United States Navy ("Navy") under Other Than Honorable Discharge by Reason of Misconduct Due to Commission of a Serious Offense. Plaintiff had served twelve years in the United States Navy at the time of his discharge. Having first enlisted in 1979, Perez worked as a petty officer on active duty and, at the time of his discharge, held the rank of petty officer second class. As defendants readily acknowledge, Perez was an outstanding sailor. Indeed, throughout his service with the Navy, Perez received numerous excellent evaluation reports, and was regularly recommended for advancement. [citation ommitted]. In July 1985, plaintiff married Petty Officer Kathleen Pedigo ("Pedigo") who, like plaintiff, was also on active duty at the time of the events in question. Together, they had one child, Blake Perez ("Blake"). On March 9, 1990, plaintiff and Pedigo were divorced

and Pedigo was awarded custody of Blake. She subsequently requested, and was granted, permission to transfer to Italy. In late October 1990, Perez also requested a transfer to Italy to be near his son. [citation ommitted]. He received letters in support of his transfer request from several Navy counsellors. [citation ommitted].

On Nov. 5, 1990, while at a military day care center in Italy, a day care worker, Marisa Minton, claimed to have found Blake imitating anal intercourse with another one of the children. [citation ommitted]. Blake was four years old at the time. When Ms. Minton asked Blake about what he was doing, he reportedly said: "My daddy does it to me all the time. He hugs me and tells me not to tell my Mommy." [citation ommitted]. After being informed of her son's statements and conduct, Pedigo claimed that Blake had twice before made comments to her indicating that he may have been sexually abused by his father. According to Pedigo, Blake told her in July 1990 that "Daddy touched my pee-pee" and on another occasion said that "Daddy puts his pee-pee in my mouth." [citation ommitted]. Initially, the allegations against plaintiff were investigated by the Naval Criminal Investigative Service (NCIS). After this preliminary investigation, plaintiff's Commanding Officer, Personnel Support Activity, Great Lakes, Illinois ("Commanding Officer") preferred charges against Perez. Plaintiff was charged with one count of sodomy under 10 U.S.C. @ 925 and six counts of indecent acts or liberties with a child under 10 U.S.C. @ 934.

In September 1991, the Commanding Officer convened a pretrial investigation in accordance with 10 U.S.C. @ 832 ("Article 32 investigation") to determine whether a general court-martial was warranted under the circumstances. [citation omitted]. The investigation lasted three days and plaintiff was represented by military counsel throughout the proceeding. At the investigation NCIS Investigating Officer Ursala Pedrillo and Pedigo testified. [citation ommitted]. Statements from the social worker and counselor involved with Blake Perez were admitted and made part of the record as were clinical notes of treatment, letters from the plaintiff to Blake, statements from people who had contact with Blake at the day care center. [citation ommitted]. After the Article 32 hearing, the Investigating Officer, Ursula Pedrillo, recommended that charges not be referred to a General Court Martial. Consequently, the Commanding Officer chose an administrative separation procedure, instead of convening a general court martial or taking no action whatsoever. [footnote omitted].

In January 1992, an Administrative Discharge Board was convened to hear the charges against plaintiff. [citation ommitted]. The government counsel introduced eight exhibits including the transcript of the earlier Article 32 pretrial investigation. [citation ommitted]. The government counsel also introduced testimony by a social worker, Mr. Malo, who managed the Navy Family Advocacy program. Malo explained the program's procedures for handling cases where child molestation has been alleged, and how he handled the Perez case. [citation ommitted]. The plaintiff introduced eleven exhibits. [citation ommitted]. Plaintiff's witnesses included his attorney who handled the divorce action and friends who testified about his relationship with his son Blake and his ex-wife Pedigo. [citation ommitted]. Perez also testified on his own behalf, describing his relationship with this son, his consultations with the social worker, Mr. Malo,

and his attempts to have a polygraph examination. [citation omitted]. Following the conclusion of the hearing, the Board deliberated for ten minutes and found, by a vote of 3 to 0 that plaintiff had committed misconduct due to commission of a serious offense for which he should be separated from the Navy with an Other Than Honorable Discharge. [citation omitted]. These recommendations, along with Perez' counsel's letter of deficiencies were then forwarded to Perez' Commanding Officer. The Commanding Officer adopted the recommendations, and on May 5, 1992 the Chief of Naval Personnel ordered that Perez be separated from the Naval Service with Other than an Honorable Discharge. PN2 Perez was ultimately discharged on August 5, 1992.

Following his discharge, plaintiff filed suit in this court requesting review of the Board's decision. . . .

DISCUSSION

. . . .

A. Due Process

Plaintiff alleges that his administrative discharge from the Navy violated his right to procedural due process. Conceding that the Navy regulations governing administrative discharges are facially valid, Perez asserts that he was nevertheless deprived of his due process rights through the Navy's failure to advise him of the nature of the charges against him, and its denial of his rights to confront his accusers, to be effectively represented by counsel, and to be tried by a fair and impartial jury. He also alleges that the Board's failure to make special findings of fact in support of its decision similarly constituted a violation of due process. (Pl. Response at 10-11). The government in turn responds that as an initial matter, Perez has no due process rights in his continued employment that could have been violated, and even if he did, the hearing Perez was afforded here more than satisfied the requirements of procedural due process requirements. [footnote omitted].

"The requirements of procedural due process apply only to the deprivation of interests encompassed by the Fourteenth Amendment's protection of liberty and property." *Board of Regents v. Roth*, 408 U.S. 564, 569, 33 L. Ed. 2d 548, 92 S. Ct. 2701 (1972). Thus, as a threshold matter, the court must decide whether Perez has a property or liberty interest in his assignment with, or discharge from, the United States Navy. The court finds that he has both.

Property Interest

"To have a property interest in a benefit, a person clearly must have more than an abstract need or desire for it. He must have more than a unilateral expectation of it. He must, instead, have a legitimate claim of entitlement to it. . . ." *Board of Regents v. Roth*, 408 U.S. 564, 577, 33 L. Ed. 2d 548, 92 S. Ct. 2701 (1972). *See also Patkus v. Sangamon-Cass Consortium*, 769 F.2d 1251, 1262 (7th Cir. 1985). As the Court explained in *Roth*, "property interests are created and their dimensions are defined by existing rules or understandings that stem from an independent source such as state law—rules or understandings that secure certain benefits." *Roth*, 408 U.S. at 577.

Numerous courts have examined the question of whether members or prospective members of the armed services have property interests in their employment in the military. As one would expect, the answer to this question has varied depending on the context in which it is raised. For example, courts have universally held that re-

servists do not have property interests in their continued employment. These cases hold that under 10 U.S.C. @ 681(a),[1] reservists serve at the pleasure of the Secretary concerned and thus can have no legitimate expectation of continued employment. The same rationale has supported similar rulings in cases where military officers have asserted property interests in their employment with the armed forces. "It is well-established law that military officers serve at the pleasure of the President and have no constitutional right to be promoted or retained in service and that the services of an officer may be terminated with or without reason." *Pauls*, 457 F.2d at 297 (1st Cir. 1972) (citing *Reaves v. Ainsworth*, 219 U.S. 296, 306, 55 L. Ed. 225, 31 S. Ct. 230 (1911); *Orloff v. Willoughby*, 345 U.S. 83, 93-94, 97 L. Ed. 842, 73 S. Ct. 534 (1953). Courts have also held that there is no constitutional right to enlist or re-enlist in the armed forces. *See Lindenau v. Alexander*, 663 F.2d 68, 72 (10th Cir. 1981) ("well established that there is no right to enlist in this country's armed services"). *See also Gant v. Binder*, 596 F. Supp. 757, 767 (D. Neb. 1984); *Shaw v. Gwatney*, 584 F. Supp. 1357 (E.D. Ark. 1984), aff'd in part vacated in part, 795 F.2d 1351 (8th Cir. 1986).

Property interests have, however, been found to exist in an enlisted member's continued employment with the military. *See, e.g., May*, 708 F. Supp. at 721. Unlike reservists, military officers who serve at the pleasure of the President or the Secretary of their branch of the service, enlisted members of the armed forces can only be discharged pursuant to the conditions set forth in 10 U.S.C. @ 1169. This statute provides:

---

[1]10 U.S.C. @ 681(a) provides that: "Except as otherwise provided in this title, the Secretary concerned may at any time release a Reserve under his jurisdiction from active duty."

No regular enlisted member of an armed force may be discharged before his term of service expires, except—(1) as prescribed by the Secretary concerned; (2) by sentence of a general or special court-martial; or (3) as otherwise provided by law.

10 U.S.C. @ 1169. Though clearly providing the military with wide latitude in fashioning disciplinary mechanisms, this statute by its express terms limits the circumstances under which enlisted members of the armed forces like Perez can be discharged. In so providing, it gives rise to a legitimate expectation, not merely an "abstract need or desire," that these members of the armed forces will only be discharged under the prescribed conditions. As the May court explained, This provision effectively limits the scope of any property interest in continued military employment. However, the phraseology of the statute does not completely defeat the recognition of such a property interest and may be considered within the protection of the Due Process Clause. *May*, 708 F. Supp. at 721. Accordingly, the court finds that PN2 Perez has a property interest, albeit a limited one, in his retention as a petty officer in the United States Navy.

Liberty Interest

The "liberty" guaranteed by the Fourteenth Amendment "denotes not merely freedom from bodily restraint but also the right of the individual to contract, to engage in any of the common occupations of life . . . and generally to enjoy those privileges long recognized . . . as essential to the orderly pursuit of happiness by free men." *Roth*, 408 U.S. at 572 (quoting *Meyer v. Nebraska*, 262 U.S. 390, 399, 67 L. Ed. 1042, 43 S. Ct. 625 (1923). As the Seventh Circuit has explained, a government employee's dismissal infringes a liberty interest where:

"(1) the individual's good name, reputation, honor or integrity are at stake by such charges as immorality, dishonesty, alcoholism, disloyalty, Communism, or subversive acts; or (2) the state imposes a stigma or other disability on the individual which forecloses other opportunities.'" *Hannon v. Turnage*, 892 F.2d 653, 660 (7th Cir. 1990).

Several courts have held that service member's liberty interests may be infringed where the service member is discharged under circumstances that might affect his or her future employment prospects. For example, in *United States ex rel Karr v. Castle*, 746 F. Supp. 1231, 1241 (D. Del. 1990), held that a former member of the National Guard had established a liberty interest where he alleged that he had been less than honorably discharged on the basis of a false claim of substandard performance. Similarly, in *Casey v. United States*, 8 Cl. Ct. 234,241 (1985), the court found that liberty interests were at stake where plaintiff was discharged for drug abuse. The court explained, "[a] 'stigma' may attach to a service member's discharge either from the characterization of the discharge or from the reasons recorded for the discharge, if such reasons present a 'derogatory connotation to the public at large.'" *Id.* at 241 (quoting *Birt v. United States*, 180 Ct. Cl. 910, 914 (1967)). *See also, May*, 708 F. Supp. at 722 (finding a liberty interest where plaintiff was discharged after allegedly failing a urinalysis test).

Here, Perez has been discharged under other than honorable circumstances for sexually abusing his four-year old son. He denies the charges. His good name, reputation, honor, and community standing are clearly at stake. Accordingly, the court finds that Perez has additionally established a liberty interest in his assignment with, and discharge from, the Navy.

Once it is determined that plaintiff is entitled to constitutional due process protections, "the question remains what process is due." *Morrissey v. Brewer*, 408 U.S. 471, 481, 33 L. Ed. 2d 484, 92 S. Ct. 2593 (1972). "The essential requirements of due process . . . are notice and an opportunity to respond. The opportunity to present reasons, either in person or in writing, why proposed action should not be taken is a fundamental due process requirement." *Cleveland Board of Education v. Loudermill*, 470 U.S. 532, 546, 84 L. Ed. 2d 494, 105 S. Ct. 1487 (1985). "The timing and content of the notice and the nature of the hearing will depend on appropriate accommodation of the competing interests involved." *Goss v. Lopez,* 419 U.S. 565, 579, 42 L. Ed. 2d 725, 95 S. Ct. 729 (1975). "The very nature of due process negates any concept of inflexible procedures universally applicable to every imaginable situation." *Cafeteria & Restaurant Workers Union v. McElroy*, 367 U.S. 886, 895, 6 L. Ed. 2d 1230, 81 S. Ct. 1743 (1961). "Consideration of what procedures due process may require under any given set of circumstances must begin with a determination of the precise nature of the government function involved as well as of the private interest that has been affected by governmental action." *Cafeteria Workers*, 367 U.S. at 895.

Plaintiff alleges that his due process rights were violated on several grounds. The court will address each in turn.

1. Notice of Charges

Plaintiff claims that the Navy failed to notify him of the charges against him prior to his discharge hearing. [citation ommitted]. Though plaintiff received the pre-hearing notice required under @ 3640300, this notice merely stated (in pertinent part) "you are being considered for an administrative discharge from the Naval Service by reason of Misconduct due to Commission of a Serious Offense." [citation ommitted]. It did not detail the underlying charges. Nevertheless, after carefully reviewing the Administrative Record, the court finds that plaintiff was well aware of the nature of the charges against him at the time of the separation proceeding.

Initially, the court notes that by January 1992, when the separation proceeding began, plaintiff had been the subject of a 16-month investigation focusing on his alleged sexual abuse of his son. In addition to having received copies of the charge sheet detailing the alleged conduct [citation ommitted], Perez was present throughout the three-day pretrial investigation hearing held in September 1991 where both live testimony and written evidence was offered regarding Perez' alleged sexual abuse of his son. [citation ommitted].

His familiarity with the charges against him is also evidenced by his lawyer's conduct at the January 1992 proceeding. At voir dire, his lawyer asked questions intended to elicit information about the board members' potential bias against accused sex offenders. [citation ommitted]. Questioning focused on issues surrounding children, visitation with children by non-custodial parents, and the sexual abuse of children. (*Id.*). She asked one member, "Have you had any background or experiences on Administrative Discharge Board [sic] or other experiences within the Navy that might cause you to have formed opinion [sic] on allegations of child sexual abuse?" [citation ommitted]. She asked another about any potentially relevant personal experiences:

Counsel: Did you have an acrimonious divorce or do you have any personal experience such as the one which might be presented today?

CWO2 Fryer: Your [sic] talking about with child abuse?

Counsel: Yes.

Finding substantial evidence in the record indicating that both plaintiff and his lawyer were well aware of the nature of the charges against him, the court rejects Perez' assertion that the Navy failed to provide him with adequate notice of the basis for the discharge proceedings as meritless.

2. Right to Confront His Accusers, Trial By Jury

Perez claims that his due process rights were also infringed through the Navy's denial of his "right" to confront his accusers and to a trial by jury. (Pl. Response at 10). As discussed below, these Sixth Amendment rights do not apply in the administrative discharge context. Procedural due process generally requires notice and some form of pre-deprivation hearing. *See Zinermon v. Burch*, 494 U.S. 113, 127, 108 L. Ed. 2d 100, 110 S. Ct. 975 (1990) (citing *Loudermill*, 470 U.S. at 542). While the hearing should normally be sufficiently structured to allow the plaintiff an opportunity to be heard and to respond to the charges against him, it need not provide him with the same protections afforded defendants in criminal trials. *C.f. Rew v. Ward*, 402 F. Supp. 331, 344 (D. N.M. 1975) (fact that a proceeding does not afford "the right to confront [one's] accusers and cross-examine them does not mean the procedures fall short of due process"). Defendant's refusal to allow Perez to confront all of the witnesses' against him or provide him with a trial by jury did not violate procedural due process.

3. Ineffective Representation

Plaintiff asserts that his right to effective assistance of counsel was "stripped from him" at his separation proceeding. While the court appreciates plaintiff's vivid characterization of the alleged wrong, it is nonplussed by his failure to provide any specific support for his claim. [footnote omitted]. As the government points out, Perez' lawyer "cross-examined government witnesses, presented [her] own witnesses and attacked Kathleen Pedigo's credibility and character." Perez' claim of ineffective assistance of counsel in violation of his right to procedural due process is denied.

. . . .

C. Sixth Amendment Right to Confront Witnesses

The Sixth Amendment to the United States Constitution requires that, "In all criminal prosecutions, the accused shall enjoy the right . . . to be confronted with the witnesses against him. . . ." U.S. Constitution, amend. VI.

The plain language of the Sixth Amendment contemplates its application only in criminal proceedings. Furthermore, relevant case law makes it abundantly clear that Sixth Amendment rights do not attach in non-criminal proceedings. *Castadena-Suarez v. Immigration and Naturalization Serv.*, 993 F.2d 142, 144 (7th Cir. 1993)("deportation hearings are deemed civil proceedings and thus aliens have no constitutional right to counsel under the Sixth Amendment."); *Camp v. United States*, 413 F.2d 419, 421 (5th Cir. 1969) (Sixth Amendment right to counsel does not attach in non-criminal administrative proceedings before the Selective Service Board); *Schultz v. Wellman*, 717 F.2d 301, 304 (6th Cir. 1983) (Sixth Amendment right to confront witnesses or compulsory processes was not applicable to administrative discharge proceedings of National Guard member because proceedings were not criminal in nature); *Savina Home Indus., Inc v. Secretary of Labor*, 594 F.2d 1358 (10th Cir. 1979) (Sixth Amendment jury trial protections did not apply in administrative proceedings of Occupational

Safety and Health Administration). Nor is it enough that the same conduct which led to plaintiff's discharge could be the subject of criminal proceedings. *Argiz v. United States Immigration*, 704 F.2d 384, 387

Members of the armed forces may be subjected to "criminal prosecutions" through the Uniform Code of Military Justice, 10 U.S.C. @@ 801-940. This was not the basis of plaintiff's discharge. Instead, plaintiff was the subject of an administrative discharge procedure in accordance with Chapter 36 of the MILPERSMAN. "An administrative military discharge is not criminal or quasi-criminal in nature, but is governed by traditional administrative law doctrine, tempered by reference to the unique circumstances of the military." *Schowengerdt v. United States*, 944 F.2d 483, 490 n.9 (9th Cir. 1991). Consequently plaintiff was not entitled to any Sixth Amendment protections in his discharge proceedings. Clearly, absent such a right, plaintiff's claim of its violation necessarily fails. . . .

Summary judgement for defendant . . . is appropriate.

Note from *Perez* that an administrative discharge board is convened by the commander of the service member's unit. It is made up of at least three commissioned, warrant, or non-commissioned officers (of the grade E-7 or higher and senior to the respondent). A majority of the board must be commissioned or warrant officers, and at least one member of the board must be an officer of the grade O-4 or higher. As *Perez* holds, this system has been deemed to provide sufficient procedural protections for service members. However, is there any guarantee that a board will not be improperly influenced by the commander convening the board? Representation by counsel will guard against illegal influence to some degree; however, the counsel cannot protect against all abuses. The military must, therefore, rely upon its officers to act appropriately.

A procedure without a hearing, the notification procedure, is used for all separations not involving a negative characterization of service, homosexuality or a member who has six or more years of service. If the notification procedure is utilized, a general discharge is the least favorable characterization of service. A service member processed using these procedures is entitled to the following rights under Naval Military Personnel Manual 3640200.4:

    a.   To consult with counsel. . . .

    b.   To present verbal or written statements in your own behalf.

    c.   To obtain documents . . . supporting the basis for the recommended separation.

    . . . .

    h.   To a minimum of 2 working days to respond to this notice.

Is the process provided by the notification procedure sufficient to protect the interests of the service member? The decision below considers that question.

Rigoberto Guerra, Jr., Private, United States Army, Plaintiff-Appellee, v. Hugh F. Scruggs, Colonel, Commanding Officer, 7th Special Forces Group, United States Army, et. al.
United States Court of Appeals for the Fourth Circuit
942 F.2d 270
August 9, 1991

OPINION: Ervin, Chief Judge

Private Rigoberto Guerra brought suit against Col. Hugh F. Scruggs, Commanding Officer of the 7th Special Forces Group at Fort Bragg, and Michael Stone, Secretary of the Army, in the United States District Court for the Eastern District of North Carolina. He sought a temporary restraining order and a preliminary injunction to prevent his discharge from the Army. Guerra challenged the procedures by which Col. Scruggs decided to discharge Guerra with a general discharge under honorable conditions for cocaine usage and absence from duty due to alcohol intoxication. Guerra alleged that the procedures violated the Due Process Clause and the Equal Protection Clause.

The district court first granted a temporary restraining order and then granted a preliminary injunction against the defendants, enjoining them from "discharging or separating plaintiff from active duty with the United States Army pending a disposition of this action on its merits or the granting of a meaningful hearing before the administrative elimination board pursuant to Army Regulation 635-200." Scruggs and Stone appealed from this order.

We find that the district court erred in granting the injunction in this case. Therefore, we reverse.

I

Private Guerra was a member of D Company, 2d Battalion, 7th Special Forces Group (Airborne), stationed at Fort Bragg. He received the Army Achievement Medal on two occasions and was named as the "Soldier of the Year" for Fiscal Year 1990 in his military organization at Fort Bragg. However, on October 29, 1989, Guerra missed a P.T. formation due to alcohol intoxication. On April 23, 1990, Guerra tested positive for cocaine use. Guerra accepted nonjudicial punishment pursuant to Article 15 of the Uniform Code of Military Justice (UCMJ) for his cocaine use. The punishment was as follows: reduction in rank, 45 days restriction and extra duty, and forfeiture of one-half of his monthly basic pay for a period of two months.

Under Article 15, UCMJ, Guerra could have refused the nonjudicial proceedings and demanded trial by court-martial. Manual for Courts-Martial, United States, para. 3 (1984). If Guerra had made such a demand, he would have been entitled to a court-martial before any punishment could be imposed. Guerra did not demand a court-martial. Rather, he voluntarily accepted proceedings under Article 15. After the Article 15 proceedings were completed, Guerra received a notice of proposed separation from Captain Akers, Commanding Officer of D Company. Grounds for the proposed separation were the positive test for cocaine use and the missed P.T. formation due to alcohol intoxication. Captain Akers stated that he would recommend a general discharge. The notice of proposed separation informed Guerra of the following procedural rights:

5. You have the right to consult with a military counsel at no cost, and with civilian counsel at no expense to the Government within a reasonable time (not less than 3 duty days).

6. You may submit written statements in your behalf.

7. You may obtain copies of documents that will be sent to the separation authority supporting the proposed separation. (Classified documents may be summarized.).

In response to the notice of proposed separation, Guerra did not deny using cocaine, but instead pleaded that his mistake had been paid for by the Article 15 punishment. Guerra requested a hearing before an administrative elimination board. Because he had not served in the Army for at least 6 years, he was not entitled to such a hearing. Army Reg. 635-200 @ 2-2d (1989). Guerra submitted ten statements from other soldiers in support of his plea of leniency. After reviewing these statements, Colonel Scruggs, Commanding Officer of the 7th Special Forces Group, approved the recommendation for a general discharge of Guerra.[1]

. . . .

The first factor to be considered is the nature and strength of Guerra's challenge to the military determination. Mindes, 453 F.2d at 201-02. Guerra raises essentially two constitutional challenges: (1) a Due Process challenge, and (2) an Equal Protection challenge. We will address each in turn.

"Procedural due process imposes constraints on governmental decisions which deprive individuals of 'liberty' or 'property' interests within the meaning of the Due Process Clause of the Fifth or Fourteenth Amendment." *Mathews v. Eldridge*, 424 U.S. 319, 332, 96 S. Ct. 893, 901, 47 L. Ed. 2d 18, 31 (1976). Thus, in order for Guerra to have a Due Process claim, he must first establish that he has a property or liberty interest.

The district court found that Guerra did not have a property interest. Property interests are . . . created and their dimensions are defined by existing rules or understandings that stem from an independent source such as state law—rules or understandings that secure certain benefits and that support claims of entitlement to those benefits. [citation omitted]. In *Perry v. Sindermann*, the Supreme Court stated that a property right cannot emanate from a mere subjective expectancy. 408 U.S. 593, 603, 92 S. Ct. 2694, 2700, 33 L. Ed. 2d 570, 580 (1972). Here, the statute on which Guerra relies to create a property interest shows that it does not create one. 10 U.S.C. @ 1169 provides:

No regular enlisted member of an armed force may be discharged before his term of service expires, except—

(1) as prescribed by the Secretary concerned;

(2) by sentence of a general or special court martial; or

(3) as otherwise provided by law.

10 U.S.C.A. @ 1169 (1983). The language of the statute, particularly subsection (1),

---

[1] Army Regulations provide: "A general discharge is a separation from the Army under honorable conditions. When authorized, it is issued to a soldier whose military record is satisfactory but not sufficiently meritorious to warrant an honorable discharge." Army Regulation 635-200, Section III, @ 3-7b(1).

shows that the Army has discretion to discharge enlisted personnel and that Guerra has no property interest. *See Rich v. Secretary of Army*, 735 F.2d 1220, 1226 (10th Cir. 1984) (holding that Rich had no property right in continued employment with the Army because of the discretion afforded the Secretary under 10 U.S.C. @ 1169(1)). Further, even if we found that Guerra had a property interest at one time, we note that he would no longer have a property interest because his term of enlistment has now expired.

Although Guerra does not have a property interest, the district court found that he did have a liberty interest which afforded him due process rights. "Liberty" as referred to in the Due Process Clause of the Fourteenth Amendment includes the right of "an individual to contract, to engage in any of the common occupations of life, to acquire useful knowledge . . . and generally to enjoy those privileges long recognized . . . as essential to the orderly pursuit of happiness by free men." [citation omitted]. From the broad notion of liberty has sprung the concept that "where a person's good name, reputation, honor, or integrity is at stake because of what the government is doing to him, notice and an opportunity to be heard are essential." *Wisconsin v. Constantineau*, 400 U.S. 433, 437, 91 S. Ct. 507, 510, 27 L. Ed. 2d 515, 519 (1971). The purpose of such notice and hearing is to provide the person an opportunity to clear his name. [citation omitted]. In the abstract, Guerra might have a liberty interest in his good name. The stigma attached to a general discharge related to a drug offense is well documented. *See Casey v. United States*, 8 Cl. Ct. 234, 242-43 (1985) (holding that a discharge for "personal abuse of alcohol and other drugs" was stigmatizing). However, merely having a liberty interest in one's good name does not make out a claim of a Due Process violation. "A critical element of a claimed invasion of a reputational liberty interest . . . is the falsity of the gov-

ernment's asserted basis for the employment decision at issue." [citations omitted]. Here, Guerra never denied that he had used cocaine. In fact, he voluntarily underwent disciplinary procedures under Article 15 without demanding a court-martial to contest the drug test results. Therefore, Guerra has failed to make out an essential element of his Due Process claim: he cannot show that the stated reason for his discharge—cocaine use—was untrue. Thus, we find that Guerra had no liberty interest.

. . . .

Guerra also raised an Equal Protection claim challenging the requirement that a serviceman must serve in the Army for 6 years before being entitled to a hearing before the ABCMR. *See* Army Reg. 635-200 @ 2-2d (1989). Guerra asserted that the 6 year requirement bears no rational relationship to a legitimate government objective and that it is arbitrary and capricious. Unless a statute or regulation impinges upon a fundamental right or involves a suspect classification, a minimal level of scrutiny is applied under the rational basis test. *See San Antonio Independent School District v. Rodriguez*, 411 U.S. 1, 17, 93 S. Ct. 1278, 1288, 36 L. Ed. 2d 16, 33 (1973). Since no fundamental right or suspect classification is involved here, we must apply the rational basis test.

Under the rational basis test, a regulation need only bear some rational relationship to legitimate governmental purposes. *See id.* at 40, 93 S. Ct. at 1300, 36 L. Ed. 2d at 47. The deference afforded to the government under the rational basis test is so deferential that even if the government's actual purpose in creating classifications is not rational, a court can uphold the regulation if the court can envision some rational basis for the classification. In *McGowan v. Maryland*, 366 U.S. 420, 81 S. Ct. 1101, 6 L. Ed. 2d 393 (1961), the Supreme Court stated that "[a] statutory discrimination will not be set aside if any state of facts reasonably may be conceived to justify it." *Id.* at 426, 81 S. Ct. at 1105, 6 L. Ed. 2d at 399.

In the case at bar, the Army explained the reason for the 6 year requirement as follows:

Six years is the maximum enlistment in the United States Army. So any soldier who has served beyond six years is by definition serving beyond his initial tour of enlistment . . . The rights of the procedures that are afforded to those soldiers are not a recognition they possess a property right to continue service in the military, but merely out of the fact that they have served beyond that initial enlistment period.

We are saying that we will afford these soldiers because of their term of service these procedures when they are considered for administrative elimination or separation from the service. And secondly, as expressed in AR 635-200 in its purpose paragraph, it is for the purpose of maintaining the readiness and the competence of a fighting force.

The Army has an investment by virtue of the time and the training possessed and invested in that soldier who serves six years or more. So it is not all for the soldier; it is there too to protect the investment of the service, again, a rational basis for determining what procedures are afforded to who [sic]. Under the exceedingly deferential rational basis test, this stated purpose of the 6 year classification is rational and does not violate the Equal Protection Clause.

. . . .

Guerra's proposed discharge was at the request of Captain Akers, who was the commanding officer of Guerra's Company D. Apparently, he believed that Guerra's actions could not be tolerated in the military context. While we might conclude that the Army should forgive Guerra and give him a second chance, we are not in a position to evaluate how this type of behavior impacts on a military unit, especially a special forces unit. . . . .

[W]e conclude that the district court should not have granted an injunction on these facts. Accordingly, we reverse the district court's order granting the injunction.

Reversed.

Why did Private Guerra not have a right to a discharge hearing in the first place? The commander in *Guerra* elected to process the accused for a general discharge only. The Army convicted Private Guerra of drug use at a nonjudicial proceeding. Therefore, the commander could have processed Private Guerra for an other than honorable discharge, but he elected not to do so. Because Private Guerra did not have six or more years of service, he was not entitled to a hearing procedure. This mirrors the procedures used by the Navy and Marine Corps, as well. *See Administrative Separation Procedures* above.

CHARACTERIZATIONS OF DISCHARGE

When a member is administratively separated, his or her service is always characterized. There are four possible characterizations of service discussed below.

An honorable discharge is awarded when "[T]he quality of the enlisted member's service has for the most part met acceptable standards of conduct and performance of duty." *See* Naval Military Personnel Manual 3610300.3.a. The vast majority of enlisted members who leave the service receive an honorable discharge.

A general discharge is issued when the performance of a service member "has been honest and faithful but significant negative aspects of the member's conduct or performance of duty outweigh positive aspects of the member's service." *See* Naval Military Personnel Manual 3610300.3.b. A general discharge is "under honorable conditions," thereby entitling a member to virtually the same benefits received by virtue of an honorable discharge. Some grounds for discharge will result in a characterization of "type warranted by service record." This means that the member will receive either an honorable or general characterization, depending on his or her evaluation marks.

An other than honorable discharge is the most negative administrative discharge issued by the armed forces. It is issued if there "have been one or more acts or omissions that constitute a significant departure from expected conduct," (i.e., the service member committed misconduct). *See* Naval Military Personnel Manual 3610300.3.c. *Compare* an other than honorable discharge with a bad conduct or a dishonorable discharge. Only a court-marital can award a bad conduct or dishonorable discharge. Which type of discharge sounds the most serious? Note that an other than honorable discharge causes a member to lose entitlements to VA benefits and the GI Bill. Because of the seriousness of receiving an other than honorable discharge, a service member always has the right to request an administrative board in cases where it is a possible characterization.

Service members are in an entry level "status" for the first 180 days of uninterrupted active duty, and administrative discharge processing initiated during that period qualifies a member for an entry level separation. However, service members who would otherwise be eligible for an entry level characterization may receive one of the other types of administrative discharges, including an other than honorable characterization, if warranted by the circumstances of the case.

GROUNDS FOR ADMINISTRATIVE DISCHARGES

There are numerous grounds for separating a service member. This section will consider those grounds relating to misconduct and to separations on the basis of homosexuality. Although the focus of this section will be the basis for administrative discharge, procedural considerations such as counseling and mandatory processing are also discussed. Figure 4-E on the next page summarizes the procedures used for each of the different grounds for discharge discussed in this section.

Misconduct

There are several grounds for separation which fall into the category of "misconduct." Members discharged under any of these bases may receive an other than honorable characterization. The Naval Military Personnel Manual 3630600 explains one of these bases.

Misconduct due to a Pattern of Misconduct

(1) A pattern of misconduct is defined as discreditable involvement with civil and military authorities. The member must have violated counseling prior to initiating counseling. Such a pattern may include both minor and serious infractions as evidenced by:

(a) Three or more civilian convictions within the current enlistment.

(b) Three or more punishments under the UCMJ within the current enlistment.

(c) Any combination of three civilian convictions or punishments under the UCMJ within the current enlistment.

(d) Three or more periods of unauthorized absence of more than three days duration within the current enlistment.

Discharge processing for a pattern of misconduct requires documented counseling. For Navy personnel, this is usually accomplished via a "page 13" service record entry. *See The Counseling Requirement* below.

Misconduct for purposes of administrative separations can also be established by commission of a serious offense. Naval Military Personnel Manual 3630600 provides:

Misconduct Due to Commission of a Serious Offense (processing not mandatory).

An individual may be processed for administrative separation when a punitive discharge would be authorized by the Manual for Courts-Martial for the same or a closely related offense. . . .

Misconduct Due to Commission of a Serious Offense (processing mandatory)

(1) An individual must be processed for administrative separation when the commanding officer believes by a preponderance of the evidence that the individual committed extremely serious misconduct that either resulted in or had the potential to result in death, or serious bodily injury. . . .

FIGURE 4-E

SUMMARY OF ADMINISTRATIVE DISCHARGES AND PROCEDURES

Basis For Processing	Procedure	Least Favorable Discharge	Mandatory Processing	Counseling Required
MISCONDUCT				
–Pattern	Admin Board	OTH	No	Yes
–Serious Offense	Admin Board	OTH	No (when a punitive discharge would be authorized by the MCM)	No
			Yes (resulted in death or serious bodily injury, or involved sexual perversion or aggravated sexual harassment)	No
–Drug Abuse	Admin Board	OTH	Yes	No
Homosexuality	Admin Board	OTH (if: by force, w/a person under 16, w/a subordinate, openly in public view, for compensation, aboard a naval vessel or a/c); otherwise TWSR.	Yes	No

(2) Sexual Perversion. An individual must be processed for administrative separation when an incident involves sexual behavior that deviates from socially acceptable standards of morality and decency. . . .

(3) Sexual Harassment. An individual must be processed for administrative separation following punitive action if appropriate, on the first substantiated incident of sexual harassment involving any of the following circumstances:

    (a) threats or attempts to influence another's career or job for sexual favors;

    (b) rewards in exchange for sexual favors; or

    (c) physical contact of a sexual nature. . . .

Note that a civilian conviction for an offense that could result in a punitive discharge under the MCM is also the basis for nonmandatory processing. Likewise, processing is mandatory for a civilian conviction for an offense involving death or serious bodily injury. *See* Naval Military Personnel Manual 3630600.1e and 3630600.1f. The military has significantly increased the number of situations where processing is mandatory (drugs, serious offenses, sexual harassment, etc.). What has caused this to occur? Do you think the Tailhook debacle played a part? Mandatory processing clearly reduces the discretion of commanders. Is this a positive or negative trend?

It is not necessary that there be a nonjudicial or court-martial conviction for a member to be processed for commission of a serious offense. Thus, a commanding officer may decide to forego punitive action (nonjudicial punishment or court-martial) and process the member immediately. Administrative processing under this category cannot be based on an offense for which a member was acquitted (found not guilty) at trial. Processing is not precluded, however, in situations where a service member was tried, but escaped conviction for reasons other than an acquittal. What if a service member is convicted at court-martial, but not awarded a punitive discharge? May the military still process the member? The Naval Military Personnel Manual permits processing in such cases for offenses that are a "serious offense" as defined above.

Drug Abuse

Drug abuse in the military results in mandatory processing for separation. Naval Military Personnel Manual 3630600 defines drug abuse.

Drug Abuse. The illegal or wrongful use or possession of controlled substance(s).

Drug Paraphernalia. All equipment, products, and materials that are used, or intended for use, or designed for use in injecting, ingesting, inhaling, or otherwise introducing into the human body controlled substances into the human body.

Drug Trafficking. The sale, transfer, or possession with intent to sell or transfer, controlled substance(s).

The Navy and Marine Corps have a "zero tolerance" policy towards drug abuse. Does that policy mean that every service member convicted of a drug-related offense will be separated? Note that all service members processed for misconduct have a right to an administrative separation board. May a board retain a respondent even though the board found he or she committed misconduct? *See Administrative Separation Procedures* above.

Homosexuality

The military's policy is that "[H]omosexual orientation is not a bar to service entry or continued service. Homosexual conduct, however, is grounds for separation. . . ." Naval Military Personnel Manual 3630400 provides:

> Basis for separation: Homosexual conduct is grounds for separation from the naval service. Homosexual conduct includes homosexual acts, a statement by a member that demonstrates a propensity or intent to engage in homosexual acts, or a homosexual marriage or attempted marriage. . . . [S]eparation processing is mandatory if the commanding officer believes that, by a preponderance of the evidence that homosexual conduct . . . has occurred.

In cases involving the commission of homosexual acts, a service member may be retained if it is found that the acts were not accomplished by force or coercion, the member is unlikely to engage in future homosexual acts, and such acts were a departure from the member's usual and customary behavior. Likewise, in cases based on statements by the member that he or she is a homosexual or bisexual, retention may occur if it is found that the member is not a person who engages in, has a propensity to engage in, or intends to engage in, homosexual acts.

The military's policy on separation of homosexuals has created significant controversy. Note that the current "don't ask, don't tell" policy instituted by President Clinton did not alter the military's basic policy of discharging homosexuals. Its only affects the procedure for initiating investigations of homosexual conduct. The following case considers separation of a service member on the basis of a statement that the member is a homosexual.

**Joseph C. Steffan, Appellant, v. William J. Perry,
Secretary of Defense, et al., Appellees
United States Court of Appeals for the District of Columbia Circuit
41 F. 3d 677
November 22, 1994**

OPINION: Silberman, Circuit Judge

Joseph Steffan, a former Navy midshipman who admitted to being a homosexual, appeals from the judgment of the district court sustaining the constitutionality of the regulations pursuant to which he was discharged from the Naval Academy. We affirm.

I.

Midshipmen enrolled in the Naval Academy are subject to at least two sets of regulations relevant to homosexuality: the Naval Academy's own regulations and the Directives of the Department of Defense applicable to the armed forces generally.

Academy regulations provide a number of "separation criteria" applicable to the "small minority of midshipmen" who "either [do] not perform to standards" or who "possess certain traits which are undesirable in commissioned officers." United States Naval Academy Regulation, COMDTMIDN Instruction 1610.6F Ch-2.15.1 (July 16, 1987).[1] A number of such deficiencies are considered to be "sufficient in and of themselves to warrant separation from the Naval Academy." *Id.* at Ch-2.15.3. The Academy regulations provide a "listing" of those shortcomings, explaining that the "listing is not all-inclusive, but rather serves as examples which severely limit a midshipman's aptitude and potential for commissioned service." *Id.* With regard to "homosexuality," one such concern, the regulations state:

The basis for separation may include previous, prior service or current service conduct or statements. Homosexuality includes the member engaging in, attempting to engage in or soliciting another to engage in a homosexual act or acts. It also includes statements by the member that he or she is homosexual or bisexual, or the member marrying or attempting to marry a person known to be

of the same biological sex. *Id.* at Ch-2.15.3.c (emphasis added). The Academy regulations do not further define the term "homosexual."

The Department of Defense Directives applicable to homosexuality are more detailed. They begin with a statement describing their "basis" which provides:

Homosexuality is incompatible with military service. The presence in the military environment of persons who engage in homosexual conduct or who, by their statements, demonstrate a propensity to engage in homosexual conduct, seriously impairs the accomplishment of the military mission. The presence of such members adversely affects the ability of the Military Services to maintain discipline, good order, and morale; to foster mutual trust and confidence among service members; to ensure the integrity of the system of rank and command; to facilitate assignment and worldwide deployment of service members who frequently must live and work under close conditions affording minimal privacy; to recruit and retain members of the Military Services; to maintain the public acceptability of military service; and to prevent breaches of security. DOD Directive 1332.14.H.1.a, 32 C.F.R. Pt. 41, App. A (1991) (superseded).

The Directives mandate that a "member shall be separated . . . if one or more of the following approved findings is made." *Id.* at 1332.14.H.1.c. One such finding is that "the member has stated that he or she is a homosexual . . . unless there is a further finding that the member is not a homosexual." *Id.* at 1332.14.H.1.c.(2). And the

---

[1] The Academy regulations found in the record postdate Steffan's separation from the Academy. The parties agree, however, that these regulations are identical, so far as relevant to this appeal, to the version existing at the time of the events, giving rise to Steffan's suit.

term "homosexual" is defined as "a person, regardless of sex, who engages in, desires to engage in, or intends to engage in homosexual acts." *Id.* at 1332.14.H.1.b.(1).

Joseph Steffan enrolled in the Naval Academy in 1983 and successfully completed three of his four years of training, consistently being ranked near the top of his class. During the fall of his senior year, Steffan confided in two fellow midshipmen that he was a homosexual. One of the two reported Steffan's conversation to Academy officials and on the basis of this report the Naval Investigative Service began an investigation of Steffan's homosexuality. Steffan was informed of that inquiry by a fellow midshipman in March 1987. When questioned by Naval investigators, Steffan "invoked his right to remain silent," but did confide his homosexuality to a chaplain in the Academy. Subsequently, in a meeting with the Commandant of the Academy, Steffan stated that he was a homosexual.

On March 24, 1987, the Academy convened a meeting of its Performance Board. At that hearing, Steffan was asked, "I'd like your word, are you a homosexual?" He replied, "Yes, sir." Steffan was then asked whether he had "anything else to add at this point," and he answered "no." Based on this hearing, the Performance Board recommended to the Commandant of the Academy that "Steffan be separated from the Naval Academy due to insufficient aptitude for commissioned service." The Board did not state explicitly whether it was relying on the Academy's regulations or the Directives, although its conclusion appears to paraphrase the Academy regulation's wording. The Commandant accepted this recommendation and forwarded it to the Academic Board, chaired by the Superintendent of the Academy. That Board met on April 1 and voted to recommend Steffan's discharge from the Academy to the Secretary of the Navy,

again based on "insufficient aptitude for commissioned service."

Following that meeting, Steffan, who was advised by counsel, reached an agreement with the Navy, the terms of which were embodied in a "statement of understanding" signed by Steffan. Steffan acknowledged in the statement that based upon the recommendation of the Academic Board, the Superintendent of the Academy would recommend his discharge. Steffan had been given a choice: either submit a "qualified resignation" or litigate and risk recommendation of a discharge. The official transcript of a midshipman who submits a "qualified resignation" reads "Resigned" rather than "Discharged" as the cause of separation. But the qualified resignation itself includes an acknowledgement by the midshipman that he will be recommended for discharge by the Superintendent if he does not resign. Had Steffan chosen to appeal—presumably to the Secretary of the Navy—and had the Secretary decided that discharge was in order, Steffan's transcript would have revealed "Discharged" as the reason for his termination. Steffan chose the first option and resigned from the Academy. The statement of understanding provided that by choosing to submit his resignation, Steffan forfeited "his right to show cause to higher authority why he should not be disenrolled from the Naval Academy." The Secretary of the Navy accepted Steffan's resignation on May 28, 1987. Subsequently, the Naval Investigative Service terminated its uncompleted investigation into possible conduct-related criminal and regulatory violations by Steffan.

Roughly a year and a half after submitting his resignation, Steffan wrote the Secretary of the Navy seeking to withdraw his resignation and resume his studies at the Academy. The Superintendent of the Academy "strongly" recommended to the Secretary that he deny the request. The

Superintendent's letter noted that Steffan had made an informed decision to resign following the conclusion of all the hearings to which he was entitled under Academy regulations. As for the merits of Steffan's request, the Superintendent pointed out that Steffan's admission that he was a homosexual constituted a basis for separation under the Academy regulations, and that the DOD Directives provided that "homosexuality" was incompatible with military service. The Secretary disapproved Steffan's request to withdraw his resignation "in accordance with the recommendation of the Superintendent."

Following that denial, Steffan brought suit in district court. Perhaps because of uncertainty as to whether his discharge was based on the Academy regulations or the DOD Directives, Steffan's complaint sought a declaration generally that "the regulations pursuant to which the Naval Academy acted are unconstitutional on their face and as applied to the Plaintiff herein." Steffan also sought an order "enjoining Defendants from prohibiting [him] from graduating and receiving his diploma from the Academy" and "from denying [him] his commission in the United States Navy." The district court entered summary judgment in favor of the government, and Steffan appealed.[2]

Steffan, whose brief focuses almost entirely on the DOD Directives, argues that the military regulations lack a rational ba-

sis because they are simply an attempt to cater to the prejudices of members of the military and because they "punish" homosexuals simply on the basis of their "status" and "thoughts" rather than on the basis of conduct. Steffan concedes—and this concession frames the dispute—that the military may discharge those who engage in homosexual conduct whether on or off duty. The government contends that the regulations are a rational attempt to exclude from the military individuals who engage in, or demonstrate a propensity to engage in, homosexual conduct. The government also asserts that admission into the military of those who engage in such conduct would undermine unit cohesion. And the government defends the regulations as an attempt to protect the privacy of service members.

. . . .

[W]e will consider the constitutionality of both the Academy regulations and the DOD Directives, as if each alone had provided the basis for Steffan's discharge.

II. Naval Academy Regulations

The familiar parameters of rational basis review were recently reiterated by the Supreme Court in *Heller v. Doe*, 125 L. Ed. 2d 257, 113 S. Ct. 2637 (1993).[3] "Rational-basis review in equal protection analysis 'is not a license for courts to judge the wisdom, fairness, or logic of legislative choices.'" *Id.* at 2642. [citations

---

[2] A panel of this court reversed the district court decision in Steffan v. Aspin, 303 U.S. App. D.C. 404, 8 F.3d 57 (D.C. Cir. 1993). The full court then vacated the panel's judgment and ordered that the case be reheard en banc.

[3] We dismiss Steffan's oblique suggestion, made only in a sketchy footnote and apparently abandoned during oral argument, that heightened scrutiny should be applied because homosexuals constitute a "suspect class" under the Supreme Court's test for identifying such classes. *See Padula v. Webster*, 261 U.S. App. D.C. 365, 822 F.2d 97, 103-04 (D.C. Cir. 1987). As we explained in *Padula*, if the government can criminalize homosexual conduct, a group that is defined by reference to that conduct cannot constitute a "suspect class." *See id.* Indeed, Steffan as much as concedes the point by agreeing that the military can ban those who engage in homosexual conduct.

omitted]. The government, "moreover, has no obligation to produce evidence to sustain the rationality of a [regulatory] classification." *Id.* Because "a classification neither involving fundamental rights nor proceeding along suspect lines is accorded a strong presumption of validity," *id.*, "the burden is on the one attacking the [governmental] arrangement to negative every conceivable basis which might support it,' whether or not the basis has a foundation in the record." *Id.* at 2643. [citations omitted]. This presumption of rationality does not apply merely to congressional or state legislative schemes, but extends to administrative regulatory action as well, such as the military regulations at issue here. See *Pacific States Box & Basket Co. v. White*, 296 U.S. 176, 186, 80 L. Ed. 138, 56 S. Ct. 159 (1935). The classification "is not subject to courtroom factfinding and may be based on rational speculation unsupported by evidence or empirical data." *FCC v. Beach Communications, Inc.*, 124 L. Ed. 2d 211, 113 S. Ct. 2096, 2098 (1993). The dissent is quite mistaken in asserting that under rational basis review, the government's position is weakened if it does not produce evidence to support ("demonstrate") its regulatory proposition. *See* dissent at 18. It is hard to imagine a more deferential standard than rational basis, but when judging the rationality of a regulation in the military context, we owe even more special deference to the "considered professional judgment" of "appropriate military officials." *Goldman v. Weinberger*, 475 U.S. 503, 509, 89 L. Ed. 2d 478, 106 S. Ct. 1310 (1986).

Under this line of precedent we are required to ask two questions of the regulations. First, are they directed at the achievement of a legitimate governmental purpose? Second, do they rationally further that purpose? The first of these questions is not even in dispute in this case. As we have noted, Steffan concedes that the military may constitutionally terminate service of all those who engage in homosexual conduct—wherever it occurs and at whatever time the conduct takes place. [footnote omitted]. Counsel at oral argument further admitted, in connection with a discussion focused on the DOD Directives, that the military could ban even those who reveal an "intention" to engage in such conduct. It is common ground, then, that the regulations would be serving a legitimate purpose by excluding those who engage in homosexual conduct or who intend to do so.[4]

The dispute between the parties is thus limited to the question of whether the regulations (focusing now on the Academy regulations), by requiring the discharge of those midshipmen who describe themselves as homosexual—whether or not the Academy has information establishing that an individual has engaged in homosexual conduct or intends to do so—are rational. Steffan first argues that there is no necessary factual connection between such self-description and such conduct. But Steffan relies primarily on a more subtle and novel argument. Even if the government could rationally, as a factual matter, draw a connection between the statement and the conduct, other legal considerations prevent the government from so doing. The military

---

[4]The regulations state that homosexuality "limits a midshipman's aptitude and potential for commissioned service" (emphasis added), which might suggest that it would be particularly troublesome for an officer to be a declared homosexual. But the government at oral argument expressly denied that the regulations were crafted with any specific concern for officers. In light of Goldman's admonition that we owe special deference to the "considered professional judgment" of the military officials, we do not think it open to us to draw any distinction between officers and enlisted members.

may not, according to Steffan, "punish" homosexuals solely on the basis of their "status." Nor may the military presume that self-declared homosexuals will actually engage in homosexual conduct, for such conduct is illegal under the Code of Military Justice. (Sodomy is prohibited under 10 U.S.C. @ 925 (1988).) Such a presumption—that someone will actually break the law—is inconsistent, he argues, with our legal traditions.

We consider first whether the Academy regulation has a rational factual basis. The appropriate question, it seems to us, is whether banning those who admit to being homosexual rationally furthers the end of banning those who are engaging in homosexual conduct or are likely to do so. The Academy can treat someone who intends to pursue homosexual conduct in the same manner as someone who engages in that conduct, because such an intent is a precursor to the proscribed conduct and makes subsequent homosexual conduct more likely than not. And the military may reasonably assume that when a member states that he is a homosexual, that member means that he either engages or is likely to engage in homosexual conduct. The inference seems particularly valid in this case because Steffan made no attempt to clarify what he meant by the term. He did not specify (nor was he asked by the Board) whether he had engaged in homosexual conduct in the past, whether he was presently engaged in homosexual conduct, whether he intended to engage in homosexual conduct in the future, or whether all three were true. Indeed, as we noted, he had previously invoked his right to remain silent when questioned on these subjects. Nor did Steffan ever indicate that his answer to the Board referred to homosexual orientation as a concept implicating only wants or thoughts unrelated to conduct—a meaning that he now suggests was a possible interpretation of the term and which the dissent embraces. He left it to the Board to draw what he apparently thought

were the ordinary inferences the term homosexual suggests. These ordinary inferences are reflected in the Academy regulations and were the apparent bases for the Board's conclusions. [footnote omitted]. The dissent's deconstruction of Steffan's terse response overlooks the obvious point that Steffan assumed that the Board would fully understand what he meant.

Admittedly, it is conceivable that someone would describe himself as a homosexual based on his orientation or tendencies (and, perhaps, past conduct), notwithstanding the absence of any ongoing conduct or the probability of engaging in such conduct. That there may be exceptions to the assumption on which the regulation is premised is irrelevant, however, so long as the classification (the regulation) in the run of cases furthers its purpose, and we readily conclude that it does. As then-Judge Kennedy pointed out in *Beller v. Middendorf*, 632 F.2d 788 (9th Cir. 1980), *cert. denied*, 454 U.S. 855 (1981):

> Nearly any statute which classifies people may be irrational as applied in particular cases. Discharge of the particular plaintiffs before us would be rational, under minimal scrutiny, not because their particular cases present the dangers which justify Navy policy, but instead because the general policy of discharging all homosexuals is rational. *Id.* at 808 n.20

The rule of law presupposes the creation of categories. The military thus may rely on presumptions that avoid the administratively costly need to adduce proof of conduct or intent, so long as there is a rational basis for believing that the presumption furthers that end. And the military certainly furthers its policy of discharging those members who either engage in, or are likely to engage in, homosexual conduct when it discharges those who state that they are homosexual. The special deference we owe the military's judgment necessarily affects the scope of the court's inquiry into the rationality of the military's policy. *Compare* dissent at 17. Whether a certain course of conduct is rational does not depend solely upon the degree of correlation that exists between a surface characteristic and a corresponding hidden trait. For the question whether the degree of correlation justifies the action taken—*i.e.*, whether it is rational—necessarily depends on one's assessment of the magnitude of the problem the action seeks to avoid. The military is entitled to deference with respect to its estimation of the effect of homosexual conduct on military discipline and therefore to the degree of correlation that is tolerable. Particularly in light of this deference, we think the class of self-described homosexuals is sufficiently close to the class of those who engage or intend to engage in homosexual conduct for the military's policy to survive rational basis review.

Because removing from the military all those who admit to being homosexual furthers the military's concededly legitimate purpose of excluding from service those who engage in homosexual conduct, Steffan's argument at bottom must be based on the notion that the classification drawn by the military is impermissibly over-inclusive—that the military may not presume that all admitted homosexuals will engage in homosexual conduct because some homosexuals would not. However, courts are compelled under rational-basis review to

accept a legislature's generalizations even when there is an imperfect fit between means and ends. A classification does not fail rational-basis review because it "is not made with mathematical nicety or because in practice it results in some inequality." "The problems of government are practical ones and may justify, if they do not require, rough accommodations—illogical, it may be, and unscientific." [citations omitted].[5]

The Ninth Circuit accepted Meinhold's characterization that the class of persons at issue was those "who say they are gay but have not acted in accordance with their propensity in the past." In our view, however, the proper characterization of the class is persons who say they are gay, but as to whom the military has no additional evidence as to their conduct. The Meinhold court also did not consider the rationality of treating all persons who identify themselves as homosexuals as likely violators of the prohibition on homosexual conduct.

Steffan seeks to end-run this analysis by arguing that a prohibition triggered simply by an admission of homosexuality is one based on "status" rather than conduct, and therefore is legally impermissible regardless of its rational relationship, as a factual matter, to the military's objective. As the panel that initially decided this case put the point, "America's hallmark has been to judge people by what they do, and not by who they are." *Steffan v. Aspin*, 303 U.S. App. D.C. 404, 8 F.3d 57, 70 (D.C. Cir.

---

[5]In *Meinhold v. United States Dept. of Defense*, 1994 WL 467311 (9th Cir. Aug. 31, 1994), the court addressed the "desires" portion of the DOD Directive in a case involving a serviceman who said on national television, "Yes, I am in fact gay." A discharge panel was convened to consider Meinhold's statement and as far as we can determine Meinhold did not appear before the Board. The Ninth Circuit construed the "desires" language to mean something akin to intent, and therefore concluded that separation could be based on a statement identifying oneself as a homosexual only when it was accompanied by evidence of conduct or intent. Finding that Meinhold's televised announcement failed to provide any such evidence, *compare infra* at 28 n.18 (discussing the appropriateness of the Meinhold court's factual finding), the court determined that Meinhold's discharge was illegal under the Navy's own regulations.

1993), vacated and rehearing en banc granted (D.C. Cir. Jan. 7, 1994). In our view, however, Steffan's attempt to invoke a rule against "punishment" based on "status" is unavailing, because it derives from a misunderstanding of constitutional law.

It is true that the Constitution forbids criminal punishments based on a person's qualities—we assume that this is what is meant by "status"—rather than on his or her conduct. *See Robinson v. California,* 370 U.S. 660, 8 L. Ed. 2d 758, 82 S. Ct. 1417 (1962). Yet, this proposition has never meant that employment decisions—which is what this case is about—cannot be made on such a basis. One cannot be put in jail for having been born blind (although a blind person who drives a truck and kills someone could be jailed for his act). But it obviously would be constitutional for the military to prohibit blind people from serving in the armed forces, even though congenital blindness is certainly a sort of "status." The logic of Steffan's argument and of the original panel's decision—that "America's hallmark" prohibits "punishment" (which term is meant to encompass discharge decisions) based on a person's "status"—would mean that the military acts unconstitutionally if it refuses to enlist blind individuals.

It is asserted that one does not choose to be homosexual and that therefore it is unfair for the military to make distinctions on that basis. But whether or not one's homosexuality is genetically predetermined, one's height certainly is. Steffan conceded at oral argument that the Navy's maximum height restrictions are constitutional because they rationally further a legitimate naval purpose. That concession amounts to an admission that employment decisions based on a person's characteristics are subject to the same analysis as decisions based on a person's conduct. Both are tested to see whether they rationally further a legitimate purpose.

. . . .

[I]n this case, the possible existence of some self-identified homosexuals who do not and would not act on their desires in a military or civilian setting does not render irrational a regulation that reaches the class as a whole. Just as age can be used as a rough proxy for diminishing physical capacities, here we think that a statement that one is a homosexual can rationally be used by the Navy as a proxy for homosexual conduct—past, present, or future.

. . . .

To be sure, it would not pass even rational basis review for the military to reject service members because of characteristics—such as race or religion or the lack of inherited wealth—that have absolutely no bearing on their military service.[6] Homosexuality, by contrast, is not irrelevant to homosexual conduct. And once Steffan concedes that the military may constitutionally seek to prevent the latter, his analogy to a hypothetical exclusion of those of a particular race or religion fails.

Nevertheless, Steffan, in order to make his point, would have us see homosexual status—which is all that he should be thought to have acknowledged—as conceptually unrelated to homosexual conduct. Although there may well be individuals who could, in some sense, be described as homosexuals based strictly on an inchoate orientation, certainly in the great majority of cases those terms are coterminous. [footnote omitted]. Homosexuality, like all forms of sexual orientation, is tied closely to sexual conduct.

---

[6]Classifications based on race or religion, of course, would trigger strict scrutiny.

. . . .

The dissent would employ the military's new policy, adopted in 1993, (which of course is not formally before the court) as an indication that the military has implicitly conceded that the Academy regulations (and former DOD Directives) were irrational. That proposition is a non sequitur. In light of the extremely deferential nature of rational basis review, there would always be a range of policy choices that would meet that standard. A shift from one of those choices to another hardly suggests that the government believes the former was unconstitutional. In any event, under the new policy, Steffan's statement—which we again emphasize is what this case is about—would be taken to mean just what the Academy Board apparently thought it meant. The new Directives provide that a "statement by a Service member that he or she is a homosexual . . . creates a rebuttable presumption that the Service member engages in homosexual acts or has a propensity or intent to do so." DOD Directive 1332.14.H.1.b.(2) (Dec. 22, 1993). To be sure, under the new policy, the government explicitly disavows any concern with a service member's totally private homosexual "orientation," meaning his "sexual attractions"; but however that language might be applied in future cases, it obviously would have no relevance to a service member who, like Steffan, has disclosed that he is a homosexual.

Certainly, individuals like Steffan who identify themselves as homosexual in a military setting—where a declaration of homosexuality is grounds for discharge—convey the impression that they are not in doubt as to the direction of their sexual drive. The inference drawn by the government in this sort of case is thus even stronger than it might be in civilian life, where it is more conceivable that an individual would experiment with such an identification. The dissent asserts that the fear of discharge would prevent a self-identified homosexual from actually engaging in homosexual conduct, see dissent at 24, but its reasoning overlooks the point that such fears, if present, would presumably also have discouraged the initial statement, particularly if a person were unsure of his or her identification and its relationship to the military's definition. Given that the military's response is the same in each case—discharge—it is unclear why the dissent thinks the deterrent would affect only the later decision.

Even if the assumption that declared homosexuals will engage in homosexual conduct is reasonable in certain contexts, Steffan maintains that it is nevertheless impermissible for the military to act on that assumption; it implies that service members will engage in criminal misconduct—violate the Uniform Code of Military Justice. Steffan argues that such an assumption flies in the face of core traditions of American jurisprudence. Although Steffan's argument has a certain superficial attractiveness, it seems to us that upon close examination it is more clever than real. First of all, the Academy regulations reach all homosexual conduct—a category of actions that may include conduct that is not illegal under the Code, which proscribes sodomy. More important, we think that when a service member declares or openly admits that he is a homosexual without any explanation, the Academy may rationally take that statement, at least for purposes unrelated to criminal enforcement, as highly likely to be an admission of homosexual conduct or intent. In a discharge proceeding, the Navy need not conduct an inquisition to test whether a particular midshipman possesses an idiosyncratic view of the term. When an individual's statement can reasonably be taken to evidence a propensity to engage in certain conduct, the military may certainly take that individual at his word.

. . . .

We recognize that the government's basic policy—that homosexuals (using the ordinary meaning) may not serve in the armed forces—is quite controversial. The issue is politically decisive. We think, however, that Steffan's claim that the government cannot rationally infer that one who states he or she is a homosexual is a practicing homosexual, or is at least likely to engage in homosexual acts, is so strained a constitutional argument as to amount to a basic attack on the policy itself. [footnote omitted]. And we think that the language used by the dissent—its invocation of "discrimination," dissent at 29 n.20, "fundamental due process," *id.*, and "fundamental impediments deeply rooted in our constitutional jurisprudence," *id.* at 18—represents a rhetorical effort to break out of the narrow constraints of the court's role on rational basis review.

III. DOD Directives

A.

The DOD Directives use somewhat different wording to define a homosexual than does the Academy regulation: Homosexual means a person, regardless of sex, who engages in, desires to engage in, or intends to engage in homosexual acts. . . . DOD Directive 1332.14.H.1.b.(1), 32 C.F.R. Pt. 41, App. A (1991) (superseded). Steffan's lawsuit takes aim primarily at the Directives because the phrase "desires to engage in" is claimed to extend the definition of homosexual into the realm of a service member's private thoughts. The DOD regulations are unconstitutional, Steffan argues, because they allow for the expulsion of service members on the basis of their inner feelings alone. They are irrationally overbroad—and thus fail rational basis review—because they define the class of excludable persons to reach those who merely harbor homosexual impulses, without requiring any indications that such

impulses are likely to be reflected in admittedly impermissible homosexual conduct. Steffan's complaint purports to challenge the Directives as applied and on their face (although his brief is ambiguous on the point).

As we have noted, however, Steffan's counsel, agreed at oral argument that the Directives constitutionally could be applied to a service member who stated that he was a homosexual and who meant by the statement that he actually engaged in homosexual conduct. This concession, that some situations exist to which the Directives may constitutionally be applied, renders Steffan's facial challenge defective. . . .

. . . .

Steffan insists that the Navy never alleged that he engaged in homosexual acts or intended to do so. That is true but, it seems to us, quite beside the point. After all, the Navy never alleged that Steffan had homosexual "desires." Steffan openly admitted his homosexuality, and under the circumstances there was no reason for the Navy to proceed further. If Steffan had wished to explain that his admission was based only on his desires—and not his conduct or intentions—he could have done so and joined the issue. The government would have been obliged, in that event, either to rest on his explanation (more naturally, he would have been at least asked what he meant by "desires") or to pursue further evidence of intent or conduct. In that manner, one could subsequently determine whether the Navy had relied on only the desires portion of the definition and therefore whether it had actually been applied to Steffan.

Indeed, the government in its brief before this court, while conceding that the word "desires" may be ambiguous "in isolation," tells us that the Department of Defense interprets the term as "conduct related," *i.e.*, bordering on intent, and referring to the actual "prospect of future acts." If the Directives were interpreted in this way—notwithstanding their different language—to mean essentially the same as the Academy regulations, then, as we have already held, it would pass constitutional muster. If, instead, the word "desires" were interpreted to extend the definition of homosexual to persons not likely to engage in homosexual conduct, a different question would be presented; but Steffan has not indicated, in his framing of the case, that he is affected by that possible (if far-fetched) definition.

. . . .

For the foregoing reasons, the judgment of the district court is affirmed.

So ordered.

Other cases have held the opposite of *Steffan*. In *Meinhold v. United States, Dept. of Defense*, 808 F. Supp. 1455, 1458 (C.D. Cal. 1993), the court permanently enjoined the Department of Defense "from discharging or denying enlistment to any person based on sexual orientation in the absence of sexual conduct which interferes with the military mission of the armed forces of the United States." The Ninth Circuit concluded that separation could be based on a statement identifying oneself as a homosexual only when it was accompanied by evidence of conduct or intent. The court found that Petty Officer Meinhold's televised announcement that he was gay failed to provide any such evidence. As the court pointed out in *Steffan*, a declaration of homosexual status is still a basis for separation under the terms of the current Department of Defense policy (although *Meinhold* found this to be unconstitutional). Ultimately, the Supreme Court will have to resolve the issue of homosexuals in the armed services.

Service members discharged for homosexual conduct receive a type warranted by service record discharge characterization. However, an other than honorable discharge is possible in certain situations. Naval Military Personnel Manual 3630400.4 explains those circumstances:

a. by using force, coercion, or intimidation;

b. with a person under sixteen years of age;

c. with a subordinate in circumstances that violate customary naval superior-subordinate relationships;

d. openly in public view;

e. for compensation;

f. aboard a naval vessel or aircraft;

g. in another location subject to naval control under aggravating circumstances that have an adverse impact on good order, discipline, or morale. . . .

In all homosexuality separations, the service member has the right to an administrative board, even if an other than honorable characterization is not possible. Why does the military have this special rule? *See Selland v. Aspin*, 832 F. Supp. 12 (D.C. 1993) (court noted stigmatizing nature of an honorable discharge on the basis of homosexuality). Finally, homosexual conduct is still a violation of the UCMJ. *See Steffan* and Article 125, UCMJ (sodomy).

THE COUNSELING REQUIREMENT

Evidence that the member has previously been counseled concerning the basis for separation is a prerequisite for discharge processing in many separation cases. For example, counseling is required in separations for misconduct due to a pattern of misconduct. Failure to adhere to the counseling requirement will preclude administrative processing. The counseling must include: (1) notification concerning the deficiency or impairment to be corrected; (2) specific recommendations for corrective action; (3) assistance available to the member; (4) a comprehensive explanation of consequences for failure to successfully undertake the corrective action; and (5) a reasonable period provided to allow the member an opportunity to correct the deficiency. If counseling is required, it must be documented in writing in the member's service record. *See* Figure 4-F on the next page for an example of a Navy page 13 counseling entry.

FIGURE 4-F

ADMINISTRATIVE REMARKS
NAVPERS 1070/613 (REV. 10-81)
S/N 0108-LF-010-9991

SHIP OR STATION USS ALWAYS GONE (CVN 72)

15 March 19XX

1. You are being retained in the naval service, however, the following deficiencies in your performance and/or conduct are identified:

> Here outline in a brief paragraph specific *performance* deficiencies such as failure to complete required PQS courses, poor attitude in the work center, lack of care in performing required tasks, failure to learn minimum required skills necessary to complete assigned tasks, poor grooming habits, etc. Also outline *conduct* deficiencies such as lack of proper respect for supervisors, periods of UA from the work center, specific offenses for which the member has been punished at NJP or court-martial.

2. The following are recommendations for corrective action:

> Here specify how the member should correct the problems you outlined in the first paragraph. For example: "Adopt a more positive attitude toward your work and your supervisors. Obtain a reliable alarm clock and ask a friend to ensure that you are up each morning in time to make muster. Since many of your disciplinary problems appear to be related to alcohol abuse, acquire hobbies and pursue recreation activities which do not involve drinking."

3. Assistance is available through:

> Here indicate the availability of counseling from the member's leading petty officer, work center supervisor, leading chief, and division officer. If the member exhibits signs of drug or alcohol abuse, outline the availability of help from the command CAAC counselor. Indicate that the Command Master Chief and Chaplain are also available to provide counseling on personal problems. The member might also be referred to the Career Counselor if he is dissatisfied in his current rating and would like to discuss other options.

4. You are advised that any further deficiencies in your performance and/or conduct will terminate the reasonable period of time for rehabilitation that this counseling/warning entry infers and may result in disciplinary action and in processing for administrative separation. All deficiencies previously cited and/or misconduct during your current enlistment, both prior to and subsequent to the date of this action will be considered. Subsequent violation(s) of the UCMJ or conduct resulting in civilian conviction could result in an administrative separation under other than honorable conditions.

5. This counseling/warning entry is made to afford you an opportunity to undertake the recommended corrective action. Any failure to adhere to the guidelines cited above, which is reflected in your future performance and/or conduct, will make you eligible for administrative separation action.

Witnessed: _____   Acknowledged: _____
          M division officer   SN Juan Moore Chance

Name (Last, First, Middle)	SSN	BRANCH AND CLASS
CHANCE, Juan Moore	123-45-6789	USN

A counseling is like a contract with the service member in the sense that the government promises not to discharge the member if he or she complies with its provisions. What happens if the government breaches this compact? *See Perez* and *Ruiz* in previous chapters, which relate to a service member's right to have the military comply with its own procedures.

STUDY QUESTIONS

1. What is the purpose of nonpunitive measures? What are the types of nonpunitive measures? Who has authority to deprive a member of liberty?

2. What is the difference between punitive and nonpunitive censure?

3. Who has the authority to impose nonjudicial punishment? May the authority be delegated?

4. What is a "minor offense" for purposes of nonjudicial punishment? Why is the definition important?

5. An enlisted accused attached to a vessel has all of the following rights at a nonjudicial punishment hearing *EXCEPT:*

    a. The right to examine any evidence on which the commanding officer intends to rely in deciding whether to make a finding on guilt or innocence.

    b. The right to present matters in defense, extenuation or mitigation.

    c. The right to be fully represented at the hearing by military counsel and/or civilian counsel.

    d. The right to speak privately with the commanding officer during the hearing about matters of a personal or embarrassing nature.

    e. The right to be advised of his right to appeal, if nonjudicial punishment is awarded.

6. When does an accused have the right to refuse nonjudicial punishment?

7. What is the standard of proof at nonjudicial punishment?

8. What punishments may be awarded at nonjudicial punishment? What are the limitations on combining punishments?

9. HM3 McCoy (an E-4) was apprehended by shore patrol as a result of a bar brawl. He was returned to the USS ENTERPRISE and put on report for being drunk and disorderly. Which of the following punishments may the commanding officer (an 0-6) NOT award to HM3 McCoy?

    a. 3 days bread and water, 10 days restriction and reduction in rate to E-3

b. 45 days restriction, 45 days extra duty and forfeiture of one-half month's pay for two months

c. 3 days bread and water, forfeiture of one week's pay and reduction in rate to E-3

d. 30 days correctional custody, reduction in rate to E-3

e. None of the above; they are all permissible punishments.

10. What actions may a commander take following imposition of nonjudicial punishment? May a commanding officer ever increase the punishment following the hearing? What are a service member's appeal rights following nonjudicial punishment? What actions may the appeal authority take on an appeal?

admin. discharge: Hon, Gen, OTH *punitive discharges*

11. How do administrative separations relate to nonjudicial punishment and courts-martial?

BCD, DD
any issue of misconduct, can come after NJP & CM

12. Describe the types of procedures used to administratively service members. When is the administrative board procedure used? When is the notification procedure appropriate? What are a service member's rights at a discharge board?

LON Adsep
Gen 5 mand. grounds
XCOB OTH

13. BM3 Smith is being processed for administrative separation under the notification procedure. The **LEAST FAVORABLE** possible characterization of his discharge is:

Misconduct
-COSO
patterns...
if max pun. is discharge
-civilian conviction

a. Discharge under other than honorable conditions.

b. Discharge with a dishonorable discharge.

c. Discharge with a general discharge.

d. Discharge with an honorable discharge.

e. Discharge with a bad conduct discharge.

14. Certain bases for administrative separation require mandatory processing. What are those bases?

15. When is processing mandatory for commission of a serious offense? What is a "serious offense" for purposes of administrative separation?

16. Assuming that each case has appropriately documented counselling, which of the following situations provides the grounds for separation due to a pattern of misconduct?

    a. Two nonjudicial punishments for unauthorized absence.

    b. Two civilian convictions for drunk and disorderly conduct.

    c. Two court-martial convictions for assault.

    d. Three nonjudicial punishments for dereliction of duty.

16. How does the "don't ask, don't tell" policy affect separation of service members on the basis of homosexuality? Does a declaration of homosexuality provide grounds for administrative separation? When can a member separated for homosexuality receive an other than honorable discharge?

17. What are the requirements for a valid counseling? What grounds for administrative separation require a counseling? Which do not?

CHAPTER V

MILITARY CRIMES

That Code [UCMJ] cannot be equated to a civilian criminal code. It, and the various versions of the Articles of War which have preceded it, regulate aspects of the conduct of members of the military which in the civilian sphere are left unregulated. While a civilian criminal code carves out a relatively small segment of potential conduct and declares it criminal, the Uniform Code of Military Justice essays more varied regulation of a much larger segment of the activities of the more tightly knit military community.

Parker v. Levy, 417 U.S. 733, 739 (1974)

NATURE OF MILITARY CRIMES

This chapter focuses on certain crimes under the UCMJ that are unique to the military. These purely military offenses generally have no civilian counterpart—they exist solely because of the unique mission of the military and its need to maintain good order and discipline. The military-specific offenses discussed in this chapter include: absences; disrespect; orders violations; dereliction of duty; and fraternization. Because of the military's strong position on drug involvement by service members, controlled substance crimes are also addressed.

For the most part, the military and its courts have developed the law surrounding the crimes discussed in this chapter. The result of this is twofold. First, the principles used to interpret military offenses are in many ways unparalleled in civilian criminal law. This means that courts in the armed services primarily look to other military decisions to decide cases involving purely military offenses. Second, the purpose behind uniquely military crimes—the maintenance of good order and discipline in the armed services—is a primary consideration of courts in interpreting such offenses. As a result, military courts must weigh fairness to accused service members against the aim of preserving order and control over soldiers and sailors. In reading the cases below, consider how these two principles are reconciled in each opinion.

ABSENCE OFFENSES

There are three types of absence offenses under the UCMJ: absence without leave (Article 86); desertion (Article 85); and missing movement (Article 87). These offenses are discussed below.

ABSENCE WITHOUT LEAVE

Paragraph 10c, Article IV, of the MCM explains the nature of Article 86.

> In general. This article [Article 86] is designed to cover every case not elsewhere provided for in which any member of the armed forces is through the member's own fault not at the place where the member is required to be at a prescribed time.

Paragraph 10b, Article IV of the MCM provides:

Article 86—Absence without leave

b.   Elements.

   (1) Failure to go to appointed place of duty.

      (a) That a certain authority appointed a certain time and place of duty for the accused;

      (b) That the accused knew of that time and place; and

      (c) That the accused, without authority, failed to go to the appointed place of duty at the time prescribed.

. . . .

   (3) Absence from unit, organization, or place of duty.

      (a) That the accused absented himself or herself from his or her unit, organization, or place of duty at which he or she was required to be;

      (b) That the absence was without authority from anyone competent to give him or her leave; and

      (c) That the absence was for a certain period of time. [Note: If the absence was terminated by apprehension, add the following element]

      (d) That the absence was terminated by apprehension.

Based on the elements listed above, what are the primary differences between the two types of absence without leave offenses? Which do you think is the most commonly violated? Which is most serious? *See* Appendix 2, the MCM Maximum Punishment Chart. Failure to go to appointed place of duty requires that a specific time and place of duty be assigned to the accused, and that the accused not appear as ordered. Thus, the government must prove actual knowledge of the duty assignment. Actual knowledge is not an element of absence from unit, organization or place of duty. Consider how specific must the order to go be as to time and place. What are the best ways to ensure an order is sufficiently specific as to time and place?

Inception and Termination of Absence Without Leave

Paragraph 10c, Article IV of the MCM provides:

> (8) Duration. Unauthorized absence under Article 86(3) is an instantaneous offense. It is complete at the instant an accused absents himself or herself without authority. Duration of the absence is a matter in aggravation for the purpose of increasing the maximum punishment authorized for the offense. . . . If the duration is not alleged or if alleged but not proved, an accused can be convicted of and punished for only a day of unauthorized absence. . . .
>
> . . . .
>
> (10) Termination—methods of return to military control.
>
> (a) Surrender to military authority. A surrender occurs when a person presents himself or herself to any military authority, whether or not a member of the same armed force, notifies that authority of his or her unauthorized absence status, and submits or demonstrates a willingness to submit to military control. Such a surrender terminates the unauthorized absence.
>
> (b) Apprehension by military authority. Apprehension by military authority of a known absentee terminates an unauthorized absence.
>
> (c) Delivery to military authority. Delivery of a known absentee by anyone to military authority terminates the unauthorized absence.
>
> (d) Apprehension by civilian authorities at the request of the military. When an absentee is taken into custody by civilian authorities at the request of military authorities, the absence is terminated.
>
> (e) Apprehension by civilian authorities without prior military request. When an absentee is in the hands of civilian authorities for other reasons and these authorities make the absentee available for return to military control, the absence is terminated when the military authorities are informed of the absentee's availability.

The above language addresses how absence without leave is terminated. The following case addresses the relationship between leave and unauthorized absence.

United States v. Marcus G. Ringer, Seaman Apprentice, U.S. Naval Reserve
United States Navy-Marine Corps Court of Military Review
14 M.J. 979
November 17, 1982

OPINION: Byrne, Judge

Seaman Apprentice Ringer was convicted of two specifications of unauthorized absence in violation of Article 86 of the Uniform Code of Military Justice (UCMJ), 10 U.S.C. @ 886 at a special court-martial. The military judge sentenced him to be confined at hard labor for three months, to forfeit $350 per month for three months, to be reduced to pay grade E-1, and to be discharged from the naval service with a bad-conduct discharge.

Seaman Apprentice Ringer pled not guilty to one of the two unauthorized absence specifications. As to this specification, a service record entry [Record of Unauthorized Absence (P601-6R)] showed his unauthorized absence began at 1900 on March 18, 1981, and terminated at 1415 on November 6, 1981, the dates alleged in the specification.

To rebut the Government's service record entry, trial defense counsel offered a tattered Leave Authorization form (3065R1). The form stated Seaman Apprentice Ringer was authorized fifteen days leave, beginning at 1530 on March 23, 1981, and ending at 0700 on April 6, 1981, a period of time located in the middle of his alleged unauthorized absence period.

The authorization to take leave was signed by Lieutenant Commander Griggs. Other completed boxes on the Leave Authorization, signed by Aviation Storekeeper Third Class Wooten, state that Seaman Apprentice Ringer departed on leave at 1020 on March 18, 1981; five days before the leave was to take effect and approximately nine hours before the official documents previously mentioned declared him to be an unauthorized absentee.

To authenticate the Leave Authorization form, the defense counsel called his only witness, Petty Officer Wooten. One of Petty Officer Wooten's duties as a yeoman in the command's Supply Department was to state, on the form, the time and day of departure of Navy personnel authorized leave and to then sign them out on leave on the form. Although Petty Officer Wooten did not specifically remember signing Seaman Apprentice Ringer out on leave, he did identify his own signature and that of Lieutenant Commander Griggs on the Leave Authorization. [footnote omitted].

Petty Officer Wooten also testified as follows:

> I remember the name "Ringer," sir, but as far as remembering signing, no, sir. It depends—like, I sign so many, like, you know, they come into the office and they say, "Sign my leave papers," they come in to pick up their leave papers and I turn it in to them, you know—well, they say, "I'm going on leave such and such a date" and I go ahead and just sign them out.

We assume the departure signature on the Leave Authorization was obtained by Seaman Apprentice Ringer in the manner described by Petty Officer Wooten.

DID THE STATEMENT THAT APPELLANT DEPARTED ON LEAVE PRIOR TO THE SPECIFIED BEGINNING DATE ON HIS LEAVE AUTHORIZATION

AUTHORIZE AN EARLY LEAVE DEPARTURE?

It did not. Petty Officer Wooten's duties were to type up leave papers and sign Navy personnel out on leave. There is no indication he possessed authority to authorize early departures. We conclude that Petty Officer Wooten's signature indicating an early departure on leave did not authorize additional leave beyond that specified in the Leave Authorization.

DID THE SIGN-OUT OF APPELLANT ON LEAVE ON MARCH 18, 1981, EFFECTUATE A DEPARTURE ON LEAVE FIVE DAYS LATER WHILE APPELLANT WAS IN AN UNAUTHORIZED ABSENCE STATUS?

It did not.

Initially, we note that the Leave Authorization form specifying the hour and date of departure states "Departed on Leave." Obviously, since Seaman Apprentice Ringer could not have departed on leave prior to 1530 on March 23, 1981 (the day and hour specified in his Leave Authorization for his leave to begin), a statement that he departed at an earlier time did not change his status.

Further, Petty Officer Wooten testified that the procedure used for checking Navy personnel out on leave in the Supply Department of the command relied upon a statement from the individual taking leave as to when his leave began. Abuse of such a check-out system, no matter how lax, cannot be translated into a valid check-out for the day authorized. To hold otherwise would be to benefit those few personnel whose personal word cannot be relied upon—a circumstance that is counterproductive to the interests of high morale, good order and discipline in the naval service.

DID THE APPROVED LEAVE AUTHORIZATION TERMINATE APPELLANT'S UNAUTHORIZED LEAVE STATUS?

It did not.

Once an unauthorized absence begins, it is presumed to continue until terminated by the exercise of military control over the absentee. [citations omitted].[1] The approved leave authorization did not, by itself, return Seaman Apprentice Ringer to military control. [footnote omitted].

Leave authorizations are always subject to revocation because of unexpected operational requirements or other military exigencies. They can also be revoked by placing a serviceman on restriction in lieu of arrest pending appropriate disciplinary action—which could well have happened to Seaman Apprentice Ringer if he had returned to military control from his unauthorized absence. *See United States v. Wheeler,* 21 C.M.R. 456, 457 (A.B.R.1956). Suffice it to say that there are many legitimate military reasons for revoking leave, either before the authorization date or during the leave period itself. To permit a service member to obtain irrevocable leave by absenting himself without authority would adversely affect the interests of high morale, good order and discipline in the military services.

This case falls in line with *United States v. Klunk,* 3 U.S.C.M.A. 92, 11 C.M.R. 92 (1953) wherein it was held that expiration of an unauthorized absentee's enlistment did not terminate his absence without leave. The Court stated:

Absence without leave is not a continuing offense, but is complete when the individual first so absents himself. *United States v. Lovell,* 7 U.S.C.M.A. 445, 22 C.M.R. 235 (1956). But, absence without leave is of a continuing duration. *United States v. Skipper,* 1 C. M.R. 581 (C.G.B.R.1951).

Hence—until the regular processes of discharge have been completed, a Naval enlisted man's status as one subject to military control remains unchanged, the expiration of his enlistment through lapse of time notwithstanding. *Id.* at 94.

Like the serviceman in *Klunk*, Seaman Apprentice Ringer had certain acts that had to be completed before he would have been authorized to depart on leave: he had to terminate his unauthorized absence and he had to properly check-out on leave sometime after the time specified for his leave to begin.

Since Seaman Apprentice Ringer did not terminate his unauthorized absence or properly check-out on leave, the observation of the United States Court of Military Appeals in *Klunk* applies to this case:

> One who renders impossible the accomplishment of these procedures through his own unauthorized absence is without standing to complain.

The findings and sentence as approved on review below are affirmed.

Which type of absence without leave was Seaman Apprentice Ringer accused of having committed? Did you get a sense in reading the case that Seaman Apprentice Ringer was trying to pull the wool over the eyes of the command in leaving the ship early? *See Affirmative Defenses To Absence Offenses* below regarding defenses to unauthorized absence. The following case considers how an unauthorized absence is terminated.

United States, Appellee, v. Private Milton B. Coglin, United States Army, Appellant.
United States Army Court of Military Review
10 M.J. 670
January 6, 1981

OPINION: Jones, Senior Judge

The appellant pleaded guilty to an unauthorized absence of two weeks duration but was convicted of an absence of 19 weeks, as charged.[1] The issue raised below and again before this Court is whether appellant, by his presence on a military installation and his contacts with military personnel, terminated his absence at a time

earlier than that charged. We hold that he did not and we affirm.[2]

Four records of nonjudicial punishment were admitted in aggravation. Two were more than two years old (appellant's absences being considered) and should not have been admitted. We find no prejudice from this error, however.

---

[1] Violation of Article 86, Uniform Code of Military Justice, 10 U.S.C. @ 886.

[2] The sentence adjudged and approved was a bad-conduct discharge, confinement at hard labor for four months, forfeiture of $150.00 pay per month for four months, and reduction to Private (E-1).

At the completion of his tour of duty in Korea, the appellant was reassigned to Fort Carson, Colorado. Instead of reporting to his new duty station, he went to Fort Benning, Georgia, his place of assignment prior to Korea and an installation much closer to his home in Florida. The appellant remained at Fort Benning for two or three weeks, living wherever he could find a spare bed in the barracks (with permission of the room occupant but without permission of a unit commander or first sergeant). During his stay at Fort Benning, appellant sometimes wore his uniform and sometimes wore civilian clothes. 10 M.J. 670, 671. The appellant went to Fort Benning to obtain a compassionate reassignment from Fort Carson. He spoke to an "E-7" at "personnel" who advised him of the appropriate procedure. Eventually the "E-7" told appellant that he did not have sufficient reasons to obtain a compassionate reassignment. Appellant contends that he advised the "E-7" of his absentee status.

The appellant went to Finance with his records in an unsuccessful attempt to be paid, and he spoke to the current first sergeant of his former company in an effort to get reassigned to that unit, to no avail. He identified himself properly to the individuals at Finance and to the first sergeant but he did not disclose to them that he was absent without leave. When he was unable to obtain pay or a compassionate reassignment, he departed Fort Benning and remained absent almost four more months before surrendering to military authorities at Fort Dix, New Jersey.

Supporting appellant's factual recitation was the stipulated testimony of a Sergeant Montgomery who was appellant's squad leader during most of appellant's tour of duty in Korea. Sergeant Montgomery was subsequently transferred to Fort Benning. By stipulation he testified that he saw appellant on several occasions during a two-week period shortly after he arrived at Fort Benning and that he advised appellant on how to obtain a compassionate reassignment. The stipulated testimony does not indicate whether Sergeant Montgomery knew appellant was AWOL when he was at Fort Benning. Assuming, as appellant maintains, that Sergeant Montgomery knew he was AWOL, it is significant that appellant states he left Fort Benning when Sergeant Montgomery advised him to turn himself in or he, the sergeant, would turn him in.

It has long been a principle of military law that an unauthorized absence may be terminated by any proper exercise of military control over an absentee. *United States v. Jackson*, 1 U.S.C.M.A. 190, 2 C.M.R. 96 (1952). For a voluntary termination initiated by the absentee to become effective, several factors must be present.

First, the absentee must present himself to competent military authority with the intention of returning to military duty. [citations omitted]. He must present himself personally, a phone call being insufficient, *United States v. Acemoglu*, 21 U.S.C.M.A. 561, 45 C.M.R. 335 (1972), but he need not report to a military installation; a recruiting office and a selective service office being sufficient for the purpose. [citations omitted]. Even a return to a military reservation does not automatically result in a termination as an absentee's casual presence on an installation for his own private purpose will not satisfy this requirement. [citations omitted]. Additionally, the competent military authority to whom the absentee must present himself must be someone with authority to apprehend, *e.g.*, a commissioned officer, *United States v. Raymo*, *supra*; a noncommissioned officer, *United States v. Kitchen*, *supra*; a military policeman, *see United States v. Reeder*, 22 U.S.C.M.A. 11, 46 C.M.R. 11 (1972). *See* paragraph 19a, Manual for Courts-Martial, United States, 1969 (Revised edition).

The second requirement that must be present for the termination of an absence is that the absentee must identify himself properly and must disclose his status as an absentee. [citations omitted]. Both identity as a member of the military and status as an absentee must be divulged. Furnishing information on the former while at the same time concealing, misrepresenting or even remaining silent on the latter would not suffice to supply the requisite degree of knowledge. An exception to this requirement that the absentee must affirmatively divulge his identity and status would be in those situations where the competent military authority was already aware of the absentee's status or, having a duty to inquire, could have determined the status by reasonable diligence. [citations omitted].

The final necessary requirement for the termination of an absence is that the military authority, with full knowledge of the individual's status as an absentee, exercises control over him. *United States v. Raymo, supra.* The measure of military control exercised may be as seemingly unimportant as referring the absentee to some other individual to solve his problem. Again an exception would occur if the military authority declined to exercise control over the absentee or was slow in the exercise of such control. In that event, the Government would not be permitted to deny a termination of absence because of the failure to exercise control. [citations omitted].

In applying the facts of the instant case to the requirements discussed above, we find a deficiency in each of the three categories. First, the appellant did not present himself to competent military authorities with the intention of terminating his absence and returning to military duty. His whole purpose at Fort Benning was a private one—to obtain a compassionate reassignment and to get paid. He spoke to the E-7, the first sergeant, Sergeant Montgomery, and others for these reasons only. An intention to return to duty would not have arisen until appellant obtained the reassignment.

Although the appellant apparently identified himself properly, we find, contrary to his contention, that he did not divulge his status as an absentee to the E-7. Appellant testified that he told the E-7 that he was "late reporting to Fort Carson."[3] In evaluating appellant's testimony we are convinced that he misrepresented his true status to the E-7. Only through deception could he have continued his discussion for a 3 week period with an E-7 in personnel concerning a compassionate reassignment, issuance of a Transportation Request, and casual or partial pay without that noncommissioned officer turning him in. To accept appellant's examination, we would have to conclude that the E-7 advised him for this extended period without apprehending him or even counselling him to turn himself in. Our credulity does not stretch that far.

The appellant testified that he told Sergeant Montgomery, his former squad leader, that he was AWOL, and that Sergeant Montgomery responded that appellant should turn himself in or he (Sergeant Montgomery) would turn him in. The stipulated testimony of Sergeant Montgomery was silent as to his knowledge of appellant's status. Accepting appellant's statement that he divulged his absentee status to Sergeant Montgomery as true, appellant still did not submit to military control when Sergeant Montgomery

---

[3]We discount the equivocal statement of appellant on redirect examination that he told the E-7 he was AWOL, especially in view of his negative response to a question by the military judge on the same issue.

attempted to exercise such control. He departed the post instead. The first sergeant and the E-7, having no knowledge of appellant's status, made no effort to exercise military control over him.

In summary, appellant did not present himself to competent military authority at Fort Benning with the intention of returning to military duty, did not disclose his status as an absentee to two of the three noncom-missioned officers with whom he had dealings, and thwarted the attempted exercise of military control by the noncommissioned officer to whom he disclosed his status. Under these circumstances, the appellant did not terminate his absence by his interlude at Fort Benning.

The findings of guilty and the sentence are affirmed.

What are the factors that will determine whether the military has exercised control over an absentee? Did you believe Private Coglin's contention that he had informed senior enlisted personnel of his AWOL status and that they had done nothing to terminate his absence? Figure 5-A demonstrates when an unauthorized absence terminates.

FIGURE 5-A

WHEN UA TERMINATES

SITUATION	UA TERMINATES
Apprehension by military authorities	At the apprehension
Surrender to military authorities	At the surrender
Civilian arrest for UA	At the civilian arrest
Civilian arrest for civilian crime	When military is informed that the accused is available for pick-up

How does a civilian arrest affect unauthorized absence? Paragraph 10c, Article IV, MCM, discusses control over military personnel by civilian authorities.

(5) Control by civilian authorities. A member of the armed forces turned over to the civilian authorities upon request under Article 14 (see R.C.M. 106) is not absent without leave while held by them under that delivery. When a member of the armed forces, being absent with leave, or absent without leave, is held, tried, and acquitted by civilian authorities, the member's status as absent with leave, or absent without leave, is not thereby changed, regardless how long held. The fact that

a member of the armed forces is convicted by the civilian authorities, or adjudicated to be a juvenile offender, or the case is "diverted" out of the regular criminal process for a probationary period does not excuse any unauthorized absence, because the member's inability to return was the result of willful misconduct. If a member is released by the civilian authorities without trial, and was on authorized leave at the time of arrest or detention, the member may be found guilty of unauthorized absence only if it is proved that the member actually committed the offense for which detained, thus establishing that the absence was the result of the member's own misconduct. . . .

Figure 5-B demonstrates the relationship between unauthorized absence and civilian charges.

Once UA
Always UA

FIGURE 5-B

RELATIONSHIP BETWEEN UA STATUS AND CIVILIAN CRIMINAL CHARGE

SITUATION*	UA	NOT UA	DURATION
UA, civ. arrest; acquit.	X		For the entire period
UA, civ. arrest; no trial	X		For the entire period
UA, civ. arrest; convict.	X		For the entire period
On Leave; arrest; acquit.		X	No "authorized" absence
On Leave; arrest; no trial	X		*If accused "at fault" (for all the time over leave)
Leave; arrest; convicted	X		**All the time over leave
Military turnover to civilians		X	Always "authorized"

*NOTE: ONCE UA, ALWAYS UA

DESERTION

Paragraph 9b, Article IV, MCM provides the elements of desertion offenses.

(1) Desertion with intent to remain away permanently.

    (a) That the accused absented himself or herself from his or her unit, organization, or place of duty;

    (b) That such absence was without authority;

    (c) That the accused, at the time the absence began or at some time during the absence, intended to remain away from his or her unit, organization, or place of duty permanently; and

    (d) That the accused remained absent until the date alleged.

    [Note: If the absence was terminated by apprehension, add the following element]

    (e) That the accused's absence was terminated by apprehension.

(2) Desertion with intent to avoid hazardous duty or to shirk important service.

    (a) That the accused quit his or her unit, organization, or other place of duty;

    (b) That the accused did so with the intent to avoid a certain duty or shirk a certain service;

    (c) That the duty to be performed was hazardous or the service important;

    (d) That the accused knew that he or she would be required for such duty or service; and

    (e) That the accused remained absent until the date alleged.

(3) Desertion before notice of acceptance of resignation.

    (a) That the accused was a commissioned officer of an armed force of the United States, and had tendered his or her resignation;

    (b) That before he or she received notice of the acceptance of the resignation, the accused quit his or her post or proper duties;

    (c) That the accused did so with the intent to remain away permanently from his or her post or proper duties; and

    (d) That the accused remained absent until the date alleged.

    [Note: If the absence was terminated by apprehension, add the following element]

    (e) That the accused's absence was terminated by apprehension.

Based upon the above elements, what are the differences between the three types of desertion? Which do you think is most common? Paragraph 9c, Article IV, of the MCM, explains several aspects of desertion offenses.

(1) Desertion with intent to remain away permanently.

    (a) In general. Desertion with intent to remain away permanently is complete when the person absents himself or herself without authority from his or her unit, organization, or place of duty, with the intent to remain away therefrom permanently. A prompt repentance and return, while material in extenuation, is no defense. It is not necessary that the person be absent entirely from military jurisdiction and control.

    (b) Absence without authority—inception, duration, termination. *See* paragraph 10c.

    (c) Intent to remain away permanently.

        (i) The intent to remain away permanently from the unit, organization, or place of duty may be formed any time during the unauthorized absence. The intent need not exist throughout the absence, or for any particular period of time, as long as it exists at some time during the absence.

        (ii) The accused must have intended to remain away permanently from the unit, organization, or place of duty. When the accused had such an intent, it is no defense that the accused also intended to report for duty elsewhere, or to enlist or accept an appointment in the same or a different armed force.

        (iii) The intent to remain away permanently may be established by circumstantial evidence. Among the circumstances from which an inference may be drawn that an accused intended to remain absent permanently are: that the period of absence was lengthy; that the accused attempted to, or did, dispose of uniforms or other military property; that the accused purchased a ticket for a distant point or was arrested, apprehended, or surrendered a considerable distance from the accused's station; that the accused could have conveniently surrendered to military control but did not; that the accused was dissatisfied with the accused's unit, ship, or with military service; that the accused made remarks indicating an intention to desert; that the accused was under charges or had escaped from confinement at the time of the absence; that the accused made preparations indicative of an intent not to return (for example, financial arrangements); or that the accused enlisted or accepted an appointment in the same or another armed force without disclosing the fact that the accused had not been regularly separated, or entered any foreign armed service without being authorized by the United States. On the other hand, the following are included in the circumstances which may tend to negate an inference that the accused intended to remain away permanently: previous long and excellent service; that the accused left valuable personal property in the unit or on the ship; or that the accused was under the influence of alcohol or drugs during the absence. These lists are illustrative only.

        (iv) Entries on documents, such as personnel accountability records, which administratively refer to an accused as a "deserter" are not evidence of intent to desert.

(v) Proof of, or a plea of guilty to, an unauthorized absence, even of extended duration, does not, without more, prove guilt of desertion.

(2) Quitting unit, organization, or place of duty with intent to avoid hazardous duty or to shirk important service.

(a) Hazardous duty or important service. "Hazardous duty" or "important service" may include service such as duty in a combat or other dangerous area; embarkation for certain foreign or sea duty; movement to a port of embarkation for that purpose; entertainment for duty on the border or coast in time of war or threatened invasion or other disturbances; strike or riot duty; or employment in aid of the civil power, in, for example, protecting property, or quelling or preventing disorder in times of great public disaster. Such services as drill, target practice, maneuvers, and practice marches are not ordinarily "hazardous duty or important service." Whether a duty is hazardous or a service is important depends upon the circumstances of the particular case, and is a question of fact for the court-martial to decide.

(b) Quits. "Quits" in Article 85 means "goes absent without authority."

(c) Actual knowledge. Article 85a(2) requires proof that the accused actually knew of the hazardous duty or important service. Actual knowledge may be proved by circumstantial evidence.

Based on the above, a service member who only intends to desert the command and not the service still has violated Article 85(1). Also, the intent to remain away permanently may be formed at any time during the absence. When a member has been UA for thirty days (or less, if the command has evidence of a desertion intent), he or she is administratively declared a "deserter." This action is administrative, resulting in the issuance of a DD Form 553 (federal arrest warrant for deserters). The DD 553 is filed on the NCIC (National Crime Information Center) computer, and is available to all law enforcement officials nationwide. The issuance of a DD 553 does not mean that a service member is guilty of desertion. Can the DD 553 be used as evidence of intent to remain away permanently?

The following case considers the evidence required to prove desertion.

United States, Appellee, v. Thaddeus E. Thun, Specialist, U.S. Army, Appellant.
United States Court of Military Appeals
36 M.J. 468
April 29, 1993

OPINION: Wiss, Judge

Despite not-guilty pleas, a military judge sitting alone as a general court-martial convicted appellant of desertion, in violation of Article 85, Uniform Code of Military Justice, 10 USC @ 885, and sentenced him to a dishonorable discharge, confine-

ment for one year, total forfeitures, and reduction to the lowest enlisted grade. The
convening authority approved these results, and the Court of Military Review affirmed without opinion on February 24,
1992.

At appellant's personal request, *see United
States v. Grostefon*, 12 M.J. 431 (C.M.A.
1982), this Court specified the following
issue of law for further review:

WHETHER THE GOVERNMENT MET
ITS BURDEN OF PROOF FOR CON-
VICTION OF DESERTION.

Now, having fully considered the record in
light of the arguments of the parties, we
affirm.

By exceptions and substitutions in the
specification, the military judge convicted
appellant of having "quit his unit, about to
deploy . . . to Saudi Arabia, then a combat
zone," at 0845 hours, January 18, 1991,
"with intent to shirk important service,
namely: participation in Operation Desert
Storm . . . and did remain so absent in desertion until 1200 hours" that same day.
See Art. 85(a)(2). To sustain this conviction in the face of appellant's broadside
challenge, we must be convinced that, "after viewing the evidence in the light most
favorable to the prosecution, any rational
trier of fact could have found the essential
elements of the crime beyond a reasonable
doubt." *Jackson v. Virginia*, 443 U.S. 307,
319, 99 S. Ct. 2781, 2789, 61 L. Ed. 2d
560 (1979).

In this case, the statute that appellant was
charged with violating reflects two essential elements, tailored to the specifics of
this case: that appellant was absent from
his unit without authority from 8:45 a.m.
until noon on January 18, 1991, *see* generally *United States v. Bondar*, 2
U.S.C.M.A. 357, 359-60, 8 C.M.R. 157,
159-60 (1953) ("It is our conclusion that

the word 'quits' is used in Article 85 as a
word of art legally synonymous with 'goes
absent without authority.'"); and secondly,
that he did so with intent to shirk important service. The latter element of intent,
in turn, requires that the service intended
to be shirked was "important service," *see
United States v. Willingham*, 2 U.S.C.M.A.
590, 10 C.M.R. 88 (1953); *United States v.
Shull*, 1 U.S.C.M.A. 177, 2 C.M.R. 83
(1952), and that appellant had actual
knowledge that he would be required for
that important service, *see United States v.
Stabler*, 4 U.S.C.M.A. 125, 15 C.M.R. 125
(1954). All of these are questions of fact.

Here, there was evidence that appellant,
realizing for several weeks that he and his
unit were marked as replacement troops in
the United States' Operation Desert Storm,
repeatedly made statements indicating that
he did not want to be a part of such a mission and that he thought the whole effort
was a misguided war over oil. Three military superiors of appellant testified that
they had informed appellant, as well as
other members of his unit, about the danger and the importance of their military
duty regarding this mission.

The prosecution's evidence indicated that,
on January 16, 1991, First Lieutenant Davenport, appellant's platoon leader, told appellant and others that their unit should
"be prepared to deploy to Saudi Arabia no
later than midnight" of January 17. On
January 17, Davenport told the unit to continue to work, to pack their bags, and to
make sure that everything was prepared for
deployment the next day to Saudi Arabia
and Operation Desert Storm.

At the formation at 6:30 a.m. on January
18, 1991, First Sergeant Ortiz told the unit
that the last thing to be done before de-
ploying was to weigh everyone's bags. After Ortiz had released the platoons,
appellant's platoon sergeant, Sergeant
First Class Anderson, ordered appellant

and the rest of the platoon to return at 8:45 a.m. that same morning to weigh their bags for deployment. At that scheduled weigh-in, appellant's packed bag was present—but appellant was not. The evidence indicated that no one in appellant's immediate chain of command had given appellant permission not to be present, as he had been ordered to be.

We acknowledge, as appellant has urged, that this case was not especially well prosecuted and that other evidence tended in some ways to mitigate the evidence summarized above. We acknowledge, as well, that the time period of which appellant was convicted of being absent was unusually short for a charge of desertion. *See United States v. Cothern*, 8 U.S.C.M.A. 158, 23 C.M.R. 382 (1957); *United States v. McCrary*, 1 U.S.C.M.A. 1, 1 C.M.R. 1 (1951).

Nevertheless, it is not the duration of appellant's absence that is telling, but its timing. "It is well established in military law that absence without leave with knowledge of immediate overseas movement is sufficient [evidence] from which a court may find desertion predicated on the intent to shirk important service." *United States v. Hemp*, 1 U.S.C.M.A. 280, 287, 3 C.M.R. 14, 21 (1952). Under the particular facts of a given case, the imminence of the overseas duty may be the decisive factor in a desertion case. *Compare United States v. McCrary*, *supra*, with *United States v. Logas*, 2 U.S.C.M.A. 489, 9 C.M.R. 119 (1953).

Considering the evidence in a light most favorable to the Government, as we must do, the evidence summarized above is a sufficient basis upon which rational factfinders could find all of the elements of the charged crime beyond a reasonable doubt. *See Jackson v. Virginia*, *supra*. Accordingly, appellant's challenge in this Court to the legal sufficiency of the evidence of his guilt fails.

The decision of the United States Army Court of Military Review is affirmed.

What was the important service Specialist Thun was charged with shirking? What factors did the court examine to determine whether the accused had the intent to shirk important service? *See* Paragraph 9c, Part IV, MCM, above regarding the factors that will bear on the issue of the intent to desert and *United States v. Kirby* in Chapter II. Note the length of Specialist Thun's absence (less than four hours). How could the court find a violation of Article 85 when the accused was only absent for such a short period?

MISSING MOVEMENT

The below provisions from the MCM describe the crime of missing movement. Paragraph 11, Article IV, MCM, provides:

b.   Elements.

(1)   That the accused was required in the course of duty to move with a ship, aircraft or unit;

    (2) That the accused knew of the prospective movement of the ship, aircraft or unit;

    (3) That the accused missed the movement of the ship, aircraft or unit; and

    (4) That the accused missed the movement through design or neglect.

c. Explanation.

    (1) Movement. "Movement" as used in Article 87 includes a move, transfer, or shift of a ship, aircraft, or unit involving a substantial distance and period of time. Whether a particular movement is substantial is a question to be determined by the court-martial considering all the circumstances. Changes which do not constitute a "movement" include practice marches of a short duration with a return to the point of departure, and minor changes in location of ships, aircraft, or units, as when a ship is shifted from one berth to another in the same shipyard or harbor or when a unit is moved from one barracks to another on the same post.

    (2) Mode of movement.

        (a) Unit. If a person is required in the course of duty to move with a unit, the mode of travel is not important, whether it be military or commercial, and includes travel by ship, train, aircraft, truck, bus, or walking. The word "unit" is not limited to any specific technical category such as those listed in a table of organization and equipment, but also includes units which are created before the movement with the intention that they have organizational continuity upon arrival at their destination regardless of their technical designation, and units intended to be disbanded upon arrival at their destination.

        (b) Ship, aircraft. If a person is assigned as a crew member or is ordered to move as a passenger aboard a particular ship or aircraft, military or chartered, then missing the particular sailing or flight is essential to establish the offense of missing movement.

    (3) Design. "Design" means on purpose, intentionally, or according to plan and requires specific intent to miss the movement.

    (4) Neglect. "Neglect" means the omission to take such measures as are appropriate under the circumstances to assure presence with a ship, aircraft, or unit at the time of a scheduled movement, or doing some act without giving attention to its probable consequences in connection with the prospective movement, such as a departure from the vicinity of the prospective movement to such a distance as would make it likely that one could not return in time for the movement.

    (5) Actual knowledge. In order to be guilty of the offense, the accused must have actually known of the prospective movement that was missed. Knowledge of the exact hour or even of the exact date of the scheduled movement is not required. It is sufficient if the approximate date was known by the accused as long as there is a causal connection between the conduct of the accused and

the missing of the scheduled movement. Knowledge may be proved by circumstantial evidence.

Actual knowledge of the movement is an element of missing movement. *See Specific Intent* discussed in Chapter II regarding specific and general intent crimes. How would you prove actual knowledge? What is the difference between missing movement through neglect and missing movement by design? Does knowledge of the movement effect whether the offense was through neglect or design? The following case addresses what a "substantial movement" is for purposes of Article 87.

United States, Appellee, v. Guillermo Quezada, Operations Specialist Seaman Apprentice, U.S. Navy, Appellant
United States Court of Military Appeals
40 M.J. 109
August 17, 1994

OPINION: Sullivan, Chief Judge

Appellant was tried by a special court-martial composed of a military judge sitting alone on October 24, 1991, at the Naval Legal Service Office, Subic Bay, Republic of the Philippines. This court-martial was convened by the Commanding Officer, USS Independence (CV 62). Appellant pleaded guilty to missing movement through neglect and two specifications of unauthorized absence, in violation of Articles 87 and 86, Uniform Code of Military Justice, 10 USC @@ 887 and 886, respectively. He was sentenced to a bad-conduct discharge, confinement and forfeiture of $500.00 pay per month for 2 months. On January 13, 1992, the convening authority approved the sentence. The Court of Military Review affirmed these results in an unpublished opinion on January 29, 1993.

This Court, on August 9, 1993, granted review of the following issue raised by appellate defense counsel:

WHETHER AN EIGHT-HOUR DEPENDENTS' CRUISE IS A MOVEMENT FOR PURPOSES OF ARTICLE 87.

We hold that such a cruise is a movement within the meaning of Article 87 and that appellant's pleas of guilty to this military offense were valid. [citation omitted].

Appellant was charged with and pleaded guilty to the following offense under Article 87:

Specification: In that [appellant] did, at Naval Air Station North Island, San Diego, California, on or about 29 June 1991, through neglect, miss the movement of the USS Independence with which he was required in the course of duty to move.

The military judge questioned appellant about this offense as follows:

The elements of the offense alleged in the Specification to Charge II are as follows:

First, that you were required in the course of duty to move with the USS INDEPENDENCE;

Second, that you knew of the prospective movement of the ship;

Third, that at the Naval Air Station North Island, San Diego, California, on or about 29 June 1991, you missed the movement of the ship; and,

Fourth, that you missed the movement through neglect.

MJ: You're advised that the term "movement" as used in this Specification, means a major transfer of a ship involving a substantial distance and period of time. The word does not include minor changes in the location of a ship. You're advised that the term "through neglect" means the omission to take such measures as are appropriate under the circumstances to assure presence with the ship at the time of a scheduled movement, or doing some act without giving attention to its probable consequences in connection with the perspective movement to such a distance as would make it likely that you could not return in time for the movement. . . .

MJ: Now, turning your attention to the Specification to Charge II. You've told me that you were a member of the USS INDEPENDENCE and that on the morning of the 29th of June you began a period of unauthorized absence. Did—was the USS INDEPENDENCE scheduled to move on the 29th of June?

ACCUSED: Yes, sir.

MJ: And where was it scheduled to move to?

ACCUSED: It was a dependents' cruise, sir.

MJ: And this was a dependents' cruise. How long was the dependents' cruise?

ACCUSED: Approximately 8 hours just about. Less than a day, sir.

MJ: So, this was a one-day cruise to familiarize dependents with the USS INDEPENDENCE?

ACCUSED: Yes, sir.

MJ: So this was more than just a minor change in the location of a ship?

ACCUSED: Yes, sir.

MJ: It was not just moving from pier to pier, but it was pulling out to sea for some period of hours?

ACCUSED: Yes, sir.

MJ: And are you satisfied that is a— constitutes a movement of the USS INDEPENDENCE?

ACCUSED: Yes I do, sir.

MJ: And you've discussed that with your counsel?

ACCUSED: Yes, sir.

MJ: And are you satisfied that indeed that was a movement?

ACCUSED: Yes, sir.

MJ: Now, did the USS INDEPENDENCE actually move on the 29th of June?

ACCUSED: Yes, sir.

The Court of Military Review stated, inter alia:

We hold that an aircraft carrier's movement out to sea albeit for only a period of eight hours does constitute a "substantial" movement, even when such a movement involves a dependents' cruise. We are aware that a duty section or skeleton crew is capable of moving a ship from pier to pier. However, for an underway beyond the breakwater and into the open seas the considerations of safety for ship and crew are much the same as they would be for a longer deployment. As reflected in the Government's brief, additional safeguards aboard the carrier are required by the addition of large numbers of dependents aboard ship. Thus, the demands placed on the crew require the presence of all those scheduled to go to sea for the event.

Appellant, for the first time before the Court of Military Review, argued that his pleas of guilty to missing movement must be set aside. He asserted that his responses to the guilty-plea inquiry do not establish this military offense as a matter of law because he only admitted to missing an insubstantial movement of his ship, *i.e.*, "an 8-hour dependents' cruise." Before us, he argues that Article 87 only prohibits missing the movement of a ship in the special military situations encountered in World War II. We disagree.

We note that Article 87 states:

Any person subject to this chapter who through neglect or design misses the movement of a ship, aircraft, or unit with which he is required in the course of duty to move shall be punished as a court-martial may direct.

The plain language of this codal provision centers on appellant's duty to move with a ship, not with the purpose of the ship's movement. *See United States v. Graham*, 16 M.J. 460, 462 (C.M.A. 1983). *See generally Conroy v. Aniskoff*, 123 L. Ed. 2d 229, U.S. , 113 S.Ct. 1562 (1993). Moreover, the prior experience of the Navy with this type of military misconduct has not deterred this Court from giving this language its full and natural meaning. *See*

United States v. Graham, 16 M.J. at 462-63 n.3; *see also United States v. Smith*, 26 M.J. 276 (C.M.A. 1988). Finally, appellant pleaded guilty to this offense and agreed that the 8-hour "dependents' cruise" was a movement within the meaning of Article 87. M.J. at (5-6). [citation omitted]. Such action precluded the need for any proof that the prosecution might have had concerning the additional missions of the aircraft carrier during the movement in question. *See United States v. Burnette*, 35 M.J. 58, 61 (C.M.A. 1992) (appellant's pleas precluded prosecution from putting its entire case on record and fully developing facts).

Paragraph 11, Part IV, Manual for Courts-Martial, United States, 1984, explains the word "movement" in Article 87, Uniform Code of Military Justice, 10 USC @ 887, as follows:

c. Explanation.

(1) Movement. "Movement" as used in Article 87 includes a move, transfer, or shift of a ship, aircraft, or unit involving a substantial distance and period of time. Whether a particular movement is substantial is a question to be determined by the court-martial considering all the circumstances. Changes which do not constitute a "movement" include practice marches of a short duration with a return to the point of departure, and minor changes in location of ships, aircraft, or units, as when a ship is shifted from one berth to another in the same shipyard or harbor or when a unit is moved from one barracks to another on the same post.

To the extent this explanation accurately reflects substantive military criminal law (*see United States v. Mance*, 26 M.J. 244, 252 (C.M.A.), *cert. denied*, 488 U.S. 942, 102 L. Ed. 2d 356, 109 S. Ct. 367 (1988)), we agree that the movement of an aircraft carrier for 8 hours cannot in any reasonable sense be considered "minor."

Thus, the granted issue is without merit.

Quezada holds that the purpose of the ship's movement does not control whether a movement is significant under Article 87. Given this holding, most movements by a ship will fall within the parameters of Article 87. In what situation will a movement not be substantial? *See* paragraph 11c, Article IV, MCM, above.

AFFIRMATIVE DEFENSES TO ABSENCE OFFENSES

In criminal jurisprudence, an affirmative showing of certain facts will constitute a defense to some crimes. These sets of facts are known as affirmative defenses. Examples of affirmative defenses include self-defense, temporary insanity, and defense of others. There are two affirmative defenses to absence offenses: impossibility and duress. These defenses are discussed below.

Impossibility

Paragraph 11c(6), Part IV, MCM, explains the defense of impossibility.

(6) Inability to return. The status of absence without leave is not changed by an inability to return through sickness, lack of transportation facilities, or other disabilities. But the fact that all or part of a period of unauthorized absence was in a sense enforced or involuntary is a factor in extenuation and should be given due weight when considering the initial disposition of the offense. When, however, a person on authorized leave, without fault, is unable to return at the expiration thereof, that person has not committed the offense of absence without leave.

Note that "impossibility" refers to absences caused by misfortunes that are not foreseeable and occur through no fault of the absentee. What situations are foreseeable? Acts of nature, acts of third parties and physical disability are the three situations that are considered to be unforeseeable. Note also that impossibility cannot arise after an absence without leave has commenced.

Duress

The following case considers the defense of duress.

United States v. Lance Corporal Riofredo, U.S. Marine Corps
United States Navy-Marine Corps Court of Military Review
30 M.J. 1251
May 11, 1990

OPINION: Judge Strickland

Contrary to his pleas, appellant was found guilty of an unauthorized absence of nearly 8 1/2 months in violation of Article 86, Uniform Code of Military Justice (UCMJ), 10 U.S.C. @ 886. He was sentenced to a bad-conduct discharge, confinement for a period of 75 days, forfeiture of $200.00 pay per month for 3 months and reduction to pay grade E-1. The military judge recommended that the bad-conduct discharge and reduction below pay grade E-2 be suspended for a period of one year from the date of the convening authority's action. The convening authority approved the adjudged sentence and suspended reduction below E-2 and the bad-conduct discharge in accordance with the military judge's recommendation. Subsequently, proceedings were held in accordance with Rule for Courts-Martial (R.C.M.) 1109, and the suspended portions of the sentence were vacated.

Appellant asserted, both at trial and on appeal, that his absence was the result of duress. The duress defense was raised as a result of two confrontations between appellant and his staff noncommissioned officer-in-charge. Apparently, a less than amicable relationship existed between the two leading up to the first confrontation, which appellant described as follows:

Q. Did you ever have any physical altercations with Staff Sergeant Lowery?

A. Yes, I did, sir.

Q. How many times?

A. Twice, sir.

Q. Approximately when was the first one in relation to 22 June?

A. Approximately three weeks before, sir.

Q. And what happened?

A. I was physically struck by Staff Sergeant Lowery and thrown across a desk, and up against a wall, sir.

Q. And where did this happen?

A. In the back room of the chow hall, sir.

Q. And was it during the working day or—when did this happen?

A. It was towards the end of our working shift, sir.

Q. Were you alone in the room with Staff Sergeant Lowery?

A. Yes, sir.

Following this altercation, appellant reported the incident to his chain of command, up through and including the Battalion Sergeant Major. The command responded by formally counseling Staff Sergeant Lowery and placing a page 11 counseling entry in his service record book.

Subsequently, a second confrontation occurred off-base between appellant and Staff Sergeant Lowery. This occurred on 22 June 1988, the same day appellant is alleged to have commenced his unauthorized absence. This confrontation and its aftermath are recounted by appellant in this colloquy:

Q. And what happened that day?

A. I was sitting on my motorcycle in the parking lot of Rocking H Video out in town. Staff Sergeant Lowery ran into me there. He pulled me off my motorcycle and threw me on the ground. When I picked myself up off the ground I was struck on the left side of my face, which resulted in having a tooth of mine—my back tooth broken.

Q. Were you scared of Staff Sergeant Lowery?

A. Yes, sir.

Q. What did—were you supposed to go to work that day?

A. Yes, sir.

Q. And why didn't you go to work that day?

A. I felt threatened and I was scared of Staff Sergeant Lowery, sir.

Q. What did you do?

A. I packed my bags and I left, sir.

Q. Why didn't you—the second altercation with Staff Sergeant Lowery, why didn't you report that to somebody? Why did you leave?

A. In my opinion, sir, I felt that it was obvious that nothing was being done. I felt further threatened by Staff Sergeant Lowery for trying to cause more trouble.

Evidence was also presented that Staff Sergeant Lowery was significantly larger in stature than was appellant and that Lowery lifted weights. Further evidence indicated that Lowery had recently reported to the command and appellant believed he would remain indefinitely.

Appellant contends that he had a reasonably grounded fear of serious bodily harm, that his attempts to resolve the matter with his chain of command had not prevented his injury in the second attack, and that he, therefore, could not avoid the absence without subjecting himself to this threatened danger. The Government asserts that there was no threat of immediate death or serious bodily harm as contemplated by R.C.M. 916(h), arguing that "[a]ppellant's situation in no way approaches the life-threatening experience contemplated in R.C.M. 916(h)," and that appellant could have avoided his absence by reporting the matter to his chain of command.

We reject the Government's argument that the harm threatened in this instance is not of the magnitude contemplated in R.C.M. 916(h). The threat of serious injury is sufficient to raise the duress defense, and the threat of a beating, *United States v. Roby*, 23 U.S.C.M.A. 295, 49 C.M.R. 544 (1975), and of an initiation, *United States v. Roberts*, 14 M.J. 671 (N.M.C.M.R. 1982), has been held to be justification for a reasonably grounded fear of receipt of serious bodily injury. Serious injury had already been inflicted on appellant, particularly in the second assault, which caused one of appellant's teeth to be broken.

The question in this case is not whether appellant had a reasonably grounded fear of serious bodily harm, but whether appellant could have avoided commencing his unauthorized absence without subjecting himself to a further assault. Appellant argues that he could not have avoided this absence because reporting the first assault to his chain of command did not prevent the occurrence of the second assault, citing Roberts. This case is distinguishable, however, because in Roberts the threat of serious bodily harm had been reported to the chain of command and no action was taken. In this instance, the command took positive action following appellant's report of the first assault. The action taken was not merely a perfunctory one, but rather was a formal counseling which resulted in an adverse entry in the service record book of his assailant, a Staff Sergeant. Such an entry has a lasting impact on the record of a staff noncommissioned officer.[1]

The real issue in this case is not whether command action prevented the second assault, but whether appellant could have reasonably expected that the command would have taken action after the second assault, which would have precluded the occurrence of further assaults. If there was such a reasonable expectation, appellant was obligated to inform his command instead of initiating self-help measures. The Court of Military Appeals has stated: "The immediacy element of the defense is designed to encourage individuals promptly to report threats rather than breaking the law themselves." [citations omitted]. Where one has a reasonable opportunity to

avoid committing an offense without subjecting himself to the threatened harm, the defense of duress does not apply. R.C.M. 916(h).

We believe that the testimony of record indicates that there was a reasonable expectation that the chain of command would have taken further action against Staff Sergeant Lowery had appellant reported the second assault and that the action taken would have precluded the occurrence of additional assaults. Given the strong command response to the first assault, we are convinced the command's response to the second assault would have been even stronger and that affirmative steps would have been taken to bring a halt to this matter.[2] Instead of packing his bags and leaving, appellant could have immediately returned to base, sought whatever medical assistance he needed and promptly made the command aware of the situation.[3] Such prudent action would have ensured that appellant not be required to go to work with Staff Sergeant Lowery later that day and would have enabled appropriate measures to be instituted by the command. Appellant's actions were not excusable where he had an opportunity to avoid his absence by seeking the assistance of his command. [citation omitted]. Under all of the facts and circumstances of this case we are con-

---

[1] A counseling entry by a commander or his designated representative is considered adverse matter reflecting unfavorably upon a Marine's mental, moral, or professional qualifications and this material is microfiched and placed in the Marine's official military personnel file (OMPH) at Headquarters Marine Corps in addition to being entered in the Marine's field service record book. *See* Paragraph 1000, Marine Corps Individual Records Administration Manual (IRAM), MCO P1070.12, 22 February 1990.

[2] This could have been accomplished in a number of ways, such as placing Staff Sergeant Lowery on restriction pending disciplinary action or by removing appellant or Staff Sergeant Lowery from duties in the chow hall. We note that the initial command action did prevent a second assault from occurring on base since the second altercation occurred out in town.

[3] Appellant could also have reported the second assault to the local law enforcement agencies since this assault occurred off-base. Given the injury inflicted upon appellant, it is likely that charges would have been brought against Staff Sergeant Lowery which would have deterred him from similar conduct off-base in the future.

vinced beyond a reasonable doubt that the duress defense did not exist.

Appellant additionally argues that his sentence to a bad-conduct discharge was inappropriately severe for the offense committed given the extenuating circumstances motivating his absence, together with evidence of his rehabilitative potential as attested to by his superiors. We have weighed these matters against appellant's record, which includes evidence of two prior nonjudicial punishments and counseling entries relating to deficient performance, testimony concerning his lack of rehabilitative potential, and the lengthy absence of which appellant was convicted, and are convinced that a bad-conduct discharge is appropriate under all of the facts and circumstances of this case.

We have concluded that the findings and sentence are correct in law and fact and that no error materially prejudicial to the substantial rights of the appellant was committed. Accordingly, the findings and the sentence are affirmed.

Riofredo holds that the threat to the accused be immediate. What must the accused fear? Lance Corporal Riofredo was absent for eight months after leaving his command. What affect do you think the length of absence had on the court's decision?

OFFENSES AGAINST AUTHORITY

Under the UCMJ, there are two categories of crimes against authority, disrespect offenses and order violations. These two types of offenses are discussed below.

DISRESPECT OFFENSES

Disrespect is defined as behavior that detracts from the respect and/or authority due to another person. It may consist of acts, omissions, or language, and may refer to another person, *i.e.*, the "victim," either as an officer/noncommissioned officer/petty officer, or as a private individual.

Paragraph 13a, Article IV, MCM, provides the elements of disrespect toward a superior commissioned officer, Article 89.

    (1) That the accused did or omitted certain acts or used certain language to or concerning a certain commissioned officer;

    (2) That such behavior or language was directed toward that officer;

    (3) That the officer toward whom the acts, omissions, or words were directed was the superior commissioned officer of the accused;

(4) That the accused then knew that the commissioned officer toward whom the acts, omissions, or words were directed was the accused's superior commissioned officer; and

(5) That, under the circumstances, the behavior or language was disrespectful to that commissioned officer.

Paragraph 13c, Article IV, MCM, explains the elements of Article 89.

(1) Superior commissioned officer.

    (a) Accused and victim in same armed force. If the accused and the victim are in the same armed force, the victim is a "superior commissioned officer" of the accused when either superior in rank or command to the accused; however, the victim is not a "superior commissioned officer" of the accused if the victim is inferior in command, even though superior in rank.

    (b) Accused and victim in different armed forces. If the accused and the victim are in different armed forces, the victim is a "superior commissioned officer" of the accused when the victim is a commissioned officer and superior in the chain of command over the accused or when the victim, not a medical officer or a chaplain, is senior in grade to the accused and both are detained by a hostile entity so that recourse to the normal chain of command is prevented. The victim is not a "superior commissioned officer" of the accused merely because the victim is superior in grade to the accused.

    (c) Execution of office. It is not necessary that the "superior commissioned officer" be in the execution of office at the time of the disrespectful behavior.

(2) Knowledge. If the accused did not know that the person against whom the acts or words were directed was the accused's superior commissioned officer, the accused may not be convicted of a violation of this article. Knowledge may be proved by circumstantial evidence.

(3) Disrespect. Disrespectful behavior is that which detracts from the respect due the authority and person of a superior commissioned officer. It may consist of acts or language, however expressed, and it is immaterial whether they refer to the superior as an officer or as a private individual. Disrespect by words may be conveyed by abusive epithets or other contemptuous or denunciatory language. Truth is no defense. Disrespect by acts includes neglecting the customary salute, or showing a marked disdain, indifference, insolence, impertinence, undue familiarity, or other rudeness in the presence of the superior officer.

(4) Presence. It is not essential that the disrespectful behavior be in the presence of the superior, but ordinarily one should not be held accountable under this article for what was said or done in a purely private conversation.

Compare the above provisions with the following sections contained in paragraphs 15a and 15c, Article IV, MCM, pertaining to Article 91:

a. Text.

    Any warrant officer or enlisted member who—

(1) strikes or assaults a warrant officer, non-commissioned officer, or petty officer, while that officer is in the execution of his office;

(2) willfully disobeys the lawful order of a warrant officer, non-commissioned officer, or petty officer while that officer is in the execution of his office; shall be punished as a court-martial may direct.

c.   Explanation.

(1) In general. Article 91 has the same general objects with respect to warrant, noncommissioned, and petty officers as Articles 89 and 90 have with respect to commissioned officer, namely, to ensure obedience to their lawful orders, and to protect them from violence, insult, or disrespect. Unlike Articles 89 and 90, however, this article does not require a superior-subordinate relationship as an element of any of the offenses denounced. This article does not protect an acting noncommissioned officer or acting petty officer, nor does it protect military police or members of the shore patrol who are not warrant, noncommissioned, or petty officers.

(2) Knowledge. All of the offenses prohibited by Article 91 require that the accused have actual knowledge that the victim was a warrant, noncommissioned, or petty officer. Actual knowledge may be proved by circumstantial evidence.

(3) Striking or assaulting a warrant, noncommissioned, or petty officer. For a discussion of "strikes" and "in the execution of office," *see* paragraph 14c. For a discussion of "assault," *see* paragraph 54c. An assault by a prisoner who has been discharged from the service, or by any other civilian subject to military law, upon a warrant, noncommissioned, or petty officer should be charged under Article 128 or 134.

(4) Disobeying a warrant, noncommissioned, or petty officer. *See* paragraph 14c(2) for a discussion of lawfulness, personal nature, form, transmission, and specificity of the order, nature of the disobedience, and time for compliance with the order.

(5) Treating with contempt or being disrespectful in language or deportment toward a warrant, noncommissioned, or petty officer. "Toward" requires that the behavior and language be within the sight or hearing of the warrant, noncommissioned, or petty officer concerned. For a discussion of "in the execution of his office," *see* paragraph 14c. For a discussion of disrespect, *see* paragraph 13c.

The above provisions define a "superior commissioned officer" for purposes of Article 89. Based on that definition, could an enlisted member of the Navy be disrespectful to an Army officer? If no, are there other orders offenses that may apply? *See Failure To Obey A Lawful General Order or Regulation* and *Failure To Obey An Other Lawful Order* below under Article 92. Note that the Navy and Marine Corps are considered part of the same armed force. The military continues to increase its emphasis on jointness between the different services. This trend has significantly increased joint operations, exercises and commands. Is it time for Congress to amend the UCMJ to account for this significant trend in the nature of the armed services? Consider that the JAG Manual now permits a multiservice commander to impose nonjudicial punishment on all members of the command, regardless of service.

A superior officer need not be in the execution of his or her office, or even be present, at the time of the disrespectful conduct. *Compare* those rules with Article 91 discussed previously. Why is there a difference between the two provisions? Paragraph 13c discusses a defense commonly referred to as "abandonment of rank."

> (5) Special defense—unprotected victim. A superior commissioned officer whose conduct in relation to the accused under all the circumstances departs substantially from the required standards appropriate to that officer's rank or position under similar circumstances loses the protection of this article. That accused may not be convicted of being disrespectful to the officer who has so lost the entitlement to respect protected by Article 89.

The following case considers this defense as it applies to a victim who is a noncommissioned officer.

United States v. Airman Basic Bobby L. Cheeks
United States Air Force Court of Military Review
43 C.M.R. 1013
April 21, 1971

OPINION: Brewer, Judge

The accused was tried by general court-martial on two specifications of wrongful possession of LSD, in violation of AFR 35-6 (Specifications 1 and 3 of Charge I); two specifications of wrongful transfer of LSD, in violation of the same regulation (Specifications 2 and 4 of Charge I); one specification alleging disrespectful and contemptuous language and deportment toward his superior noncommissioned officer (Specification 1 of Charge II); one specification of willful disobedience of an order issued by the same noncommissioned officer (Specification 2 of Charge II); and one specification of willful destruction of Government property (Charge III and its specification). Having pleaded not guilty to all charges and specifications, the accused was convicted of each of the four drug offenses and the disrespect offense. As to the specification alleging willful disobedience, he was convicted, by appropriate exceptions, of the lesser included offense of failure to obey a lawful order. He was acquitted of the offense of willful destruction of Government property. The approved sentence provides for bad conduct discharge, confinement at hard labor for 18 months and total forfeitures.

. . . .

Our disposition turns on the first supplemental assertion of error by appellate defense counsel, which urges that:

> "AS A MATTER OF LAW, THE EVIDENCE WAS INSUFFICIENT TO SUPPORT A FINDING OF GUILTY OF SPECIFICATION 1 OF CHARGE II."

The specification at which this assignment of error is directed alleges in pertinent part that on 24 July 1970, while confined as a prisoner in the detention facility at Shaw Air Force Base, South Carolina, the accused "was disrespectful and contemptuous in language and deportment toward Staff Sergeant Levon Skipper, his superior noncommissioned officer, who was then in the execution of his office, by saying to him, 'I'm not going to do a damned thing,' 'you don't tell me what to do,' 'Get fucked,' or words to that effect, and by slamming the cell block door and saying, 'You will see who goes to work,' or words to that effect."

At trial, it was the contention of defense counsel that on the occasion in question, as well as during a very substantial period of time prior thereto, Sergeant Skipper had systematically subjected the accused to vile and degrading verbal abuse, as a consequence of which the accused had been "provoked, harassed, badgered and baited" into the behavior alleged in the specification. Expanding on that theme here, appellate defense counsel urge that the repeated abuse visited upon the accused by Skipper, as overwhelmingly established by the evidence, was so patently reprehensible as to divest Sergeant Skipper of his cloak of authority and thus strip him of any right, on the occasion in question, to be accorded the respect otherwise due him as a noncommissioned officer in the execution of his office. In order for us to properly assess that contention, a brief recitation of the evidence is essential.

The picture which this record portrays of Sergeant Skipper is nothing short of appalling. The uncontroverted evidence establishes a disgraceful history of sustained prisoner abuse on the part of Skipper. It was shown, and indeed acknowledged by Skipper, that on one prior occasion he had been punished under Article 15 for physically abusing a prisoner. On yet another occasion, while in a drunken rage, Skipper struck a prisoner in the face, knocking him to the ground, following which he kicked him repeatedly in the chest, shouting—"I'm going to stomp the hell out of you." The brutality and general dereliction shown by Skipper on that occasion resulted in a high level investigation which apparently resulted in some further disciplinary action of an undisclosed nature. Unsurprisingly, by the time of trial, Skipper was no longer performing duties of any kind in the confinement facility.

As regards this accused, Skipper was apparently content to restrict himself to verbal abuse. The record shows that he repeatedly cursed the accused and systematically ridiculed him by constantly addressing him as "Shits" or "Airman Shits." Becoming ever more sensitive to that degrading treatment, the accused frequently requested Skipper to address him properly. Skipper, however, continued to regularly address the accused in that loathsome fashion, professing that he "couldn't pronounce" the accused's simple and uncomplicated name of Cheeks. That pattern of abuse prevailed for a period of several months immediately prior to the episode which gave rise to the accused's alleged disrespectful behavior.

In the early morning hours of 24 July 1970, Sergeant Michael Mulliken, who was then performing supervisory duties at the confinement facility, assigned the accused to a buffer machine cleaning detail in a nearby building. Approximately 20 minutes later, the accused returned to the confinement facility and informed Mulliken that the buffer insert had worn out and that a new one would be needed. Mulliken instructed the accused to return to the situs of the cleaning detail and busy himself with other chores. Mulliken indicated that in the meantime he would attempt to locate a new buffer. A short while later, the accused returned once again to the confinement facility and inquired of Mulliken if he had yet located another buffer. On this occasion, for no apparent reason, Sergeant Skipper intervened, directing the accused to discontinue the cleaning detail to which he had earlier been assigned and to clean the latrine instead. Somewhat aggravated by that development, the accused nevertheless grudgingly complied.

Some 15 minutes later, a Technical Sergeant Harris arrived at the confinement facility to obtain a prisoner detail for work at Base Operations. Whereupon, Sergeant Skipper directed the accused to accompany Sergeant Harris on that work detail. As recounted by several witnesses, Skipper addressed the accused as "Shits" on that occasion as he had on past occasions. According to one version, Skipper shouted, "Shits, fall out to go on detail." Another version recounts Skipper as saying, "Shits, get up here, you are going on detail now." All agree that Skipper used the word "Shits" at several junctures during the episode.

Angered by Skipper's continued insistence upon addressing him in that manner, the accused responded—"I'm not moving until you call me Cheeks." Thus triggered, the exchange quickly escalated in intensity, with Skipper and the accused "both yelling at each other." During the course of the exchange, it is undisputed that the accused did speak and behave in the manner alleged in the specification. As for Skipper, his demeanor during the exchange is variously described as "losing control of himself"; "swearing and cursing"; and "yelling and screaming and going crazy." One witness recounted that Skipper approached the accused in a menacing manner with uplifted "balled up fist" and that "it looked like he was going to hit him."

In the face of that overwhelming showing of Sergeant Skipper's own gross misconduct, we have no hesitation in concluding,

as urged by appellate defense counsel, that during the course of the episode described, Skipper forfeited the special privilege which Article 91 confers upon a noncommissioned officer to be treated with respect in the execution of his office. Indeed, the degrading term which Skipper insisted upon using in addressing the accused, both on the occasion in question and throughout several months prior thereto, was palpably a violation of Article 117 of the Code, for which Skipper himself might well have been prosecuted. Under those circumstances, the accused's behavior, as alleged in the specification, was without criminality and his conviction of the alleged offense of using disrespectful and contemptuous language to a superior noncommissioned officer cannot be permitted to stand. [citations omitted].

We decline, however, to extend the application of that principle to the disobedience offense of which the accused was also convicted. While we recognize that some forms of misbehavior on the part of a noncommissioned officer in the purported execution of his office could conceivably rise to such magnitude as would divest him even of his authority to exact obedience from subordinates, we are satisfied that verbal abuse would not, standing alone, serve to vitiate a legitimate order. It is one thing to conclude, out of simple considerations of human dignity, that a superior forfeits his right to be treated with respect by a subordinate upon whom he has heaped verbal abuse. It is quite another matter, however, to conclude that a subordinate is vested with a license to disobey any order administered in a verbally abusive manner. We are simply not prepared to risk the devastation of discipline likely to be visited upon the military establishment as a consequence of such a conclusion. As cogently observed by Judge Finkelstein in his concurring and dissenting opinion in *United States v. Johnson, supra,* "[w]ords, no matter how hateful, when employed by a [superior] in an effort to require compliance with an order which may even involve hardship and possible death, would not excuse disobedience."

Here there can be no doubt that the order administered by Sergeant Skipper to the accused was, on its face, a perfectly valid one. Moreover, it is not open to controversy that however much the accused was verbally abused on that occasion, the order was administered by Skipper in the clear execution of his office. We conclude, therefore, that neither the provocative and abusive manner in which the order was administered, nor any other aspect of the attendant circumstances, would serve to legally excuse the accused's disobedience.

For the reasons heretofore indicated, we find the evidence insufficient in law and

fact to support the accused's conviction of the offense of disrespectful and contemptuous behavior toward a noncommissioned officer in the execution of his office. Accordingly, the finding of guilty of Specification 1 of Charge II is set aside and that specification is ordered dismissed. Having reassessed the sentence in light of our partial disaffirmance, and on the basis of the entire record, we find appropriate only so much of the sentence as provides for bad conduct discharge, confinement at hard labor for 12 months, and total forfeitures.

The findings of guilty and the sentence, both as modified herein, are

Affirmed.

Note that abandonment of rank applies to disrespect offenses, but not to orders violations. The court in *Cheeks* refused to extend the defense to disobedience because of the "devastation of discipline" that such a ruling would cause.

ORDERS OFFENSES

There are five types of orders offenses under the UCMJ: (1) willful disobedience of a superior commissioned officer, Article 90; (2) willful disobedience of a warrant, noncommissioned or petty officer, Article 91; (3) failure to obey a lawful general order or regulation, Article 92(1); (4) failure to obey an other lawful order, Article 92(2); and dereliction of duty, Article 92(3). Each of these offenses is discussed below.

A fundamental principle of the law of military orders is that only lawful directives may be enforced. In order to be lawful, the order must relate to some military duty. This includes "all activities reasonably necessary to safeguard and protect morale, discipline and usefulness of the members of a command." *See United States v. Martin*, 5 C.M.R. 102 (C.M.A. 1952). The order may not, without such a valid military purpose, interfere with private rights or personal affairs, nor may it conflict with the statutory or constitutional rights of the person receiving the order. As a general rule, service members may assume that the orders issued to them are lawful. However, this assumption will not apply to a patently illegal order, such as one that directs a subordinate to perform an act of personal servitude for the superior, or directs the subordinate to commit a crime. *See United States v. Calley* in Chapter XI concerning an order to kill civilian noncombatants. The next case addresses the lawfulness of an order that affects the private life of a service member.

United States, Appellee, v. Marc A. Dumford, Senior Airman, U.S. Air Force, Appellant
United States Court of Military Appeals
30 M.J. 137
May 10, 1990

OPINION: PER CURIAM

Appellant stands convicted, pursuant to his pleas, of two specifications: Willfully disobeying the command of a commissioned officer not to engage in sexual activity without informing his partner that he was infected with the Human Immunodeficiency Virus (HIV) and taking precautions against spreading the virus; and assault with a means likely to produce death or grievous bodily harm, in violation of Articles 90 and 128, Uniform Code of Military Justice, 10 USC @@ 890 and 928, respectively. We granted his petition for review [footnote omitted] to determine whether the order was overbroad. After considering the contents of the order and the context of the violation, we uphold the decision of the Court of Military Review. 28 M.J. 836 (1989).

In *United States v. Womack*, 29 M.J. 88, 89 (C.M.A. 1989), we concluded that, in general, issuing a "safe sex" order to a service member infected with HIV, which "is a progenitor to the Acquired Immune Deficiency Syndrome (AIDS) disease," is a valid exercise of military authority. The order here is similar in content to the one challenged in *Womack*. It is equally clear, definite, and certain as to its requirements. The only question is whether a valid military necessity existed as to scope because the order required appellant to warn civilians as well as service members.

In Womack the sexual activity consisted of an act of nonconsensual homosexual sodomy with a fellow service member. Because the armed forces have an interest in preserving the health and readiness of their service members, the order there had a clear military purpose. *See also United States v. Negron*, 28 M.J. 775, 778 (A.C.M.R.), *aff'd*, 29 M.J. 324 (C.M.A. 1989).

Appellant argues that, as applied to consensual, nondeviant, sexual intercourse with a female civilian, the order restricts his personal rights. However, as we noted in Womack, many states have enacted statutes limiting the personal liberties of those persons who carry HIV, statutes which are far more restrictive than the present order. 29 M.J. at 90. This order did not prohibit sexual contact; rather, it set forth terms under which appellant could engage in such activities. Thus, even to the extent that the order may have limited appellant's freedom, it is not so broadly drawn as to warrant invalidating the order.

Appellant's argument that the order lacks any valid military purpose is without merit. In *United States v. Stewart*, 29 M.J. 92 (C.M.A. 1989), we took note of the dangers of unprotected sexual intercourse by those infected with HIV. Consequently, we are certain that, when a service member is capable of exposing another person to an infectious disease, the military has a legitimate interest in limiting his contact with others, including civilians, and otherwise preventing the spread of that condition.

See United States v. Johnson, 30 M.J. 53 (C.M.A. 1990).[1]

The decision of the United States Air Force Court of Military Review is affirmed.

Willful Disobedience Offenses

Paragraph 14a, Part IV, MCM, provides the elements of willful disobedience of a superior commissioned officer, Article 90.

(1) That the accused received a lawful command from a certain commissioned officer;

(2) That this officer was the superior commissioned officer of the accused;

(3) That the accused then knew that this officer was the accused's superior commissioned officer; and

(4) That the accused willfully disobeyed the lawful command.

Paragraph 15a, Part IV, MCM, provides the elements of willful disobedience of a warrant, noncommissioned or petty officer, Article 91.

(1) That the accused was a warrant officer or enlisted member;

(2) That the accused received a certain lawful order from a certain warrant, noncommissioned, or petty officer;

(3) That the accused then knew that the person giving the order was a warrant, noncommissioned, or petty officer;

(4) That the accused had a duty to obey the order; and

(5) That the accused willfully disobeyed the order.

The order involved in a willful disobedience charge must be personally and individually directed to the accused. Orders to a unit as a whole, be it oral or written, are not personal to the accused; therefore, "unit" or "group" orders are not punishable under Articles 90 and 91 (although they may be punishable under Article 92).

The definition of a superior commissioned officer used in Article 89 also applies to disobedience offenses. As with disrespect, willful disobedience of the order of a warrant, noncommissioned, or petty officer does not require "superior" status. *See*

---

[1] We have absolutely no doubt that preventing a service member who has HIV from spreading it to the civilian population is a public duty of the highest order and, thus, is a valid military objective. It is clear to us that such conduct could be found to be service-discrediting. Art. 134, Uniform Code of Military Justice, 10 USC @ 934; *see also United States v. Woods*, 28 M.J. 318-19 (C.M.A. 1989).

the discussion in *Disrespect* earlier in this chapter regarding situations where an enlisted member can violate the order of an enlisted member junior in rank.

The disobedience must be intentional, not through neglect or incompetence. Will the failure to immediately carry out an order constitute a willful disobedience? Consider the following case.

United States, Appellee, v. Specialist Alisa Schwabauer, United States Army, Appellant
United States Army Court of Military Review
34 M.J. 709
February 6, 1992

OPINION: Naughton, Senior Judge

A military judge sitting as a special court-martial at Log Base Echo, Saudi Arabia and Iraq, convicted the appellant, consistent with her pleas, of willfully disobeying the lawful order of a noncommissioned officer and wrongful disposition of military property, in violation of Articles 91 and 108, Uniform Code of Military Justice [hereinafter UCMJ], 10 U.S.C. @@ 891 and 908 (1982), respectively.[1] The appellant was sentenced to a bad-conduct discharge, confinement for three months, forfeiture of $ 400.00 pay per month for three months, and reduction to Private E1. The convening authority approved the sentence but remitted the unexecuted portion of the sentence adjudging confinement effective 1 May 1991.

The appellant contends that the military judge erred in accepting her plea of guilty to willful disobedience of a lawful order since the appellant complied with the order within a reasonable time. The appellant also contends that the military judge erred in accepting the appellant's plea of guilty to wrongful

disposition of military property where the property never left government control. Further, the appellant contends that her bad-conduct discharge should be set aside because she was illegally confined for twenty-nine days after her sentence to confinement was remitted. We disagree with the appellant's first two contentions, but do agree as to the latter contention that the appellant is entitled to sentence relief.

In January 1991, the appellant and her husband, Specialist Steven P. Schwabauer deployed with their unit from Germany to Saudi Arabia for Operation Desert Shield/Storm. On 4 February 1991, Command Sergeant Major (CSM) Cook, was approached by the appellant and her husband and asked whether he was available for a private conversation. After a short delay, the conversation began and the appellant and her husband told of the appellant's fears of being forward deployed as a member of a contact team engaged in repairing intelligence equipment and of going into combat. According to the stipulation of fact, they both stated words to the effect that "we are sick of this, we

---

[1] The appellant pleaded not guilty and was found not guilty of disrespect toward a noncommissioned officer in violation of Article 91, UCMJ. The appellant also pleaded not guilty to misbehavior before the enemy, in violation of Article 99, UCMJ, but guilty by exceptions and substitutions to wrongful disposition of military property in violation of Article 108, UCMJ.

can't take any more, we want to quit the Army." CSM Cook attempted to resolve the situation, but the appellant became emotional and upset. The appellant and her husband then placed their M16A2 rifles on a folded tent, dropped their bayonets on the ground, turned, and began walking away. CSM Cook ordered the appellant and her husband to "stop and come back here" but they continued to walk away. The appellant and her husband continued to walk for another several feet and CSM Cook again told them to "stop." They stopped walking after the second order, but did not return to CSM Cook.

According to the providence inquiry and the stipulation of fact, the appellant admitted that she understood the first order to stop and return, that it was a lawful order requiring immediate compliance, that she had a duty to obey the order, and that she willfully disobeyed it. The appellant also acknowledged that she had previously been given an order to keep her weapon in her physical possession and control at all times while in the 3d Armored Division Tactical Assembly Area.

Citing *United States v. Dellarosa*, 27 M.J. 860 (A.F.C.M.R. 1989), aff'd, 30 M.J. 255 (C.M.A. 1990), the appellant contends that the short delay in compliance between CSM Cook's first order and second order to stop does not constitute disobedience and that the appellant was entitled to a reasonable time to comply with the order to stop. In *United States v. Wilson*, 17 M.J. 1032, 1033 (A.C.M.R. 1984), . . . this Court adopted the analysis of *United States v. McLaughlin*, 14 M.J. 908, 913 (N.M.C.M.R. 1982), *petition denied*, 15 M.J. 405 (C.M.A. 1983), and stated "That immediate compliance is required by any order which does not explicitly or implicitly indicate that delayed compliance is authorized or directed." A direct order to "stop and come back here" is clear and unambiguous. It requires immediate obedience. [footnote omitted]. Under the circumstances of this case, there is nothing in CSM Cook's order that permitted or implied a reasonable time to obey or authorized delayed compliance. [citation omitted].

. . . .

The findings of guilty are affirmed.

In *Schwabauer*, the order given was meant for immediate execution. The ruling adheres to the principle that a declaration by the accused that he or she will not obey an order constitutes disobedience. What about the same declaration concerning an order that does not require action until some time in the future? Such an order cannot be violated until the time for performance arrives. *See United States v. Williams*, 39 C.M.R. 78 (C.M.A. 1968).

Failure to Obey a Lawful General Order or Regulation, Article 92(1)

Paragraph 16a, Part IV, MCM, states the three elements to this offense.

(1) That there was in effect a certain lawful general order or regulation;

(2) That the accused had a duty to obey it; and

(3) That the accused violated or failed to obey the general order or regulation.

Paragraph 16c, Part IV, MCM, explains who can issue general orders.

(1) Officers having general court-martial convening authority;

(2) General or flag officers in command; or

(3) Commanders superior to GCM convening authorities/flag officers.

An example of an officer who can issue general orders is the Commanding General of Marine Corps Base Camp Pendleton, California—a brigadier general. As a general officer in command (and general court-martial convening authority), he has the authority to issue general orders and regulations. Other examples of general orders or regulations are: SECNAVINST 5300.26B (sexual harassment), SECNAVINST 5300.28B (drug abuse paraphernalia), and Article 1165 of U.S. Navy Regulations (fraternization). These regulations are all issued by the Secretary of the Navy. Why does the military only give authority to issue general orders to high ranking officers?

Knowledge of the order is oftentimes a key issue in cases involving violation of an order. Consider the knowledge aspect of general orders as explained in Paragraph 16c, Part IV, MCM.

(1) Violation of or failure to obey a lawful general order or regulation.

(d) Knowledge. Knowledge of a general order or regulation need not be alleged or proved, as knowledge is not an element of this offense and a lack of knowledge does not constitute a defense.

Note that a directive must be "punitive" in nature to constitute a general order. Paragraph 16c(1), Part IV, MCM, explains the status of policy statements or instructions under Article 92.

(e) Enforceability. Not all provisions in general orders or regulations can be enforced under Article 92(1). Regulations which only supply general guidelines or advice for conducting military functions may not be enforceable under Article 92(1).

Failure to Obey an Other Lawful Order, Article 92(2)

This offense includes all other lawful orders not covered by Articles 90, 91, and 92(1). Its elements are:

(1) That a member of the armed forces issued a certain lawful order;

(2) That the accused had knowledge of the order;

(3) That the accused had a duty to obey the order; and

(4) That the accused failed to obey the order.

Paragraph 16c, Part IV, MCM, explains this offense.

(2) Violation of or failure to obey other lawful order.

(a) Scope. Article 92(2) includes all other lawful orders which may be issued by a member of the armed forces, violations of which are not chargeable under Article 90, 91, or 92(1). It includes the violation of written regulations which are not general regulations. . . .

(b) Knowledge. In order to be guilty of this offense, a person must have had actual knowledge of the order or regulation. Knowledge of the order may be proved by circumstantial evidence.

(c) Duty to obey order.

(i) From a superior. A member of one armed force who is senior in rank to a member of another armed force is the superior of that member with authority to issue orders which that member has a duty to obey under the same circumstances as a commissioned officer of one armed force is the superior commissioned officer of a member of another armed force for the purposes of Articles 89 and 90.

(ii) From one not a superior. Failure to obey the lawful order of one not a superior is an offense under Article 92(2), provided the accused had a duty to obey the order, such as one issued by a sentinel or a member of the armed forces police. *See* paragraph 15b(2) if the order was issued by a warrant, noncommissioned, or petty officer in the execution of office. A member who violates any order of which he has knowledge and a duty to obey may be punished under Article 92(2). The order may be oral or in writing, and need not have been directed to the accused personally. This paragraph provides the ability to punish group-directed orders that may not punished as willful disobedience and lawful orders issued by an authority lacking rank or status to issue "general orders." Failure to obey an "other lawful order" may be committed by simple negligence. Actual knowledge of the order is, however, required, and it will not be sufficient for a successful prosecution to show that the accused "should have known" of the order.

Article 92(2) provides a method to charge service members for orders violations that do not meet the criteria of willful disobedience or failure to obey a general order. Consider when this would be possible.

Dereliction of Duty, Article 92(3)

Though technically not an orders offense, the crime of dereliction of duty is so closely related to the overall concept of disobedience that it is included within Article 92. Its elements are:

(1) That the accused had certain duties;

(2) That the accused knew or reasonably should have known of the duties; and

(3) That the accused was (willfully)(through neglect or culpable inefficiency) derelict in the performance of those duties.

Paragraph 16c, Part IV, MCM, explains this offense.

(a) Duty. A duty may be imposed by treaty, statute, regulation, lawful order, standard operating procedure, or custom of the service.

(b) Knowledge. Actual knowledge of duties may be proved by circumstantial evidence. Actual knowledge need not be shown if the individual reasonably should have known of the duties. This may be demonstrated by regulations, training or operating manuals, customs of the service, academic literature or testimony, testimony of persons who have held similar or superior positions, or similar evidence.

(c) Derelict. A person is derelict in the performance of duties when that person willfully or negligently fails to perform that person's duties or when that person performs them in a culpably inefficient manner. "Willfully" means intentionally. It refers to the doing of an act knowingly and purposely, specifically intending the natural and probable consequences of the act. "Negligently" means an act or omission of a person who is under a duty to use due care which exhibits a lack of that degree of care which a reasonably prudent person would have exercised under the same or similar circumstances. "Culpable inefficiency" is inefficiency for which there is no reasonable or just excuse.

(d) Ineptitude. A person is not derelict in the performance of duties if the failure to perform those duties is caused by ineptitude rather than by willfulness, negligence, or culpable inefficiency, and may not be charged under this article, or otherwise punished. For example, a recruit who has tried earnestly during rifle training and throughout record firing is not derelict in the performance of duties if the recruit fails to quality with the weapon.

The following case discusses the nature of dereliction of duty.

United States v. Allen V. Lawson, First Lieutenant, U.S. Marine Corps
United States Navy-Marine Corps Court of Military Review
33 M.J. 946
October 31, 1991

OPINION: Mitchell, Senior Judge

Appellant stands convicted by members at a contested general court-martial of failure to obey the lawful order of a superior officer to submit a roster of checkpoint Marines before posting them, dereliction of duty by failing to post as a pair Lance Corporals Rother and Key at a tactical exercise road checkpoint, and conduct unbecoming an officer by driving a motor vehicle while drunk, while his driving privileges were revoked and while possessing an open malt beverage container. The dereliction of duty and order offenses arose during a tactical Combined Arms Exercise (CAX) conducted in the California desert. The approved sentence extends to a dismissal, forty-nine days confinement, and forfeiture of all pay and allowances.

Before this court in normal course of review appellant asserts that he was the victim of unlawful command influence from the pretrial statements and actions of the Commandant of the Marine Corps, that his conduct in regard to the posting of the Marines did not support the findings of dereliction of duty, that the opinions of two superior officers were improperly considered during the sentence hearing, that evidence of the desert search for the lost Lance Corporal Rother and of his death was improperly admitted, and that the sentence is inappropriately severe. We disagree and affirm.

I. BACKGROUND

On 20 June 1988, appellant went to battalion nonjudicial punishment (NJP) for speeding, driving on a revoked license, and drunk driving. In July 1988, he received NJP from the Commanding General, 2d Marine Division (CG, 2d MarDiv) for other driving offenses and lying to the arresting military police. On 1 August 1988, the CG, 2d MarDiv sent a letter to Headquarters, U.S. Marine Corps (HQMC), recommending that appellant be expeditiously separated, and that he not be tendered a reserve commission.

On 30 August 1988, appellant was temporarily deployed with his battalion to a training site at Marine Corps Air-Ground Combat Training Center, Twentynine Palms, California (29 Palms). While there, he was detailed to post road guides along a route for a motorized night march. At the conclusion of the march, a road guide, Lance Corporal Rother, was not picked up. His unit did not report his absence to the battalion headquarters for about 1 1/2 days. When the situation was reported, the battalion commander, suspecting that Lance Corporal Rother had been left in the desert, ordered a massive search for him. The search was unsuccessful.

. . . .

III. DERELICTION OF DUTY

A. The Facts of the Offenses

During the ill-fated CAX, appellant participated in mock tactical operations. Toward the end of training, he was assigned uncomplicated duties of (1) posting road guards in pairs along a route designated for a battalion-sized motorized night movement, (2) obtaining a roster of Marines posted as road guides, and (3) providing the roster to Captain Edwards, the appellant's superior coordinator for this movement.

Appellant was Heavy Machine Gun Platoon Commander, 3d Battalion, 2d Marine Regiment (3/2). He had no prior desert training but had 20 months' experience as an infantry officer. The battalion commander, Lieutenant Colonel Robeson, was a new and inexperienced battalion commander. All company commanders were also new. Nonetheless, Lieutenant Colonel Robeson had stressed personnel accountability at all times because of harsh desert conditions and the number of key new people in the battalion. To conduct the critical movement, Lieutenant Colonel Robeson decided to use newly available terrain to move the battalion to the objective. Consequently, no plan for this movement had been written or practiced in advance. The exercise evolved as follows.

The CAX was to be conducted over two and one-half days. The first two days of objectives were taken. At the second objective, Lieutenant Colonel Robeson received and, in turn, gave a fragmentary order for a third objective. The battalion was very disorganized at this time. Timing afforded a period from 1730 to 2300 to jump off on the third objective. Lieutenant Colonel Robeson gave a short (15-minute) brief to command personnel on the myriad of things to be done and decided to short-cut normal preparedness so that the battalion could get underway before dark. It was understood that appellant had some discretion in posting guides in that he could add road guides, but they all had to be posted in pairs and on the movement route.

Lieutenant Colonel Robeson's extant policy was that following briefings, officers were to ask questions of him if they did not understand something or had any doubts about the subject matter. The appellant claims he stayed after this brief and asked some questions, but he provided no details for the record. Lieutenant Colonel Robeson testified that the appellant did not stay and did not ask mission questions. We conclude that even if appellant asked questions, they were not on matters pertinent to the road guide operation. Road guide details were set out on maps that no one in the command had seen before this time. For purposes of battalion control, Lieutenant Colonel Robeson used a unique system of two command teams—gold and scarlet. The critical events occurred on the night of 30 August 1988.

Specifically, appellant was detailed to reconnoiter the route of advance and to post road guides at four predetermined checkpoints at major road intersections. He was to post two guides at each location, a buddy system. The road guides were to prevent convoys from turning from the line of advance and getting lost. Captain Edwards was detailed to place a unit in trace of the battalion and conduct road guide recovery operations. Captain Edwards tasked appellant with providing a list of names of guides and posting points to him for use as a checklist. The roster was to be delivered before appellant departed the area to post the road guides. Appellant understood these leadership obligations but did not discharge them.

In his briefing, Lieutenant Colonel Robeson initially said road guides could be singly posted because of vehicle space limitations, but later in the brief changed his mind on this and directed paired road guides. In any event, it was clear at the end of the briefing that guides were to be posted in pairs and not separated. This was consistent with established battalion policy and, at the moment, driven by darkness and desert safety concerns. Specific and detailed instructions for road guide posting and recovery operations were not given to Captain Edwards or appellant by the battalion commander. Appellant, however, knew that another battalion, 1st Battalion, 10th Marine Regiment (1/10), which was also to use the same route and follow his battalion, was also going to post road guides.

Fragmentary orders are not well-known in civilian life, but are common to military activities in general and tactical operations and exercises specifically. Fragmentary orders, being captives of short time periods and fast-paced movements, are not detailed and are children of a much more detailed operations order. A fragmentary order contains only the most essential information necessary to the conduct of the movement to which it relates. *See* Joint Publication 1-02, Department of Defense Dictionary of Military and Associated Terms, pg. 151. An order directs that a job be done, but does not specify how it will be done. Noel and Beach, Naval Terms Dictionary, 4th Ed. Logically, then, fragmentary orders, being less than full operations orders, rely for effectiveness on the provisions of the operations order upon which they are ultimately based, the clarity of the objective assigned, and the training, experience, judgment, and common sense of those charged with executing them. We conclude that this commander's fragmentary order in regard to the conduct of the movement and his guidance on posting road guides were adequate in detail to fix the main obligations and establish responsibility for execution.

The terrain and scheme of maneuver for this movement, as revealed in the record, are as follows. The exercise was conducted in remote and rough desert terrain in California, during late August. The exercise covered a line of movement of approximately forty miles, largely through valleys surrounded by rugged mountains. It was a straightline exercise that did not contemplate revisiting terrain through which the maneuvering commands had previously moved. There was no built-up area beyond the initial line of departure at day 1 that was within a minimum of about ten miles of any point on the route of advance. Maps reveal no apparent natural or artificial water sources. It is difficult to imagine a more remote, barren, and dangerous environment than the terrain over which this exercise was conducted. The fatal third movement covered about twenty-three miles of administrative and operational movement. Once a command passed a point, it left behind and alone in this environment anything that did not move with the commands that passed over the particular road assigned for that portion of the exercise. Thus, if Lance Corporal Rother was not picked up by his battalion and his whereabouts were totally unknown to the tracing battalion, he was on his own against the harsh desert.

At the outset of appellant's assignment, things were not smooth. One company refused to provide guides as required, leaving appellant short two guides. Scarlet leader, the battalion executive officer (Major Holm), then in control, learned of this when he found appellant still at the second objective at 1845 and facing a 1900 launch time. Major Holm told appellant to go to the offending company, get the guides and immediately get on the road. At the time appellant had been talking with a Lieutenant Liddy. Lieutenant Liddy had advised

appellant to go to the offending company and pick up the guides, make a list of all guides, and post a staff noncommissioned officer (SNCO) at the rear of battalion with the list to check the recovery. Appellant apparently was unable to locate the offending unit and did not know whether their guides were on the way. He did know that he was under orders to leave before dark. Appellant still did not know what to do (even though he had seventeen Marines in his own platoon he could have used) when Major Holm found him. He finally got on the road 20 minutes late. Appellant left to post the road guides two Marines short of the requisite manpower and without having made a list of road guides and their posts. Appellant did not provide any guide list to Captain Edwards.

Marines Rother, McAdams, Adamson and Key were designated guides by Kilo Company. Their executive officer briefed them on their duty and told them they were to stay in pairs. None of them saw appellant before departure, and their names were not taken by appellant when they reported to him. When they reported for guide duty, they were simply told to board the vehicles and go.

Appellant put his best navigator, Sergeant Gardner, on the point of his column of several vehicles, while he stayed in the rear apparently because he thought that would enhance his control of his column. He told Sergeant Gardner that appellant was directed to post two guides at designated spots on the map. The column then departed on the mission. Before Checkpoint 1, Sergeant Gardner misread a rock formation and wrongly veered north (right) off the main road. The road began to thin out and soon looked nothing like a main road. He ultimately returned to the main road at Checkpoint 1 by cutting across rough terrain. Appellant followed Sergeant Gardner but stopped where the navigator turned to rejoin the main road. At first, appellant posted two guides, Lance Corporals Key and Rother at that spot, wrongly believing it to be Checkpoint 1. After scouting the bogus road for a distance, appellant became uncertain about the checkpoint. He returned to the site and picked up Lance Corporal Key. He left Lance Corporal Rother there posted at a rock about 200 yards off the main road and some four hundred yards from the designated Checkpoint 1.

Appellant then proceeded across open terrain to the real Checkpoint 1 where he joined Sergeant Gardner. He posted Lance Corporal Key there. He also drove down the plainly identifiable main supply road a short distance and talked with Sergeant Gardner, who was parked in front of an intersection sign that marked the checkpoint and, hence, the main road. We are convinced that by this time appellant knew that Lance Corporal Rother was not posted at the correct checkpoint. We also find that mission performance and speed of movement were the paramount concerns to him despite the safety emphasis in the battalion. He realized that he was behind schedule and he did not take the time to go back to Lance Corporal Rother and re-post him with Lance Corporal Key at Checkpoint 1. He did nothing about Rother until much later at the final assembly area, when he realized that this was only an exercise and not real war and that safety concerns were important.

Appellant did not record Lance Corporal Rother's name or his location when he posted him at the rock. He ignored warnings about posting in pairs given by Lance Corporals Adamson and Key, reminding them that he was the senior. He did not give any instructions about the circumstances under which either guide could leave his post or how each was to consolidate for pick up after the battalion main column passed. Appellant told both guides to keep the battalion convoy on the main road, but did not tell Lance Corporal Rother where Checkpoint 1 was located (at that time appellant did not know). He told neither Marine what course directions to give the battalion if it passed by him.

At trial, appellant testified that by splitting the two guides, he intended to see that the battalion would not veer off the main road the way his column had done. However, initially he testified that he thought the petered out road was really the main road. If so, there was no reason to split the guides, as they were on the main road. He did not split guides at any other nondesignated intersection. If preventing a battalion wrong turn off the main road was his motive, it was not reasonable to post one guide well beyond the main intersection where the main road and the bogus road met and past two other road branches. The obvious place to prevent a wrong turn of the battalion was the main intersection, not the middle of nowhere. It made even less sense to post guides for such a purpose and provide to them no instructions for giving route-correcting directions to the battalion column.

Appellant also testified that he did not think Rother was in jeopardy because he was posted in close proximity to Lance Corporal Key. They were both left with chemical lights, rations, and water. Lance Corporal Key at Checkpoint 1 was about 400 yards from Lance Corporal Rother and could see him in daylight. At night, Lance Corporal Key could see Lance Corporal Rother's chemical light. We do not know whether Lance Corporal Rother saw Lance Corporal Key. The appellant apparently did not see Rother from Checkpoint 1 and it is unlikely that anyone not specifically looking at his position would see him in daylight or darkness. Appellant was not concerned that the guides might be afraid or in danger. Lost to his concern, however, was the effect of his changing the game plan in midstream when none of the necessary coordinating and guide recovery parties knew about it. This was the jeopardy of being left behind in the desert. At least the recovering party expected to look for and find guides on the main road. But what did they know of a second route? This danger should also have occurred to appellant when First Sergeant Floyd later asked him at Checkpoint 3 if appellant was posting his road guides in pairs. Appellant said he was doing that, implying that appellant knew it was an important policy, knew that he was not following orders, and knew that he did not want to admit that to the First Sergeant.

At Checkpoint 2, appellant found that the planned north route to Checkpoint 3 was impassable, so he and his navigator decided to lead the battalion along the south route. Since he was short two road guides, he left only chemical lights at that checkpoint and went on.

At Checkpoint 3, appellant posted two guides and by 2200 reached Checkpoint 4, where he posted his last 2 guides. He told these Marines that he would either pick them up or have a vehicle get them. Appellant then proceeded to the final assembly area at the north end of the route of march. Arriving there between 2200 and 2300, he told his navigator, Sergeant Gardner, to go back along the route with a vehicle, post two of his heavy machine gun platoon Marines as guides at Checkpoint 2 (manned only by chemical lights) and drop off a chemical light at each checkpoint on the road. He also told the navigator that he had split guides at Checkpoint 1 (Lance Corporals Rother and Key). Appellant told Sergeant Gardner to go there and tell Lance Corporals Rother and Key that the guide who does not have the convoy pass him is to walk over to the place where the other guide was posted. Appellant testified that he gave these orders because, on reflection, the safety of the Marines was of prime importance, though he earlier believed that his mission was first priority.

The navigator told appellant that he would have to do this via administrative movement (with vehicle lights on) to have time to do it all because the main body of the battalion would be on the move up the road.

The navigator left two chemical lights at Checkpoints 4 and 3 but did not post guides at Checkpoint 2. He did not reach Checkpoint 1 because he met the battalion proceeding tactically under night vision (no lights), and he did not want to blind them with his vehicle lights. The navigator turned around and went back to the assembly area and reported to appellant. Appellant testified, however, that he thought his navigator found no Marines at Checkpoint 1.

The battalion began its tactical movement at 2300. Captain Edwards designated Lieutenant Fossett to draw a truck, pick one of his better drivers, hang chemical lights on the vehicle, assign it to follow in the rear of the battalion convoy and recover road guides who were posted in pairs along the road. Captain Edwards told Lieutenant Fossett that there were guides at the checkpoints along the road, but he did not say how many, who they were, or what companies they came from because Captain Edwards, not possessed of any roster, did not know. Nor did he appear to know what to do after recovery. Captain Edwards told him to pick up all Marines on side of road and they would sort out the recovery operation the next morning. Lieutenant Fossett briefed drivers and Staff Sergeant Dozier, the motor transport chief. Staff Sergeant Dozier picked Lance Corporal Barrett to drive the recovery vehicle. Staff Sergeant Dozier briefed Lance Corporal Barrett but made no mention of any road guides off the main road (he didn't know of any split guide posting). Neither Lieutenant Fossett, Staff Sergeant Dozier or Lance Corporal Barrett had a list of guides to recover. This created minimized accountability and maximized risk to the troops.

The recovery operation started when the battalion began moving north along the road. As is not at all uncommon in such things, especially short-fused night tactical movements, there was significant overall confusion. Pertinently, no battalion vehicles went by the off-road position where Lance Corporal Rother was posted. The recovery operation was done hastily so that the recovery team would not lose contact with the battalion and become lost. Speed generated more problems. One guide described the pickup as the guides being told to "get on" the vehicle without concern for what unit they belonged to, apparently in the belief that only 3/2 guides were on the road. People were dragged aboard the vehicles. Lance Corporal Key was apparently picked up by 4th vehicle from the end instead of a recovery vehicle. Road guides posted by 1/10 (the following battalion) were also picked up by the 3/2 column.

Lance Corporal Key was picked up at Checkpoint 1. He was told by the driver of the vehicle to get on or be left behind. Lance Corporal Key told the driver that Lance Corporal Rother was also "out there." The driver said that Lance Corporal Key could go get him but he (Key) would be left behind. Some 1/10 Marines were on the vehicle and told Key that 1/10 might pick up Lance Corporal Rother since 3/2 had picked up some of 1/10's Marines. Lance Corporal Key, believing that 1/10 would pick up Lance Corporal Rother, got on. Another guide, Lance Corporal Adamson, waved down a vehicle and was picked up by the first vehicle in the 3/2 column. Lieutenant Fossett did not account for any of the Marines picked up (most of them left the pickup vehicles before the last stop). Captain Edwards was not debriefed by Lieutenant Fossett and assumed that all got back to their units.

Appellant watched all battalion vehicles pass through the release point. He did not see the chemically lighted pickup vehicle so he stopped Staff Sergeant Dozier. Staff Sergeant Dozier told appellant that he had picked up 6 guides, because it seemed that many jumped on the vehicle. Appellant, thinking that two guides were still at Checkpoint 4, went there and picked up two guides and took them to their company. He did not personally check the recovery vehicle for names of guides, nor did he account for them in any specific way.

At 0700 on 31 August, appellant saw Major Holm, the battalion executive officer, and asked him if all Marines had returned, a peculiar question to ask him, considering the known lack of accounting the previous night. Major Holm said everything was fine as far as he knew and that the march was smooth. Appellant did not discuss the failure to pair guides at Checkpoint 1 or the list deficiency. However, Lance Corporal Adamson, who had been a road guide during the battalion movement, noticed at weapon turn-in that Lance Corporal Rother's rifle card was still not claimed at the end of the exercise. He reported it to Platoon and was told that Lance Corporal Rother was gone on a guard detail. We conclude that this was an unfortunate misunderstanding.

The night of 31 August, the battalion commander met with his officers and stressed that three things were to be accounted for—"people, weapons and communication security material system gear"—and reports filed with him that night. At 1000 on 1 September, Lance Corporal Rother had still not turned in his weapon, so Lance Corporal Adamson reported this to his Company headquarters. At 1730, 1 September, appellant revealed Lance Corporal Rother's split posting at Checkpoint 1 when Captain Henderson, Lance Corporal Rother's company commander, confronted appellant about the missing Rother. Lance Corporal Rother was later found dead.

B. Dereliction of Duty: Discussion

The circumstances in which the appellant found himself on movement night, while a somewhat pressured, fast-moving and confusing situation, are common to tactical operations and exercises of this size and kind. Some of appellant's difficulties were of his own creation, particularly his failure to pick two of his own men and mount out with a complete unit on time. The circumstances of this exercise were not, as the court members also decided by their findings, of such magnitude as to excuse appellant from responsibility for his failures to follow his orders. Likewise, without regard to the derelictions, criminal or otherwise, of other officers, staff noncommissioned officers and other Marines involved in the fatal tactical movement, we are convinced, as were the court members, that appellant's failure to follow his orders with a good measure of plain common sense, was a key failure in a chain of events that could have been expected to and did result in leaving a Marine in the desert, alone, at night, with no apparent capacity to link up to his own or any other command.

While not a certainty in all cases, it was foreseeable that if the appellant did not follow his orders a Marine could be left behind at night in a harsh environment, get lost, become disoriented, and die. The obedience to the orders and the application of due care were especially important where appellant knew that 1/10 was to use the same road in trace of 3/2, creating a potential for confusion. Command safety policies and pairing guidance were more than adequate to alert appellant to the importance of following orders and the dangers of a failure to comply with them and exercise good judgment in the process. Common sense had to tell him that without a roster in the hands of the recovery detail and without proper guide posting, recovery operations would be haphazard and uncontrolled. No one was in a position to verify who was posted and who was recovered. A detailed roster would have been mandated as a matter of judgment without regard to specific features of the fragmentary order.

We put substantial distance between our view of the traditional plain meaning of dereliction of duty proscribed by Article 92, UCMJ. *See* Manual for Courts-Martial, United States, 1984, para. 16b(3), 16c(3), and dicta in the precedent of this Court, suggesting that the only standard applicable to a professional charged with a negligence-based offense is gross negligence. *Compare United States v. Billig*, 26 M.J. 744, 760 (N.M.C.M.R. 1988) (citing *State v. Weiner*, 41 N.J. 21, 25-26, 194 A.2d 467 (1963), applying a state statutory gross negligence standard to a medical manslaughter case) with Manual for Courts-Martial, United States, 1984, Part IV, para. 16b(3), 16c(3).

C. Dereliction of Duty: Conclusion

We conclude that the evidence is legally sufficient to sustain the findings of guilty. We, as were the court members, are convinced beyond a reasonable doubt that appellant is guilty of the offenses of which he now stands convicted.

. . . .

V. DISPOSITION

Accordingly, the findings and sentence as approved on review below are affirmed.

What duty was First Lieutenant Lawson derelict in performing? The MCM states that the "duty" can be imposed by regulation, order or custom of the service. Who or what imposed the duty on the accused in *Lawson*? Is it possible for a service member to be derelict in performance of a duty that he or she was unaware existed? A "should have known" standard is normally applied to dereliction of duty cases, making it possible to convict a member of dereliction of duty for failing to properly perform a task that he or she should have known about.

DRUG OFFENSES

ARTICLE 112A, UCMJ

Article 112a prohibits certain activities involving illegal drugs, or "controlled substances." Paragraph 37, Part IV, MCM explains the offenses under Article 112a.

37. Article 112a—Wrongful use, possession, etc., of controlled substances

a. Text.

(a) Any person subject to this chapter who wrongfully uses, possesses, manufactures, distributes, imports into the customs territory of the United States, exports from the United States, or introduces into an installation, vessel, vehicle, or aircraft used by or under the control of the armed forces a substance described in subsection (b) shall be punished as a court-martial may direct.

(b) The substances referred to in subsection (a) are the following:

(1) Opium, heroin, cocaine, amphetamine, lysergic acid diethylamide, methamphetamine, phencyclidine, barbituric acid, and marijuana, and any compound or derivative of any such substance.

(2) Any substance not specified in clause (1) that is listed on a schedule of controlled substances prescribed by the President for the purposes of this article.

(3) Any other substance not specified in clause (1) or contained on a list prescribed by the President under clause (2) that is listed in schedules I through V of section 202 of the Controlled Substances Act (21 U.S.C. 812).

The list of controlled substances is very lengthy, but the most commonly abused controlled substances in the naval service are marijuana, cocaine, amphetamines, methamphetamine, heroine, and lysergic acid diethylamide (LSD). The activities prohibited by Article 112a include the wrongful possession, use, distribution, introduction and manufacture of such controlled substances. There are two fundamental elements for each drug offense: (1) that the accused possessed/used/distributed/introduced/ manufactured a controlled substance; and (2) that the possession/use/distribution/introduction/manufacture was wrongful. Paragraph 37c(5), Part IV, MCM, explains the aspect of wrongfulness in drug cases.

> Wrongfulness. To be punishable under Article 112a, possession, use, distribution, introduction, or manufacture of a controlled substance must be wrongful. Possession, use, distribution, introduction, or manufacture of a controlled substance is wrongful if it is without legal justification or authorization. Possession, use, distribution, introduction, or manufacture of a controlled substance is not wrongful if such act or acts are: (A) done pursuant to legitimate law enforcement activities (for example, an informant who receives drugs as part of an undercover operation is not in wrongful possession); (B) done by authorized personnel in the performance of medical duties; or (C) without knowledge of the contraband nature of the substance (for example, a person who possesses cocaine, but actually believes it to be sugar, is not guilty of wrongful possession of cocaine). Possession, use, distribution, introduction, or manufacture of a controlled substance may be inferred to be wrongful in the absence of evidence to the contrary. The burden of going forward with evidence with respect to any such exception in any court-martial or other proceeding under the code shall be upon the person claiming its benefit. If such an issue is raised by the evidence presented, then the burden of proof is upon the United States to establish that the use, possession, distribution, manufacture, or introduction was wrongful.

Article 112a sets forth several types of offenses involving controlled substances. The following sections discuss some of those offenses.

Possession

Paragraph 37c(2), Part IV, MCM, discusses the nature of possession.

> Possess. "Possess" means to exercise control of something. Possession may be direct physical custody like holding an item in one's hand, or it may be constructive, as in the case of a person who hides an item in a locker or car to which that person may return to retrieve it. Possession must be knowing and conscious. Possession inherently includes the power or authority to preclude control by others. It is possible, however, for more than one person to possess an item simultaneously, as when several people share control of an item. An accused may not be convicted of possession of a controlled substance if the accused did not know that the substance was present under the accused's control. Awareness of the presence of a controlled substance may be inferred from circumstantial evidence.

Based on the above, an owner of a house in which drugs are found may or may not be guilty of possession of a controlled substance. What factors will bear on this issue?

Distribution

Paragraph 37c(3), Part IV, MCM, defines distribution under Article 112a.

> Distribute. "Distribute" means to deliver to the possession of another. "Deliver" means the actual, constructive, or attempted transfer of an item, whether or not there exists an agency relationship.

The above definition appears to construe the term "distribute" very broadly. Does every transfer of a controlled substance amount to a distribution? If a member is convicted of distribution, should the nature of the transfer affect the sentence awarded? Consider the following case.

United States, Appellee, v. Thomas R. Ratleff, Private First Class U.S. Army, Appellant
United States Court of Military Appeals
34 M.J. 80
February 21, 1992

OPINION: Cox, Judge

Appellant was tried at Garlstedt, Federal Republic of Germany, by a military judge sitting as a special court-martial. Pursuant to his pleas, he was convicted of three specifications of distributing marijuana and one specification of using marijuana (in the hashish form), in violation of Article 112a, Uniform Code of Military Justice, 10 USC @ 912a. He was sentenced to a bad-conduct discharge, confinement and forfeiture of $482.00 pay per month for 4 months, and reduction to E-1.

The convening authority approved the adjudged sentence, and the Court of Military Review affirmed the findings and sentence in a short-form decision dated October 17, 1990.

This Court granted appellant's petition for review of the following issue:

WHETHER THE MILITARY JUDGE SHOULD HAVE DISMISSED A DRUG-DISTRIBUTION SPECIFICA- TION BECAUSE CONGRESS NEVER INTENDED TO MAKE APPELLANT'S TRANSFER OF THE DRUG A CRIMINAL DISTRIBUTION UNDER UCMJ ART. 112a.

After oral argument and a review of the appellate briefs, we decide that dismissal of the drug-distribution specification (4 of the Charge) is not warranted.

The facts of the case are not in dispute. The relevant portion of the stipulation of fact agreed to by both parties reads as follows:

6. The accused used marijuana in the hashish form, on 18 December 1989, with PFC Jaundoo in the accused's room. The accused had accompanied PFC Jaundoo to the mess hall, where PFC Jaundoo had hidden a can with hashish in it. PFC Jaundoo extracted the can, then he and the accused went back to the accused's room. The accused ripped the can open, extracted the hashish, and gave it to PFC Jaundoo. The accused and PFC Jaundoo then smoked the hashish. The hashish was smoked by pok-

ing holes in a soft drink can, setting the hashish in an indentation made in the can, lighting the substance, and inhaling the resulting smoke into the lungs.

These facts formed the basis for specification 3, alleging use, and specification 4, alleging distribution, of hashish.

We note at the outset that appellant pleaded guilty to all four specifications alleging either use or distribution of marijuana in the hashish form. Our inquiry focuses on specification 4, alleging distribution.

At trial, the military judge questioned whether appellant's mere action of passing the hashish to Private First Class Jaundoo constituted distribution within the meaning of Article 112a. A discussion ensued with both counsel, after which the military judge ruled:

> MJ: Well, that now—Well, there's a difference we've got to make between when we have the crime of distribution and how aggravated it is for purposes of sentencing.
>
> DC: Yes, sir.
>
> MJ: I'll say this. I'll put this on the record, and, of course, I don't know what all the facts are and I won't know until I go through the entire providence inquiry, but if the facts are as stated in the stipulation, and if they're not close we've got other problems, but I'll consider this as a distribution but the punishment will be based on the fact of use—of a use with another soldier as opposed to a distribution to another soldier. Do you understand—
>
> DC: Yes, sir.
>
> MJ: Do you have any problem—

> DC: No, sir.
>
> MJ: With that?
>
> DC: No, sir, I don't have any problem with that.
>
> MJ: In other words, the fact that there was a distribution will be given no particular—The fact that the crime of distribution occurs will be given no particular weight. It will be considered by me on sentencing as a use with another soldier.

The military judge then addressed the providence of appellant's pleas. Regarding specification 4, the military judge reviewed all the elements of the offense, and appellant reasserted his guilt. The military judge then addressed the issue of distribution under specification 4 and its relation to specification 3 to determine if they were multiplicious for sentencing:

> MJ: Now, I'm going to consider the incidents of the 18th of December to be multiplicious for sentencing purposes, and even though I consider it to be a technical distribution, I'm really considering it as an aggravated use. That is, a use with another soldier as opposed to a distribution to another soldier. And, really, for purposes of sentencing I consider the facts as opposed to the actual conviction of a particular crime.

The military judge subsequently held appellant's guilty pleas provident and found him guilty.

Appellant asserts the facts do not support a conviction under specification 4. We disagree. Article 112a requires the Government to prove: "(a) That the accused distributed a certain amount of a controlled substance; and (b) That the distribution . . . was wrongful." Para. 37b(3)(a) and (b), Part IV, Manual for Courts-Martial,

United States, 1984. Distribution has been explained as meaning "to deliver to the possession of another." Para. 37c(3). *See United States v. Zubko*, 18 M.J. 378, 385-86 (C.M.A. 1984). In this case the military judge held that, as far as specification 4 was concerned, appellant was guilty of distributing hashish.

From our review of the undisputed record, appellant took possession of the hashish while it was in its container, ripped open the container, retrieved the hashish, and handed it to Private First Class Jaundoo. Given this set of facts, appellant, by passing the hashish to Private First Class Jaundoo, is guilty of distribution. [citations omitted].

Appellant has argued that this set of facts suggests only that he and PFC Jaundoo jointly possessed the hashish or that only Jaundoo could be found guilty of the distribution. *See United States v. Swiderski,* 548 F.2d 445 (2d Cir.1977). We reject these arguments. The plain, ordinary construction of Article 112a of the Code requires us to conclude that appellant "delivered" the hashish to his friend, a fact readily admitted by appellant in his guilty pleas. *See United States v. Tuero, supra; United States v. Hill,* 25 M.J. 411 (C.M.A. 1988). In any event, the military judge was not asleep at the switch. He recognized that the distribution charge was based upon a technical construction of the statute and that the essence of the offenses was appellant's joint use of the drug with his fellow soldier. In view of the entire record of this guilty-plea case, we conclude that appellant is not entitled to further relief. Art. 59(a), UCMJ, 10 USC @ 859(a).

The decision of the United States Army Court of Military Review is affirmed.

Manufacture of a Controlled Substance

Paragraph 37c(4), Part IV, MCM, explains "manufacture" under 112a.

> Manufacture. "Manufacture" means the production, preparation, propagation, compounding, or processing of a drug or other substance, either directly or indirectly or by extraction from substances of natural origin, or independently by means of chemical synthesis or by a combination of extraction and chemical synthesis, and includes any packaging or repackaging of such substance or labeling or relabeling of its container. "Production," as used in this subparagraph, includes the planting, cultivating, growing, or harvesting of a drug or other substance.

The above definition is very broad in the sense that it includes labeling and packaging of a drug. Is such an expansive reading consistent with the interpretation of "distribution" discussed above?

Use of a Controlled Substance

To "use" a controlled substance means to ingest it into the human body by smoking, snorting, eating, injecting, etc. The vast majority of wrongful use cases come about because of the military's urinalysis program. Urinalysis testing essentially looks for the presence of certain chemical by-products of illegal drugs (called "metabolites") in each specimen tested. If such metabolites are found, the laboratory sends a message back to the command reporting the positive result of the analysis. *See* OPNAVINST 5350.4B (the Navy's drug testing instruction). What are the bases for conducting a urinalysis? Fourth Amendment considerations do apply to urinalysis. *See Unger v. Zemniack* in Chapter VII regarding the legal basis for ordering a urinalysis.

A positive urinalysis normally raises the inference of a wrongful use on the part of the accused. *See* Paragraph 37c(5), Part IV, MCM, discussed above. The burden is then on the member to show that the collection or testing procedures were flawed or that his or her ingestion of the controlled substance was not wrongful, (e.g., the cocaine was unknowingly slipped in the member's drink or use of controlled substances is so out of character the ingestion could not have been wrongful). Court-martials are sometimes reluctant to convict a member based only on a positive urinalysis. Why would this be?

Introduction of a Controlled Substance

This offense is committed by bringing any amount of a controlled substance onto a vessel, aircraft, vehicle, or installation used by or under the control of the armed forces. A member is not guilty of introduction if he or she receives or distributes a controlled substance while already on board property under control of the armed forces. The member must actually bring the substance on board the naval station, etc. Also, the member must have knowledge that he or she is introducing the substance. If a service member borrows a friend's jacket that has LSD in the pocket, will she be guilty of introduction if she goes on board a Navy ship? What factors will the court consider to decide the issue of wrongfulness?

Defenses to Drug Offenses

As discussed above, the absence of wrongfulness on the part of the accused will result in an acquittal. What other defenses may an accused raise? Consider the following case regarding the entrapment defense.

United States, Appellee, v. Staff Sergeant Orlando Cortes, United States Army, Appellant
United States Army Court of Military Review
29 M.J. 946
January 3, 1990

OPINION: Neurauter, Judge

Contrary to his plea, appellant was convicted by a military judge sitting as a general court-martial of distribution of cocaine in violation of Article 112a, Uniform Code of Military Justice, 10 U.S.C. @ 912a (Supp. IV 1986)[hereinafter UCMJ].

The convening authority approved the adjudged sentence of a dishonorable discharge, confinement for five years, forfeiture of all pay and allowances, and reduction to Private E1.

I

Appellant now asserts that the special defense of entrapment was raised at his trial and that the government failed to prove beyond a reasonable doubt that he was not entrapped. We disagree.

The Manual for Courts-Martial, United States, 1984, Rule for Courts-Martial [hereinafter R.C.M.] 916(g) provides that "[i]t is a defense that the criminal design or suggestion to commit the offense originated in the Government and the accused had no predisposition to commit the offense." The Manual further provides that:

> The "Government" includes agents of the Government and persons cooperating with them (for example, informants). The fact that persons acting for the Government merely afford opportunities or facilities for the commission of the offense does not constitute entrapment. Entrapment occurs only when the criminal conduct is the product of the creative activity of law enforcement officials.

R.C.M. 916(g) discussion.

We must first determine whether there was evidence presented at this court-martial which would raise the defense of entrapment. Once the defense is placed into issue by some evidence, the prosecution has the burden of proving beyond reasonable doubt that the defense did not exist. *See* R.C.M. 916(b).

After weighing the evidence in the record, we are convinced beyond a reasonable doubt that appellant did commit the offense of distribution of cocaine on 29 December 1988. UCMJ art. 66(c); *United States v. Turner,* 25 M.J. 324 (C.M.A. 1987). We also conclude that the testimony of the appellant is sufficient to raise both elements of the defense of entrapment. *See United States v. Ferguson,* 15 M.J. 12 (C.M.A. 1983). Appellant claimed that the suggestion to commit the offense originated with SGT L, a government agent, and that he had no predisposition to commit the offense given his lack of prior involvement with drugs.

Accordingly, we must now determine whether the prosecution sustained its burden to prove beyond reasonable doubt that the defense did not exist. Once the defense is raised, the Government must prove that the appellant was predisposed to commit the offense and needed only the opportunity to commit the crime. In this case, it is appropriate that the issue be resolved by the fact finder. *See United States v. Vanzandt,* 14 M.J. 332 (C.M.A. 1982). The court in *Vanzandt* stated:

> [T]he subjective test of entrapment involves balancing the accused's resistance to temptation against the amount of government inducement. The focus is on the accused's latent predisposition to commit the crime, which is triggered by the government inducement. The existence of reasonable suspicion by the police is immaterial, so there is no occasion to offer or receive evidence establishing whether or why any suspicion existed. *United States v. Vanzandt,* 14 M.J. at 344.

In the case now before us, the trial defense counsel argued to the military judge, as the fact finder, that the appellant did distribute cocaine on 29 December, but that he should be acquitted based upon the entrapment defense. [footnote omitted]. The military judge was not requested to make special findings and no such findings appear in the record. [footnote omitted].

In applying the subjective test in this case, we first note the following statement of the court in *Vanzandt*:

> The latitude given the Government in "inducing" the criminal act is considerably greater in contraband cases (drugs, liquor)—which are essentially "victim-less" crimes—than would be permissible as to other crimes, where commission of the acts would bring injury to members of the public. It would appear that, in giving such latitude, courts recognize that the Government needs more leeway in detecting and combating these illicit enterprises.

United States v. Vanzandt, 14 M.J. at 344. Here, although appellant testified that SGT L approached him approximately ten times over a two-month period with requests to bring cocaine back to Fort Drum from New York City, appellant also stated that he just put SGT L off and said he would think about it. SGT L testified that when he asked appellant if he could "get some drugs for me," that appellant responded that he wasn't sure, he would let SGT L know, and that he (appellant) used to sell drugs but that he had "retired" from that. Finally, when asked by his trial defense counsel why he finally decided to purchase the cocaine and then distribute it at Fort Drum, appellant referred to pressures of his job, his family problems (appellant's divorce was pending at the time), and his financial situation.

At the time of the offense, appellant had served more than eight years in the Army, was a staff sergeant, had been a noncommissioned officer more than three years, and was twenty-eight years old. SGT L, the government informant, was junior to appellant, and, according to the testimony of both appellant and SGT L, they were merely acquaintances, for they were neither friends nor did they work together. The record clearly establishes and appellant admits that, when the distribution took place, appellant bragged about the quality of the cocaine ("taste it, it's real good-it's the best in the city"), he stated there would be no problem supplying the buyer with cocaine on a regular basis, and he anticipated making at least $500.00 from the transaction. In addition, SGT L testified that appellant wanted him to sell drugs for appellant and was guaranteed at least $400.00 per week.

The establishment of a profit motive, in and of itself, does not establish the appellant's predisposition to commit the offense of distribution of cocaine. *United States v. Meyers*, 21 M.J. 1007 (A.C.M.R. 1986). In applying the balancing test enunciated in *Vanzandt,* however, it is one factor which may be considered along with the other evidence in the case. Even accepting without question the testimony of appellant, SGT L, the government informant, did not practice any form of deceit, nor did he engage in any egregious activity in attempts to overcome appellant's resistance to distribute cocaine. Appellant did not convey to the informant an outright refusal to engage in such activity, and when the opportunity arose and the circumstances were favorable, appellant freely and willingly purchased the cocaine, transported it to Fort Drum, and distributed it to a police undercover agent. We are convinced beyond a reasonable doubt that, although the suggestion to commit the offense originated with the government, the appellant was, in fact, predisposed to commit the offense.

. . . .

The findings of guilty and the sentence are affirmed.

The court in *Cortes* stated that the government is given considerable latitude in "inducing" the criminal act in "contraband cases (drugs, liquor)—which are essentially 'victim-less' crimes—than would be permissible as to other crimes, where commission of the acts would bring injury to members of the public." Do you agree with this principle? Such a statement suggests the difficulty in successfully using the defense of entrapment in drug cases. What did the court say in *Cortes* about the accused's contention that he was not predisposed to commit the charged offense?

FRATERNIZATION

The military has historically relied upon custom and tradition to define the bounds of acceptable personal relationships among its members. The following cases discusses the history and development of fraternization rules.

United States, Appellee, v. Dennis A. Tedder, Captain U.S. Marine Corps, Appellant.
United States Court of Military Appeals
24 M.J. 176
July 6, 1987

OPINION: Everett, Chief Judge

A general court-martial found Captain Tedder guilty of one specification of conduct unbecoming an officer and a gentleman, as well as one specification of obstructing justice and two specifications of wrongful fraternization with an enlisted woman Marine, in violation of Articles 133 and 134, Uniform Code Military of Justice, 10 U.S.C. @@ 933 and 934, respectively. Appellant was sentenced to dismissal, confinement for 1 year, and total forfeitures.

Except for reducing the confinement to 45 days, the convening authority approved these results. The Court of Military Review set aside the finding of guilty to one specification of wrongful fraternization; but, upon reassessment, it affirmed the sentence as approved by the convening

authority. 18 M.J. 777 (N.M.C.M.R.1983). We granted review of these issues:

. . . .

II

WHETHER SPECIFICATION 2 OF CHARGE III [WRONGFUL FRATERNIZATION WITH LANCE CORPORAL CHIRIBOGA] FAILS TO STATE AN OFFENSE AND IS, IN ANY EVENT, VOID FOR VAGUENESS.

III

WHETHER THE SPECIFICATION UNDER CHARGE II [CONDUCT UNBECOMING AN OFFICER BY SOLICITING NAMED WOMEN MARINES TO ARRANGE A DATE WITH CORPORAL MCCOY] FAILS TO

STATE AN OFFENSE, AND IS IN ANY EVENT, VOID FOR VAGUENESS.

I

Tedder was the unit legal officer for a squadron.[1] Lance Corporal Germaine Chiriboga, a 19-year-old woman Marine in the same squadron, testified that in early November 1982 she had consulted appellant about allegations of homosexual conduct lodged against her. Subsequently, he had conversed with her while she was on watch as assistant staff duty officer. At this time, he mentioned that he frequented the Northwoods Tavern, a bar near the air station at Cherry Point, North Carolina, where both were stationed.[2] According to Chiriboga, appellant told her that, if he saw her there, he would buy her a beer. She had responded that he could do so; and Tedder then informed her that he would probably be there the next weekend.

Accompanied by another woman Marine lance corporal, she had gone to eat at the Northwoods on the next Saturday. After dinner, she went into the bar to see if appellant would arrive. Shortly thereafter, he and several friends entered the bar; and he approached her and stood next to her for about an hour. During this time, they each consumed alcoholic beverages and conversed on a first-name basis. Chiriboga testified that Tedder had told her that, if anyone asked her to explain this meeting, she should say that "it was just plain that he said that if he saw me in Northwoods, he would buy me a beer, and that was the end of it."

In the following week, appellant and Chiriboga had another conversation in which he advised her that he would be at the Northwoods on Friday evening. Again he offered to buy her a beer. Chiriboga replied that this would be acceptable; but, before going to the tavern on this occasion, she asked Sergeant Stephanie Canady of the squadron administrative office if there were Marine Corps orders concerning fraternization. Chiriboga told Canady that she was concerned because she had a date with an officer. At trial, she explained that she had been concerned that both she and Tedder might be violating some directive by their meeting.

Chiriboga then went to the Northwoods alone. She met Tedder at the bar where he and his friends purchased drinks for her. After some conversation and drinking, she accompanied him to a private club he belonged to. Later they drove to his house where they had sexual intercourse.

Appellant again instructed Chiriboga to tell anyone who inquired that he had agreed to buy her a drink if he met her at the Northwoods but not to say anything further. When the Naval Investigative Service (NIS) commenced an investigation into his conduct, he told her not to discuss the events of the evening beyond their meeting at the Northwoods. In particular, he wanted her to deny that there had been any "date" or prearrangement between them on the night in question.

Chiriboga's testimony was corroborated by that of Lance Corporal Sharon Stanton, who told the court-martial that she had accompanied Chiriboga to the Northwoods

---

[1] Appellant was not a judge advocate of the Marine Corps, but his position as legal officer was a non-lawyer billet like that of the courts-and-boards officers in some Army units.

[2] The Northwoods Tavern appears to have been frequented by Marines of all ranks; and this circumstance led the Court of Military Review to set aside the finding of guilty to the specification which charged that Tedder had wrongfully fraternized with Chiriboga by meeting her there and consuming alcoholic beverages with her.

Tavern on November 13, 1982. Before leaving the base, Chiriboga had told her that she would be meeting Captain Tedder, the legal officer for their squadron, but not to mention this to anyone because he had said that "if anybody found out that he could get in trouble." Chiriboga had told her that it was not "a date" but that Tedder was going to "buy her a beer" "if they happened to meet" at the Northwoods. She also stated that Chiriboga had remarked, "We don't want anyone to know that we are meeting." They had alcoholic beverages at the Northwoods that evening with appellant and others; but neither Stanton nor Chiriboga paid for them.

Corporal Danielle Guidry testified that on November 13, Chiriboga had been riding with her. Upon seeing appellant's car at the squadron office, Chiriboga remarked that she was supposed to meet him at the Northwoods Tavern that evening. According to Guidry, she had counseled Chiriboga against that meeting. Guidry also testified that, during the course of a subsequent investigation into fraternization by appellant, Chiriboga had told her that appellant wanted Chiriboga to refrain from discussing the matter with NIS.

The Government also called Private Carol Brown, another woman Marine in the squadron to which Tedder and Chiriboga were assigned.[3] Brown worked in the same unit with Tedder; and at one time he had shared an office with her boss. On several occasions, he had asked her to get him a date with Sergeant Catherine McCoy, another woman Marine. Brown had complained to NIS that Chiriboga had threatened "to rip my face off my head"; and, according to her, appellant had attempted to dissuade her from pursuing this complaint. His initial contact with her had been by telephone, when he told her, "I want you to drop the charges against Chiri-

boga, or else"; and he had instructed her to come to his office the next morning. When she did so, he warned Private Brown not "to ever threaten" Chiriboga "or badmouth her again or even mention her name in a conversation or there will be charges brought against you that you don't want." Moreover, Tedder told Brown "not to tell anybody about this conversation, and if I did, he would deny it, and no one would believe me." Nonetheless, Private Brown did report the conversation to NIS; and as a result, she was fitted with a device to record future conversations with Tedder.

Subsequently, in a recorded conversation, appellant had brought up the allegation that he had been wrongfully fraternizing with Lance Corporal Chiriboga; but he added that he was not being investigated any longer, and that money talks, and that they were intimidated, and he had planned on filing in civil court and suing them. He said something about a million dollars; if he sued for a million dollars, and they defaulted, they would have to pay him a million dollars, and therefore they were going to stop the investigation because they didn't want to have to hire a civilian attorney.

Lance Corporal Michelle Rottman testified that appellant had been her "officer in charge when I was assigned to the mail room" in July through October 1982. During this time, Sergeant McCoy, then a corporal, came into the unit. On "the day that she checked in," Tedder commented to her that McCoy "was good looking and she was pretty and she seemed like a nice young lady." Almost "every other day for about 2 weeks," appellant talked to Rottman about Sergeant McCoy. At one point he made "the statement that if he wasn't an officer and if she wasn't an enlisted, he wouldn't mind seeing her, but under the circumstances, he wasn't able

---

[3]Private Brown had been a sergeant but had been reduced by the sentence at a court-martial.

to." Appellant, "in a round-about way," asked Corporal Rottman "to check out McCoy." On at least one occasion she had mentioned to Sergeant McCoy that appellant "said that she was good looking and that he wouldn't mind going out with her."

Sergeant McCoy testified that she had known appellant, Private Brown, and Lance Corporal Rottman while she had been assigned to their unit at Cherry Point. According to her, "There were approximately two occasions when I talked with Lance Corporal Rottman, and she had mentioned the fact to me that Captain Tedder wanted to know if his future wife had checked in and if I would go to lunch with him." Although Brown had been present on these occasions, there were three other times when Private Brown had asked Sergeant McCoy "along the same lines. She hadn't mentioned anything about [his] future wife. She had just said that he wanted to know if I wanted to go out to lunch with him, and he was on Cloud Nine because I spoke to him."

The defense offered evidence which in various ways tended to refute the Government's case; [footnote omitted] but Captain Tedder himself did not testify. The defense did not argue that appellant had been unaware of any Marine Corps policy or custom which would have prohibited his dating Chiriboga or McCoy. Instead, he contended that any meetings between appellant and Chiriboga were happenstance; that nothing serious transpired; and that appellant's conduct was neither service-discrediting, prejudicial to good order and discipline, nor conduct unbecoming an officer. [footnote omitted].

. . . .

III

In *Parker v. Levy*, 417 U.S. 733, 94 S. Ct. 2547, 41 L. Ed. 2d 439 (1974), the Supreme Court considered the constitutionality of Articles 133 and 134 of the Uniform Code of Military Justice. With respect to the contention that these Articles were void for vagueness, the Court decided that, due to the special needs of the unique military society, a different test should be applied to these Articles than would be used for a penal statute on which was based a prosecution in a federal district court or a state court.

Nonetheless, penal statutes applicable to service members and military directives intended to govern their conduct must convey some notice of the standards of behavior they require. [citations omitted]. We have recognized that "not every social conduct between an officer and an enlisted man is or even can reasonably be prohibited." [citation omitted].[4] In the opinion in *Pitasi*, this Court urged that appropriate directives be drafted to govern the relationships between officers and enlisted persons. In this way, notice would be provided.

The Air Force did not take this suggestion. Moreover, according to the determination of the Air Force Court of Military Review in Johanns, there was no custom of the service in the Air Force which prohibited dating or consensual sexual intercourse with enlisted women who were not under the accused's command or supervision. Therefore, we held that, for want of constitutionally adequate notice, Captain Johanns could not be prosecuted successfully under Articles 133 and 134 of the Uniform Code for fraternization with an enlisted person who was not under his command or

---

[4]In *United States v. Lovejoy*, 20 U.S.C.M.A. 18, 21, 42 C.M.R. 210, 213 (1970), Judge Darden, writing separately, noted his reservation as to whether "this practice" of fraternization was subject to prosecution.

supervision, when the alleged misconduct consisted only of consensual sexual intercourse.

The Army, on the other hand, has issued some directives which give notice as to various prohibited relationships between officers and certain enlisted personnel. Thus, in *United States v. Mayfield*, 21 M.J. 418 (C.M.A. 1986), this Court affirmed the conviction of an officer for wrongfully fraternizing with a female enlisted trainee assigned to his company—although not under his direct supervision—by asking her for a date. Mayfield did not contend that he was unaware of the restrictions on the relationship he had attempted to establish. Moreover, he admitted on cross-examination that he had been well aware of the command policy which prohibited dating between the command cadre and the trainees.

In *United States v. Adames*, 21 M.J. 465 (C.M.A. 1986), the accused—executive officer of a training company which included female soldiers—was convicted of conduct unbecoming an officer by reason of his "socializing with" the trainees. *Id.* at 466. Several of the trainees testified that the accused as an officer had been lowered in their esteem by this action. Most importantly, we recognized that the Army had set rules of behavior restricting social relationships between a senior and a subordinate—especially when one was a trainee being supervised by the other.

The Commandant of the Marine Corps has also attempted to provide guidance for his officers about the correct relationships with their subordinates. Paragraph 1100.4 of the Marine Corps Manual (1980) provides:

> Relations Between Officers and Enlisted Marines. Duty relationships and social and business contacts among Marines of different grades will be consistent with traditional standards of good order and discipline and the mutual respect that has always existed between Marines of senior grade and those of lesser grade. Situations which invite or give the appearance of familiarity or undue informality among Marines of different grades will be avoided or, if found to exist, corrected.[5] (Emphasis added.)

Subsequent paragraphs quote observations on leadership by former Commandant, Major General John A. Lejeune, which appeared in the 1921 edition of the Marine Corps Manual. They compare the relationship between Marine officers and enlisted persons to "that of teacher and scholar . . . partak[ing] of the nature of the relation between father and son."[6] The Manual also observes that a large portion of those persons who enlist "are under twenty-one years of age" and "in the formative period of their lives."[7]

The Marine Corps Development and Education Command has prepared a lesson plan on fraternization; and this plan, which makes reference to the Marine Corps Manual, observes that certain relationships between an officer and an enlisted person—such as that which developed be-

---

[5]The introductory paragraphs of the Marine Corps Manual (1980) state that it is the basic publication of the United States Marine Corps issued by the Commandant of the Marine Corps and approved by the Secretary of the Navy. It is a regulatory publication for the Department of the Navy as defined in U.S. Navy Regulations.

[6]At the time this passage was written, there were no women in the Marine Corps. Consequently, General Lejeune spoke of the relationship "between officers and enlisted men."

[7]Indeed, as already noted, Lance Corporal Chiriboga was 19 years old at the time of these offenses.

tween appellant and Chiriboga—are inconsistent with good order and discipline. Moreover, the Court of Military Review found that the custom of the service which prohibited an intimate relationship between officers and enlisted persons still exists in the Naval Service. *See United States v. Tedder, supra* at 781. This finding was grounded on the publication of the Manual for Courts-Martial, United States, 1984, which specifically recognized wrongful fraternization as a serious offense,[8] and on the prior case law in the Naval Service. *See, e.g., United States v. Free,* 14 C.M.R. 466 (N.B.R. 1953).

In his capacity as unit legal officer for the squadron, Tedder had some official duties that pertained to Chiriboga. Indeed, he first met her while performing those duties. Although the specification on fraternization under Article 134 does not allege that she was a "subordinate member" of his command as did the allegations in *Adames,* it appears that in some respects Tedder was her supervisor. Certainly he was in a position to affect her career by his recommendations as to appropriate action in connection with certain accusations that had been made against her.

As described in Lance Corporal Chiriboga's testimony, Tedder's own course of conduct made it clear that he did not believe that he could lawfully maintain an intimate sexual relationship with a woman Marine who was in his unit. We also observe that appellant did not contend at trial that Articles 133 and 134 were being applied to him unconstitutionally because of a lack of notice.

Although Tedder was well aware that he should not institute a sexual relationship with Lance Corporal Chiriboga, he did so anyway and thereby prejudiced good order and discipline. Therefore, the finding of guilty of the specification alleging wrongful fraternization with Chiriboga in violation of Article 134 is valid.

IV

Lance Corporal Rottman and Private Brown were subordinates of appellant in his squadron. Nonetheless, he solicited their assistance in arranging a date for him with still another woman Marine, Sergeant (then Corporal) McCoy. Appellant never contended at trial that he was not aware that this could be conduct unbecoming an officer in violation of Article 133. Indeed, one of his remarks to Private Brown revealed his doubts that he could ever have a date with McCoy.

Long ago, the Court of Claims noted that with military officers "there is a higher code termed honor which holds . . . [them] to stricter accountability." *Fletcher v. United States,* 26 Ct.Cl. 541, 563 (1891). Because of an officer's special status, a higher standard of conduct may be required of him. *United States v. Means,* 10 M.J. 162 (C.M.A. 1981); *see also United States v. Scott,* 21 M.J. 345 (C.M.A. 1986). We are unable to reconcile these standards of behavior with appellant's attempt to utilize military subordinates in his unit to procure a date for him with another enlisted person in the unit. Under the circumstances, we see no reason to disturb the finding of guilty of unbecoming conduct.

V

The decision of the United States Navy-Marine Corps Court of Military Review is affirmed.

---

[8]Of course, this Manual was published after appellant's trial.

Captain Tedder was also convicted of conduct unbecoming an officer (Article 133, UCMJ) for having enlisted female Marines obtain dates for him. Was this an inappropriate use of subordinate personnel? *Compare Tedder* with *United States v. Robinson* in Chapter VI. One of the issues in *Tedder* was whether the Marine Corps had a custom prohibiting personal relationships among officers and enlisted members. In reaching its decision, the court relied upon regulations promulgated by the Commandant of the Marine Corps. Note that in *Robinson*, the Air Force Court of Military Review found there was no custom in the Air Force which prohibited dating or consensual sexual intercourse with enlisted women who were not under the accused's command or supervision. In *Tedder*, the accused was charged with fraternization under Article 134, UCMJ. Because of the difficulty of showing that particular associations violate the custom of the service, the Navy has issued general orders defining prohibited relationships.

OPNAVINST 5370.2A

Commander Naval Operations Instruction 5370.2A (OPNAVINST 5370.2A) prohibits the following relationships:

(1) Any personal relationship between an officer and an enlisted member that is unduly familiar and does not respect differences in rank and grade; and

(2) When prejudicial to good order and discipline or of a nature to bring discredit on the naval service, personal relationships between officer members or between enlisted members that are unduly familiar and that do not respect differences in grade or rank.

The above explains that unduly familiar officer-enlisted relationships are always prohibited under OPNAVINST 5370.2A. For an unduly familiar relationship between officer members or between enlisted members to be prohibited, however, it must prejudice good order and discipline or discredit the naval service. OPNAVINST 5370.2A explains that prejudice to good order and discipline or discredit results from circumstances which:

(1) call into question a senior's objectivity;

(2) result in actual or apparent preferential treatment;

(3) undermine the authority of a senior; or

(4) compromise the chain of command.

What circumstances satisfy the above criteria? The instruction explains that unduly familiar relationships between officer members or between enlisted members in the same chain of command normally undermine the leadership authority of the senior and compromise the chain of command, and that relationships between chief petty officers (E-7 to E-9) and junior enlisted (E-1 to E-6) at the same command (but not in the same direct chain of command) also typically prejudice good order and discipline or discredit the naval service. The instruction further provides that personal relationships that are unduly familiar between staff/student personnel at training commands are also prejudicial to good order and discipline. Relationships between officer members and between enlisted members outside of the situations described above must be analyzed on a case by case basis to determine if they are prejudicial to good order and discipline or discredit the naval service.

What activities are "unduly familiar?" OPNAVINST 5370.2A explains that dating, cohabitation, sexual relationships, and private business relationships are considered unduly familiar. Note that a fraternization case is not excused by a subsequent marriage between the offending parties. Is fraternization a gender-neutral concept? The answer is "yes." Its focus is on the detriment to good order and discipline resulting from unduly familiar senior-subordinate relationships, not from the gender of the members involved.

As discussed above, OPNAVINST 5370.2A is punitive in nature and violations of its provisions, discussed above, may be charged as violation of a lawful general order under Article 92, UCMJ. The Secretary of the Navy, in Article 1165 of the U.S. Navy Regulations, also prohibits unduly familiar relationships between officer and enlisted members and unduly familiar relationships between officer members and between enlisted members that are prejudicial to good order and discipline or of a nature to bring discredit on the naval service. Article 1165, U.S. Navy Regulations, is a lawful general order, as well. May an officer be charged with both fraternization and conduct unbecoming an officer for engaging in a prohibited relationship with an enlisted person? *See* the discussion in the next section regarding Article 133, UCMJ, and *United States v. Gauglione.*

CONDUCT UNBECOMING AN OFFICER

Paragraph 59a, Part IV, MCM, sets forth the elements of Article 133, UCMJ.

(1) That the accused did or omitted to do certain acts; and

(2) That, under the circumstances, these acts or omissions constituted conduct unbecoming an officer and gentleman.

Paragraph 59c, Part IV, MCM, defines a "gentleman" and attempts to explain the nature of conduct unbecoming an officer.

(1) Gentleman. As used in this article, "gentleman" includes both male and female commissioned officers, cadets, and midshipmen. The elements of this offense under Article 133 are quite broad.

(2) Nature of offense. Conduct violative of this article is action or behavior in an official capacity which, in dishonoring or disgracing the person as an officer, seriously compromises the officer's character as a gentleman, or action or behavior in an unofficial or private capacity which, in dishonoring or disgracing the officer personally, seriously compromises the person's standing as an officer. There are certain moral attributes common to the ideal officer and the perfect gentleman, a lack of which is indicated by acts of dishonesty, unfair dealing, indecency, indecorum, lawlessness, injustice, or cruelty. Not everyone is or can be expected to meet unrealistically high moral standards, but there is a limit of tolerance based on customs of the service and military necessity below which the personal standards of an officer, cadet, or midshipman cannot fall without seriously compromising the person's standing as an officer, cadet, or midshipman or the person's character as a gentleman. This article prohibits conduct by a commissioned officer, cadet, or midshipman which, taking all the circumstances into consideration, is thus compromising. This article includes acts made punishable by any other article, provided these acts amount to conduct unbecoming an officer and a gentleman. Thus, a commissioned officer who steals property violates both this article and Article 121. Whenever the offense charged is the same as a specific offense set forth in this Manual, the elements of proof are the same as those set forth in the paragraph which treats that specific offense, with the additional requirement that the act or omission constitutes conduct unbecoming an officer and gentleman.

Article 133 has been attacked for vagueness in defining conduct that is unbecoming. The Supreme Court addressed this issue in the following case.

Parker v. Levy
Supreme Court of the United States
417 U.S. 733
June 19, 1974

OPINION: Mr. Justice Rehnquist

Appellee Howard Levy, a physician, was a captain in the Army stationed at Fort Jackson, South Carolina. He had entered the Army under the so-called "Berry Plan," [footnote omitted] under which he agreed to serve for two years in the Armed Forces if permitted first to complete his medical training. From the time he entered on active duty in July 1965 until his trial by court-martial, he was assigned as Chief of the Dermatological Service of the United States Army Hospital at Fort Jackson. On

June 2, 1967, appellee was convicted by a general court-martial of violations of Arts. 90, 133, and 134 of the Uniform Code of Military Justice, and sentenced to dismissal from the service, forfeiture of all pay and allowances, and confinement for three years at hard labor.

The facts upon which his conviction rests are virtually undisputed. The evidence admitted at his court-martial trial showed that one of the functions of the hospital to which appellee was assigned was that of training Special Forces aide men. As Chief of the Dermatological Service, appellee was to conduct a clinic for those aide men. In the late summer of 1966, it came to the attention of the hospital commander that the dermatology training of the students was unsatisfactory. After investigating the program and determining that appellee had totally neglected his duties, the commander called appellee to his office and personally handed him a written order to conduct the training. Appellee read the order, said that he understood it, but declared that he would not obey it because of his medical ethics. Appellee persisted in his refusal to obey the order, and later reviews of the program established that the training was still not being carried out.

During the same period of time, appellee made several public statements to enlisted personnel at the post, of which the following is representative:

"The United States is wrong in being involved in the Vietnam War. I would refuse to go to Vietnam if ordered to do so. I don't see why any colored soldier would go to Vietnam: they should refuse to go to Viet Nam and if sent should refuse to fight because they are discriminated against and denied their freedom in the United States, and they are sacrificed and discriminated against in Viet Nam by being given all the hazardous duty and they are suffering the majority of casualties. If I were a colored soldier I would refuse to go to Viet Nam and if I were a colored soldier and were sent I would refuse to fight. Special Forces personnel are liars and thieves and killers of peasants and murderers of women and children."

Appellee's military superiors originally contemplated nonjudicial proceedings against him under Art. 15 of the Uniform Code of Military Justice, 10 U. S. C. @ 815, but later determined that court-martial proceedings were appropriate. The specification under Art. 90 alleged that appellee willfully disobeyed the hospital commandant's order to establish the training program, in violation of that article, which punishes anyone subject to the Uniform Code of Military Justice who "willfully disobeys a lawful command of his superior commissioned officer." [footnote omitted]. Statements to enlisted personnel were listed as specifications under the charges of violating Arts. 133 and 134 of the Code. Article 133 provides for the punishment of "conduct unbecoming an officer and a gentleman," [footnote omitted] while Art. 134 proscribes, inter alia, "all disorders and neglects to the prejudice of good order and discipline in the armed forces."[1]

The specification under Art. 134 alleged that appellee "did, at Fort Jackson, South Carolina, . . . with design to promote disloyalty and disaffection among the troops, publicly utter [certain] statements to divers enlisted personnel at divers times. . . ."[2]

---

[1] Article 134 of the Uniform Code of Military Justice, 10 U. S. C. @ 934, provides:

"Though not specifically mentioned in this chapter, all disorders and neglects to the prejudice of good order and discipline in the armed forces, all conduct of a nature to bring discredit upon the armed forces, and crimes and offenses not capital, of which persons subject to this chapter may be guilty, shall be taken cognizance of by a general, special, or summary court-martial, according to the nature and degree of the offense, and shall be punished at the discretion of that court."

[2] The specification under Art. 134 (Charge II) alleged in full:

"In that Captain Howard B. Levy, U.S. Army, Headquarters and Headquarters Company, United States Army Hospital, Fort Jackson, South Carolina, did, at Fort Jackson, South Carolina, on or

Appellee was convicted by the court-martial, and his conviction was sustained on his appeals within the military. [footnote omitted]. After he had exhausted this avenue of relief, he sought federal habeas corpus in the United States District Court for the Middle District of Pennsylvania, challenging his court-martial conviction on a number of grounds. The District Court, on the basis of the voluminous record of the military proceedings and the argument of counsel, denied relief. It held that the "various articles of the Uniform Code of Military Justice are not unconstitutional for vagueness," citing several decisions of the United States Court of Military Appeals. [footnote omitted]. The court rejected the balance of appellee's claims without addressing them individually, noting that the military tribunals had given fair consideration to them and that the role of the federal courts in reviewing court-martial proceedings was a limited one.

The Court of Appeals reversed, holding in a lengthy opinion that Arts. 133 and 134 are void for vagueness. 478 F.2d 772 (CA3 1973). The court found little difficulty in concluding that "as measured by contemporary standards of vagueness applicable to statutes and ordinances governing civilians," the general articles "do not pass constitutional muster." It relied on such cases as *Grayned v. City of Rockford*, 408 U.S. 104 (1972); *Papachristou v. City of Jacksonville*, 405 U.S. 156 (1972); *Giaccio v. Pennsylvania*, 382 U.S. 399 (1966); *Coates v. City of Cincinnati*, 402 U.S. 611

(1971), and *Gelling v. Texas*, 343 U.S. 960 (1952). The Court of Appeals did not rule that appellee was punished for doing things he could not reasonably have known constituted conduct proscribed by Art. 133 or 134. Indeed, it recognized that his conduct fell within one of the examples of Art. 134 violations contained in the Manual for Courts-Martial, promulgated by the President by Executive Order. [footnote omitted]. Nonetheless, relying chiefly on *Gooding v. Wilson*, 405 U.S. 518 (1972), the Court found the possibility that Arts. 133 and 134 would be applied to future conduct of others as to which there was insufficient warning, or which was within the area of protected First Amendment expression, was enough to give appellee standing to challenge both articles on their face. While it acknowledged that different standards might in some circumstances be applicable in considering vagueness challenges to provisions which govern the conduct of members of the Armed Forces, the Court saw in the case of Arts. 133 and 134 no "countervailing military considerations which justify the twisting of established standards of due process in order to hold inviolate these articles, so clearly repugnant under current constitutional values." Turning finally to appellee's conviction under Art. 90, the Court held that the joint consideration of Art. 90 charges with the charges under Arts. 133 and 134 gave rise to a "reasonable possibility" that appellee's right to a fair trial was prejudiced, so that a new trial was required.

---

about the period February 1966 to December 1966, with design to promote disloyalty and disaffection among the troops, publicly utter the following statements to divers enlisted personnel at divers times: 'The United States is wrong in being involved in the Viet Nam War. I would refuse to go to Viet Nam if ordered to do so. I don't see why any colored soldier would go to Viet Nam; they should refuse to go to Viet Nam and if sent should refuse to fight because they are discriminated against and denied their freedom in the United States, and they are sacrificed and discriminated against in Viet Nam by being given all the hazardous duty and they are suffering the majority of casualties. If I were a colored soldier I would refuse to go to Viet Nam and if I were a colored soldier and were sent I would refuse to fight. Special Forces personnel are liars and thieves and killers of peasants and murderers of women and children,' or words to that effect, which statements were disloyal to the United States, to the prejudice of good order and discipline in the armed forces."

Appellants appealed to this Court pursuant to 28 U. S. C. @ 1252. We set the case for oral argument, and postponed consideration of the question of our jurisdiction to the hearing on the merits. 414 U.S. 973 (1973). [footnote omitted].

This Court has long recognized that the military is, by necessity, a specialized society separate from civilian society. We have also recognized that the military has, again by necessity, developed laws and traditions of its own during its long history. The differences between the military and civilian communities result from the fact that "it is the primary business of armies and navies to fight or be ready to fight wars should the occasion arise." United States ex rel. *Toth v. Quarles*, 350 U.S. 11, 17 (1955). In re *Grimley*, 137 U.S. 147, 153 (1890), the Court observed: "An army is not a deliberative body. It is the executive arm. Its law is that of obedience. No question can be left open as to the right to command in the officer, or the duty of obedience in the soldier." More recently we noted that "the military constitutes a specialized community governed by a separate discipline from that of the civilian," *Orloff v. Willoughby*, 345 U.S. 83, 94 (1953), and that "the rights of men in the armed forces must perforce be conditioned to meet certain overriding demands of discipline and duty. . . ." *Burns v. Wilson*, 346 U.S. 137, 140 (1953) (plurality opinion). We have also recognized that a military officer holds a particular position of responsibility and command in the Armed Forces:

"The President's commission . . . recites that 'reposing special trust and confidence in the patriotism, valor, fidelity and abilities' of the appointee he is named to the specified rank during the pleasure of the President." *Orloff v. Willoughby, supra*, at 91.

Just as military society has been a society apart from civilian society, so "military law . . . is a jurisprudence which exists separate and apart from the law which governs in our federal judicial establishment." *Burns v. Wilson, supra*, at 140. And to maintain the discipline essential to perform its mission effectively, the military has developed what "may not unfitly be called the customary military law" or "general usage of the military service." *Martin v. Mott*, 12 Wheat. 19, 35 (1827). As the opinion in *Martin v. Mott* demonstrates, the Court has approved the enforcement of those military customs and usages by courts-martial from the early days of this Nation:

". . . Courts Martial, when duly organized, are bound to execute their duties, and regulate their modes of proceeding, in the absence of positive enactments. Upon any other principle, Courts Martial would be left without any adequate means to exercise the authority confided to them: for there could scarcely be framed a positive code to provide for the infinite variety of incidents applicable to them." *Id.*, at 35-36.

An examination of the British antecedents of our military law shows that the military law of Britain had long contained the forebears of Arts. 133 and 134 in remarkably similar language. The Articles of the Earl of Essex (1642) provided that "all other faults, disorders and offenses, not mentioned in these Articles, shall be punished according to the general customs and laws of war." One of the British Articles of War of 1765 made punishable "all Disorders or Neglects . . . to the Prejudice of good Order and Military Discipline . . ." that were not mentioned in the other articles. [footnote omitted]. Another of those articles provided:

"Whatsoever Commissioned Officer shall be convicted before a General

Court-martial, of behaving in a scandalous infamous Manner, such as is unbecoming the Character of an Officer and a Gentleman, shall be discharged from Our Service." [footnote omitted].

In 1775 the Continental Congress adopted this last article, along with 68 others, for the governance of its army. [footnote omitted]. The following year it was resolved by the Congress that "the committee on spies be directed to revise the rules and articles of war; this being a committee of five, consisting of John Adams, Thomas Jefferson, John Rutledge, James Wilson and R. R. Livingston. . . ." [footnote omitted]. The article was included in the new set of articles prepared by the Committee, which Congress adopted on September 20, 1776. [footnote omitted]. After being once more re-enacted without change in text in 1786, it was revised and expanded in 1806, omitting the terms "scandalous" and "infamous," so as to read:

"Any commissioned officer convicted before a general court-martial of conduct unbecoming an officer and a gentleman, shall be dismissed [from] the service." [footnote omitted]. From 1806, it remained basically unchanged through numerous congressional re-enactments until it was enacted as Art. 133 of the Uniform Code of Military Justice in 1951.

The British article punishing "all Disorders and Neglects . . ." was also adopted by the Continental Congress in 1775 and re-enacted in 1776.[3] Except for a revision in 1916, which added the clause punishing "all conduct of a nature to bring discredit upon the military service,"[4] substantially the same language was preserved through-

out the various re-enactments of this article too, until in 1951 it was enacted as Art. 134 of the Uniform Code of Military Justice.

Decisions of this Court during the last century have recognized that the longstanding customs and usages of the services impart accepted meaning to the seemingly imprecise standards of Arts. 133 and 134. In *Dynes v. Hoover*, 20 How. 65 (1857), this Court upheld the Navy's general article, which provided that "all crimes committed by persons belonging to the navy, which are not specified in the foregoing articles, shall be punished according to the laws and customs in such cases at sea." The Court reasoned:

"When offenses and crimes are not given in terms or by definition, the want of it may be supplied by a comprehensive enactment, such as the 32d article of the rules for the government of the navy, which means that courts martial have jurisdiction of such crimes as are not specified, but which have been recognized to be crimes and offenses by the usages in the navy of all nations, and that they shall be punished according to the laws and customs of the sea. Notwithstanding the apparent indeterminateness of such a provision, it is not liable to abuse; for what those crimes are, and how they are to be punished, is well known by practical men in the navy and army, and by those who have studied the law of courts martial, and the offenses of which the different courts martial have cognizance." *Id.*, at 82. In *Smith v. Whitney*, 116 U.S. 167 (1886), this Court refused to issue a writ of prohibition against Smith's court-martial trial on charges of "scandalous conduct tending to the destruction of good mor-

---

[3]Article L of the American Articles of War of 1775; Art. 5 of section XVIII of the American Articles of War of 1776; Winthrop, *supra*, at 957, 971.

[4]Act of Aug. 29, 1916, c. 418, 39 Stat. 619, 666.

als" and "culpable inefficiency in the performance of duty." The Court again recognized the role of "the usages and customs of war" and "old practice in the army" in the interpretation of military law by military tribunals. *Id.*, at 178-179.

In *United States v. Fletcher*, 148 U.S. 84 (1893), the Court considered a court-martial conviction under what is now Art. 133, rejecting Captain Fletcher's claim that the court-martial could not properly have held that his refusal to pay a just debt was "conduct unbecoming an officer and a gentleman." The Court of Claims decision which the Court affirmed in Fletcher stressed the military's "higher code termed honor, which holds its society to stricter accountability" [footnote omitted] and with which those trained only in civilian law are unfamiliar.

. . . .

II

The differences noted by this settled line of authority, first between the military community and the civilian community, and second between military law and civilian law, continue in the present day under the Uniform Code of Military Justice. That Code cannot be equated to a civilian criminal code. It, and the various versions of the Articles of War which have preceded it, regulate aspects of the conduct of members of the military which in the civilian sphere are left unregulated. While a civilian criminal code carves out a relatively small segment of potential conduct and declares it criminal, the Uniform Code of Military Justice essays more varied regulation of a much larger segment of the activities of the more tightly knit military community. In civilian life there is no legal sanction—civil or criminal—for failure to behave as an officer and a gentleman; in the military world, Art. 133 imposes such

a sanction on a commissioned officer. The Code likewise imposes other sanctions for conduct that in civilian life is not subject to criminal penalties: disrespect toward superior commissioned officers, Art. 89, 10 U. S. C. @ 889; cruelty toward, or oppression or maltreatment of subordinates, Art. 93, 10 U. S. C. @ 893; negligent damaging, destruction, or wrongful disposition of military property of the United States, Art. 108, 10 U. S. C. @ 908; improper hazarding of a vessel, Art. 110, 10 U. S. C. @ 910; drunkenness on duty, Art. 112, 10 U. S. C. @ 912; and malingering, Art. 115, 10 U. S. C. @ 915.

But the other side of the coin is that the penalties provided in the Code vary from death and substantial penal confinement at one extreme to forms of administrative discipline which are below the threshold of what would normally be considered a criminal sanction at the other. Though all of the offenses described in the Code are punishable "as a court-martial may direct," and the accused may demand a trial by court-martial, [footnote omitted] Art. 15 of the Code also provides for the imposition of nonjudicial "disciplinary punishments" for minor offenses without the intervention of a court-martial. 10 U. S. C. @ 815. The punishments imposable under that article are of a limited nature. With respect to officers, punishment may encompass suspension of duty, arrest in quarters for not more than 30 days, restriction for not more than 60 days, and forfeiture of pay for a limited period of time. In the case of enlisted men, such punishment may additionally include, among other things, reduction to the next inferior pay grade, extra fatigue duty, and correctional custody for not more than seven consecutive days. Thus, while legal proceedings actually brought before a court-martial are prosecuted in the name of the Government, and the accused has the right to demand that he be proceeded against in this manner before any sanctions may be imposed upon him, a range of minor sanctions for lesser infractions are often imposed administratively. Forfeiture of pay, reduction in rank, and even dismissal from the service bring to mind the law of labor-management relations as much as the civilian criminal law.

In short, the Uniform Code of Military Justice regulates a far broader range of the conduct of military personnel than a typical state criminal code regulates of the conduct of civilians; but at the same time the enforcement of that Code in the area of minor offenses is often by sanctions which are more akin to administrative or civil sanctions than to civilian criminal ones.

The availability of these lesser sanctions is not surprising in view of the different relationship of the Government to members of the military. It is not only that of lawgiver to citizen, but also that of employer to employee. Indeed, unlike the civilian situation, the Government is often employer, landlord, provisioner, and lawgiver rolled into one. That relationship also reflects the different purposes of the two communities. As we observed in re *Grimley*, 137 U.S., at 153, the military "is the executive arm" whose "law is that of obedience." While members of the military community enjoy many of the same rights and bear many of the same burdens as do members of the civilian community, within the military community there is simply not the same autonomy as there is in the larger civilian community. The military establishment is subject to the control of the civilian Commander in Chief and the civilian departmental heads under him, and its function is to carry out the policies made by those civilian superiors.

Perhaps because of the broader sweep of the Uniform Code, the military makes an effort to advise its personnel of the contents of the Uniform Code, rather than depending on the ancient doctrine that everyone is presumed to know the law. Article 137 of the Uniform Code, 10 U. S. C.

@ 937, requires that the provisions of the Code be "carefully explained to each enlisted member at the time of his entrance on active duty, or within six days thereafter" and that they be "explained again after he has completed six months of active duty. . . ." Thus the numerically largest component of the services, the enlisted personnel, who might be expected to be a good deal less familiar with the Uniform Code than commissioned officers, are required by its terms to receive instructions in its provisions. Article 137 further provides that a complete text of the Code and of the regulations prescribed by the President "shall be made available to any person on active duty, upon his request, for his personal examination."

With these very significant differences between military law and civilian law and between the military community and the civilian community in mind, we turn to appellee's challenges to the constitutionality of Arts. 133 and 134.

III

Appellee urges that both Art. 133 and Art. 134 (the general article) are "void for vagueness" under the Due Process Clause of the Fifth Amendment and overbroad in violation of the First Amendment. We have recently said of the vagueness doctrine:

"The doctrine incorporates notions of fair notice or warning. Moreover, it requires legislatures to set reasonably clear guidelines for law enforcement officials and trier of fact in order to prevent 'arbitrary and discriminatory enforcement.' Where a statute's literal scope, unaided by a narrowing state court interpretation, is capable of reaching expression sheltered by the First Amendment, the doctrine demands a greater degree of specificity than in other contexts." *Smith v. Goguen*, 415

U.S. 566, 572-573 (1974). Each of these articles has been construed by the United States Court of Military Appeals or by other military authorities in such a manner as to at least partially narrow its otherwise broad scope.

The United States Court of Military Appeals has stated that Art. 134 must be judged "not in vacuo, but in the context in which the years have placed it," [citation omitted] Article 134 does not make "every irregular, mischievous, or improper act a court-martial offense," [citation omitted] but its reach is limited to conduct that is "'directly and palpably—as distinguished from indirectly and remotely—prejudicial to good order and discipline.'" [citation omitted] only to calls for active opposition to the military policy of the United States, [citation omitted], and does not reach all "disagreement with, or objection to, a policy of the Government." [citation omitted].

The Manual for Courts-Martial restates these limitations on the scope of Art. 134. [footnote omitted]. It goes on to say that "certain disloyal statements by military personnel" may be punishable under Art. 134. "Examples are utterances designed to promote disloyalty or disaffection among troops, as praising the enemy, attacking the war aims of the United States, or denouncing our form of government." [footnote omitted]. Extensive additional interpretative materials are contained in the portions of the Manual devoted to Art. 134, which describe more than sixty illustrative offenses.

. . . .

But the Court of Appeals found in this case, and we agree, that Arts. 133 and 134 are subject to no such sweeping condemnation. Levy had fair notice from the language of each article that the particular conduct which he engaged in was punishable. This is a case, then, of the type adverted to in *Smith v. Goguen*, in which the statutes "by their terms or as authoritatively construed apply without question to certain activities, but whose application to other behavior is uncertain." 415 U.S., at 578. The result of the Court of Appeals' conclusion that Levy had standing to challenge the vagueness of these articles as they might be hypothetically applied to the conduct of others, even though he was squarely within their prohibitions, may stem from a blending of the doctrine of vagueness with the doctrine of overbreadth, but we do not believe it is supported by prior decisions of this Court.

. . . .

Because of the factors differentiating military society from civilian society, we hold that the proper standard of review for a vagueness challenge to the articles of the Code is the standard which applies to criminal statutes regulating economic affairs. Clearly, that standard is met here, for as the Court stated in *United States v. National Dairy Corp.*, 372 U.S. 29, 32-33 (1963):

> "The strong presumptive validity that attaches to an Act of Congress has led this Court to hold many times that statutes are not automatically invalidated as vague simply because difficulty is found in determining whether certain marginal offenses fall within their language. [citations omitted]. Indeed, we have consistently sought an interpretation which supports the constitutionality of legislation. [citations omitted].

> "Void for vagueness simply means that criminal responsibility should not attach where one could not reasonably understand that his contemplated conduct is proscribed. *United States v. Harriss*, 347 U.S. 612, 617 (1954). In determining the sufficiency of the notice a statute must of necessity be examined in the light of the

conduct with which a defendant is charged. *Robinson v. United States*, 324 U.S. 282 (1945)."

Since appellee could have had no reasonable doubt that his public statements urging Negro enlisted men not to go to Vietnam if ordered to do so were both "unbecoming an officer and a gentleman," and "to the prejudice of good order and discipline in the armed forces," in violation of the provisions of Arts. 133 and 134, respectively, his challenge to them as unconstitutionally vague under the Due Process Clause of the Fifth Amendment must fail.

We likewise reject appellee's contention that Arts. 133 and 134 are facially invalid because of their "overbreadth." In *Gooding v. Wilson*, 405 U.S., at 520-521, the Court said:

"It matters not that the words appellee used might have been constitutionally prohibited under a narrowly and precisely drawn statute. At least when statutes regulate or proscribe speech and when 'no readily apparent construction suggests itself as a vehicle for rehabilitating the statutes in a single prosecution,' *Dombrowski v. Pfister*, 380 U.S. 479, 491 (1965), the transcendent value to all society of constitutionally protected expression is deemed to justify allowing 'attacks on overly broad statutes with no requirement that the person making the attack demonstrate that his own conduct could not be regulated by a statute drawn with the requisite narrow specificity.' . . ."

While the members of the military are not excluded from the protection granted by the First Amendment, the different character of the military community and of the military mission requires a different application of those protections. The fundamental necessity for obedience, and the consequent necessity for imposition of discipline, may render permissible within the military that which would be constitutionally impermissible outside it. Doctrines of First Amendment overbreadth asserted in support of challenges to imprecise language like that contained in Arts. 133 and 134 are not exempt from the operation of these principles. The United States Court of Military Appeals has sensibly expounded the reason for this different application of First Amendment doctrines in its opinion in *United States v. Priest*, 21 U. S. C. M. A., at 570, 45 C. M. R., at 344:

"In the armed forces some restrictions exist for reasons that have no counterpart in the civilian community. Disrespectful and contemptuous speech, even advocacy of violent change, is tolerable in the civilian community, for it does not directly affect the capacity of the Government to discharge its responsibilities unless it both is directed to inciting imminent lawless action and is likely to produce such action. *Brandenburg v. Ohio*, .S. 444 (1969)]. In military life, however, other considerations must be weighed. The armed forces depend on a command structure that at times must commit men to combat, not only hazarding their lives but ultimately involving the security of the Nation itself. Speech that is protected in the civil population may nonetheless undermine the effectiveness of response to command. If it does, it is constitutionally unprotected. *United States v. Gray*, [20 U. S. C. M. A. 63, 42 C. M. R. 255 (1970)]."

. . . .

There is a wide range of the conduct of military personnel to which Arts. 133 and 134 may be applied without infringement of the First Amendment. While there may lurk at the fringes of the articles, even in the light of their narrowing construction by the United States Court of Military Appeals, some possibility that conduct which would be ultimately held to be protected by the First Amendment could be included within their prohibition, we deem this insufficient to invalidate either of them at the behest of appellee. His conduct, that of a commissioned officer publicly urging enlisted personnel to refuse to obey orders which might send them into combat, was unprotected under the most expansive notions of the First Amendment. Articles 133 and 134 may constitutionally prohibit that conduct, and a sufficiently large number of similar or related types of conduct so as to preclude their invalidation for overbreadth.

IV

Appellee urges that should we disagree with the Court of Appeals as to the constitutionality of Arts. 133 and 134, we should nonetheless affirm its judgment by invalidating his conviction under Art. 90. He contends that to carry out the hospital commandant's order to train aide men in dermatology would have constituted participation in a war crime, and that the commandant gave the order in question, knowing that it would be disobeyed, for the sole purpose of increasing the punishment which could be imposed upon appellee. The Court of Appeals observed that each of these defenses was recognized under the Uniform Code of Military Justice, but had been resolved against appellee on a factual basis by the court-martial which convicted him. The court went on to say that:

"In isolation, these factual determinations adverse to appellant under an admittedly valid article are not of constitutional significance and resultantly, are beyond our scope of review." 478 F.2d, at 797.

See *Whelchel v. McDonald*, 340 U.S. 122 (1950). We agree with the Court of Appeals.

Reversed.

The Supreme Court's holding in *Parker v. Levy* firmly establishes the constitutionality of Article 133. Although vagueness was a significant issue in the case, the Court concluded that Captain Levy was on sufficient notice that his conduct was improper. The MCM provides the following specific examples of unbecoming conduct:

(1) Knowingly making a false official statement;

(2) Dishonorable failure to pay a debt;

(3) Cheating on an exam;

(4) Opening and reading a letter of another without authority;

(5) Using insulting or defamatory language to another officer in that officer's presence or about that officer to other military persons;

(6) Being drunk and disorderly in a public place;

(7) Public association with known prostitutes;

(8) Committing or attempting to commit a crime involving moral turpitude; and

(9) Failing without good cause to support the officer's family.

Outside of these specific examples, how can an officer know if his or her conduct violates Article 133? The following case considers this issue.

United States, Appellee, v. Donato J. Guaglione, First Lieutenant, U.S. Army, Appellant.
United States Court of Military Appeals
27 M.J. 268
November 16, 1988

OPINION: Everett, Chief Judge

Contrary to his pleas, First Lieutenant Guaglione was convicted by a general court-martial of one specification of wrongful use of marijuana, and three specifications of conduct unbecoming an officer—namely, by fraternizing with enlisted soldiers during a visit to a house of prostitution, by allowing enlisted men to use hashish in his presence, and by himself using hashish in the presence of enlisted men, in violation of Articles 112a and 133, Uniform Code of Military Justice, 10 USC @@ 912a and 933, respectively. The members sentenced appellant to be dismissed from the Army; and the convening authority approved this sentence.

The Court of Military Review concluded that the specification alleging wrongful use of marijuana was necessarily included in that which alleged use of marijuana in the presence of enlisted men. Therefore, it set aside the findings of guilty to the former and dismissed the Article 112a charge and its specification. The remaining findings and the sentence were affirmed.

We granted appellant's petition to consider these issues:

I

WHETHER THE EVIDENCE IS SUFFICIENT AS A MATTER OF LAW TO SUPPORT A FINDING OF GUILTY

TO SPECIFICATION 1 OF CHARGE II (CONDUCT UNBECOMING AN OFFICER).

. . . .

I

This case had its beginnings in the late summer of 1984 at Bad Hersfeld, Federal Republic of Germany, when appellant's unit formed a softball team. The team included Guaglione, a number of other officers, a warrant officer, and several enlisted soldiers. Among the enlisted members were Privates First Class Kennedy, Diaz, and Sawyer. Despite the natural closeness engendered by such activity, proper military courtesy was observed; and the junior members of the team referred to appellant as "Lieutenant G." Neither Kennedy, Diaz, nor Sawyer was directly subordinate to appellant.

In September of that year the team entered a tournament sponsored by the unit's parent command. This contest was held in Darmstadt, some distance from their assigned installation. After the team had been eliminated on September 6, the members arranged car pools among themselves for the return trip to Bad Hersfeld; and Kennedy, Diaz, and Sawyer rode back with Lieutenant Guaglione. En route, the passengers bought and consumed an alcoholic beverage. Guaglione did not partake thereof—presumably because he was driving.

The parties stopped in Frankfurt for food. After consuming hamburgers at a fast-food outlet, they decided to visit the nearby "red light district." The houses of prostitution in this area were legal; and one witness at the trial described them as being "a tourist attraction." There was no evidence that the area had been declared off-limits by any military commander.

The four men remained for about an hour. During this period, Kennedy and Diaz partook of the services available, and Sawyer purchased some hashish. Guaglione entered two of the houses of prostitution; but, while there, he did nothing more than look and comment on the physical charms of the hostesses. After the visit to the brothels, the journey to Bad Hersfeld resumed.

. . . .

Testifying in his own behalf, Guaglione denied any criminal misconduct, although he admitted visiting the houses of prostitution. This visit he attributed to his own "personal curiosity," that is, "[t]o to see what those houses looked like, what was there, what was available." In this connection, he asserted that, although his enlisted passengers had been in the "red-light district" before, he had never before seen "legalized prostitution." Guaglione asserted that he had not allowed the soldiers to smoke marijuana or to visit his quarters. Although he admitted to preservice experimentation with marijuana while in high school and due to peer pressure, he denied use of the substance on September 6, 1984. Guaglione's defense attorneys presented evidence of his excellent military character and Sawyer's lack of credibility.

Appellant's battery and battalion commanders testified that his conduct in visiting the houses of prostitution had displayed "poor judgment" but had not demeaned him as an officer. The battalion commander, Lieutenant Colonel Leverett, an officer of some 23 years' military service, refused to describe appellant's conduct as "unbecoming" despite trial counsel's repeated attempts to so characterize it during cross-examination. Also, the former first sergeant of the battery to which Guaglione was assigned testified that, on the basis of his own experience and knowledge of the customs and standards of the Army, appellant's act was only "[p]oor judgment." This witness had served in the Army for 27 years at the time of trial.

The Government's only rebuttal witness was the brigade commander, Colonel A. W. Schulz. Testifying in response to a hypothetical question based on the facts of this case, he stated on direct examination, "I do not believe the conduct is acceptable." When asked whether the visit to the house of prostitution "rises to the level . . . that would disgrace him as an officer," he responded, "I think it comes very close. It might be very, very poor judgment and it is [sic] certainly borderlines on conduct unbecoming."

II

The first specification alleges unbecoming conduct, in that Guaglione was "fraternizing with Private First Class Thomas A. Sawyer, Private First Class Michael M. Diaz, and Private First Class Kevin N. Kennedy, while visiting an establishment known for prostitution activities, on terms of military equality . . ." To prove that appellant violated Article 133, the Government was required to show not only that Guaglione had visited the brothels with the three enlisted members but also "[t]hat, under the circumstances [this] . . . constituted conduct unbecoming an officer and gentleman." Para. 59b(2), Part IV, Manual, *supra*.

According to Colonel Winthrop, unbecoming conduct was that which not only disgraced the accused personally but seriously compromised his standing as an officer. W. Winthrop, Military Law and

Precedents 713 (2d ed. 1920 Reprint). The most recent edition of the Manual for Courts-Martial has adopted this formulation almost without change. Para. 59c(2), Manual, *supra. See* also J. Snedeker, Military Justice Under the Uniform Code 889 (1953); G. Davis, A Treatise or the Military Law of the United States 470 (1913).

In determining whether Guaglione's visit to the house of prostitution constituted such conduct, we accept the premise that a commissioned officer may be held to a higher standard of accountability for his conduct than an enlisted member or a civilian. [citations omitted]. However, not every delict or misstep warrants punishment under Article 133. In general, it must be so disgraceful as to render an officer unfit for service. [citations omitted]. This requirement for conviction is consistent with the mandatory dismissal of an officer that was prescribed by the Articles of War (AW) for unbecoming conduct. *See* AW 95 (1916); AW 61 (1874); AW 83 (1806); *see* also para. 457, Naval Courts and Boards, 1937, at 237.

There is no evidence that Guaglione participated in any sexual activity while in the Frankfurt "red-light district" or that he encouraged any of the enlisted members to do so. They already were familiar with this district, while Guaglione had never seen "legalized prostitution" before. There is also no evidence that, while they were in the houses of prostitution, any of the three soldiers addressed Guaglione in any familiar way, failed to show him military courtesy, or committed a breach of military decorum. Moreover, no American commander had attempted to prohibit American service members from entering these brothels by declaring them off-limits; and they were lawful under German law.

Among the examples of unbecoming conduct listed in the Manual for Courts-Martial is "public association with known prostitutes." Para. 59c(3), Manual, *supra. Cf. United States v. Hooper,* 9 U.S.C.M.A. 637, 646-47, 26 C.M.R. 417, 426-27 (1958) (specification alleging that retired rear admiral had "publicly associate[d] with persons known to be sexual deviates, to the disgrace of the armed forces" held sufficient under Article 133).[1] Moreover, in one case, the Army Board of Review affirmed the conviction of an officer who visited a house of prostitution, *United States v. Rice,* 14 C.M.R. 316, *pet. denied,* 4 U.S.C.M.A. 725, 15 C.M.R. 431 (1954).

We do not conclude, however, that "public association" within the contemplation of the Manual occurs when a young officer not in uniform merely walks through a German "red-light district" or even enters a house of prostitution. For one thing, "public" denotes something that is open or generally known, *see* Webster's Ninth New Collegiate Dictionary 952 (Merriam Webster 1988); and Guaglione's activity in Frankfurt on September 6 was not either generally known at the outset or intended to be generally known. More importantly, we do not believe that ogling the wares in a brothel constitutes "association"; instead, the contact must be physical or, if not physical, must be continued over a substantial period of time.

We recognize that an officer's conduct may be "unbecoming" for purposes of Article 133 even though it is private and even though it may not violate some other punitive article. *United States v. Norvell,* 26 M.J. 477 (C.M.A. 1988). However, the disgraceful aspect of the "association with known prostitutes" is apparently that it is "public" and so represents an open flouting of com-

---

[1] *See* also *Hooper v. Laird,* 19 U.S.C.M.A. 329, 41 C.M.R. 329 (1970); *Hooper v. United States,* 164 Ct.Cl. 151, 326 F.2d 982, *cert. denied,* 377 U.S. 977, 84 S. Ct. 1882, 12 L. Ed. 2d 746 (1964); *Hooper v. Hartman,* 163 F. Supp. 437 (S.D.Cal.1958), *aff'd,* 274 F.2d 429 (9th Cir.1959).

munity morals. Here, Guaglione's conduct was quite lawful insofar as the local community was concerned.

The *Rice* decision is distinguishable. There, the accused was charged with entering the house of prostitution in the company of enlisted men for the purpose of engaging in sexual intercourse. The evidence showed that his entire purpose in making the expedition of that evening was to purchase sex. Moreover, the house of ill fame was in an area which was clearly marked as being off-limits and had been so designated by a general officer.

Despite the high standards of accountability to which an officer is held, it still is necessary that, through custom, regulation, or otherwise, he be given notice that his conduct is unbecoming. [citations omitted]. In this connection, we recognize that participation on an athletic team tends to be an equalizer and that the members of the team tend to evaluate one another in terms of athletic ability rather than military rank. When officers and enlisted members play on the same team, it is inevitable that some relaxation of usual military decorum will occur and that there will be some modification of ordinary military relationships. Obviously, military authorities have come to the conclusion that, whatever the disadvantage of this relaxation may be, there are many offsetting advantages; and we are well aware that many military units have teams on which both officers and enlisted persons participate. The camaraderie that results under these circumstances must be taken into account in determining whether unlawful "fraternization" has occurred in violation of service custom.

With this in mind, we cannot ignore the testimony of Guaglione's own battery commander and battalion commander—persons from whom he would be expected to receive guidance as to his military responsibilities—that his conduct constituted no more than "poor judgment." Likewise, the first sergeant, with extensive military experience, was unwilling to characterize appellant's conduct as unbecoming. The testimony even of Colonel Schultz, appellant's brigade commander, who was a rebuttal witness, is so equivocal as to undermine the Government's position.

We conclude that the Government has failed to show that Guaglione had been given the requisite notice that his conduct would be considered "unbecoming." *Cf. United States v. Johanns, supra.* Accordingly, appellant's conviction under specification 1 of Charge II for fraternizing in violation of Article 133 cannot stand.

STUDY QUESTIONS

Boatswain's Mate Third Class (BM3) Daniels and Boatswain's Mate Seaman (BMSN) Beam both were authorized liberty from 1630, 17 Feb (Friday) through 0730 20 Feb (Monday), and they had plans to meet after Liberty Call before going out for the weekend. At about 1200 on Friday, Daniels decided that he had better things to do than to stay on board USS BERT berthed at Naval Station, San Diego; therefore, he left the ship at 1200 and went to their favorite off-base club. Beam waited until Liberty Call to leave the ship and showed up at the club at 1700. The guys were having a great time until Beam was arrested by the San Diego police at 2100, 18 Feb (Saturday night) for DUI. The San Diego police notified the BERT at 2200, 18 Feb of Beams's whereabouts. Beam was put in jail and remained there until he plead guilty to the DUI on 21 Feb (Tuesday). At 1600, 21 Feb the police notified the BERT that Beam was available for pickup. Daniels arrived at BERT at 0730, 20 Feb ready for a full week of work.

1. Which of the following correctly states the period of BMSN Beam's unauthorized absence?

   a. 1630, 17 Feb–0730, 20 Feb

   b. 1630, 17 Feb–2200, 18 Feb

   c. 0730, 20 Feb–1600, 21 Feb

   d. 2200, 18 Feb–1600, 21 Feb

   e. 2200, 18 Feb–0730, 20 Feb

2. Which of the following correctly states the period of BM3 Daniel's unauthorized absence?

   a. 1630, 17 Feb–0730, 20 Feb

   b. 1200, 17 Feb–2200, 18 Feb

   c. 1200, 17 Feb–1630, 17 Feb

   d. 1200, 17 Feb–0730, ~~21~~ 20 Feb

   e. He was never in an unauthorized absence status.

The USS NANTUCKET, located at Charleston, SC, was scheduled to shift berths (piers) at Naval Station Charleston at 1300, Friday, 31 Nov. BM3 Helen

Chambers was authorized liberty from 1630, 31 Nov until 0730 3 Dec and had plans to go to Atlanta for the weekend. At 1200 on Friday, 31 Nov, BM3 Chambers intentionally left the ship early to avoid the mundane tasks associated with shifting berths and headed for Atlanta.Unbeknownst to BM3 Chambers, the ship's XO came over the 1MC (ship's public address system) at 1500 and announced to all hands that the NANTUCKET would be getting underway on Monday, 3 Dec 93 at 0800 for a three day training exercise. BM3 Chambers, who was having a great weekend in Atlanta, had every intention of returning by quarters at 0700 on Monday morning but was caught by a severe, unexpected ice storm that developed in Atlanta late Sunday afternoon. Despite her best efforts, she was not able to get back to Naval Station Charleston until 1600 on Monday, 3 Dec. Upon her arrival at the pier, she was surprised to find the NANTUCKET gone. BM3 Chambers immediately reported into the Squadron Duty Office.

3. Which of the following offenses did BM3 Chambers commit by leaving the NANTUCKET at 1200 on 31 Nov?

   a. Unauthorized Absence From Unit or Organization, Art 86, UCMJ

   b. Missing Movement Through Design, Art 87, UCMJ

   c. Missing Movement Through Neglect, Art 87, UCMJ

   d. Both (a) and (b) above

   e. None of the above

4. Which of the following correctly states the period of BM3 Chambers' unauthorized absence?

   a. 1200 31 Nov–1630 31 Nov

   b. 1630 31 Nov–1600 3 Dec

   c. 0700 3 Dec–1600 3 Dec

   d. 1200 31 Nov–0700 3 Dec

   e. 1200 31 Nov–1600 3 Dec

5. What factors will tend to prove the crime of desertion?

6. Which of the following is *TRUE* regarding the case of *United States v. Riofredo*?

    a. LCPL Riofredo successfully asserted the defense of impossibility.

    b. LCPL Riofredo successfully asserted the defense of mistake of fact.

    c. LCPL Riofredo unsuccessfully asserted the defense of duress.

    d. LCPL Riofredo unsuccessfully asserted the defense of impossibility.

    e. None of the above are true.

Per U.S. Navy Uniform Regulations, ADM Jackson, Commander in Chief, U.S. Naval Forces, Europe (CINCUSNAVEUR)is a prescribing authority for uniform policy within the CINCUSNAVEUR area of responsibility. As a prescribing authority, ADM Jackson has the authority to decide whether male sailors can wear earrings or nose-rings off base while on liberty in the CINCUSNAVEUR area of responsibility. Pursuant to this authority, he signed and issued the following:

a. The wearing of earrings or nose-rings by male personnel in the naval service within the CINCUSNAVEUR area of responsibility is strictly prohibited. Male personnel are prohibited from wearing earrings and nose-rings while on duty or while on leave or liberty. This prohibition applies irrespective of whether a member is in military or civilian attire.

b. Violations of this directive may result in administrative or punitive action.

USS NASHVILLE was in port in Holy Loch, Scotland. While on liberty out in town, Operations Specialist First Class (OS1) Brooks, a crewmember of the NASHVILLE, decided to wear his favorite set of gold earrings and a subtle (but stylish) silver and turquoise nose-ring. OS1 Brooks was aware of the prohibition on wearing earrings in European foreign ports but had no idea that nose-rings were not allowed.

7. Based on the above facts, which orders offenses, if any, did OS1 Brooks commit by wearing the earrings and nose-ring?

The Commanding Officer of the USS NASHVILLE, CDR Travis, USN (an O-5), had also promulgated his own written instruction on the subject. This order, NASHVILLEINST 5100.2A, dated 1 January 1995, also prohibited the wearing of earrings or nose-rings while on liberty in foreign ports, and applied to all service members attached to or embarked on the NASHVILLE. The instruction clearly stated that violations were punishable under the UCMJ. Shortly before the current deployment, CDR Travis included the provisions of NASHVILLE-INST 5100.2A in several consecutive issues of the ship's plan of the day (POD). OS1 Brooks had been on leave immediately before the deployment and was unaware of the new instruction.

8. Which of the following statements is **TRUE**?

    a. By violating NASHVILLEINST 5100.2A, OS1 Brooks is guilty of failure to obey an other lawful order, Art 92, UCMJ.

    b. By violating NASHVILLEINST 5100.2A, OS1 Brooks is guilty of willful disobedience of a superior commissioned officer, Art 90, UCMJ.

    c. NASHVILLEINST 5100.2A is not a lawful order since it does not serve a valid military purpose and is overly broad.

    d. Both (a) and (b).

    e. OS1 Brooks is not guilty of violating NASHVILLEINST 5100.2A because he lacked actual knowledge of the instruction.

    When OS1 Brooks returned to the Holy Loch Naval Station, he was still wearing the earrings and nose-ring. Consequently, he was confronted by the gate guard, Master at Arms Third Class (MA3) Gill, an E-3, whose duties included enforcement of proper uniform standards. MA3 Gill immediately told OS1 Brooks to remove the earrings and nose-ring. OS1 Brooks responded by screaming at MA3 Gill, "You stupid camouflaged piece of #$@%&*^$. There is no way I am taking out my earrings and nose-ring. You are a worthless !@#$%^&*!" MA3 Gill responded by asking OS1 Brooks the name of his division officer on board the NASHVILLE. OS1 Brooks responded by screaming at the top of his lungs, "His name is LTJG Strait and he is the biggest !@#$%& loser in the entire civilized world!" LTJG Strait was out in town on liberty at the time of the incident.

9. If OS1 Brooks is charged with disrespect toward a petty officer, Article 91, UCMJ, which of the following would be a **VALID** defense?

    a. His statements to MA3 Gill fit within the "purely private conversation" doctrine.

    b. OS1 Brooks is senior to MA3 Gill.

    c. The earrings and nose-ring were legal; therefore, he was legally justified in chewing out MA3 Gill.

    d. The wearing of the earrings and nose-ring was legal; therefore, MA3 Gill was not properly in the execution of his office at the time.

e. None of the above would be a valid defense.

10. If OS1 Brooks is charged with disrespect toward a superior commissioned officer, Article 89, UCMJ, which of the following would be a *VALID* defense?

   a. LTJG Strait was not present to hear the statement.

   b. His statement about LTJG Strait fits within the "purely private conversation" doctrine.

   c. He did not intend the statement to be disrespectful.

   d. LTJG Strait was on liberty and not in the execution of his office when the statement was made.

   e. None of the above would be a valid defense.

11. What are the differences between the charges of disrespect towards a superior commissioned officer, Article 89, and disrespect towards a petty officer (ART 91).

   Boatswain's Mate Chief (BMC) Biggins, USN, was the Leading Chief Petty Officer for the deck division on board the USS SANDPIPER, underway in the Pacific. While inspecting the division berthing spaces one morning, he discovered three marijuana cigarettes on Boatswain's Mate Seaman Apprentice (BMSA) Hackett's rack. BMSA Hackett had purchased the marijuana cigarettes from Machinist's Mate Third Class (MM3) Mather the night before on the fantail of the SANDPIPER. The marijuana had come from MM3 Mather's marijuana farm in the backyard of his off-base apartment. Prior to the deployment, MM3 Mather brought a large amount of marijuana on board the SANDPIPER for himself and any of his shipmates who might want to buy some for their own use. BMC Biggins picked up the three marijuana cigarettes and turned them over to the Master-at-Arms (MAA).

12. Based on the above scenario, which of the offenses did BMSA Hackett commit?

13. Based on the above scenario, which of the offenses did MM3 Mather commit?

14. If BMC Biggins is charged with wrongful possession of marijuana, Article 112a, UCMJ, which of the following statements would be *TRUE*?

   a. He is guilty since he knew the substance was marijuana.

   b. He is guilty since he knew he was in possession of marijuana.

c. His is not guilty since he took possession of the marijuana in the course of his official duties; such possession is not wrongful.

d. He is guilty since he should not have picked up the marijuana cigarettes in the first place. He should have left them on BMSA Hackett's rack while he went to search for the MAA.

e. None of the above.

15. All of the following are examples of Conduct Unbecoming an Officer and Gentleman, Article 133, UCMJ, *EXCEPT*:

a. An Army First Lieutenant tutors a fellow lieutenant in platoon leadership at the request of his battery commander, but charges the lieutenant over $2,000 for the professional "extra instruction" sessions.

b. A female Ensign requests the assistance of her enlisted subordinates in getting dates with a male Petty Officer.

c. An Army First Lieutenant is a member of his unit's softball team that includes several enlisted soldiers.

d. A midshipman at the Naval Academy cheats on his electrical engineering exam.

e. A Navy Lieutenant is drunk and disorderly at the annual Tailhook convention at the Las Vegas Hilton hotel.

16. OPNAVINST 5370.2A is the Navy's Fraternization Policy. What kind of order is the instruction? Describe the relationships it prohibits.

CHAPTER VI

GOVERNMENT ETHICS

Ethical government means much more than laws. It is a spirit, an imbued code of conduct, an ethos. . . . Laws and rules can never be fully descriptive of what an ethical person should do. . . . Compulsion by law is the most expensive way to make people behave.

President's Commission on Federal Ethics Law Reform,
To Serve with Honor, 1 (1989).

INTRODUCTION

As the above quotation implies, government ethics laws seek to compel government employees, both civilians and members of the armed forces, to behave ethically. Some have suggested, as is also implied above, that law alone, in the absence of a sense of personal honor, cannot effectively and efficiently promote and ensure ethical conduct. Conversely, for those who possess such a sense, ethics laws become superfluous—such people behave ethically without regard to the compulsion of law. Perhaps a better view is that law reinforces honor, and honor empowers the law, so that each gives force and power to the other, thus better inducing the ethical behavior required by both. Whatever is true, however—whether ethics laws are superfluous, ineffective, empowering, or simply necessary to ensure public trust and confidence in government—they exist, and are important to the naval officer in that he or she must comply with them and ensure that his or her subordinates do the same.

The rules in this area are sophisticated and complex, and sometimes counter-intuitive even for those with a strong sense of honor. To comply with ethics rules requires knowledge and understanding of the laws and regulations, and a feel for when to check the rule book before taking an action that may turn out to be inappropriate or even illegal. To begin the process of acquiring this required knowledge and understanding, this chapter traces the development of laws regulating conduct of government employees and discusses the purposes behind them. The discussion then focuses on the contemporary law of government ethics, and reviews those laws and derivative regulations of frequent concern to naval personnel.

DEVELOPMENT OF ETHICS LAWS

Corruption in American government has existed since the establishment of the United States, and, as a consequence, attempts to limit the conduct of government employees have also existed since that time.[1] In the nineteenth century, extensive bribery and graft provoked the enactment of criminal laws addressing such abuses, particularly in the area of procurement fraud. Surprisingly, however, these statutes are not the primary source of contemporary government ethics laws, which focus on preventing conflicts of interest.[2] Contemporary ethics law was born out of a desire to curb the use of public office for private gain. Professor A. Allen King explains in *Symposium Ethics in Government: Ethics in Government and the Vision of Public Service*, 58 Geo. Wash. L. Rev. 417, 419 (1990) [footnotes deleted].

> Corruption has accompanied American political life from the founding of the Constitution. For example, Jefferson's Postmaster General lobbied openly for the advancement of land companies in which the Postmaster had invested. Moreover, the spoils system defined public employment in terms of patronage, where obligations to political patrons replaced other loyalties, and rebates of salary and requirements of personal service were commonly perceived as conditions of employment. Following the Civil War, the buying and selling of offices was commonplace, and the purchasers often used these offices for personal gain. Corruption served as one of the period's motifs.
>
> Bribery and graft, the crudest forms of corruption, provoked the enactment of criminal penalties and criminal statutes addressing these derelictions and specific abuses of governmental authority, particularly involving procurement, in the mid-nineteenth century preceding and following the Civil War. The regulation of ethics in government, however—controlling conflicts of interest, as opposed to graft and bribery—is linked historically and conceptually to the civil service reform movement of the late nineteenth century and to the Civil Service Act of 1883. . . .
>
> The spoils system invited, if not required, personal corruption, and placed the powers of government in the hands of persons who used and manipulated that power for their own gain. In addition, the lack of ethical principles in government permitted unfair and inequitable application of the laws, and subjected citizens to not only inefficient but abusive government as well. . . .
>
> [T]he reform movement sought to create politically neutral public employees by emphasizing competence and professionalism. . . . [it desired public employees to

---

[1]58 Geo. Wash. L. Rev. 417, 419(1990).

[2]58 Geo. Wash. L. Rev. at 420.

be] able to perform their jobs free of requirements to support political officials and free of pressures to base government decisions on personal or partisan motives.

The reform movement required a personal morality for public employees. These employees, freed from corrupting influences, had to exercise personal restraint and be honest and fair. Ethical guidance, however, did not extend beyond these general ideas. The reform movement's preoccupation with removing the sources of political corruption admonished the employee principally to administer the service for the public good, rather than the private or individual one.

[T]his vision of politically neutral public employees conditioned the development of public service ethics and provided the context and premises upon which ethics regulation relied. It established the premise that an employee was an agent for broadly defined public interests; it created special responsibilities; and it emphasized the importance of public employment, creating a moral calling for public service.

. . . .

The moral calling of public employment depended upon service of not one group or position, but of the broader public interest. This obligation required the subordination of one's personal interests, perceptions, and biases to recognize that one was working on behalf of others, serving the public. This obligation required self-restraint; it emphasized the morality of role.

Thus, regulation of ethics in government since the passage of the Civil Service Act of 1883 has been premised on the concept of "public service" by politically neutral employees, who do not have private interests conflicting with their obligations of public service. In the early 1960's, new statutes addressed conflicts of interest in three important areas: (1) conflicting financial interests; (2) outside compensation; and (3) post-government service employment. In 1965, Congress delegated extensive authority to federal agencies to issue and enforce comprehensive ethics regulations. Consequently, from 1965 to 1993, federal employees (including military personnel) were governed to a large extent by their agency's own rules relating to ethics and standards of conduct. Thus, the Department of the Navy had its own standards of ethical conduct contained in an instruction issued by the Secretary of the Navy (the SECNAVINST 5370.2 series). In 1978, Congress again modified existing ethics statutes, and added new ethics laws by the Government Ethics Act of 1978. Each agency, however, retained authority to create its own ethics regulations within the statutory framework. In 1989, at least in part motivated by unethical conduct associated with the Iran-Contra affair, President George Bush established a commission to study federal ethics law. This commission recommended a single set of standards for all executive branch employees (including military personnel). In 1992, the Office of Government Ethics (OGE) made this recommendation reality by issuing the *Standards of Ethical Conduct for Employees of the Executive Branch,* which became effective in February 1993. Pursuant to the *OGE Standards of Ethical Conduct*, the Department of Defense issued the *Department of Defense Joint Ethics Regulation 5500.7R (JER)* to supplement the OGE regulation. This instruction superseded the Navy's Ethics instruction, SECNAVINST 5370.2J. The OGE and DOD regulations will be discussed below in further detail.

In the last decade, public awareness regarding government ethics has heightened significantly because of several high profile cases, the most notable of which are the cases arising out of the Iran-Contra investigation in 1985-86. Before you study particular standards of conduct, consider the following facts. Do you think Lieutenant Colonel North acted unethically? Illegally? Does it matter which?

United States of America v. Oliver S. North
United States District Court for the District of Columbia
713 F. Supp. 1448 (D. D.C. 1989)

. . . .

The Government has introduced substantial evidence in this case from which a reasonable jury could—and, in the Government's view, should find that Oliver North accepted or agreed to receive the gratuity at issue in Count Ten.

FACTUAL BACKGROUND

The evidence shows that, by May, 1986, defendant North had spent the prior 18 months or more in his secret effort "to keep the Contras together body and soul." [citations omitted]. Although he accomplished this goal in a number of different ways, a key part of North's project was to direct the opening up of a Southern front in Nicaragua with the assistance of Richard Secord and his organization acting under North's direction. [citations omitted]. In 1986, North expanded the operation by enlisting Secord to assist with the Iran initiative.

The North-Secord relationship, which is the crux of the charge in Count Ten, thus had its locus in North's position as NSC staff member in Washington, D.C.

It was through this position that North directed both Contra-related and Iran-related business to [Army General (ret.) Richard] Secord, and North's continued employment at the NSC was essential to the continuation of Secord's involvement in these projects. . . . In late April, 1986, Secord told Glenn Robinette, a security consultant whose office is in Washington, that North and his family had been the object of threats, . . . [citations omitted]. He solicited Robinette's assistance to "give some support" to North in this connection. [citation omitted]. On April 30, 1986, Robinette went to the North household, met Mrs. North, and walked through the North home to determine what "could be used" to provide the family with increased security. [citation omitted]. Robinette then "contacted several security equipment suppliers" to determine what equipment was available and how much it would cost. [citation omitted]. Although there is no direct testimony that North knew about Robinette's visit, a jury could reasonably find—especially in light of North's professed concern about the security of his household—that North knew of Robinette's intended visit and approved it in advance.

On May 5, 1986, North, Secord, and Robinette met in North's office at the OEOB in Washington, D.C. [citation omitted]. Robinette at this time had completed his "preliminary review" and "was prepared to discuss what [Robinette] thought should be done" with respect to a security system. [citation omitted]. Robinette told North that he wanted to install a security system to "frighten away or scare any intruders or people coming to the home." [citation omitted]. At the end of the meeting, North "seemed to accept what [Robinette] told him as a preliminary plan, equipment and plans and procedures." [citation omitted].

North said "something to [the] effect" of "go ahead and keep working on it." [citation omitted]. Robinette accordingly continued his work on the system, and was recompensed for his time by Secord. On May 10, there was another meeting at which more specific plans were discussed, and the security system—paid for entirely by Secord [using his own private, non-government funds]—was installed [at North's private home] the following month.

. . . .

Secord was also charged with a federal crime. The former general was charged with conspiracy to give and with giving a gratuity to a government official. In discussing Secord's case, the Federal District Court for the District of Columbia noted that the relevant federal law concerning giving and receiving gratuities concerned, among other things, the issue of whether Secord gave official things of value because of the official position held by Lieutenant Colonel North. *See United States v. Secord*, 726 F. Supp. 845 (D. D.C. 1989).

Look at the federal law excerpted below, Title 18 United States Code section 201 (1994). Does this affect your thinking as to whether Lieutenant Colonel North acted unethically, illegally or both?

201. Bribery of public officials and witnesses. . . .

(b) Whoever . . .

    (2) being a public official . . . directly or indirectly, corruptly demands, seeks, receives, accepts, or agrees to receive or accept anything of value personally or for any other person or entity, in return for:

    (A) being influenced in the performance of any official act; . . .

(c) Whoever . . .

    (1) otherwise than as provided by law for the proper discharge of official duty . . .

    (B) being a public official, . . ., otherwise than as provided by law for the proper discharge of official duty, directly or indirectly demands, seeks, receives, accepts, or agrees to receive or accept anything of value personally for or because of any official act performed or to be performed by such official or person; . . .

shall be fined under this title or imprisoned for not more than two years, or both.

In analyzing how the above excerpts from section 201 of Title 18 applies to the *North* facts described above, it might be helpful to consider the reason for the rule. According to the United States Court of Appeals for the Fifth Circuit, one purpose of section 201 is to reach any situation in which the judgment of a government agent might be clouded because of payments or gifts made to him by reason of his position, because even if corruption is not intended by either party, there may remain a tendency in such a situation for the government agent to provide conscious or unconscious preferential treatment to the gift giver, and so result in inefficient management of public affairs. *See United States v. Evans* 572 F.2d 455 (5th Cir. 1978). Would, or could, the gift of the security fence to Lieutenant Colonel North from General (ret.) Secord have clouded Lieutenant Colonel North's judgment such that he might have provided General (ret.) Secord's private business venture preferential treatment over competing private businesses seeking to do business with the government? Is there a potential appearance of impropriety, such that the public confidence in honest and fair government might be affected?

PURPOSE OF ETHICS LAWS

The above section discussed how ethics regulations developed out of concern over abuses by government employees motivated by conflicting private and public obligations, and how such abuses impaired government function. Professor King states the following in this regard:

> Corruption and conflict of interest violations undercut public confidence in government because they indicate a bureaucracy out of control and raise the specter that public employees will use the power of government for their own purposes. Abuse of power and abuse of the public can follow closely upon one another. Therefore, bureaucracies have an interest in controlling and regulating corruption and conflicts of interest. If members of the bureaucracy cannot show self-restraint, other methods of control must be sought. 58 Geo. L. Rev. at 432.

Professor King argues that the moral force implicit in the concept of public service as a public trust has diminished in the last twenty years, and warns against the use of laws to make up for this loss of moral force. He argues this point as follows:

> Too great a reliance on legal regulation can have side effects, like a drug too frequently used. By converting ethical problems into legal ones, the law becomes the sole judge of propriety. What can be done becomes what should be done. If what is legal continues to seem improper, additional conduct is made illegal, reinforcing the perception that what is legal constitutes what is proper. Soon ethics has limited significance apart from legal command and enforcement structures and sanctions become increasingly important. 58 Geo. L. Rev. at 432-33.

Do you agree with Professor's King's contention that the public service vision—that is, a moral or ethical code requiring public servants to act for the public good, rather than for their own—has lost importance as the motivator of government employees to act ethically? What about the notion that the legal regulation of ethics actually damages the promotion of ethics in government? Consider the following statement of Navy Inspector General Vice Admiral Bennett:

> We have so many obscure and confusing directives that most of us are in violation of something most of the time. I'm not suggesting ignoring directives in our daily professional lives. A good approach is to ask ourselves: What are we really trying to do; what is the most efficient way to accomplish the task; what, if anything, do I need to change; whose endorsement or permission do I need; how do I explain it to my troops and my boss. Most of our tasks are relatively simple when reduced to their essence. The common sense approach almost always works. Living in fear of making an honest mistake or of being criticized is not why any of us was hired. Our fear should be that we won't have the courage of our convictions, won't be worthy of the trust of those we lead or won't be ready when we are needed. [quoted from *Surface Sitrep, Vol X, No. 4, August/September 1994*, a publication of the Surface Navy Association]

SOURCES AND ENFORCEMENT OF CURRENT ETHICS LAWS AND REGULATIONS

As discussed above, there are several sources of ethics rules, including federal criminal statutes and regulations issued by the OGE and DOD.

Title 18 of the United States Code contains several statutes pertaining to bribery, corruption and conflicts of interest. As stated by the Federal District Court for the Northern District of California, the purpose of these statutes (Title 18 United States Code sections 201 through 208) is to protect the government from corruption and self-interested financial dealing, and their function is to protect the public from corrupting influences that might be brought to bear upon government agents who are financially interested in business transactions which they are conducting on behalf of government. *San Francisco v. United States* 443 F. Supp 1116 (N.D. Cal. 1977) *aff'd* (9th Cir. 1980) 615 F.2d 498. For example, as to bribery, 18 United States Code section 201(b) (discussed above with respect to the *North* case) provides:

> [E]mployees are prohibited from, directly or indirectly, giving, offering, promising, demanding, seeking, receiving, accepting, or agreeing to receive anything of value to influence any official act, to influence commission of fraud

on the United States, to induce committing or omitting any act in violation of a lawful duty. . . .

With regard to conflicts of interest, Section 208 of Title 18 prohibits executive branch and independent agency officers and employees from substantially, personally and officially participating in any governmental activity in which they know that they have a private financial interest. This is not a new concept. For example, a 1942 Opinion of the Attorney General of the United States held that an Army officer should not have been assigned to maintain liaison with private corporation of which he was officer and stockholder, because a person whose duty it was to serve the public should not have been put into position where he could also serve his selfish interests. 40 Op Atty. Gen. 168 (1942).

The criminal statutes contained in Title 18 are independent of agency regulations, and create criminal penalties under federal law for their violation.

The *Standards of Ethical Conduct* issued by OGE in 1993 is a comprehensive agency ethics regulation applicable to all employees of the executive branch, including military officers. It incorporates the criminal conflict of interest statutes of Title 18 (such as the one quoted above) and sets forth numerous other standards of conduct. It also requires government agencies to "initiate appropriate disciplinary or corrective action in individual cases," and authorizes federal agencies, such as DOD, to issue regulations supplementing its provisions, as well. Pursuant to this authorization, DOD issued the *Joint Ethics Regulation* (JER) to supplement the OGE regulation in 1994. The JER explains and amplifies the OGE *Standards of Ethical Conduct*, as well as the criminal statutes in Title 18. It provides a single source of standards of ethical conduct and ethics guidance for DOD personnel. The JER applies to all civilian employees and military personnel, including officers and midshipmen, and makes the OGE *Standards of Ethical Conduct* applicable to enlisted personnel, as well. It covers such activities as gifts (giving and receiving), conflicts of interest, impartiality in performing duties, outside activities and employment, misuse of position, travel, gambling, political activities, honoraria and post-government service employment.

The JER is a lawful general order. Failure to obey the rules prescribed by the JER is, therefore, a violation of Article 92, UCMJ. *See* Chapter V. As with all general orders, ignorance of the regulation is not a valid defense. Violations of the JER may be punished at court-martial or by nonjudicial punishment, or be addressed through nonpunitive measures (e.g., nonpunitive letters of caution or letters of instruction). *See* Chapter IV. As noted above, an ethics violation may subject the violator to separate federal criminal or civil sanctions as provided in the particular statute involved, as well.

Are there other UCMJ articles under which a military member be prosecuted for an ethics violation? (*See* Chapter V and *United States v. Robinson* below).

CURRENT ETHICS RULES

GENERAL PRINCIPLES AND STANDARDS

There are a host of ethics rules that apply to military members. Although it is improbable that a member will know all of these rules, it is essential that they be aware of certain standards. The basic, or fundamental principles from which the more specific rules are derived, are of special importance. If a member understands and applies these general ethical principles, it reduces the chances of unknowingly violating some more technical rule. The following regulation from the OGE *Standards of Ethical Conduct* lays out the fourteen fundamental tenets of ethical conduct.

Section 2635.101 Basic obligation of public service.

(a) Public service is a public trust. Each employee has a responsibility to the United States Government and its citizens to place loyalty to the Constitution, laws and ethical principles above private gain. To ensure that every citizen can have complete confidence in the integrity of the Federal Government, each employee shall respect and adhere to the principles of ethical conduct set forth in this section, as well as the implementing standards contained in this part and in supplemental agency regulations.

(b) General principles. The following general principles apply to every employee and may form the basis for the standards contained in this part. Where a situation is not covered by the standards set forth in this part, employees shall apply the principles set forth in this section and determining whether their conduct is proper.

    (1) Public service is a public trust, requiring employees to place loyalty to the constitution, the laws and ethical principles above private gain.

    (2) Employees shall not hold financial interests that conflict with the conscientious performance of duty.

    (3) Employees shall not engage in financial transactions using nonpublic Government information or allow the improper use of such information to further any private interest.

    (4) An employee shall not, except as permitted by subpart B of this part, solicit or accept any gift or other item of monetary value from any person or entity seeking official action from, doing business with, or conducting activities regulated by the employee's agency, or whose interests may be substantially affected by the performance or nonperformance of the employee's duties.

    (5) Employees shall put forth honest effort in the performance of their duties.

    (6) Employees shall not knowingly make unauthorized commitments or promises of any kind purporting to bind the Government.

    (7) Employees shall not use public office for private gain.

(8) Employees shall act impartially and not give preferential treatment to any private organization or individual.

(9) Employees shall protect and conserve Federal property and shall not use it for other than authorized activities.

(10) Employees shall not engage in outside employment or activities, including seeking or negotiating for employment, that conflict with official Government duties and responsibilities.

(11) Employees shall disclose waste, fraud, abuse and corruption to appropriate authorities.

(12) Employees shall satisfy in good faith their obligations as citizens, including all just financial obligations, especially those—such as Federal, State, or local taxes—that are imposed by law.

(13) Employees shall adhere to all laws and regulations that provide equal opportunity for all Americans regardless of race, color, religion, sex, national origin, age, or handicap.

(14) Employees shall endeavor to avoid any actions creating the appearance that they are violating the law or the ethical standards set forth in this part. Whether particular circumstances create an appearance that the law or these standards have been violated shall be determined from the perspective of a reasonable person with knowledge of the relevant facts.

Query whether the above rules reflect the public service concept that motivated the Civil Service reform movement of the nineteenth century? Do you agree that a member who abides by the above standards will not run afoul of other more specific ethics regulations? Consider some of the more specific rules set forth below.

EXAMPLES OF SPECIFIC RULES

Gifts Between Superiors and Subordinates

As with the rest of society, military members commonly exchange gifts. Ethical problems arise when the giving or receipt of a gift raises the appearance of favoritism. The OGE *Standards of Ethical Conduct* contains the following rules regarding gifts.

Section 2635.302 General standards.

(a) Gifts to superiors. Except as provided in this subpart, an employee may not:

(1) Directly or indirectly, give a gift to a or make a donation toward a gift for an official superior; or

    (2) Solicit a contribution from another employee for a gift to either his own or the other employee's official superior.

      (b) Gifts from employees receiving less pay. Except as provided in this subpart, an employee may not directly or indirectly, accept a gift from an employee receiving less pay then himself unless:

    (1) The two employees are not in a subordinate-official superior relationship; and

    (2) There is personal relationship between the two employees that would justify the gift.

      (c) Limitation on use of exceptions. Notwithstanding any exception provided in this subpart, an official superior shall not coerce the offering of a gift from a subordinate.

Consider these problems, drawn from *Dangerous Dilemmas*, a standards of conduct training game published by the Office of Government Ethics [the entire game, and answers, can be obtained via internet. Log in to *FedWorld* by typing *telnet fedworld.gov*. Choose D from the main menu, and then D again from the Gateway menu. Choose #91 from Govt sys/database. The version quoted below was downloaded in August 1994].

1. Ensign Karen Anjinsan is good friends with her department head, Lieutenant Anita Toronaga. Lieutenant Toronaga is getting married and Ensign Anjinsan has chosen a $25 wedding gift for her. Ensign Anjinsan has also been asked by her coworkers to contribute towards a group gift for the Lieutenant. The Ensign may:

    a. Choose a gift worth $10 or less for Lieutenant Toronaga but not contribute towards the group gift.

    b. Not worry about the ethics rules because the Lieutenant is a personal friend.

    c. Not give Lieutenant Toronaga a personal gift, but contribute towards the group gift.

    d. Give the $25 wedding gift. She may also contribute towards the group gift.

Answer:

In general, § 2635.302(a) prohibits employees from giving gifts to or donating towards a gift for an official superior. The $25 gift and the contribution towards a group item are defined as "gifts" by subpart C of part 2635. However, there are exceptions to the prohibition, such as weddings or other infrequent occasions of personal significance that would cover Lieutenant Toronaga's wedding. Answer "d" is the best answer, because it recognizes that Ensign Anjinsan may choose both options for the Lieutenant's gift. The Ensign may give a personal gift, and may make a voluntary nominal contribution towards an appropriate group gift. (Appropriate gifts are defined by section 2635.304(c)(1)). Answer "a" recognizes that there are limitations on gift giving between employees and their official superiors. However, only if this were a "recurring occasion" (such as Christmas or the Lieutenant's birthday), would Ensign Anjinsan be limited to a gift worth $10 or less (2635.304(a)(1). Also, remember that you cannot make voluntary contributions for gifts for such "recurring occasions." Answer "b" is wrong; unfortunately, personal friendship is not a factor when the recipient is in the employee's "chain of command."

2. The Colonel, and Battalion Commanding Officer, is retiring. His executive officer has invited all battalion officers (there are ten) and their spouses to a $25 per person dinner given in the Colonels' honor. He is collecting money to buy the shotgun that the Colonel has always wanted. The executive officer may:

  a. Tell the officers they have to contribute $30 for the shotgun and buy a $25 dinner ticket.

  b. Suggest a $30 contribution, but make it clear that the officers may contribute whatever they want. Also, collect $25 from anyone attending the dinner.

  c. Not give the shotgun, but may suggest the officers take the Colonel to a local deli for lunch.

  d. Require the officers (including those not attending the dinner) to pay at least $55 since this is a "once-in-a-lifetime" event for the Colonel.

Answer:

The executive officer may solicit voluntary contributions of *nominal* amounts for an appropriate gift for the commanding officer and may recommend a *nominal* contribution (§ 2635.304(c)). However, the recommendation must be accompanied by a statement that the officers are free to contribute less or nothing at all (§ 2635.303(f)). Answer "b" is the best answer because it recognizes that the executive officer may suggest a $30 contribution for the gift, but has to make it clear that the contribution is voluntary and the contributors may decide how much they wish to contribute. In addition, he may collect $25 from anyone freely choosing to attend the dinner (knowing the cost in advance). Answer "c" describes an acceptable "gift" under the standards of conduct, but fails to cover all of the issues. Answer "a" is wrong because it fails to recognize that the contribution was not voluntary because the amount was not determined by the contributing employee (§ 2635.303(f)). Answer "d" is wrong because it fails to recognize that the executive officer may not coerce a gift or contributions for a gift to the retiring commanding officer. The fact that this is a "once-in-a-lifetime" event for the commanding officer has no bearing on the amount the executive officer is permitted to solicit.

Misuse of Official Position

One of the most common violations of ethics rules occurs when a government employee uses his or her position or government property for personal benefit or for the benefit of relatives, friends or other private organizations.

Section 2635.702 Use of public office for private gain.

An employee shall not use his public office for his own private gain, for the endorsement of any product, service or enterprise, or for the private gain of friends, relatives, or persons with whom the employee is affiliated in a nongovernmental capacity, including nonprofit organizations of which the employee is an officer or member, and persons with whom the employee has or seeks employment or business relations. The specific prohibitions set forth in paragraphs (a) through (d) of this section apply this general standard, but are not intended to be exclusive or to limit the application of this section.

(a) Inducement of coercion of benefits. An employee shall not use or permit the use of his government position or title or any authority associated with his public office in a manner that is intended to coerce or induce another person, including a subordinate, to provide any benefit, financial or otherwise, to himself or to friends, relatives, or persons with whom the employee is affiliated in a nongovernmental capacity.

(b) Appearance of governmental sanction. Except as otherwise provided in this part, an employee shall not use or permit the use of his government position or title or any authority associated with his public office in a manner that could reasonably be construed to imply that his agency or the government sanctions or endorses his personal activities or those of another. When teaching, speaking, or writing in a personal capacity, he may refer to his official title or position only as permitted by Section 2635.807(b). He may sign a letter of recommendation using his official title only in response to a request for any employment recommendation or a character reference based upon personal knowledge of the ability or character of an individual with whom he has dealt in the course of Federal employment or whom he is recommending for Federal employment.

(c) Endorsements. An employee shall not use or permit the use of his government position or title or any authority associated with his public office to endorse any product, service or enterprise except:

   (1) In furtherance of statutory authority to promote products, services or enterprises; or

   (2) As a result of documentation of compliance with agency requirements or standards or as the result of recognition for achievement given under an agency program of recognition for accomplishment in support of the agency's mission.

(d) [omitted]

(e) Use of terms of address and ranks. Nothing in this section prohibits an employee who is ordinarily addressed using a general term of address, such as "The Honorable," or a rank, such as a military or ambassadorial rank, from using that term of address or rank in connection with a personal activity.

This rule prohibits, among other things, use of public office to obtain private "benefits," "financial or otherwise," from subordinates. Consider the following case decided by the Air Force Court of Military Review regarding the definition of what is a "benefit" under the Air Force's standards of conduct regulation.

United States v. Staff Sergeant Gordon T. Robinson, Jr., United States Air Force
United States Air Force Court of Military Review
37 M.J. 588
May 10, 1993

OPINION: Snider, Judge

Contrary to his pleas, appellant was convicted, by general court-martial, of committing an indecent assault and violating a general regulation, in violation of Articles 134 and 92, UCMJ, 10 USC 934, 992 (1988). He was sentenced to a bad-conduct discharge and reduction to E-2. He raises three assignments of error, which we resolve adversely to him and affirm.

I

Two of the claimed errors are related and involve Charge III, specification 1, which alleges a violation of *Air Force Regulation (AFR) 30-30, Standards of Conduct, paragraph 8 (May 1989).* Appellant first asserts the specification fails to state an offense. It reads as follows:

> Did . . . on divers occasions, . . . violate a lawful general regulation . . . by influencing a subordinate, Airman [K], through the use of his Air Force rank and position to enter an isolated portion of their duty section to assist and facilitate his making sexual advances toward the said Airman [K].

AFR 30-30, paragraph 8, reads as follows:

USING OFFICIAL AIR FORCE POSITION. Air Force personnel must not use their Air Force positions to induce, coerce, or influence a person (including subordinates) in any way to provide any personal benefit, financial or otherwise, to themselves or others.

Relying on the same basis as his trial defense counsel, appellant avers that acquiring the opportunity for the "sexual advances" alleged in the specification does not constitute a "personal benefit," and, therefore, no reasonable reading or interpretation of AFR 30-30 reaches the conduct of which he was convicted. As did the trial judge, we disagree with appellant's assertion.

To support his averment, appellant emphasizes the fact that *AFR 30-30* defines the term, "gratuity," but does not define "benefit." He argues that this fact reflects the drafters' intent to restrict *AFR 30-30* to commercial or financial transactions. This assertion is plainly incorrect. Paragraph 8, by its very terms, clearly addresses benefits other than those of a financial nature. Further, none of our precedents construing *AFR 30-30* suggest its reach is confined to financial or commercial situations and transactions. *See United States v. Smith,*

16 M.J. 694 (A.F.C.M.R. 1983) and cases cited therein.

The trial judge was entirely correct in applying the plain meaning of the term, "benefit," which includes "anything that is advantageous or for the good of a person or thing," as well as financial situations. *Random House College Dictionary, Rev. Ed. (1980).* Consequently, specification 1, Charge III, alleges acts which fall within the terms of the regulation's prohibition and it placed appellant on notice of what he was required to defend against. We find it states an offense under Article 92, UCMJ, 10 USC 992 (1988).

II

A brief recitation of the facts will assist in placing the next assignment of error in perspective. The facts regarding Charge III, specification 1, are not in dispute. Appellant disputed only his intent. Although not the official Noncommissioned Officer In Charge, appellant was a shift supervisor of a software maintenance complex section located at Falcon AFB, Colorado. Airman K was a female airman assigned to appellant's shift. The work area contained tall mainframe computers as well as a room in the rear portion of the work area. The common practice was that a superior conducted counselling in the rear room, while other corrective action, such as brief oral rebukes or on-the-spot corrections, were provided behind the mainframes. This practice was followed to avoid embarrassment in front of peers.

On three to six occasions during duty hours, appellant appeared in the work area and asked Airman K to step behind the mainframes so he could talk to her.

After they went behind the mainframes, appellant proceeded to hug Airman K. On these occasions, appellant did not speak to Airman K at all (as he did during actual counselling), but merely smiled and walked away after hugging her. Appellant did not order, or demand, Airman K to step behind the mainframes, but Airman K stated she instinctively assumed appellant was acting in his superior and supervisory capacity when he asked her to step back there, as well as assuming it was for an official work purpose. She never asked the purpose of appellant's requests before responding, nor did she hesitate, for she did not desire to appear insubordinate to a superior. Airman K stated that, on each occasion, she remained rigid with her arms at her side, not responding in any manner, in hopes appellant would realize his actions were unwelcomed.

Against this factual background, appellant attacks *AFR 30-30, paragraph 8,* as unconstitutionally vague, and therefore, void, as applied to him. However, although appellant couches this assignment of error in terms of unconstitutional vagueness, the essence of his brief, and arguments on this issue, is an attack on the punitiveness of *AFR 30-30* and the factual sufficiency of the evidence that he violated *AFR 30-30, paragraph 8.* We disagree with both assertions.

We first address the letter of appellant's assignment of error. *AFR 30-30, paragraph 8,* is nearly identical to its predecessor *AFR 30-30, paragraph 3a(2) (1978),* which we held was punitive and constitutional. We hold likewise with regards to paragraph 8. [citation omitted].

We now address the substance of appellant's attack on his conviction of violating *AFR 30-30,* namely, his conduct did not fall within the prohibition of paragraph 8. He argues three bases in support of his assertion: (1) this Court has ruled other provisions of *AFR 30-30* insufficiently definite and certain for punitive application, (2) his conduct more properly could have been charged under Article 93,

UCMJ, 10 USC 993 (1988) [cruelty and maltreatment] [footnote omitted], and (3) his conduct is similar to the factual situation in *Smith*, and the result in *Smith* requires setting aside appellant's conviction. Appellant's first two assertions, plainly, are insufficient reasons to vitiate his conviction. They have no impact on whether his conduct violated paragraph 8. Appellant's third assertion also falls short.

The situation addressed in *Smith* involved a lieutenant colonel (Lt. Col.) who requested subordinates, some of whom were personal friends, to drop by his office at their convenience. When they appeared, he requested a loan of money, sometimes successfully, sometimes not. The loans ranged from the nominal to substantial. *See Smith*, 16 M.J. at 702. During these events, there were times when he was the temporary commander of his unit. The majority's decision devoted significant emphasis, perhaps too much, to whether paragraph 8's predecessor prohibited a superior's borrowing from a subordinate, regardless of circumstances. *Smith*, 16 M.J. at 701-702. After an extensive discussion of the distinction between inducement, influence, and coercion, the majority concluded the Government failed to prove beyond reasonable doubt that Lt. Col. Smith used his Air Force position to influence his subordinates to loan him money.

Appellant's reliance and asserted application of *Smith* at trial and before us, although not unreasonable, are nevertheless misplaced.

First, uncertainty regarding certain legal issues existent when *Smith* was decided has been clarified. [citations omitted]. How one uses rank or position to obtain a personal benefit in violation of paragraph 8, *i.e.*, inducement, coercion, influence, or any combination thereof, is irrelevant. When testing for a violation of *AFR 30-30, paragraph 8*, the focus is on whether one uses his or her official position to obtain a personal benefit. The factfinder must apply an objective test in assessing all of the surrounding circumstances to determine if one's office was, in fact, used and, if so, whether it was used to obtain the personal benefit in question. [footnote omitted].

. . . .

The instant case is an example of the Government proving the allegations without evidence of a blatant use of rank or position, or by showing stroking or cajolery, etc. However, the evidence clearly shows appellant used his official position to acquire Airman K's presence in a secluded location for unwelcomed hugs. Given the de facto supervisory, as well as the superior-subordinate relationship between them, appellant used the force of his position when he indicated his desire to speak with Airman K. Subtly directing her behind the mainframes to effect his desire to hug her out of the view of co-workers provided him a personal benefit in violation of *AFR 30-30, paragraph 8*. [footnote omitted].

One other matter merits comment. *Department of Defense Directive (DOD Dir.) 5500.7 (May 1987)* is the means by which the Secretary of Defense directs the Departments of the Army, Navy, and Air Force, to implement various statutes and executive orders which address personal conduct and ethics. *AFR 30-30* implements DODDIR. 5500.7. As Congress has passed increasingly more legislation in those areas, the implementing regulations unavoidably have grown in length and complexity. Consequently, in view of the fact *AFR 30-30* contains advisory and hortatory provisions as well as prohibitions, perhaps the time has arrived for *AFR 30-30's* drafters to designate a separate section for all its putative punitive prohibitions, or designate a specific paragraph within each section for that purpose [footnote omitted]. Such a method probably would save considerable appellate resources. . . .

The findings and sentence are correct in law and fact, Article 66(c), UCMJ, 10 USC 866(c) (1988), and they are hereby,

AFFIRMED.

Do you agree with the court's conclusion? *Compare* the Air Force instruction with the Section 2635.702 of the OGE *Standards of Ethical Conduct.* Would the same result be reached under both sections? Note in *Robinson* that the Air Force Court of Military Review comments on the "length and complexity" of the Air Force standards of conduct instruction and suggests revision in order to clarify the "punitive" provisions. Consider the following provision in the OGE *Standards of Ethical Conduct.*

Section 2635.705 Use of official time.

(b) Use of a subordinate's time. An employee shall not encourage, direct, coerce, or request a subordinate to use official time to perform activities other than those required in the performance of official duties or authorized in accordance with law or regulation.

Could Staff Sergeant Robinson have been convicted under this provision?

Misuse of Government Property

Related to the rules concerning misuse of position is the prohibition on using government property for other than official purposes. Both derive from the prohibition against using public office for private gain.

Section 2635.704 Use of Government property.

(a) Standard. An employee has a duty to protect and conserve government property and shall not use such property, or allow its use, for other than authorized purposes.

(b) Definitions. For purposes of this section:

(1) Government property includes any form of real or personal property in which the government has an ownership, leasehold, or other property interest as well as any right or other intangible interest that is purchased with government funds, including the services of contractor personnel. The term includes office supplies, telephone and other telecommunications equipment and services, the government mails, automated data processing capabilities, printing and reproduction facilities, government records, and government vehicles.

(2) Authorized purposes are those purposes for which government property is made available to members of the public or those purposes authorized in accordance with law or regulation.

Should this section be read as broadly as the court in *Robinson* interpreted *AFR 30-30,* paragraph 8? Would it make any difference if the use of government property was for charitable or philanthropic purposes? Consider the following problems drawn from *Dangerous Dilemmas.*

1. Chief Douglas is the sponsor for her daughter's high school debate team. The team does several special projects during the school year to finance the program's "extras." Many times Chief Douglas needs copies of letters and letter-sized posters for various reasons. She uses the office copier for these small items. She may:

   a. Make 20 copies at a time and not exceed the 50-copy deminimis limit per month.

   b. Not use the copier for anything other than government-authorized copying required by her job.

   c. Use the office copier to make copies on her own time (during lunch, or before or after work).

   d. Copy only official debate team letters, but not posters and other publicity materials.

Answer:

This situation involves misuse of government property as outlined in § 2635.704(b)(1) and (2). government property, including printing and reproduction equipment, may be used only for agency authorized purposes. Answer "b" is the only correct answer. The only possible action is to discontinue the copying immediately. Chief Douglas should use the copier to reproduce only government-authorized documents required by her employment. There is not a de minimis exception for misuse of government equipment. Don't confuse this with the de minimis exception for gifts. The use of government equipment is either authorized or it is not. The fact that Chief Douglas used her own time to make the copies is irrelevant. The copier may be used only for government-authorized purposes. The purpose of the debate team documents is not at issue.

2. Commander Powell is involved in scouting with his children. A co-leader suggested that Commander Powell borrow a projector from work for use at a scout meeting. He borrowed it on Friday and returned it first thing Monday morning. The Commander also replaced a defective switch at his own expense while he had the projector. On Monday morning he told his executive officer what he had done. What should his executive officer do now?

   a. She should be happy that he replaced the switch. It takes forever to get machinery repaired through normal procurement channels.

   b. Insist that next time he should tell her before he borrows the projector.

   c. She should tell him to be sure to return things he borrows in the original condition so as not to disrupt the government supply and repair systems.

   d. She should make sure he knows that he should not use government equipment for personal use and require that he not do it again.

Answer:

This situation involves misuse of government property (§ 2635.704). However, it is not alleviated by the replacement/repair of the equipment, no matter how hard it is to get repairs done through "the system." Answer "d" is the best answer. The executive officer must tell him not to misuse government equipment. At her discretion, he may still be subject to administrative action, but the improper behavior has ended. As to answer "a", you get NO points for having a big heart. A misguided employee might think that he was making up for borrowing the equipment by repairing it. Without specific authority, the executive officer may not allow employees to borrow government equipment for other than official purposes.

Financial Responsibilities

Should the government regulate whether its employees handle their financial obligations in a responsible manner? If an employee does not, is it right for the government to prosecute the individual? Take a look at this section of the OGE *Standards of Ethical Conduct.*

Section 2635.809 Just financial obligations.

Employees shall satisfy in good faith their obligations as citizens, including all just financial obligations, especially those such as Federal, State or local taxes that are imposed by law. For purposes of this section, a just financial obligation acknowledged by the employee or reduced to judgment by a court. In good faith means an honest intention to fulfill any just financial obligation in a timely manner. In the event of a dispute between an employee and an alleged creditor, this section does not require an agency to determine the validity or amount of the disputed debt or to collect a debt on the alleged creditor's behalf.

Will a provision such as section 2635.809 cause employees to handle their money matters in a more responsible manner? *See Administrative Separations* in Chapter IV regarding separation of Navy members who exhibit a "set pattern of failure to pay just debts" (MILPERSMAN 3630600b(2)(a)). Also look at Paragraph 71, Article, UCMJ (debt, dishonorable failure to pay).

Gambling

DOD also has very restrictive rules regarding gambling by its employees.

2-302. Gambling

a. A DoD employee shall not participate while on Federally-owned or leased property or while on duty [for military members, this means, in this context, present for duty] for the Federal government in any gambling activity prohibited by 5 C.F.R. 735.208 (reference (i)) except:

    (1) Activities necessitated by a DoD employee's law enforcement duties;

    (2) Activities by organizations composed of DoD employees or their dependents when transacted entirely among their own members and approved by the Head of the DoD Component or designee; or

    (3) Private wagers among DoD employees if based on a personal relationship and transacted entirely within assigned Federal government living quarters and within the limitations of local laws.

Note that military organizations are not permitted to have fund raising events such as casino nights, while Indian Reservations (also on federal property) are allowed to run gambling casinos. What are the policy considerations in the two situations?

CONCLUSION

In concluding this discussion of ethics in government, consider the following remarks regarding the relationship between ethics, leadership and military readiness, excerpted from a speech entitled *The Privilege of Leadership—The Courage of Character*, given by Secretary of the Navy John Dalton at the United States Naval Academy on April 29, 1994:

What is the tie between leadership and ethics? Between ethics and readiness? Quite simply, the main element of effective leadership is trust. To trust someone to be a leader—to accept the changes and often the hardships they bring—requires the leader to be worthy of trust. We most trust the individual who we consider consistently able to act in an ethical, honest manner. And even if we can't always define every aspect of ethics and honesty, we know it when we see it.

Without ethical leadership in our Armed Forces, there can be no trust by subordinates in the orders of their superiors. There can be none of the special esprit or bonding that we consider essential to the teamwork required for a sound defense. And there would be little confidence by the American people in the rightness of our actions. Without trust and confidence, there cannot be an effective military for America . . . that is the ultimate measure of readiness. . . .

A leader stands for something . . . and that something is character. People choose to follow because they believe that that individual, that leader, has the personal principles to make the right choice, the ethical choice, when it comes to making a tough decision. They choose to follow because they believe that when faced with an ethical dilemma, their leader will make the decision that is in their best interests . . . not the leader's personal best interest . . . but in his or her follower's best interests. You do not have to believe in exactly the same things that the leader does . . . you don't have to have exactly the same perspective . . . no two people have exactly the same thoughts. No, what makes people follow a leader—even if they disagree about this idea or that—is the belief that the leader will do his or her best for the collective good. . . .

I have seen that the men and women of the naval service have joined and stayed with us not only because they have discipline and personal ambition but also because service in the Navy and Marine Corps holds out to them the ideal of personal and professional responsibility as something to believe in and to live out. . . .

They come to us because we represent the possibility of . . . a life that nurtures and requires the exercise of personal honor and integrity, sacrifice in the service of others, and commitment to a community that deeply values such sacrifice. The Navy and Marine Corps are attractive precisely because we insist that there is a good higher than our individual pleasures and achievements. . . .

Secretary Dalton believes that the relationship between ethics, leadership and readiness—that is, that ethics and honor require a military leader to place the interests of others before his or her own personal interests, and in so doing inspire trust and confidence in those to be led, thus impelling them to follow through sacrifice and hardship to teamwork, readiness, and sound defense. Are his views much different from the purposes underlying ethics laws and regulations as discussed in this chapter?

STUDY QUESTIONS

1. A supply officer at a naval station is asked by a friend to determine why his firm's bid on a construction project at the naval station has not been accepted. At a department-level staff meeting, the supply officer employee raised as a matter for official inquiry the rejection of the bid and asked that the particular license be expedited.

2. A department head on a destroyer is asked to provide a letter of recommendation for a former division officer in his department. The department head wants to use official stationery and sign the letter using his official title. What if the recommendation is for a personal friend with whom he has not dealt in the Navy?

3. Can a commanding officer appear in a television commercial in which she endorses an appliance used in the galley of her ship, stating that it has been found by the Navy to be safe for residential use?

4. May the Judge Advocate of the Navy use his official title or refer to his government position in a book jacket endorsement of a novel about organized crime written by an author whose work he admires? May he do so in a book review published in a newspaper?

5. May a Sailor may make a personal long distance call charged to her personal calling card?

6. The computer of a disbursing officer at a Marine Corps Base gives her access to a commercial service providing information for investors. May she use it for personal investment research?

7. May a Navy command hold a raffle in which the proceeds are to pay for renovating the enlisted club?

8. May an executive officer of a Marine battalion order his yeoman to type his personal correspondence during duty hours? What if the executive officer asks and the yeoman agrees to do the work? What if the arrangement is entirely voluntary and appropriate compensation is paid, and the yeoman types the correspondence at home on his own time? What if the compensation were inadequate?

CHAPTER VII

SEARCH AND SEIZURE

When we assumed the soldier, we did not lay aside the citizen.

George Washington
26 June 1775

INTRODUCTION

The Fourth Amendment, contained in the Bill of Rights, guarantees:

> The right of the people to be secure in their persons, houses, papers, and effects, against unreasonable searches and seizures, shall not be violated, and no Warrants shall issue, but upon probable cause, supported by Oath or affirmation, and particularly describing the place to be searched, and the persons or things to be seized.

How much protection does the Fourth Amendment provide service members? The Court of Military Appeals in *United States v. Jacoby*, 29 C.M.R. 244, 247-47 (C.M.A. 1960) stated:

> It is apparent that the protections in the Bill of Rights, except those which are expressly or by necessary implication inapplicable, are available to members of our armed forces.

As the above quotation implies, the military environment does modify the protections of the Fourth Amendment. This is true in large measure because the expectation of privacy in the military is different than in the civilian sector. This chapter focuses on the extent of the military's impact on the protections of the Fourth Amendment.

FOURTH AMENDMENT REQUIREMENTS

SEARCHES WITHIN THE FOURTH AMENDMENT

The Fourth Amendment's protection against unreasonable search and seizure applies to searches that meet certain requirements. The case below addresses the question of when the Fourth Amendment applies.

United States, Appellee, v. Robert F. Baker, Staff Sergeant, U.S. Army, Appellant
United States Court of Military Appeals
30 M.J. 262
August 1, 1990

OPINION: Everett

A special court-martial composed of officer and enlisted members tried Staff Sergeant Baker at Fort Lewis, Washington. Contrary to his pleas, he was convicted of charges that on April 22, 1988, he had stolen two stereo components worth $510 from the Army and Air Force Exchange Service and that he had been disorderly, in violation of Articles 121 and 134, Uniform Code of Military Justice, 10 USC @@ 921 and 934, respectively. He was sentenced to a bad-conduct discharge and reduction to Private E-1. The sentence was approved by the convening authority. The Court of Military Review affirmed the larceny conviction but set aside the conviction for disorderly conduct and dismissed that charge. Upon reassessment, the court affirmed the sentence. 28 M.J. 902 (1989).

In turn, upon appellant's petition, we granted review of these three issues:

I

WHETHER THE MILITARY JUDGE ERRED BY DENYING THE DEFENSE MOTION TO SUPPRESS PROSECUTION EXHIBITS 1-4 AND BY RULING THAT THE SEARCH BY A STORE DETECTIVE OF THE POST EXCHANGE WAS A "PRIVATE" SEARCH IN LIGHT OF *UNITED STATES v. QUILLEN*, 27 M.J. 312 (C.M.A. 1988).

. . . .

III

WHETHER THE ARMY COURT OF MILITARY REVIEW ERRED IN HOLDING THAT APPELLANT HAD NO REASONABLE EXPECTATION OF PRIVACY IN AN OPAQUE CONTAINER WHICH WAS TAPED SHUT.

I

Before pleading, the defense moved to suppress a box containing the two stereo components which were the subject of the larceny charge and claimed that this evidence was the product of an illegal search. Only one witness testified on this motion—Mrs. Mary Holmes, who was called by the prosecution. On April 22, 1988, she had been working "as an exchange detective" for the Army and Air Force Exchange System (AAFES) at Fort Lewis, Washington. When she first saw Sergeant Baker, he had a shopping cart which contained one huge like packing box, brown packing box, . . . and he was strolling from the stereo area by stationery and heading up towards the cashier's cage and the brown box was on top of the shopping cart, and then he had a stereo item on the very bottom of the shopping cart and was just pushing it down the aisle.

Mrs. Holmes followed him around and noticed Baker had went [sic] over into the boy's area and pushed his shopping cart in between two racks of children's—little boy's—jeans. And he proceeded to take the brown box off the top of the shopping cart and open it up and then take the stereo item from underneath the shopping cart and tried to stick it inside this brown box, but the stereo item wouldn't fit. So, he put the stereo item back onto the bottom of the shopping cart and then he closed the big box back up and ran his hand over the tape that was on top of it and picked it up . . . and put it on top of the shopping cart again.

Subsequently, Baker repeated his effort to put the stereo item into the box; but again he was unsuccessful. "[T]hen he took the stereo item and laid it kind of on the carpet and then he taped back up the brown box and placed it back on top of the shopping cart and instead of putting the stereo item back underneath the shopping cart, he

placed it underneath" some clothing. Thereafter, he again placed the stereo item back in the cart; but, finally he "put it back on the shelf where all the like items were, and then he turned around and left out of the area and at [that] time I went, and kind of waited for him to come out on the mall."

After appellant had gone "through the central check out area and came out through the two main doors" into a mall area, Mrs. Holmes approached Baker and identified herself as an exchange detective. After telling him that she wished to "do a parcel . . . check of different items to make sure" the "cashiers with our new system in have properly rung up the merchandise," Mrs. Holmes told Baker, "I would like to check his package. And he handed me a small brown bag and I said, 'No,' I said, 'I'd like to check this big brown one here if I can.'" Baker claimed that it only contained his "wife's clothing," whereupon Mrs. Holmes asked him to go with her and two other exchange employees back into the store.

As they proceeded back to an office, Baker became "belligerent." Ultimately, "a brawl" ensued as Mrs. Holmes enlisted the aid of others to get appellant back into an office. As she opened up the box, he explained, "That box doesn't belong to me. I've never seen it before." Mrs. Holmes "just ignored him . . . and called the military police."

Baker was not wearing a uniform; and Mrs. Holmes did not know "if he was active duty military." She looked into the box "[b]ecause he had tried to conceal the stereo item inside that box, and I figured if he had tried to put one, then maybe there might be other items in there of the same likeness, because the stereo items come in a complete unit." She had not seen Baker when he had first come into the store, and she did not know how long he had been there at that time.

Mrs. Holmes testified that, according to the guidelines provided her, "we are just a detaining unit. We have no authority to apprehend—as a matter of fact, even when we go out on the mall and ask, and after we identify ourselves and ask for their ID card, they do not need to give it to us. They do not need to come with us. They can turn around and walk out the door and just act like we aren't even there. We have no authority whatsoever."

Mrs. Holmes maintained that, as an exchange detective, she had no more "authority than any other store employee" and no more "than any other private citizen that would be in the area."

Mrs. Holmes identified the "big brown box" that Baker had been carrying in the shopping cart and the box containing stereo components worth $ 510 which were inside the brown box. On examination by the military judge, she testified that the box on Baker's shopping cart did "not appear to be an Army and Air Force Exchange Service type of packaging." When "a customer brings a box into the exchange from outside," an "ID checker would" have affixed "an AAFES security thank you sticker," with the date and the initials of the checker; and such a sticker was on appellant's box.

The military judge found that, "as a store detective," Mrs. Holmes had as "her main purpose . . . to protect the exchange system and safeguard its customers from pilferage." However, she had "no power to arrest or apprehend. Her duties are not related to direct law enforcement and she does not represent the commander's punitive or disciplinary power." Most importantly, the judge found that her "actions constituted a private search conducted by a person who was not an agent of the gov-

ernment, therefore, the provisions of Military Rule of Evidence 311, and the Fourth Amendment were not triggered by her actions on 22 April 1988." Accordingly, the motion to suppress was denied.

The Government subsequently called Mrs. Holmes and two other post-exchange employees to testify on the merits; and their description of events conformed substantially to that given in connection with the motion to suppress. Appellant's defense was that he had been so intoxicated on April 22 that he did not remember the incident at the post exchange and that he did not have a felonious intent.

II

A

The Fourth Amendment is a restriction only against government action; and the fruits of a search and seizure by a private person are not subject to the exclusionary rule. *Burdeau v. McDowell*, 256 U.S. 465, 41 S. Ct. 574, 65 L. Ed. 1048 (1921); *United States v. Volante*, 4 U.S.C.M.A. 689, 16 C.M.R. 263 (1954). Since the military judge found that Mrs. Holmes had been acting as a private person, he concluded that the Fourth Amendment did not apply to her search of Baker's box.

However, in *United States v. Quillen*, 27 M.J. 312 (C.M.A. 1988), we determined that a store detective—indeed, the same Mrs. Holmes involved in the present case—had been acting "as an instrument of the military," *id.* at 314 (footnote omitted), when she interrogated a suspect about a shoplifting incident. As we observed there, "post exchanges . . . are arms of the government deemed by it essential for the performance of governmental functions. They are integral parts of the War Department, [and] share in fulfilling the duties entrusted to it . . ." *Id.* at 314, quoting *Stand-*

ard Oil Co. of California v. Johnson, 316 U.S. 481, 485, 62 S. Ct. 1168, 1170, 86 L. Ed. 1611 (1942).

Military authorities controlled the Army and Air Force Exchange Service and the local post exchange at Fort Lewis. Accordingly—just as in *Quillen*—Mrs. Holmes' "position as a store detective at a base exchange was not private, but governmental in nature and military in purpose." 27 M.J. at 314 (footnote omitted).

According to her own testimony, Mrs. Holmes was authorized only "to detain" and not "to apprehend" and had no "more authority than any other private citizen that would be in the area." Therefore, she may not have been an "investigative or law enforcement officer[]" under the Federal Tort Claims Act, so the United States might not be liable if she committed an "assault, battery, false imprisonment, false arrest, malicious prosecution, abuse of process, libel, slander, misrepresentation, deceit, or interference with contract rights." 28 USC @ 2680(h).

However, the protection of the Fourth Amendment is not limited to searches and seizures by investigators or law-enforcement personnel. It also extends to searches and seizures performed by many other governmental officials. [citations omitted]. We conclude that—in light of *Quillen*, which was decided after the trial of this case—the military judge erred in concluding that the search by Mrs. Holmes was made by a private person. This, however, is only the beginning of the inquiry.

B

No Fourth Amendment protection is granted unless the person claiming it had a reasonable expectation of privacy. Thus, open fields are unprotected by the Fourth Amendment even if enclosed by fences, because there is no reasonable expectation

of privacy in an open field. [citations omitted]. Likewise, there is no expectation of privacy in bank records, checks, and other negotiable instruments, *United States v. Miller*, 425 U.S. 435, 96 S. Ct. 1619, 48 L. Ed. 2d 71 (1976); or in the telephone numbers which one calls, *Smith v. Maryland*, 442 U.S. 735, 99 S. Ct. 2577, 61 L. Ed. 2d 220 (1979). There is no expectation of privacy in the movement of a car on a highway, so that warrantless use of a beeper to trace the car does not violate the Fourth Amendment. [citation omitted]. A prisoner has no reasonable expectation of privacy in his cell and so enjoys no Fourth Amendment protection there. [citation omitted]. The Supreme Court has held that even a dog's sniffing around someone's baggage to discover drugs does not violate any privacy expectation and is not a search under the Fourth Amendment. [citation omitted].

The Court of Military Review applied a similar rationale in upholding the military judge's denial of the defense motion to suppress. In its view, Baker had no reasonable expectation of privacy because "no reasonable person should expect to carry a large box with easily opened flaps into a store, walk about, place items in the box, and then have its contents remain inviolate." 28 M.J. at 903.

We agree generally with the conclusion of the court below; and certainly we recognize that if a person's actions make clear that he has no reasonable expectation of privacy, then he is not entitled to avail himself of Fourth Amendment protections. *Cf. United States v. Burnette*, 29 M.J. 473 (C.M.A. 1990). However, it may be worthwhile to spell out our reasoning in some detail.

By entering a post exchange to shop, a person does not automatically forfeit Fourth Amendment protection and become subject to inspection of his purse or wallet. This is particularly true when no sign or notice is posted to inform the customer that his belongings may be searched at the will of store detectives[1] and when, unlike the situation with some public buildings, [footnote omitted] no published regulations give notice that the parcels of patrons may be inspected.

Although we conclude that the customer entering a post exchange or other government operated store has a privacy interest which entitles him to Fourth Amendment protection, we also recognize that the Fourth Amendment only safeguards against "unreasonable searches and seizures." *See United States v. Middleton*, 10 M.J. 123, 127 (C.M.A. 1981). Moreover, not every search or seizure is unreasonable because it is performed without a warrant or with less than probable cause. [citations omitted].

In determining which warrantless searches and seizures are reasonable, the scope of expectations of privacy is again a major factor to be considered. Thus, in *South Dakota v. Opperman*, 428 U.S. 364, 96 S. Ct. 3092, 49 L. Ed. 2d 1000 (1976), one of the reasons advanced for allowing automobile searches without a warrant was that a lesser expectation of privacy exists in a

motor vehicle than in a private home. Likewise, a partial justification for upholding a warrantless search of an automobile junkyard under authority of a state statute was that a reduced expectation of privacy exists in such a "closely regulated" industry. [citation omitted].

. . . .

These precedents lead us to conclude that the search and seizure of Baker's brown box, as well as his physical detention, were "reasonable" for purposes of the Fourth Amendment. In our view, a person who brings a big box into a post exchange and opens it in a furtive or surreptitious manner has a reduced expectation of privacy in comparison with a customer who walks through the exchange with a sealed box or closed purse. Furthermore, whatever might have been Baker's subjective expectation of privacy, the reasonableness of that expectation must also be considered.

. . . .

The decision of the United States Army Court of Military Review is affirmed.

The opinion in *Baker* discussed who the Fourth Amendment restricts in conducting searches and in what situations a person has an expectation of privacy. Military Rule of Evidence 311 addresses these issues, as well.

(a) General rule. Evidence obtained as a result of an unlawful search or seizure made by a person acting in a governmental capacity is inadmissible against the accused if:

. . . .

(2) Adequate interest. The accused had a reasonable expectation of privacy in the person, place or property searched; the accused had a legitimate interest in the property or evidence seized when challenging a seizure; or the accused would otherwise have grounds to object to the search or seizure under the Constitution of the United States as applied to members of the armed forces.

---

[1] Prior notice is a factor relevant to the reasonableness of a search and tends to reduce the intrusion on privacy occasioned by the search. *See National Treasury Employees Union v. Von Raab*, 489 U.S. 656 n. 2, 109 S. Ct. 1384, 1394 n. 2, 103 L. Ed. 2d 685, 706 n. 2 (1989).

Is Military Rule of Evidence 311 consistent with *Baker*? The next case considers where an expectation of privacy exists in the military.

United States, Appellee, v. William E. Portt, Jr., Airman First Class U.S. Air Force, Appellant.
United States Court of Military Appeals
21 M.J. 333
February 17, 1986

OPINION: Cox, Judge

Contrary to his pleas, appellant was convicted, by a military judge sitting alone as a special court-martial, of possession, distribution, use, and introduction of marihuana, in violation of Article 134, Uniform Code of Military Justice, 10 U.S.C. @ 934. His sentence to confinement at hard labor for 4 months, forfeiture to $350 pay per month for 2 months, reduction to pay grade E-1, and a bad-conduct discharge was approved by the convening authority. The supervisory authority disapproved the finding of guilty as to the introduction offense, modified the findings as to the use and possession offenses, reassessed the sentence, and approved the sentence as adjudged. The Court of Military Review affirmed. 17 M.J. 911 (1984). This Court granted review of the following specified issue:

> WHETHER THE MILITARY JUDGE ERRED BY DENYING A DEFENSE MOTION TO SUPPRESS PROSECUTION EXHIBITS 1-7 BY RULING THAT THE REOPENING OF APPELLANT'S LOCKER WAS A CONTINUATION OF THE INITIAL ENTRY AND WAS AN ACT INCLUDED WITHIN THE PLAIN VIEW DOCTRINE.

We hold that under the circumstances of this case appellant had no legitimate expectation of privacy in the unlocked locker located in a common area and affirm.

The facts are not in dispute. Airman Scott Garner and Airman Ronald Coolidge were assigned to clean the security police guard-mount room on the morning of May 8, 1983. This room was used for briefings and contained desks, chairs, and small wall lockers. The lockers were assigned by request to individual security policemen who wanted one for their own use. Each user was required to provide a padlock for his locker at his own expense.

Airman Garner noticed that one of the lockers, A-44, was unlocked, with the padlock just hanging on it. He testified that he opened the locker because he was "curious" and observed only a mitten lying on top of a white piece of paper and what appeared to be a yellow shot record. He surmised that it was a "junk" locker and not assigned to anyone.

Airman Garner then removed the mitten and threw it at Airman Coolidge, who found a crushed soda can inside it. After examining the can, they suspected that it had been used as a device to smoke marihuana. Becoming nervous at the prospect of being found in the possession of contraband, they put the can back inside the mitten, returned the mitten to the locker, closed the door, and reported their findings to the flight chief. Law-enforcement authorities were notified and responded with a drug dog and handler, and a security police investigator.

Although the dog did not alert on locker A-44, the locker was opened by law-enforcement officials and searched, apparently to determine whose locker it was. Records of the locker assignments were kept on cards by the six flight chiefs, but the card reflecting the assignment of locker A-44 was unavailable at the time. Appellant's name appeared on the shot record discovered in the locker, which led the security police to appellant. Upon questioning, appellant admitted that locker A-44 was assigned to him, although he had not used it in six months, and confessed that he frequently used and distributed marihuana. Furthermore, he consented to a search of his barracks room, urine, and automobile.

Prior to pleas, appellant sought to suppress the resulting physical evidence and confessions as tainted by the illegal entry into his locker. The military judge denied the motion to suppress, finding that the initial entry into the locker was not a governmental intrusion, but the act of a private individual, and the subsequent opening of the locker was simply a continuation of that entry. We agree that the initial invasion of the locker by Airman Garner was that of a private individual not acting as an agent of the Government. A private invasion, whether "accidental or deliberate," "reasonable or unreasonable," does "not violate the Fourth Amendment because of . . . [its] private character." *United States v. Jacobsen*, 466 U.S. 109, , 104 S. Ct. 1652, 1657, 80 L. Ed. 2d 85 (1984) (footnote omitted).

The question is whether the Fourth Amendment required the law-enforcement officials to obtain a search authorization before they opened the locker a second time and examined the contents. Appellant can successfully invoke the Fourth Amendment's prohibition against unreasonable searches only if he had a reasonable "expectation of privacy" in the locker which

has been violated by the search that occurred. [citation omitted]. The determination of whether a reasonable expectation of privacy existed is a legal conclusion. [citation omitted]. In considering reasonableness, we must determine whether a person invoking the protection of the Fourth Amendment took normal precautions to maintain his privacy—that is, precautions customarily taken by those seeking privacy.

Rakas v. Illinois, 439 U.S. 128, 152, 99 S. Ct. 421, 435, 58 L. Ed. 2d 387 (1978) (Powell, J., concurring).

The Supreme Court has applied the two-point test articulated by Justice Harlan in *Katz v. United States*, 389 U.S. 347, 360, 88 S. Ct. 507, 516, 19 L. Ed. 2d 576 (1967) (Harlan, J., concurring), to determine whether an accused had a legitimate expectation of privacy:

> [F]irst that a person have exhibited an actual (subjective) expectation of privacy and, second, that the expectation be one that society is prepared to recognize as "reasonable."

[citations omitted].

We doubt that appellant maintained a subjective expectation of privacy in locker A-44. His failure to secure the lock, keep any valuables in it, or even go near the locker in six months indicates as much. Even if appellant satisfied the first part of Justice Harlan's test, however, the facts do not satisfy the second and most important part.

Generally, a warrantless search of a government locker assigned for the personal use of a military member, particularly if the locker were located in living quarters, would be unreasonable, as such lockers are in a class of effects in which there exists a legitimate expectation of privacy. The locker here, however, was located in a common area. Moreover, the initial private invasion of the locker revealed that it was an apparently abandoned "junk" locker, with the only contents being a crushed soda can inside a mitten and two scraps of paper. The law-enforcement officials were free to avail themselves of this information. "Once frustration of the original expectation of privacy occurs, the Fourth Amendment does not prohibit governmental use of the now-non-private information." *United States v. Jacobsen*, 466 U.S. at, 104 S. Ct. at 1658.

In addition to the information obtained through the private action, the law-enforcement officials knew that no name was on the locker and that it was left unlocked

Compare *Portt* with the following case.

in a common area where all the other lockers were routinely locked. Thus, appellant had failed to take the most elementary precaution, one that was taken by the other locker users to maintain their privacy. Based on the facts as they existed at the time of the governmental intrusion into the locker, we conclude that appellant retained no reasonable expectation of privacy in the locker.*

. . . .

The decision of the United States Air Force Court of Military Review is affirmed.

Chief Judge EVERETT concurs.

United States, Appellee, v. John V. Battles, Storekeeper Seaman Apprentice U.S. Navy.
United States Court of Military Appeals
25 M.J. 58
September 24, 1987

OPINION: Sullivan, Judge

Appellant was tried by military judge sitting alone as a general court-martial at Naval Station, Treasure Island, San Francisco, California, in March and April 1985. After mixed pleas, he was found guilty of possession of phenobarbital with intent to distribute, use of phenobarbital, use of marijuana, and receiving stolen property, in violation of Articles 112a and 134, Uniform Code of Military Justice, 10 U.S.C. @@ 912a and 934, respectively. Appellant was sentenced to a dishonorable discharge, confinement for 2 years, total forfeitures, and reduction to the lowest enlisted grade. The convening authority approved, and Court of Military Review

affirmed, the findings of guilty and the sentence.

This Court granted review of both an assigned and specified issue:

I

WHETHER THE UNITED STATES NAVY-MARINE CORPS COURT OF MILITARY REVIEW ERRED WHEN IT AFFIRMED THE MILITARY JUDGE'S DENIAL OF APPELLANT'S MOTION TO SUPPRESS THE EVIDENCE FOUND DURING AN "INSPECTION" HELD OUTSIDE THE SCOPE OF MIL.R.EVID. 313.

. . . .

We hold that the government action challenged in this case was constitutional, and the drugs discovered were admissible as evidence at appellant's court-martial under Mil.R.Evid. 314(d), Manual for Courts-Martial, United States, 1984.[1] *See* Mil.R.Evid. 314(a). . . .

At trial, the parties stipulated to the following facts:

> On Sunday, 9 September 1984, both Storekeeper Seaman Apprentice [SKSA] Battles and Seaman [SN] Troy W. Lipmyer were berthed in S-8 berthing on board USS ENTERPRISE. At approximately 0200 that morning the Commanding Officer had ordered to be searched a postal package addressed to SN Lipmyer; when this package was opened, 92 hits of LSD were discovered. Subsequently, at approximately 0300-0400 the Executive Officer ordered a "health and comfort inspection" of S-8 berthing. SKSA Battles and other personnel sleeping in the berthing area were awakened, taken out of the berthing area into a void, searched and then ordered into their working spaces while the "inspection" was being conducted. During this "inspection" a box bearing SKSA Battles' name was found by a maintenance locker; when this box was opened, phenobarbital and USS ENTERPRISE cigarette lighters were discovered inside.

The ENTERPRISE executive officer, CAPT Dantone, ordered the "health and comfort inspection;" he testified at SN Lipmyer's court-martial that:

> Prior to 9 September 1984 "we had several masts that included people from S-8. I had several indicators from informants on the ship that there was a larger amount of drug activity in S-8 than we had throughout the rest of the ship";

> "[T]he names Battles and Babb were familiar to me well prior to the discovery of the phenobarbital";

> "Battles had been to mast for drug use and I believe Babb had also and I interviewed them personally. So those two prior to this whole time were known to me to ha[ve] at least had involvement in drugs."

Appellant asserts that the "health and comfort inspection" noted above was no more than a subterfuge search designed to locate evidence for later use in disciplinary proceedings. Mil.R.Evid. 313(b). In support of his contention, he notes the early hour of the inspection, its occurrence 2 hours after discovery of other drugs, the pre-existing suspicions with respect to appellant and his berthing mates, and the executive officer's intent to initiate disciplinary action against anyone violating drug laws. Appellant argues that these facts preclude a finding that a legitimate inspection oc-

---

[1] Mil.R.Evid. 314 provides:

(d) Searches of government property. Government property may be searched under this rule unless the person to whom the property is issued or assigned has a reasonable expectation of privacy therein at the time of the search. Under normal circumstances, a person does not have a reasonable expectation of privacy in government property that is not issued for personal use. Wall or floor lockers in living quarters issued for the purpose of storing personal possessions normally are issued for personal use; but the determination as to whether a person has a reasonable expectation of privacy in government property issued for personal use depends on the facts and circumstances at the time of the search.

curred as defined in Mil.R.Evid. 313(b) and require suppression under Mil.R.Evid. 313(a). [citation omitted]. His argument further implies that this search required probable cause, which was lacking [citation omitted] and was so unreasonable as to otherwise violate the Fourth Amendment. [citation omitted].

The first question we must ask is whether appellant had a reasonable expectation of privacy in berthing area S-8 on the USS ENTERPRISE while this naval vessel was underway in the Pacific Ocean. Appellant shared this berthing area with approximately sixty other crewmembers. The berthing area was subject to a great deal of traffic during shift changes, as well as unit inspections and other operational demands. The box in which drugs were found was not located in the limited storage area assigned to appellant on board this ship but near a maintenance locker in a common space in the berthing area. In this context, we hold that appellant cannot reasonably claim that his expectation of privacy in berthing area S-8 was so great as to bar other naval personnel from accessing its common spaces. [citations omitted].

This type of situation was noted by the Supreme Court in *O'Connor v. Ortega, supra*; *cf. United States v. Muniz*, 23 M.J. 201 (C.M.A.1987); *United States v. Weshenfelder*, 20 U.S.C.M.A. 416, 421-22, 43 C.M.R. 256, 261-62 (1971). The Supreme Court held that government employees had a limited privacy interest in the workplace. However, a plurality recognized that the scope of this expectation of privacy depended in part on the demands of the workplace and its openness to em-

ployees and the public. *O'Connor v. Ortega, supra* 107 S. Ct. at 1498. It further intimated that probable cause to access certain parts of the workplace was not needed. The stated reason was that society was not reasonably prepared to expect privacy for the individual in these circumstances or that searches of these areas were not unreasonable. *Id.* at 1506 (Scalia, J., concurring in the judgment). A berthing area on a naval ship is more like a workplace than a home or barrack's environment. We hold that operational realities and common sense dictate that, at the very least, appellant had no reasonable expectation of privacy in the common spaces of such a berthing area. *See* generally *United States v. Hessler*, 7 M.J. 9, 10 (C.M.A.1979).

Appellant also had no reasonable expectation of privacy in the box which contained the illegal drugs. *United States v. Ellis*, 24 M.J. at 372 (C.M.A.1987); *cf. O'Connor v. Ortega, supra* at 1497 (plurality opinion). The box, with his name on it, was found in a common area near a maintenance locker, and it was unsealed and open. Its location and unprotected condition lead us to conclude that appellant failed to take reasonable precautions to insure his privacy rights in the contents of the box. As a result, we conclude that appellant relinquished[2] any possible expectation of privacy in this box prior to its examination by the inspection team. [citations omitted].

The decision of the United States Navy-Marine Corps Court of Military Review is affirmed.

---

[2]Appellant asserted later in his trial that, prior to this inspection he had collapsed this box and thrown it in the trash.

PROBABLE CAUSE SEARCHES

Search Authorizations

If a service member has a reasonable expectation of privacy in a particular place, the Fourth Amendment protects that private area from an unreasonable search. The consequence of a privacy expectation is that a search authorization based upon probable cause is generally required. Miliary Rule of Evidence 315 describes who has the authority to issue search authorizations.

> (d) Power to authorize. Authorization to search pursuant to this rule may be granted by an impartial individual in the following categories:
>
> > (1) Commander. A commander or other person serving in a position designated by the Secretary concerned as either a position analogous to an officer in charge or a position of command, who has control over the place where the property or person to be searched is situated or found, or if that place is not under military control, having control over persons subject to military law or the law of war; or
> >
> > (2) Military judge. A military judge or magistrate if authorized under regulations prescribed by the Secretary of Defense or the Secretary concerned.

The above language indicates that the commander issuing a search authorization must be neutral and detached. When, if ever, is a commander impartial for purposes of the Fourth Amendment? The next case considers that issue.

United States, Appellee, v. Elijah D. Ezell, et al.
United States Court of Military Appeals
6 M.J. 307
April 9, 1979

OPINION: Perry, Judge

We granted review in these cases to consider identical claims, made by the appellants, that evidence leading to their convictions was seized during searches authorized by commanding officers who, by reason of their involvement in ferreting out evidence of crime, were not neutral and detached magistrates and that hence the evidence was obtained in violation of the Fourth Amendment to the Constitution of the United States. A further claim is made that military commanders are inherently devoid of neutrality and detachedness because of a conflict between their attendant duties as commanding officers and the requirement of the Fourth Amendment that search warrants be issued only by neutral and detached magistrates. We are, therefore, urged to rule that for these and other reasons commanding officers are per se disqualified to authorize searches and seizures of evidence of crime. The importance of that question throughout the military services is underscored by the arguments set forth in the splendid briefs filed on behalf of the parties and by the various amici curiae. For the reasons set forth herein, we decline to hold that commanding officers are per se disqualified to serve as neutral and detached magistrates. . . . In the case of *United States v. Ezell*, Number 31,304, we have determined that the commander acted as an impartial magistrate and that decision is, accordingly, affirmed.

I

We consider first the appellants' contention that military commanders are inherently incapable of being neutral and detached as required by the Fourth Amendment. At the forefront of that consideration is the very language of the Fourth Amendment:[1]

The right of the people to be secure in their persons, houses, papers, and effects, against unreasonable searches and seizures, shall not be violated, and no Warrants shall issue, but upon probable cause, supported by Oath or affirmation, and particularly describing the place to be searched, and the persons or things to be seized.

The fundamental inquiry in considering Fourth Amendment issues is whether or not a search or seizure is reasonable under all the circumstances. . . . The judicial warrant has a significant role to play in that it provides the detached scrutiny of a neutral magistrate, which is a more reliable safeguard against improper searches than the hurried judgment of a law enforcement officer "engaged in the often competitive enterprise of ferreting out crime." *Johnson v. United States,* 333 U.S. 10, 14, 68 S. Ct. 367, 369, 92 L. Ed. 436 (1948). . . .

Inherent in the warrant requirement is the prerequisite that it be issued "by a neutral and detached magistrate." [citations omitted].

The point of the Fourth Amendment, which often is not grasped by zealous officers, is not that it denies law enforcement the support of the usual inferences which reasonable men draw from evidence. Its protection consists in requiring that those inferences be drawn by a neutral and detached magistrate instead of being judged by the officer engaged in the often competitive enterprise of ferreting out crime. Any assumption that evidence sufficient to support a magistrate's disinterested determination to issue a search warrant will justify the officers in making a search without a warrant would reduce the Amendment to a nullity and leave the people's homes secure only in the discretion of police officers. . . . When the right of privacy must reasonably yield to the right of search is, as a rule, to be decided by a judicial officer, not by a policeman or Government enforcement agent.

To emphasize the importance of the requirement that the officer who issues the warrant in fact be neutral and detached, the Supreme Court has stated:[2]

The Fourth Amendment does not contemplate the executive officers of Government as neutral and disinterested magistrates. Their duty and responsibility is to enforce the laws, to investigate, and to prosecute. . . . But those charged with this investigative and prosecutorial duty should not be the sole judges of when to utilize constitutionally sensitive means in pursuing their tasks.

. . . .

---

[1]U.S. Const. amend. IV.

[2]*Id.* 407 U.S. at 317, 92 S. Ct. at 2136.

Therefore, minimum requirements for officials issuing warrants for purposes of the Fourth Amendment are being (1) "neutral and detached" [footnote omitted] as well as (2) "capable of determining" the existence of probable cause to arrest or search. "If . . . detachment and capacity do conjoin," the Court emphasized, "the magistrate has satisfied the Fourth Amendment's purpose." [footnote omitted].

. . . .

II

In these cases, the appellants contend that, for a variety of reasons, military commanders are inherently devoid of neutrality and detachedness. [footnote omitted]. We are, therefore, urged to announce a per se rule of disqualification of the commander as an appropriate official to exercise the warrant authority of the Fourth Amendment. We proceed here to discuss that contention together with the various arguments of the parties.

. . . .

Finally, the appellants contend that commanding officers are so involved in the business of investigating criminal conduct that they are devoid of neutrality and detachedness. The very objective of command, it is argued, is the maintenance of law, order, and discipline. Therefore, to effectuate that command objective, it is said that the commander necessarily becomes a law-enforcement official. The appellants remind us that commanding officers have the authority to arrest. Article 7(b), UCMJ, 10 U.S.C. @ 807(b); paragraph 19a, Manual, *supra*. We are also reminded that this Court has had occasion to pass upon conduct of the commander which underscores the law enforcement function of command. *United States v. Seay*, 1 M.J. 201 (C.M.A. 1975) (commander questioning a suspect); *United States v. Hall*, 1 M.J. 162 (C.M.A.

1975) (commander questioning an accused). *See also United States v. Holmes*, 43 C.M.R. 430 (A.C.M.R. 1970), pet. denied 43 C.M.R. 413 (1971) (commander conducting a lineup). Indeed, it is clear that military commanders have statutory and Manual authority to perform many functions that are properly classified as law enforcement in nature. Yet, under paragraph 152 of the Manual for Courts-Martial, commanders are charges with the duty to authorize searches.

The military commander must himself or through subordinates perform a variety of duties. These included the concomitant authority to enforce the law, [footnote omitted] authorize prosecutions for offenses allegedly committed, [footnote omitted] maintain discipline, [footnote omitted] investigate crime, [footnote omitted] authorize searches and seizures, [footnote omitted] as well as train and fashion those under his command into a cohesive fighting unit. [footnote omitted]. These duties provide the basis for a persuasive argument against the notion that he may at the same time be neutral and detached as contemplated by the Fourth Amendment. Indeed, no official in the civilian community having similarly combined functions could qualify as a neutral and detached magistrate under Fourth Amendment jurisprudence. *Shadwick v. Tampa; United States v. United States District Court; Coolidge v. New Hampshire*, all *supra*. We decline, however, to hold that military commanders are per se disqualified to act as neutral and detached magistrates. Our declination results not only for the reasons previously stated, *see United States v. Staggs, supra*, [footnote omitted] but in deference to the President's designation of the commander as the authorized person to issue the search authorization. [footnote omitted] Our deference to paragraph 152 of the Manual, is, we believe, not ill-founded, for Congress has conferred powers upon some military commanders which are judicial or quasi-judicial in nature.

[footnote omitted]. And this Court has from time to time interpreted functions of the commander as judicial, [footnote omitted] preferring to review the exercise of those judicial powers against established principles of law which pertain to the exercise of judicial functions [footnote omitted] with respect to the exercise of his paragraph 152 powers. [footnote omitted]. We have recognized that the military commander is capable of neutrality when he is not actively involved in the investigative or prosecutorial functions which are otherwise clearly within the perimeters of command authority. *United States v. Staggs*, *supra*. We have also held that, when the military commander becomes personally involved as an active participant in the gathering of evidence or otherwise demonstrates personal bias or involvement in the investigative or prosecutorial process against the accused, that commander is devoid of neutrality and cannot validly perform the functions envisioned by paragraph 152 of the Manual for Courts-Martial. [footnote omitted]. These approaches, properly applied, will, we believe, continue to provide for the men and women of the armed services the protection of the Fourth Amendment.

Whether an authorization to search is made by a commanding officer, or . . . by his delegate, the act of authorizing a search on the basis of probable cause is a 'judicial function.' *United States v. Drew*, 15 U.S.C.M.A. 449, 454, 35 C.M.R. 421, 425 (1965). "[S]earches conducted outside the judicial process, without prior approval by judge or magistrate, are per se unreasonable under the Fourth Amendment—subject only to a few specifically established and well-delineated exceptions." *Katz v. United States*, 389 U.S. 347, 357 [88 S. Ct. 507, 19 L. Ed. 2d 576] (1967) (footnotes omitted). One well-recognized exception to the requirement that a magistrate or judicial officer must authorize certain searches is found in the military practice permitting commanding officers or their delegates to authorize searches upon probable cause. Paragraph 152, MCM. Nevertheless, we have held that a commanding officer "stands in the same position as a Federal magistrate issuing a search warrant." *United States v. Sam*, 22 U.S.C.M.A. 124, 127, 46 C.M.R. 124, 127 (1973).

Consequently, the military officer's decision to authorize a search on probable cause must be made with "a magistrate's neutrality and detachment." *Id.* Or, to put it in the words of the Manual in describing the necessary quality of an officer delegated the power to authorize searches, the magistrate function in the military must be exercised by an "impartial person." Paragraph 152, MCM. The search authority must be exercised with "a 'judicial' rather than a 'police' attitude to the examination of the operative facts." *United States v. Drew*, *supra* at 454, 35 C.M.R. at 426.

In light of what has been stated, we hold that obtaining information to be used as the basis for requesting authorization to search is a law-enforcement function and involvement in that information-gathering process would disqualify the commander from authorizing the search. Specifically included in this process are such actions as approving or directing the use of information, the use of drug detection dogs except in gate searches, [footnote omitted] the use of controlled buys, surveillance operations and similar activities. It is noted that there is no constitutional requirement for judicial approval of any of these activities before they may be conducted.

Once the law enforcement agency decides that there is a sufficient basis for requesting search authorization, then the information available to them may be presented to the commander for his judicial determination. At this point the commander may require the agency to provide such additional information as he deems necessary. This would be an exercise of his judicial function since he is passing upon the sufficiency of a completed application. It must be emphasized that agencies must not use the request to search as a subterfuge by presenting a clearly deficient requests to that the commander may help fill in the gaps. Finally, we consider that anyone present during the search is engaged in law-enforcement activities, so we expect that the commander will not be present at the scene of the search. Presence would indicate to us that the commander has been engaged in law-enforcement activities throughout his participation in the entire authorization process, except in very extraordinary situations, which we will deal with on a case-by-case basis.

III

We proceed now to consider the pertinent facts of each case, together with the context in which the crucial issues arose.

A. *United States v. Ezell*, # 31,304

On June 21, 1974, at about 10:20 a.m., Captain Morris and Special Agent West of the Criminal Investigation Division (CID) approached Lieutenant Colonel Cross, the commander for the 326th Engineer Battalion at Fort Campbell, Kentucky, and sought permission to search the barracks rooms occupied by Pvt. E-2 Elijah Ezell, Jr., an enlisted member assigned to the 326th Engineer Battalion. They advised Colonel Cross that an informant had made a sworn statement that he (the informant) had purchased a quantity of heroin from Ezell that morning in Ezell's barracks room and had observed additional heroin and a pistol in the

room. They also advised Colonel Cross that they had the heroin in their possession and that the informant was willing to testify that the sale had occurred. They further stated that they (the CID) had formulated a plan by which the informant was to make a second purchase of heroin from Ezell later that day. Colonel Cross thereupon authorized a search of Ezell's barracks room. Pursuant to that authorization, CID agents subsequently conducted the search of Ezell's barracks room and seized a quantity of heroin and a pistol. Ezell was arrested and charged with two specifications of distributing heroin to the CID informant prior to the search; possession of heroin with intent to distribute (Charge I, specification 3); possession of drug paraphernalia; and the failure to deposit a nongovernment owned firearm for safekeeping (Charge III, specification 2), in violation of Articles 134 and 92, UCMJ, 10 U.S.C. @ @ 934 and 892, respectively.

During his trial, Ezell challenged the seizure of the heroin and the pistol by the agents during the search of his room on Fourth Amendment grounds. He contended there and here that (1) Colonel Cross was biased against him as evidenced by the fact that one month prior to the search authorization Colonel Cross had ordered that Ezell be administratively discharged as unsuitable for military service; and (2) that military commanders are inherently devoid of neutrality. During the hearing on the challenge, Colonel Cross testified concerning what he knew about Ezell and how he made the finding of probable cause on which the search authorization was made.[3] He denied that he was "after Ezell" but admitted that he would prefer

---

[3]Colonel Cross testified during proceedings on the challenge to the search: "Well, the accused had been on the periphery. His name had come up a number of times during the year or the period I had been in command. We never had any hard evidence that he was involved in drug traffic before that we were able to prosecute or anything. . . . Based on the character of the individual and his associations, I felt that it was probably so that he was selling heroin."

to see Ezell out of his unit.[4] Because of the "pattern" of Ezell's minor transgressions and "illegal activities," Colonel Cross had, he admitted, "signed off" on the Chapter 13 (administrative) discharge. The military judge rejected the challenge and, resultantly, Ezell was convicted of offenses involved in this review. [footnote omitted]. He was sentenced to dishonorable discharge, confinement for 25 years, total forfeitures, and reduction to the lowest enlisted grade. The United States Army Court of Military Review reduced the confinement to 9 years, but in all other respects, affirmed the findings and the sentence. [footnote omitted].

We conclude that the while Colonel Cross was aware of Ezell's presence in the unit and of allegations that he had been involved in some "illegal activities," there is no showing that Colonel Cross was personally biased against Ezell or that he involved himself in the investigative or prosecutorial function. While performing the traditional command function of maintaining his troops in a state of readiness to perform any mission required of them, Colonel Cross remained severed and disengaged from activities of law enforcement and prosecution. We reject the contention that because Colonel Cross had been informed that Ezell had been involved in some illegal activities and that he would prefer not to have Ezell in his unit, he was biased. Colonel Cross was, therefore, not disqualified to issue the authorization to search Ezell's barracks room. Thus, there

was no error in admitting the heroin and the pistol seized in the search.

B. *United States v. Boswell*, # 32,414

On December 3, 1974, Major Moi, Company Commander of Headquarters Company, First Support Brigade, Headquarters Commandant and the Assistant Installation Coordinator of Panzer Kaserne, was told by an informant[5] that Private Phil Boswell, a member of the command, was, later that day, going to sell a quantity of marihuana to two other enlisted men then working as gate guards. The informant stated that he had overheard Boswell and the gate guards discussing the anticipated sale and that the transfer sale would occur somewhere in the barracks and that the informant believed that a search of the gate guards' room would lead to the discovery of marihuana. The informant also stated that he, on several occasions, had been in Boswell's room and that he had observed quantities of marihuana while there. He further stated that on the previous day (December 2, 1974) he was in Boswell's room and had observed marihuana in the "right hand drawer" of the desk therein.[6] Major Moi thereupon authorized searches of the gate guards' rooms and of Boswell's room. Major Moi personally conducted the search of Boswell's room in the presence of Boswell and another enlisted man. He proceeded to examine the desk where the informant had said the marihuana was seen the previous day. Nothing pertinent here was found in the drawer. Major Moi then

---

[4]Colonel Cross' tacit admission that he would prefer to see Ezell out of his unit and his personal approval of an administrative discharge undoubtedly constituted evidence that Colonel Cross regarded Ezell as a disciplinary problem and, indeed, that Ezell was unsuitable for further military service. On the other hand, there is no showing that Colonel Cross was involved in the investigative process (see note 10), or that he personally dispatched the informant to Ezell's room or that he was otherwise involved in the business of ferreting out evidence of crime. His role in this case was well within the recognized function of command.

[5]Major Moi's testimony reveals that he knew the informant and had received information from the informant during the period of "at least four, five months" which involved several investigations.

[6]At the time of this search, Boswell resided in the room alone.

looked under some coats on a sofa and discovered a packet containing mandrax tablets. A piece of paper was found on the floor which contained a small amount of what appeared to be hashish. He proceeded to examine a cupboard in which he found a coffee can which contained hashish and mandrax tablets.

At his trial on charges that he possessed marihuana and methaqualone, in violation of Article 92 and 134, *supra*, Boswell challenged use of the evidence seized by Major Moi during the search of the room. [footnote omitted]. While testifying on the challenge, Major Moi stated that prior to the search of Boswell's room, he had received information from several sources that Boswell was dealing in narcotics; and that he had administered nonjudicial punishment to Boswell about 3 months prior to this incident on account of the possession of marihuana. He further testified that about 2 weeks prior to this search, he had entered Boswell's room and caught Boswell and others in the midst of a "pot party." However, he stated, he "blew that one" since he should have searched the room at that time. Finally, Major Moi stated that there was "no doubt in my mind at all" that marihuana would be found in Boswell's room. The military judge rejected the challenge and, resultantly, Boswell was convicted as charged by special court-martial. He was sentenced to a

bad-conduct discharge, forfeiture of $200 pay per month for 2 months, and confinement at hard labor for 2 months. The sentence was approved by the convening authority. The Court of Military Review found the charges multiplicious for sentencing purposes, and after reassessing the sentence based on this error, affirmed the same sentence.

. . . .

We conclude that under the circumstances of this case, Major Moi was not neutral and detached but that, instead, he was involved in the "often competitive enterprise of ferreting out [evidence of] crime." *United States v. Johnson, supra.* [footnote omitted]. By personally conducting [footnote omitted] the search and seizing the items whose admission was challenged, Major Moi revealed that he had been engaged in law enforcement activities throughout his participation in the entire authorization process. In addition his attitude resulting from the failure of the earlier search of the accused's room to support action against the accused raised the spectra of bias which must be avoided if the authorizing official is to remain neutral and detached. Accordingly, the commander was disqualified from authorizing the search since he was not neutral and detached, and the products of the search were inadmissible in evidence.

Military Rule of Evidence 315 amplifies the decision in *Ezell*:

> (d) . . . An otherwise impartial authorizing official does not lose that character merely because he or she is present at the scene of a search of is otherwise readily available to person who may seek the issuance of a search authorization; nor does such an official lose impartial character merely because the official previously and impartially authorized investigative activities. . . .

The following case addresses the scope of a commander's authority to issue a search authorization.

United States, Appellee, v. Raenell A. Chapple, Disbursing Clerk Seaman Apprentice, U.S. Navy, Appellant.
United States Court of Military Appeals
36 M.J. 410
April 19, 1993

OPINION: Gierke, Judge

A military judge sitting as a special court-martial convicted appellant, contrary to his pleas, of failing to obey a regulation; larceny of a checkbook and attempted larceny of $800; and forgery of a check, in violation of Articles 92, 121, 80, and 123, Uniform Code of Military Justice, 10 USC @@ 892, 921, 880, and 923, respectively. The military judge sentenced appellant to a bad-conduct discharge, confinement and forfeiture of $400.00 pay per month for 4 months, and reduction to the lowest enlisted grade. The convening authority approved the sentence.

. . . .

We granted review of the following issue:

WHETHER THE COMMANDING OFFICER, NAVAL SUPPORT ACTIVITY [NAVSUPPACT], NAPLES, WAS EMPOWERED TO AUTHORIZE A SEARCH OF AN OVERSEAS OFF-BASE APARTMENT WHERE NEITHER APPELLANT NOR THE LESSOR OF THE APARTMENT WERE IN HIS CHAIN OF COMMAND.

On January 5, 1988, several crew members of the USS BELKNAP, including Lieutenant Commander (LCDR) McConahy and Disbursing Clerk (DK3) Dacey, reported that their checks had been stolen and that checks drawn on their accounts had been forged and cashed at the USS BELKNAP disbursing office. The Naval Investigative Service (NIS) initiated an investigation and listed appellant as a suspect since he was assigned to the disbursing office during the time the stolen checks were negotiated. The NIS attempted to interview appellant, but he invoked his right to counsel.

On September 19, 1988, the NIS received the report of a handwriting examiner who opined that there were "strong indications" that appellant had forged one of the stolen checks belonging to DK3 Dacey. On September 22, 1988, appellant, wearing Navy dungarees with "R.A. Chapple" stenciled on the shirt, presented LCDR McConahy's checkbook to a teller at the Navy Federal Credit Union in Naples, Italy. Appellant told the teller that LCDR McConahy was his boss and that LCDR McConahy had sent him to obtain additional checks. The teller took one of the deposit slips from the checkbook to verify LCDR McConahy's account, but when she returned appellant had departed the credit union. The teller reported what had happened to the credit union manager, who advised the teller that LCDR McConahy had reported his checks missing and had been transferred from the area approximately 6 months earlier. Appellant's actions at the credit union were reported to the NIS.

The NIS also learned that appellant lived off-base with his fiance, Radioman Seaman (RMSN) Victoria Johns, in an apartment leased by RMSN Johns from an Italian landlord. Her lease was negotiated and prepared through the housing referral office operated by NAVSUPPACT.

The NIS requested authorization from Captain Paron, USN, Commanding Officer, NAVSUPPACT, to search RMSN Johns' apartment for the stolen checks. After being provided with an affidavit relating the foregoing information and consulting with his staff judge advocate, Captain Paron authorized the search. Neither appellant nor RMSN Johns was assigned to NAVSUPPACT. Appellant was assigned to Commander Task Force 63 (CTF 63), and RMSN Johns was assigned to Naval Communications Area Master Station Mediterranean (NAVCAMSMED). However, Captain Paron was designated by Commander-in-Chief United States Naval Forces Europe Instruction (CINCUS-NAVEURINST) 5450.21D as Senior Officer Present (Administration) for Naples (para. 3c) and the local coordinator for the Naples area, with responsibility for supporting both CTF 63 and NAVCAMSMED.

The NIS agents initially did not rely on the search authorization because RMSN Johns executed a written consent to the search of her apartment. However, she was not able to admit the NIS agents into the apartment because she had left her keys in the apartment. The NIS agents brought appellant to the apartment, ordered him to unlock the entrance, searched the apartment, and found the stolen checks.

CINCUSNAVEURINST 5450.21D tasks NAVSUPPACT to provide numerous support functions to station, tenant, and supported activities, including CTF 63 and NAVCAMSMED. According to paragraph 2 of Enclosure (1) to this Instruction, those support functions include the following:

c. Facilities support.

. . . .

(6) Operate a housing referral office to provide referrals and accompany prospective tenants to housing areas and to assist with utilities and service contracts, lease negotiations, rental agreements and terminations for U.S.

personnel and authorized NATO personnel in the Naples and Gaeta areas.

. . . .

j. Security.

. . . .

(2) Provide physical security for NAVSUPPACT Naples facilities, installations and aircraft from unauthorized access, sabotage, espionage, theft, or other criminal acts; enforce internal security regulations; investigate crimes and prepare investigation reports; maintain good order and discipline; provide for the safety and security of personnel and property; act as liaison with Italian police.

(3) Provide law enforcement support for NAVSUPPACT Naples compounds and areas to include traffic control and accident investigations.

(4) Provide and maintain Military Working Dog kennels and provide detection services for narcotics and explosives to support activities.

. . . .

(8) Provide fire prevention and inspection of all buildings utilized by NAVSUPPACT Naples, tenant and supported activities. . . .

(9) Provide motor vehicle registration in compliance with Italian law. . . .

(10) Operate a central motor vehicle registration office. . . .

(11) Provide a motor vehicle safety program. . . .

At trial, appellant contested Captain Paron's authority to authorize a search of the apartment, arguing that Captain Paron was neither RMSN Johns' commander nor appellant's, and that he did not have authority over the property, which was a privately-owned apartment leased and occupied by RMSN Johns.

. . . .

The military judge ruled that Captain Paron had authority to authorize the search because his authority as local coordinator "requires him to operate [a] Housing Referral Office" and to "investigate crimes and prepare investigation reports; maintain good order and discipline; provide for the safety and security of personnel and property. . . ."

Mil.R.Evid. 315(d)(1), Manual for Courts-Martial, United States, 1984, provides that a search may be authorized by:

> A commander or other person serving in a position designated by the Secretary concerned as either a position analogous to an officer in charge or a position of command, who has control over the place where the property or person to be searched is situated or found, or, if that place is not under military control, having control over persons subject to military law or the law of war. . . .

A commander's search authority extends to nonmilitary property in foreign countries. Mil.R.Evid. 315(c)(4)(B). Even if the search is in violation of a treaty, the North Atlantic Treaty Organization Status of Forces Agreement in this case, that subsection states that appellant has no standing to object on that basis. [citations omitted].

Captain Paron's authority to authorize the search of RMSN Johns' apartment must be based on either his control over RMSN Johns' apartment or his command relationship with RMSN Johns or appellant. We hold that Captain Paron did not have "control" over RMSN Johns' apartment, as that term is used in Mil.R.Evid. 315(d)(1). The sole authority relied upon by the Government, both at trial and before this Court, is Captain Paron's responsibility under CINCUSNAVEURINST 5450.21D to operate a housing referral office. While that directive required Captain Paron to provide assistance to military personnel in finding and contracting for housing, it does not confer any authority over the property leased through the housing referral office.

Turning next to Captain Paron's command relationship with RMSN Johns and appellant, it is undisputed that Captain Paron was not in the chain of command for RMSN Johns' unit or appellant's. We hold that Captain Paron's law enforcement support responsibilities under CINCUSNAVEURINST 5450.21D do not make his position analogous to an officer in charge or a position of command. The directive tasks him to provide police and fire protection for supported units but does not vest him with command authority over those units. To the contrary, the directive on which CINCUSNAVEURINST 5450.21D is based, Secretary of the Navy Instruction 5400.14A, directs area coordinators to exercise their authority "through the appropriate chains of command." (Para. 10b.) His responsibility is to support members of tenant and supported units, not to command them. Unlike the "Deputy Subcommunity Commander" in *United States v. Bunkley*, 12 M.J. 240, 242 (C.M.A. 1982), Captain Paron was not given specific authority to exercise command or to authorize searches with respect to members of supported units.

. . . .

The decision of the United States Navy-Marine Corps Court of Military Review is affirmed.

When a search is authorized by a commander, the authorization must specifically describe the place to be searched and the things to be seized. How particular must the search authorization be? This question is considered in the following case.

United States v. Robert E. Abernathy, III, Corporal, U.S. Marine Corps.
United States Navy Court of Military Review
6 M.J. 819
December 28, 1978

OPINION: Gladis, Judge

Appellant was tried by a general court-martial military judge, sitting alone. Contrary to his pleas, appellant was convicted of one specification of selling military property without authority (two red toolboxes) and one specification of larceny of United States Government property (one gray toolbox), in violation of Articles 108 and 121, Uniform Code of Military Justice, 10 U.S.C. @@ 908, 921. He was sentenced to a bad conduct discharge, confinement at hard labor for 9 months, forfeiture of all pay, and reduction to pay grade E-1. The convening authority approved the findings and sentence; however, by a later supplemental action, he remitted a portion of the confinement at hard labor.

The evidence presented by the prosecution at trial indicates that appellant sold the two red toolboxes to a Corporal (now Sergeant) Logan and had previously stated to Sergeant Logan that the two red toolboxes would be obtained from the warehouse aboard Camp Lejeune where appellant worked. Sergeant Logan, a military policeman, had provided information to the Naval Investigative Service concerning the forth-coming sale and had made the purchase with funds provided by the Naval Investigative Service. Sergeant Logan also provided information that other Government property was located at appellant's quarters aboard Camp Lejeune. On the basis of this information, authorization to search appellant's quarters for "items of stolen Government property and other items identified as contraband" was granted by the Chief of Staff for Marine Corps Base, Camp Lejeune. The gray toolbox was among the items seized from appellant's quarters.

Appellant has assigned the following errors before this Court:

I. THE COMMAND AUTHORIZED SEARCH OF APPELLANT'S QUARTERS FAILED TO SATISFY THE REQUIREMENTS OF THE FOURTH AMENDMENT TO THE UNITED STATES CONSTITUTION.

We find merit in the third assignment of error and reject the others.

I

The appellant contends that the search of his residence was illegal because the information upon which the command authorization . . . was overbroad. These contentions lack merit.

. . . .

Construing the search authorization in light of the request for authorization to search, we do not find it to be overbroad. The request for authorization to search appellant's residence and seize items of stolen U.S. Government property and other material which might be identified as contraband recited that appellant had admitted to the informant stealing and selling various items of Government property, that on the previous evening at his residence appellant had sold two toolboxes he had stolen from his place of duty to the informant, and that the informant had observed an additional quantity of toolboxes of the same description at the residence. The authorization to search appellant's residence authorized seizure of items of stolen Government property and other items identified as contraband. In determining whether an authorization to search is overbroad resort may be had to the request. *Cf. United*

States v. Carter, 16 U.S.C.M.A. 277, 284, 36 C.M.R. 433, 440 (1966); *United States v. Hartsook*, 15 U.S.C.M.A. 291, 35 C.M.R. 263 (1965). There is no room for a grudging or negative attitude by reviewing courts towards command authorizations. Requests must be tested and interpreted in a common sense and realistic fashion. Technical requirements of elaborate specificity once exacted under common law pleadings have no proper place in this area. *See United States v. Ventresca, supra*, 380 U.S. at 108, 85 S. Ct. 741. Examining the authorization in the light of the request, we construe the authorization to authorize only a search for the tool boxes observed by the informant and seizure of any contraband observed during the search for the tool boxes.[1] The authorization was not overbroad and the seizure of the gray toolbox was legal.

Abernathy emphasizes that the request for the search will determine in large measure the specificity required in the search authorization. Where can a law enforcement official look in searching for the items described in the search authorization? The next decision ponders the legal scope of a search.

United States, Appellee, v. Sadat-Abdul Jasper, Private First Class U.S. Army, Appellant.
United States Court of Military Appeals
20 M.J. 112
May 28, 1985

OPINION: Cox, Judge

Contrary to his pleas, a general court-martial composed of officer members convicted appellant of desertion and stealing $95,000 in currency and also stealing, on another occasion, a gold necklace, in violation of Articles 85 and 121, Uniform Code of Military Justice, 10 U.S.C. @@

885 and 921, respectively. His sentence to a dishonorable discharge, confinement at hard labor for 8 years and 6 months, forfeiture of all pay and allowances, and reduction to E-1, was approved by the convening authority. The Court of Military Review affirmed the findings and sentence. 16 M.J. 786 (1983).

---

[1]An agent executing a search warrant may lawfully seize contraband not described in the warrant which he observes. [citations omitted].

This Court granted review of the following issue:

> WHETHER THE MILITARY JUDGE AND THE ARMY COURT OF MILITARY REVIEW ERRED BY FINDING THAT THE INVENTORY OF THE APPELLANT'S ROOM DID NOT CONSTITUTE AN ILLEGAL SEARCH AND THAT SERGEANT KOS DID NOT EXCEED THE SCOPE OF THE SEARCH BY LOOKING INSIDE AN ENVELOPE AND READING A LETTER IT CONTAINED.

We hold that they did not and affirm.

While appellant was working as a mail clerk in February 1980 at Kelly Barracks, Federal Republic of Germany, a package containing $95,000 in American Express funds was stolen from the mails. Appellant was questioned concerning the theft and consented to a search of his off-post apartment. No evidence incriminating appellant was found at that time.

In early June, appellant was informed that charges were pending against him for adultery; he had been living with Private First Class Gwendolyn Battle, a female soldier who was not his wife. Although he apparently was still a suspect in the theft from the mails, he was not then charged with larceny. On June 11, 1980, appellant went on ordinary leave, flying by commercial airline to the United States to "work on a divorce." He failed to return to his unit upon termination of his leave on June 24, 1980.

On July 25, 1980, appellant's unit commander sent Staff Sergeant Bennie Kos, the unit supply sergeant, with an inventory team to appellant's off-post apartment to inventory his effects, to box them up, and to transport them to the unit for storage and safekeeping. They obtained a key to the apartment from another soldier with whom appellant had left a key when he went on leave.

While at the apartment, Sergeant Kos found an opened envelope addressed to Major John V. Lewin from Captain and Mrs. David V. Olson. On the face of the envelope was an insured sticker and a customs tag with a notation that the envelope contained a chain. Sergeant Kos looked inside the envelope and read the enclosed letter, which indicated that a gold necklace had been forwarded in the envelope. No necklace was then in the envelope. Sergeant Kos took the letter and envelope to the unit and turned them over to the authorities. On the motion to suppress the letter and envelope, Sergeant Kos testified, in part, as follows:

> When we first went in, we went in there and weren't quite positive whether the stuff belonged to him or the landlord. What we done was we started with all the clothing and this type of stuff first, and went through and inventoried the majority of all the small stuff and later on went back and picked up the large items after we confirmed it with the landlady of what stuff was hers. . . . I found the letter in the bedroom. It was laying on the floor, right next to the closet. I was pulling something out of the closet and there were other papers laying on the bottom of the closet, and as I slid it out these papers came out, and when I reached down and finished picking up the rest of the papers and stuff I noticed it laying there. I picked it up and inspected it and found out that the item was registered and it was not addressed to Jasper or Battle.

Staff Sergeant Kos then read the letter:

> Because I was curious to find out what reasoning would he have of having the mail there, and that's when I found that it contained the necklace—or was to

contain the necklace. I was not instructed to search for anything. We were
sent there to inventory his personal effects by regulation.

The military judge denied the motion to
suppress, finding that the evidence was
lawfully obtained as a result of a reasonable inventory. The United States Army
Court of Military Review held that the
"commander has a legitimate interest in
conducting an inventory of" a service
member's personal property located in an
off-post apartment outside the United
States when the "service member . . . is
dropped from the rolls due to" unauthorized absence. The court below concluded
that "[u]nder the facts of this case . . . the
inventory," including the reading of the
letter, "was reasonable and did not exceed
the scope of the command authority." 16
M.J. at 788. We agree with this conclusion.

The regulations on which trial counsel relied in this case[2] required the unit commander to inventory the personal effects,
clothing, and government property of a
service member dropped from the rolls of
the unit. Although the current Army regulation specifically provides that the inventory procedures apply only if the absent

service member resides in government
quarters,[3] this limitation was not in effect
at the time appellant was dropped from the
rolls of his unit.

. . . .

Because we have determined that Sergeant
Kos was properly in appellant's apartment
to conduct an inventory, we must next consider whether he exceeded the scope of
that inventory by looking inside the envelope and reading the enclosed letter. We
held in *United States v. Brown*, 12 M.J.
420 (C.M.A. 1982), that opening a folded
piece of paper in the accused's pocket exceeded the scope of the health-and-welfare
inspection being conducted where none of
the purposes of the inspection were served
by that activity. In this case, however, the
purposes of the inventory procedure were
to identify, inventory, and transport appellant's belongings to the unit for storage.
Although Sergeant Kos testified that he
read the letter because he was "curious"
after noticing that the envelope was registered and was not addressed to either appellant or the other person known to have
occupied the apartment, his characterization of his subjective motive is not
controlling. Rather, an objective assessment of the facts and circumstances known

---

[2]Army Regulation (AR) 630-10, Personnel Absences—Absence Without Leave and Desertion
(January 15, 1980), referring to AR 700-84, Logistics-Issue and Sale of Personal Clothing (February
15, 1980) and Procedure 5-25, Department of the Army Pamphlet 600-8, Military Personnel
Office-Management and Administrative Procedures (May 31, 1971). Paragraph 12-12, AR 700-84,
provides in part as follows:

Clothing of absentees. a. Inventory. The abandoned property of a member absent from the unit
without authority will be inventoried as shown in (1) and (2) below.

(1) The unit commander will designate an officer, warrant officer, or noncommissioned officer (E5
through E9) to make the inventory. He or she will assure the inventory officer that the clothing
abandoned actually belongs to the absent member.

Step 7a of Procedure 5-25, DA Pam 600-8, provides in part that when a service member is
determined to be absent without authorized leave, the unit commander is required to "Inventory
personal effects, clothing, and Government property charged to the individual . . ."

[3]Para. 12-12, AR 700-84, Logistics-Issue and Sale of Personal Clothing (June 1, 1983).

to him at the time is necessary to determine the reasonableness of his actions. *Scott v. United States*, 436 U.S. 128, 98 S. Ct. 1717, 56 L. Ed. 2d 168 (1978).

Sergeant Kos was there to inventory only property that actually belonged to appellant. The inventory team removed all property from the apartment that was determined to belong to appellant and left behind items determined to belong to the landlady. Because the envelope on its face did not belong to appellant and appeared to have contained something of value, opening the envelope and reading the letter was a reasonable way to establish ownership. *See United States v. Law, supra* at

239 ("[r]eading the note" in the suitcase "was a logical way to identify the suitcase's owner"); *United States v. Strahan*, 674 F.2d 96 (1st Cir.), *cert. denied*, 456 U.S. 1010, 102 S. Ct. 2304, 73 L. Ed. 2d 1306 (1982) (when conducting inventory of van, permissible to read documents on floor to determine ownership).

We conclude that the envelope and letter were discovered during a valid inventory that was conducted in a reasonable manner and the evidence was admissible. Accordingly, the decision of the United States Army Court of Military Review is affirmed.

In some cases, the time necessary to obtain a search authorization may result in the loss or destruction of the evidence. Military Rule of Evidence 315 addresses such exigent circumstances.

(g) Exigencies. A search warrant to search authorization is not required under this rule for a search based on probable cause when:

(1) Insufficient time. There is a reasonable belief that the delay necessary to obtain a search warrant or search authorization would result in the removal, destruction, or concealment of the property or evidence sought;

(2) Lack of communications. There is a reasonable military operational necessity that is reasonably believed to prohibit or prevent communication with a person empowered to grant a search warrant or authorization and there is a reasonable belief that the delay necessary to obtain a search warrant or search authorization would result in the removal, destruction, or concealment of the property or evidence sought;

(3) Search of operable vehicle. An operable vehicle is to be searched, except in the circumstances where a search warrant or authorization is required by the Constitution of the United States, this Manual, or these rules;

While the exigent circumstances exception eliminates the search authorization requirement, it does not do away with the need for probable cause. Why are searches of automobiles *per se* exempt from the warrant requirement? Consider the following quotation from the United States Supreme Court in *Chambers v. Maroney*, 399 U.S. 42 (1970):

[T]he guaranty of freedom from unreasonable searches and seizures by the Fourth Amendment has been construed, practically since the beginning of the Government, as recognizing a necessary difference between a search of a store, dwelling house or other structure in respect of which a proper official warrant readily may be obtained, and a search of a ship, motor boat, wagon or automobile, for contraband goods, where it is not practicable to secure a warrant because the vehicle can be quickly moved out of the locality or jurisdiction in which the warrant must be sought. [*quoting Carroll v. United States,* 267 U.S. 132, 153-54 (1925)].

Probable Cause

When does probable cause exist? Military Rule of Evidence 315 addresses this issue.

(f) Basis for search authorizations.

(1) Probable cause requirement. A search authorization issued under this rule must be based upon probable cause.

(2) Probable cause determination. Probable cause to search exists when there is a reasonable belief that the person, property, or evidence sought is located in the place or on the person to be searched. A search authorization may be based upon hearsay evidence in whole or in part. A determination of probable cause under this rule shall be based upon any or all of the following:

(1) Written statements communicated to the authorizing officer;

(2) Oral statements communicated to the authorizing official in person, via telephone, or by other appropriate means of communication; or

(3) Such information as may be known by the authorizing official that would not preclude the officer from acting in an impartial fashion.

The factors set forth above are considered in the next case.

United States v. Kenneth C. Queen, Electronics Technician Third Class, U.S. Navy
United States Navy-Marine Corps Court of Military Review
20 M.J. 817
June 28, 1985

OPINION: Gregory, Senior Judge

Appellant was tried by a general court-martial constituted with officer members. Pursuant to his guilty pleas, he was convicted of two specifications of violating U.S. Navy Regulations, 1973, by loaning money to shipmates at an excessive rate of interest, in violation of Article 92, Uniform Code of Military Justice (UCMJ). In addition, contrary to his pleas of not guilty, he was found guilty of two other violations of U.S. Navy Regulations, 1973, by wrongfully possessing a dangerous weapon (Liberty Arms Derringer .357 and four bullets) and by wrongfully possessing drug abuse paraphernalia (Zig-Zag papers), in violation of Article 92, UCMJ; wrongful appropriation of U.S. Navy tools of some value, in violation of Article 121, UCMJ;

and possession of some amount of marijuana, possession of some amount of methamphetamines, distribution of one-quarter ounce of marijuana, communication of a threat to a Seaman Recruit Hatfield, and communication of a threat to a Seaman Recruit McNutt, in violation of Article 134, UCMJ. Appellant was sentenced to a bad conduct discharge, confinement at hard labor for 18 months, forfeiture of $380.00 per month for 18 months, and reduction to pay grade E-1. The convening authority disapproved the finding of guilty as to the alleged distribution of marijuana; however, he approved the sentence as adjudged.

I

The first question we consider is whether the military judge erred in denying the defense motion to suppress the fruits of a search of appellant's automobile located aboard Naval Station, Long Beach, California. Captain Barnhart, Commanding Officer, Naval Station, Long Beach, authorized the search on the basis of information provided by LCDR Peck, Executive Officer of USS JOHN YOUNG (DD-973), the ship to which appellant was attached. LCDR Peck had telephoned Captain Barnhart and advised him that several crew members had been recently threatened by appellant and were frightened since a crew member had previously seen a gun in appellant's car. LCDR Peck did not identify the crew members threatened or the informants; however, he did advise Captain Barnhart that one of these sailors who reported this was under oath and he (LCDR Peck) believed what he was hearing. Captain Barnhart was further advised that appellant lived aboard USS JOHN YOUNG and had not checked the gun in with the ship's armory. Captain Barnhart was not informed that these informants had been previously involved in drug transactions, had multiple nonjudicial punishments, were awaiting administrative discharge,

one had been promised assistance toward a better discharge for information about drug dealing aboard the ship, and one was indebted to appellant. The search of appellant's automobile uncovered the dangerous weapon, the drugs and drug-related items, and the U.S. Navy tools.

. . . .

In addition, it was further noted in *Illinois v. Gates* that "[T]he traditional standard for review of an issuing magistrate's probable cause determination has been that so long as the magistrate had a 'substantial basis . . . for conclud[ing]' that a search would uncover evidence of wrongdoing, the Fourth Amendment requires no more." 103 S. Ct. at 2331.

In the case sub judice, Captain Barnhart was aware that crew members of USS JOHN YOUNG had reported threats involving use of a firearm and that another crew member had seen a weapon in appellant's vehicle about six weeks earlier. He also knew that appellant lived aboard USS JOHN YOUNG and had not checked a firearm into the ship's armory. From this, it was reasonable for Captain Barnhart to deduce that appellant did possess a firearm and that it would probably still be located in his vehicle. Captain Barnhart testified at trial that he also felt an expediency present because the vehicle was currently located aboard the Naval Station, it was late in the work day, and he could not be sure of appellant's intentions.

Captain Barnhart was not aware of the informants' poor reputations aboard USS JOHN YOUNG; however, he had been advised that the informants had come forward and reported these matters to their Executive Officer. The Court of Military Appeals has recognized the unique "truth-telling effect" of a service member giving information to a superior officer, *United States v. Land*, 10 M.J. 103 (C.M.A.

1980), and the degree of accountability in military society not always found in civilian society. *United States v. Tipton, supra.*

We concede that the question of probable cause in this case is a close one. Examining the totality of circumstances surrounding the case, however, we find the information available to Captain Barnhart, including the accountability of the less than savory informants, sufficient to find probable cause for the ordered search. On this basis, we would find the military judge to have been correct in denying the motion to suppress.

Even beyond the "totality of the circumstances" in this case, however, an additional basis exists for upholding the legality of the search. The record of trial establishes that the mechanism used to accomplish the search was a written search authorization (Appellate Exhibit I) signed by Captain Barnhart and directed to Master-at-Arms First Class C.A. Berit, U.S. Navy. The record of trial also clearly establishes that Petty Officer Berit relied in "good faith" on this facially sufficient search authorization. The facts of this case are remarkably similar to those in *United States v. Leon*, 468 U.S. 897, 104 S. Ct. 3405, 82 L. Ed. 2d 677 (1984). In *Leon*, a confidential informant of questionable reliability informed police that two persons were selling cocaine. The informant indicated that he had witnessed a sale five months earlier. The U.S. District Court ruled that the information was unsupported by probable cause and fatally stale. The United States Supreme Court ultimately determined that the Fourth Amendment exclusionary rule does not bar use of evidence obtained by law enforcement officers acting in objectively reasonable and good faith reliance on a facially valid search warrant issued by a detached and neutral magistrate, even though the warrant may be ultimately found to be unsupported by probable cause. In *United States v. Postle, supra*, Judge Barr set forth an excellent rationale toward the conclusion that the "good faith" exception enunciated in *Leon* applies in military jurisprudence. 20 M.J. at 642-47.

. . . .

Petty Officer Berit had no previous involvement in the case and no conversation with Captain Barnhart concerning the circumstances leading up to issuance of the search authorization. There is no indication that Captain Barnhart abandoned his neutral and detached status or that he was provided information known to be false or in reckless disregard of the truth. The search authorization was explicit as to the search of appellant's car for a handgun and ammunition. Petty Officer Berit expeditiously carried out the search in reliance on this facially sufficient search authorization.

In summary, we find that *Leon* is dispositive in this instance. Petty Officer Berit clearly acted reasonably and in good faith and any technical deficiencies as to the establishment of probable cause for the search authorization issued do not require exclusion of the fruits of the search. On this basis also, the ruling of the military judge was correct.

The *Queen* case utilized the "totality of the circumstances" test to determine whether probable cause existed. *Illinois v. Gates* discussed in *Queen* established this test as the method to assess whether probable exists that contraband or evidence of a crime will be found in a particular place. In what other situations is a "totality of the circumstances" test utilized? *See United States v. Goudy* below.

THE PLAIN VIEW DOCTRINE

As noted in the *Abernathy* case, an "agent executing a search warrant may lawfully seize contraband not described in the warrant which he observes." The Fourth Amendment, therefore, does not apply to evidence observed in "plain view." To seize items in plain view it is not necessary to have a search authorization, probable cause, or any other basis to conduct the search. The following case discusses the elements of the "plain view" doctrine.

United States, Appellee, v. Donald J. Kaliski, Second Lieutenant U.S. Air Force, Appellant
United States Court of Military Appeals
37 M.J. 105
June 1, 1993

OPINION: Gierke, Judge

A military judge sitting as a general court-martial convicted appellant, contrary to his pleas, of conduct unbecoming an officer by committing acts of adultery and sodomy with the wife of a staff sergeant, in violation of Article 133, Uniform Code of Military Justice, 10 USC @ 933. The military judge sentenced appellant to a dismissal, forfeiture of $500.00 pay per month for 2 months, and a reprimand. The convening authority approved the dismissal and the forfeitures, but not the reprimand. The Court of Military Review affirmed the findings and sentence in an unpublished opinion dated August 24, 1992. This Court granted review of the following issue:*

WHETHER THE AIR FORCE COURT OF MILITARY REVIEW ERRED WHEN THEY HELD THAT THE TESTIMONY OF MRS. S WAS NOT TAINTED BY THE ILLEGAL SEARCH OF THE SPI [SECURITY POLICE INVESTIGATORS], AND THUS INEVITABLY DISCOVERABLE.

* We heard oral argument in this case at the United States Air Force Academy, Colorado Springs, Colorado, on Tuesday, April 13, 1993, as part of "Project Outreach." *See United States v. Stinson*, 34 M.J. 233, 234 (C.M.A. 1992).

Appellant was a public affairs officer at Vandenberg Air Force Base, California. Mrs. S was employed by a local newspaper and regularly conducted business at the base public affairs office. She was married to a staff sergeant assigned to the base hospital and the mother of two children, ages 11 and 8.

Appellant's co-worker and neighbor observed Mrs. S's car outside appellant's Bachelor Officer's Quarters (BOQ) on numerous occasions, suspected they were having an affair, and reported his suspicions to the security police on June 25, 1990. Appellant's BOQ was a duplex on Vandenberg Air Force Base, with a private entrance at the front and a sliding glass door leading to a private patio at the rear.

On Friday evening, June 29, 1990, appellant's neighbor called the security police to advise them that Mrs. S's car was once again parked outside appellant's BOQ. At about 10:15 p.m., two investigators, Staff Sergeants Hagans and Pennywitt, rode by appellant's quarters on bicycles while investigating an unrelated complaint of animal mutilation. They noticed Mrs. S's car parked in front of the BOQ, but the curtains were drawn and the interior appeared to be dark. When they rode by again at about 11:00 p.m., the scene was unchanged. They returned shortly before midnight and rode their bicycles into an open field behind appellant's BOQ. From a distance of about 60 feet they noticed a light and movement inside appellant's BOQ. Sergeant Pennywitt went to the front of the BOQ, determined that Mrs. S's car was still parked in front, and verified that they were looking into appellant's BOQ. Sergeant Pennywitt returned to the rear of the building. He and Hagans then advanced onto the patio, within three feet of the patio door, and peeked through an 8-to 10-inch gap in the curtains. They watched appellant and Mrs. S for about 35 minutes, during which they witnessed appellant and Mrs. S engaging in oral sodomy. Shortly after midnight, they saw Mrs. S looking directly at them. Thinking they had been seen peering through the curtains, they ran from the area, leaving their bicycles behind.

Sergeants Hagans and Pennywitt had been told "to handle the situation with a great deal of professionalism" because it involved an officer. They ran from the scene because they "didn't feel that [they] should go ahead and cause an embarrassing moment between an officer and an enlisted person's wife."

On the following Monday morning, the security police called Mrs. S to the police station and interviewed her. Sergeant Pennywitt testified that he told Mrs. S that they "were investigating an allegation with Lieutenant Kaliski and herself." He testified that he did not tell her that he had personally "observed the activity," but he told

her that he and Sergeant Hagans "knew some things and that we wanted to interview her to confirm or deny it."

Sergeant Pennywitt testified that Mrs. S asked if they had observed her activity with appellant. Sergeant Pennywitt testified that he was "not real positive" whether he told Mrs. S what they had observed before or after her statement was written, but he "believe[d] it was after the statement was written."

Mrs. S testified that on the night of June 29-30, while with appellant in his BOQ, she observed someone looking into the BOQ from the patio. Regarding her interview by Sergeants Hagans and Pennywitt, Mrs. S testified as follows:

Q. Now after you observed the face in the window, when did you next become aware of the fact that somebody had observed your activities that evening?

A. Only once.

Q. Were you later called in and questioned by security police officers concerning the incident that evening?

A. Yes, I was.

Q. Did they tell you that they had observed the activities that were going on in the premises?

A. After I was there. I mean they didn't tell me until I got there.

A. But when you did get there they told you they had observed what was going on that evening on the 29th of June?

A. Yes.

Q. And did they describe in detail what they had observed?

A. Pretty much in detail.

Q. As a result of the fact that they called you and confronted you with this, did you give a statement to the police officers?

A. Yes, they had told me about the details after I gave them my statement.

At trial appellant moved to suppress all evidence obtained from the surveillance of his BOQ and any evidence derived from the observations of the security police, including Mrs. S's testimony. The military judge found that "Sergeants Hagans and Pennywitt were not trespassing at the time they made their observations," and that the activities of appellant and Mrs. S "were in plain view." C.M.R. unpub. op. at 4. He ruled that Sergeants Hagans and Pennywitt did not violate appellant's Fourth Amendment rights by peering through his patio window. *Id.* at 5. The Court of Military Review disagreed, holding that Sergeants Hagans and Pennywitt had engaged in an unlawful search of appellant's BOQ, *id.* at 6-7, but holding further that Mrs. S's statement and subsequent testimony would have been inevitably discovered. *Id.* at 8-9. We agree with the Court of Military Review that Sergeants Hagans and Pennywitt conducted an unlawful search of appellant's BOQ, but we disagree with the Court of Military Review on the question of inevitable discovery. Accordingly, we reverse the decision of that court.

The Surveillance

The Fourth Amendment protects citizens from unreasonable governmental intrusion into their homes. *Silverman v. United States*, 365 U.S. 505, 511, 81 S.Ct. 679, 682, 5 L.Ed.2d 734 (1961). A tenant has the same protection as an owner. *Chapman v. United States*, 365 U.S. 610, 81 S.Ct.

776, 5 L.Ed.2d 828 (1961). Military law recognizes a privacy right in government quarters. *See United States v. Figueroa*, 35 M.J. 54 (C.M.A. 1992) (probable-cause analysis for search inside government quarters); *United States v. Thatcher*, 28 M.J. 20 (C.M.A. 1989) (recognizing expectation of privacy in barracks room). *Cf.*

RCM 302(e)(2), Manual for Courts-Martial, United States, 1984 (authorization required to make apprehension in private government quarters). The Fourth Amendment protects not only the interior of a home, but also the land "immediately adjacent" to the dwelling. [citations omitted].

Looking into the window of a private residence is a search. *See McDonald v. United States*, 335 U.S. 451, 69 S.Ct. 191, 93 L.Ed. 153 (1948) (looking through transom of door in rooming house); *Texas v. Gonzales, supra* (looking into window); *Brock v. United States*, 223 F.2d 681 (5th Cir.1955) (looking into bedroom window). Where, as in this case, such a visual search occurs, the question is whether the search was reasonable. A plain view observation does not constitute an unreasonable search if made from a place where the observer has a right to be. [citations omitted].

We agree with the Court of Military Review that Sergeants Hagans and Pennywitt had no right to be on appellant's patio, peeking through his patio door. They were not in a public area, but on a private patio on which appellant had a reasonable expectation of privacy. When Sergeants Hagans and Pennywitt peeked through the almost-closed curtain in the middle of the night and observed his sexual activities with Mrs. S, they had no search authorization or other justification for their visual search of appellant's quarters. Accordingly, we agree with the Court of Military Review that Sergeants Hagans and Pennywitt conducted an unlawful search of appellant's quarters.

EXAMINATIONS NOT WITHIN THE FOURTH AMENDMENT

INSPECTIONS AND INVENTORIES

The analysis to Military Rule of Evidence 313 discusses inspections in the military in relation to the Fourth Amendment.

> The intent of the Framers [of the Constitution], the language of the amendment itself, and nature of military life render the application of the Fourth Amendment to a normal inspection questionable. As the Supreme Court has often recognized, the "military is, 'by necessity, a specialized society separate from civilian society.'" . . . "Military personnel must be ready to perform their duty whenever the occasion arises. To ensure that they always are capable of performing their mission promptly and reliably, the military services 'must insist upon a respect for duty and a discipline without counterpart in civilian life.'" . . . An effective armed force without inspections is impossible—a fact amply illustrated by the unfettered right to inspect vested in commanders throughout the armed forces of the world.

Military Rule of Evidence 313 defines an "inspection" and explains the admissibility of evidence obtained during the course of an inspection.

    (a) General rule. Evidence obtained from inspections and inventories in the armed forces conducted in accordance with this rule is admissible. . . .

    (b) Inspections. An "inspection" is an examination of the whole or part of a unit, organization, installation, vessel, aircraft, or vehicle, including an examination conducted at entrance and exit points, conducted as an incident of command the primary purpose of which is to determine and to ensure the security, military fitness, or good order and discipline of the unit, organization, installation, vessel, aircraft, or vehicle. An inspection may include but is not limited to an examination to determine and to ensure that any or all of the following requirements are met: that the command is properly equipped, functioning properly, maintaining proper standards of readiness, sea or airworthiness, sanitation and cleanliness, and that personnel are present, fit, and ready for duty. An inspection also includes an examination to locate and confiscate unlawful weapons and other contraband. An order to produce body fluids, such as urine, is permissible in accordance with this rule. An examination made for the primary purpose of obtaining evidence for use in a trial by court-martial or in other disciplinary proceedings in not an inspection within the meaning of this rule. If a purpose of an examination is to locate weapons or contraband, and if: (1) the examination was directed immediately following a report of a specific offense in the unit, organization, installation, vessel, aircraft, or vehicle and was not previously scheduled; (2) specific individuals are selected for examination; or (3) persons examined are subjected to substantially different intrusions during the same examination, the prosecution must prove by clear and convincing evidence that the examination was an inspection within the meaning of this rule.

Inspections shall be conducted in a reasonable fashion and shall comply with Mil. R. Evid. 312, if applicable. Inspections may utilize any reasonable natural or technological aid and may be conducted with or without notice to those inspected. Unlawful weapons, contraband, or other evidence of crime located during an inspection may be seized.

Use of an inspection as a guise to obtain evidence against a particular person within a unit is unlawful. The following case addresses that principle as it applies to berthing spaces on board ships.

United States, Appellee, v. Greg S. Thatcher, Private, U.S. Marine Corps, Appellant.
United States Court of Military Appeals
28 M.J. 20
February 28, 1989

OPINION: Everett, Chief Judge

In this appeal from a special court-martial conviction for larceny,[1] appellant argues that the military judge erred in denying a defense motion to suppress as evidence the pilfered items which had been seized during an alleged "health-and-comfort" inspection pursuant to Mil.R.Evid. 313(b), Manual for Courts-Martial, United States, 1984. Specifically, appellant urges that the "inspection" was a subterfuge to search for criminal evidence without probable cause. We agree.

I

One Monday morning in January 1985, Corporal Cerullo, the Company Police Sergeant, discovered missing from the police shed "a gray metal tool box containing assorted tools, . . . a green Army first-aid kit, containing his own assorted tools, and a green metal trunk (with a 'The Who'

sticker on the side)." 21 M.J. 909. All of these items had been in the shed the previous Friday, but none had been logged out. After Cerullo unsuccessfully had searched the barracks' common areas, he reported the incident to Gunnery Sergeant McKay. Major Talbott, the company commander, joined the conversation, and both McKay's and Talbott's initial reaction was that the property probably had been misplaced. Further search of the police shed and the surrounding area, however, proved fruitless.

Noting that, previously, property had been removed from the police shed without being logged out properly, Talbott surmised that possibly one of the persons assigned to a working party that had been in the area the week before had checked out the property and had left it in a working area or in his room. The Court of Military Review found factually that, at this point,

---

[1]Despite Thatcher's pleas of not guilty, he was convicted of stealing various items in total value "in excess of $100.00," in violation of Article 121, Uniform Code of Military Justice, 10 USC @ 921. Therefore, he was sentenced to a bad-conduct discharge, confinement for 4 months, and forfeiture of $400.00 pay per month for 4 months. The convening authority approved these results, and the Court of Military Review affirmed. 21 M.J. 909 (1986).

Talbott "had no knowledge . . . whether the property had been stolen." *Id.* at 910.

However, when Talbott was advised that Thatcher had been a member of the working party, he grimaced. Cerullo testified:

> I went down the list and I told him that we'd had Private Thatcher. You know, he looked at me like—like, you know, he'd been in a lot of trouble before. You know, the Major knows that he's been caught—not caught, but he's been—well, he has been caught but not charged with taking things.

As Talbott himself later testified, "It just seems like whenever something negative happens around the company, Private Thatcher's name is involved."

Talbott instructed Cerullo to check the possibility of a mixup with another marine, who he knew owned a trunk similar to the missing one. He also instructed McKay and Cerullo "to track these people down" who had been in the working party and "to look in their rooms to see if the tool boxes were in their rooms." As McKay put it, Talbott had "informed Corporal Cerullo and I to find out who was on the working party that week, and to go over into their rooms and search for the tools." McKay testified that "Cerullo relayed back to" him that "First Sergeant Poffenroth [had] stat[ed] something about 'Go over to Thatcher's room. He's been caught stealing before.'"

At this point, it should be noted that, for the preceding 8 months, there had been a routine of conducting daily health-and-comfort inspections of this unit to check for cleanliness and to ensure that all pilferable items were secured in wall lockers. Usually, such inspections were done in the morning, but occasionally they were held during the lunch hour. All rooms were inspected, whether locked or unlocked and whether the occupants were present or away. During the inspections, McKay was not authorized to open or to break into secured wall lockers. Only if a wall locker was unlocked was he to enter it—and then only to identify to whom it belonged.

Talbott indicated at trial that he had intended his check of the working party personnel's rooms for the tools to be part of that day's health-and-comfort inspection. However, he conceded that he never formally advised McKay to conduct this check in connection with the daily inspection.

So, as Sherlock Holmes might have said, the game was afoot. Passing by a head (latrine) and another person's room, McKay and Cerullo went directly to Thatcher's room, where they knocked on the closed door. Before receiving a response, however, they entered the room and found Thatcher standing next to his open wall locker, packing the locker's contents into his open seabag in anticipation of his scheduled discharge the next day. While "inspecting" the room, McKay advised Thatcher that he was looking for the missing tools.

At this point, Cerullo spotted a green metal trunk with a "The Who" sticker on its side inside the open wall locker. After Cerullo had advised McKay of his discovery, McKay directed Thatcher to remove the trunk and to remove the trunk's contents. Inside, McKay discovered the gray metal tool box and tools and the green Army first-aid kit and tools that they were looking for.

Later that same day, in the afternoon, the health-and-comfort inspection was conducted of the remainder of the barracks.

II

A

It is time-honored precedent of this Court that a service member possesses a Fourth-Amendment right to protection against unreasonable searches and seizures. As was stated in the lead opinion[2] in *United States v. Stuckey*, 10 M.J. 347, 349 (C.M.A. 1981) (Everett, C.J.):

> The time is long past when scholars disputed the applicability of the Bill of Rights to service personnel. Instead, our premise must be "that the Bill of Rights applies with full force to men and women in the military service unless any given protection is, expressly or by necessary implication, inapplicable" and, therefore, that the Fourth Amendment does shield the American serviceperson. *United States v. Middleton*, 10 M.J. 123, 126 (C.M.A. 1981) (footnote omitted); *United States v. Ezell*, [6 M.J. 307] at 313 [C.M.A. 1979]; *United States v. Hartsook*, 15 U.S.C.M.A. 291, 35 C.M.R. 263 (1965).

Of course, it is only unreasonable searches and seizures against which a service member—or a civilian—is protected by the Fourth Amendment. What is unreasonable depends substantially on the circumstances of the intrusion; and this Court has recognized that, in some instances, an intrusion that might be unreasonable in a civilian context not only is reasonable but is necessary in a military context.

Thus, we long have recognized that unit inspections are necessary and legitimate exercises of command responsibility. *See, e.g., United States v. Gebhart*, 10 USMCA 606, 610 n. 2, 28 C.M.R. 172,

176 n. 2 (1959). Accord *United States v. Middleton*, 10 M.J. 123 (C.M.A. 1981). However, we steadfastly have admonished that any "inspection" which is, in reality, a subterfuge for a traditional search for evidence of crime will be seen for what it is; and, if conducted without probable cause or in an unreasonable manner, will be condemned. *See, e.g., United States v. Lange*, 15 U.S.C.M.A. 486, 35 C.M.R. 458 (1965). Moreover, we have insisted that persons conducting military "inspections must be ever faithful to the bounds of a given inspection, in terms both of area and purpose." *United States v. Brown*, 12 M.J. 420, 423 (C.M.A. 1982).

When the Manual for Courts-Martial, United States, 1951, mentioned searches "made in accordance with military custom" (see para. 152), it undoubtedly contemplated the health-and-welfare inspections traditional in all the armed services. *See United States v. Middleton, supra* at 127. The Manual for Courts-Martial, United States, 1969 (Revised edition), stated that the restriction which limits the objects of a search "does not apply to administrative inspections or inventories conducted in accordance with law, regulation, or custom" (para. 152). Once again administrative inspections—which, under many names, always have been conducted in the military establishment—were intended to be included in this reference. *See United States v. Middleton, supra* at 127.

When the President promulgated the Military Rules of Evidence in 1980, he decided to be more explicit in the treatment of "[i]nspections and inventories in the armed forces." *See* Mil.R.Evid. 313, 1969 Man-

---

[2]Judge Fletcher's opinion concurring in the result, 10 M.J. 347, at 365-66, reflects agreement with the excerpt quoted from the lead opinion, *infra*.

ual, *supra*. This rule allowed an inspection to be "conducted as an incident of command the primary purpose of which is to determine and to ensure the security, military fitness, or order and discipline of the unit, organization, installation, vessel, aircraft, or vehicle" being examined. According to the rule as it then existed, an "inspection" includes "an examination to locate and confiscate unlawful weapons and other contraband"—if certain conditions were met.

Subsequently, Mil.R.Evid. 313(b) was amended by the President; and, among other things, it now states:

> An inspection also includes an examination to locate and confiscate unlawful weapons and other contraband. . . . An examination made for the primary purpose of obtaining evidence for use in a trial by court-martial or in other disciplinary proceedings is not an inspection within the meaning of this rule. If a purpose of an examination is to locate weapons or contraband, and if: (1) the examination was directed immediately following a report of a specific offense in the unit, organization, installation, vessel, aircraft, or vehicle and was not previously scheduled; (2) specific individuals are selected for examination; or (3) persons examined are subjected to substantially different intrusions during the same examination, the prosecution must prove by clear and convincing evidence that the examination was an inspection within the meaning of this rule.

1984 Manual, *supra*.

In *New York v. Burger*, 482 U.S. 691, 107 S. Ct. 2636, 96 L. Ed. 2d 601 (1987), the Supreme Court reaffirmed that administrative inspections are within the purview of the Fourth Amendment and that, to be constitutional, the inspections must meet several criteria. Mil.R.Evid. 313(b) passes constitutional muster under Burger, because it restricts the scope of administrative inspections to reasonable bounds. *See United States v. Flowers*, 26 M.J. 463, 466 (C.M.A. 1988) (Everett, C.J., concurring in the result). However, appellant claims that in his case those bounds were ignored, because the intrusion into his room was not really an "inspection" but instead was a classic search for evidence of a crime.

B

Preliminarily, however, the Government seeks to forestall any consideration of appellant's claim by contending that Thatcher lacks standing to complain of the intrusion. The Government's argument is that, because his room was subject to a daily health-and-comfort inspection, Thatcher lacked any "legitimate expectation of privacy" therein against intrusion by command. [citations omitted].

To the extent this theory implies that a commander's daily routine of inspecting the rooms of his subordinates automatically cancels any reasonable expectation of privacy by them with respect to their rooms, we reject the notion. The circumstance that one is subject to a lawful inspection does not preclude him from complaining about an inspection which violates the requirements imposed by the President. [citation omitted]. To accept the Government's argument would obliterate service members' Fourth Amendment rights with respect to their rooms and their property; and in so doing, we would be overruling our established precedents recognizing those rights. In short, if an intrusion on privacy is really an "inspection" and complies with Mil.R.Evid. 313, no reasonable expectation of privacy has been violated; but if the purported inspection is only a subterfuge for a search or is not properly conducted, then a violation has occurred.[3]

C

In ruling on the defense motion to suppress evidence seized as a result of the entry into appellant's room, the military judge initially considered what burden of proof would apply. He found that the purpose of the examination of the accused's room was to locate contraband; specifically, missing tools, toolboxes, et cetera which Gunnery Sergeant McKay and the company commander were aware of early in the morning of 28 January 1985. Moreover, a specific individual was selected for examination; that is, the accused, as his name had been mentioned by Corporal Cerullo to the CO and also mentioned by the first sergeant.

Consequently, he concluded that the Government should be "held to the burden of proving by clear and convincing evidence that this was an inspection."[4]

It has been suggested that the Government should not have been required to shoulder so heavy a burden, because the stolen property was not "contraband" within the meaning of Mil.R.Evid. 313(b). We reject this suggestion, for we are convinced that the term "contraband," as used in Mil.R.Evid. 313(b), was intended to include stolen property. According to

Black's Law Dictionary 291 (5th ed. 1979), "contraband" means "any property which is unlawful to . . . possess. Goods exported from or imported into a country against its laws."

We doubt that the President intended for the term "contraband" to be limited to the meaning it has in connection with customs laws—items whose importation or exportation is forbidden. Instead, we believe that it includes all items which are not lawfully possessed. Under this interpretation, stolen property is "contraband" because the possessor is not entitled to retain possession of such property.

A broad interpretation of "contraband" conforms to the obvious purpose of Mil.R.Evid. 313(b) to ensure that "inspections" are not used as "subterfuge[s for] searches." *See* Drafters' Analysis to Mil.R.Evid. 313(b), 1984 Manual, *supra* at A22-17 to A22-20. This danger is as great in the present case—where stolen property is involved—as it would be if the more typical "contraband," like drugs, were involved. Therefore, it is unlikely that the President would have intended for a lower standard of proof to apply here.

D

Although the military judge conducted a meticulous inquiry and applied the correct

---

[3]As noted earlier, what is reasonable depends upon the circumstances of the intrusion. As we recognized in *United States v. Middleton*, 10 M.J. 123, 128 n.8 (C.M.A. 1981), "The armed services have made increasing efforts to provide privacy for service members in their dormitories and barracks." This transition from open bays to semi-private rooms evolved largely to make military life more palatable and, accordingly, more attractive to potential recruits. There is a much greater expectation of privacy in such a lifestyle than there is in large bays holding large numbers of individuals and having no walls or barriers between bunks and lockers. While there still is no reasonable expectation of privacy from all intrusions where command responsibility dictates otherwise, in other circumstances substantial expectations do arise from these living conditions.

[4]The military judge also ruled on the Government's contention that, if the inspection were illegal, the stolen property would nonetheless have been inevitably discovered. [citations omitted]. In this instance he properly utilized a preponderance-of-the-evidence burden of proof, as authorized by *Kozak*. Applying this standard, he ruled against the Government on the inevitable-discovery issue.

standard of proof, we disagree with his conclusion that the Government established by the requisite "clear and convincing" evidence that the intrusion into Thatcher's room was a lawful military inspection under Mil.R.Evid. 313, rather than a prohibited criminal search without probable cause.

In the first place, Thatcher was the prime suspect with respect to the possible theft of the tools and boxes. He was awaiting imminent discharge from the Marine Corps, and he had been in the working party so he might have had an opportunity to steal the property. He was thought by his commander and others to have stolen things before, even though for some reason he had never been charged therewith. Indeed, Thatcher's reputation was such that Major Talbott, his commander, "grimaced" when he learned that Thatcher had been in the working party. Talbott knew that Thatcher always was involved somehow in any trouble in the unit.[5]

Although the barracks was inspected daily, on this occasion McKay and Cerullo passed by the head and another room and went straight to Thatcher's room. Moreover, after the stolen property had been seized in Thatcher's room in the morning, no further examination of the barracks took place until that afternoon. Thus, it appears that when McKay and Cerullo went to the barracks, they had in mind not the routine daily inspection (which could have included looking for the missing items, if done in a neutral fashion) but instead a search of the suspect's quarters. This inference is supported by this testimony of Gunnery Sergeant McKay on direct examination:

Q. Exactly what was it the commanding officer told you that morning?

A. The commanding officer told Corporal Cerullo and myself, sir, to find out who was on the working parties and go over and search their rooms for the possible tools that were missing.

Furthermore, although both McKay and Cerullo gave detailed statements to the Naval Investigative Service (NIS) on the day after the stolen property was recovered, neither of those statements made any reference to an "inspection" or gave any indication that Cerullo and McKay were making an inspection rather than a search. According to McKay's testimony, he first mentioned an "inspection" in a conversation with trial counsel or defense counsel a few days before trial—and some 2 months after his earlier statement.

Thus, it appears that the sequence of events on January 28, 1985 was this: Initially Cerullo thought some items of property in the shed had been misplaced; so he examined the shed and common areas. After this effort proved unsuccessful, he proceeded on the hypothesis that a member of the working party had inadvertently taken the tools, without any intent to steal them, and that the members of the working party should be approached and asked about this possibility. At this point, however, the incident took on a different flavor: Thatcher was identified as a member of the working party, and because of his poor record in the unit and his impending discharge, suspicion developed that he had stolen the property. When this possibility was discussed with Major Talbott, the unit commander, he told McKay and Cerullo to go

---

[5]During the hearing on the motion to suppress, there was also a reference to Thatcher's incarceration by civilian authorities at some time not long before the alleged theft occurred. Also, it seems clear from other testimony that at one time he had been a corporal and thereafter had been reduced to private—presumably through nonjudicial punishment for misconduct.

search for the missing tools. They went directly to the most likely suspect— Thatcher—and by-passed other areas of the barracks that would have been examined during the routine daily barracks inspection. When that examination proved fruitful, the exercise ceased; and the routine inspection of the barracks occurred later that day.

This evidence is not "clear and convincing," as required by Mil.R.Evid. 313(b); thus the Government has failed to establish that the incriminating evidence was found as the result of a lawful inspection. Instead, that evidence is inadmissible because it was the product of an unlawful intrusion into Thatcher's room.

III

The decision of the United States Navy-Marine Corps Court of Military Review is reversed. The findings of guilty and the sentence are set aside. The record of trial is returned to the Judge Advocate General of the Navy. A rehearing may be ordered.

Military Rule of Evidence 313 states that an order to produce body fluids is an inspection subject to the same requirements as all inspections. The following case considers the lawfulness of the military's urinalysis program.

Elizabeth Susan Unger, Lieutenant, U.S. Navy, Appellant, v. Daniel Ziemniak, Captain, U.S. Navy, Military Judge, Appellee.
United States Court of Military Appeals
27 M.J. 349
January 27, 1989

OPINION: Everett, Chief Judge

In August 1988, Lieutenant Unger was charged with willfully disobeying the lawful order of a superior commissioned officer that she comply with a Naval directive—OPNAV Instruction 5350.4A— by giving a urine sample under direct observation by a female enlisted service member. *See* Art. 90, Uniform Code of Military Justice, 10 USC @ 890. After a pretrial investigation had been conducted pursuant to Article 32 of the Code, 10 USC @ 832, the charge was referred for trial by a special court-martial.

After arraignment, Lieutenant Unger made several motions contesting the legality of the order and seeking dismissal of the charge. The military judge denied the motions, whereupon Lieutenant Unger petitioned the United States Navy-Marine Corps Court of Military Review for extraordinary relief. Her petition was dismissed without prejudice. In turn, she petitioned this Court for extraordinary relief. We treated the petition as a writ-appeal petition, ordered a stay in her trial and thereafter heard oral argument to determine whether she was entitled to relief. 27 M.J. (Daily Journal, Nov. 21, 1988).

I

Facts

Lieutenant Unger is a Naval Academy graduate with 8 years of unblemished service. In July 1988, she was required to provide a urine sample at Great Lakes Naval

Training Center in connection with the drug-testing program authorized by OPNAVINST 5350.4A. That directive calls for "direct observation" of the private parts of a person who is giving a urine specimen. Para. 1c, App. B to Encl. (4), OPNAVINST 5350.4A. Accordingly, a female chief petty officer insisted that Lieutenant Unger "disrobe from the waist down, sit on a toilet, and urinate into a collection bottle" while being observed from a distance of approximately 18 inches. Lieutenant Unger refused to comply with the conditions—although, without direct observation, she provided a sample which ultimately tested negative for drugs.

Because of her refusal to be directly observed, Lieutenant Unger was given "a direct oral order from" her executive officer "to comply with OPNAVINST 5350.4A and provide another sample under direct visual observation of" her "private parts." She refused this order because of her claimed constitutional rights to privacy and to freedom from unreasonable searches and seizures and also because, in her view, the direct observation by an enlisted person constituted fraternization and demeaned her status as an officer. Her refusal gave rise to the charge filed against her after she refused punishment under Article 15, UCMJ, 10 USC @ 815.

. . . .

IV

Merits

A

In *United States v. Trottier*, 9 M.J. 337 (C.M.A. 1980), this Court emphasized the significance of the drug program for the armed services. We pointed out:

As military equipment has become more sophisticated, there is the concomitant increased risk that an operator will be unable to handle the complicated weapons system with which he is entrusted and upon which his safety and that of others may depend. This risk, disturbingly, often cannot be obviated by keeping a person under the influence of a drug off the job for, unlike use of alcohol, there frequently are only marginally visible indications of the influence of drugs. Even when the user is not then under the influence, there may be dangerous psychological pressures on him which, themselves, could affect his performance adversely. Moreover, all this may be said of the serviceperson performing what may be perceived as the most routine and mundane duty, for there is no individual in our modern armed forces whose performance may not touch others in a significant way.

Without the maintenance of a credible armed force, the United States is at a serious military and geopolitical disadvantage. The need is overwhelming to be prepared to field at a moment's notice a fighting force of finely tuned, physically and mentally fit men and women—and satisfaction of that need is not compatible with indiscriminate use of debilitating drugs.

Id. at 345-46 (footnotes omitted). These observations made in *Trottier* in 1980 are still accurate now.

In *Murray v. Haldeman, supra,* we considered the constitutionality of compulsory urinalysis under a drug-testing program that had been instituted in the armed services late in December 1981. Our conclusion was that, although the questioned testing involved a "seizure" of urine within the meaning of the Fourth Amendment, this seizure was reasonable.[1] In reaching this conclusion, we relied especially on the adverse effect of drugs on performance of the military mission and the great value of compulsory urinalysis in detecting and deterring drug abuse.

The premises on which that case relied also are still valid. The experience of recent years makes clear that mandatory drug testing of service members contributes substantially to reduction of drug use in the armed services and to making the military community drug free.[2] In our view, compulsory urinalysis is appropriate and necessary to maintain the effectiveness of the military establishment.[3]

Lieutenant Unger insists, however, that even if mandatory drug testing is reasonable, her superiors sought to make her provide a urine specimen under conditions that were humiliating and degrading and, so, violated the guidelines established by *Murray v. Haldeman, supra.* In effect, she is contending that, by use of a direct order, her military superiors were attempting to accomplish an unreasonable—and therefore unconstitutional—"seizure" of her urine.

In this connection, she insists that it was unreasonable to require that she give a urine specimen under "direct observation." As Lieutenant Unger emphasizes, "direct observation" is not required currently in civilian drug-testing programs, unless there is reason to believe that a particular individual to be tested may substitute a urine specimen. *See* Federal Personnel Manual, FPM Letter 792-16 (November 28, 1986). Moreover, until recently direct observation was only required in collecting the urine specimens of male service members, and alternate procedures were employed for female service members.[4]

Undoubtedly, for many persons it is unpleasant and disagreeable to urinate while being directly observed by someone else. However, we also realize that there are cavities in the body where small quantities of urine can be secreted for purposes of substitution in the event of a drug test; and only by direct observation can this tactic be prevented. Indeed, many tricks have been used to avoid detection by compulsory urinalysis. There are reports of persons who sell drug-free urine to others who, in turn, will substitute pure urine for their own urine when a specimen is being collected. A leading athlete has described how he concealed some drug-free urine on

---

[1]Similarly, in *United States v. Middleton*, 10 M.J. 123 (C.M.A. 1981), we had concluded that the traditional military inspection constituted a "search" for Fourth-Amendment purposes but that this "search" was reasonable.

[2]Evidence offered in this proceeding indicates that the reduction in the use of drugs among service members since 1982 has been about 90 percent. Even though drug testing undoubtedly does not deserve sole credit for this improvement, we are convinced that it performed a significant role.

[3]Because of the impact of drug abuse on the performance of the military mission, we believe that mandatory drug testing in the military community is not necessarily subject to the same limitations that would be applicable in the civilian society. [citations omitted].

[4]Paragraph IVD.1 of DOD Instruction 1010.1, dated April 4, 1974, provides that "urine specimens . . . for male service members" must be collected "under direct observation"; but "alternate procedures which insure that a valid specimen is obtained may be used for female service members." Paragraph 1c to Enclosure 1 of OPNAV Instruction 5355.1, dated January 25, 1975, provided that "[urine] specimens shall be collected under direct observation for male service members," but for female members they should be collected "under conditions of sufficient security to ensure that a valid specimen has been submitted."

his body for purposes of substitution if he was required by the National Football League to submit a urine specimen. *See* L. Taylor and D. Falkner, L.T.: Living on the Edge (Times Books, New York, 1987). Only recently, we reviewed the case of a female commissioned officer who had devised still another scheme to defeat the Air Force's drug-testing program. *See United States v. Norvell,* 26 M.J. 477 (C.M.A. 1988).

In view of the varied tactics which may be employed to evade drug testing, we conclude that it is not unreasonable per se for the Navy to require "direct observation" when urine specimens are collected. Otherwise, the temptation and opportunity for evasion are too great.

Lieutenant Unger also complains that she was to be directly observed by an enlisted person while she provided the urine specimen. Although her pleadings are phrased in terms of fraternization, her real complaint is that, in the hierarchical military society, it is demeaning and degrading for an officer to be observed by an enlisted person while she performs an activity that typically is performed in private.

However disagreeable it may be for an officer to be observed under such circumstances by an enlisted person, we believe that the need to prevent evasion of the drug-testing program justifies the surveillance. We recognize the importance of maintaining the military hierarchical structure reflected in rank, but we doubt the practicality of requiring that a person giving a urine specimen be of lower rank than the observer.

Furthermore, to exempt officers entirely from the requirement of "direct observation" would ignore the lesson that officers, like enlisted persons, may yield to the temptation of drugs and use tricks to avoid detection. The armed services are sufficiently egalitarian that every person in the armed services may be required to provide a urine specimen under direct observation. Although rank has its privileges, favored treatment in drug testing is not one of them.[5]

Lieutenant Unger insists that, for physiological and psychological reasons, the requirement for "direct observation" is more offensive and degrading for a female than for a male. We recognize that in the military context males and females are not totally fungible.[6] Therefore, Congress has limited the use of women for combat purposes and does not require them to register for the draft. *See Rostker v. Goldberg*, 453 U.S. 57, 101 S. Ct. 2646, 69 L. Ed. 2d 478 (1981). Furthermore, for many years, the armed services apparently allowed use of alternatives to the direct observation of females giving urine specimens.

Our conclusion, however, is that, even though as a policy matter the armed services could modify the current procedures for collecting urine from female service members, they may require direct observation for females as well as for males. In our opinion, such observation of females does not inevitably transmute collection of urine specimens into an unreasonable "seizure" of the urine.

Although we reject Lieutenant Unger's claim that direct observation of the collection of urine from females is unconstitu-

---

[5] Evidence in this proceeding indicates that the female observer who was assigned to observe Lieutenant Unger had also directly observed a female admiral who was providing a urine specimen.

[6] However, in *United States v. Smith*, 27 M.J. 242, 249 (C.M.A. 1988), we rejected a government contention that the "experience" of females is so unique that they may be specially selected to serve as court members in certain kinds of cases.

tional, a caution is in order. Direct observation can be performed in different ways and from different distances. If the eyes of the observer are too close to the genitalia of the person giving the urine specimen, the process of obtaining this specimen would be unduly humiliating and degrading and would violate the precepts of *Murray v. Haldeman, supra*. Likewise, even though a male gynecologist may examine a woman's vagina for medical purposes, we believe it would be clearly unreasonable for male service members—even if medical corpsmen—to serve as "observers" of women who have been required to give urine specimens.[7]

B

In a prosecution for disobedience, lawfulness of the command is an element of the offense. *See* Arts. 90(2), 91(2), and 92(1) and (2), UCMJ, 10 USC @@ 890(2), 891(2), and 892(1) and (2), respectively. An order is presumed to be lawful, *see United States v. Austin,* 27 M.J. 227, 231-32 (C.M.A. 1988); but the presumption may be rebutted. Thus, an order requiring the recipient to provide a urine specimen is illegal—and therefore unenforceable—if the order provided for collection of urine under humiliating and degrading conditions, as proscribed by *Murray v. Haldeman, supra*, and authorities relied on therein. If, in a trial for disobedience, the military judge determines from undisputed facts that the order was illegal, he should dismiss the charge.

If, in a trial by members, the military judge determines that no evidence has been offered to rebut the presumed legality of the order to provide a urine specimen, he need not advise the members as to what facts might rebut the presumption. If, however, he concludes from all the evidence that an issue exists as to whether the service member had been ordered to provide the specimen under unreasonable conditions, he should submit the issue to the court members for their consideration. In that event, his instruction would be that, unless the members have been convinced beyond a reasonable doubt that the requirements for producing the urine specimen—including the manner in which the direct observation was to be performed—were reasonable and not unduly humiliating or degrading, the order was illegal and the accused should be acquitted. Of course, in a trial by military judge alone, he must determine beyond a reasonable doubt that the order contemplated "seizure" of the urine specimen under reasonable conditions.

In this case, the military judge apparently did not conclude from the evidence before him that the order was illegal. Therefore, he did not dismiss the charges; and on the record before us, we agree with this decision.

At trial the evidence may raise the issue of the legality of the order received by Lieutenant Unger.[8] In that event, unless trial by members has been waived, the judge should instruct the members that they must

---

[7] OPNAV Instruction 5350.4A provides that "the direct observation" shall be performed by a person "of the same sex as the member providing the" urine specimen. Para. 1c, App. B to Encl. 4 of OPNAVINST. 5350.4A.

[8] There was testimony that, although usually it is easier for a female to urinate into a bottle with a wider opening than would customarily be used in obtaining a specimen from a male, and although the Navy has authorized use of such bottles for collecting urine specimens from women, a container with a narrow opening was being used for both males and females at Lieutenant Unger's military installation. On the other hand, we do not know if at trial there will be evidence as to whether, in order to assuage her concerns, Lieutenant Unger was offered any alternative procedures—such as direct observation by a doctor or a strip search or cavity search for a concealed urine specimen immediately before providing her specimen.

determine whether the order given to Lieutenant Unger required her to provide a urine specimen under conditions that were not humiliating and degrading.

denying the petition for extraordinary relief without prejudice is affirmed. The stay of court-martial proceedings is dissolved. The case is returned to the military judge for further proceedings.

V

The decision of the United States Navy-Marine Corps Court of Military Review

Lieutenant Unger was given "a direct oral order" from her executive officer to comply with OPNAVINST 5350.4A and provide a sample under direct visual observation of her "private parts." She refused this order because, in her view, the direct observation by an enlisted person constituted fraternization and demeaned her status as an officer. Does observation of an officer by an enlisted person during a urinalysis constitute an "unduly familiar" relationship? *See* the discussion of fraternization in Chapter V. Lieutenant Unger also argued that direct observation of females is more intrusive and degrading than for males. Is such a distinction viable in light of a gender-neutral approach to assignment of personnel in the military?

INVENTORIES

Military Rule of Evidence 313 provides:

> (c) Inventories. Unlawful weapons, contraband, or other evidence of crime discovered in the process of an inventory, the primary purpose of which is administrative in nature, may be seized. Inventories shall be conducted in a reasonable fashion. . . . An examination made for the primary purpose of obtaining evidence for use in a trial by court-martial or in other disciplinary proceedings is not an inventory within the meaning of this rule.

Evidence discovered in the process of a proper inventory may be seized and admitted into evidence at court-martial. As with inspections, the purpose of the inventory must be to ensure health and welfare, or some other administrative purpose. In *United States v. Jasper* above, the examination of the accused's off-base apartment overseas was an inventory that resulted from the accused's deserter status. Inventories of the property of deserters and confined personnel, and general seabag inspections, are three of the most common types of inventories. A seabag inspection is an inventory to ensure that the member has the prescribed types and amount of uniform items. The deserter inventory involves the packing of any personal items in order to store them until the deserter returns. The incarceration inventory occurs when a member is confined and his or her personal items must be stored during the period of confinement.

SEARCHES NOT REQUIRING PROBABLE CAUSE

BORDER SEARCHES AND SEARCHES ON INSTALLATIONS OVERSEAS

Military Rule of Evidence 314 sets forth those searches not requiring probable cause. Included in the list of such searches are border searches and searches upon exit or entry of United States military property abroad.

> (b) Border searches. Border searches for customs or immigration purposes may be conducted when authorized by Act of Congress.

> (c) Searches upon entry to or exit from United States installations, aircraft, and vessels abroad. In addition to the authority to conduct inspections . . ., a commander of a United States military installation, enclave, or aircraft on foreign soil, or in foreign or international airspace, or a United States vessel in foreign or international waters, may authorize appropriate personnel to search persons or the property of such persons upon entry to or exit from the installation, enclave, aircraft, or vessel to ensure the security, military fitness, or good order and discipline of the command. A search made for the primary purpose of obtaining evidence for use in a trial by court-martial or other disciplinary proceeding is not authorized by this subdivision.

The following case discusses both types of searches described above.

United States, Appellee, v. Julio E. Rivera, Airman First Class, U.S. Air Force, Appellant.
United States Court of Military Appeals
4 M.J. 215
February 20, 1978

OPINION: Fletcher, Chief Judge

The appellant was convicted by a general court-martial of larceny and possession of heroin in violation of Articles 121 and 134, Uniform Code of Military Justice, 10 U.S.C. @@ 921 and 934, respectively. The findings and sentence to confinement at hard labor for twelve months, forfeitures of $200.00 pay per month for twelve months, and reduction to the lowest enlisted grade were approved by the convening authority and the United States Air Force Court of Military Review. We granted review to determine whether the heroin seized was the product of an unlawful search, and hence inadmissible. [footnote omitted]. Counsel for the appellant argue that the random gate search program utilized at Korat Royal Thai Air Force Base was constitutionally infirm because it was too vague, undefined, and unlimited in scope and application to pass muster under the Fourth Amendment. I have determined, however, that this case, because of the foreign situs, must be resolved under the "border search" line of cases from the Supreme Court, and that application of that doctrine leads to the conclusion that the heroin was lawfully seized.[1]

The heroin in question was the product of two separate seizures. On the night of August 31, 1974, the appellant arrived at gate one of the base riding in a civilian (Thai) taxi; the gate guard, at the direction of a Sergeant Blackmore, the handler for the marihuana detection dog stationed at the gate, directed the taxi driver to pull over to the side of the road and stop. The occupants were removed, and Sergeant Blackmore led the dog into the vehicle whereupon it "alerted" towards the back seat. The dog was led into the back seat area and it "alerted" even more strongly where the appellant had been sitting. Sergeant Blackmore then asked the two passengers for their military identification cards. The appellant, whose hands and legs were visibly shaking, was placed under apprehension after the dog "alerted" upon him, and taken to the gate guard shack and read his rights. A search of his pants pocket revealed a small plastic vial containing the heroin which was the basis for the first charge of possession of heroin.

On October 22, 1974, the appellant and another serviceman were entering the base through gate number one; at Sergeant Blackmore's direction the civilian taxi was stopped and ordered to pull over to the side of the road. As the passengers alighted from the taxi, the marihuana dog "alerted" on the other serviceman; Sergeant Blackmore then proceeded to search the car. When the sergeant noticed the appellant,[2] he took the dog out of the car and asked both the appellant and the other serviceman for their military identification cards. After the dog "alerted" on both men, Sergeant Blackmore informed both that they were being detained. At that point the appellant started to move behind the other passenger and appeared to Sergeant Blackmore to be attempting to place a white container in his mouth. After a struggle, the sergeant was able to force the appellant to spit out the pieces of the container, analysis of which revealed heroin which was the basis for the second possession charge.

I start with the proposition recently reaffirmed by the Supreme Court in *United States v. Ramsey*, 431 U.S. 606, 616-8, 97 S. Ct. 1972, 52 L. Ed. 2d 617 (1977), that searches made at the border, [footnote omitted] pursuant to the longstanding right of the sovereign to protect itself by stopping and examining persons and property crossing into the country, are reasonable simply because they occur at the border. [footnote omitted]. This exception to the search warrant requirement is not based upon the doctrine of exigent circumstances, but instead is the result of historical recognition by both the Congress and the Court of the distinctions between those activities occurring at the border and those occurring elsewhere. The Supreme Court in *Boyd v. United States*, 116 U.S. 616, 6 S. Ct. 524, 29 L. Ed. 746 (1886), set forth the doctrinal basis for the exception by

---

[1] Our decision, therefore, will be concerned with, and limited to, searches occurring at entry point onto American military installations/ enclaves from foreign soil. We further limit our inquiry, and the holding of this case, to those procedures which permit an external search of the suspect and his clothing as well as the vehicle and its contents.

[2] I find nothing, however, in the record to indicate that the sergeant adopted a different procedure upon recognizing the appellant; instead, he continued to search in accordance with the standard procedures.

noting that from the commencement of our government, customs agents have had the power to make searches and seizures without the normal prerequisites of probable cause or a search warrant. The Court emphasized that the very Congress which proposed the Bill of Rights enacted the first customs statute granting such powers to those entrusted with protection of the international borders.

. . . .

Travelers may be so stopped in crossing an international boundary because of national self-protection reasonably requiring one entering the country to identify himself as entitled to come in, and his belongings as effects which may be lawfully brought in. [footnote omitted].

Clearly the Court in recognizing this exception concluded that Congress had, by enacting the 1789 Act virtually contemporaneously with its proposal of the Bill of Rights, already considered and balanced the conflicting societal interests [footnote omitted] involved, and that this balancing passed constitutional muster.

I recognize that a distinction between the problem posed by this case and that addressed by the Supreme Court in the *Boyd* line of decisions is the absence of Congressional action granting this custom power to the military as to points of entry onto American installations in foreign countries. [footnote omitted]. Yet, I feel that the essential underlying rationale remains applicable, and that the factual similarities between an international border and the entrance onto an American military installation overseas compels adoption of the border search exception for this situation. [footnote omitted].

Examining the facts of this case, I am satisfied that the procedures utilized were reasonable and sufficiently non-intrusive to comply with the standards enunciated by the Supreme Court. The magnitude of the service's need—to maintain the security of the installation on foreign soil and to combat an ever increasing drug traffic problem [footnote omitted]—when coupled with the reasonableness of the procedures I would authorize [footnote omitted] persuade me that each search meets the requirements of the Fourth Amendment. The decision of the United States Air Force Court of Military Review is affirmed.

Note that searches at the entry or exit point of a base, aircraft or ship located in the United States must be all-inclusive or random. These types of examinations are considered to be inspections. What difference is there between a search at an exit or entry point of a military installation overseas and an inspection? Is the purpose of both types of searches the same?

SEARCHES OF GOVERNMENT PROPERTY

Military Rule of Evidence 314 addresses searches of government property.

(d) Searches of government property. Government property may be searched under this rule unless the person to whom the property is issued or assigned has a reasonable expectation of privacy therein at the time of the search. Under normal circumstances, a person does not have a reasonable expectation of privacy in government property that is not issued for personal use. Wall or floor lockers in living quarters issued for the purpose of storing personal possessions normally are issued for personal use; but the determination as to whether a person has a reasonable expectation of privacy in government property issued for personal use depends on the facts and circumstances at the time of the search.

The legality of a search of government property will turn on whether the item was issued for personal use as described above What factors will bear on that determination? The next case considers that issue.

United States, Appellee, v. Felix A. Muniz, Captain
U.S. Air Force, Appellant.
United States Court of Military Appeals
23 M.J. 201

OPINION: Cox, Judge

Appellant was charged with signing a false official document (a leave request form); conduct unbecoming an officer by making a false statement to a noncommissioned officer (that he had to go on leave to Puerto Rico); and drunk driving, in violation of Articles 107, 133, and 111, Uniform Code of Military Justice, 10 U.S.C. @@ 907, 933, and 911, respectively. At trial, he made an unsuccessful motion to suppress the fruits of a search of his office credenza and any information derivative thereof. The military judge denied the motion on the grounds that appellant "did not have a reasonable expectation of privacy . . . [in] the credenza in his office; and that the evidence was not obtained as a result of unlawful search or seizure."

Thereafter, appellant entered conditional pleas of guilty[1] to the false-document and false-statement charges and unconditional pleas of guilty to the drunk-driving charge.

A general court-martial comprised of members sentenced him to dismissal from the service. The convening authority approved the sentence. [footnote omitted]. In its unpublished opinion, the Court of Military Review did not decide whether appellant had a reasonable expectation of privacy in the credenza. Instead, the court affirmed on the ground that the intrusion was justified by an emergency.

. . . .

[T]he questions now before the Court are whether appellant had a reasonable expectation of privacy in the contents of a government-owned credenza drawer and, if so, whether the intrusion into it was nonetheless justified. Under the circumstances of this case, I conclude that he did not have such an expectation—at least vis-a-vis his commander—and, in any event, we hold that exigent circumstances justified the intrusion. The following facts are essentially undisputed.

----

[1]R.C.M. 910(a)(2), Manual for Courts-Martial, United States, 1984, provides:

With the approval of the military judge and the consent of the Government, an accused may enter a conditional plea of guilty, reserving in writing the right, on further review or appeal, to review of the adverse determination of any specified pretrial motion. If the accused prevails on further review or appeal, the accused shall be allowed to withdraw the plea of guilty. The Secretary concerned may prescribe who may consent for the Government; unless otherwise prescribed by the Secretary concerned, the trial counsel may consent on behalf of the Government.

I

Appellant was second in command of the 96th Munitions Maintenance Squadron, Dyess AFB, Texas. During the last week of September and the first week of October, 1983, appellant's commander, Lieutenant Colonel John M. Rhoads, was on leave. Appellant was in charge of the squadron. Appellant, though married and the father of a young daughter, had evidently established some sort of relationship with Captain S, a female Air Force officer, not appellant's wife, who was stationed at Greenham Common RAF Base, England. Apparently, appellant made the acquaintance of this officer in Aviano, Italy, where they both had been stationed previously.

In late September 1983, during Lieutenant Colonel Rhoads' leave, appellant called Captain S and told her (falsely) that he had been granted leave and (accurately) that he would be coming to visit her for two weeks. Several days later, appellant told the unit first sergeant, Master Sergeant Thomas Little, that he had to go on leave to Puerto Rico because his uncle had died and he needed to care for his ailing mother (it was this statement that constituted the conduct-unbecoming charge). Indeed, it appears that appellant's uncle had recently died, but taking care of his mother was not what was animating appellant. His only purpose in saying this to Master Sergeant Little was to set the stage for his clandestine trip to England. To be consistent with the story he told his wife, appellant also asked the first sergeant to tell her, should she inquire, that he was on a temporary duty assignment. The reason given for requesting this service was purportedly to not upset her because of his uncle's death.

A few days later, but still before the commander returned, appellant filled out and signed a leave request indicating a leave address, without telephone number, in Puerto Rico (this action resulted in the false-official-document charge). Placing the document on the commander's desk for his signature, appellant departed for England only hours before the commander returned. In accordance with appellant's instructions, the first sergeant duly briefed the commander on the crisis; and the request was approved. But for an untimely ear infection, nobody might have been the wiser.

What appellant could not anticipate was that his infant daughter would develop an ear infection of such proportions as to require surgery. Confronted with this situation, Mrs. Muniz came in to see Lieutenant Colonel Rhoads to enlist his assistance in getting in touch with appellant. The exact degree of medical urgency is not documented in the record, and it does not appear that Rhoads was so informed. Nonetheless, the impression was unmistakably conveyed to Rhoads that the situation was serious and that it was urgent that Mrs. Muniz consult with appellant before giving her consent to the operation. As can be imagined, Rhoads and Little sprang into action.

Through Red Cross and security police channels, all efforts were employed to contact appellant at his supposed leave address in Puerto Rico. When it was discovered that the address appellant left was insufficient, they sent for appellant's file from the personnel office and got a better address. Of course, the efforts to contact him in Puerto Rico were to no avail, as he was in England. It is certain that appellant's relatives in Puerto Rico were actually contacted because Mrs. Muniz received at least one phone call from a relative in Puerto Rico asking why the security police were coming around looking for appellant. Having no idea at the time that her husband was supposedly in Puerto Rico, Mrs. Muniz became quite upset and called Lieutenant Colonel Rhoads about it.

Again she impressed on him the urgency of contacting appellant.

Confronted with this turn of events, Rhoads and Little began to realize that appellant was not where he said he would be. Still motivated by the overriding need to put him in contact with his wife about his daughter, however, they began to play long shots. They both knew appellant had only recently arrived at the unit from his previous assignment in Italy. Master Sergeant Little also recalled that appellant had been receiving letters at the unit, through distribution, with an APO return number. Thinking that there might be a connection between his unexplained absence and the letters—or perhaps because they simply had nothing better to go on—the two "sleuths" decided to look in his office for the letters, on the chance that they might provide a clue. Not having any luck on the surfaces or in the unlocked drawers, they "jimmied" the lock on a drawer of appellant's credenza.

In the drawer, they found a stack of letters bearing an APO return address. According to their testimony, they merely copied the APO number, along with a "PSE box," leaving the letters in the drawer. Both Rhoads and Little insisted that they did not open the letters or even remove them from the drawer. As no sender's name appeared with the return address, they consulted a directory and found that the number corresponded to Greenham Common RAF Base, England. It so happened that another member of the unit, Staff Sergeant Prentiss, had also been assigned at Aviano. Rhoads and Little asked Prentiss if he knew of anyone who had been at Aviano but who was now at Greenham Common. Prentiss identified Captain S.

The effort then shifted to contacting Captain S. By dint of considerable persistence, they got through to her duty section but found that she was on leave (she was touring the country with appellant). They left the message that, if appellant were there, he was to call Lieutenant Colonel Rhoads or Mrs. Muniz immediately, as there had been an emergency. When appellant and Captain S returned from their travels several days later, they found the note; appellant promptly called Lieutenant Colonel Rhoads. By then, the surgery had been successfully completed, and appellant was so informed. Rhoads also ordered appellant to return to base, which he did.[2]

II

There is no question that the Fourth Amendment to the Constitution applies to service members. *See United States v. Stuckey*, 10 M.J. 347, 349 (C.M.A. 1981). That amendment provides:

> The right of the people to be secure in their persons, houses, papers, and effects, against unreasonable searches and seizures, shall not be violated, and no Warrants shall issue, but upon probable cause, supported by Oath or affirmation, and particularly describing the place to be searched, and the persons or things to be seized.

The classic remedy for an illegal government search or seizure is the suppression at trial of the improperly obtained evidence and any other evidence derived therefrom. [footnote omitted] [citations omitted]. Formerly, before an accused could avail himself of such remedies, he had the burden of establishing that he had "standing." In the context of searches, standing generally depended on the closeness and strength of one's connection to

---

[2]Captain S, who, unlike appellant, employed no deception in obtaining leave, evidently was counseled "for dating a married man" for her part in the escapade.

the premises or item searched. [citations omitted]. Under the present view, however, an accused must demonstrate a "legitimate expectation of privacy" in the place searched. [citations omitted]. Whether an accused had such an expectation appears to be a legal conclusion. [citations omitted].

The evidence taken regarding the privacy conditions in the office was also essentially uncontroverted. Appellant, as second in command, had a separate office. This office and the credenza therein were government property. The principal purpose of the facility was to conduct military business. Though the door to the office was lockable, both the commander and the first sergeant had access to it by key. The credenza was allocated to appellant's exclusive use. It had recently arrived at the unit and had come equipped with a set of keys. Appellant had never been asked to turn in any of the keys, and no unit policy had been formulated concerning the nature of items unit members might keep in their work areas. From time to time in the course of their official duties, various staff members would enter each other's work areas, notwithstanding the absence of the occupant, to obtain work products. Appellant's office had previously been so entered, despite his absence, for such purposes. No one had ever entered his locked credenza drawers.

Like the earlier civilian cases, our earlier military cases tended to emphasize the ownership interests in the property in question. [citations omitted]. It is now clear, however, in the civilian context that people can acquire legitimate expectations of privacy vis-a-vis law-enforcement authorities in property they do not own. [citations omitted]. Thus, the fact that the credenza was government-owned does not automatically exclude the possibility that appellant may have acquired a legitimate expectation of privacy in its contents.

Nonetheless, the ownership status of property unquestionably plays a significant role in the expectation of privacy which society is willing to regard as reasonable. See Rakas v. Illinois, 439 U.S. at 143-44 n. 12, 99 S. Ct. at 430-31 n. 12. It goes without saying that one has a much greater expectation of privacy in one's own property, on one's own premises, than in property owned by someone else, on that person's premises, for use in that person's business. Thus, in Mancusi v. DeForte, supra, the Court pointed out that Mancusi's expectation of privacy in the property seized (union records) related only to the police. There was no question that the "union higher ups" had access to it. There also seems to have been no doubt that a business supervisor could consent to the search of company property in the custody of a subordinate. [citations omitted]. Rhoads, as appellant's commander, was clearly such a business supervisor, and there appears to be no reason why he could not have had access to the government property in appellant's constructive custody.[3]

The only seemingly complicating factor in the military is that sometimes business-supervisor and law-enforcement authority

---

[3]The government property was the drawer itself. Assuming the legitimacy of that entry, the return address, on what was undeniably private property, could apparently be seen in plain view. See Illinois v. Andreas, 463 U.S. 765, 771, 103 S. Ct. 3319, 3324, 77 L. Ed. 2d 1003 (1983). Moreover, it may be that an expectation of privacy cannot be maintained as to the external portion of an envelope that has been transmitted through the mails. [citations omitted]. Further, in view of the various justifications for the entry into the drawer, see infra, it may well be that, even if Rhoads and Little had read the contents of the letters and thereby discovered appellant's location, such action would have been lawful under the circumstances.

merge in the person of the commander. That fact should not detain us, however. For one thing, the commander, as supervisor, should be in no worse position than his civilian counterpart with respect to access to "company" property. Certainly, it can potentially be far more critical for a military commander to have access to the assets under his supervision than a civilian supervisor. More importantly, the issue is the legitimacy of the individual's claim to privacy, not which hat the commander happens to be wearing that day.

In that regard, we note that the credenza, like any other item of government property within the command, was subject at a moment's notice to a thorough inspection. *United States v. Middleton*, 10 M.J. 123 (C.M.A. 1981). That omnipresent fact of military life, coupled with the indisputable government ownership and the ordinarily nonpersonal nature of military offices, could have left appellant with only the most minimal expectation—or hope—of privacy in the drawer vis-a-vis his commander. This minimal expectation must be distinguished from an unquestionably greater expectation of privacy and security vis-a-vis the rest of the world.

Additionally, it should be borne in mind that Rhoads, above all, was appellant's military commander. That particular relationship imposes a much greater degree of responsibility—in both directions—than is true of most civilian analogs. [footnote omitted]. As commander, Rhoads had a compelling duty to notify his subordinate of his child's trouble—if for no other reason than to permit him to return home and comfort her. Had Rhoads simply given up at the first dead end, had he merely contented himself with sitting on his hands and not even bothering to exert the minimal effort of breaking into this government-owned drawer, we would have had serious reservations about his fitness to command. *Cf. State v. Hetzko*, 283 So.2d

49, 52 (Fla. App. 1973) (officers would have been derelict in their duty if they acted otherwise). A service member has a right to expect that, if he is killed in battle, his leaders will not willingly surrender his body to the enemy. He should have no less reason to trust that, if his dependents are in trouble, his leaders will exert every human effort to find him. By not being where he led his commander to believe he would be, appellant virtually invited his commander to look in his credenza drawer if it became necessary to contact him. Just as the rescuer's actions are foreseeable in the civil law, W. Prosser, Handbook of the Law of Torts @ 44 (4th ed. 1971), appellant should have foreseen Rhoads' actions. Viewed in this light, it was really appellant's misconduct that dispersed whatever lingering remnants of privacy, vis-a-vis his commander, he may have retained in the drawer.

There is another potentially relevant aspect of command responsibility, although not specifically invoked by Rhoads here. That is, a commander has a duty at all times to be able to account for his people. By appellant's breaching his duty to his commander, and by that fact coming to the commander's attention, Rhoads' obligation to account for him was triggered. Just as above, this obligation should have been foreseen by appellant. For this reason also, appellant cannot reasonably insist that the contents of his government-issued credenza should have remained inviolate. Indeed, it is mildly ironic that appellant should think he could leave behind some sacrosanct aura of privacy in his government-supplied credenza, while he himself was free to run about the world and deceive his superiors about his location.

For these several reasons, the military judge was correct in concluding that appellant had no grounds to complain of a violation of his Fourth Amendment rights against unreasonable searches and seizures.

III

Even if appellant had possessed a legitimate expectation of privacy in the drawer, he would still not have prevailed. In this respect, we agree also with the Court of Military Review that the emergency, as reasonably perceived by Rhoads and Little, justified the entry. The Fourth Amendment consists of two main components. The first part refers to the right of the people to be free of unreasonable searches. The second part describes the circumstances under which warrants may issue. The interrelationship between the two parts has historically been expressed in terms such that searches without a valid warrant are unreasonable, unless they fall within one of the recognized exceptions to the warrant requirement; and the burden is on the Government to show that the search fits within an exception. [citations omitted]. [footnote omitted].

In addition, we have held that military conditions justified several types of warrantless intrusions into what, in other circumstances, might have involved protected privacy rights. *Murray v. Haldeman,* 16 M.J. 74 (C.M.A. 1983) (compulsory urinalysis); *United States v. Middleton*, 10 M.J. 123 (C.M.A. 1981) (inspections); *United States v. Harris,* 5 M.J. 44 (C.M.A. 1978) (random gate searches); *United States v. Kazmierczak,* 16 U.S.C.M.A. 594, 37 C.M.R. 214 (1967) (inventory of confined service member's belongings). This catalog suggests that "[t]he ultimate standard set forth in the Fourth Amendment is reasonableness," *Cady v. Dombrowski, supra* 413 U.S. at 439, 93 S. Ct. at 2527; *see South Dakota v. Opperman, supra* 428 U.S. at 370 and n. 5, and 373, 96 S. Ct. at 3097 and n. 5, and 3099, as opposed to some previously frozen list of "exceptions."

One such exception that is clearly established is the "emergency" doctrine, the basis upon which the Court of Military Review found that Lieutenant Colonel Rhoads' actions were reasonable. A classic statement of that doctrine is found in *Wayne v. United States*, 115 U.S. App. D.C. 234, 318 F.2d 205, 212 (D.C. Cir.), *cert. denied*, 375 U.S. 860, 84 S. Ct. 125, 11 L. Ed. 2d 86 (1963), where then Judge Burger stated for the court:

[A] warrant is not required to break down a door to enter a burning home to rescue occupants or extinguish a fire, to prevent a shooting or to bring emergency aid to an injured person. The need to protect or preserve life or avoid serious injury is justification for what would be otherwise illegal absent an exigency or emergency. Fires or dead bodies are reported to police by cranks where no fires or bodies are to be found. Acting in response to reports to "dead bodies," the police may find the "bodies" to be common drunks, diabetics in shock, or distressed cardiac patients. But the business of policemen and firemen is to act, not to speculate or meditate on whether the report is correct. People could well die in emergencies if police tried to act with the calm deliberation associated with the judicial process. Even the apparently dead often are saved by swift police response. A myriad of circumstances could fall within the terms "exigent circumstances" . . . . *e.g.*, smoke coming out a window or under a door, the sound of gunfire in a house, threats from the inside to shoot through the door at police, reasonable grounds to believe an injured or seriously ill person is being held within.

See also Root v. Gauper, 438 F.2d 361 (8th Cir. 1971).

In all candor, there is some question in our minds as to whether the need to contact appellant rose to the level of a true emergency in the sense of *Wayne v. United States, supra.* Assuming that the operation itself was a medical necessity, Mrs. Muniz was present and able to consent to the operation, as she evidently later did in appellant's absence. There is no suggestion that she was so irrational as to be unable to make a responsible decision. Moreover, we cannot simply assume that the local medical authorities would have refused, or been precluded, from operating in a true emergency. Certainly, there have been many cases where judicial authorities have ordered necessary medical treatment for minors, even over the objections of the parents. *See* Annot., 97 A.L.R. 3d 421 (1980); Annot., 52 A.L.R. 3d 1118 (1973). In other words, it was not established that the operation could not have been authorized but for appellant's approval.

However, whether a true emergency actually existed is beside the point. Like the courts below, we must examine the circumstances as they appeared to Rhoads and Little at the time they acted. *United States v. Erb,* 596 F.2d 412, 419 (10th Cir.), *cert. denied,* 444 U.S. 848, 100 S. Ct. 97, 62 L. Ed. 2d 63 (1979). Based on the information presented to them, we can hardly fault them for electing not to gamble on the well-being of the child. Up to and including the time when the credenza was searched and the call to England was placed, there appears to be no doubt that Rhoads and Little were operating with the best of intentions and on the assumption that obtaining appellant's consent, or at least advice, was imperative. Therefore, we also agree with the Court of Military Review that the search of the drawer was reasonable under the emergency exception to the Fourth Amendment.

The decision of the United States Air Force Court of Military Review is affirmed.

The issue in *Muniz* was whether the accused had an expectation of privacy in a locked desk. What factors did the court consider in making its ruling? Is there a privacy expectation in other types of government property? *See United States v. Battles* above for a discussion of the privacy expectation in barracks. The Court of Military Appeals also upheld the search of Captain Muniz' locker as a lawful "emergency" search. Military Rule of Evidence 314 discusses emergency situations:

> (i) Emergency searches to save life or for related purposes. In emergency circumstances to save life or for a related purpose, a search may be conducted of persons or property in a good faith effort to render immediate medical aid, to obtain information that will assist in the rendering of such aid, or to prevent immediate or ongoing personal injury.

A valid emergency search does not require probable cause to conduct the search. *Compare* emergency searches with the exigent circumstances exception to the search authorization requirement discussed above. Do the two principles go hand in hand? Where does probable cause come into play in the exigent circumstances exception? In the O.J. Simpson murder trial, the police claimed that they feared for the safety of Mr. Simpson and his children. Is this a legitimate emergency under military law? Consider the following case.

United States v. Technical Sergeant Marvin J. Walker, United States Air Force
United States Air Force Court of Military Review
Slip Opinion
October 3, 1985

OPINION: PER CURIAM

Before a general court-martial consisting of members, the accused was convicted, pursuant to mixed pleas, of wrongful possession of marijuana with intent to distribute* and wrongful use of marijuana. The approved sentence was a bad conduct discharge, forfeiture of $413.00 per month for 30 months, confinement for 30 months, and reduction to E-1.

* The appellant entered a conditional guilty plea to wrongfully possessing marijuana, a lesser included offense of wrongfully possessing marijuana with the intent to distribute, *see* paragraph 37d(6), MCM 1984, choosing to contest only the allegation that his possession was with the intent to distribute. Additionally, he entered an unconditional guilty plea to wrongfully using marijuana.

On appeal, the appellant contends that the military judge erred in denying his motion to suppress evidence of a letter addressed to his wife seized by an OSI agent during a warrantless search of his off base quarters.

The facts are not in dispute. On 4 January 1985, while on leave in the Philippines, the appellant was apprehended by Air Force Security Police for wrongful possession of marijuana. He was allowed to return to his duty station at Kadena Air Base the following day. On 10 January 1985 the OSI Superintendent of Investigative Operations on Kadena AB, Mr. Louis F. Breaux, Jr., received a telephone call from the Security Police Desk Sergeant that there was a possible homicide at an off base residence of an Air Force member.

Agent Breaux proceeded to the scene. The Security Police Flight Chief, other Security Police representatives, local law enforcement officials, the appellant's First Sergeant, and hospital personnel were there when he arrived. The OSI agent learned that the situation involved the appellant, the same sergeant who was recently apprehended for possession of marijuana in the Philippines. Meanwhile the medics were inside the appellant's residence rendering aid. The OSI agent looked through a window and saw the appellant lying in a bath tub. At about this time some medics came out and asked if they could move certain items to affect the appellant's removal from the apartment. Agent Breaux knew that a knife was either in the bath tub or near to it, however, since it was necessary to save the appellant's life he voiced no objections to the appellant's removal from his residence. Agent Breaux saw the medics remove the appellant from the apartment on a stretcher. He then proceeded to discuss the case with the Okinawan officials at the scene and did not enter the appellant's residence until 10 to 15 minutes after he had witnessed him removed therefrom. Agent Breaux then entered the apartment for the express purpose of investigating whether there had been a suicide or homicide attempt. The OSI Agent was asked by defense counsel (during the preliminary inquiry on the defense motion to suppress a letter, contained in a sealed envelope, to the accused's wife) "so your entrance then into the apartment was not to render any kind of emergency aid to, you know, in assistance to Sgt Walker, was it?" Answer: "no."

In his ruling on the defense motion the Military Judge found that Agent Breaux entered the appellant's apartment without his consent, "but under a good faith belief and with probable cause within the meaning of Military Rules of Evidence 314(i), and that the OSI agent's seizure of the envelope described above was still within the guidelines of MRE 314(i)." Having made these findings, he then denied the defense motion to suppress the envelope and letter. (An ambiguous paragraph of that letter could be construed to mean Sgt Walker intended to distribute for profit the marijuana he was apprehended with in the Philippines.)

Given these facts, we find that the warrantless search of appellant's residence did not qualify as a search conducted pursuant to the emergency circumstances envisioned by M.R.E. 314(1). In the case at bar, the OSI agent knew the appellant had already been removed from his residence by the medics when he entered some 10 to 15 minutes later. His stated delayed purpose in going into Sgt Walker's residence was clearly not a good faith effort to render immediate medical aid or to obtain information that would assist in the rendering of such aid, or to prevent immediate or ongoing personal injury, but to seek evidence to establish whether there had been a suicide attempt. This court has held that such a warrantless intrusion was not "an emergency search" under M.R.E. 134(i), and that such an intrusion violated the appellant's rights under the Fourth Amendment. *United States v. Smeal*, 49 C.M.R. 75, (C.M.A. 1975); *United States v. Hays*, 16 M.J. 636 (A.F.C.M.R. 1983). *Also see United States v. Gammon*, 16 M.J. 646 (A.F.C.M.R. 1983).

Having concluded the search of the appellant's house was improper and that the trial judge erred in not suppressing the only evidence suggesting the appellant's planned involvement in the distribution of marijuana, we find insufficient evidence to support a finding of possessing marijuana with intent to distribute. Accordingly, a conviction for this offense cannot stand. However, the appellant's guilty plea to the lesser included offense of wrongfully possessing marijuana was provident and is affirmed. The remaining findings of guilty are affirmed. Reassessing the sentence in light of the error discussed above, we find appropriate only so much of the sentence as provides for a bad conduct discharge, confinement for 24 months, and forfeiture of $413.00 per month for 24 months. The findings of guilty and the sentence, both as modified, are

AFFIRMED.

CONSENT SEARCHES

Military Rule of Evidence 314 addresses consent searches.

  (e) Consent searches.

   (1) General rule. Searches may be conducted of any person or property with lawful consent.

   (2) Who may consent. A person may consent to a search of his or her person or property, or both, unless control over such property has been given to another. A person may grant consent to search property when the person exercises control over that property.

(3) Scope of consent. Consent may be limited in any way by the person granting consent, including limitations in terms of time, place, or property and may be withdrawn at any time.

(4) Voluntariness. To be valid, consent must be given voluntarily. Voluntariness is a question to be determined from all the circumstances. Although a person's knowledge of the right to refuse to give consent is a factor to be considered in determining voluntariness, the prosecution is not required to demonstrate such knowledge as a prerequisite to establishing a voluntary consent. Mere submission to the color of authority of personnel performing law enforcement duties or acquiescence in an announced or indicated purpose to search is not a voluntary consent.

(5) Burden of proof. Consent must be shown by clear and convincing evidence. The fact that a person was in custody while granting consent is a factor to be considered in determining the voluntariness of the consent, but it does not affect the burden of proof.

Whether a consent is lawful depends on the voluntariness of the permission to search. *United States v. Goudy* below addresses the factors used to determine whether a consent is voluntary.

United States, Appellee, v. Stephen A. Goudy, Lance Corporal, U.S. Marine Corps, Appellant
United States Court of Military Appeals
32 M.J. 88
February 5, 1991

OPINION:

A special court-martial (military judge alone) convicted appellant, contrary to his pleas, of stealing a television, a graphic equalizer, and assorted clothing of a fellow service member—violations of Article 121, Uniform Code of Military Justice, 10 USC @ 921. Thereafter, the judge sentenced appellant to a bad-conduct discharge, confinement and forfeiture of $447.00 pay per month for 6 months, and reduction to the lowest enlisted grade. The convening authority approved these results.

In its review, the Court of Military Review specified for briefs and argument an issue that addresses the same matters upon which we ultimately granted review. In the end, though, the court affirmed the findings and sentence in a memorandum opinion.

On appellant's petition, we agreed to consider whether his consent to a search of his wall locker, his car, and his living quarters was voluntary under the totality of the circumstances and, if it was not, whether the illegal search tainted his subsequent written and testimonial admissions. [footnote omitted]. See Mil.R.Evid. 311, Manual for Courts-Martial, United States, 1984. The Government has conceded in this Court that, if the consent was involuntary, appellant's admissions were, indeed, tainted. Accordingly, the beginning and the end of our inquiry is whether appellant's consent was voluntary. We now decide that it was.

. . . .

I

Major Harrison, appellant's company commander, suspected that appellant had stolen a number of items of personal property belonging to other members of the unit. Apparently, appellant earlier had made incriminating statements to two people concerning their missing property, and Harrison was aware of these statements. Accordingly, he arranged for Sergeant Laird, an apprentice investigator with the Criminal Investigation Division, to come to his office to look into the matter.

When appellant arrived for work at 6:30 a.m., his supervisor advised him that he was to report to Major Harrison's office at 8:00 a.m.; in the meantime, he was told to carry out his normal duties but was admonished that he would be under the "strict guide" of one of the company's sergeants. Specifically, although appellant's usual routine was undisturbed, he was not to go anywhere or do anything except in the presence of the named sergeant.

At the appointed hour, the sergeant escorted appellant to Harrison's office, where appellant reported to his commander in the position of attention. Laird and Staff Sergeant Hudson, another investigator, also were in the room, and Harrison introduced them to appellant. Preliminarily, Harrison advised appellant that he suspected him of selling a television that did not belong to him and of stealing personal property of other Marines in the barracks. He asked generally whether appellant understood his rights under Article 31 of the Code, 10 U.S.C. @ 831, to which appellant replied that he did.

Harrison observed that the best way to clear up the matter would be to search appellant's room. He advised appellant that "he needed" his "consent" to do so and suggested that, if appellant "had nothing to hide, there was no reason" not to give that consent by signing a consent-to-search form.

As is implied in our granted issues, of course, appellant did ultimately sign the form. After Harrison had made the comments set out above, appellant responded, "'Okay,' or 'Yes,' something like that, in that nature," and Harrison "then . . . just gave him to" Laird. Laird described what happened at that point:

> I filled it [the consent form] out and I went step-by-step over all this with him, telling him where to initial, where I had marked out parts that had nothing to do with what we were looking for. Had him read it, then I asked him, "Do you understand everything about this form?" That he didn't have to give his consent to search because that part of the form, it says that you don't have to give your consent to search, and he said, "Okay." Finally, just before appellant signed the form, Laird again asked, "'Do you understand everything on this form?,' and he said, 'Yes.'"

Appellant acknowledged that he was not under arrest or apprehension at the time, only under escort. While Harrison's voice was "authoritative,", appellant conceded that at no time did Harrison raise his voice, scream, or make any threats or promises. Laird described Harrison as "cool, calm, and collected. Just wanted to find out what was going on." Laird also testified that appellant's physical and mental appearance seemed normal at the time, with no indications that he was under the influence of any alcohol or drug that might impair his understanding.

Appellant, however, testified that he took Harrison's request for consent as an "implied order." He explained that an "implied order" is "[s]omething you don't have to do, but sometimes it would be better if you did." He amplified that "you don't have to" obey an implied order, but "presumably" "it would go better for you if you did."

Additionally, appellant could not recall specifically being advised by Laird, while going over the form, that he did not have to give his consent. The prosecutor pointed out that he had initialed and signed the form that gave this advice, but appellant asserted that he had not read the form. When asked why, he responded, "It didn't seem relevant to me, sir." In an effort to better define the ambiguity of this answer, the prosecutor initiated the following exchange:

Q. It didn't seem relevant to you?

A. I was being told that it was a consent to search. A search would be the best way to clear the incident. I wasn't concerned with what the statement said. I understood that it was a consent to search.

Q. So basically you knew that the best chance, the best way to get out of this, you thought was the consent to search. Is that correct?

A. That's what I was instructed by the CO.

Q. You thought it was going to help you out?

A. The CO said that if I didn't have anything to hide there was no reason to not consent to search, sir.

Q. And that was the reason why you consented to the search?

A. That is true, sir.

Q. Because you didn't think you had anything to hide?

A. Yes, sir.

Appellant's stated motivation for signing the consent form is probably best summed up in this brief colloquy between himself and his counsel at the end of his testimony:

Q. Why did you sign this consent-to-search form?

A. Because I was instructed that if I had nothing to hide then there was no reason why I should not. Therefore implying that I should sign it.

Q. Did the Major tell you he needed it?

A. Yes, sir, he did.

Q. When superior officers tell you they need something, what do you do?

A. I do what they ask, sir.

II

If the Government relies upon consent to justify the lawfulness of a search, *see Katz v. United States*, 389 U.S. 347, 88 S. Ct. 507, 19 L. Ed. 2d 576 (1967); Mil.R.Evid. 314(e), it has the burden of proving that consent was freely and voluntarily given. [citations omitted]. Whether such consent was voluntary must be determined from the totality of the circumstances, [citations omitted], and "must be shown by clear and convincing evidence," Mil.R.Evid. 314(e)(5). The person's knowledge of the right to refuse consent, *see Schneckloth v. Bustamonte, supra; United States v. Stoecker*, 17 M.J. 158, 162 (C.M.A. 1984), and the fact that the person is in some form of custody at the time consent is requested, *see United States v. Wallace*, 11 M.J. 445, 448 (C.M.A. 1981), are important factors to be considered. Neither, however, is fully determinative, one way or the other. Mil.R.Evid. 314(e)(4) and (5). To reiterate, the question of consent must be answered from the totality of the circumstances.

Viewing the evidence in the light most favorable to the Government, *see United States v. Lowry*, 2 M.J. 55, 59 (C.M.A. 1976), we conclude from the totality of the circumstances that appellant's consent was voluntarily given. *See* factors discussed in *United States v. Watson*, 423 U.S. 411, 424-25, 96 S. Ct. 820, 828, 46 L. Ed. 2d 598 (1976), and *United States v. Middleton, supra* at 133.

First, appellant acknowledged to Harrison an awareness of his rights under Article 31. Certainly, Harrison's general inquiry in this regard would not be sufficient to meet the requirements for admissibility of a subsequent statement.[1] In the context of a consent to search, however, it does suggest that appellant was alerted to the fact that this confrontation with his commander was one in which his rights as a criminal suspect would be respected.

Second, by appellant's own admission, Harrison never overtly ordered appellant's compliance with his request for consent. We recognize that Goudy had been brought to Harrison's office under escort and that, under many circumstances, a request from a major in the Marine Corps likely would be met with a response of "aye, aye, sir."

However, granting appellant's plea to this Court to view these circumstances as an "implied order," even in the context just discussed in the first consideration above, would virtually establish a "bright-line" rule against a military commander's personally asking a subordinate for his consent to search unless the commander did so informally and without any of the usual trappings of military courtesy that accompany such a meeting. That is neither the law nor logic, much less both.

Third, beyond this, appellant was orally admonished by Laird that he did not have to give his consent, and the form which he signed reiterated that advice. Appellant claims that he did not read the form before signing it; if true, however, he omitted to do so at his own peril. In any event, he received the advice orally from Laird.

Fourth, Harrison told Goudy that he needed his consent in order to search. Accordingly, other than appellant's "implied order" argument addressed above, there is no basis for a claim that appellant's consent was merely acquiescence to a claim of lawful authority. *See generally Bumper v. North Carolina, supra* 391 U.S. at 548-50, 88 S. Ct. at 1791-92 (where searching official first asserted he possessed a warrant, the consent which followed was merely acquiescence to lawful authority, rather than true consent). The message was clear: Appellant, by virtue of his consent, held the key to his privacy.

Fifth, Goudy was a 20-year-old high school graduate, with a GT/GCT score of 129[2] and 2 years of experience in the Marine Corps. Moreover, his testimony at trial—at least so far as can be discerned from the printed pages—was well articu-

---

[1]Unlike a situation in which a statement is sought from a suspect, there is no absolute requirement that a rights warning under Article 31(b), Uniform Code of Military Justice, 10 USC @ 831(b), be given before seeking or obtaining a valid consent to search. [citations omitted].

[2]To put appellant's score in perspective, we are informed by government counsel that the minimum GT score to enlist in the Marine Corps is 80. Further, counsel has advised this Court that an "EL" score of 115 qualifies the subject for certain officer programs; appellant's EL score is 131.

lated and assertive, not at all reflective of an uncertain or submissive person. All this makes it even less likely that appellant— alerted to his statutory rights as a criminal suspect and forthrightly advised that he did not have to consent—would have merely rolled over in the face of an "implied order," as opposed to deciding for himself that his best chance lay in voluntarily consenting.

Sixth, nothing in Harrison's message or demeanor could have overcome appellant's own free choice. The commander was calm and his voice was conversational, not overbearing in any manner. Further, Harrison made no obvious or subtle threats or promises to induce appellant to do something that he had not decided for himself was in his own best interest.

Instead, we agree with the Government's analysis in its final brief in this Court:

> Using the totality of the circumstances test, it is apparent that appellant's consent was more likely based upon his guilty conscience and/or resignation to the inevitable. Acquiescence to one's circumstances is certainly distinguishable from acquiescence to authority. The facts show that appellant had previously (recently) been confronted by the owner of the trousers which appellant had stolen. Appellant had returned them after admitting to the owner that he had stolen them. He had also been recently confronted by the person who had purchased the television from appellant. It seemed as though the true owner of the television had taken issue with the fact that appellant had sold the television. Appellant had made admissions to the purchaser which were incriminatory. Appellant must have realized that things did not look very good for him at the time he was called into the commanding officer's office and advised that he was a suspect of those very crimes, as well as other thefts.

> Whether he believed that he was caught and might as well give up or whether he hoped to bluff his way out of the situation by agreeing to the search to demonstrate that he had nothing to hide—either way, it does not amount to coercion or any overwhelming of appellant's free choice.

. . . .

The decision of the United States Navy-Marine Corps Court of Military Review is affirmed.

Is it always best to attempt to obtain consent prior to conducting a search? What impact would the mental or physical condition of the person granting consent have on the decision to seek permission? From the prosecution's standpoint, written consent is preferable to oral consent. Does *Goudy* illustrate this point? How much control does the person consenting have over the scope of the search? As a general rule, consent may be withdrawn at any time before or during the search and the area or possessions to be searched may be limited.

SEARCHES INCIDENT TO APPREHENSION

Military Rule of Evidence 314 discusses the authority to search following a lawful apprehension.

> (g) Searches incident to a lawful apprehension.
>
> > (1) General rule. A person who has been lawfully apprehended may be searched.
>
> > (2) Search for weapons and destructible evidence. A search may be conducted for weapons or destructible evidence in the area within the immediate control of a person who has been apprehended. The area within the person's "immediate control" is the area which the individual searching could reasonably believe that the person apprehended could reach with a sudden movement to obtain such property; provided, that the passenger compartment of an automobile, and containers within the passenger compartment may be searched as a contemporaneous incident of the apprehension of an occupant of the automobile, regardless of whether the person apprehended has been removed from the vehicle.

The above rule is intended to protect law enforcement officials and to preserve evidence. The following case demonstrates the mechanics of a search incident to an apprehension.

United States, Appellee, v. Anderson Wallace, Jr.
Staff Sergeant U.S. Army, Appellant
U.S. Court of Military Appeals
34 M.J. 353
July 30, 1992

OPINION: Wiss, Judge

Despite appellant's not-guilty pleas, a general court-martial consisting of a military judge alone convicted him of three specifications alleging multiple instances of wrongful distribution of cocaine, *see* Art. 112a, Uniform Code of Military Justice, 10 USC @ 912a. The judge sentenced him to a bad-conduct discharge, confinement for 12 years, and reduction to the lowest enlisted grade. The convening authority approved these results, and the Court of Military Review affirmed in an unpublished opinion.

On appellant's petition, this Court granted review of the following three issues:

I

WHETHER THE MILITARY JUDGE ERRED IN FAILING TO SUPPRESS SLIPS OF PAPER SEIZED FROM APPELLANT DURING THE WARRANTLESS SEARCH OF HIS WALLET, AND THE DERIVATIVE EVIDENCE THEREOF.

. . . .

Now, after full consideration of the record, we affirm.

I

A

The Army Criminal Investigation Command (CID) received an anonymous tip that Specialist Robin Farrar was distributing cocaine from her quarters. In response, the CID instructed Sergeant Sermons, who was a CID confidential source, to make friends with Farrar and to attempt to purchase cocaine from her.

At some point, a meeting between Sermons and Farrar for this purpose was arranged for March 10, 1989, and the CID made all necessary preparations for a controlled buy on that occasion. When Sermons arrived at Farrar's quarters, she advised him that she did not have the cocaine at the moment but that her source would arrive with it soon.

Shortly thereafter, surveilling agents saw a black man and woman drive up to Farrar's quarters in a car that agents learned was registered to appellant. The couple left the car and went into Farrar's quarters.

Inside, Sermons remained alone while the couple and Farrar went to the rear of the quarters. After a short period of time, Farrar returned to Sermons with two bags of cocaine, which Sermons bought. Sermons, however, did not see either of the couple in possession of the cocaine or see either one deliver it to Farrar.

Farrar was apprehended on April 26. During her interrogation, she gave two statements involving appellant in her drug operation and identifying him as the black male whom Sermons had seen on March 10. Apparently, some subsequent efforts were made to set up transactions in which appellant actually would deliver the drug to the agent/buyer, but none was successful. In any event, the CID finally decided to apprehend appellant, and on June 9, 1989, Agent Cobb sent for him. Command

Sergeant Major Boseman escorted appellant to the CID office. The following direct examination of Agent Cobb reveals what happened upon appellant's arrival:

Q. Why did you—why were you having him brought over by the unit, what was the purpose in that?

A. To be formally apprehended.

Q. What happened once the accused got to CID?

A. He arrived in the waiting room, I was told by my clerk that he was here, I went downstairs—

Q. How long do you think he was in the waiting room?

A. 3, 4, no more than 5 minutes, 5 minutes at the most.

Q. Alright *[sic]*, what happened after that?

A. I asked him if he was Staff—Staff Sergeant Wallace, he said that he was, I showed him my identification, I told him he was under apprehension for offenses of wrongful possession, distribution of cocaine, and conspiracy.

Q. Is there any doubt in your mind if you told him he was under apprehension for those offenses?

A. I told him he was under apprehension and I also asked him if he understood what those offenses meant, or if he understood what those offenses were and he nodded in the affirmative. He didn't say anything; he nodded in the affirmative.

Q. Was the accused free to leave your office at that point?

A. No.

Q. Did he seem surprised about what you were saying to him?

A. No, he did not.

Q. What happened next?

A. Uh, I told Staff Sergeant Wallace to empty his pockets, which he did. I told him to stand against the wall and I conducted a pat down search of his body.

Q. Then what did you do?

A. I sat him down, completed a interview worksheet on him, advised him of his rights for the offenses of wrongful possession, distribution of cocaine.

Q. Let's back up a little bit; did you search his wallet at all?

A. Yes, I did.

Q. When?

A. After he had been patted down.

Q. And what did you say to him?

A. I told Sergeant Wallace, I said "watch me as I go through your wallet," we do that sometimes—a lot of times there's currency in there and we don't want any problems or someone to say my money was missing after CID searched my wallet. He was on one side of the table; I was on the other.

Q. Why were you searching the wallet?

A. Any weapons, any destructible evidence that he might have had in the wallet at the time.

Q. How long between the time you searched his wallet, how long was it from the time you told him he was apprehended to the time you searched his wallet.

A. 30 seconds, 45 seconds at the most.

Q. I show you what have been marked as Prosecution Exhibits 1 through 4 for identification [hands documents to witness]; can you tell me what those are?

A. [Examines.] These are photostatic copies of pieces of paper that I removed from Staff Sergeant Wallace's wallet on the day that he was apprehended in my office [returns documents to counsel].

Q. Why did you seize these pieces of paper?

A. We had reason to believe that Sergeant Wallace was a distributor of cocaine, and from the dollar amounts and the names on it, it appeared to be a list of money that was owed for cocaine transaction or drug deals.

Q. What—what was the 1—can you describe to the judge what the list is?

A. . . . It would have like for example, Johnny $100.00, Mary Smith $75.00. Some of the papers contained phone numbers and dollar amounts also.

Q. What—do you know approximately how many names were on these lists?

A. Approximately 23, 24, 25 names.

Q. And approximately what the dollar value was beside these various names?

A. Approximately $2,300.00.

Q. What did you do with these pieces of paper?

A. The originals or the photostatic copies?

Q. The originals?

A. After they were xeroxed they were returned to Staff Sergeant Wallace.

* * *

Q. What happened after that?

A. I advised Sergeant Wallace of his constitutional rights, he—he elected not to waive his rights at that time. He was fingerprinted; attempt to make—attempt to photograph him was made, the camera was inoperable. At that time he was taken to the Military Police Station for subsequent release to his unit.

Q. How was he released to the MPs; was it on a actual form, a release form?

A. I took him to the Military Police and directed that they release him to the unit on a DD Form 629 or DA Form 629.

Q. Your purpose in having the accused come to your office on the 9th of June 1989 was to apprehend him?

A. The only reason was to apprehend him, that's correct.

Subsequently, CID agents attempted to contact the people whose names were on the list

copies; two of them agreed to cooperate in the investigation and implicated appellant in drug distributions. Their trial testimony, as well as the list copies, were admitted against appellant over his objection.

B

The Court of Military Review held that the challenged search of appellant's wallet was incident to his apprehension and that the apprehension was supported by probable cause. We agree.

. . . .

[T]his Court stated in *United States v. Schneider*, 14 M.J. 189, 194 (C.M.A. 1982), that probable cause for apprehension exists where "the facts and circumstances within . . . [the officers'] knowledge and of which they had reasonably trustworthy information [are] sufficient in themselves to warrant a man of reasonable caution in the belief that" an offense has been or is being committed.

. . . .

Measured against this standard, we conclude that the Government is correct when it argues that "it cannot be seriously contended that SA Cobb lacked probable cause to apprehend the accused." Answer to Final Brief at 7. When Sermons entered Farrar's quarters to purchase cocaine, Farrar told him she had none but that her supplier would be there shortly. A few minutes later, a man driving a car registered to appellant arrived and accompanied Farrar to a back room. Shortly, Farrar returned to Sermons with two bags of cocaine. Finally, when she was apprehended several weeks later, Farrar herself expressly fingered appellant as her cocaine source in her drug business and as the man Sermons had seen in her apartment on March 10.

In response, appellant points to the fact that he was not apprehended until June 9— 6 weeks after Farrar had implicated him and 3 months after Sermons' purchase from Farrar. He argues, "It is not well settled that the justification for a search incident to apprehension still apply [sic] three months after the crime." Final Brief at 5. On this basis, he concludes, "The probable cause to arrest was stale and the probable cause to search must be considered in the same light." *Id*. at 6.

Of course, a full search incident to apprehension does not, itself, depend upon probable cause to search; instead, its validity flows from the lawfulness of the apprehension. [citations omitted]. Moreover, appellant fails to cite any authority at all for his novel supposition that probable cause to apprehend, like probable cause to search, can become fatally stale with the mere passage of time. Consideration of the bases of these probable-cause determinations quickly reveals the illogic of such a proposition.

Probable cause to search is based upon belief that evidence will be found in a particular place; because evidence does not necessarily stay put, time may be a factor in determining probable cause to believe whether the evidence sought will be found in the place to be searched. In contrast, probable cause to apprehend is based upon a belief that a crime has been committed by the apprehendee. Once a crime has been committed, it stays committed—that fact is unaffected by the passage of time; and probable cause to believe that the apprehendee is the one who committed it "normally would not grow stale as easily as that which supports a warrant to search a particular place for particular objects." *United States v. Watson*, 423 U.S. 411, 432 n. 5, 96 S. Ct. 820, 832 n. 5, 46 L. Ed. 2d 598 (1976) (Powell, J., concurring). Accordingly, passage of time since commission of the offense usually is not relevant to probable cause to apprehend or to the lawfulness of a search incident to apprehension.

Additionally, appellant's argument erroneously implies that the challenged search was based upon probable cause; instead, as was made clear earlier, the prosecution's theory throughout—and the basis of the decision below—was that the search was proper as being incident to a lawful apprehension.

Moreover, appellant's fanciful arguments notwithstanding, no rational conclusion can be permitted but that the search was incident to an apprehension. According to Agent Cobb's testimony, he sent for appellant for the very purpose of formally apprehending him; upon arrival, Cobb promptly informed appellant that he was under apprehension and the reasons therefor, *see* RCM 302(d)(1). Within seconds thereafter, appellant's pockets were emptied, his body patted down, and his wallet searched—all directed at locating any weapons or "destructible evidence." Appellant was then fingerprinted and finally taken to the Military Police Station for formal release to his unit. These circumstances leave no room at all to doubt Cobb's testimony that "the only reason" he had sent for appellant "was to apprehend him."

Finally, appellant's contention that the search of his wallet was outside the lawful scope of a search incident to apprehension misses the mark. A search for weapons or destructible evidence "within the 'immediate control' area" of the arrestee—without regard to whether there is probable cause to believe that the person has a weapon or is about to destroy evidence—is reasonable, at least so long as the search is not "remote in time or place from the arrest." [citations omitted].

. . . .

C

. . . .

In sum, then, we conclude that Agent Cobb had probable cause to apprehend appellant; that he did lawfully apprehend appellant; and that the challenged search of appellant's wallet was incident to the apprehension.

The decision of the United States Army Court of Military Review is affirmed.

The U.S. Supreme Court in *New York v. Belton*, 453 U.S. 545 (1981), held that a lawful apprehension of passengers in a vehicle authorizes a search of not only the entire passenger compartment of the vehicle, but also any container found therein, whether such container is open or closed. Even if the vehicle occupants are under arrest and outside the automobile, the vehicle's passenger compartment and containers may be searched. Note that a search incident to an apprehension does not authorize the search of the vehicle's trunk, only the passenger compartment and containers located therein. Why are law enforcement officials given such broad authority to search a vehicle following an arrest? *Compare* the authority to search incident to an apprehension with the exigent circumstances exception to the warrant requirement. Is there ever a situation in which a search authorization is required to search a car?

STUDY QUESTIONS

1. Airman Hatfield is popularly known as a ready source of a illegal drugs. His commander has requested that NCIS investigate several rumors about Airman Hatfield. One day at 1245, NCIS Agent Helmsman hurriedly approaches the commanding officer with a request for authorization for a search of Airman Hatfield's car. He relates to the commanding officer that Petty Officer McCoy has come to him with information he has overheard in the head. Airman Hatfield and a cohort were planning to replenish their supply of high grade marijuana, meeting their supplier at lunch time. According to Petty Officer McCoy, they were going to leave the ship at 1200 and drive around the base in a white 1966 Mustang until no one was watching, and then make the transfer.

   Helmsman reports that a records check has verified that Airman Hatfield owns a white 1966 Mustang. Furthermore, he and a person matching the description provided by Petty Officer McCoy were observed leaving the ship in the same car just a few minutes before 1200. The two returned to the pier in the Mustang at 1235. Both suspects are back on board the ship. Agent Helmsman says that since the vehicle returned, it has been under constant supervision by other NCIS agents.

   a. What is the most important issue for the commander to consider in granting or denying Agent Helmsman's search request?

   b. What information regarding Petty Officer McCoy should the commanding officer elicit from Agent Helmsman? For what purpose?

   c. If the commanding officer is not satisfied that the information provided by Petty Officer McCoy is sufficient to constitute probable cause, what could NCIS do to bolster its information?

   d. The executive officer suggests that whether or not they have probable cause, it is perfectly all right to search Hatfield's car anywhere on base because of the signs posted at all gates that "Entry grants consent to search of all persons and vehicles on board this installation." Is this good advice?

   e. Suppose that Airman Hatfield eases through a stop sign and is apprehended for a traffic violation. May NCIS then search his car for drugs?

   f. Suppose a valid search of Airman Hatfield's car yields four pounds of high quality marijuana laced with opium. Can Agent Helmsman then request authority to search Airman Hatfield's room in the barracks, arguing that it is only logical that if he has it in his car, he probably has it in his barracks room as well?

g. Suppose that the commanding officer concludes there is no probable cause to search Airman Hatfield's car. Agent Helmsman then seizes the initiative, and when Airman Hatfield returns to AIMD, he asks Airman Hatfield for consent to search his car. What procedures should Agent Helmsman use to ensure he conducts a valid consent search?

2. What are the requirements for a legitimate seizure of property under the "plain view" doctrine?

3. Quarterdeck searches on a United States ship in a foreign port are considered equivalent to what other type of examination?

4. You are the duty officer of a shore command and your duties require you to make periodic "walk through" inspections of the enlisted barracks. While walking through the barracks one evening, you smell what you believe to be the strong odor of marijuana emanating from behind the locked door of an enlisted room. You notice that the bottom of the door appears to have been sealed off on the inside by something, perhaps a rolled-up rug. These observations, along with your experience, lead you reasonably to believe that marijuana is being consumed inside that particular room. What should you do?

a. Immediately call the Commanding Officer, inform him of all the facts, and wait for him to prepare his written search authorization based upon probable cause.

b. Immediately enter the barracks room using the duty officer's master key; once inside you may seize the marijuana and make the appropriate apprehensions.

c. Immediately knock on the door and wait for the occupants to open the door. Then advise them of their Article 31(b) rights and their right to consent to a search of their room.

d. Immediately knock on the door, but enter *only if* you hear a window being opened or a toilet being flushed.

e. Continue on with your walk-through of the barracks, since the occupants of the room have a reasonable expectation of privacy in their barracks room.

Lieutenant Sharp was talking to his division chief, Electrician's Mate Chief (ETC) Hawkeye, on the messdecks of the USS TICONDEROGA (CG-55). As he was talking, he saw a Third Class Petty Officer (PO3) pass something to the sailor sitting next to him at the table. Lieutenant Sharp did not know the name of the PO3, but he did recognize the other sailor as Electrician's Mate Fireman ETFN Smart. The PO3 looked suspicious to Lieutenant Sharp because he looked around several times and took great care to conceal the item that was being passed. Lieutenant Sharp was aware that several enlisted members of the TI-CONDEROGA had recently been identified through the command's urinalysis program as abusers of cocaine.

5. Based on the above facts, what may Lieutenant Sharp *LAWFULLY* do?

   a. Thoroughly search both sailors for weapons and destructible evidence.

   b. Temporarily detain both sailors; he may then ask the PO3 to identify himself and to explain his suspicious conduct.

   c. Apprehend the PO3 based on his reasonable suspicion that criminal activity "was afoot."

   d. Immediately request that the Commanding Officer authorize an inspection of both sailors' berthing spaces.

   e. None of the above; they would all be unlawful.

While Lieutenant Sharp was contemplating what he could lawfully do under the circumstances, ETFN Smart approached him. ETFN Smart was one of Lieutenant Sharp's most trustworthy and reliable subordinates. ETFN Smart told Lieutenant Sharp that the PO3 had just given him a small bag containing a white powdery substance that the PO3 claimed was cocaine. The PO3 had asked ETFN Smart to try it out as a free sample and had told ETFN Smart that if he liked it, there was plenty more where that came from, since he had another half-ounce of cocaine in his locker. ETFN Smart then immediately handed Lieutenant Smart the bag of cocaine. Based on ETFN Smart's report, as well as the bag of cocaine, Lieutenant Sharp promptly and lawfully apprehended the PO3 who was still on the messdecks. The PO3 identified himself as Hull Technician Third Class Felony. Lieutenant Sharp then conducted a thorough search of HT3 Felony that resulted in his seizure of two more bags of cocaine from HT3 Felony's pockets.

6. The two bags of cocaine seized from HT3 Felony's pockets are:

   a. Inadmissible since Lieutenant Sharp did not have probable cause to search HT3 Felony's pockets.

   b. Admissible as the result of a search incident to a lawful apprehension.

   c. Admissible as the result of a lawful "frisk" for drugs.

   d. Inadmissible since Lieutenant Sharp did not obtain proper search authorization.

e. Inadmissible since HT3 Felony never consented to a search of his pockets.

After informing the Commanding Officer of the above events and the report of ETFN Smart, Lieutenant Sharp obtained verbal search authorization from the commanding officer to search HT3 Felony's locker on board the TICON-DEROGA. This search yielded a half-ounce of cocaine.

7. The half-ounce of cocaine seized from HT3 Felony's locker is:

   a. Inadmissible since HT3 Felony had a reasonable expectation of privacy in his locker.

   b. Admissible as the result of a search incident to a lawful apprehension.

   c. Inadmissible since there were no exigent circumstances present.

   d. Admissible as the result of a lawful search based on probable cause.

   e. Admissible as the result of a lawful inspection of HT3 Felony's locker.

8. What is a valid purpose for a inspection? Are unlawful weapons, contraband or other evidence of crime seized during the course of a lawful inspection admissible at court-martial?

9. What are the requirements for a lawful command search? What is the role of the commander who has control over the place where the property or person to be searched is located? How does "probable cause" factor into a command search?

10. What are the requirements for a valid gate or quarterdeck inspection in the United States (purpose, procedure, etc.)? May evidence seized during a valid gate or quarterdeck inspection be admitted in a trial by court-martial?

CHAPTER VIII

SELF-INCRIMINATION

Because of a subordinate military person's obligation to respond to the command of his superior, Congress enacted Article 31[UCMJ] to serve as a protection against the inherent tendency of that relationship, either directly or subtly, to induce an accused to respond to a question by the superior. . . .

United States v. Lewis, 12 M.J. 205, 206-07 (C.M.A. 1982)

INTRODUCTION

The military is an authoritarian environment. As such, military superiors generally expect subordinates to respond immediately to their inquiries. Because military leaders also perform significant law enforcement functions, there is a natural tension between the obligation to provide information and the privilege against self-incrimination. While service members are protected by both statutory and constitutional safeguards, the nature of the military nevertheless places significant day-to-day pressures on the privilege against self-incrimination. This chapter addresses the parameters of right against self-incrimination in the armed forces and focuses on the effect that military life has on the protections of that right.

SOURCES OF THE RIGHT AGAINST SELF-INCRIMINATION

The Fifth Amendment to the Constitution provides:

No person . . . shall be compelled in any criminal case to be a witness against himself. . . .

Article 31, UCMJ provides as follows:

> (a) No person subject to this chapter may compel any person to incriminate himself or to answer a question, the answer to which may intend to incriminate him.

What is the difference between Article 31(a) and the Fifth Amendment? The Court of Appeals for the Armed Forces in *United States v. Armstrong*, 9 M.J. 374 (C.M.A. 1980), stated that "[T]he clearly manifested intent of Congress in enacting Article 31(a) was merely to afford the serviceperson a privilege against self-incrimination which parallel[s] the constitutional privilege."

SCOPE OF THE RIGHT AGAINST SELF-INCRIMINATION

What does the privilege against self incrimination protect? Military Rule of Evidence 301 states:

> (a) General Rule. The privileges against self-incrimination provided by the Fifth Amendment to the Constitution of the United States and Article 31 are applicable only to evidence of a testimonial or communicative nature.

The above rule codifies the Supreme Court's holdings to the effect that the privilege against self-incrimination only protects individuals from creating evidence against themselves. *See Schmerber v. California*, 384 U.S. 757 (1966). Because verbal or written statements or testimony are "created" by an accused in response to questioning by investigators or prosecutors, such evidence is subject to the safeguards of the Fifth Amendment. Whether the compulsion of other types of evidence violates the Fifth Amendment and Article 31(a) depends on its "testimonial or communicative nature." The following case considers this issue with respect to blood samples.

United States v. Ralph M. Armstrong, Specialist Five,
U.S. Army, Appellant.
U.S. Court of Military Appeals.
9 M.J. 370
Oct. 27, 1980.

OPINION: Everett, Chief Judge

On his plea of not guilty appellant was tried by special court-martial, consisting of military judge alone, on charges of involuntary manslaughter, reckless driving resulting in injury, fleeing the scene of a collision and possession of marijuana. The first and second charges were alleged as violations of Articles 119 and 111, Uniform Code of Military Justice, 10 U.S.C. Sections 919 and 911, respectively; the other two, as violations of Article 134, 10 U.S.C. Section 934. Appellant was acquitted of fleeing the scene of the collision, but he was found guilty of the remaining charges. The military judge then sentenced him to a bad-conduct discharge, forfeiture of $250 pay per month for 6 months, and reduction to the lowest enlisted grade. The convening authority approved the sentence, and, in turn, the United States Army court of Military Review affirmed the findings and sentence without opinion. On April 6, 1979, the Court granted appellant's petition for review in order to consider two issues. 7 M.J. 41.

The first issue concerns the admissibility in evidence of a blood specimen extracted from the appellant at a military hospital soon after the automobile accident, which gave rise to the charge of involuntary manslaughter.

. . . .

I

On the evening of January 29, 1978, appellant drove with three passengers in his Mercedes automobile to a night club in Bremerhaven, Germany. While there they consumed a substantial amount of beer. After they had departed the night club, appellant's automobile crashed into the rear of a trailer-container parked on a city street. The passenger seated beside the appellant on the front seat was killed; the other passengers were injured to various degrees.

Appellant ran from the scene of the accident and was apprehended in flight by the German police. Shortly thereafter, he was confronted by Sergeant Luis of the American military police who detected a strong odor of alcohol on appellant's breath. Luis accompanied the appellant to an American hospital. However, the appellant was advised that "if you refuse to take the blood alcohol test, your USAREUR permit would be revoked." Moreover, Luis explained to appellant that the German police could transport him to a German medical facility where a blood specimen could be drawn from him by force and, if necessary, used in any subsequent German court proceedings. Thereupon, appellant agreed to take the blood alcohol test.

Because of the need to treat other persons injured in the crash, a delay of some three hours occurred before the blood was drawn. Just before the appellant took the blood test, he was re-advised of his rights and once again agreed to submit to the test. Two blood specimens were taken-one for use by American military authorities and the other for the German police.

At trial, defense counsel objected to the receipt in evidence of the blood-test results. After considering the evidence and hearing extensive argument, the military judge concluded that the test results were not within the protection of Article 31, UCMJ, 10 U.S.C. Section 831, and should be admitted. This ruling gives rise to the first issue we shall consider.

After the accident, appellant's Mercedes was transported by the German fire brigade to a lot in Bremerhaven which they regularly used to impound vehicles. According to stipulated testimony, no inventory was conducted at the time of the impoundment, as would have been customary if the Germans had planned to take any inventory. Early on the morning of January 21—only a few hours after the accident—two American military policemen looked at the outside of the car, took some pictures, and then left. Approximately two hours late, other military police arrived, whereupon the German custodian of the impoundment lot began looking into the contents of the car. The military police were present at the search, in which the marijuana and pipe were found. These items were turned over to the military police and subsequently were the subject of testimony at the trial. The legality of the search and seizure of the contraband was contested by defense counsel at trial. The military judge's receipt of evidence concerning the marijuana and pipe gave rise to the second issue.

. . . .

III

Even if use of appellant's blood specimen is not precluded by Article 31(b), is it barred by Article 31(a), which provides that no one subject to the Code "may compel any person to incriminate himself"? It will be recalled that Sergeant Luis, a military policeman, advised appellant that, if he refused to submit to a blood-alcohol test, he would lose his USAREUR driving permit and would be subject to extraction of blood by the German police, who had taken him into custody after the accident. Under the circumstances of this case, this warning from Sergeant Luis—at least to the extent that it threatened a revocation of appellant's own driving permit—might be construed as compulsion for purposes of Article 31(a). [citations omitted]. Of course, *California v. Byers*, 402 U.S. 424, 91 S.Ct. 1535, 29 L.Ed.2d 9 (1971), upheld requirements that an accident be reported despite the argument that the reporting requirement compelled possible self-incrimination. However, in *Byers* the reporting might be construed as much more directly related to the State's regulatory functions than to prosecution for criminal offenses; in the case at hand the obtaining of the blood specimen from appellant was closely intertwined with the prospect that he would be prosecuted for homicide.

Whether the words of Sergeant Luis wold constitute compulsion for purposes of Article 31(a) need not be determined, for the statutory language providing that no person may be compelled to "incriminate himself" was not intended to go beyond the scope of the Fifth Amendment. Hence it has no relevancy to blood specimens or other body fluids since, under the currently dominant "testimonial compulsion" approach to interpretation of the Fifth Amendment, such evidence is not subject to self-incrimination safeguards as it lacks the qualities of a communication by the suspect.

. . . .

In (a) we have just reiterated again the right not to incriminate himself. [Part](b) incidentally, covers a wider scope in that you can't force a man to incriminate himself beforehand—not just on the trial, if you will. And this in addition, since it prohibits any person trying to force a person accused or one suspected, would make it a crime for any officer or any person who tries to force a person to do that. So not only do we retain the constitutional protections again self-incrimination and this evidentiary protection against degrading yourself unless it is material, but it goes further and provides that if anybody tries to force you to incriminate yourself then he has committed an offense. In providing for all those ideas we have different language.

The commentary to Article 31(a) in the Index and Legislative History of the Code again verifies that this subdivision merely "extends the privilege against self-incrimination to all persons under all circumstances," since under then current "Army and Navy provisions only persons who [were] witnesses [were] specifically granted the privilege."

. . . .

Therefore, we conclude that, in enacting the compulsory self-incrimination provision of Article 31, Congress did not plan for blood samples to be covered by the privilege. Instead, the clearly manifested intent of Congress in enacting Article 31(a) was merely to afford to servicepersons a privilege against self-incrimination which paralleled the constitutional privilege. Accordingly, Article 31 did not apply to the taking of blood specimens from Armstrong since body fluids are not within the purview of the Fifth Amendment.

WARNINGS CONCERNING SELF-INCRIMINATION

WARNINGS REQUIRED UNDER *MIRANDA V. ARIZONA*

The Supreme Court held in *Miranda v. Arizona*, 384 U.S. 436, 444 (1966):

[T]he prosecution may not use statements, whether exculpatory or inculpatory, stemming from custodial interrogation of the defendant unless it demonstrates the use of procedural safeguards effective to secure the privilege against self-incrimination. By custodial interrogation, we mean questioning initiated by law enforcement officers after a person has been taken into custody or otherwise deprived of his freedom of action in any significant way. As for the procedural safeguards to be employed, unless other fully effective means are devised to inform accused persons of their right of silence and to assure a continuous opportunity to exercise it, the following measures are required. Prior to any questioning, the person must be warned that he has a right to remain silent, that any statement he does make may be used as evidence against him, and that he has a right to the presence of an attorney, either retained or appointed. The defendant may waive effectuation of these rights, provided the waiver is made voluntarily, knowingly and intelligently. If, however, he indicates in any manner and at any stage of the process that he wishes to consult with an attorney before speaking there can be no questioning. Likewise, if the individual is alone and indicates in any manner that he does not wish to be interrogated, the police may not question him. The mere fact that he may have answered some questions or volunteered some statements on his own does not deprive him of the right to refrain from answering any further inquiries until he has consulted with an attorney and thereafter consents to be questioned.

Following the *Miranda* decision, the military was faced with the issue of whether the holding applied to service members. The next case addressed that issue.

United States, Appellee, v. Michael L. Tempia
Airman Third Class, U.S. Air Force, Appellant
United States Court of Military Appeals
16 U.S.C.M.A. 629; 37 C.M.R. 249
April 25, 1967

OPINION: Ferguson, Judge

This case, certified by the Judge Advocate General, United States Air Force, presents important questions concerning the administration of military justice. Basically, it inquires whether the principles enunciated by the Supreme Court in *Miranda v. Arizona*, 384 U.S. 436, 16 L ed 2d 694, 86 S Ct 1602 (1966), apply to military interrogations of criminal suspects. We hold that they do.

. . . .

I

The accused was tried by general court-martial at Dover Air Force Base, Delaware, and convicted of taking indecent liberties with females under the age of sixteen, in violation of Uniform Code of Military Justice, Article 134, 10 USC @ 934. He was sentenced to bad-conduct discharge, forfeiture of all pay and allowances, confinement at hard labor for six months, and reduction. Intermediate appellate authorities affirmed, and the case was, as indicated above, certified to this Court on the question:

"WAS THE BOARD OF REVIEW CORRECT IN ITS DETERMINATION THAT THE ACCUSED'S PRETRIAL STATEMENT WAS PROPERLY RECEIVED IN EVIDENCE?"

The accused's trial commenced on June 14, 1966, one day after the effective date of applying the principles set forth in *Miranda, supra*. *See Johnson v. New Jersey*, 384 U.S. 719, 16 L ed 2d 882, 86 S Ct 1772 (1966). The testimony of the witnesses therein disclosed the following evidence.

On May 1, 1966, accused accompanied an Airman Keitel to the base library. Upon request, Keitel pointed out the location of the latrine. Accused left Keitel in the reading room and returned in five or six minutes.

From other testimony, it appears he went to the ladies' rest room, stood in its partially opened door, and made obscene proposals to three young girls. The victims left the library, returned with one of their parents and the Air Police, and pointed accused out in the reading room. Accused was asked "to come back to the office" by one of the policemen. He did so.

At the Air Police office, accused was advised by Agent Blessing that he was suspected of taking indecent liberties with children; of his rights under Code, *supra*, Article 31, 10 USC @ 831; and "'that you may consult with legal counsel if you desire.'" Agent McQuary assisted Agent Blessing in the interview. It was immediately terminated, as Tempia stated "'he wanted counsel.'" He was released from custody.

On May 3, 1966, Tempia was again called to the "OSI Office" where he was once more advised by Blessing, in the presence of Agent Feczer, of his rights and entitlement to consult with counsel. Accused "'stated he had not yet received legal counsel.'" Blessing thereupon called Major Norman K. Hogue, Base Staff Judge Advocate, and made an appointment for Tempia.

Blessing's interview with Tempia terminated at 8:50 a.m., and the latter proceeded to Major Hogue's office. Hogue informed him he was the Staff Judge Advocate and "that I could not accept an attorney-client relationship with him because if I did, it would disqualify me from acting in my capacity as Staff Judge Advocate." He further stated to Tempia that he would nevertheless "advise him of his legal rights and explained to him that this was different than acting as his defense counsel in that I did not want to hear any of his story, but I would answer any legal questions he had after I explained some rights to him."

Major Hogue also told accused he could not make a military lawyer available to him "as his defense counsel during that OSI investigation," but that he had the right to employ civilian counsel; would be given a reasonable time to do so; and that civilian counsel would be entitled to appear with him at the investigation. In addition, Hogue advised him of his rights under Code, *supra*, Article 31, and explained those rights to him, but:

"... As I say, I told him no military lawyer would be appointed to represent him during the OSI investigation or any investigation by the law enforcement agents on this base. I told him that if charges are preferred—in his case, referred to trial by special court-martial or general court-martial, where it's referred to an investigation under Article 32b, he would be furnished a military lawyer at that time, one certified under Article 27b of the Uniform Code of Military Justice."

In addition, accused filled out a written form in which it was indicated he had been advised:

a. That he had the right to retain civilian counsel at his own expense;

b. That no military lawyer would be appointed to represent him while under investigation by law enforcement agents;

c. That he would be furnished military counsel if charges were preferred and referred to trial or a pretrial investigation convened;

d. Of his rights under Code, *supra*, Article 31;

e. Of the maximum punishment involved; and,

f. That he had not discussed his guilt or innocence or any of the facts involved with Major Hogue.

Following his session with Major Hogue, Tempia returned to the Office of Special Investigations, at 9:24 a.m. He "was then called in . . . readvised of his rights, readvised of the nature of the investigation and of his rights to seek legal counsel the second time." He stated he had consulted with Major Hogue, and did not desire further counsel as "they could not help him. . . . He said, 'They didn't do me no good.'" Thereafter, he was interrogated by Blessing and Feczer, to whom he began to dictate his confession.

At the trial, defense counsel sought exclusion of the statement on the basis of the Supreme Court decision in Miranda, *supra*, as he had found it reported in the press. The law officer overruled his timely objection and admitted Tempia's confession in evidence.

II

. . . .

Thus, it will be seen that both the Supreme Court and this Court itself are satisfied as to the applicability of constitutional safeguards to military trials, except insofar as they are made inapplicable either expressly or by necessary implication. The Government, therefore, is correct in conceding the point, and the Judge Advocate General, United States Navy, as amicus curiae, is incorrect in his contrary conclusion. Indeed, as to the latter, it would appear from the authorities on which he relies that the military courts applied what we now know as the constitutional protection against self-incrimination in trials prior to and contemporaneous with the adoption of the Constitution.

. . . .

The point need not, however, be belabored. Sufficient has been said to establish our firm and unshakable conviction that Tempia, as any other member of the armed services so situated, was entitled to the protection of the Bill of Rights, insofar as we are herein concerned with it.

. . . .

IV

We turn, therefore, to the merits of the controversy before us. *Miranda v. Arizona, supra,* explicitly and at length lays down concrete rules which are to govern all criminal interrogations by Federal or State authorities, military or civilian, if resulting statements are to be used in trials commencing on and after June 13, 1966. We commend a reading of that opinion to all involved in the administration of military criminal law as well as the undertaking of educative measures to see that its precepts are not violated in pretrial interrogations.

. . . .

We now proceed to examine the facts presented in this record, in light of the foregoing requirements.

a. Custodial Interrogation.

The Government urges upon us the proposition that the accused was not in custody, and, hence, the need for appropriate advice and assistance did not arise. We may at once dispose of this contention. The accused was apprehended on May 1, 1966; freed to seek counsel; recalled for interrogation on May 3, 1966; an appointment was made for him with Major Hogue, following which, he immediately returned to the Office of Special Investigations, where his interrogation was successfully completed. The test to be applied is not whether the accused, technically, has been taken into custody, but absent that, whether he has been "otherwise deprived of his freedom of action in any significant way." *Miranda, supra,* at page 444. Here, the accused was clearly summoned for interrogation. Had he not obeyed, he would have undoubtedly subjected himself to being penalized for a failure to repair. Code, *supra,* Article 86, 10 USC @ 886; Manual for Courts-Martial, United States, 1951, paragraph 127b. In the military, unlike civil life, a suspect may be required to report and submit to questioning quite without regard to warrants or other legal process. It ignores the realities of that situation to say that one ordered to appear for interrogation has not been significantly deprived of his freedom of action. *See People v. Kelley,* 57 West's Cal Rptr 363, 424 P2d 947 (1967). Hence, we conclude there was "custodial interrogation" in this case.

b. The Warning.

The accused was fully advised of his rights under Code, *supra,* Article 31, and of his right to consult with counsel. On indicating a desire to speak with counsel, he was initially freed and, ultimately, on May 3, was referred to Major Hogue for further advice concerning his rights. But that officer went no further than to emphasize to the accused that he could not form an attorney-client relationship with him; to advise him again of his rights under Code, *supra*, Article 31; and to inform him he could retain civilian counsel at his own expense, who could appear at his interrogation. He specifically told accused no military lawyer would be appointed "to represent him during the OSI investigation or any investigation by the law enforcement agents on this base."

Miranda, *supra*, squarely points out "the person must be warned that he has a right to remain silent, that any statement he does make may be used as evidence against him, and that *he has a right to the presence of an attorney, either retained or appointed.*" (Emphasis supplied.) In addition, if the accused "indicates in any manner and at any stage of the process that he wishes to consult with an attorney before speaking there can be no questioning. Likewise, if the individual is alone and indicates in any manner that he does not wish to be interrogated, the police may not question him."

Undoubtedly, the advice given Tempia under Code, *supra*, Article 31, sufficed to inform him both of his right to remain silent and the purpose for which any statement he might make could be used. The advice as to counsel, however, was deficient.

First, accused was only warned by the agents that he was entitled to consult with counsel. When Major Hogue elaborated on this proposition, he limited the availability of counsel to private attorneys employed by the accused at his own expense. He specifically told accused no attorney would be appointed to represent him in any law en-forcement investigation. This is exactly contrary to the information which, under *Miranda*, *supra*, must be preliminarily communicated to the accused.

. . . .

The point need not, however, be belabored. Sufficient has been said to establish our firm and unshakable conviction that Tempia, as any other member of the armed services so situated, was entitled to the protection of the Bill of Rights, insofar as we are herein concerned with it.

. . . .

In sum, we are not persuaded by our brother's views that we have anticipated the Supreme Court in this area, nor that the military picture is as rosy as he paints it. What does concern us is our duty to follow the interpretation by the Supreme Court of the Constitution of the United States insofar as it is not made expressly or by necessary implication inapplicable to members of the armed forces. It is well to remember that we, "like the state courts, have the same responsibilities as do the federal courts to protect a person from a violation of his constitutional rights." *Burns v. Wilson*, *supra*, at page 142. We necessarily must effectuate that mandate by holding *Miranda v. Arizona*, *supra*, applicable in military prosecutions.

The decision of the board of review is reversed, and the record of trial is returned to the Judge Advocate General of the Air Force. A rehearing may be ordered.

ARTICLE 31(B) WARNINGS

The military justice system has a long history of providing warnings to service members—much longer, in fact, than most civilian criminal systems. The 1917 MCM, for example, recognized the inherently coercive atmosphere that may exist between superiors and subordinates and advised investigators to "warn the person investigated that he need not answer any question that might tend to incriminate him." By 1921, the MCM expanded the protection by requiring investigators and other military superiors to give warnings regarding self-incrimination. Under the Elston Act of 1948 and the 1949 MCM, a failure to provide warnings caused the exclusion of an accused's statement at court-martial, unless the government could show that the accused was otherwise aware of the right to remain silent. This tradition of broad protections against self-incrimination played a significant role in the adoption of Article 31(b) in its current form.

> (b) No person subject to this chapter may interrogate, or request any statement from an accused or a person suspected of an offense without first informing him of the nature of the accusation and advising him that he does not have to make any statement regarding the offense of which he is accused or suspected and that any statement made by him may be used as evidence against him in a trial by court-martial.

The language of Article 31(b) indicates that an accused must be warned if he or she is "suspected" of an offense. In contrast, *Miranda* warnings are necessary when an accused is undergoing "custodial interrogation." Also, the Article 31(b) warning does not mention the right to counsel, while *Miranda* provides the right to have an attorney present during questioning. Which, if either, provides greater protection? Which warning will likely occur first?

Note that the military courts construe Articles 31(a) and (b) in significantly different ways. The Court of Military Appeals explained in *United States v. Ravenel*, 26 M.J. 344, 349 (C.M.A. 1988):

> [T]his Court clearly is on record that, while Article 31(a) and the Fifth Amendment coincide in scope and while Article 31(b) was enacted to serve the purpose of avoiding coerced statements in violation of both provisions, unique factors in the military environment—unknown in the civilian setting—lead us to interpret Article 31(b) as being broader in the scope of its protection than is the mandate of *Miranda*. Both the subtleties of the superior-subordinate relationship and the conditioned response, consciously created from the first day of basic training, to respond almost unthinkingly to the wishes of a military superior can permit no other result.

Thus, the military courts hold that Article 31(a) is identical in scope to the Fifth Amendment, but that the protections of Article 31(b) are broader than those in *Miranda*. How is Article 31(b) broader in its protections than *Miranda*? Does the answer hinge on when a person must be warned under Article 31(b)?

When Must Article 31(b) Warnings be Given

Following enactment of Article 31(b), the military courts initially construed the provision in a literal manner. In *United States v. Wilson*, 8 C.M.R. 48, 54-55 (C.M.A. 1953), the Court of Military Appeals concluded that a "person suspected of an offense" must be warned without regard to the purpose or nature of the questioning. Do you foresee problems with such a standard? In *United States v. Duga*, 10 M.J. 206 (C.M.A. 1981), the Court of Military Appeals addressed the "literal interpretation" standard established in *Wilson* as follows.

> Careful consideration of the history of the requirement of the warning, compels a conclusion that its purpose is to avoid impairment of the constitutional guarantee against compulsory self incrimination. Because of the effect of superior rank or official position upon one subject to military law, the mere asking of a question under certain circumstances is the equivalent of a command. A person subjected to these pressures may rightly be regarded as deprived of his freedom to answer or to remain silent. Under such circumstances, we do not hesitate to reverse convictions whenever the accused has been deprived of the full benefit of the rights granted him by Congress. [citations omitted]. By the same token, however, it is our duty to see to it that such rights are not extended beyond the reasonable intendment of the Code at the expense of substantial justice and on the grounds that are fanciful or unsubstantial.

Based on the above reasoning, the Court of Military Appeals held that Article 31(b) "applies only to situations in which, because of military rank, duty, or other similar relationship, there might be subtle pressure on a suspect to respond to an inquiry." When would such a situation exist? The following case considers that issue.

United States v. Airman John G. Loukas,
United States Air Force
Court of Military Appeals
29 M.J. 385
February 13, 1990

OPINION: Sullivan, Judge

During August 1987, the accused was tried by a general court-martial composed of a military judge sitting alone at Pope Air Force Base, North Carolina. Contrary to his pleas, he was found guilty of wrongfully using cocaine and being incapacitated for duty, in violation of Articles 112a and 134, Uniform Code of Military Justice. He was sentenced to a dishonorable discharge, confinement for 8 months, total forfei-

tures, and reduction to the lowest enlisted grade.

. . . .

[The below facts are from the decision of the Air Force Court of Military Review overturning the accused's conviction]. To restate the pertinent facts briefly, the appellant was the loadmaster aboard a C-130 flight bound for Trinidad, Bolivia, where it was to receive certain unspecified cargo.

The assistant crew chief, who was alone in the empty cargo section with the appellant at one point in the flight, noticed that the latter was acting in a decidedly irrational manner, pointing and calling out to invisible persons. The appellant handed the assistant crew chief his sidearm, a .38 calibre pistol, while urging that he take it. The assistant crew chief did so and reported the incident to his immediate superior, the aforementioned SSgt Dryer. SSgt Dryer confronted the appellant and observed that he was continuing to hallucinate. This behavior and the appellant's general appearance, caused SSgt Dryer to suspect that the appellant was under the influence of a drug. He was concerned for the security of the aircraft and its crew. Accordingly, he asked whether the appellant had taken drugs. The appellant responded that he had not. SSgt Dryer asked in a more insistent tone what the appellant had taken, or words to that effect. The appellant, in reply, acknowledged that he had used cocaine the evening before.

. . . .

The stated premise of the Court of Military Review majority opinion . . . was that Sergeant Dryer was obligated by Article 31(b) to warn the accused of his rights before questioning him about possible drug use. This legal conclusion was drawn on the basis of the decision of this Court in *United States v. Duga*, 10 M.J. 206 (C.M.A. 1981), and a finding of fact that Sergeant Dryer was acting officially and not simply out of "idle curiosity." 27 M.J. 792. We disagree as a matter of law because the crew chief's inquiry was not a *law-enforcement or disciplinary* investigation which is also required before Article 31(b) becomes applicable.

. . . .

In the case before us, Sergeant Dryer was the crew chief of an operational military aircraft who was similarly responsible for the plane's safety and that of its crew, including the accused, his military subordinate. In addition, his questioning of the accused was limited to that required to fulfill his operational responsibilities, and there was no evidence suggesting his inquiries were designed to evade constitutional or codal rights. [citations omitted]. Finally, the unquestionable urgency of the threat and immediacy of the crew chief's response underscore the legitimate operational nature of his queries. [citations omitted]. Under our precedents, the prosecution satisfactorily showed that Article 31 warnings were not required in this operational context.

. . . .

The decision of the United States Air Force Court of Military Review setting aside the findings of guilty and sentence is reversed.

The reasoning used in *Loukas* renders investigations with no law enforcement and disciplinary purpose exempt from Article 31(b). For example, the Court of Military Appeals concluded that a Army pediatrician did not have to give Article 31(b) warnings to an accused when questioning him about injuries to his four-year old son. *See United States v. Bowerman*, 39 M.J. 219 (C.M.A. 1994). In what other situations are Article 31(b) warnings required? *See* Chapter IV concerning nonjudicial punishment and administrative separation hearings.

Who Must Provide Article 31(b) Warnings

The above discussion tells us generally when warnings are necessary based on the purpose of the questioning. However, the UCMJ provides that only persons "subject to the code" [the UCMJ] must comply with Article 31. Active duty personnel are always subject to the UCMJ and therefore have to abide by Article 31 at all times. Military Rule of Evidence 305(b)(1) also explains that "a person subject to the code' includes a person acting as a knowing agent of a military unit or of a person subject to the code." Who is a "knowing agent?" As a general rule, civilian and foreign law-enforcement personnel are not agents of the military. The military courts hold, however, that civilians who act as "instruments of the military" are subject to Article 31 requirements. *See United States v. Quillen*, 27 M.J. 312 (C.M.A. 1988) (exchange store detective required to provide Article 31(b) warnings to soldier suspected of shoplifting).

REMEDIES FOR VIOLATIONS OF THE RIGHT AGAINST SELF-INCRIMINATION

What happens to evidence that is obtained in contravention of Article 31 or the Fifth Amendment? Article 31(d) explains the ramifications:

> (d) No statement obtained from any person in violation of this article . . . may be received in evidence against him in a trial by court-martial.

Like Article 31, a violation of the Fifth Amendment renders evidence inadmissible at court-martial. This prohibition on the introduction of evidence is known as the "exclusionary rule." It applies to the unlawful compulsion of evidence in violation of Article 31(a) and the Fifth Amendment and a failure to provide *Miranda* or Article 31(b) warnings. Does the exclusionary rule apply at forums other than courts-martial? *See* Chapter IV.

A failure to comply with Article 31 is also a violation of the UCMJ. Article 98 provides that "[a]ny person . . . who . . . knowingly and intentionally fails to enforce or comply with any provision of this chapter regulating the proceedings before, during, or after trial of an accused; shall be punished as a court-martial may direct." The intent of Congress in enacting Article 98 was to protect the procedural rights of service members, and, in particular, to enforce respect for the right against self-incrimination.

STUDY QUESTIONS

1. Which, if either, provides broader protections, Article 31(a) or the Fifth Amendment?

2. Which of the following may lawfully be required of a suspect *without* advising the suspect of his or her rights under Article 31(b), UCMJ?

   a. Provide fingerprints.

   b. Provide urine samples.

   c. Submit to the taking of a blood sample.

   d. Provide voice exemplars (samples).

   e. All of the above may lawfully be required.

3. When must the *Miranda* warning be provided to a service member? How is "custodial interrogation" defined by the Supreme Court? Why is it important?

4. What is the difference between *Miranda* warnings and Article 31(b) advisements? When are Article 31(b) warnings required? Does the purpose of the questioning affect whether Article 31(b) applies?

5. Before requesting a statement from a service member whom a naval officer suspects has committed an offense under the UCMJ (but who is not in custody or otherwise being deprived of his freedom of action in any significant way), she must first do which of the following?

   a. Inform him of the nature of the offense.

   b. Advise him that he does not have to make any statement regarding the offense and that any statement he does make may be used against him in trial by court-martial.

   c. Inform him he has the right to consult with counsel before questioning and to have counsel present during questioning.

   d. Both (a) and (b).

   e. All of the above.

6. What is the "exclusionary rule?" Where and when does it apply?

CHAPTER IX

MILITARY INVESTIGATIONS

One of the primary purposes of conducting investigations of any type is to identify ways to improve the effectiveness and efficiency of the Department or of its components. Investigations alone, however, do not achieve that purpose. Put differently, investigations are means, not ends.

JAG Manual 0203

INTRODUCTION

The number and types of investigations conducted by the military is rivaled by few institutions in the United States. This is due in large measure to the tight control that the military must maintain over its personnel and property. This strong oversight interest of the military results in investigations of damage to military personnel or property, as well as probes into violations of the laws and regulations of the services. While military investigations serve different purposes, many of these probes share similar characteristics. This chapter will discuss the most common varieties of investigations conducted in the armed forces and the relationship between those inquiries.

CRIMINAL INVESTIGATIONS

The Navy and Marine Corps divide criminal offenses into two categories: major and minor crimes. This distinction is important not only because it impacts the forum where the offense is adjudicated (*see* Chapters IV and V), but also because it determines who will conduct the inquiry.

MAJOR CRIMINAL OFFENSES

SECNAVINST 5520.3B describes the responsibility for investigating major criminal offenses in the Navy and Marine Corps.

    a. Major Criminal Offenses

        (1) Within the Department of the Navy, Naval Criminal Investigative Service (NCIS) is primarily responsible for investigating actual, suspected or alleged major criminal offenses committed against a person, the United States Government, or private property, including the attempts or conspiracies to commit such offenses. A major criminal offense (felony) is defined for purposes of this instruction as one punishable under the Uniform Code of Military Justice by confinement for a term of more than 1 year, or similarly framed federal statutes, state, local or foreign laws or regulation. Incidents of actual, suspected or alleged major criminal offenses coming to command attention must be immediately referred to NCIS whether occurring on or off an installation or ship and regardless of whether they are being investigated by state, local or other authorities. The referral to NCIS should be made before any substantive investigative steps are considered by the command, such as interrogation of suspect(s) or conducting searches of property, as to which individuals have an expectation to privacy, unless such steps are necessary to protect life or property or to prevent the destruction of evidence. Command investigations conducted under the Manual of the Judge Advocate General . . . must not compromise or otherwise impede the NCIS investigation. . . .

Why is there a concern that commands will conduct an inquiry into a major offense prior to notifying NCIS? Note that the "fruit of the poisonous tree" doctrine may cause the exclusion of evidence derived from illegally obtained evidence. *See* Chapter VI. Is NCIS concerned that its investigation of a major offense will be tainted by mistakes made by the command involved?

SECNAVINST 5520.3B also explains how criminal investigations among different agencies are coordinated.

        (4) A major criminal offense, as defined, may constitute a violation of both military and civil law, and may involve both military personnel and civilians. Primary or concurrent jurisdiction may also rest with another agency outside of the Department of the Navy. Only NCIS has the authority to make investigative referrals in these instances. When Department of the Navy commands or personnel are contacted by other law enforcement organizations in connection with investigative matters, the matter must be referred to NCIS for coordination. This policy includes inquiries by federal, state, local and foreign law enforcement or investigative agencies when the matter involves security or major criminal offenses, as previously defined. This does not preclude Department of the Navy commands from conferring with law enforcement organizations of physical security, loss prevention issues and other matters of mutual concern.

The above sections discusses jurisdiction of the military and civilian agencies. Does jurisdiction of courts-martial depend on the location of the crime? *See United States v. Solario* discussed in Chapter III.

MINOR CRIMINAL OFFENSES

SECNAVINST 5520.3B provides guidance on investigation of minor offenses.

b. Minor Criminal Offenses. A minor criminal offense . . . is defined as one punishable under the Uniform Code of Military Justice by confinement of 1 year or less, or carrying similar punishment by federal, state, local or foreign statute or regulation, and lacking any of the considerations enumerated in the discussion of major criminal offenses above.

c. Use of Command Investigators

(1) Many Navy and Marine Corps commands maintain an investigative capability. Use of command investigators for criminal and security investigations shall be limited to minor offenses, as defined in this instruction, except when NCIS has declined jurisdiction. . . . This stipulation does not preclude command investigations in those instances where NCIS is not investigating or where the offense is purely military in nature (*e.g.* unauthorized absence).

Note that "command investigators" are personnel specifically trained in criminal investigative techniques. In the Navy, these personnel are usually Masters-at-Arms. In addition to command investigators, officers and senior enlisted also conduct inquiries into minor offenses. These "preliminary inquires" provide the information to dispose of cases at nonjudicial punishment or through nonpunitive measures. As with NCIS agents and command investigators, preliminary inquiry officers gather evidence of the suspected offense. However, they also provide information regarding an accused's military performance and behavior, and any other information that will provide the command with a full understanding of both the case and the accused. Finally, the preliminary inquiry officer includes a specific recommendation concerning disposition and punishment. *See* Figures 4-B and 4-C in Chapter IV. The preliminary inquiry officer normally interviews all material witnesses, as well as the accused. Does the Fourth Amendment apply to a search conducted by a preliminary inquiry officer? What about the Fifth Amendment or Article 31(b)? *See* Chapters IV, VII and VIII.

INTELLIGENCE AND SECURITY INVESTIGATIONS

SECNAVINST 5520.3B addresses the conduct of criminal intelligence investigations.

d. Criminal Intelligence Operations. Criminal intelligence operations are defined as formalized programs targeting persons or organizations whose criminal activity significantly affects the naval establishment, or those activities designed to gain information of a criminal intelligence nature for law enforcement purposes. A high degree of specialized training and experience is necessary for the successful accomplishment of these operations, and, to the extent that they are undertaken within the Department of the Navy, they will be done exclusively by NCIS, regardless of location.

The following case considers the nature of criminal intelligence inquiries.

United States, Appellee, v. Clayton J. Lonetree, Sergeant U.S. Marine Corps, Appellant.
U.S. Court of Military Appeals
35 M.J. 396
September 28, 1992

SENTELLE, Circuit Judge

Sergeant Clayton Lonetree was a Marine Corps embassy guard on duty in Moscow when he met Soviet agent Violetta Seina in a subway station. He began a romantic liaison with Seina and eventually passed confidential information to a Soviet agent named Yefimov (a.k.a. "Uncle Sasha"). Ignorant of his activities, the Marine Corps transferred Lonetree to guard duty at the U.S. Embassy in Vienna, where he continued his contact with the Soviets through an agent named Lyssove (a.k.a. "George"). His double life came to an end on December 14, 1986, when, in the first of a series of meetings with two Vienna-station U.S. intelligence agents known as "Big John" and "Little John" ("the Johns"), Lonetree disclosed his involvement with the Soviet agents.

The Naval Investigative Service (NIS) took over questioning Lonetree from the Johns on December 24, 1986, and obtained a more detailed account of the information Lonetree had passed to the Soviets. Based on Lonetree's confessions to the Johns and the NIS, as well as verification through a U.S. government agent known as "John Doe" of Lonetree's relationship with George, a general court-martial found Lonetree guilty of conspiracy to commit espionage, disobeying Navy security regulations, disclosing the identities of covert agents, willfully communicating information in violation of the Federal Espionage Act, and committing espionage. Though the general court-martial sentenced Lonetree to confinement for 30 years, the convening authority reduced the sentence to 25 years in exchange for Lonetree's cooperation in damage assessment.

I

Unlawful Inducement of Lonetree's Confessions

Lonetree argued at his court-martial and to the Court of Military Review that his confessions should have been suppressed because they were induced by false promises of confidentiality made by the Johns, promises the Johns violated by sharing Lonetree's statements with the NIS. It is uncontroverted that Lonetree first approached Big John at the U.S. Embassy in Vienna on December 14, 1986, and explained that he had become "deeply involved" with Soviet agents. Big John had his subordinate, Little John, maintain a dialogue with Lonetree, during which Lonetree provided ever-increasing details about his work and contacts with the Soviets. The prosecution concedes that "[i]n the interest of gaining [Lonetree's] trust [Little John] assured appellant that any information would be treated as 'confidential'." Answer to Final Brief at 14 (citing testimony of Little John: "What I said to [Lonetree] was that his information would be held in confidence."). Despite this assurance, the Johns divulged Lonetree's confidences to NIS investigating agents brought in to interrogate Lonetree and testified at Lonetree's trial about the statements he made.

At his court-martial, Lonetree moved to suppress the confessions, in part because the Johns had unlawfully induced his cooperation. The judge denied this motion, and the Court of Military Review affirmed the denial. The Court of Military Review, however, did not address the merits of Lonetree's argument but simply agreed with the Government that "Little John, while advising appellant that it was in his best interest to cooperate in the debriefings, *never made any promises to appellant*; instead, he repeatedly emphasized to appellant that someone else would decide whether to initiate criminal charges." 31 M.J. at 866 (emphasis added). Since Little John's uncontested testimony establishes beyond peradventure that a promise of confidentiality was made to Lonetree, we infer that the Court of Military Review construed Lonetree's complaint as solely an assertion that the Johns had offered prosecutorial or use immunity in exchange for his confession. Having granted review of Lonetree's unanswered argument that the had been unlawfully induced to confess, we focus now on this claim.

Generally, a confession is not admissible unless it has been made voluntarily, considering the totality of the circumstances surrounding the confession. *Arizona v. Fulminante*, 111 S.Ct. 1246, 1251-52, 113 L.Ed.2d 302 (1991) (reviewing voluntary-confession standard and holding that admission of involuntary confessions may satisfy a harmless-error analysis). Under federal criminal law, a confession made in reliance on a promise not to use the information against the confessor can be found involuntary and therefore inadmissible. *See Streetman v. Lynaugh*, 812 F.2d 950, 957 (5th Cir. 1987) (observing in dicta that "certain promises, if not kept, are so attractive that they render a resulting confession involuntary. A promise of immediate release or that any statement will not be used against the accused is such a promise.") (citation omitted). Military criminal law incorporates the voluntariness inquiry through Article 31(d), UCMJ, 10 USC Section 831(d), which prohibits use of any confession that was obtained "through the use of coercion, unlawful influence, or unlawful inducement."

In support of his argument, Lonetree directs us to *United States v. Churnovic*, 22 M.J. 401 (C.M.A. 19886), in which this Court applied Article 31(d) to an induced confession. In *Churnovic*, a senior Navy Non-commissioned Officer (NCO) promised Churnovic that, if he told what he knew about drugs on board a ship, the seaman would not "get in trouble" with the chain of command. *Id.* at 406. Churnovic relied on this promise and told the NCO where some drugs were located, which prompted the ship's captain to initiate an investigation leading to the seaman's conviction on drug charges.

This Court, with then-Judge Sullivan not participating, entered two separate opinions, each recognizing merit in Churnovic's argument. Chief Judge Everett concluded that the record did not contain sufficient information about the authority given to the NCO for him to rule on whether the NCO could grant Churnovic transactional immunity. However, he did state that the NCO's assurances "encompassed a promise that [the accused's] statements would not be used against him as evidence in a trial." Chief Judge Everett therefore deemed inadmissible the NCO's testimony regarding Churnovic's confession, since "use of such a promise to obtain a statement but not honoring that promise constitutes an 'unlawful inducement' for purposes of Article 31(d)." Additionally, Churnovic's subsequent confession given to a Navy investigator was also ruled inadmissible because "[clearly the later statement would never have been made if earlier Churnovic had not made his inadmissible statement to" the NCO. *Id.* at 408.

In a concurring opinion, Judge Cox explained that he would determine voluntariness by assessing whether a confession was "'the product of an essentially free and unconstrained choice.'" *Id.* at 409 (Cox, J., concurring in the result)(quoting *Schneckloth v. Bustamonte,* 412 U.S. 218, 225, 93 S. Ct. 2041, 2046, 36 L.Ed.2d 854 (1973)). Since Churnovic relied on the senior NCO's promise that he would not "get in trouble" with "the chain of command on the ship" if he cooperated, Judge Cox concluded that Churnovic's statements should have been suppressed. *Id.* (citing *United States v. Dalrymple,* 14 U.S.C.M.A. 307, 34 C.M.R. 87 (1963)).

The lesson we take from *Churnovic* is that, when a superior, acting with the apparent approval of the chain of command, makes an assurance of confidentiality to a subordinate, an incriminating statement springing from that assurance may not be the product of a free and unconstrained choice. *United States v. Washington,* 9 U.S.C.M.A. 131, 133, 25 C.M.R. 393, 395 (1958) (holding inadmissible a confession obtained from a suspect by a promise of confidentiality from the suspect's company commander, explaining that the company commander "occupied a position of responsibility where his assurance could

be given credence by the accused, and the overall effect of the promise created in the mind of the accused a belief that his disclosures would not be made the basis for a prosecution"). Given that military superiors often act as law enforcement investigators within their commands the lesson of *Churnovic* derives naturally from a long line of military cases involving promises of confidentiality by law enforcement agents to suspects. Citations omitted.

However, appellant can point to no military case holding a confession involuntary because a non-police agent made a false promise of confidentiality. No such cases are to be found in civilian federal criminal law, in large part because under the totality of the circumstances courts have found that non-police agents do not exert the same coercive force or custodial constraint as do law enforcement agents. 3 W. Ringel, *Searches & Seizures, Arrests and Confessions* Section 26.5(a) at 26-23 (1991) (in context or requirement to issue *Miranda* warnings, suggesting that "questioning by non-law enforcement personnel will occur in a less coercive setting than would be the case with law enforcement agents"). [citations omitted].

Consistent with both military and civilian authority, we agree that, for an inducement to be unlawful under Article 31(d) and thus render the resulting confession involuntary, an inducement must be made by someone acting in a law enforcement capacity or in a position superior to the person making the confession.

Lonetree does not attempt to convince us that the Johns were somehow his superiors, asserting instead that, because Little John was a U.S. government official, his false promissory inducement was unlawful. As explained above, though, Lonetree needs to show more than that the Johns were affiliated with the U.S. government; he must show that the Johns were acting in a law enforcement capacity when they made their inductive promise of confidentiality. *Colorado v. Connelly*, 479 U.S. at 165-66, 107 S.Ct. at 521. The record below demonstrates that the Johns displayed none of the indicia of law enforcement actors: They did not engage in custodial or coercive discussions with Lonetree; they made clear they did not represent the command or law enforcement entities; and they did not attempt to restrict Lonetree's movements or suggest they possessed the authority to do so. In fact, all the meetings between Lonetree and the Johns were arranged with Lonetree's approval, and he even cancelled one scheduled meeting. Lonetree does not refute this. Because Lonetree does not provide a scintilla of evidence indicating that the Johns were engaged in a law enforcement activity when they made their promise of confidentiality, we hold that Lonetree's confession was voluntary, so it was properly admitted at his court-martial.

II

Need for Rights Warnings

Lonetree next argues that the Johns were obligated, but failed, to give an Article 31(b) warning before interrogating him. As is common learning, a military questioner must give a military suspect an Article 31 warning when the questioner is "acting or could reasonably be considered to be acting in an official law-enforcement or disciplinary capacity." *United States v. Good*, 32 M.J. 105, 108 (C.M.A. 1991)(footnote and citations omitted). Giving bite to this obligation, Article 31(d) creates an exclusionary rule for statements obtained in violation of a service member's Article 31(b) rights. And though Article 31 obligations usually attach only to military questioners, this Court has recognized that civilian investigators must give Article 31 warnings in at least two situations:

(1) When the scope and character of their cooperative efforts demonstrate "that the two investigations merged into an indivisible entity"; and (2) when the civilian investigator acts "in furtherance of any military investigation, or in any sense as an instrument of the military."

United States v. Penn, 18 U.S.C.M.A. 194, 199, 39 C.M.R. 194, 199 (1969) (citations omitted).

Blurring these tow prongs, Lonetree asserts that, by operation of Executive Order No. 12333, the Johns' damage-assessment investigation "merged" into an indivisible entity with the NIS's criminal investigation and that the Johns became instruments of the NIS. Lonetree argues that the Johns knew of their authority under Executive Order No. 12333 to cooperate with law enforcement officials and that the Johns did in fact assist the NIS by providing them with all the information Lonetree had given and by introducing the NIS agents to Lonetree at his final meeting with the Johns on December 24, 1986. Indeed, Lonetree suggests that Executive Order No. 12333 mandates that this Court adopt a bright-line rule prohibiting use in courts-martial of any statements obtained by intelligence agents when those agents did not first give a suspect an Article 31 warning.

Lonetree made the same argument to the Court of Military Review, which unpacked his claims and, after an exhaustive review of the trial record and the relevant case law, concluded that the Johns' damage assessment did not merge with the separate NIS criminal investigation, 31 M.J. at 867-68, and that the Johns had not become instruments of the NIS. *Id.* at 868-69. We agree.

As to Lonetree's indivisible-entity claim, the Court of Military Review began by observing that, to determine if a civilian and a military criminal investigation have merged, "military courts consider the purpose of each of the two investigations and whether they act independently." *Id.* at 867. That court's examination of the trial record led it to conclude that "Big John and Little John analyzed appellant's activities for the purpose of ascertaining what damage may have occurred to the security of the United States and not for the purpose of perfecting a criminal prosecution." *Id.* at 868. In fact, the court remarked in a footnote that the Johns were statutorily prohibited "from conducting a criminal investigation or possessing law enforcement powers," *Id.* at 868 n. 18, a prohibition which the court found was not violated.

Our review of the record confirms the conclusions of the Court of Military Review. The Johns did not coordinate their activities with any military authorities but stayed within their own agency's communications channels. Lonetree does not assert that the Johns requested or sought the advice or guidance of the NIS. Moreover, the Johns' investigation did not begin as a coordinated effort with the NIS, and it was not influenced by military authorities; in fact, the NIS did not know about the Johns' investigation until over a week after it began on December 14. The Johns first met with NIS agents on the morning of December 24, when it was decided that the NIS would take Lonetree into custody after he appeared for a meeting with Little John previously scheduled for that evening. The NIS did not advise Little John on how to conduct this final meeting, and they did not instruct him to obtain any general or specific type of information from Lonetree.

In sum, we agree with the Court of Military Review that this record cannot support a finding that the Johns' investigation merged into an indivisible entity with the NIS's investigation. [citation omitted].

As to the separate claim that the Johns became an instrument of the military, Lonetree relies on this Court's decision in *United States v. Quillen*, 27 M.J. 312 (C.M.A. 1988). In *Quillen*, a base exchange civilian store detective stopped a service member suspected of shoplifting, showed the suspect her detective's badge, and then proceeded to question the suspect without giving an Article 31 warning. The *Quillen* Court held that the store detective, though a civilian, was an "instrument of the military" acting "at the behest of military authorities" and was therefore obligated to give an Article 31 warning. 27 M.J. at 314. In so holding, the Court explained that the store detective's job was military in purpose and service regulations required the store detective to work closely with military police since shoplifting crimes were command responsibilities. *Id.* at 314-15. Analogizing *Quillen* to his case, Lonetree argues that Executive Order No. 12333 required the Johns to work closely with military investigators and that, therefore, they were instruments of the military and under a duty to give an Article 31 warning.

Finding no merit in this claim, the Court of Military Review pointed out the "obvious factual differences" between *Quillen* and Lonetree's case. 31 M.J. at 868. The court explained that the Johns were not employed by or under the direction of military authorities and that they were prohibited from engaging in law enforcement activities. Though Executive Order No. 12333 authorized cooperation between the Johns and military law enforcement agents, cooperation in and of itself does not necessarily convert someone into an instrument of the military. *United States v. Jones*, 6 M.J. 226, 229 (C.M.A. 1979). The Executive Order did not make the Johns subordinate to, or under the control of, the military, and the Executive Order did not compel the Johns to conduct their investigation "at the behest of military authorities [or] in furtherance of [the military's] duty to investigate crime." *United States v. Quillen*, 27 M.J. at 314.

Finally, when the Johns met with the NIS and arranged for Lonetree's apprehension, the Johns did not assume a subordinate relationship to the NIS; they did not schedule a special meeting with Lonetree to effect his arrest; and they did not take direction from the NIS on how to conduct the final meeting. In agreement with the Court of Military Review, ten, we believe these facts do not demonstrate that military authorities used "the services of a person not subject to the [UCMJ] as an instrument for eliciting disclosures without warning." *United States v. Grisham*, 4 U.S.C.M.A. 694, 696, 16 C.M.R. 268, 270 (1954).

Accordingly, we conclude that the Johns, as civilians not subject to the UCMJ conducting an independent investigation without serving as an instrument of the military, had no obligation to give Lonetree an Article 31 warning prior to their meetings with him. *United States v. Penn*, 18 U.S.C.M.A. at 198-99, 39 C.M.R. at 198-99 (stating that "civilian investigators, acting entirely independent of military authority, need not as persons not subject to the [UCMJ], preliminarily advise an accused of his rights under Article 31*/*). Though the bright-line rule urged by Lonetree, by definition, would provide some certainty as to when intelligence agents who question a service member must give Article 31 warnings, we are convinced that, outside the special circumstances establishing an agency relationship discussed above, Article 31 does not require a civilian investigator to give rights warning.

. . . .

Affirmed.

The *Lonetree* case refers to Article 31(d) which provides in part that "no statement obtained from any person in violation of this article, or through the use of coercion, unlawful influence, or unlawful inducement may be received in evidence against him in a trial by court-martial." The case also discusses Article 31(b). When are rights warnings under 31(b) necessary? *See* Chapter VIII. Is the court's holding in *Lonetree* consistent with *United States v. Loukas* in Chapter VIII?

There are also special requirements for investigating compromises of classified documents. Chief of Naval Operations Instruction (OPNAVINST) 5510.1H requires an immediate preliminary inquiry in every case where classified information has been "lost, compromised or subjected to compromise." Following completion of the preliminary inquiry, the command with custodial responsibility over the material must convene a JAG Manual investigation and notify NCIS if it suspects:

> [T]hat a compromise of classified information may have occurred and that one or more of the following conditions are also true: (1) the probability of harm to the national security cannot be discounted; (2) significant security weaknesses may have been revealed; or (3) punitive disciplinary action is contemplated. . . .

A JAG Manual investigation of a possible compromise addresses all aspects of the possible security violation, including accountability, procedures and harm to the national security. JAG Manual investigations are discussed in the next section.

ADMINISTRATIVE INVESTIGATIONS

The Navy and Marine Corps also conduct inquiries primarily focused not on criminal culpability, but on issues such as efficient command administration, claims for or against the government, safety, training, leadership and injuries to personnel. These inquiries serve to collect and record information and are purely advisory in nature. The findings of such inquiries do not constitute final determinations or legal judgments, and their recommendations are not binding. The report of an administrative investigation may, however, become the basis for actions such as reevaluation of operational practices or standards, redesign and improvement of material, modification or adoption of instructions, regulations, and procedures, disciplinary action and reply to inquiries concerning incidents of public interest. The types of inquiries discussed in this section are all administrative in nature; however, each variety of investigation (JAG Manual

USS *Maine* Court of Inquiry. The *Maine* exploded and sunk in Havana Harbor in 1898. Photo courtesy of U.S. Naval Historical Society.

investigations, line of duty determinations and safety inquiries) serve a different purpose.

JAG MANUAL INVESTIGATIONS

Chapter II of the JAG Manual contains the regulations concerning administrative fact-finding bodies (JAG Manual investigations). There are three types of administrative fact-finding bodies in Chapter II: command investigations; litigation report investigations, and courts or boards of inquiries. Before deciding which variety of fact-finding body to convene, a preliminary inquiry into the matter is usually necessary. JAG Manual 0204 describes a preliminary inquiry.

> b. Purpose. A preliminary inquiry serves as an analytical tool to determine whether additional investigation is warranted and, if so, how it is to be conducted. The preliminary inquiry is the foundation for the subsequent exercise of the convening authority's (CA) discretion and is not intended to develop facts extensively or to serve as a medium for analyzing facts.
>
> . . . .
>
> d. Responsibility
>
>> (1) Generally, an officer in command (including an officer-in-charge) is responsible for initiating preliminary inquiries into incidents occurring within, or involving personnel of, the command.
>>
>> (2) In the event of a major incident, however, the officer exercising general court-martial convening authority over the command involved, if a flag or general officer, or the first flag or general officer in the chain-of-command, or any superior flag or general officer in the chain-of-command, will immediately take cognizance over the case as the CA.
>
> e. Method. A convening authority may conduct a preliminary inquiry personally or through designees. The preliminary inquiry may be accomplished in *any* manner considered sufficient by the CA. No particular format is required, but the convening authority may choose to document the outcome in writing.

The preliminary inquiry is a screening method to determine if a JAG Manual investigation is necessary. As noted above, there are three types of JAG Manual investigations. JAG Manual 0209a describes the most common of these inquiries, the command investigation:

> A command investigation functions to gather, analyze, and record relevant information about an incident or event of primary interest to command authorities. Most investigations be will of this nature. Command investigations may, *for example*, be used to inquire into—

(1) significant property losses (minor property losses may be adequately documented through other means in most cases), other than damage to or destruction of public quarters since such incidents are likely to result in claims against or for the Government and, consequently, require a litigation-report investigation;

(2) incidents in which a member of the naval service, as a result of possible misconduct, incurs a disease or injury that may result in a permanent disability or a physical inability to perform duty for a period exceeding 24 hours (distinguished from a period of hospitalization for evaluation or observation);

(3) deaths of military personnel, or of civilian personnel occurring aboard an activity under military control, apparently caused by suicide or under other unusual circumstances; and

(4) aircraft incidents, groundings, floodings, fires, and collisions not determined to be major incidents.

Paragraph 0209c describes the responsibilities of commanders to convene command investigations.

(1) Generally, an officer in command (including an officer-in-charge) is responsible for initiating command investigations into incidents occurring within, or involving personnel of, the command.

(2) If a commander believes that the investigation of an incident is impractical or inappropriate for the command to investigate, another command may be requested to conduct the investigation. . . .

(3) Whenever more than one command is involved in an incident requiring investigation, a single investigation should be conducted. Such an investigation may be convened by the officer in command of any of the activities concerned, and all the activities shall cooperate in the investigation. . . .

. . . .

(5) Incidents involving Marine Corps personnel—

(a) When an investigation of a training or operational incident causing serious injury or death (other than a major incident or aviation mishap) is required, the senior commander in the chain-of-command to the organization involved will consider convening the investigation and appointing the investigating officer at that level. No member of the organization suffering the incident, nor any member of the staff of a range or other training facility involved in the incident, shall be appointed to conduct the investigation without the concurrence of the next senior commander.

Paragraph 0209e provides the procedures for conducting a command investigation.

(1) A command investigation—

(a) is convened in writing;

(b) is conducted by one or more persons in the Department;

(c) collects evidence by personal interviews, telephone inquiries, or written correspondence;

(d) is documented in writing in the manner prescribed by the CA in the convening order;

(e) does not involve hearings; and

(f) may contain sworn statements signed by witnesses.

Line officers without significant training in investigations and legal matters conduct command investigations. What are the advantages/disadvantages of using such investigators? In certain situations, the investigating officer must interview persons suspected of violations of the UCMJ. Should the investigating officer advise such persons of the right to remain silent under Article 31(b)? Does it make any difference that a JAG Manual investigation is an administrative inquiry? *See* Chapter VIII.

Following completion of a command investigation, the commander convening the inquiry may act on the results of the inquiry in one of several ways. JAG Manual 0209g sets forth the commander's options.

A convening authority may determine that the investigation is of no interest to anyone outside the command, and, unless otherwise directed by superior authority, may choose to treat it as an internal report. If the convening authority intends to forward the report of investigation—

(1) Upon receiving a command investigation report, the convening authority shall review or have the report reviewed, and either endorse the report in writing or return it to the investigating officer for further investigation. In the endorsement, the convening authority may approve, disapprove, modify, or add to the findings of fact, opinions, and recommendations. The convening authority may also concur in or disagree with recommendations which the convening authority cannot implement at the convening authority's level. If the convening authority did not require opinions and recommendations in the convening order, then the convening authority shall state such opinions and make such recommendations as deemed appropriate. The convening authority shall also indicate what corrective action, if any, is warranted and has been or will be taken. . . .

(2) The convening authority shall retain a copy of the report and forward the original, through the chain-of-command (including area coordinators when appropriate), to the officer who exercises general court-martial convening authority (GCMCA) over the convening authority. The subject matter and facts found will dictate the routing of the report for further review. (Note: The GCMCA may, by regulation, direct subordinate commands not to forward investigations into certain categories or types of incidents.) The convening authority shall

also provide copies of the report to other commands which may have an interest, such as the Naval Safety Center, the local legal service office, or the Office of the Judge Advocate General. The convening authority shall maintain copies of all command investigations for a minimum of 2 years.

JAG Manual 0209h addresses review of completed command investigations:

(1) A GCMCA superior to the convening authority must review any command investigation which has been forwarded. Thus if the first reviewer is not a GCMCA, the investigation will require additional review. (Note: Superior commanders may, by regulation or on an *ad hoc* basis, provide direction concerning review and forwarding of investigations consistent with this chapter.) The subject matter and facts found will dictate the routing of the report for additional review.

. . . .

(4) Copies of the report should be made available to all superior commanders who have a direct official interest in the recorded facts. Area coordinators or designated subordinate commanders have a direct official interest in incidents that affect their command responsibility or occur in their geographic area.

Based on the above, when will a commander treat a command investigation as an internal report? Do you think commanders generally prefer keeping inquiries internal? The JAG Manual also provides specific requirements for the investigation of certain types of incidents (e.g., aircraft accidents, vehicle accidents, ship groundings and collisions and stranding of ships). *See* JAG Manual 0226-0227 and 0230-0237 for the requirements of investigating these specific varieties of incidents.

The second variety of JAG Manual inquiry, the litigation report investigation, is described in JAG Manual 0210.

a. Purpose. Investigations serve many purposes but when an incident or event is likely to result in claims or civil litigation against or for DON or the United States . . . the primary purpose of the resulting investigation is often to prepare to defend the legal interests of the Department and the United States. A command should contact a judge advocate at the earliest opportunity prior to commencing a litigation-report investigation to determine if a litigation-report investigation is the appropriate type of investigation to be conducted under the circumstances. Investigations into such incidents must be conducted under the direction and supervision of a judge advocate, and protected from disclosure to anyone who does not have an official need to know. When investigations are conducted in anticipation of litigation but are not conducted under the direction and supervision of a judge advocate or are handled carelessly, they cannot be legally protected from disclosure to parties whose litigation interests may be adverse to the interests of the United States. . . .

b. Comparison with Command Investigations

(1) Unlike a command investigation, a litigation-report investigation must be—

(a) convened only after consultation with a cognizant judge advocate;

(b) conducted under the direction and supervision of that judge advocate;

(c) conducted primarily in anticipation of claims or litigation; and

(d) forwarded to the Judge Advocate General.

(2) Like a command investigation, a litigation-report investigation—

(a) may not be used to investigate a major incident;

(b) may not have designated parties; and

(c) does not involve hearings.

c. Responsibilities

(1) After consulting a judge advocate, an officer in command is responsible for initiating litigation-report investigations into incidents involving the command or its personnel. The cognizant judge advocate, however, is responsible for supervising the conduct of the investigation. This does *not* mean that the judge advocate is the investigating officer, but it does mean that the investigating officer works under the direction and supervision of the judge advocate while conducting the investigation.

Why do litigation-report inquiries involve naval lawyers? What types of incidents may result in a claim for or against the government? JAG Manual 0210e describes the procedures for conducting a litigation report investigation:

(1) A litigation-report investigation shall—

(a) be convened in writing;

(b) be conducted by one or more persons in DON [Department of the Navy] under the direction and supervision of the cognizant judge advocate;

(c) collect evidence by personal interviews, telephone inquiries, written correspondence, or other means;

(d) be documented in writing in the manner prescribed by the cognizant judge advocate . . .; and

(e) shall *not* contain statements signed by witnesses. (Signed statements are subject to discovery and release to opposing parties in civil litigation even if provided to an attorney.)

(2) During the course of a litigation-report investigation, the investigating officer shall be guided by the cognizant judge advocate and shall consult frequently as the investigation progresses. When it is necessary to obtain evidence such as expert analyses, outside consultant reports, and so forth, the judge advocate should sign the necessary requests. The investigating officer shall present the preliminary findings to the judge advocate for review. The judge advocate may direct the investigating officer to provide opinions and recommendations or may write the opinions and recommendations.

(3) When the report is compiled, it shall be marked "FOR OFFICIAL USE ONLY: LITIGATION/ATTORNEY WORK PRODUCT" and be signed by both the investigating officer *and* the cognizant judge advocate.

The third variety of JAG Manual investigation, the court or board of inquiry, is a formal procedure to investigate "major incidents." Following the gun turret explosion on board the USS IOWA in 1989, the Navy convened a one-officer inquiry (then known as an informal investigation) to probe into the tragedy. The

Taken from the bridge of USS *Iowa* at the time of an explosion in #2 turret on 19 Apr 89, as the ship was operating off the coast of Puerto Rico. Photo by Lt. Thomas Jarrell, USN; courtesy of U.S. Naval Institute.

RADM R.D. Milligan, the investigating officer of the USS *Iowa* explosion, points to two powder bags during a Pentagon press conference called to release the findings of the Navy's official investigation. Following the *Iowa* inquiry, the Navy amended its investigative rules to require that a Courts of Inquiry investigate "major incidents." Photo by JO3 Oscar L. Sosa (5 Sep 89); courtesy of U.S. Naval Institute.

two-star admiral conducting the inquiry concluded that the explosion was most probably caused by a detonation device placed in the turret by a troubled sailor. The media and Congress criticized both the findings of the investigation and the Navy's selection of a relatively informal fact-finding procedure to delve into the incident. As a result of this reaction, the Navy revised the JAG Manual to ensure that a court or board of inquiry is convened for all events considered to be "major" and for serious and significant acts.

Appendix A-2-a of Chapter II of the JAG Manual defines a "major incident."

> Major Incident. An extraordinary incident occurring during the course of official duties resulting in multiple deaths, substantial property loss, or substantial harm to the environment where the circumstances suggest a significant departure from the expected level of professionalism, leadership, judgment, communication, state of material readiness, or other relevant standard. Substantial property loss or other harm is that which greatly exceeds what is normally encountered in the course of day to day operations. These cases are often accompanied by national public and press interest and significant congressional attention. They may also have the potential of undermining public confidence in the Naval service. That the case is a major incident may be apparent when it is first reported or as additional facts become known.

South China Sea—A view of the damaged bow of the Australian aircraft carrier HMAS *Melbourne*. It collided with the destroyer USS *Frank E. Evans* during Seato exercises in the South China Sea on 3 Jun 69. The Evans broke into two pieces. Such an incident would be considered a "major incident" under current administrative investigations regulations. Photo courtesy of U.S. Naval Institute.

JAG Manual 0211b describes the characteristics of a court of inquiry:

(1) Convened by persons authorized to convene general courts-martial or so designated by the Secretary of the Navy. (See Article 135, UCMJ.)

(2) Consists of at least three commissioned officers as members and also has appointed legal counsel for the court. It may also include advisors appointed to assist the members. (See subsection d below for additional information on advisors.)

(3) Convened by written appointing order.

(4) Uses a hearing procedure. Takes all testimony under oath and records all open proceedings verbatim, except arguments of counsel, whether or not directed to do so in the appointing order.

(5) Designates as parties persons subject to the UCMJ whose conduct is subject to inquiry.

(6) Designates as parties persons subject to the UCMJ or employed by the Department of Defense who have a direct interest in the subject under inquiry and request to be so designated:

(7) Has the power to order military personnel to appear, testify, and produce evidence, and the power to subpoena civilian witnesses to appear, testify, and produce evidence. (Article 47, UCMJ, provides for prosecution of civilian witnesses in U.S. district court for failing to appear, testify, or produce evidence.)

Less formal than a court of inquiry is a board an inquiry. JAG Manual 0211c details the characteristics of a board of inquiry:

(1) Convened by persons authorized to convene general courts-martial.

(2) Consists of one or more commissioned officers, and should have appointed legal counsel for the board. It may also include advisors appointed to assist the members. (See subsection d below for additional information on advisors.)

(3) Convened by written appointing order, which should direct that all testimony be taken under oath and all open proceedings, except counsel's argument, recorded verbatim. Persons whose conduct is subject to inquiry or who have a direct interest in the subject of the inquiry may be designated parties by the convening authority in the appointing order. The convening authority may also authorize the board to designate parties during the proceedings.

(4) Uses a hearing.

(5) Does not possess power to subpoena civilian witnesses unless convened under Article 135, UCMJ, and Chapter IV, but can order naval personnel to appear, testify, and produce evidence.

The responsibility for convening courts and boards of inquiry is discussed in JAG Manual 0211e.

(1) The officer exercising general court-martial convening authority over the command most involved in a major or serious incident, if a flag or general officer, or the first flag or general officer in the chain-of-command, or any superior flag officer in the chain-of-command, will immediately take cognizance over the case as the convening authority.

(2) Whenever more than one command is involved in a major or serious incident requiring formal investigation, a single investigation shall be conducted. The common superior commander shall convene the investigation in such cases, unless that officer's conduct or performance of duty may be subject to inquiry, in which case the next superior in the chain-of-command shall convene the investigation.

Based on the above, what are the differences between a court of inquiry and a board of inquiry? Consider which investigative body has the power to subpoena civilians. Note that a court of inquiry must designate persons as "party," and a board of inquiry may do so. Appendix A-2-b to Chapter II of the JAG Manual defines a "party" and explains the rights of a person so designated:

a. Party. A "party" is an individual who has properly been designated as such in connection with a court of inquiry or a fact-finding body required to conduct a hearing whose conduct is either the subject of the inquiry or has a direct interest in the inquiry.

b. Subject to inquiry. A person's conduct or performance of duty is "subject to inquiry" when the person is involved in the incident or event under investigation in such a way that either disciplinary action may follow, that his rights or privileges may be adversely affected, or that his personal reputation or professional standing may be jeopardized.

c. Direct interest. A person has a "direct interest" in the subject of inquiry:

(1) When the findings, opinions, or recommendations of the fact-finding body may, in view of his relation to the incident or circumstances under investigation, reflect questionable or unsatisfactory conduct or performance of duty; or

(2) When the findings, opinions, or recommendations may relate to a matter over which the person has a duty or right to exercise official control.

d. Rights. A person duly designated a party before a fact-finding body shall be advised of and accorded the following rights:

(1) To be given due notice of such designation.

(2) To be present during the proceedings, but not when the investigation is cleared for deliberations.

(3) To be represented by counsel.

(4) To examine and to object to the introduction of physical and documentary evidence and written statements.

(5) To object to the testimony of witnesses and to cross-examine witnesses other than his own.

(6) To introduce evidence.

(7) To testify as a witness.

(8) To refuse to incriminate himself; and, if accused or suspected of an offense, to be informed of the nature of the accusation and advised that he does not have to make any statement regarding the offense of which he is accused or suspected; and that any statement made by him may be used as evidence against him in a trial by court-martial.

(9) To make a voluntary statement, oral or written, to be included in the record of proceedings.

(10) To make an argument at the conclusion of presentation of evidence.

(11) To be properly advised concerning the Privacy Act of 1974.

(12) To challenge members.

Compare the procedural protections of a party with an accused at court-martial. Who has more rights? *See* Chapter III.

JAG Manual 0211j addresses review of courts and boards of inquiry:

(1) Upon receiving a report from a court or board of inquiry, the convening authority shall review it or cause it to be reviewed, and either endorse the report in writing or return it for further investigation. In the endorsement, the convening authority may approve, disapprove, modify, or add to the findings of fact, opinions, and recommendations. The convening authority shall also indicate what corrective action, if any, is warranted and has been or will be taken. The convening authority shall state in the endorsement, however, where the original evidence is preserved and provide the name and telephone number of the responsible official (see section 0215 for further information on the safekeeping of evidence).

LINE OF DUTY DETERMINATIONS

When service members incur an injury that might result in permanent disability, or that results in the physical inability to perform duty for a period exceeding 24 hours, a finding concerning the member's responsibility for the injury is necessary. For members of the naval service, these findings are known as line of duty determinations.

JAG Manual 0222 explains why line of duty determinations are necessary:

a. General. Line of duty/misconduct determinations are extremely important since they control several personnel actions, the most important of which is the awarding of disability retirement and severance pay. These determinations will also effect extensions of enlistment; changes in longevity, severance, and retirement pay multipliers; forfeitures of pay; Reserve incapacitation pay and medical care entitlement; and benefits administered by the Department of Veterans Affairs.

JAG Manual 0221 provides the specifics on when line of duty findings are required.

a. General. If a member incurs a disease or injury that may result in a permanent disability or that results in the member's physical inability to perform duty for a period exceeding 24 hours (as distinguished from a period of hospitalization for evaluation or observation), then determining whether the disease or injury was incurred in the line of duty or as the result of misconduct is very important. An injury or disease suffered by a member of the naval service will, however, be presumed to have been incurred in the line of duty and not as a result of misconduct unless contrary findings are made.

b. Warning Required. Any person in the Armed Forces, prior to being asked to sign any statement relating to the origin, incidence, or aggravation of any disease or injury that he or she has suffered, shall be advised of the right not to sign such a statement. *See* 10 U.S.C. § 1219. The spirit of this section will be violated if a person, in the course of an investigation, obtains the member's oral statements and reduces them to writing, unless the above advice was given first. Compliance with this section must be documented.

Note that injury warnings are in addition to Article 31(b) warnings. Is the injury warning based on constitutional principles, or is it required solely by statute? *See* Chapter VIII. JAG Manual 0229 discusses the relationship of line of duty determinations to disciplinary action.

An adverse line of duty/misconduct determination is not a punitive measure. If warranted, commanders should take independent disciplinary action. Similarly, a favorable line of duty/misconduct determination does not preclude separate disciplinary action. Nor is such a favorable determination relevant or binding on the issue of guilt or innocence of the member in a separate disciplinary proceeding.

JAG Manual 0223 sets forth what constitutes an injury incurred not in the line of duty.

a. General. . . . injury or disease incurred by naval personnel while in active service will be considered to have been incurred "in line of duty" except when incurred under one or more of the following circumstances:

(1) as a result of the member's own misconduct as determined under the regulations contained in this chapter;

(2) while avoiding duty by deserting;

(3) while absent without leave and such absence materially interfered with the performance of required military duties (see subsection c below);

(4) while confined under sentence of a court-martial that included an unremitted dishonorable discharge; or

(5) while confined under sentence of a civil court following conviction of an offense that is defined as a felony by the law of the jurisdiction where convicted.

"Misconduct" as discussed in JAG Manual 0223a(1) is explained in JAG Manual 0224.

a. Generally. "Misconduct," as used in this chapter, is a term of art. It is more than just inappropriate behavior. An injury or disease is the result of a member's misconduct if it is either intentionally incurred or is the result of willful neglect which demonstrates a reckless disregard for the foreseeable and likely consequences of the conduct involved. Simple or ordinary negligence, or carelessness, standing alone, does not constitute misconduct. The fact that the conduct violates law, regulation, or order, or is engaged in while intoxicated, does not, of itself, constitute a basis for a misconduct determination.

b. Presumption. An injury or disease suffered by a member of the naval service is presumed to have been incurred in the line of duty and not to be the result of misconduct. Clear and convincing evidence (see section 0215) is required to overcome this presumption.

"Clear and convincing evidence" is a higher standard of proof than preponderance of the evidence, but less than beyond a reasonable doubt. *See* Chapters III and IV. Why is there a more difficult burden in line of duty cases than in nonjudicial punishment? *See* JAG Manual 0222 above, which addresses the ramifications of a finding of not in the line of duty. JAG Manual 0225 discusses the relationship between misconduct and line of duty.

a. General. For purposes of these regulations, "misconduct" can never be "in line of duty." Hence, a finding or determination that an injury was incurred as a result of the member's own misconduct must be accompanied by a finding or determination that the member's injury was incurred "not in line of duty." It is permissible, however, to find that an injury was incurred "not as a result of misconduct" and "not in line of duty." As an example, a member who is absent without authority may be injured by a felonious assault or struck by a vehicle driven by a drunken driver. Obviously, the injury was incurred through no fault of the member, but if the absence materially interfered with the performance of his required military duties a finding of "not in line of duty" must result.

b. Possible Findings. The only possible combinations of findings are:

(1) "In line of duty" and "not due to the member's own misconduct;"

(2) "Not in line of duty" and "not due to the member's own misconduct;" and

(3) "Not in line of duty" and "due to the member's own misconduct."

Which of the above findings is favorable for the service member? The above section references the connection between unauthorized absence and line of duty determinations. JAG Manual 0225c specifically addresses this issue:

(1) Whether absence without leave materially interferes with the performance of required military duties necessarily depends upon the facts of each situation, applying a standard of reality and common sense. No definite rule can be formulated as to what constitutes "material interference." Generally speaking, absence in excess of 24 hours constitutes a material interference unless evidence to the contrary exists. Similarly, an absence of shorter duration will not be considered a material interference unless there is clear and convincing evidence to establish the contrary. A statement of the individual's commanding officer, division officer, or other responsible official, and any other available evidence to indicate whether the absence constituted a material interference with the performance of required military duties, should be included in the record whenever appropriate.

Note that under 10 USC § 1207, a service member is ineligible for physical disability retirement or physical disability severance benefits if the disability was incurred during a period of unauthorized absence, regardless of the length of such absence and regardless of whether such absence constituted a material interference with the performance of required military duties.

The method of transcribing line of duty findings depends on the determination itself. JAG Manual 0230 provides the methods for recording line of duty determinations.

a. General. As noted above, injuries or disease suffered by naval personnel are presumed to have been incurred in the line of duty and not as a result of a member's misconduct. Each injury or disease requiring line of duty/ misconduct determinations (see 0221) *must* be the subject of a preliminary inquiry. If, however, following a preliminary inquiry the conditions set forth in subparagraph c below are met, then the member's command need *not* convene an investigation and need *not* report the line of duty/misconduct determinations separately. Thus, if appropriate entries in the member's health or dental records are made, and the command does not convene an investigation, then the presumption that the member's injuries or disease was incurred in the line of duty and was not a result of the member's misconduct will *not* be rebutted.

b. Reporting. If the command completing the preliminary inquiry is *not* a GCMCA, the command will report the circumstances surrounding the injury . . . using the Personnel Casualty Report system (see MILPERSMAN 4210100). Unless the GCMCA directs otherwise, the command will provide a copy of this preliminary inquiry report to the appropriate medical department for inclusion in the health or dental record as part of the entry described in subparagraph c. Of course, the GCMCA may review the preliminary inquiry and order an investigation.

c. Entry in Health or Dental Record. An investigation need not be convened and a report need not be forwarded concerning misconduct and line of duty when, in the opinion of the medical officer (or senior representative of a medical department), with the concurrence of the commanding officer, the injury or disease was incurred "in line of duty" and "not as a result of the member's own misconduct" *and* appropriate entries to this effect have been made in the member's health or dental record.

d. Command Investigations. A command must convene an investigation and make findings concerning misconduct and line of duty when—

(1) the injury was incurred under circumstances which suggest a finding of "misconduct" might result. These circumstances include, but are not limited to, all cases in which a qualifying injury was incurred—

(a) while the member was using illegal drugs;

(b) while the member's blood alcohol content was of .10 percent by volume or greater. This does not preclude the convening of an investigation if the blood-alcohol percentage is lower than .10, if the circumstances so indicate; and

(c) as a result of a bona fide suicide attempt;

(2) the injury was incurred under circumstances that suggest a finding of "not in line of duty" might result;

(3) there is a reasonable chance of permanent disability and the commanding officer considers the convening of an investigation essential to ensure an adequate official record is made concerning the circumstances surrounding the incident; or

The authority convening the inquiry and a general court-martial convening authority take certain actions on completed investigations. JAG Manual 0231 describes these actions.

a. Action by Convening Authority. Unless the report is returned for further inquiry, the convening authority will make a line of duty/misconduct determination by taking one of the following actions:

(1) If the convening authority concludes that an injury or disease was incurred "in line of duty" and "not due to the member's own misconduct" (or that clear and convincing evidence is not available to rebut the presumption of in line of duty/not due to misconduct), this conclusion shall be expressed in the action on the record of proceedings. This action may be taken regardless of whether it differs from or concurs with an opinion expressed by the investigating officer.

b. Action by General Court-Martial Convening Authority.

(1) Unless the convening authority is empowered to convene general courts-martial, the report shall be forwarded via the chain-of-command to an officer empowered to convene general courts-martial with an assigned judge advocate. This officer may take any action on the report that could have been taken by the convening authority. With respect to conclusions concerning misconduct and line of duty, the GCMCA shall indicate approval, disapproval, or modification of such conclusions unless the record is returned for further inquiry.

(2) The investigation should not normally be forwarded to the Judge Advocate General.

Compare review of line of duty reports with review of administrative investigations, in general. Is there any difference? It is important to understand that line of duty findings are oftentimes part of administrative investigations into incidents that involve other issues. That is, the investigation may consider safety, operational, disciplinary and procedural questions, as well as make findings regarding the line of duty status of injured service members.

SAFETY AND MISHAP INVESTIGATIONS

Apart from criminal and JAG Manual inquiries, the Navy and Marine Corps conduct investigations that focus solely on safety issues. JAG Manual 0244 explains the relationship between safety investigations and other types of probes:

> (2) Mishap Investigation Reports. For the sole purpose of safety and mishap prevention, the Chief of Naval Operations has issued special instructions . . . for the conduct, analysis, and review of investigations of mishaps that occur aboard ships or submarines. These investigations are conducted by mishap investigation boards appointed for that purpose and the results are documented in mishap investigation reports (MIRs).
>
> (3) JAGMAN Investigations. When an afloat mishap results in death or serious injury, extensive damage to Government property, or the possibility exists that a claim may be filed by or against the Government, a JAGMAN investigation shall be appointed to investigate and determine the cause and responsibility for the mishap, nature and extent of any injuries, description of all damage to property, and any and all attendant circumstances. These JAGMAN investigations are in addition to, and separate from, the mishap investigation boards. . . .

Paragraph 204 of OPNAVINST 5102.1C explains the procedures for conducting mishap investigations:

CONDUCTING THE MISHAP INVESTIGATION. Some of the many factors involved in the investigation of mishaps are listed below. These are not all inclusive, but will serve as a basis from which to proceed.

a. Steps should be taken to preserve and/or photograph the material evidence.

. . . .

c. Individuals interviewed during investigations conducted under this instruction shall not testify under oath and shall be advised that their statements (oral or written) are for one purpose only—the prevention of further mishaps. That assurance is necessary to obtain complete and candid information regarding the circumstances surrounding a mishap. Information obtained during any investigation conducted under this instruction shall not be the basis for any administrative, regulatory, disciplinary, or criminal proceeding within the Department of the Navy. This paragraph does not bar appropriate discipline when a management offi-

A helo lifts personnel off the bow of the destroyer USS *Frank Knox* shortly after running aground (23 Aug 65). Chapter II of the JAG Manual contains special rules for investigating incidents such as ship groundings. The Navy also conducts separate and independent safety and mishap inquiries. Photo courtesy of U.S. Naval Institute.

cial, superior to the individual, obtains facts surrounding a mishap from source different than an investigation conducted under this paragraph.

Aircraft mishap investigations have a similar purpose as discussed in paragraph 602 of OPNAVINST 3750.6Q:

602. PURPOSE OF AIRCRAFT MISHAP INVESTIGATIONS

The purpose of aircraft mishap investigations is hazard detection, to identify the cause factors of the mishap and the damage and/or injury occurring in the course of the mishap. Cause factors of mishaps, and cause factors of injury and damage occurring in the course of a mishap, can be two different matters, but both are the subject of aircraft mishap investigations. Other, less important reasons for conducting aircraft mishap investigations include determination of the extent of damage and injury resulting from the mishap and demonstration of the safety commitment of the organization conducting the investigation. All naval aircraft mishap investigations are conducted solely for safety purposes.

Paragraph 603 of OPNAVINST 3750.6Q illustrates the relationship between safety inquiries and JAG Manual probes:

d.   JAG Manual Investigations. A mishap involving naval aircraft may require an investigation pursuant to the JAG Manual in addition to the aircraft mishap investigation. These investigations are conducted for legal or administrative action; such as property damage, possible negligence, culpable performance of duty, etc. Such investigations will be completely independent and separate from any safety investigations.

A common characteristic of all safety investigations is that statements provided by witnesses are privileged from disclosure and from use in disciplinary proceedings. Paragraph 606 of OPNAVINST 3750.6Q explains the privilege and its purpose in relation to aircraft mishap investigations:

a.   Limited Use. . . . [the mishap investigation] shall not be used for any other purposes, which include, but are not limited to, the following (prohibited) uses:

   (1) In making any determination affecting the interest of an individual making a statement under an assurance of confidentiality or involved in a mishap.

   (2) As evidence or to obtain evidence in determining the misconduct or line of duty status of killed or injured personnel.

   (3) As evidence to determine the responsibility of personnel from the standpoint of discipline.

   (4) As evidence to assert affirmative claims on behalf of the government.

   (5) As evidence to determine the liability of the government for property damage caused by a mishap.

   (6) As evidence before administrative bodies, such as Naval Aviator/Naval Flight Officer Evaluation Boards (USN) or Field Flight Performance Boards (USMC).

   (7) In any other punitive or administrative action taken by the DON.

b.   The Purpose of Designating Information as Privileged. The actions above are taken to:

   (1) Overcome any reluctance of an individual to reveal complete and candid information pertaining to the circumstances surrounding a mishap.

   (2) Encourage aircraft mishap boards and endorsers of aircraft mishap investigative reports to provide complete, open and forthright information, opinions and recommendations regarding a mishap.

c. Rationale. If privileged information were allowed to be used for purposes other than safety, vital safety information might be withheld:

(1) Individuals may be reluctant to reveal information pertinent to a mishap because they believe certain uses of the information could be embarrassing or detrimental to themselves, their fellow service members, their command, their employer, or other. They may also elect to withhold information by exercise of their constitutional rights to avoid self incrimination. Individual members of the armed forces must be assured that they may confide in others for the mutual benefit of fellow service members without incurring personal jeopardy in the process. . . .

(2) If aircraft mishap boards and endorsers of mishap investigative reports believed that their deliberations, opinions and recommendations could be used for other than safety purposes, they might be reluctant to develop, or include in their report and endorsements, information which would be vital for safety.

In a 1995 message to the entire Navy, the Chief of Naval Operations, Admiral Boorda, explained the nature and significance of privileged safety investigations as it related to the inquiry into the death of the Navy's first female combat pilot, Lieutenant Kara Hultgreen. The safety report of the crash causing her death was released to the media without authority. He stated:

Most of you have probably seen the continuing accounts of the investigations into last fall's F-14 crash that killed LT Hultgreen. As you know, JAG Manual investigations and aviation mishap reports (MIRs) are very different approaches with very different objectives. They deal with the same facts and because of that, should agree (they do in this case but they are also different). The JAGMAN report establishes cause and accountability. The MIR is much more detailed and, because it is intended to serve aviation safety and instructional needs, it examines every factor and reports in the bluntest of terms. . . . One or more people have taken it upon themselves to release all or part of one of the Navy's most consistently safeguarded investigation reports, the MIR. The effectiveness and integrity of the entire mishap safety investigation process rests on our ability to have a frank discussion of accident causes and what might be done to prevent such accidents in the future. Those doing MIR's must be free to discuss in very direct terms not only what happened but all the things that might have been done to prevent or lessen the mishap. . . . Unauthorized disclosures really damage this system.

Admiral Boorda emphasized the importance of maintaining the confidentiality and privileged nature of safety inquiries. Based on his comments, what is the effect of an improper release of a mishap investigation? Outside of the safety investigation situation, communications by service personnel are normally not privileged from use in future disciplinary proceedings. However, certain relationships do protect against such use. For example, attorney-client communications are privileged, as are discussions with clergy personnel and between spouses. *See* Military Rule of Evidence 501-504. Note, however, that the doctor-patient privilege does not exist in the military.

STUDY QUESTIONS

1. Who investigates major criminal offenses in the Navy and Marine Corps? Who handles the inquiry into minor violations?

2. What is the purpose of criminal intelligence operations? How are such investigations different than criminal inquiries?

3. What are the three types of JAG Manual investigations? When should a preliminary inquiry be done prior to convening a JAG Manual investigation?

4. Who has authority to convene a command investigation? Litigation report investigation? A court or board of inquiry?

5. When is a command investigation appropriate? What is the purpose of such an inquiry?

6. What is a "major incident?' Which fact-finding body should inquire into a major incident?

7. While on patrol in the Atlantic Ocean, USS CAINE collides with an oil tanker. Admiral Quigg convenes an investigation and appoints one Rear Admiral and two Captains to look into the incident. The fact-finding body has subpoena power and a JAG officer is assigned to act as the legal advisor. This type of administrative fact-finding body is:

   a. A formal investigation.

   b. A command investigation.

   c. An informal investigation.

   d. A court of inquiry.

   e. A litigation report investigation.

PC3 Claven and DK3 Peterson are both attached to the USS BOSTON, homeported in Norfolk, Virginia. One evening while on liberty together, they stopped at a convenience store and purchased two 6-packs of beer. After the beer was gone, PC3 Claven kept the party going by smoking some crack cocaine. While stopped at a red light just outside the Norfolk city limits, DK3 Peterson's car was crushed from behind by an "18-wheeler" whose driver had fallen asleep at the wheel. Both DK3 Peterson and PC3 Claven had been wearing their seat belts, but nevertheless suffered severe injuries as a result of the force of the impact. They were taken to Portsmouth Naval Hospital for treatment, but PC3 Claven died from his injuries shortly after their arrival. The autopsy on PC3 Claven revealed a blood alcohol content (BAC) of .21% and the presence of cocaine metabolite in his bloodstream. DK3 Peterson survived, but was hospitalized for several months for treatment of his injuries. DK3 Peterson is now permanently disabled and will require extensive physical therapy. Laboratory analysis of DK3 Peterson's blood revealed a BAC of .19%, well above the legal limit in Virginia.

8. What is the proper line of duty (LOD)/misconduct determination for PC3 Claven?

   a. In the LOD, not due to misconduct.

   b. Not in the LOD, not due to misconduct.

   c. Not in the LOD, due to misconduct.

   d. In the LOD, due to misconduct.

   e. No LOD/misconduct determination should be made.

9. What is the proper line of duty (LOD)/misconduct determination for DK3 Peterson?

   a. In the LOD, not due to misconduct.

   b. Not in the LOD, not due to misconduct.

   c. Not in the LOD, due to misconduct.

   d. In the LOD, due to misconduct.

   e. No LOD/misconduct determination should be made.

10. What are the three possible line of duty/misconduct determinations? When is each type appropriate? When should a command investigation be used to record a line of duty determination?

11. How does unauthorized absence affect the line of duty status of an injured service member?

12. What is the purpose of safety investigations? How are they different than criminal investigations and JAG Manual inquires? For what purpose can a safety investigation be used?

CHAPTER X

APPREHENSION AND RESTRAINT

SIGNIFICANCE OF APPREHENSION AND RESTRAINT IN THE MILITARY

The military's need to maintain good order and discipline requires that service personnel perform many functions typically handled by police or law enforcement officials in the civilian sector. Apprehension and restraint are good examples of this unique aspect of military law. Because of order and discipline considerations, the military delegates the authority to apprehend or restrain service members to a broad segment of its personnel. To ensure that this important authority is used properly, extensive procedures and limitations affecting apprehension and restraint exist. This chapter discusses the authority and grounds to restrict the movement of service members, as well as the consequences of resisting or challenging such restrictions.

Apprehending or restraining a service member also has important ramifications from both a constitutional and procedural standpoint. For example, confining a service member begins the running of several procedural clocks, including the accused's statutory and constitutional right to a speedy trial. This chapter also addresses the procedural implications related to apprehension and restraint.

APPREHENSION

Rules for Court-Martial (RCM) 302(a) defines "apprehension" as the term is used in the military:

(1) Definition. Apprehension is the taking of a person into custody.

(2) Scope. This rule applies only to apprehensions made by persons authorized to do so . . . with respect to offenses subject to trial by court-martial. Nothing in this rule limits the authority of federal law enforcement officials to apprehend

persons, whether or not subject to trial by court-martial, to the extent permitted by applicable enabling statutes and other law.

The military term "apprehension" has a statutory meaning, *see* Article 7(a), UCMJ, and is not synonymous with the civilian term, "arrest." *See generally United States v. Kinane*, 1 M.J. 309 (C.M.A. 1976). Based on RCM 302, an apprehension in the military will oftentimes occur well before what is considered an arrest in civilian criminal law. What is the distinction between arrests, apprehensions and detentions? Why is the distinction important? *See Rights of the Pretrial Confinees* below concerning rights of service members following apprehension. RCM 302 does not affect apprehensions of persons not subject to trial by court-martial. A base commander may order the apprehension of persons not subject to the UCMJ by military law enforcement personnel. He or she may do so as part of the inherent authority of commanders to maintain law and order on a military installation.

AUTHORITY TO APPREHEND

RCM 302(b) describes who has the authority to apprehend in the military:

> (b) Who may apprehend. The following officials may apprehend any person subject to trial by court-martial:
>
> > (1) Military law enforcement officials. Security police, military police, master at arms personnel, members of the shore patrol, and persons designated by proper authorities to perform military criminal investigative, guard, or police duties, whether subject to the code or not, when, in each of the foregoing instances, the official making the apprehension is in the execution of law enforcement duties;
> >
> > (2) Commissioned, warrant, petty, and noncommissioned officers. All commissioned, warrant, petty, and noncommissioned officers on active duty or inactive duty training;
> >
> > (3) Civilians authorized to apprehend deserters. . . . any civilian officer having authority to apprehend offenders under laws of the United States or of a State, Territory, Commonwealth, or possession, or the District of Columbia, when the apprehension is of a deserter from the armed forces.

Based on the above section, commissioned and warrant officers may be apprehended by noncommissioned or petty officers. Do you foresee a problem with enlisted personnel apprehending officers? Does it help or hurt good order and discipline to give this important authority to junior personnel? The discussion to RCM 302 explains that "[n]oncommissioned and petty officers not otherwise performing law enforcement duties should not apprehend a commissioned officer unless directed to do so by a commissioned officer or in order to prevent disgrace to the service or the escape of one who has committed a serious offense." This same rule applies to Naval Criminal Investigative Service (NCIS) agents, as well. *See* JAG Manual 0168. Note that enlisted personnel who are not petty officers or noncommissioned officers may only apprehend if they are performing law enforcement duties.

BASES AND PROCEDURES TO APPREHEND

RCM 302(c) sets forth the grounds and procedures for apprehending persons.

> (c) Grounds for apprehension. A person subject to the code or trial thereunder may be apprehended for an offense triable by court-martial upon probable cause to apprehend. Probable cause to apprehend exists when there are reasonable grounds to believe that an offense has been or is being committed and the person to be apprehended committed or is committing it. Persons authorized to apprehend under subsection (b)(2) of this rule (commissioned, warrant, petty, and noncommissioned officers) may also apprehend persons subject to the code who take part in quarrels, frays, or disorders, wherever they occur.
>
> (d) How an apprehension may be made.
>
> > (1) In general. An apprehension is made by clearly notifying the person to be apprehended that person is in custody. This notice should be given orally or in writing, but it may be implied by the circumstances.
> >
> > (2) Warrants. Neither warrants nor any other authorization shall be required for an apprehension under these rules except as required in subsection (e)(2) of this rule.
> >
> > (3) Use of force. Any person authorized under these rules to make an apprehension may use such force and means as reasonably necessary under the circumstances to effect the apprehension.
>
> (e) Where an apprehension may be made.
>
> > (1) In general. An apprehension may be made at any place, except as provided in subsection (e)(2) of this rule.
> >
> > (2) Private dwellings. A private dwelling includes dwellings, on or off a military installation, such as single family houses, duplexes, and apartments. The quarters may be owned, leased, or rented by the residents, or assigned, and may be occupied on a temporary or permanent basis. "Private dwelling" does not include the following, whether or not subdivided into individual units: Living areas in military barracks, vessels, aircraft, vehicles, tents, bunkers, field encampments, and similar places. No person may enter a private dwelling for the purpose of making an apprehension under these rules unless:
> >
> > > (A) Pursuant to consent . . .;
> > >
> > > (B) Under exigent circumstances . . .;
> > >
> > > (C) In the case of a private dwelling which is military property or under military control, or nonmilitary property in a foreign country,
> > >
> > > > (i) if the person to be apprehended is a resident of the private dwelling, there exists, at the time of the entry, reason to believe that the person

to be apprehended is present in the dwelling, and the apprehension has been authorized by an official . . . upon a determination that probable cause to apprehend the person exists; or

(ii) if the person to be apprehended is not a resident of the private dwelling, the entry has been authorized by an official . . . upon a determination that probable cause exists to apprehend the person and to believe that the person to be apprehended is or will be present at the time of the entry;

Probable cause that an offense has been or is being committed provides the basis for an apprehension. "Offenses", as used in RCM 302, refers only to crimes under the UCMJ. Apprehensions for civilian crimes sometimes occur on board military installations. This occurs through coordination with the base or unit commander by civilian law enforcement authorities. Note that civilian authorities must have an arrest warrant and agree to deliver the member back to his or her unit once the charges are resolved before Navy and Marine Corps personnel will be delivered. *See* Article 14, UCMJ; JAG Manual 0603, 0607. RCM 302(c) also provides authority to apprehend service members who are involved in disturbances. Why is this provision necessary? What action may a service member take for being wrongly apprehended? *See* Article 138, UCMJ (complaint of wrongs).

Except in private dwellings, a warrant is not required to apprehend a service member. This rule is a codification of longstanding military law. *See United States v. Kinane*, 1 M.J. 309 (C.M.A. 1976). *See also United States v. Sanford*, 12 M.J. 170 (C.M.A. 1981). Is this inconsistent with the Fourth Amendment protection against unlawful searches and seizures? RCM 302(e)(2) defines a "private dwelling" for purposes of the warrant requirement. This definition is based upon those areas where service members are considered to have an expectation of privacy. *See* Chapter VII regarding constitutional restraints on search and seizure. If a warrant is not needed to apprehend a service member located in a barracks, does this also do away with the need for probable cause? RCM 302(d)(3) authorizes the use of force to apprehend. Does this include the use of "deadly force?"

APPREHENSION AND CUSTODY OFFENSES

Resisting Apprehension

Article 95, UCMJ makes "resisting apprehension" a military offense. Paragraph 19b, Part IV, MCM details the elements of the offense.

(a) That a certain person attempted to apprehend the accused;

(b) That said person was authorized to apprehend the accused; and,

(c) That the accused actively resisted the apprehension.

Note that the person attempting to apprehend must be authorized to do so. *See Authority to Apprehend* above regarding who has such authority. It is a defense that the accused held a reasonable belief that the person attempting to apprehend did not have authority to do so. What if the accused believed that no basis existed for the apprehension, i.e., he or she did not commit the offense? This is not a defense. *See* Paragraph 19c(1)(d), Part IV, MCM. The following case considers conduct that constitutes actively resisting apprehension.

United States, Appellee, v. Richard Burgess, Specialist, U.S. Army, Appellant
United States Court of Military Appeals
32 M.J. 446
July 11, 1991

OPINION: Cox

Pursuant to his pleas, appellant was convicted, among other things, [footnote omitted] of resisting apprehension by an armed forces policeman who was authorized to apprehend him, in violation of Article 95, Uniform Code of Military Justice, 10 USC @ 895. The findings and sentence were affirmed by the Court of Military Review in a short-form opinion dated April 13, 1990.

In addition to resisting apprehension, a military judge sitting alone as a general court-martial convicted appellant of distributing and attempting to distribute cocaine, in violation of Articles 112a and 80, Uniform Code of Military Justice, 10 USC @ @ 912a and 880, respectively. He was sentenced to a dishonorable discharge, confinement for 8 years, and reduction to pay grade E-1. Pursuant to a pretrial agreement, the convening authority approved the sentence but reduced the confinement to 5 years.

Appellant petitioned this Court for further review, contending that his pleas of guilty for resisting apprehension must be set aside because his conduct constituted only flight, not resisting apprehension. We granted his petition to determine if the record of trial established a factual basis sufficient to support a conviction of resisting apprehension under Article 95 of the Uniform Code. After careful review, we hold that it did not and that appellant's "flight" was not a violation of Article 95. *United States v. Harris*, 29 M.J. 169 (C.M.A. 1989).

I

On June 9, 1989, in Clarksville, Tennessee, appellant met with a prospective cocaine buyer. Unbeknownst to him, the buyer actually was an undercover agent of the CID (Criminal Investigation Command) who was part of a drug suppression team investigating appellant's recent drug activity.[1] The rendezvous took place in the parking lot of a local retail store; both appellant and the agent remained in their re-

---

[1] The undercover agent had become acquainted with appellant through a confidential source, and they had engaged in two previous drug transactions. The first transaction occurred on May 24, 1989, when appellant sold the agent 3 grams of cocaine; the second took place on May 30, when he sold the same agent over 5 grams of cocaine.

spective cars during the meeting. A surveillance team consisting of military agents and Tennessee State Police was also at the site, waiting and prepared to apprehend appellant when the drug deal was completed.

Appellant and the agent had previously negotiated the sale of one ounce of cocaine, but when appellant noticed a police car near the scene, he became hesitant. The agent suggested that they move elsewhere (each man still remained in his own automobile), and appellant agreed. The two cars began to move; appellant's car followed the agent's.

As this was occurring, the surveillance team watched for the undercover agent's prearranged signal—the illumination of the brake lights on the agent's car—indicating that the deal was done and that they should act. Consequently, when the agent's car moved and the brake lights brightened, the surveillance team incorrectly assumed that the signal had been given, and they moved in to arrest appellant. One CID agent "jumped out of a vehicle and yelled, 'Police, you're under arrest!'"

Appellant ignored the agent and drove off in his car. According to a stipulation of fact, "He was immediately pursued by several [military and state police] vehicles," with sirens blaring and lights flashing. It was this flight by appellant that formed the basis of the resisting-apprehension charge.

II

"Resisting apprehension" is proscribed by Article 95. The elements of the offense are:

(a) That a certain person attempted to apprehend the accused;

(b) That said person was authorized to apprehend the accused; and,

(c) That the accused actively resisted the apprehension.

Para. 19b(1), Part IV, Manual for Courts-Martial, United States, 1984 at IV-33.

The record reveals that the first two elements of the Article 95 offense were satisfied. The agent who jumped out of the car did in fact attempt to apprehend appellant—surely, the language: "Police, you're under arrest," yields no other conclusion. Furthermore, the military agents clearly were authorized to perform criminal apprehensions, and the agent who first tried to apprehend appellant was wearing "a . . . jacket with the CID emblem visible." Moreover, during the providence inquiry, appellant admitted that he had recognized the person who attempted to apprehend him to be a military policeman who had the authority to arrest him.

The key to resolving this case lies in whether the third element of the Article 95 offense exists. We must determine whether appellant "actively resisted" the attempted apprehension by driving away from a police officer who had communicated to appellant that he was under arrest. The Government contends that appellant's flight (driving away and leading authorities on a chase) alone was sufficient to constitute resisting apprehension under Article 95. We disagree.

III

The Manual explains the "nature of the resistance" as a type that "must be active, such as assaulting the person attempting to apprehend. . . ." Likewise, the explanation states that "flight" constitutes resisting apprehension. Para. 19c(1)(c), Part IV, Manual, *supra*. However, in *United States v. Harris, supra*, we rejected this view. We concluded: (1) "that the drafters of the Uniform Code never contemplated that 'flight' from attempted apprehension would constitute a violation of Article 95," *id.* at 172; and (2) "'fleeing or eluding a police officer is not a residuum of elements of Article 95, UCMJ.' *United States v. Kline*, 15 M.J. 805, 806 (1983), *aff'd on other grounds*, 21 M.J. 366 (C.M.A. 1986)." 29 M.J. at 173. We are not persuaded to change this view.

We emphasize however, that such conduct (flight from an arresting officer) does not leave military authorities helpless:

> Failure to obey the lawful order of one not a superior is an offense under Article 92(2), 10 U.S.C. @ 892(2), provided the accused had a duty to obey the order, such as one issued by a sentinel or a member of the armed forces police.

Para. 16c(2)(c)(ii), Part IV, Manual, *supra* (emphasis added); *see United States v. Harris, supra* at 173. In addition, military installations may promulgate general regulations that require automobiles to stop when being pursued by police vehicles with sirens or lights on. Violators would then be subject to prosecution under Article 92, UCMJ, 10 USC @ 892. Moreover, state statutes [footnote omitted] may also provide deterrence to such behavior on military bases under the Assimilative Crimes Act, 18 USC @ 13. *United States v. Harris, supra.*

Finally, once one is in custody, any type of flight would be covered by Article 95 as an escape from custody.[2]

Conclusion

The decision of the United States Army Court of Military Review as to Charge I and its specification is reversed. The findings of guilty thereon are set aside and that Charge is dismissed. The record of trial is returned to the Judge Advocate General of the Army for remand to that court for reassessment of the sentence based on the remaining findings of guilty.

Based on *Burgess*, how active must the resistance be to violate Article 95? The court in *Burgess* alluded to Article 92, UCMJ, as another provision which may apply to fleeing from an attempted apprehension. *See* Chapter V regarding orders violations. It also noted that a commander can issue an order prohibiting flight from officials attempting to effect an apprehension. Would an accused have to know of such an order? Finally, the court stated that once a service member is in custody, any attempt to flee violates Article 95. *See* the following section for the elements of fleeing custody under Article 95.

Escape from Custody or Confinement

Article 95 also proscribes escaping from custody or confinement. The elements of escape from custody are contained in Paragraph 19b, Part IV, MCM.

   (a) That a certain person apprehended the accused;

---

[2]We recognize that, in close cases or where the evidence is conflicting, it may be necessary to charge some of these theories in the alternative.

(b) That said person was authorized to apprehend the accused;

(c) That the accused freed himself or herself from custody before being released by proper authority.

The elements of escape from confinement are also contained in Paragraph 19b, Part IV, MCM.

(a) That a certain person ordered the accused into confinement;

(b) That said person was authorized to order the accused into confinement;

(c) That the accused freed himself or herself from confinement before being released by proper authority.

Custody occurs following apprehension of a service member. *See Apprehension,* above, regarding the definition of "apprehension." Confinement, however, is physical restraint imposed either as a pretrial measure or as punishment following disciplinary proceedings. Although escaping from custody and confinement are both part of the same UCMJ article, the distinction between the two restraints is important. The following case discusses the difference between custody and confinement and the importance of the distinction in properly charging the offense.

United States, Appellee, v. Richard P. Ellsey, Private, U.S. Marine Corps, Appellant
United States Court of Military Appeals
16 U.S.C.M.A. 455; 37 C.M.R. 75
December 23, 1966

Ferguson, Judge

Convicted below by special court-martial of a number of offenses in violation of the Uniform Code of Military Justice, the accused sought our review, and we granted his petition upon the following issues:

. . . .

2. WHETHER THERE IS A FATAL VARIANCE BETWEEN THE ALLEGATIONS AND THE PROOF OF THE SPECIFICATION OF ADDITIONAL CHARGE II.

. . . .

The Government . . . urges there is no substantial difference between the offenses of escape from custody and escape from confinement and, hence, imply no prejudice resulted from the unauthorized action of the trial counsel. We deem it necessary, therefore, as well as desirable, to reach the second question before us and inquire whether there is presented a fatal variance between the allegation that accused escaped from lawful confinement and the proof. In order to do so, a brief sketch of the evidentiary background is obviously necessary.

The accused was taken from the battalion adjutant's office by a guard, who was there furnished with a written confinement order directing his incarceration in the brig. En route to the confinement facility, accused was accompanied to his barracks in order to pack his gear. While at the latter place, accused evaded his guard and disappeared. Based on these facts, the accused was, as noted above, charged with escape from custody and convicted, because of the alteration of the count, of escape from confinement. The question of variance before us thus turns on the difference between "custody" and "confinement."

Code, *supra*, Article 95, 10 USC @ 895, under which the accused stands convicted, provides for the punishment of "Any person subject to this chapter who resists apprehension or breaks arrest or who escapes from custody or confinement." (Emphasis supplied.) It is urged that the emphasized portion of the statute creates but the single offense of escape which may be proven to be committed—regardless of the allegations—from either custody or confinement, both being mere forms of physical restraint. We cannot agree, for we believe the argument overlooks essential differences between the two statuses.

Confinement is defined by the Uniform Code of Military Justice as "the physical restraint of a person." Code, *supra*, Article 9, 10 USC @ 809. It may be imposed upon an enlisted person only by a commissioned officer, and by a warrant officer, petty officer, or noncommissioned officer only when such authority is conferred upon them by a commanding officer. It may be imposed upon a commissioned or warrant officer or civilian "only by a commanding officer to whose authority he is subject." Such authority may not be delegated. Code, *supra*, Article 9. It may not ordinarily be executed if an accused is charged with an offense normally tried by summary court-martial, Code, *supra*, Article 10, 10 USC @ 810, nor may it be carried out "in immediate association with enemy prisoners or other foreign nationals." Code, *supra*, Article 12, 10 USC @ 812. Where imposed by a court-martial, it begins to run from the date the sentence is adjudged. Code, *supra*, Article 57, 10 USC @ 857. Confinement cannot be refused "when the committing officer furnishes a statement, signed by him, of the offense charged against the prisoner," and must be reported by the custodian, "within twenty-four hours after that commitment or as soon as he is relieved," to the commanding officer. Code, *supra*, Article 11, 10 USC @ 811.

On the other hand, custody is defined only inferentially by the Code, which declares "Apprehension is the taking of a person into custody." Code, *supra*, Article 7, 10 USC @ 807. The Manual, *supra*, elaborates upon this by declaring, in paragraph 174d:

> ". . . Custody is that restraint of free locomotion which is imposed by lawful apprehension. The restraint may be corporeal and forcible or, once there has been a submission to apprehension or a forcible taking into custody, it may consist of control exercised in the presence of the prisoner by official acts or orders."

Unlike confinement, "Any person authorized under regulations governing the armed forces" may apprehend members of the services and thus impose the status of custody upon them. So, also, may officers, warrant officers, and noncommissioned officers quell disorders and "apprehend persons subject to this chapter who take part therein." Code, *supra*, Article 7. In short, as the Manual, *supra*, points out, "There is a clear distinction between the authority to apprehend and the authority to arrest or confine." Manual, *supra*, paragraph 19d. Moreover, those empowered to apprehend are only authorized "to secure the custody of an alleged offender until proper authority may be notified." Manual, *supra*, paragraph 19d.

Thus, it will be seen that custody and confinement are entirely different in nature. The first results from apprehension and lasts "until proper authority may be notified." Manual, *supra*, paragraph 19d. It may be imposed by any person empowered by departmental regulations. Confinement, on the other hand, absent authorization by a commanding officer, may be ordered only by a commissioned officer. Its execution before and after trial is subjected to strict control. Finally, while custody may of necessity be maintained by physical restraint, it also suffices to utilize no more than moral suasion. Hence, far from being identical to confinement, it is an altogether different condition.

Indeed, the legislative history evidences the intent of Congress to create two different types of restraint in dealing with custody and confinement. By the enactment of the pertinent Articles of the Code, a "certain duality of meaning in the words 'arrest,' 'restraint,' 'confinement,' and words of that character," was found and "we adopted this scheme to clarify the definitions of those words and started off with 'apprehension' in article 7." Hearings before House Armed Services Committee on H.R. 2498, 81st Congress, 1st Session, pages 901-902.

What was intended by custody was the temporary form of restraint imposed upon an individual subject to the Code by his lawful apprehension. *United States v. West*, 1 C.M.R. 770. It was to continue until "proper authority may be notified." Manual, *supra*, paragraph 19d. At that time, such authority may take cognizance of the circumstances and order the individual into confinement—"a screening out process will occur here in reference to a more permanent status." Hearings, *supra*, at page 904. As was said in *United States v. West*, *supra*, at page 773:

". . . Such status [custody] thereafter may be altered by the arrest, confinement, restriction, or release of the individual. After confinement has been effected in a lawful manner (MCM, 1951, par 20d (3)), by competent authority (Art 9 (b) (c); MCM, 1951, par 21a) (which is 'confinement' as contemplated by Article 95 and MCM, 1951, par 174c, and is something more than mere restraint within a confinement facility), such confinement is not a continuation of custody but a new and different form of restraint. Nor does confinement include custody in this sense, because confinement may be imposed in cases where there has been no apprehension and resultant custody."

Applied to the facts before us, the fatal variance between the evidence and the "charge" upon which the accused was tried becomes apparent. The accused had been duly ordered into confinement. It appears he was then taken into custody for delivery to the confinement facility. Before that delivery could be effected and confinement actually imposed upon him, the accused made his escape. Hence, his offense was breach of lawful custody of his guard and not of a confinement in which he never entered. Poetically speaking, "Stone walls do not a prison make, nor iron bars a cage;"[1] practically and legally, they do.

The findings of guilty of Additional Charge II and its specification are set aside. The decision of the board of review is reversed and the record of trial is returned to the Judge Advocate General of the Navy. The board may reassess the sentence on the remaining findings of guilty or order a rehearing on a proper charge and the penalty.

---

[1]Lovelace, To Althea from Prison, stanza 4.

Private Ellsey was charged at trial with escape from custody, but convicted of escape from confinement. In *Ellsey*, the trial counsel amended the charge from escape from confinement to escape from custody without approval from the convening authority (this information was removed for purposes of this text). Why would the trial counsel make such a change? Do you think the convening authority was pleased with the trial counsel's action?

Breaking Arrest and Restriction

The following case discusses the difference between the offenses of breaking arrest under Article 95 and breaking restriction under Article 134.

United States v. Bascom Brooks Hughes, Airman Apprentice, U.S. Navy
United States Navy Board of Review
11 C.M.R. 600
June 5, 1953

OPINION: Albrink, McNemar, and Lauerman, Judges

Specification 1 of Charge II, violation of the Uniform Code of Military Justice, Article 95, alleges that the accused, "having been duly placed in arrest in a Prisoner At Large Status at the U.S. Naval Air Technical Training Center, Norman, Oklahoma, did, at . . . [said center] . . . at or about 2100 hours, on or about 10 January 1953, break said arrest." The accused was convicted after a plea of not guilty to this specification. (He was convicted on a number of other counts as well, but these are not material to this discussion.)

A prosecution's witness testified that he was the athletic officer of the center and that while on duty on 3 January 1953 as Officer of the Day he put the accused in a "prisoner at large status" by advising the accused orally that he "would be a PAL," having him read and sign a certain form, and giving the accused a copy thereof. The witness used the piece of paper involved to refresh his memory during direct examination. On cross-examination the defense had the witness identify the piece of paper in-

volved, and it was received into evidence as Defense Exhibit "A."

This exhibit reads:

"NAVAL AIR TECHNICAL TRAINING CENTER NORMAN, OKLAHOMA

3 JAN 1953
(DATE)

From: Discipline Officer

To: HUGHES, Bascom B.
(NAME)

499 87 73
(SERVICE NO.)

AA
(RATE)

USN
(CLASS)

Subj: Restriction to limits of Station/Extra Duty; notification of

1. You are hereby notified that you have been:

   (a) Restricted to the limits of the Naval Air Technical Training Center for a period of

   (b) Awarded Extra Duty for a period of : as a result of approved on

2. You will report to the CMAA, NATTC at Barracks #39 for instructions upon receipt and acknowledgment of this notice.

3. While in Restraint, you WILL NOT INDULGE IN THE USE OF INTOXICATING BEVERAGES of any kind.

4. You are warned not to violate the terms of restraint or you will be subject to severe disciplinary action.

5. Men on Restriction will muster at the following times at Barracks #39.

   WEEK DAYS: 0645, 1700, 1900, 2130 bunk check and SAT., SUN., and HOLIDAYS: 0645, 1100, 1400, 1700, 1900, and 2130 bunk check. [*602]

6. Men having Extra Duty will muster at the following times at Barracks #39.

   WEEK DAYS: 1800 and 2000 SAT., SUN., and HOLIDAYS: 0800 and 1000.

7. The period of restraint will expire on and the Master-at-Arms is hereby directed to automatically remove you on that date.

8. I have READ and UNDERSTAND the above.

BASCOM B. HUGHES

(SIGNATURE)

/s/ R. E. GOSS, LT.

R. E. GOSS, LT, O.O.D.

A CERTIFIED TRUE COPY:

/s/ Charles M. Sodersten

CHARLES M. SODERSTEN, LTJG, USNR, TRIAL COUNSEL

The term "prisoner at large" is a term familiar to naval law under the Articles for the Government of the Navy. *See United States v. Coyle* (N.C.M. 20), 1 C.M.R. 483. Although the term does not appear anywhere in the Uniform Code of Military Justice and is conspicuously absent from Chapter V, Apprehension and Restraint, of the Manual for Courts-Martial, United States, 1951, it has continued to be used from time to time with resulting needless confusion. Such use should be discontinued. In the case of *United States v. Lowery* (No. 683), 2 U.S.C.M.A. 315, 8 C.M.R. 115, decided March 13, 1953, the United States Court of Military Appeals held that a "prisoner at large" is a person in the status of arrest. Arrest and restriction are separate forms of authorized restraint; breach of arrest is pleaded under Article 95, UCMJ, and breach of restriction is pleaded under Article 134, UCMJ; breach of arrest has a greater maximum legal limit of punishment than breach of restriction; breach of restriction is a lesser included offense of breach of arrest. *See* paragraphs 20, 127c Section A, and 174, and Appendix 12, MCM, 1951. Notification to the accused of the imposition of restraint, of the type of restraint being imposed, and of the limits of the restraint as well as a legal power to impose restraint of the type used are parts of the element of due imposition of restraint common to both arrest and restriction. Such notice should be clear and unambiguous, and the accused should not be compelled to speculate as to his status. While the parole evidence rule has no place in criminal law, we are of the opinion that if a person being placed under restraint is simultaneously given a written notification pertaining to his status, the written notice governs, unless there is an express cancellation or negation, either written or oral, of the provisions thereof. Defense Exhibit "A" clearly imposes only restriction, and the finding on the first specification of Charge II should be reduced to the lesser included offense of breach of restriction, a violation of Article 134, UCMJ. The sentence is appropriate for the findings as thus reduced.

Restriction is a more commonly used form of restraint than is arrest. The elements of restriction are set forth in paragraph 102, Part IV, MCM:

(1) That a certain person ordered the accused to be restricted to certain limits;

(2) That said person was authorized to order said restriction;

(3) That the accused knew of the restriction and the limits thereof;

(4) That the accused went beyond the limits of the restriction before being released therefrom by proper authority; and

(5) That, under the circumstances, the conduct of the accused was to the prejudice of good order and discipline in the armed forces or was of a nature to bring discredit upon the armed forces.

PRETRIAL RESTRAINT

RCM 304 describes the types of restraint imposable prior to disposition of an offense:

(a) Types of pretrial restraint. Pretrial restraint is moral or physical restraint on a person's liberty which is imposed before and during disposition of offenses. Pretrial restraint may consist of conditions on liberty, restriction in lieu of arrest, arrest, or confinement.

(1) Conditions on liberty. Conditions on liberty are imposed by orders directing a person to do or refrain from doing specified acts. Such conditions may be imposed in conjunction with other forms of restraint or separately.

(2) Restriction in lieu of arrest. Restriction in lieu of arrest is the restraint of a person by oral or written orders directing the person to remain within specified limits; a restricted person shall, unless otherwise directed, perform full military duties while restricted.

(3) Arrest. Arrest is the restraint of a person by oral or written order not imposed as punishment, directing the person to remain within specified limits; a person in the status of arrest may not be required to perform full military duties such as commanding or supervising personnel, serving as guard, or bearing arms.

The status of arrest automatically ends when the person is placed, by the authority who ordered the arrest or a superior authority, on duty inconsistent with the status of arrest, but this shall not prevent requiring the person arrested to do ordinary cleaning or policing, or to take part in routine training and duties.

(4) Confinement. Pretrial confinement, is physical restraint, imposed by order of competent authority, depriving a person of freedom pending disposition of offenses.

RCM 304 also details the authority to impose restraint prior to disposition of an offense:

(b) Who may order pretrial restraint:

(1) Of civilians and officers. Only a commanding officer to whose authority the civilian or officer is subject may order pretrial restraint of that civilian or officer.

(2) Of enlisted persons. Any commissioned officer may order pretrial restraint of any enlisted person.

(3) Delegation of authority. The authority to order pretrial restraint of civilians and commissioned and warrant officers may not be delegated. A commanding officer may delegate to warrant, petty, and noncommissioned officers authority to order pretrial restraint of enlisted persons of the commanding officer's command or subject to the authority of that commanding officer.

RCM 304 explains when pretrial restraint is appropriate.

(c) When a person may be restrained. No person may be ordered into restraint before trial except for probable cause. Probable cause to order pretrial restraint exists when there is a reasonable belief that:

(1) An offense triable by court-martial has been committed;

(2) The person to be restrained committed it; and

(3) The restraint ordered is required by the circumstances.

(d) Procedures for ordering pretrial restraint. Pretrial restraint other than confinement is imposed by notifying the person orally or in writing of the restraint, including its terms or limits. The order to an enlisted person shall be delivered personally by the authority who issues it or through other persons subject to the code. The order to an officer or a civilian shall be delivered personally by the authority who issues it or by another commissioned officer. Pretrial confinement is imposed pursuant to orders by a competent authority by the delivery of a person to a place of confinement.

(e) Notice of basis for restraint. When a person is placed under restraint, the person shall be informed of the nature of the offense which is the basis for such restraint.

(f) Punishment prohibited. Pretrial restraint is not punishment and shall not be used as such. No person who is restrained pending trial may be subjected to punishment or penalty for the offense which is the basis for that restraint. Prisoners being held for trial shall not be required to undergo punitive duty hours or training, perform punitive labor, or wear special uniforms prescribed only for post-trial prisoners. This rule does not prohibit minor punishment during pretrial confinement for infractions of the rules of the place of confinement. Prisoners shall be afforded facilities and treatment under regulations of the Secretary concerned.

(g) Release. Except as otherwise provided in R.C.M. 305, a person may be released from pretrial restraint by a person authorized to impose it. Pretrial restraint shall terminate when a sentence is adjudged, the accused is acquitted of all charges, or all charges are dismissed.

(h) Administrative restraint. Nothing in this rule prohibits limitations on a service member imposed for operational or other military purposes independent of military justice, including administrative hold or medical reasons.

What factors should be considered in deciding on appropriate pretrial restraint? Possible flight prior to trial is a factor which must be examined. Is the likelihood that the service member will commit another offense pertinent? What about violent or suicidal tendencies on the part of the accused? *See* RCM 305 discussed below.

Note that in cases other than pretrial confinement, the service member is not entitled to consult with counsel. If pretrial restraint is used as punishment, the remedy is meaningful sentence relief. This means that the military judge who tries the accused should reduce the sentence to compensate for the unlawful pretrial restraint. *See United States v. Pringle*, 41 C.M.R. 324 (C.M.A. 1970); *United States v. Nelson*, 39 C.M.R. 177 (1969).

PRETRIAL CONFINEMENT

RCM 305 explains the rules regarding pretrial confinement:

(a) In general. Pretrial confinement is physical restraint, imposed by order of competent authority, depriving a person of freedom pending disposition of charges.

(b) Who may be confined. Any person who is subject to trial by court-martial may be confined if the requirements of this rule are met.

. . . .

(d) When a person may be confined. No person may be ordered into pretrial confinement except for probable cause. Probable cause to order pretrial confinement exists when there is a reasonable belief that:

(1) An offense triable by court-martial has been committed;

(2) The person confined committed it; and

(3) Confinement is required by the circumstances.

Compare the above rules with the procedures for other types of pretrial restraint. *See* RCM 304, discussed above.

Confinement prior to disposition of an alleged offense triggers significant procedural rights for the confinee. RCM 302 describes those protections:

(e) Advice to the accused upon confinement. Each person confined shall be promptly informed of:

(1) The nature of the offenses for which held;

(2) The right to remain silent and that any statement made by the person may be used against the person;

(3) The right to retain civilian counsel at no expense to the United States, and the right to request assignment of military counsel; and

(4) The procedures by which pretrial confinement will be reviewed.

(f) Military counsel. If requested by the prisoner, military counsel shall be provided to the prisoner before the initial review under subsection (1) of this rule. Counsel may be assigned for the limited purpose of representing the accused only during the pretrial confinement proceedings before charges are referred. If assignment is made for this limited purpose, the prisoner shall be so informed. Unless otherwise provided by regulations of the Secretary concerned, a prisoner does not have a right under this rule to have military counsel of the prisoner's own selection.

Compare the right to counsel following pretrial confinement with an accused's counsel rights at court-martial. *See* Chapter III. In which situation does the accused have more rights to counsel?

Review of the decision to confine a member is addressed in RCM 302.

(h) Notification and action by commander.

(1) Report. Unless the commander of the prisoner ordered the pretrial confinement, the commissioned, warrant, noncommissioned, or petty officer to whose charge the prisoner was committed shall, within 24 hours after that commitment, cause to be made a report to the commander which shall contain the name of the prisoner, the offenses charged against the prisoner, and the name of the person who ordered or authorized confinement.

(2) Action by commander.

(A) Decision. Not later than 72 hours after ordering a prisoner into pretrial confinement, or after receipt of a report that a member of the commander's unit or organization has been confined, the commander shall decide whether pretrial confinement will continue.

(B) Requirements for confinement. The commander shall direct the prisoner's release from pretrial confinement unless the commander believes upon probable cause, that is, upon reasonable grounds, that:

(i) An offense triable by a court-martial has been committed;

(ii) The prisoner committed it; and

(iii) Confinement is necessary because it is foreseeable that:

  (a) The prisoner will not appear at a trial, pretrial hearing, or investigation, or

  (b) the prisoner will engage in serious criminal misconduct; and

(iv) Less severe forms of restraint are inadequate.

(i) Procedures for review of pretrial confinement.

  (1) In general. A review of the adequacy of probable cause to believe the prisoner has committed an offense and of the necessity for continued pretrial confinement shall be made within 7 days of the imposition of confinement.

  (2) By whom made. The review under this subsection shall be made by a neutral and detached officer appointed in accordance with regulations prescribed by the Secretary concerned.

  (3) Nature of review.

. . . .

  (C) Standard of proof. The requirements for confinement . . . of this rule must be proved by a preponderance of the evidence.

(j) Review by military judge. Once the charges for which the accused has been confined are referred to trial, the military judge shall review the propriety of pretrial confinement upon motion for appropriate relief.

(k) Remedy. The remedy for noncompliance with subsection (f), (h), (i), or (j) of this rule shall be an administrative credit against the sentence adjudged for any confinement served as the result of such noncompliance. Such credit shall be computed at the rate of one day credit for each day of confinement served as a result of such noncompliance. This credit is to be applied in addition to any other credit the accused may be entitled as a result of pretrial confinement served. This credit shall be applied first against any confinement adjudged. If no confinement is adjudged, or if the confinement adjudged is insufficient to offset all the credit to which the accused is entitled, the credit . . . shall be applied against hard labor without confinement, restriction, fine, and forfeiture of pay, in that order, if adjudged. For purposes of this subsection, 1 day of confinement shall be equal to 1 day of total forfeiture or a like amount of fine. The credit shall not be applied against any other form of punishment.

. . . .

(m) Exceptions.

. . . .

(2) At sea. [The rules relating to counsel and review of pretrial confinement] shall not apply in the case of a person on board a vessel at sea. In such situations, confinement on board the vessel at sea may continue only until the person can be transferred to a confinement facility ashore. Such transfer shall be accomplished at the earliest opportunity permitted by the operational requirements and mission of the vessel.

The above rules are designed to ensure that service members are not improperly confined. This explains the extensive review that occurs in pretrial confinement cases. If a member is a flight risk, then pretrial confinement is normally appropriate. "Serious criminal misconduct" is more difficult to determine. RCM 305 states that it includes intimidation of witnesses, seriously injuring others, or other offenses which pose a serious threat to the safety of the community or to the effectiveness, morale, discipline, readiness, or safety of the command, or to the national security of the United States. Does this clarify the issue?

Compare the remedies described above in RCM 305(k) for illegal pretrial confinement with the remedies for a speedy trial violation discussed below. RCM 305 does not provide a remedy for illegal confinement where the accused is acquitted or not awarded any of the punishments listed in 305(k). Are there any other remedies available to the accused? *See* Article 138, UCMJ.

SPEEDY TRIAL

The Sixth Amendment to the Constitution provides that "[i]n all criminal prosecutions, the accused shall enjoy the right to a speedy and public trial." The military has established its own rules to ensure that an accused's right to a speedy trial are not violated. RCM 707 describes the speedy trial rules in the military.

(a) In general. The accused shall be brought to trial within 120 days after the earlier of:

(1) Preferral of charges;

(2) The imposition of restraint under R.C.M. 304(a)(2).

(b) Accountability.

(1) In general. The date of Preferral of charges, the date on which pretrial restraint under R.C.M. 304(a)(2)-(4) is imposed . . . shall not count for the purpose of computing time under subsection (a) of this rule. The date on which the accused is brought to trial shall count. The accused is brought to trial within the meaning of this rule at the time of arraignment under R.C.M. 904.

    (A) Dismissal or mistrial. If charges are dismissed, or if a mistrial is granted, a new 120-day time period under this rule shall begin on the date of dismissal or mistrial for cases in which there is no repreferral and cases in which the accused is in pretrial restraint. In all other cases, a new 120-day time period under this rule shall begin on the earlier of

        (i) the date of repreferral

        (ii) the date of imposition of restraint under R.C.M. 304(a)(2)-(4)

    (B) Release from restraint. If the accused is released from pretrial restraint for a significant period, the 120-day time period under this rule shall begin on the earlier of

        (i) the date of preferral of charges;

        (ii) the date on which restraint under R.C.M. 304(a)(2)-(4) is reimposed;

(c) Excludable delays. All periods of time covered by stays issued by appellate courts and all other pretrial delays approved by a military judge or the convening authority shall be excluded when determining whether the period in subsection (a) of this rule has run.

(d) Remedy. A failure to comply with the right to a speedy trial will result in a dismissal of the affected charges. This dismissal will be with or without prejudice to the government's right to reinstitute court-martial proceedings against the accused for the same offense at a later date. The charges must be dismissed with prejudice where the accused has been deprived of his or her constitutional right to a speedy trial. In determining whether to dismiss charges with or without prejudice, the court shall consider, among others, each of the following factors: the seriousness of the offense; the facts and circumstances of the case that lead to dismissal; the impact of a reprosecution on the administration of justice; and the prejudice to the accused.

The purpose of RCM 707 is to apply speedy trial rights under the Sixth Amendment to the military. In cases of pretrial confinement, the time limit to bring the accused to trial used to be ninety days. The current version of RCM 707 eliminated this rule. The 120-day rule established in RCM 707(a) now applies to all cases, not just where the accused is not in pretrial confinement. What factors would cause the government to fail to try an accused in 120 days? The general rule is that the government is accountable for all time prior to trial unless a competent authority grants a delay. Military judges and convening authorities are required to make an independent determination as to whether there is good cause for a pretrial delay, and to grant such delays for only so long as is necessary under the circumstances. Decisions granting or denying pretrial delays will be subject to review for both abuse of discretion and the reasonableness of the period of delay granted.

Until recently, the military courts held that when an accused has been held in pretrial confinement for more than 90 days, a presumption arose that the accused's right to a speedy trial had been violated. In such cases, the government had to demonstrate due diligence in bringing the case to trial. *United States v. Burton*, 44 C.M.R. 166 (C.M.A. 1971). This rule resulted in numerous dismissals of cases based on speedy trial grounds. *See, e.g.*, *United States v. Pyburn*, 48 C.M.R. (C.M.A. 1974). Note that when an accused is released from pretrial restraint for a significant period, he or she will be treated as if no restraint had been imposed. Therefore, unless restraint is reimposed, the 120-day period will run from the date of preferral of charges, regardless of whether that event occurs before or after the accused was released from restraint. Based on this rule, are there situations where the government would want or need to release an accused from pretrial confinement? The following case considers the effect of a change in pretrial restraint on speedy trial.

United States, Appellee, v. Private Roy L. Reynolds, II, United States Army
United States Army Court of Military Review
36 M.J. 1128
March 25, 1993

OPINION: Walczak, Judge

Appellant was tried by a general court-martial composed of officer and enlisted members at Frankfurt, Germany. Contrary to his pleas, he was convicted of violating a general regulation by wrongfully carrying a concealed weapon, a lock-blade knife, in violation of Article 92, Uniform Code of Military Justice [hereinafter UCMJ], 10 U.S.C. @ 892. The court-martial sentenced the appellant to a bad-conduct discharge, and the convening authority approved the sentence.

I.

Speedy Trial

Appellant first argues that he was denied his right to a speedy trial under the Manual for Courts-Martial, United States, 1984, Rule for Courts-Martial [hereinafter R.C.M.] 707. He asserts that the government intentionally manipulated speedy trial accountability so as to bring appellant to trial in excess of the 120 days mandated by R.C.M. 707(a). We disagree.

At trial, the defense moved for dismissal of the charges for denial of speedy trial. The military judge heard evidence on the issue and made specific findings on these periods. The military judge found that appellant was first placed in restriction tantamount to confinement from 29 March to 8 April 1991, then under restriction not equivalent to confinement from 9 April to 10 May 1991, then subject to conditions on liberty from 10 May to 10 July 1991. Midway through this entire period, on 29 May 1991, charges were preferred. On 31

July 1991, the appellant was arraigned. The military judge found that appellant's earlier restraint ended on 10 May 1991, when appellant's status was changed from restriction to conditions on liberty, and that the period of 10 May to 29 May was a significant release from pretrial restraint under R.C.M. 707(b)(3)(B). Accordingly, he held that the 120-day speedy trial accountability under R.C.M. 707 began with preferral of the charges on 29 May, and ended with arraignment on 31 July 1991, for a total of 63 days attributable to the government. He found no R.C.M. 707 speedy trial violation.

Appellant contends that the government intentionally manipulated the speedy trial clock by superficially changing the conditions of appellant's restraint so that it would appear as if he had been released from restraint for a significant period of time. Appellant's argument, however, confuses conditions on liberty under R.C.M. 304(a)(1) (limits on the pass and civilian clothing privilege) with forms of restraint under R.C.M. 304(a)(2)-(4) (restriction, arrest, and confinement). The latter would constitute continuation of restraint under R.C.M. 707.

R.C.M. 707(a) requires that an accused be brought to trial within 120 days after the earlier of:

(1) Preferral of charges;

(2) The imposition of restraint under R.C.M. 304(a)(2)-(4); or

(3) Entry on active duty under R.C.M. 204.

R.C.M. 304(a)(2)-(4) define restraint as confinement, restriction, or restriction tantamount to confinement. Conditions on liberty under R.C.M. 304(a)(1), however, do not constitute restraint for purposes of triggering the 120-day rule. Further, under R.C.M. 707(b)(3)(B), if an accused is released from pretrial restraint for a significant period, the 120-day period begins on the earlier of the three events of R.C.M. 707(a) specified above.

In the present case, charges were not preferred against appellant prior to his restraint. R.C.M. 304. Moreover, in view of his subsequent release from restriction on 10 May, the 120-day accountability did not begin until 29 May 1991 with the formal preferral of charges. The period of 10 May to 29 May, when appellant was under conditions on liberty, was not a continuation of pretrial restraint under R.C.M. 707(a) and it is a significant period, under the facts of this case. Accordingly, we agree with the findings of the military judge that the 120-day speedy trial accountability imposed in R.C.M. 707 began on the date of preferral, 29 May 1991, and ended on the date of arraignment, 31 July 1991, for a total of 63 days attributable to the government.

The finding of guilty and the sentence are affirmed.

Based on *Reynolds*, will the reason why the government modifies pretrial restraint be considered in a motion to dismiss the case for a speedy trial violation? Private Reynolds sought dismissal of the charges against him. This is the usual sanction for a speedy trial violation. However, the judge may dismiss the case with or without prejudice. If it is dismissed without prejudice, the government is not precluded from filing new charges. A dismissal without prejudice is only appropriate for nonconstitutional speedy trial violations. *See Strunk v. United States*, 412 U.S. 434 (1973).

Commanding officers are given authority to restrict the liberty of members in foreign countries without having to use disciplinary procedures. This is part of the "liberty risk program" discussed in Chapter IV in *Nonpunitive Measures*. The following case considers liberty risk as a form of pretrial restraint for purposes of speedy trial.

United States v. Bobby J. Wilkes, Lance Corporal
U.S. Marine Corps
United States Navy-Marine Corps Court of Military Review
27 M.J. 571
September 21, 1988

OPINION: Riley, Senior Judge

At a general court-martial, appellant entered a conditional plea of guilty to one specification of unauthorized absence, three specifications of dishonorable failure to maintain funds, and ten specifications of uttering checks with the intent to defraud, in violation of Articles 86, 134, and 123a, respectively, of the Uniform Code of Military Justice (UCMJ). Appellant was sentenced to be confined for three years, to forfeit $658.00 pay per month for 36 months, to be reduced to pay grade E-1, and to be discharged from the Naval Service with a bad-conduct discharge. The convening authority approved only so much of the sentence as provided for a bad conduct discharge, confinement for four months, and reduction to pay grade E-1.

As a result of a previous unauthorized absence, the appellant, on 24 December 1986, received nonjudicial punishment which included, inter alia, restriction for 30 days. Appellant had served 29 days of that restriction when he left without authorization once again. On 5 February 1987, appellant surrendered to military authorities in Albany, Georgia. Appellant returned to his unit (Communications

Company, H and S Battalion, Camp Kinser, Okinawa) on 8 February 1987, and on the next day he began serving the remainder of the previously imposed restriction. On the last day of that restriction (19 February 1987), appellant was interviewed by agents of the Naval Investigative Service (NIS). In that interview, he confessed to writing 33 bad checks totaling over $10,000.00. Later that day, Lieutenant Ubalde, the appellant's acting executive officer, after learning of appellant's bad check offenses and his unauthorized absence, placed him on pretrial restriction. Appellant remained in that status until 24 February 1987, when he was placed in a "liberty risk" status, restricting him to the limits of the base. He remained in that status until his trial began 125 days later on 30 June 1987.

Before this Court, appellant argues that the liberty risk program in this instance was used as a subterfuge to avoid the strict accountability of R.C.M. 707. The Government, on the other hand, argues that the appellant was placed in the liberty risk program in order to help him with an alcohol abuse problem and to avoid alcohol-related incidents involving the appellant and foreign nationals. Accordingly, government counsel urges that the appellant's restriction was valid pursuant to Rule for Courts-Martial (R.C.M.) 304(h), and therefore did not trigger the speedy trial clock under R.C.M. 707. Both appellate government and appellate defense counsel cite to *United States v. Bradford,* 25 M.J. 181 (C.M.A. 1987), in support of their positions.

In *United States v. Bradford, supra,* the appellant was involved in a number of assaults in various foreign ports and was placed in a liberty risk status, restricting him to the confines of his ship. The "liberty risk" status was necessary, according to his command, to avoid international incidents. During the ensuing investigation into the assaults, Bradford became the prime suspect and was subsequently tried and convicted for those offenses. At trial, he moved to dismiss all charges against him, arguing that he was denied a speedy trial. The heart of his argument was that his status as a liberty risk was, in substance, pretrial restriction which triggered the running of the speedy trial clock. The military judge ruled that appellant's status as an administrative liberty risk, while properly imposed at first, was transformed into pretrial restriction under R.C.M. 707(a) by virtue of the fact that he became the prime suspect in the assaults. The judge dismissed the charges against Bradford because he was not brought to trial within 120 days. The Government appealed the judge's decision under Article 62, UCMJ, and this Court reversed the ruling. 24 M.J. 831 (N.M.C.M.R. 1986). The Court of Military Appeals affirmed our decision.

In *Bradford,* the Court of Military Appeals rejected the notion that administrative restraint is transmuted as a matter of law into pretrial restraint when the subject of the restraint becomes a criminal suspect, likely to face trial by court-martial. Such a result, according to the court, would "give

rise to a variety of unacceptable scenarios" which could potentially jeopardize international relations by forcing commanders to release subordinates "who might properly be the subject of administrative restraint such as the liberty risk program . . . [but] who would not otherwise be the subject of pretrial restraint." 25 M.J. at 186. The court cautioned, however, that "administrative restriction under R.C.M. 304(h) must not become a subterfuge whereby a commander may avoid a successful claim that speedy trial has been denied." *Id.* In this regard, the court stated that "the test is whether the primary purpose in imposing conditions on liberty is to restrain an accused prior to trial in order to assure his presence at trial or to avoid interference with the trial process." *Id.* The court went on to point out that "in applying this standard we may inquire whether the same conditions would have been imposed, even if no trial by court-martial were in prospect." *Id.*

Inasmuch as the initial restriction placed upon the appellant by Lieutenant Ubalde constituted pretrial restriction under R.C.M. 304(a)(2) and 707(a), the question presented in this appeal is just the reverse of the one generated by the Bradford fact pattern. Here, we must decide whether the transformation of appellant's status from pretrial restrictee to liberty risk candidate operated to stop the running of the speedy trial clock. Resolution of this issue hinges upon whether appellant's restriction as a liberty risk was imposed primarily for "purposes independent of military justice." R.C.M. 304(h). *See also United States v. Bradford, supra.*

As noted earlier, appellant was placed on pretrial restriction by Lieutenant Ubalde on 19 February 1987. The military judge correctly found this restriction to be pretrial restraint as contemplated by R.C.M. 304(a)(2). On 24 February, appellant was placed on the liberty risk program which, in essence, did nothing more than change the name of his continuing restriction. He still had to muster every four hours during non-working hours. At trial, appellant's commanding officer, Major Glenn, testified that he had interviewed the appellant upon appellant's arrival at Camp Kinser in December, 1986. In that interview, appellant told him that he had an alcohol problem and had recently completed a voluntary rehabilitation course at the Naval Hospital on Okinawa. Major Glenn stated that the liberty risk status was imposed because appellant "had all the indications of a recovering alcoholic" and, because the command wanted to protect the appellant from any alcohol-related problems in the surrounding community.

In answering the military judge's questions, however, Major Glenn gave some revealing information about his concept of the liberty risk program vis a vis pretrial restriction.

Q. Major Glenn, are you aware, or were you at the time as Commanding Officer, that there's a difference between restriction imposed as a punishment for nonjudicial punishment and restriction imposed as a form of pretrial restraint?

A. Oh, yes, sir.

Q. Did you ever impose restriction in your company as a form of pretrial restraint during your time as a Company Commander?

A. That's a very touchy situation, sir, and the reason I have always used the liberty risk program because of

the legal ramifications; and I can't recall ever putting someone on restriction without the result of nonjudicial punishment.

[citation omitted].

Q. Are you saying, sir, that if you applied restriction as a pretrial restraint, that the restriction with regard to confines, as you have described it, would be less?

A. That's a hard one for me to answer because like I said, sir, I cannot recall putting anyone on restriction prior to a resolution of any judicial proceedings. I try and stay away from awarding a restriction without the punishment being awarded at my level or the punishment being awarded at the Battalion Commander's level or as a result of court-martial. The liberty risk program is an administrative tool that I have used quite a bit.

[citation omitted].

Major Glenn further testified that he had neither seen nor heard of appellant having been involved in any alcohol-related incidents either on base or in the surrounding community. Additionally, there was never any indication, oral or written, to the appellant about when his liberty risk status would terminate.[1] Instead, the liberty risk restrictions remained in effect until 30 June 1987, the date of his trial.

While we may not agree with appellant's categorization of his assignment to the liberty risk program as a subterfuge to avoid

---

[1]Indeed, none of the administrative requirements of the liberty risk program, such as notification of the right of appeal, the length of the status, and the right to periodic review, were followed in the appellant's case. While this fact is not, in and of itself, determinative on the question of whether the status was appropriately imposed, it is some evidence of the command's intent behind appellant's restrictions.

R.C.M. 707, we are not convinced that concern for the appellant's safety and the maintenance of good international relations were the primary motivations behind the liberty risk restrictions. That is, while there may have been a genuine concern on the part of the commanding officer about appellant's suspected alcohol problem, we find that the liberty risk status was not imposed primarily for such purposes. It was imposed primarily to ensure his presence at trial, and, as such, did not stop the speedy trial clock, which continued to run uninterrupted for 131 days. This violated the 120-day rule of R.C.M. 707. [footnote omitted].

Accordingly, the military judge erred in denying appellant's motion to dismiss all charges for lack of a speedy trial. The finding of guilty and the sentence are set aside. All charges and specifications are dismissed.

STUDY QUESTIONS

1. Define "apprehension" as used in the military. Who has the authority to apprehend?

2. What are the grounds for apprehending a service member? How is an apprehension made? When, if ever, is a warrant required to apprehend?

3. What constitutes actively resisting apprehension?

4. What is the difference between escape from custody and escape from confinement? Why is the distinction significant?

5. What is the difference between breaking arrest and breaking restriction?

6. What are the permissible types of pretrial restraint? Who has the authority to impose pretrial restraint? When should it be used?

7. When is pretrial confinement appropriate? What are a pretrial confinee's rights? How is pretrial confinement reviewed? What is the remedy for unlawful pretrial confinement?

8. How long does the military have to bring a service member to trial? When does the speedy trial clock begin? How does release from pretrial restraint affect the speedy trial clock?

9. Which of the following will *NOT* start the "speedy trial clock?"

    a. The preferral of charges against the accused.

    b. Placing the accused on pretrial restriction.

    c. Placing conditions on the liberty of the accused.

    d. Placing the accused in pretrial confinement.

    e. Both (a) and (c).

CHAPTER XI

INTERNATIONAL LAW

International law is part of our law . . .

The Supreme Court of the United States of America

The sources of military jurisdiction include . . . international law.

Paragraph 1, Preamble to the Manual for Courts-Martial, United States

At all times, commanders shall observe, and require their commands to observe, the principles of international law. Where necessary to fulfill this responsibility, a departure from other provisions of Navy Regulations is authorized.

Article 0705, United States Navy Regulations, 1990

INTRODUCTION

Although scholars, philosophers and academicians sometimes debate whether or not such a thing as international law truly exists in the same sense as we think of domestic criminal and civil law, there can be no doubt that there occurs in the international community a body of norms, rules, processes and institutions by which conduct in the international arena is measured, judged, and to some degree, governed. The naval services of the United States operate within this international legal system, and are one of the many and varied actors in that system. Others include states such as the United States itself, international organizations such as the United Nations (UN) and the North Atlantic Treaty Organization (NATO), and international nongovernmental organizations such as the International Committee of the Red Cross, Greenpeace, Amnesty International, and Human Rights Watch. Actors in the international legal system also include transnational corporations and businesses, and in a growing number of cases, individual persons, such as those seeking relief in domestic and international courts for violations of the international law of human rights, in particular those prohibiting torture, genocide and crimes against humanity. This latter development represents a significant departure from the classical view of international law as concerned only with the actions of states with respect to each other, and which reached the conduct of individual persons only to the extent to which a state might desire to perceive an injury to one of its nationals as an injury to the state itself.

International tribunals, including courts, such as the UN's International Court of Justice, and arbitral tribunals, such as the Iran-United States Claims Tribunal, are also among the cast of players upon the international stage, yet it is largely because many of these courts and tribunals do not provide particularly effective enforcement mechanisms for violations of international law, or for resolutions of disputes by and among the other actors in the international system, at least not to the same degree as do criminal and civil courts in the domestic legal system, that some scholars argue that the norms and rules of the international system cannot be considered "law." Even these skeptical scholars, however, must recognize that the international system relies heavily in its operation upon the language and process of law. Indeed, most students of the system, which draws its rules of normative behavior from, among others, two explicitly legal primary sources—treaties and customary law—in the end agree that a system of international law does exist, and that this legal system significantly influences the behavior of the players within it. In fact, even in the absence of strong and effective judicial enforcement, nations tend to comply with international law, although often on a basis that seems to the casual observer to be essentially voluntary. In the event of apparent noncompliance, however, violators often attempt to justify their conduct as permitted by some exception to, or interpretation of, international law, which manifests the tangibility of the law even as an attempt is made to escape its effect.

Why do nations generally comply with international law and worry about it when they do not? *The Commander's Handbook on the Law of Naval Operations*, a naval warfare publication produced by the Department of the Navy, suggests the following reason:

> International law provides stability in international relations and an expectation that certain acts and omissions will effect predictable consequences. If one nation violates the law, it may expect that others will reciprocate. Consequently, failure to comply with international law ordinarily involves greater political and economic costs than does observance. In short, nations comply with international law because it is in their interest to do so.

Certainly, the United States has historically found support of the international legal system to be in its national interest. Indeed, as noted in the quotes above, the naval services require by explicit regulation that commanders observe and comply with the principles of international law. These principles include, for example, those of the international law of the sea, the law of armed conflict, and the laws regulating the use of force by states, all subjects of particular interest to professional military officers. Study and understanding of those specific principles, however, requires first an exposure to some basic concepts that provide the foundation for, and context of, international law in its broader sense. A good place to start is with the sources of international law: treaties and customary law.

INTERNATIONAL LAW

SOURCES

The American Law Institute, in its 1987 *Restatement of the Law, Third, Foreign Relations Law of the United States*, lists the following sources of international law:

(1) A rule of international law is one that has been accepted as such by the international community of states

    (a) in the form of customary law;

    (b) by international agreement; or

    (c) by derivation from general principles common to the major legal systems of the world.

(2) Customary international law results from a general and consistent practice of states followed by them from a sense of legal obligation.

(3) International agreements create law for the states parties thereto and may lead to the creation of customary international law when such agreements are intended for adherence by states generally and are in fact widely accepted.

(4) General principles common to the major legal systems, even if not incorporated or reflected in customary law or international agreement, may be invoked as supplementary rules of international law where appropriate.

So, we see that the primary sources of international law are international agreements, often called treaties, which bind only the parties to them as if parties to a contract, and customary laws. Customary international laws are rules that have evolved from the practice of nations—that is, from what states actually do and say about what they do—when that practice somehow comes to involve a perception that the practice is required by law. Customary law generally binds all states, while treaty law binds only those states party to the treaty.

TREATIES

Article VI of the Constitution of the United States declares, in part, that "... all Treaties made, or which shall be made, under the authority of the United States shall be the supreme Law of the land. ..." The kind of treaty referred to here is an international agreement made in accordance with Article II, section 2 of the Constitution—that is, pursuant to the President's power ". . . by and with the consent of the Senate to make Treaties, provided two thirds of the Senators present concur . . ." The definition of a treaty under international law, however, is much broader than that implied by the United States Constitution; international obligations, legally binding in the international system, may arise from international agreements that have not been ratified by the Senate, and which therefore cannot be considered treaties in the sense of Article VI of the Constitution. Executive Agreements made by the President, for example, although not treaties under Article VI of the Constitution, may be considered treaties under international law. Consider the following two definitions of a "treaty" under international law.

The Vienna Convention on the Law of Treaties, itself a treaty, one which entered into force in 1980 with 59 nations party to it (not including the United States), states that a " 'treaty' means an international agreement concluded between States in written form and governed by international law, whether embodied in a single instrument or in two or more related instruments and whatever its particular designation." Contrast this with the following excerpt from section 301 of *The Restatement of the Law, Third, Foreign Relations Law of the United States,* published in 1987 by the American Law Institute:

(1) "international agreement" means an agreement between two or more states or international organizations that is intended to be legally binding and is governed by international law;

(2) "party" means a state or international organization that has consented to be bound by the international agreement and for which the agreement is in force.

Comment:

a. Various designations of agreements. The terminology used for international agreements is varied. Among the terms used are: treaty, convention, agreement, protocol, covenant, charter, statute, act, declaration, concordat, exchange of notes, agreed minute, memorandum of agreement, memorandum of understanding, and modus vivendi. Whatever their designation, all agreements have the same legal status, except as their provisions or the circumstances of their conclusion indicate otherwise.

b. Form of agreement. While most international agreements are in writing, written form is not essential to their binding character. The Vienna Convention specifies (Article (2)(1)(a)) that it applies only to written agreements, but under customary international law, oral agreements are no less binding although their terms may not be readily susceptible of proof.

. . . .

f. International organizations and agreements. . . . The Vienna Convention applies only to agreements between states . . . The Vienna Convention does not apply to agreements between a state and an international organization, or between two international organizations, but the rules stated in this Part apply to such agreements also. . . .

The sources of international law, as we have said, include treaties and customary law, and here we see that a treaty, the Vienna Convention, and customary law, as reported by the *Restatement,* provide slightly differing definitions of exactly what a treaty is. The Vienna Convention excludes unwritten international agreements from its definition of a treaty, while the *Restatement* argues that oral agreements may form binding treaties under international law. Moreover, the Vienna Convention defines as treaties only those written agreements concluded between states, while the *Restatement*'s view of customary law would have it include among treaties those agreements concluded between a state and an international organization—between a state and the UN for example. The critical element common to both, however, implicit in the Vienna Convention, and explicit in the *Restatement,* is that the parties to the treaty intend to have made a legally binding agreement.

Examples of treaties important to the student of naval law include the Charter of the United Nations, the various Geneva Conventions relevant to the law of armed conflict, and the Third United Nations Convention on the Law of the Sea. Another very commonly encountered kind of treaty is the Status of Forces Agreement (SOFA), versions of which govern the use of military facilities and areas used by the United States in foreign countries, such as those in Japan, Korea, the United Kingdom and the several states of the European continent. SOFAs generally permit U.S. military personnel stationed in these foreign countries to drive with their U.S. driver's licenses, to bring their household goods and automobiles into the country without paying customs duties, and to be exempt from paying income taxes to the host government. In addition, SOFAs usually include terms governing the exercise of criminal jurisdiction over service members and their families who may commit crimes while stationed abroad. An example typical of such provisions is that found in the SOFA between The United States and Japan:

1. Subject to the provisions of this Article,

    (a) the military authorities of the United States shall have the right to exercise within Japan all criminal and disciplinary jurisdiction conferred on them by the law of the United States;

    (b) the authorities of Japan shall have jurisdiction over members of the United States armed forces, the civilian component, and their dependents with respect to offenses committed within the territory of Japan and punishable by the law of Japan.

    . . . .

3. In cases where the right to jurisdiction is concurrent the following rules shall apply:

(a) The military authorities of the United States shall have the primary right to exercise jurisdiction over members of the United States armed forces or the civilian component in relation to

    (i) offenses solely against the property or security of the United States, or offenses solely against the person or property of another member of the United States armed forces or the civilian component or of a dependent;

    (ii) offenses arising out of any act or omission done in the performance of official duty.

(b) In the case of any other offense the authorities of Japan shall have the primary right to exercise jurisdiction.

The effect of this kind of SOFA criminal jurisdiction provision is to subject U.S. service members and their family members to trial in foreign courts for any crimes they commit under the host country's criminal law, when the crimes involve nationals of the host country. In appropriate cases, convicted service members may serve sentences in the host country's jail. The United States will have primary jurisdiction only over UCMJ offenses not criminal under host country law—such as Unauthorized Absence, for example—and over offenses involving only U.S. personnel, such as an assault by one service member upon another or upon the family of another. The United States would also have primary jurisdiction over actions that would be crimes under host country law, when the actions were "done in the performance of official duty." The two cases below provide examples of how the process can work in these latter two circumstances.

Wilson, Secretary of Defense, et al. v. Girard
Supreme Court of the United States,
354 U.S. 524; 77 S. Ct. 1409
July 11,1957

Syllabus: The United States and Japan became involved in a controversy as to whether an American soldier should be tried by a Japanese court for causing the death of a Japanese woman in Japan. While on duty guarding a machine gun on a firing range, he fired from a grenade launcher an empty cartridge case which struck the Japanese woman, causing her death. American authorities took the position that he was acting at the time "in performance of official duty," within the meaning of Paragraph 3 of Article XVII of an Administrative Agreement between the United States and Japan, as amended by a Protocol, and, therefore, the United States had the "primary right" to try him in a situation of concurrent jurisdiction. Japanese authorities contended that he was acting beyond the scope of official duty and that, therefore, Japan had the "primary right" to exercise jurisdiction. After lengthy negotiations, and with the approval of the President, the Secretary of State, and the Secretary of Defense, the United States yielded to the Japanese position, and agreed, under a provision of the amended Administrative Agreement, to waive whatever jurisdiction it might have and deliver him to Japanese authorities for trial. Japan then indicted him for causing death by wounding. He sought a writ of habeas corpus . . .

OPINION OF THE COURT

Girard, a Specialist Third Class in the United States Army, was engaged on January 30, 1957, with members of his cavalry regiment in a small unit exercise at Camp Weir range area, Japan. Japanese civilians were present in the area, retrieving expended cartridge cases. Girard and another Specialist Third Class were ordered to guard a machine gun and some items of clothing that had been left nearby. Girard had a grenade launcher on his rifle. He placed an expended 30-caliber cartridge case in the grenade launcher and projected it by firing a blank. The expended cartridge case penetrated the back of a Japanese woman gathering expended cartridge cases and caused her death . . .

The United States ultimately notified Japan that Girard would be delivered to the Japanese authorities for trial. Thereafter, Japan indicted him for causing death by wounding . . .

A Security Treaty between Japan and the United States, signed September 8, 1951, was ratified by the Senate on March 20, 1952, and proclaimed by the President effective April 28, 1952. Article III of the Treaty authorized the making of Administrative Agreements between the two Governments concerning "the conditions which shall govern the disposition of aimed forces of the United States of America in and about Japan. . . ." Expressly acting under this provision, the two Nations, on February 28, 1952, signed an Administrative Agreement covering, among other matters, the jurisdiction of the United States over offenses committed in Japan by members of the United States armed forces, and providing that jurisdiction in any case might be waived by the United States. This Agreement became effective on the same date as the Security Treaty (April 28, 1952) and was considered by the Senate before consent was given to the Treaty . . .

The United States claimed the right to try Girard upon the ground that his act, as certified by his commanding officer, was "done in the performance of official duty" and therefore the United States had primary jurisdiction. Japan insisted that it had proof that Girard's action was without the scope of his official duty and therefore that Japan had the primary right to try him. . . . [In a series of high level negotiations, the United States ultimately acceded to the Japanese position, and decided to turn Girard over to Japan for trial. Girard challenged this decision, and sought an injunction to prevent the turnover.]

A sovereign nation has exclusive jurisdiction to punish offenses against its laws committed within its borders, unless it expressly or impliedly consents to surrender its jurisdiction. . . . Japan's cession to the United States of jurisdiction to try American military personnel for conduct constituting an offense against the laws of both countries was conditioned by the covenant of Article XVII, section 3, paragraph (c) of the Protocol that ". . . The authorities of the State having the primary right shall give sympathetic consideration to a request from the authorities of the other State for a waiver of its right in cases where that other State considers such waiver to be of particular importance."

The issue for our decision is therefore narrowed to the question whether, upon the record before us, the Constitution or legislation subsequent to the Security Treaty prohibited the carrying out of this provision authorized by the Treaty for waiver of the qualified jurisdiction granted by Japan. We find no constitutional or statutory barrier to the provision as applied here. In the absence of such encroachments, the wisdom of the arrangement is exclusively for the determination of the Executive and Legislative Branches. [Girard lost his case. He was tried and convicted in Japanese court of bodily injury resulting in death, and served a comparatively light sentence.]

Is the "Administrative Agreement" that defines the boundaries of criminal jurisdiction in this case a "treaty" within the meaning of Article VI of the Constitution, or is it an Executive Agreement (that is, a treaty as defined by international law, but not for the purposes of Article VI of the Constitution)? Why do you think the Japanese government took the position that Girard's action was not "in the performance of his official duty?" On what foundation could the United States rest its argument to the contrary? Consider the American Commanding Officer's Certificate as to Official Duty and the Japanese response:

COMPANY F, 8TH CAVALRY REGIMENT
7 February 1957

SUBJECT: Certificate as to Official Duty

THRU: Provost Marshal, Regional Camp Whittington

TO: Chief Procurator, Maebashi District, Maebashi City, Honshu, Japan

1. Pursuant to the provisions of paragraph 43 of the Agreed Views of the Criminal Jurisdiction Subcommittee with respect to the Protocol amending Article XVII of the Administrative Agreement between the United States and Japan, I certify that GIRARD, William S, RA 16 452 809, Specialist Third Class, Company F, 8th Cavalry Regiment, APO 201, was in the performance of his official duty at 1350 hours, 30 January 1957, Camp Weir Range Area, when he was involved in the following incident: On 30 January 1957, 2nd Battalion, 8th Cavalry Regiment, was engaged in routine training at Camp Weir Range Area. Company F was conducting blank firing exercises. Specialist Third Class William S. GIRARD was instructed by his platoon leader to move near a position near an unguarded machine gun to guard the machine gun and items of field equipment that were in the immediate area. GIRARD, following instructions, moved to the designated position near the machine gun. While performing his duties as guard, he fired an expended cartridge case, as a warning, which struck and killed SAKAI, Naka, Kami-Shinden, Somamura, Gumma Prefecture, who had entered the range area for the purpose of gathering expended cartridge cases.

2. The United States will exercise jurisdiction in this case, unless notification is given immediately that proof to the contrary exists.

3. Should this incident result in trial of the above individual by general court-martial, you will be notified of the date of trial in accordance with the provisions of paragraph 45 of the above mentioned Agreed Views.

CARL C. ALLIGOOD
1st Lt. Infantry
Commanding

MAEBASHI DISTRICT PUBLIC
PROCURATOR'S OFFICE
Maebashi, 9 February 1957

TO: Mr. CARL C. ALLIGOOD, 1st Lt Infantry, Command, F Co., 2nd Bn 8th Cavalry Regiment

Re: Notification of the existence of the contrary proof.

Dear Sir:

Reference is made to the letter from you dated on 8 February 1957, regarding to the "On Duty" status of the case involving SP3 GIRARD S. WILLIAM, which we received on 8 February 1957.

This is to inform you that this office considers the proof contrary thereto exists, basing upon our examinations.

/s/ Nagami Sakai
Chief Procurator
Maebashi Public Procurator's Office

[The Japanese summary of the facts was as follows:]

"He (Girard) and Nickel went to the gun and, about 13.15 hrs he picked up and threw expended cartridge cases in the direction of the slope south of the hill, and, beckoning Hidehara Onozeki (male) and Naka Sakai (female) who had been at a place in the south-west of Hill 655 to gather empty cartridge cases, etc., cried out to them 'PAPA-SAN, DAIJOBU,' 'MAMA-SAN, DAIJOBU' ('Old man, O.K., old lady, O.K.'), etc. in Japanese and thus let the 2 Japanese pick up expended cartridge cases he had thrown. Then he, pointing to the nearby hole for Naka Sakai, cried out to her in Japanese 'MAMA-SAN, TAKUSAN-NE'('Old lady, plenty more!'), and hinting thereby that there remained some expended cartridge cases in it, induced her to go to the hole. But, at that moment, Hideharu Onozeki who was picking up expended cartridge cases on the said slope became suspicious of the suspects behaviour and tried to run away. Then the suspect suddenly shouted to Onoseki 'GE-ROU! HEY!'and fired a blank shot towards him, placing an expended cartridge case in the grenade launcher attached to the rifle which he had carried with him. Then he cried out 'GE-ROU! HEY!'to Naka Sakai who was in the hole, and, when he saw her running off towards the north slope of the hill, he, holding the stock of the rifle under his arm, fired standing a blank shot toward her about eight (8) meters away with an expended cartridge case put in the grenade launcher, just in the same manner as he had done to Hideharu Onozeki, as the result of which he made her sustain a penetrating wound on the left side of her back which proved fatal on the spot because of the loss of blood resulting from a cut in the main artery."

... "Sp-3 William S. Girard, the suspect in this case, had been instructed to guard a machine gun and equipment at the time of occurrence of the case. It is evident, however, as shown in the above finding of facts, that the incident arose when he, materially deviating from the performance of such duty of his, wilfully threw expended cartridge cases away towards Naka Sakai and Hideharu Onozeki, and, thus inviting them to come near to him, he fired towards them. Therefore, the incident is not considered to have arisen out of an act or omission done in the performance of official duty."

What happens when the crime involves only Americans, and not, as in the *Girard* case, a national of the host country? In the following case, the civilian wives of active duty service members overseas were tried by courts-martial for murder of their husbands. Each argued that trial by court-martial denied them their constitutional right to trial by jury. The Government argued that trial by court-martial was authorized and required by the SOFAs with the host countries in which the crimes had occurred.

Reid, Superintendent of District of Columbia Jail v. Covert
Supreme Court of the United States
354 U.S. 1; 77 S. Ct. 1222
June 10, 1957

OPINION: Mr. Justice Black announced the judgment of the Court and delivered an opinion, in which the Chief Justice, Mr. Justice Douglas, and Mr. Justice Brennan join.

These cases raise basic constitutional issues of the utmost concern. They call into question the role of the military under our system of government. They involve the power of Congress to expose civilians to trial by military tribunals, under military regulations and procedures, for offenses against the United States thereby depriving them of trial in civilian courts, under civilian laws and procedures and with all the safeguards of the Bill of Rights. These cases are particularly significant because for the first time since the adoption of the Constitution wives of soldiers have been denied trial by jury in a court of law and forced to trial before courts-martial.

In No. 701 Mrs. Clarice Covert killed her husband, a sergeant in the United States Air Force, at an airbase in England. Mrs. Covert, who was not a member of the armed services, was residing on the base with her husband at the time. She was tried by a court-martial for murder under Article 118 of the Uniform Code of Military Justice (UCMJ). The trial was on charges preferred by Air Force personnel and the 1957 court-martial was composed of Air Force officers. The court-martial asserted jurisdiction over Mrs. Covert under Article 2 (11) of the UCMJ, which provides: "The following persons are subject to this code: . . . (11) Subject to the provisions of any treaty or agreement to which the United States is or may be a party or to any accepted rule of international law, all persons serving with, employed by, or accompanying the armed forces without the continental limits of the United States. . . ."

Counsel for Mrs. Covert contended that she was insane at the time she killed her husband, but the military tribunal found her guilty of murder and sentenced her to life imprisonment . . . [Mrs. Covert sought relief in Federal District Court, alleging the courts-martial denied her the civilian's constitutional right to trial by jury]. . . .

In No. 713 Mrs. Dorothy Smith killed her husband, an Army officer, at a post in Japan where she was living with him. She was tried for murder by a court-martial and despite considerable evidence that she was

insane was found guilty and sentenced to life imprisonment. The judgment was approved by the Army Board of Review . . . and the Court of Military Appeals . . . Mrs. Smith was then confined in a federal penitentiary in West Virginia. Her father, respondent here, filed a petition for habeas corpus in a District Court for West Virginia. The petition charged that the court-martial was without jurisdiction because Article 2 (11) of the UCMJ was unconstitutional insofar as it authorized the trial of civilian dependents accompanying servicemen overseas . . .

We hold that Mrs. Smith and Mrs. Covert could not constitutionally be tried by military authorities.

At the beginning we reject the idea that when the United States acts against citizens abroad it can do so free of the Bill of Rights. The United States is entirely a creature of the Constitution. Its power and authority have no other source. It can only act in accordance with all the limitations imposed by the Constitution. When the Government reaches out to punish a citizen who is abroad the shield which the Bill of Rights and other parts of the Constitution provide to protect his life and liberty should not be stripped away just because he happens to be in another land. This is not a novel concept. To the contrary, it is as old as government. . . .

At the time of Mrs. Covert's alleged offense, an executive agreement was in effect between the United States and Great Britain which permitted United States' military courts to exercise exclusive jurisdiction over offenses committed in Great Britain by American servicemen or their dependents. For its part, the United States agreed that these military courts would be willing and able to try and to punish all offenses against the laws of Great Britain by such persons. In all material respects, the same situation existed in Japan when Mrs.

Smith killed her husband. Even though a court-martial does not give an accused trial by jury and other Bill of Rights protections, the Government contends that Art. 2 (11) of the UCMJ, insofar as it provides for the military trial of dependents accompanying the armed forces in Great Britain and Japan, can be sustained as legislation which is necessary and proper to carry out the United States' obligations under the international agreements made with those countries. The obvious and decisive answer to this, of course, is that no agreement with a foreign nation can confer power on the Congress, or on any other branch of Government, which is free from the restraints of the Constitution. (. . . The [Executive Agreement then] in effect in Great Britain and the other North Atlantic Treaty Organization nations, as well as in Japan, [was] the NATO Status of Forces Agreement . . . which by its terms gives the foreign nation primary jurisdiction to try dependents accompanying American servicemen for offenses which are violations of the law of both the foreign nation and the United States . . . The foreign nation has exclusive criminal jurisdiction over dependents for offenses which only violate its laws . . . However, the Agreement contains provisions which require that the foreign nations provide procedural safeguards for our nationals tried under the terms of the Agreement in their courts. . . . Apart from those persons subject to the Status of Forces and comparable agreements and certain other restricted classes of Americans, a foreign nation has plenary criminal jurisdiction, of course, over all Americans—tourists, residents, businessmen, government employees and so forth—who commit offenses against its laws within its territory.)

Article VI, the Supremacy Clause of the Constitution, declares: "This Constitution, and the Laws of the United States which shall be made in Pursuance thereof, and all Treaties made, or which shall be made, under the Authority of the United States, shall be the supreme Law of the Land." . . . There is nothing in this language which intimates that treaties and laws enacted pursuant to them do not have to comply with the provisions of the Constitution. Nor is there anything in the debates which accompanied the drafting and ratification of the Constitution which even suggests such a result. These debates as well as the history that surrounds the adoption of the treaty provision in Article VI make it clear that the reason treaties were not limited to those made in "pursuance" of the Constitution was so that agreements made by the United States under the Articles of Confederation, including the important peace treaties which concluded the Revolutionary War, would remain in effect. It would be manifestly contrary to the objectives of those who created the Constitution, as well as those who were responsible for the Bill of Rights—let alone alien to our entire constitutional history and tradition—to construe Article VI as permitting the United States to exercise power under an international agreement without observing constitutional prohibitions. In effect, such construction would permit amendment of that document in a manner not sanctioned by Article V. The prohibitions of the Constitution were designed to apply to all branches of the National Government and they cannot be nullified by the Executive or by the Executive and the Senate combined.

There is nothing new or unique about what we say here. This Court has regularly and uniformly recognized the supremacy of the Constitution over a treaty. For example, in *Geofroy v. Riggs,* 133 U.S. 258, 267, it declared: "The treaty power, as expressed in the Constitution, is in terms unlimited except by those restraints which are found in that instrument against the action of the government or of its departments, and those arising from the nature of the government itself and of that of the States. It would not be contended that it extends so far as to authorize what the Constitution forbids, or a change in the character of the government or in that of one of the States, or a cession of any portion of the territory of the latter, without its consent."(We recognize that executive agreements are involved here but it cannot be contended that such an agreement rises to greater stature than a treaty.)

This Court has also repeatedly taken the position that an Act of Congress, which must comply with the Constitution, is on a full parity with a treaty, and that when a statute which is subsequent in time is inconsistent with a treaty, the statute to the extent of conflict renders the treaty null. It would be completely anomalous to say that a treaty need not comply with the Constitution when such an agreement can be overridden by a statute that must conform to that instrument.

In summary, we conclude that the Constitution in its entirety applied to the trials of Mrs. Smith and Mrs. Covert. Since their court-martial did not meet the requirements of Art. III, section 2 or the Fifth and Sixth Amendments we are compelled to determine if there is anything within the Constitution which authorizes the military trial of dependents accompanying the armed forces overseas. [The Court found that there was not.]

If civilian family members of active duty service members abroad cannot be tried by court-martial, must they be tried by host country courts for offenses against other members of the military community, when those offenses violate host country criminal law? What other options does an overseas Base Commander have with respect to civilians who misbehave on an overseas installation?

The preceding discussion illustrated the effect that treaty law has on the activities of military personnel at nearly every level of day-to-day life, as well as alluding to its effect upon activities related to military operations at sea, during armed conflict, and involving the threat or use of force in operations other than war. Perhaps an even more important and encompassing source of law in the international legal system, however, is customary law. *The Commander's Handbook on the Law of Military Operations,* for example, unequivocally declares that "Customary international law is the principal source of international law and is binding upon all nations."

CUSTOMARY LAW

What exactly is customary international law? Article 38 of the Statute of the International Court of Justice states that "The Court, whose function is to decide in accordance with international law such disputes as are submitted to it, shall apply . . . international custom, as evidence of a general practice accepted as law." In this definition, the custom is not itself a law, but evidence of the existence of a law—that is, because the Court can observe a custom, it may infer that the custom exists out of some sense in the international community that the custom developed and is adhered to out of a belief that it is a matter of law. What the Court—or anyone else seeking to establish a particular rule of customary international law—really looks for, then, is evidence of a perceived legal obligation. Perceived by whom? By states, and by the many other players in the international system. If the actors in the international system perceive a certain practice to be a matter of law, and behave in a manner consistent with such a perception, then the perception becomes the reality. The perception and the consistent behavior resulting from, and contributing to it, if observable, in fact become the law. This then is the essence of customary international law—a practice so commonly followed that it may be considered customary, when followed out of a sense of legal obligation.

As noted in the Reporter's notes to section 102 of the *Restatement of the Law, Third, Foreign Relations Law of the United States,* the concept is essentially circular:

> There have been philosophical debates about the very basis of the definition: how can practice build law? Most troublesome conceptually has been the circularity in the suggestion that law is built by practice based on a sense of legal obligation: how it can be asked, can there be a sense of legal obligation before the law from which the legal obligation derives has matured? Such conceptual difficulties, however, have not prevented acceptance of customary law essentially as here defined. . . . Perhaps the definition reflects a later stage in the history of international law when governments found practice and sense of obligation already in evidence, and accepted them without inquiring as to the original basis of that sense of legal obligation.

Thus, notwithstanding the "which came first?" conundrum inherent in the concept, a practice engaged in as a matter of custom may provide very persuasive evidence that the "custom" is at the same time a law; and indeed exists by virtue of this very fact. Proving that a custom establishes a rule of international law requires more, however, than simply asserting that it occurs. It requires analysis of the practice of states and other players in the international system; that is, looking at what they actually do. The process of proof also requires analysis of what they say about what they do; what is said provides evidence of whether or not the players perceive a legal obligation. Sources of evidence relevant to this inquiry include, as noted in Article 38 of the Statute the International Court of Justice, "judicial decisions and the teachings of the most highly qualified publicists of the various nations," as well as diplomatic correspondence, press releases, opinions of legal advisors, military manuals, rules of engagement, previous or related treaties, policy statements, domestic legislation, and statements of international organizations.

The following case represents the paradigmatic example of how such an analysis might be conducted. In the case of *The Paquete Habana and The Lola,* the Supreme Court of the United States found itself challenged by the need to decide whether the customary international law of armed conflict permitted U.S. warships to target Cuban coastal fishing vessels during the Spanish American War. As you read this opinion, note the evidence considered by the Court in resolving this question. Note also the role played by rules of engagement in the Court's analysis, how those rules are related to the international law of armed conflict, and the relationship of principles of humanity and of military necessity to that law.

The Paquete Habana
Supreme Court of the United States
175 U.S. 677; 44 L. Ed. 320; 20 S. Ct. 290
January 8, 1900 Decided

SYLLABUS [summary]: . . .

At the breaking out of the recent war with Spain, two fishing smacks—the one a sloop, 43 feet long on the keel and of 25 tons burden, and with a crew of three men, and the other a schooner, 51 feet long on the keel and of 35 tons burden, and with a crew of six men—were regularly engaged in fishing on the coast of Cuba, sailing under the Spanish flag, and each owned by a Spanish subject, residing in Havana . . . Each vessel left Havana on a coast fishing voyage, and sailed along the coast of Cuba about two hundred miles to the west end of the island; the sloop there fished for twenty-five days in the territorial waters of Spain; and the schooner extended her fishing trip a hundred miles farther across the Yucatan Channel, and fished for eight days on the coast of Yucatan. On her return, with her cargo of live fish, along the coast of Cuba, and when near Havana, each was captured by one of the United States blockading squadron. Neither fishing vessel had any arms or ammunition on board; had any knowledge of the blockade, or even of the war, until she was stopped by a blockading vessel; made any attempt to run the blockade, or any resistance at the time of her capture; nor was there any evidence that she, or her crew, was likely to aid the enemy. Held, that both captures were unlawful, and without probable cause. . . .

OPINION: Mr. Justice Gray

These are two appeals from decrees of the District Court of the United States for the Southern District of Florida, condemning two fishing vessels and their cargoes as prizes of war.

Each vessel was a fishing smack, running in and out of Havana, and regularly engaged in fishing on the coast of Cuba; sailed under the Spanish flag; was owned by a Spanish subject of Cuban birth, living in the city of Havana; was commanded by a subject of Spain, also residing in Havana; and her master and crew had no interest in the vessel, but were entitled to shares, amounting in all to two thirds, of her catch, the other third belonging to her owner. Her cargo consisted of fresh fish, caught by her crew from the sea, put on board as they were caught, and kept and sold alive. Until stopped by the blockading squadron, she had no knowledge of the existence of the war, or of any blockade. She had no arms or ammunition on board, and made no attempt to run the blockade after she knew of its existence, nor any resistance at the time of the capture.

The Paquete Habana was a sloop, 43 feet long on the keel, and of 25 tons burden, and had a crew of three Cubans, including the master, who had a fishing license from the Spanish Government . . . She left Havana March 25, 1898; sailed along the coast of Cuba . . . and there fished for twenty-five days . . . within the territorial waters of Spain; and then started back for Havana, with a cargo of about 40 quintals of live fish. On April 25, 1898, about two miles off Mariel, and eleven miles from Havana, she was captured by the United States gunboat Castine.

The Lola was a schooner, 51 feet long on the keel, and of 35 tons burden, and had a crew of six Cubans, including the master, and no commission or license. She left Havana April 11, 1898, and proceeded to Campeachy Sound off Yucatan, fished there eight days, and started back for Havana with a cargo of about 10,000 pounds of live fish. On April 26, 1898, near Havana, she was stopped by the United States steamship Cincinnati, and was warned not to go into Havana, but was told that she would be allowed to land at Bahia Honda. She then changed her course, and put for Bahia Honda, but on the next morning, when near that port, was captured by the United States steamship Dolphin.

Both the fishing vessels were brought by their captors into Key West. A libel for the condemnation of each vessel and her cargo as prize of war was there filed on April 27, 1898; a claim was interposed by her master, on behalf of himself and the other members of the crew, and of her owner; evidence was taken, showing the facts above stated; and on May 30, 1898, a final decree of condemnation and sale was entered, "the court not being satisfied that as a matter of law, without any ordinance, treaty or proclamation, fishing vessels of this class are exempt from seizure."

Each vessel was thereupon sold by auction; the Paquete Habana for the sum of $490; and the Lola for the sum of $800. . . .

We are . . . brought to the consideration of the question whether, upon the facts appearing in these records, the fishing smacks were subject to capture by the armed vessels of the United States during the recent war with Spain.

By an ancient usage among civilized nations, beginning centuries ago, and gradually ripening into a rule of international law, coast fishing vessels, pursuing their vocation of catching and bringing in fresh fish, have been recognized as exempt, with their cargoes and crews, from capture as prize of war.

This doctrine, however, has been earnestly contested at the bar; and no complete collection of the instances illustrating it is to be found, so far as we are aware, in a single published work, although many are referred to and discussed by the writers on international law. . . . It is therefore worth the while to trace the history of the rule, from the earliest accessible sources, through the increasing recognition of it, with occasional setbacks, to what we may now justly consider as its final establishment in our own country and generally throughout the civilized world.

The earliest **acts of any government** on the subject, mentioned in the books, either emanated from, or were approved by, a King of England.

In 1403 and 1406, Henry IV issued orders to his admirals and other officers, entitled "Concerning Safety for Fishermen—De Securitate pro Piscatoribus." By an order of October 26, 1403, reciting that it was made pursuant to a treaty between himself and the King of France . . . it was ordained that French fishermen might, during the then pending season for the herring fishery, safely fish for herrings and all other fish . . . And by an order of October 5, 1406, he took into his safe conduct, and under his special protection, guardianship and defence, all and singular the fishermen of France, Flanders and Brittany, with their fishing vessels and boats, everywhere on the sea, through and within his dominions, jurisdictions and territories . . . and it was therefore ordered that such fishermen should not be interfered with, provided they should comport themselves well and properly. . . .

The **treaty** made October 2, 1521, between the Emperor Charles V and Francis I of France, through their ambassadors, recited that a great and fierce war had arisen between them, because of which there had been, both by land and by sea, frequent depredations and incursions on either side, to the grave detriment and intolerable injury of the innocent subjects of each; and that a suitable time for the herring fishery was at hand, and, by reason of the sea being beset by the enemy, the fishermen did not dare to go out, whereby the subject of their industry, bestowed by heaven to allay the hunger of the poor, would wholly fail for the year, unless it were otherwise provided. . . . And it was therefore agreed that the subjects of each sovereign, fishing in the sea, of exercising the calling of fishermen, could and might, until the end of the next January, without incurring any attack, depredation, molestation, trouble or hindrance soever, safely and freely, everywhere in the sea, take herrings and every other kind of fish, the existing war by land and sea notwithstanding; and further that, during the time aforesaid, no subject of either sovereign should commit, or attempt or presume to commit, any depredation, force, violence, molestation or vexation, to or upon such fishermen, or their vessels, supplies, equipments, nets and fish, or other goods soever truly appertaining to fishing.

. . . .

The herring fishery was permitted, in time of war, by **French and Dutch edicts in 1536**. . . .

France from remote times, set the example of alleviating the evils of war in favor of all coast fishermen. In the compilation entitled *Us et Coutumes de la Mer*, published by Cleirac in 1661, and in the third part thereof, containing "Maritime or Admiralty Jurisdiction—la Jurisdiction de la Marine ou d'Admiraute—as well in time of peace as in time of war," article 80 is as follows: "The admiral may in time of war accord fishing truces—tresves pescheresses—to the enemy and to his subjects; provided that the enemy will likewise accord them to Frenchmen." Cleirac, 544. Under this article, reference is made to articles 49 and 79 respectively of the **French ordinances** concerning the Admiralty in 1543 and 1584, of which it is but a reproduction . . . And Cleirac adds, in a note, this quotation from Froissart's Chronicles: "Fishermen on the sea, whatever war there were in France and England, never did harm to one another; so they are friends, and help one another at need—. . ."

The same **custom** would seem to have prevailed in France until towards the end of the seventeenth century. For example, in 1675, Louis XIV and the States General of Holland, by mutual agreement, granted to Dutch and French fishermen the liberty, undisturbed by their vessels of war, of fishing along the coasts of France, Holland and England. . . . But by the ordinances of 1681 and 1692 the practice was discontinued, because, Valin says, of the faithless conduct of the enemies of France, who, abusing the good faith with which she had always observed the treaties, habitually carried off her fishermen, while their own fished in safety. . . .

The doctrine which exempts coast fishermen with their vessels and cargoes from capture as prize of war has been familiar to the United States from the time of the War of Independence.

On June 5, 1779, Louis XVI, our ally in that war, addressed **a letter to his admiral**, informing him that the wish he had always had of **alleviating, as far as he could, the hardships of war**, had directed his attention to that class of his subjects which devoted itself to the trade of fishing, and had no other means of livelihood; that he had thought that the example which he should give to his enemies, and which could have no other source than **the sentiments of humanity** which inspired him, would determine them to allow to fishermen the same facilities which he should consent to grant; and that **he had therefore given orders to the commanders of all his ships** not to disturb English fishermen, nor to arrest their vessels laden with fresh fish, even if not caught by those vessels; provided they had no offensive arms, and were not proved to have made any signals creating a suspicion of intelligence with the enemy; and **the admiral was directed to communicate the King's intentions to all officers under his control**. By a royal order in council of November 6, 1780, the former orders were confirmed; and the capture and ransom, by a French cruiser, of The John and Sarah, an English vessel, coming from Holland, laden with fresh fish, were pronounced to be illegal. . . .

Among the standing orders made by Sir James Marriott, Judge of the English High Court of Admiralty, was one of April 11, 1780, by which it was "ordered, that all causes of prize of fishing boats or vessels taken from the enemy may be consolidated in one monition, and one sentence or interlocutory, if under fifty tons burden, and not more than six in number." . . . But by the statements of his successor, and of both French and English writers, it appears that England, as well as France, during the American Revolutionary War, abstained from interfering with the coast fisheries. . . .

In the **treaty** of 1785 between the United States and Prussia, article 23, (which was proposed by the American Commissioners, John Adams, Benjamin Franklin and Thomas Jefferson, and is said to have been drawn up by Franklin), provided that, if war should arise between parties, "all women and children, scholars of every faculty, cultivators of the earth, artisans, manufacturers and fishermen, unarmed and inhabiting unfortified towns, villages or places, and in general all others whose occupations are for the common subsistence and benefit of mankind, shall be allowed to continue their respective employments, and shall not be molested in their persons; nor shall their houses or goods be burnt or otherwise destroyed, nor their fields wasted, by the armed force of the enemy, into whose power, by the events of war, they may happen to fall; but if anything is necessary to be taken from them for the use of such armed force, the same shall be paid for at a reasonable price." . . . Here was the clearest exemption from hostile molestation or seizure of the persons, occupations, houses and goods of unarmed fishermen inhabiting unfortified places. The article was repeated in the later treaties between the United States and Prussia of 1799 and 1828 . . . And Dana, in a note to his edition of Wheaton's International Law, says: "In many treaties and decrees, fishermen catching fish as an article of food are added to the class of persons whose occupation is not to be disturbed in war."

Since the United States became a nation, the only serious interruptions, so far as we are informed, of the general recognition of the exemption of coast fishing vessels from hostile capture, arose out of the mutual suspicions and recriminations of England and France during the wars of the French Revolution.

In the first years of those wars, England having authorized the capture of French fishermen, a decree of the French National Convention of October 2, 1793, directed the executive power "to protest against this conduct, theretofore without example; to reclaim the fishing boats seized; and, in case of refusal, to resort to reprisals." But in July, 1796, the Committee of Public Safety ordered the release of English fishermen seized under the former decree, "not considering them as prisoners of war."

On January 24, 1798, the English Government, by express order, instructed the commanders of its ships to seize French and Dutch fishermen with their boats . . . After the promulgation of that order, Lord Stowell (then Sir William Scott) in the High Court of Admiralty of England condemned small Dutch fishing vessels as prize of war. . . .

For the year 1800 . . . the French government, unwilling to resort to reprisals, reenacted the orders given by Louis XVI in 1780, above mentioned, prohibiting any seizure by the French ships of English fishermen, unless armed, or proved to have made signals to the enemy. On May 30, 1800, the English government, having received notice of that action of the French government, revoked its order of January 24, 1798. But, soon afterwards, the English government complained that French fishing boats had been made into fireboats at Flushing, as well as that the French government had impressed, and had sent to Brest, to serve in its flotilla, French fisherman and their boats, even those whom the English had released on condition of their not serving; and on January 21, 1801, summarily revoked its last order, and again put in force its order of January 24, 1798. On February 16, 1801, Napoleon Bonaparte, then First Consul, directed the French commissioner at London to return at once to France, first declaring to the English government that its conduct, "contrary to all the usages of civilized nations, and to the common law which governs them, even in time of war, gave to the existing war a character of rage and bitterness which destroyed even the relations usual in a loyal war," and "tended only to exasperate the two nations, and to put off the term of peace;" and that the French government, having always made it "a maxim to alleviate as much as possible the evils of war, could not think, on its part, of rendering wretched fisherman victims of a prolongation of hostilities, and would abstain from all reprisals."

On March 16, 1801, the Addington Ministry, having come into power in England, revoked the orders of its predecessors against the French fisherman; maintaining, however, that "the freedom of fishing was nowise founded upon an agreement, but upon a simple concession;" that "this concession would be always subordinate to the convenience of the moment," and that "it was never extended to the great fishery, or to commerce in oysters or in fish." And the freedom of the coast fisheries was again allowed on both sides . . .

Lord Stowell's judgment in the Young Jacob and Johanna, 1 C. Rob. 20, above cited, was much relied on by the counsel for the United States, and deserves careful consideration.

The vessel there condemned is described in the report as "a small Dutch fishing vessel taken April, 1798, on her return from the Dogger bank to Holland;" and Lord Stowell, in delivering judgment, said: "In former wars, it has not been usual to make captures of these small fishing vessels; but this rule was a rule of comity only, and not of legal decision; it has prevailed from views of mutual accommodation between neighboring countries, and from tenderness to a poor and industrious order of people. In the present war there has, I presume, been sufficient reason for changing this mode of treatment, and, as they are brought before me for my judgment, they must be referred to the general principles of this court; they fall under the character and description of the last class of cases; that is, of ships constantly and exclusively employed in the enemy's trade." And he added: "It is a farther satisfaction to me in giving this judgment to observe that the facts also bear strong marks of a false and fraudulent transaction."

Both the capture and condemnation were within a year after the order of the English government of January 24, 1798, instructing the commanders of its ships to seize French and Dutch fishing vessels, and before any revocation of that order. Lord Stowell's judgment shows that his decision was based upon the order of 1798, as well as upon strong evidence of fraud. Nothing more was adjudged in the case.

But some expressions in his opinion have been given so much weight by English writers, that it may be well to examine them particularly. The opinion begins by admitting the known custom in former wars not to capture such vessels—adding, however, "but this was a rule of comity only, and not of legal decision." Assuming the phrase "legal decision" to have been there used, in the sense in which courts are accustomed to use it, as equivalent to "judicial decision," it is true that, so far as appears, there had been no such decision on the point in England. The word "comity" was apparently used by Lord Stowell as synonymous with courtesy or good will. But the period of a hundred years which has since elapsed is amply sufficient to have enabled what originally may have rested in custom or comity, courtesy or concession, to grow, by the general assent of civilized nations, into a settled rule of international law. As well said by Sir James Mackintosh: "In the present century a slow and silent, but very substantial mitigation has taken place in the practice of

war; and in proportion as that mitigated practice has received the sanction of time, it is raised from the rank of mere usage, and becomes part of the law of nations."
. . .

The **French prize tribunals**, both before and after Lord Stowell's decision, took a wholly different view of the general question. In 1780, as already mentioned, an order in council of Louis XVI had declared illegal the capture by a French cruiser of The John and Sarah, an English vessel, coming from Holland, laden with fresh fish. And on May 17, 1801, where a Portuguese fishing vessel, with her cargo of fish, having no more crew than was needed for her management, and for serving the nets, on a trip of several days, had been captured in April, 1801, by a French cruiser, three leagues off the coast of Portugal, the Council of Prizes held that the capture was contrary to "the principles of humanity, and the maxims of international law," and decreed that the vessel, with the fish on board, or the net proceeds of any that had been sold, should be restored to her master. . . .

The English government, soon afterwards, more than once unqualifiedly prohibited the molestation of fishing vessels employed in catching and bringing to market fresh fish. On May 23, 1806, it was "ordered in council, that all fishing vessels under Prussian and other colors, and engaged for the purpose of catching fish and conveying them fresh to market, with their crews, cargoes and stores, shall not be molested on their fishing voyages and bringing the same to market; and that no fishing vessels of this description shall hereafter be molested. And the Right Honorable the Lords Commissioners of His Majesty's Treasury, the Lords Commissioners of the Admiralty and the Judge of the High Court of Admiralty are to give the necessary directions herein as to them may respectively appertain." . . .

Wheaton, in his **Digest of the Law of Maritime Captures and Prizes**, published in 1815, wrote: "It has been usual in maritime wars to exempt from capture fishing boats and their cargoes, both from views of mutual accommodation between neighboring countries, and from tenderness to a poor and industrious order of people. This custom, so honorable to the humanity of civilized nations, has fallen into disuse; and it is remarkable that both France and England mutually reproach each other with that breach of good faith which has finally abolished it." . . .

This statement clearly exhibits Wheaton's opinion that the custom had been a general one, as well as that it ought to remain so. His assumption that it had been abolished by the differences between France and England at the close of the last century was hardly justified by the state of things when he wrote, and has not since been borne out.

During the wars of the French Empire, as both French and English writers agree, the coast fisheries were left in peace. . . . De Boeck quaintly and truly adds, "and the incidents of 1800 and of 1801 had no morrow. . . ."

In the war with Mexico in 1846, the United States recognized the exemption of coast fishing boats from capture. In proof of this, counsel have referred to records of the Navy Department, which this court is clearly authorized to consult upon such a question. . . .

By those records it appears that Commodore Conner, commanding the Home Squadron blockading the east coast of Mexico, on May 14, 1846, wrote a letter from the ship Cumberland, off Brazos Santiago, near the southern point of Texas, to Mr. Bancroft, the Secretary of the Navy, enclosing a copy of **the commodore's "instructions** to the commanders of the vessels of the Home Squadron, showing the principles to be observed in the blockade of the Mexican ports," one of which was that "Mexican boats engaged in fishing on any part of the coast will be allowed to pursue their labors unmolested;" and that on June 10, 1846, those instructions were approved by the Navy Department, of which Mr. Bancroft was still the head, and continued to be until he was appointed Minister to England in September following. Although Commodore Conner's instructions and the Department's approval thereof do not appear in any contemporary publication of the Government, they evidently became generally known at the time, or soon after; for it is stated in several treatises on international law (beginning with Ortolan's second edition, published in 1853) that the United States in the Mexican War permitted the coast fishermen of the enemy to continue the free exercise of their industry. . . .

As qualifying the effect of those statements, the counsel for the United States relied on a proclamation of Commodore Stockton, commanding the Pacific Squadron, dated August 20, 1846, directing officers under his command to proceed immediately to blockade the ports of Mazatlan and San Blas on the west coast of Mexico, and saying to them, "All neutral vessels that you may find there you will allow twenty days to depart; and you will make the blockade absolute against all vessels, except armed vessels of neutral nations. You will capture all vessels under the Mexican flag that you may be able to take." . . . But there is nothing to show that Commodore Stockton intended, or that the Government approved, the capture of coast fishing vessels.

On the contrary, General Halleck, in the preface to his work on International Law or Rules Regulating the Intercourse of States in Peace and War, published in

1861, says that he began that work, during the war between the United States and Mexico, "while serving on the staff of the commander of the Pacific Squadron" and "often required to give opinions on questions of international law growing out of the operations of the war." Had the practice of the blockading squadron on the west coast of Mexico during that war, in regard to fishing vessels, differed from that approved by the Navy Department on the east coast, General Halleck could hardly have failed to mention it, when stating the prevailing doctrine upon the subject as follows:

"Fishing boats have also, as a general rule, been exempted from the effects of hostilities. As early as 1521, while war was raging between Charles V and Francis, ambassadors from these two sovereigns met at Calais, then English, and agreed that, whereas the herring fishery was about to commence, the subjects of both belligerents, engaged in this pursuit, should be safe and unmolested by the other party, and should have leave to fish as in time of peace. In the war of 1800, the British and French governments issued formal instructions exempting the Fishing boats of each other's subjects from seizure. This order was subsequently rescinded by the British government, on the alleged ground that some French fishing boats were equipped as gunboats, and that some French fishermen, who had been prisoners in England, had violated their parole not to serve, and had gone to join the French fleet at Brest. Such excuses were evidently mere pretexts, and, after some angry discussions had taken place on the subject, the British restriction was withdrawn, and the freedom of fishing was again allowed on both sides. French writers consider this exemption as an established principle of the modern law of war, and it has been so recognized in the French courts, which have restored such vessels when captured by French cruisers." . . .

That edition was the only one sent out under the author's own auspices, except . . . Elements of International Law and the Law of War, which he published in 1866, as he said in the preface, to supply **a suitable textbook** for instruction upon the subject, "not only in our colleges, but also in our two great national schools—the Military and Naval Academies." In that abridgment, the statement as to fishing boats was condensed, as follows: "Fishing boats have also, as a general rule, been exempted from the effects of hostilities. French writers consider this exemption as an established principle of the modern law of war, and it has been so recognized in the French courts, which have restored such vessels when captured by French cruisers."

In the **treaty of peace** between the United States and Mexico in 1848 were inserted the very words of the earlier treaties with Prussia, already quoted, forbidding the hostile molestation or seizure in time of war of the persons, occupations, houses or goods of fishermen. . . .

Wharton's Digest of the International Law of the United States, published by authority of Congress in 1886 and 1887, embodies General Halleck's fuller statement, above quoted, and contains nothing else upon the subject. . . .

France, in the Crimean War in 1854, and in her wars with Austria in 1859 and with Germany in 1870, by **general orders**, forbade her cruisers to trouble the coast fisheries, or to seize any vessel or boat engaged therein, unless naval or military operations should make it necessary.

Calvo says that in the Crimean War, "notwithstanding her alliance with France and Italy, England did not follow the same line of conduct, and her cruisers in the Sea of Azof destroyed the fisheries, nets, fishing implements, provisions, boats, and even the cabins, of the inhabitants of the coast." And a Russian writer on Prize Law remarks that those depredations, "having brought ruin on poor fishermen and inoffensive traders, could not but leave a painful impression on the minds of the population, without impairing in the least the resources of the Russian government." But the contemporaneous reports of the English naval officers put a different face on the matter, by stating that the destruction in question was part of a military measure, conducted with the cooperation of the French ships, and pursuant to instructions of the English admiral "to clear the seaboard of all fish stores, all fisheries and mills, on a scale beyond the wants of the neighboring population, and indeed of all things destined to contribute to the maintenance of the enemy's army in the Crimea;" and that the property destroyed consisted of large fishing establishments and storehouses of the Russian government, numbers of heavy launches, and enormous quantities of nets and gear, salted fish, corn and other provisions, intended for the supply of the Russian army.

Since the English orders in council of 1806 and 1810, before quoted, in favor of fishing vessels employed in catching and bringing to market fresh fish, no instance has been found in which the exemption from capture of private coast fishing vessels, honestly pursuing their peaceful industry, has been denied by England, or by any other nation. And the Empire of Japan, (the last State admitted into the rank of civilized nations), . . . ordained that "the following enemy's vessel's are exempt from detention"—including in the exemption "boats engaged in coast fisheries," as well as "ships engaged exclusively on a voyage of scientific discovery, philanthropy or religious mission." . . .

International law is part of our law, and must be ascertained and administered by the courts of justice of appropriate jurisdiction, as often as questions of right depending upon it are duly presented for their determination.

For this purpose, where there is no treaty, and no controlling executive or legislative act or judicial decision, resort must be had to the customs and usages of civilized nations; and, as evidence of these, to the works of jurists and commentators, who by years of labor, research and experience, have made themselves peculiarly well acquainted with the subjects of which they treat. Such works are resorted to by judicial tribunals, not for the speculations of their authors concerning what the law ought to be, but for trustworthy evidence of what the law really is.

Wheaton places, among the principal sources of international law, "Text-writers of authority, showing what is the approved usage of nations, or the general opinion respecting their mutual conduct, with the definitions and modifications introduced by general consent." . . . They are witnesses of the sentiments and usages of civilized nations . . .

Chancellor Kent says: "In the absence of higher and more authoritative sanctions, the ordinances of foreign States, the opinions of eminent statesmen, and the writings of distinguished jurists, are regarded as of great consideration on questions not settled by conventional law . . . no civilized nation, that does not arrogantly set all ordinary law and justice at defiance, will venture to disregard the uniform sense of the established writers on international law." . . .

It will be convenient, in the first place, to refer to some leading French treatises on international law. . . .

"Enemy ships," say Pistoye and Duverdy, in their Treatise on Maritime Prizes, published in 1855, "are good prize. Not all, however; for it results from the unanimous accord of the maritime powers that an exception should be made in favor of coast fishermen. Such fishermen are respected by the enemy, so long as they devote themselves exclusively to fishing." . . .

De Cussy, in his work on the Phases and Leading Cases of the Maritime Law of Nations . . . published in 1856, affirms in the clearest language the exemption from capture of fishing boats . . .

Ortolan, in the fourth edition of the Regles Internationales et Diplomatie de la Mer, published in 1864, after stating the general rule that the vessels and cargoes of subjects of the enemy are lawful prize, says: "Nevertheless, custom admits an exception in favor of boats engaged in the coast fishery; these boats, as well as their crews, are free from capture and exempt from all hostilities. The coast fishing industry is . . . wholly pacific . . .

No international jurist of the present day has a wider or more deserved reputation than Calvo, who, though writing in French, is a citizen of the Argentine Republic, employed in its diplomatic service abroad. In the fifth edition of his great work on international law, published in 1896, he observes ". . . there are generally exempted, from seizure and capture, fishing vessels." . . .

The modern German books on international law, cited by the counsel for the appellants, treat the custom, by which the vessels and implements of coast fishermen are exempt from seizure and capture, as well established by the practice of nations. . . .

De Boeck, in his work on Enemy Private Property under Enemy Flag—de la Pro-

priete Privee Ennemie sous Pavillon Ennemi—published in 1882, and the only continental treatise cited by the counsel for the United States, says "A usage very ancient, if not universal, withdraws from the right of capture enemy vessels engaged in the coast fishery. The reason of this exception is evident; it would have been too hard to snatch from poor fishermen the means of earning their bread." . . .

Two recent English text-writers, cited at the bar, (influenced by what Lord Stowell said a century since), hesitate to recognize that the exemption of coast fishing vessels from capture has now become a settled rule of international law. Yet they both admit that there is little real difference in the views, or in the practice, of England and of other maritime nations; and that no civilized nation at the present day would molest coast fishing vessels, so long as they were peaceably pursuing their calling, and there was no danger that they or their crews might be of military use to the enemy. Hall, . . . in the fourth edition of his Treatise on International Law, after briefly sketching the history of the positions occupied by France and England at different periods, and by the United States in the Mexican War, goes on to say: "In the foregoing facts there is nothing to show that much real difference has existed in the practice of the maritime countries. England does not seem to have been unwilling to spare fishing vessels so long as they are harmless, and it does not appear that any State has accorded them immunity under circumstances of inconvenience to itself. It is likely that all nations would now refrain from molesting them as a general rule, and would capture them so soon as any danger arose that they or their crews might be of military use to the enemy; and it is also likely that it is impossible to grant them a more distinct exemption." So T.J. Lawrence, in . . . his Principles of International Law, says: "The difference between the English and the French view is more apparent than real; for no civilized belligerent would now capture the boats of fishermen plying their avocation peaceably in the territorial waters of their own State; and no jurist would seriously argue that their immunity must be respected if they were used for warlike purposes, as were the smacks belonging to the northern ports of France when Great Britain gave the order to capture them in 1800."

But there are writers of various maritime countries, not yet cited, too important to be passed by without notice.

Jan Helenus Ferguson, Netherlands Minister to China, and previously in the naval and in the colonial service of his country, in his Manual of International Law for the Use of Navies, Colonies and Consulates, published in 1882, writes: "An exception to the usage of capturing enemy's private vessels at sea is the coast fishery. This principle of immunity from capture of fishing boats is generally adopted by all maritime powers, and in actual warfare they are universally spared so long as they remain harmless."

Ferdinand Attlmayr, Captain in the Austrian Navy, in his Manual for Naval Officers, put at Vienna in 1872 under the auspices of Admiral Tegetthoff, says: "Regarding the capture of enemy property, an exception must be mentioned, which is a universal custom. Fishing vessels which belong to the adjacent coast, and whose business yields only a necessary livelihood, are, from considerations of humanity, universally excluded from capture." 1 Attlmayr, 61.

Ignacio de Negrin, First Official of the Spanish Board of Admiralty, in his Elementary Treatise on Maritime International Law, adopted by royal order as a text-book in the Naval Schools of Spain, and published at Madrid in 1873, concludes his chapter "Of the lawfulness of prizes" with these words: "It remains to be added that

the custom of all civilized peoples excludes from capture, and from all kind of hostility, the fishing vessels of the enemy's coasts, considering this industry as absolutely inoffensive, and deserving, from its hardships and usefulness, of this favorable exception. It has been thus expressed in very many international conventions, so that it can be deemed an incontestable principle of law, at least among enlightened nations."

Carlos Testa, Captain in the Portuguese Navy and Professor in the Naval School at Lisbon, in his work on Public International Law, published in French at Paris in 1886, when discussing the general fight of capturing enemy ships, says: "Nevertheless, in this, customary law establishes an exception of immunity in favor of coast fishing vessels. Fishing is so peaceful an industry, and is generally carried on by so poor and so hardworking a class of men, that it is likened, in the territorial waters of the enemy's country, to the class of husbandmen who gather the fruits of the earth for their livelihood. The examples and practice generally followed establish this humane and beneficent exception as an international rule, and this rule may be considered as adopted by customary law and by all civilized nations."

No less clearly and decisively speaks the distinguished Italian jurist, Pasquale Fiore, in the enlarged edition of his exhaustive work on Public International Law, published at Paris in 1885–6, saying: "The vessels of fishermen have been generally declared exempt from confiscation, because of the eminently peaceful object of their humble industry, and of the principles of equity and humanity. The exemption includes the vessel, the implements of fishing, and the cargo resulting from the fishery. This usage, eminently humane, goes back to very ancient times; and although the immunity of fishery along the coasts may not have been sanctioned by treaties, yet it is considered to-day as so definitely established, that the inviolability of vessels devoted to that fishery is proclaimed by the publicists as a positive rule of international law, and is generally respected by the nations. Consequently, we shall lay down the following rule: (a) Vessels belonging to citizens of the enemy State, and devoted to fishing along the coasts, cannot be subject to capture. (b) Such vessels, however, will lose all right of exemption, when employed for a warlike purpose. (c) There may, nevertheless, be subjected to capture vessels devoted to the great fishery in the ocean, such as those employed in the whale fishery, or in that for seals or sea calves."

This review of the precedents and authorities on the subject appears to us abundantly to demonstrate that at the present day, by the general consent of the civilized nations of the world, and independently of any express treaty or other public act, it is an established rule of international law, founded on considerations of humanity to a poor and industrious order of men, and on the mutual convenience of belligerent States, that coast fishing vessels, with their implements and supplies, cargoes and crews, unarmed, and honestly pursuing their peaceful calling of catching and bringing in fresh fish, are exempt from capture as prize of war.

The exemption, of course, does not apply to coast fishermen or their vessels, if employed for a warlike purpose, or in such a way as to give aid or information to the enemy; nor *when military or naval operations create a necessity to which all private interests must give way.*

. . . .

This rule of international law is one which prize courts, administering the law of nations, are bound to take judicial notice of,

and to give effect to, in the absence of any treaty or other public act of their own government in relation to the matter. . . .

. . . .

To this subject, in more than one aspect, are singularly applicable the words uttered by Mr. Justice Strong, speaking for this court: "Undoubtedly, no single nation can change the law of the sea. That law is of universal obligation, and no statute of one or two nations can create obligations for the world. Like all the laws of nations, it rests upon the common consent of civilized communities. It is of force, not because it was prescribed by any superior power, but because it has been generally accepted as a rule of conduct. . . . it is recognition of the historical fact that by common consent of mankind these rules have been acquiesced in as of general obligation. Of that fact, we think, we may take judicial notice. Foreign municipal laws must indeed be proved as facts, but it is not so with the law of nations."

The position taken by the United States during the recent war with Spain was quite in accord with the rule of international law, now generally recognized by civilized nations, in regard to coast fishing vessels.

On April 21, 1898, **the Secretary of the Navy gave instructions to Admiral Sampson,** commanding the North Atlantic Squadron, to "immediately institute a blockade of the north coast of Cuba. . . . The blockade was immediately instituted accordingly. On April 22, the President issued a proclamation, declaring that the United States had instituted and would maintain that blockade, "in pursuance of . . . the law of nations applicable to such cases." . . .

On April 26, 1898, the President issued another proclamation, which, after reciting the existence of the war, as declared by

Congress, contained this further recital: "It being desirable that such war should be conducted upon principles in harmony with the present views of nations and sanctioned by their recent practice. " This recital was followed by specific declarations of certain rules for the conduct of the war by sea, making no mention of fishing vessels. . . . But the proclamation clearly manifests the general policy of the Government to conduct the war in accordance with the principles of international law sanctioned by the recent practice of nations.

On April 28, 1898, (after the capture of the two fishing vessels now in question,) Admiral Sampson telegraphed to the Secretary of the Navy as follows: "I find that a large number of fishing schooners are attempting to get into Havana from their fishing grounds near the Florida reefs and coasts. They are generally manned by excellent seamen, belonging to the maritime inscription of Spain, who have already served in the Spanish navy, and who are liable to further service. As these trained men are naval reserves, have a semi-military character, and would be most valuable to the Spaniards as artillerymen, either afloat or ashore, I recommend that they should be detained prisoners of war, and that I should be authorized to deliver them to the commanding officer of the army at Key West."

To that communication the Secretary of the Navy, on April 30, 1898, guardedly answered: "Spanish fishing vessels attempting to violate blockade are subject, with crew, to capture, and any such vessel or crew considered likely to aid enemy may be detained."

. . . . The Admiral's dispatch assumed that he was not authorized, without express order, to arrest coast fishermen peaceably pursuing their calling; and the necessary

implication and evident intent of the response of the Navy Department were that Spanish coast fishing vessels and their crews should not be interfered with, so long as they neither attempted to violate the blockade, nor were considered likely to aid the enemy.

The Paquete Habana, as the record shows, was a fishing sloop of 25 tons burden . . . She had no arms or ammunition on board; she had no knowledge of the blockade, or even of the war, until she was stopped by a blockading vessel; she made no attempt to run the blockade, and no resistance at the time of the capture; nor was there any evidence whatever of likelihood that she or her crew would aid the enemy.

In the case of the Lola, the only differences in the facts were that she was a schooner of 35 tons burden, and had a crew of six men, including the master; that after leaving Havana, and proceeding some two hundred miles along the coast of Cuba, she went on, about a hundred miles farther, to the coast of Yucatan, and there fished for eight days; and that, on her return, when near Bahia Honda, on the coast of Cuba, she was captured, with her cargo of live fish, on April 27, 1898. These differences afford no ground for distinguishing the two cases.

. . . .

The two vessels and their cargoes were condemned by the District Court as prize of war; the vessels were sold under its decrees; and it does not appear what became of the fresh fish of which their cargoes consisted.

Upon the facts proved in either case, it is the duty of this court, sitting as the highest prize court of the United States, and administering the law of nations, to declare and adjudge that the capture was unlawful, and without probable cause; and it is therefore, in each case,

Ordered, that the decree of the District Court be reversed, and the proceeds of the sale of the vessel, together with the proceeds of any sale of her cargo, be restored to the claimant, with damages and costs.

. . .

DISSENT: Mr. Chief Justice Fuller, with whom concurred Mr. Justice Harlan and Mr. Justice McKenna, dissenting.

The District Court held these vessels and their cargoes liable because not "satisfied that as a matter of law, without any ordinance, treaty or proclamation, fishing vessels of this class are exempt from seizure."

This court holds otherwise, not because such exemption is to be found in any treaty, legislation, proclamation or instruction, granting it, but on the ground that the vessels were exempt by reason of an established rule of international law applicable to them, which it is the duty of the court to enforce.

I am unable to conclude that there is any such established international rule, or that this court can properly revise action which must be treated as having been taken in the ordinary exercise of discretion in the conduct of war.

. . . .

I do not think that, under the circumstances, the considerations which have operated to mitigate the evils of war in respect of individual harvesters of the soil can properly be invoked on behalf of these hired vessels, as being the implements of like harvesters of the sea. Not only so as to the owners but as to the masters and crews. The principle which exempts the husbandman and his instruments of labor,

exempts the industry in which he is engaged, and is not applicable in protection of the continuance of transactions of such character and extent as these.

In truth, the exemption of fishing craft is essentially an act of grace, and not a matter of right, and it is extended or denied as the exigency is believed to demand.

It is, said Sir William Scott "a rule of comity only, and not of legal decision."

. . . .

In his Lectures on International Law at the Naval Law College the late Dr. Freeman Snow laid it down that the exemption could not be asserted as a rule of international law. These lectures were edited by Commodore Stockton and published under the direction of the Secretary of the Navy in 1895, and, by that department, in a second edition, in 1898, so that in addition to the well-known merits of their author they possess the weight to be attributed to the official imprimatur. Neither our treaties nor settled practice are opposed to that conclusion.

. . . .

In my judgment, the rule is that exemption from the rigors of war is in the control of the Executive. He is bound by no immutable rule on the subject. It is for him to apply, or to modify, or to deny altogether such immunity as may have been usually extended.

Exemptions may be designated in advance, or granted according to circumstances, but carrying on war involves the infliction of the hardships of war at least to the extent that the seizure or destruction of enemy's property on sea need not be specifically authorized in order to be accomplished.

Being of opinion that these vessels were not exempt as matter of law, I am constrained to dissent from the opinion and judgment of the court; and my brothers Harlan and McKenna concur in this dissent.

Professional military officers might note that the case of *The Paquete Habana and The Lola* is one which, at bottom, is concerned with the law of armed conflict; and in deciding a legal issue born of war, the Court made pronouncements about principles of international law applicable not only to legal issues associated with war, but to those associated with the international legal system in its broadest sense. This result is not at all novel; much of modern international law derives from international legal principles first developed out of an effort to ameliorate the violence, suffering and destruction associated with war by using law to induce limits. Indeed, perhaps the seminal work of modern international law, written in 1625 by the Dutch scholar, Hugo Grotius, often called "father of international law," is entitled *The Law of War and Peace*. War, an activity apparently antithetical to the notion of the rule of law, thus ironically has been a key catalyst in its formation, and such is true of the case of *The Paquete Habana and The Lola*. One of the broadly applicable portions of the Supreme Court's law of armed conflict ruling in *The Paquete Habana and The Lola* is the Court's consideration of treaties as evidence of customary international law. The treaties discussed were not ones between Spain and the United States, but were between other countries. What is the relationship between a treaty and customary international law?

The comments to section 102 of the *Restatement of the Law, Third, Foreign Relations Law of the United States* make two points relevant to understanding the relationship between treaties and customary international law:

> International agreements constitute practice of states and as such contribute to the growth of customary law . . . Some multilateral agreements may come to be law for non-parties that do not actively dissent. That may be the effect where a multilateral agreement is designed for adherence by states generally, is widely accepted, and not rejected by a significant number of important states. A wide network of similar bilateral arrangements on a subject may constitute practice and also result in customary law.

> Multilateral agreements open to all states . . . are increasingly used for general legislation, whether to make new law, as in human rights . . . or for codifying and developing customary law . . .

In another judicial decision born out of issues of armed attack, self-defense, force and violence, the International Court of Justice elaborated upon and applied these concepts in a modern context. In 1984, Nicaragua sued the United States in the International Court of Justice, alleging that the United States had, among other things, engaged in an illegal armed attack against Nicaragua's territorial sovereignty and political independence, in violation of both the Charter of the

United Nations and customary international law. Although the United States did not consent to the exercise of jurisdiction by the International Court of Justice (ICJ), and in fact refused to participate in the trial on the merits of the case, the ICJ's lengthy and comprehensive opinion is often cited in support of the broad and fundamental international law principles discussed.

International Court of Justice; Judgment On Merits In Case Concerning Military And Paramilitary Activities In And Against Nicaragua (Nicaragua v. United States) Official citation: Military and Paramilitary Activities in and against Nicaragua (Nicaragua v. United States of America), Merits, Judgment, I.C.J. Reports 1986, p. 14.

In the case concerning military and paramilitary activities in and against Nicaragua,
between
the Republic of Nicaragua,
and
the United States of America.
THE COURT,
composed as above,
delivers the following Judgment:

1. On 9 April 1984 the Ambassador of the Republic of Nicaragua to the Netherlands filed in the Registry of the Court an Application instituting proceedings against the United States of America in respect of a dispute concerning responsibility for military and paramilitary activities in and against Nicaragua . . .

"Nicaragua, reserving the right to supplement or to amend this Application and subject to the presentation to the Court of the relevant evidence and legal argument, requests the Court to adjudge and declare as follows:

(a) That the United States, in recruiting, training, arming, equipping, financing, supplying and otherwise encouraging, supporting, aiding, and directing military and paramilitary actions in and against Nicaragua, has violated and is violating its express charter and treaty obligations to Nicaragua, and in particular, its charter and treaty obligations under:

—Article 2 (4) of the United Nations Charter;

. . . .

(b) That the United States, in breach of its obligation under general and customary international law, has violated and is violating the sovereignty of Nicaragua by:

• armed attacks against Nicaragua by air, land and sea;

- incursions into Nicaraguan territorial waters;

- aerial trespass into Nicaraguan airspace;

- efforts by direct and indirect means to coerce and intimidate the Government of Nicaragua.

(c) That the United States, in breach of its obligation under general and customary international law, has used and is using force and the threat of force against Nicaragua.

(d) That the United States, in breach of its obligation under general and customary international law, has intervened and is intervening in the internal affairs of Nicaragua.

(e) That the United States, in breach of its obligation under general and customary international law, has infringed and is infringing the freedom of the high seas and interrupting peaceful maritime commerce.

(f) That the United States, in breach of its obligation under general and customary international law, has killed, wounded and kidnapped and is killing, wounding and kidnapping citizens of Nicaragua.

(g) That, in view of its breaches of the foregoing legal obligations, the United States is under a particular duty to cease and desist immediately from all use of force whether direct or indirect, overt or covert—against Nicaragua, and from all threats of force against Nicaragua;

from all violations of the sovereignty, territorial integrity or political independence of Nicaragua, including all intervention, direct or indirect, in the internal affairs of Nicaragua;

from all support of any kind—including the provision of training, arms, ammuni-tion, finances, supplies, assistance, direction or any other form of support—to any nation, group, organization, movement or individual engaged or planning to engage in military or paramilitary actions in or against Nicaragua;

from all efforts to restrict, block or endanger access to or from Nicaraguan ports;

and from all killings, woundings and kidnappings of Nicaraguan citizens.

. . . .

34. There can be no doubt that the issues of the use of force and collective self-defence raised in the present proceedings are issues which are regulated both by customary international law and by treaties, in particular the United Nations Charter. . . .

176. As regards the suggestion that the areas covered by the two sources of law are identical, the Court observes that the United Nations Charter, the convention to which most of the United States argument is directed, by no means covers the whole area of the regulation of the use of force in international relations. On one essential point, this treaty itself refers to pre-existing customary international law; this reference to customary law is contained in the actual text of Article 51, which mentions the "inherent right" (in the French text the "droit naturel") of individual or collective self-defence which "nothing in the present Charter shall impair" and which applies in the event of an armed attack. The Court therefore finds that Article 51 of the Charter is only meaningful on the basis that there is a "natural" or "inherent" right of self-defence, and it is hard to see how this can be other than of a customary nature, even if its present content has been confirmed and influenced by the Charter. Moreover the Charter, having itself recognized the

existence of this right, does not go on to regulate directly all aspects of its content. For example, it does not contain any specific rule whereby self-defence would warrant only measures which are proportional to the armed attack and necessary to respond to it, a rule well established in customary international law. Moreover, a definition of the "armed attack" which, if found to exist, authorizes the exercise of the "inherent right" of self-defence is not provided in the Charter, and is not part of treaty law. It cannot therefore be held that Article 51 is a provision which "subsumes and supervenes" customary international law. It rather demonstrates that in the field in question, the importance of which for the present dispute need hardly be stressed, customary international law continues to exist alongside treaty law. The areas governed by the two sources of law thus do not overlap exactly, and the rules do not have the same content. This could also be demonstrated for other subjects, in particular for the principle of non-intervention.

177. . . . [E]ven if the customary norm and the treaty norm were to have exactly the same content, this would not be a reason for the Court to hold that the incorporation of the customary norm into treaty-law must deprive the customary norm of its applicability as distinct from that of the treaty norm. The existence of identical rules in international treaty law and customary law has been clearly recognized by the Court in the North Sea Continental Shelf cases. To a large extent, those cases turned on the question whether a rule enshrined in a treaty also existed as a customary rule, either because the treaty had merely codified the custom, or caused it to "crystallize," or because it had influenced its subsequent adoption. The Court found that this identity of content in treaty law and in customary international law did not exist in the case of the rule invoked, which appeared in one article of the treaty, but

did not suggest that such identity was debarred as a matter of principle: on the contrary, it considered it to be clear that certain other articles of the treaty in question "were . . . regarded as reflecting, or as crystallizing, received or at least emergent rules of customary international law" (I.C.J. Reports 1969, p. 39, para. 63). More generally, there are no grounds for holding that when customary international law is comprised of rules identical to those of treaty law, the latter "supervenes" the former, so that the customary international law has no further existence of its own.

178. There are a number of reasons for considering that, even if two norms belonging to two sources of international law appear identical in content, and even if the States in question are bound by these rules both on the level of treaty-law and on that of customary international law, these norms retain a separate existence. This is so from the standpoint of their applicability. In a legal dispute affecting two States, one of them may argue that the applicability of a treaty rule to its own conduct depends on the other State's conduct in respect of the application of other rules, on other subjects, also included in the same treaty. For example, if a State exercises its right to terminate or suspend the operation of a treaty on the ground of the violation by the other party of a "provision essential to the accomplishment of the object or purpose of the treaty" (in the words of Art. 60, para. 3(b), of the Vienna Convention on the Law of Treaties), it is exempted, vis-a-vis the other State, from a rule of treaty-law because of the breach by that other State of a different rule of treaty-law. But if the two rules in question also exist as rules of customary international law, the failure of the one State to apply the one rule does not justify the other State in declining to apply the other rule. Rules which are identical in treaty law and in customary international law are also distinguishable by reference to the methods of interpretation and application. A State

may accept a rule contained in a treaty not simply because it favours the application of the rule itself, but also because the treaty establishes what that State regards as desirable institutions or mechanisms to ensure implementation of the rule. Thus, if that rule parallels a rule of customary international law, two rules of the same content are subject to separate treatment as regards the organs competent to verify their implementation depending on whether they are customary rules or treaty rules. The present dispute illustrates this point.

179. It will therefore be clear that customary international law continues to exist and to apply, separately from international treaty law, even where the two categories of law have an identical content. . . . so far from having constituted a marked departure from a customary international law which still exists unmodified, the Charter gave expression in this field to principles already present in customary international law, and that law has in the subsequent four decades developed under the influence of the Charter, to such an extent that a number of rules contained in the Charter have acquired a status independent of it. The essential consideration is that both the Charter and the customary international law flow from a common fundamental principle outlawing the use of force in international relations.

. . . .

183. In view of this conclusion, the Court has next to consider what are the rules of customary international law applicable to the present dispute. For this purpose, it has to direct its attention to the practice and

opinio juris of States; as the Court recently observed,

"It is of course axiomatic that the material of customary international law is to be looked for primarily in the actual practice and *opinio juris* of States, even though multilateral conventions may have an important role to play in recording and defining rules deriving from custom, or indeed in developing them." (Continental Shelf (Libyan Arab Jamahiriya/Malta), I.C.J. Reports 1985, pp. 29–30, para. 27.)

. . . .

186. It is not to be expected that in the practice of States the application of the rules in question should have been perfect, in the sense that States should have refrained, with complete consistency, from the use of force or from intervention in each other's internal affairs. The Court does not consider that, for a rule to be established as customary, the corresponding practice must be in absolutely rigorous conformity with the rule. In order to deduce the existence of customary rules, the Court deems it sufficient that the conduct of States should, in general, be consistent with such rules, and that instances of State conduct inconsistent with a given rule should generally have been treated as breaches of that rule, not as indications of the recognition of a new rule. If a State acts in a way prima facie incompatible with a recognized rule, but defends its conduct by appealing to exceptions or justifications contained within the rule itself, then whether or not the State's conduct is in fact justifiable on that basis, the significance of that attitude is to confirm rather than to weaken the rule.

What multilateral treaties did the ICJ look to in its analysis of customary international law? What was the relationship between these treaties and customary law? What effect does the creation of a multilateral treaty have on customary law? Do developments in customary law influence treaty formation? What is the potential effect of very widely accepted multilateral treaties on non-parties to those treaties? If particular rule of a international law is substantially the same in a multilateral treaty as it is in customary law, what incentives exist for states to sign on to the treaty? In this regard, consider that the International Court of Justice is an institution created by the UN Charter.

Among the several important points discussed in the *Nicaragua* case is one only alluded to there, but here deserving of further discussion. The ICJ noted that practice need not be universally followed to be considered general. Wide acceptance is sufficient. What happens when a state does not actively engage in a generally followed practice, but does not actually object either? Such states are said to acquiesce to the practice. Comment (b) to section 102 of *The Restatement, Third, Foreign Relations Law of the United States* states that "inaction may constitute state practice, as when a state acquiesces in acts of another state that affect its legal rights." Thus, silence in a circumstance where one might be expected to object amounts to tacit acceptance, and acceptance constitutes practice. What about states who actively dissent and object to a practice, either by diplomatic notes or other means to publicize their dissent, or by deliberately engaging in some contrary practice? Can these dissenters, by objecting, prevent a rule of customary international law from forming; or does their dissent have some less comprehensive effect? Comment (d) to section 102 says "Although customary law may be built by the acquiescence as well as by the actions of states . . . and become generally binding on all states, in principle a state that indicates its dissent from a practice while the law is still in the process of development is not bound by that rule even after it matures."

The conceptual effects of objection and acquiescence upon developing customary international law have influenced the oceans policy of the United States with respect to the international law of the sea. These ideas are more fully discussed in the section of the law of the sea chapter dealing with the United States' Freedom of Navigation Program. For our purposes here, however, consider this excerpt from *Excessive Maritime Claims*, a book published as Volume 66 of the *Naval War College International Law Studies* series.

> . . . . It is accepted international law and practice that, to prevent changes in or derogations from rules of law, States must persistently object to actions by other States that seek to change those rules. Protest 'must, at the very least, be repeated' and 'must be supported by conduct which opposes the presentations of the claimant state.' Naturally, States are not required to adopt a course of conduct which virtually negates the rights reserved by the protest. Consequently, States will not be permitted to acquiesce in emerging new rules of law and later claim exemption from them at will.
>
> Acquiescence is the tacit acceptance of a certain legal position as a result of a failure to make a reservation of rights at the appropriate juncture. For acquiescence to arise, a claim must have been made and accepted. The claim must be made in a manner, and in such circumstances, that the other State has been

placed on notice of that claim. The conduct that allegedly constitutes acquiescence, or tacit acceptance of that claim, likewise must be clear and unequivocal. The failure to make a timely protest in circumstances where it reasonably could have been expected to do so may constitute tacit acceptance of that claim.

. . . . Where the claim protested against has the effect of taking away a nation's right to use portions of the oceans, mere preservation of one's legal right to operate there is of little practical value when one chooses not to operate there except in extraordinary circumstances. Avoiding areas where a country needs to operate, or could be expected to operate, in the absence of the illegal claim gives both practical and legal effect to the excessive claim.

One of the four Geneva Conventions of 1949 establishes rules of international law requiring humane treatment of Prisoners of War (POWs). Many of these treaty law principles coexist with virtually identical rules of customary international law. Suppose the United States is engaged in armed conflict with another country, and that country is violating international law by maltreating American POWs in its custody, claiming that these captives are international criminals undeserving of POW status. Why should the United States comply with the Geneva Conventions in its treatment of any POWs it may hold, when the enemy is not? What should the United States do about the violations committed by the other side?

Suppose a state announces that a portion of the ocean off of its coast is permanently closed to foreign shipping, unless permission is asked and received from that state's government. Should the United States acquiesce to that claim? What happens if it does, and then other states make similar claims? Brazil, Iran, and India have all announced that foreign warships must request permission to operate in the waters extending 200 miles from these states' coasts. A number of other countries make outright claims of 200 mile territorial seas, and purport to restrict foreign naval operations in those waters. If the United States considers these claims to be excessive claims not supportable under the customary international law of the sea, what should it do? What could happen if the United States does nothing?

CONCLUSION

The sources of international law include international agreements and customary international law. Customary international law is formed of practice combined with *opinio juris*, that is, a perception that the practice is legally obligatory. Action is practice, and therefore has a profound influence on the development and formation of customary international law. Action may take the form of agreement to treaties, and also of military operations and the rules of engagement associated with them. The conduct of the naval services of the United States in action thus actually influences the development of international law. Failure to act, if considered acquiescence, may have similar consequences. Thus, the naval services in action—and at rest—affect the development and evolution of the customary international law of the sea and of the customary international law of armed conflict. Conversely, existing international law provides a context within which the naval services must operate. The following chapters discuss in further detail the law of the sea and the law of armed conflict, and the interaction between international law and the military activities of the United States' naval services.

Study Questions

1. What are the sources of international law?

2. Why do states comply with international law?

3. What is the difference between the Vienna Convention definition of a treaty and the customary international law definition? U.S. law definition and international law definition?

4. How is customary international law formed?

5. What provides evidence of the existence of a rule of customary international law?

6. How does treaty law affect the development of customary international law?

7. To whom or what does treaty law apply? What about customary international law?

8. What are SOFAs? What do they typically say about foreign criminal jurisdiction?

9. Why is it important for a state to object by action and deed to claims of right under customary international law with which it does not agree?

10. To whom does international law apply?

11. What effect can military rules of engagement have upon international law? Vice versa?

CHAPTER XII

WAR CRIMES

If the nations which command the great physical forces of the world want the society of nations to be governed, these principles [of the Nuremberg Charter] may contribute to that end. If those who have the power of decision revert to the concept of unlimited and irresponsible sovereignty, neither this nor any charter will save the world from international lawlessness.

Justice Robert H. Jackson, in the preface of his official report as
United States Representative to the Nuremberg Trials, Feb 1949.

NATURE OF WAR CRIMES

The term "war crime" is the technical expression for a violation of the law of war. The laws governing the conduct of armed conflict limit the means and methods of warfare. This law derives from international treaties (conventions) and custom. While not always an easy undertaking, determining whether conduct constitutes a war crime is achievable in most circumstances. The true difficulty in studying war crimes comes with understanding the political aspects of war crimes cases. Unlike domestic criminal cases, prosecution of persons for violations of the law of war requires evidence of guilt, plus the right international situation and necessary political will to carry through with the case. In many situations, these elements are not present. The result is an inconsistent history of war crimes prosecutions that may lead one to question the relevance of the law in this area. Perhaps a better view, however, is to recognize that war crimes law does exist and that an understanding of the rules will enable military officers and their subordinates to comply with those regulations. A comprehension of war crimes law will also facilitate an insight into the political circumstances and considerations that affect decisions by nations on whether to try or not try suspected war criminals.

DEVELOPMENT OF WAR CRIMES LAW

Serious legal consideration of the conduct of belligerents during war did not begin until the second half of the nineteenth century. The United States Union Army enacted General Order 100, known as the *Lieber Code*, during the American Civil War. This set of laws sought to codify international law on the treatment of prisoners of war and noncombatants. The humanitarian principles contained in the *Lieber Code* provided a substantial basis for subsequent international conventions concerning the conduct of war. The *Declaration of St. Petersburg of 1868* sought to limit the use of projectiles over a certain weight. The 1907 *Hague Convention IV* went further and placed restrictions on the use of certain inhumane weapons during armed conflict and limited the means of conducting warfare. *See* Appendix 5 for full text. Following World War I, the international community ratified several conventions concerning the conduct of war. The use of poisonous gases during World War I resulted in the *1925 Geneva Protocol for the Prohibition of the Use in War of Gases and Bacteriological Methods*. The 1929 Geneva Conventions provided protections for prisoners of war and the wounded and sick as well. The *1928 General Treaty for the Renunciation of War* (known as the *Kellogg-Briand Pact*) sought to eliminate the use of aggressive war as an instrument of foreign policy.

While international agreements and custom set up principles for the conduct of armed conflict, the war crimes trials following the end of World War I were the first large-scale attempt to try persons for actions occurring during war. Such trials had occurred, however, on a sporadic basis. For example, during the Anglo-Boer War of 1899-1902, the British tried and convicted several Boers of acts contrary to the usages of war. The British also convicted three Australian soldiers of shooting Boer prisoners in the well-known case of Lieutenant Charles Morant. Following the end of World War I, the treaty of Versailles prohibited extradition of persons accused of war crimes. The allies, therefore, agreed to permit cases against Germans to be tried by a German court at Leipzig, Germany. Department of the Army Pamphlet, 27-161-2, *International Law*, describes the results of those trials.

> The trials resulted in six convictions and six acquittals. Most of the acquittals resulted from a failure of the court to accept certain evidence as credible. Disappointment was expressed over the comparatively light sentences meted out but also over the fact the trials dealt almost exclusively with treatment of shipwrecked survivors of submarine activity and with the treatment of prisoners of war. No trials were held on the actual conduct of hostilities, such as the use of weapons and the destruction of life and property in combat. Another objection was the fact that the court itself was under pressure from the German press and German public opinion. Both were very hostile to the trials. For example, after the sentence was announced in the Llandovery Castle case, the British observers had to leave by a side door under police escort.

The offenses charged at the Leipzig trial ranged from torpedoing a hospital ship to killing prisoners of war. The most severe punishment awarded at the trials was confinement for four years.

At the close of World War II, the victorious allied nations undertook an aggressive program for the punishment of war criminals. This program began with the establishment of an international military tribunal for the trial of senior German officers and leaders in Nuremberg, Germany. The trials at Nuremberg lasted for nine and one-half months. The tribunal held 403 open sessions, heard evidence from 113 witnesses, and considered over 1900 interrogatory responses and affidavits. The tribunal handed down the following findings and sentences:

Defendant	Findings	Sentence
Goering	Guilty	Hanging
Hess	Guilty	Life
Ribbentrop	Guilty	Hanging
Fritzsche	Not Guilty	
Keitel	Guilty	Hanging
Kaltenbrunner	Guilty	Hanging
Rosenberg	Guilty	Hanging
Frank	Guilty	Hanging
Frick	Guilty	Hanging
Streicher	Guilty	Hanging
Funk	Guilty	Life
Schacht	Not Guilty	
Von Neurath	Guilty	15 years
Doenitz	Guilty	10 years
Raeder	Guilty	Life
Von Schiroch	Guilty	20 years
Sauckel	Guilty	Hanging
Jodl	Guilty	Hanging
Bormann	Guilty(tried in absentia)	Hanging
Von Papen	Not Guilty	
Seyss-Inquart	Guilty	Hanging
Speer	Guilty	20 years
Krupp	Not tried because of old age	
Ley	Suicide	

Following the trials of German leaders at Nuremberg, the allies established a second international tribunal to try senior Japanese officials. Known as the International Military Tribunal for the Far East, this court tried 28 high-ranking Japanese leaders. The tribunal convicted 25 of the accused, with two of the defendants dying during the procedures and one judged unfit to stand trial. Seven of the defendants were hanged, while 16 were sentenced to life imprisonment. The remainder of the defendants were sentenced to long prison terms. Following the dramatic and well-publicized hearings at Nuremberg and Tokyo, the allies tried other suspected war criminals using various types of tribunals, commissions and courts. The United States established military tribunals and commissions in various places in Europe and Asia. There is no complete list of all the war crimes trials held following World War II, however, it is safe to estimate that the allies tried over 24,000 persons on war crimes charges.

The accused at the Nuremberg Trials. Nineteen were convicted of war crimes. Twelve of these convicted were hanged. Photo courtesy of U.S. Naval Institute.

Judges sit on the Far Eastern War Crimes Tribunal in Tokyo. Photo courtesy of Naval Historical Society.

The experiences of World War II led the world community to codify specific international rules pertaining to war crimes in the Geneva Conventions of 1949. These conventions set forth a list of serious war crimes, termed "grave breaches." Apart from the World War II war crimes trials, prosecution of individuals for war crimes has occurred sporadically since 1945. The United States tried service members for crimes in Vietnam, *see United States v. Calley* in *Responsibility for War Crimes* below, and in Panama, *see United States v. Freed* (First Sergeant charged with murder for shooting a Panamanian prisoner acquitted at general court-martial). Recently, however, the United Nations commenced a war crimes trial for atrocities allegedly committed during the ongoing conflict in Bosnia-Hercegovina. This trial is described in the article from the Washington Post below:

THE WASHINGTON POST
THURSDAY, APRIL 27, 1995

War Crimes Tribunal Arraigns 1st Suspect

Bosnian Serb Pleads Not Guilty to Charges That He Killed Muslims at Detention Camp

By William Drozdiak

Washington Post Foreign Service

THE HAGUE, April 26—A Bosnian Serb accused of torturing and killing dozens of Muslims at a death camp three years ago appeared before a U.N. tribunal here today, the first defendant to face an international war crimes hearing since the Nuremberg and Tokyo trials after World War II.

Dusan Tadic, the only one of 22 Serbs indicted for crimes against humanity who is now in legal custody, pleaded not guilty to a long list of charges including the murder, rape and beating of Muslim and Croat neighbors during the 1992 Serb campaign of "ethnic cleansing" to drive non-Serbs from Bosnia's Prijedor region.

The hearing, presided over by Judge Gabrielle Kirk McDonald of the United States, lasted only 45 minutes. Tadic was then remanded to one of 24 cells specially built by the United Nations to house Balkan war criminals at nearby Schevenigen prison. His trial is scheduled for June.

Tadic was arrested in Germany last year and flown by helicopter here two days ago from a Munich jail to stand trial before the U.N. tribunal investigating war crimes in Yugoslavia and its former republics. The 11-judge panel was set up by the U.N. Security Council in May 1993 after its members refused to approve military force to

reverse the forced eviction of 700,000 Muslims from their homes in Bosnia.

Tadic's extradition on Monday coincided with an announcement by Justice Richard Goldstone of South Africa, the chief U.N. prosecutor, that his team was launching judicial proceedings into the "criminal responsibility" of Bosnian Serb leader Radovan Karadzic and two close associates for genocide, torture and other war crimes. Court officials said that the investigations are moving fast and that indictments may be handed up by the end of the year.

The decision by the tribunal to press ahead with its first war crimes trial and to explore prosecution of the Bosnian Serb leadership was applauded by the United States and the Muslim-led Bosnian government as a step toward bringing to justice those accused of ordering or committing the war's most serious atrocities.

Russia has criticized the tribunal's action for jeopardizing efforts to reach a peace settlement, however, and France and Britain expressed fears that it could provoke Serb reprisals against their U.N. troops in Bosnia. A fragile four-month cease-fire will end on Monday, and officials in the countries that have contributed troops to the U.N. force are concerned for their safety if the fighting escalates.

Despite the anxieties of some Security Council members, Goldstone said at a news conference this week that he is determined to take legal action on the basis of accumulating evidence, regardless of the political consequences. "My strategy is to indict those in leadership positions, both civilian and military, who are responsible for serious violations of international law," he said.

While Karadzic, Bosnian Serb military commander Ratko Mladic and former secret police chief Mico Stanisic are being investigated for masterminding the ethnic cleansing campaign, Tadic is charged with being one of its primary instruments.

The indictment presented at today's pre-trial hearing accused him of participating in a roundup of more than 3,000 Muslims and Croats forced from their homes during a Bosnian Serb offensive in May 1992, the second month of the war in Bosnia. The prisoners were taken to a former mining complex that was transformed into the notorious Omarska detention camp.

The Omarska camp housed many of Prijedor's leading Muslim and Croat intellectuals, businessmen and politicians. Conditions at the camp were described as brutal. Prisoners were crowded together and fed on starvation rations with little or no clean water. Male and female inmates were systematically beaten, humiliated and attacked with all manner of weapons, including knives, rifles, metal rods and wooden truncheons, prosecutors said.

Tadic, a 39 year old cafe owner in the Prijedor area, was identified despite the black mask he often wore because many of his victims were his former friends and neighbors. He was accused of murdering 13 people and participating in the killing of many others. He also was charged with beating many victims senseless and, in some instances, forcing them to drink motor oil or to bite off the testicles of other prisoners.

The indictment formally charges Tadic with "genocide, through the policy of ethnic cleansing, and crimes against humanity, such as assault, murder, rape and persecution based on religious grounds." If convicted, he faces life imprisonment.

Although the Serbian government and Bosnian Serb leaders say they do not recognize the tribunal's proceedings and have refused to cooperate, Tadic was represented in court today by Milan Vujin, a Belgrade lawyer, and other Serb attorneys. The defense team also includes Michael Wladimiroff, a Dutch lawyer assigned by the tribunal at Tadic's request.

Officials at the tribunal say they have little hope of bringing to trial the 21 other Serbs under indictment for war crimes, including the senior commander of the Omarska camp, Zeljko Meakic, because they are believed to have taken refuge in Serbian-dominated Yugoslavia or Serb-held parts of Bosnia and Croatia. Nonetheless, the officials said international arrest warrants will be issued for those who fail to appear at subsequent trials, a step that would inhibit them from traveling outside Yugoslavia.

While all those indicted so far are Serbs, the tribunal is investigating crimes committed by other sides in the three-year-old war. Goldstone's team is expected to issue indictments soon against 27 Bosnian Croats in an April 1993 assault on the central Bosnian village of Ahmici in which 144 Muslims were killed.

Do you agree that the greatest impediment to trying suspected war criminals in the former Yugoslavia is not the law, but political considerations? Is it easier to conduct war crimes prosecutions if there is a clear victor in the conflict? The Russians are alleged to have committed war atrocities in Chechnya. Do the international rules regarding war crimes apply to that conflict?

DEFINING WAR CRIMES

The Charter of the International Military Tribunal at Nuremberg contained the following categories of crimes:

1. Crimes Against Peace. Planning, preparation, initiation, or waging of a declared or undeclared war of aggression, or war otherwise in violation of international treaties, agreements, or assurances.

2. War Crimes. The traditional violations of the laws or customs of war.

3. Crimes Against Humanity. A collective category of major felonious crimes committed against any civilian population before or during an armed conflict.

The categories of war crimes used in the Nuremberg trials evolved from both customary and conventional law. *See* Appendix 3, NWP 9, which describes the sources of the law of war. The crime of waging aggressive war, however, was not articulated as an offense until the end of World War II. Although the 1928 Kellogg-Briand Pact renounced war as an instrument of national policy, neither it nor its predecessors declared aggressive wars to be illegal under international law. At the time of the trials, the charge of crimes against peace raised serious *ex poste facto* issues that were resolved in favor of the prosecution. United States Supreme Court Justice Robert H. Jackson, the senior prosecutor for the United States at Nuremberg, believed that the criminalization of aggression was the most important aspect of the trials. Note, however, that of the 24 accused at Nuremberg, only one was found guilty solely of crimes against peace and only two were convicted solely of crimes against humanity.

Article 2 of the United Nations Charter provides:

3. All Members shall settle their international disputes by peaceful means in such a manner that international peace and security, and justice, are not endangered.

4. All Members shall refrain in their international relations from the threat or use of force against the territorial integrity or political independence of any state. . . .

Do the above provisions outlaw aggression? In other words, if an individual were tried with crimes against peace, as in the Nuremberg cases, would he or she be charged with violating Article 2 of the United Nations Charter? If no, is there a law that proscribes aggressive war? After the World War II war crimes trials, are crimes against peace now part of customary international law? The world community charged that Iraq had committed a war crime by waging aggressive war against Kuwait. Did Iraq's invasion violate the proscription on waging wars of aggression? Is yes, then why have there been no war crimes trials involving Iraq?

Kuwait—A burning oil well spews flame and smoke into the air after it was set afire by retreating Iraqi forces during Operation Desert Storm. The United States considered these acts to be "Environmental Terrorism" in violation of the Law of Armed Conflict. Photo by CWO2 Ed Bailey, USNR, (Feb 91); courtesy of U.S. Naval Institute.

Article 50, *1949 Geneva Convention for the Amelioration of the Condition of the Wounded and Sick in Armed Forces in the Field*, lists the following grave breaches of the convention:

> Grave breaches to which the preceding Article relates shall be those involving any of the following acts, if committed against persons or property protected by the Convention: wilful killing, torture or inhuman treatment, including biological experiments, wilfully causing great suffering or serious injury to body or health, and extensive destruction and appropriation of property, not justified by military necessity and carried out unlawfully and wantonly.

The above list is not exhaustive of all serious war crimes. For example, Iraq's intentional release of oil into the Persian Gulf during the Gulf War is generally considered a grave breach type of offense. Genocide, the destruction of a national, ethnic, racial or religious group, was outlawed by the *Geneva Convention on the*

Prevention and Punishment of the Crime of Genocide. This offense is viewed as grave breach of the law of war as well.

Violations of the law of war not amounting to grave breaches constitute simple breaches. *See* Appendix 4 concerning the distinction between simple and grave breaches. Army Pamphlet 27-10, *The Law of Land Warfare*, provides examples of simple breaches of the law of war:

1. Making use of poisoned or otherwise forbidden arms or ammunition;

2. Treacherous request for quarter;

3. Maltreatment of dead bodies;

4. Firing on localities which are undefended and without military significance;

5. Abuse of or firing on the flag of truce;

6. Misuse of protected emblems;

7. Use of civilian clothing by troops to conceal their military character during battle;

8. Compelling prisoners of war to perform prohibited labor;

9. Killing without trial spies or other persons who have committed hostile acts.

RESPONSIBILITY FOR WAR CRIMES

The prosecutions at Nuremberg and in the Far East at the conclusion of World War II raised the issue of who is legally responsible for the commission of war crimes. The following cases addresses that issue and also considers the authority to convene war crimes commissions.

In Re Yamashita
Supreme Court of the United States
327 U.S. 1
February 4, 1946

OPINION: Mr. Chief Justice Stone

No. 61 Miscellaneous is an application for leave to file a petition for writs of habeas corpus and prohibition in this Court. No. 672 is a petition for certiorari to review an order of the Supreme Court of the Commonwealth of the Philippines (28 U. S. C.

@ 349), denying petitioner's application to that court for writs of habeas corpus and prohibition. As both applications raise substantially like questions, and because of the importance and novelty of some of those presented, we set the two applications down for oral argument as one case.

From the petitions and supporting papers it appears that prior to September 3, 1945, petitioner was the Commanding General of the Fourteenth Army Group of the Imperial Japanese Army in the Philippine Islands. On that date he surrendered to and became a prisoner of war of the United States Army Forces in Baguio, Philippine Islands. On September 25th, by order of respondent, Lieutenant General Wilhelm D. Styer, Commanding General of the United States Army Forces, Western Pacific, which command embraces the Philippine Islands, petitioner was served with a charge prepared by the Judge Advocate General's Department of the Army, purporting to charge petitioner with a violation of the law of war. On October 8, 1945, petitioner, after pleading not guilty to the charge, was held for trial before a military commission of five Army officers appointed by order of General Styer. The order appointed six Army officers, all lawyers, as defense counsel. Throughout the proceedings which followed, including those before this Court, defense counsel have demonstrated their professional skill and resourcefulness and their proper zeal for the defense with which they were charged.

. . . .

Our first inquiry must therefore be whether the present commission was created by lawful military command and, if so, whether authority could thus be conferred on the commission to place petitioner on trial after the cessation of hostilities between the armed forces of the United States and Japan.

General Styer's order for the appointment of the commission was made by him as Commander of the United States Army Forces, Western Pacific. His command includes, as part of a vastly greater area, the Philippine Islands, where the alleged offenses were committed, where petitioner surrendered as a prisoner of war, and where, at the time of the order convening the commission, he was detained as a prisoner in custody of the United States Army. The congressional recognition of military commissions and its sanction of their use in trying offenses against the law of war to which we have referred, sanctioned their creation by military command in conformity to long-established American precedents. Such a commission may be appointed by any field commander, or by any commander competent to appoint a general court-martial, as was General Styer, who had been vested with that power by order of the President. 2 Winthrop, Military Law and Precedents, 2d ed., 1302; *cf.* Article of War 8.

Here the commission was not only created by a commander competent to appoint it, but his order conformed to the established policy of the Government and to higher military commands authorizing his action. In a proclamation of July 2, 1942 (56 Stat. 1964), the President proclaimed that enemy belligerents who, during time of war, enter the United States, or any territory or possession thereof, and who violate the law of war, should be subject to the law of war and to the jurisdiction of military tribunals. Paragraph 10 of the Declaration of Potsdam of July 26, 1945, declared that ". . . stern justice shall be meted out to all war criminals, including those who have visited cruelties upon our prisoners." U.S. Dept. of State Bull., Vol. XIII, No. 318, pp. 137-138. This Declaration was accepted by the Japanese government by its note of August 10, 1945. U.S. Dept. of State Bull., Vol. XIII, No. 320, p. 205.

By direction of the President, the Joint Chiefs of Staff of the American Military Forces, on September 12, 1945, instructed General MacArthur, Commander in Chief, United States Army Forces, Pacific, to proceed with the trial, before appropriate military tribunals, of such Japanese war criminals "as have been or may be apprehended." By order of General MacArthur of September 24, 1945, General Styer was specifically directed to proceed with the trial of petitioner upon the charge here involved. This order was accompanied by detailed rules and regulations which General MacArthur prescribed for the trial of war criminals. These regulations directed, among other things, that review of the sentence imposed by the commission should be by the officer convening it, with "authority to approve, mitigate, remit, commute, suspend, reduce or otherwise alter the sentence imposed," and directed that no sentence of death should be carried into effect until confirmed by the Commander in Chief, United States Army Forces, Pacific.

It thus appears that the order creating the commission for the trial of petitioner was authorized by military command, and was in complete conformity to the Act of Congress sanctioning the creation of such tribunals for the trial of offenses against the law of war committed by enemy combatants.

. . . .

The charge. Neither congressional action nor the military orders constituting the commission authorized it to place petitioner on trial unless the charge preferred against him is of a violation of the law of war. The charge, so far as now relevant, is that petitioner, between October 9, 1944 and September 2, 1945, in the Philippine Islands, "while commander of armed forces of Japan at war with the United States of America and its allies, unlaw-

fully disregarded and failed to discharge his duty as commander to control the operations of the members of his command, permitting them to commit brutal atrocities and other high crimes against people of the United States and of its allies and dependencies, particularly the Philippines; and he . . . thereby violated the laws of war."

Bills of particulars, filed by the prosecution by order of the commission, allege a series of acts, one hundred and twenty-three in number, committed by members of the forces under petitioner's command during the period mentioned. The first item specifies the execution of "a deliberate plan and purpose to massacre and exterminate a large part of the civilian population of Batangas Province, and to devastate and destroy public, private and religious property therein, as a result of which more than 25,000 men, women and children, all unarmed noncombatant civilians, were brutally mistreated and killed, without cause or trial, and entire settlements were devastated and destroyed wantonly and without military necessity." Other items specify acts of violence, cruelty and homicide inflicted upon the civilian population and prisoners of war, acts of wholesale pillage and the wanton destruction of religious monuments.

It is not denied that such acts directed against the civilian population of an occupied country and against prisoners of war are recognized in international law as violations of the law of war. Articles 4, 28, 46, and 47, Annex to the Fourth Hague Convention, 1907, 36 Stat. 2277, 2296, 2303, 2306-7. But it is urged that the charge does not allege that petitioner has either committed or directed the commission of such acts, and consequently that no violation is charged as against him. But this overlooks the fact that the gist of the charge is an unlawful breach of duty by petitioner as an army commander to control the operations of the members of his command by "permitting them to commit" the extensive and widespread atrocities specified. The question then is whether the law of war imposes on an army commander a duty to take such appropriate measures as are within his power to control the troops under his command for the prevention of the specified acts which are violations of the law of war and which are likely to attend the occupation of hostile territory by an uncontrolled soldiery, and whether he may be charged with personal responsibility for his failure to take such measures when violations result. That this was the precise issue to be tried was made clear by the statement of the prosecution at the opening of the trial.

It is evident that the conduct of military operations by troops whose excesses are unrestrained by the orders or efforts of their commander would almost certainly result in violations which it is the purpose of the law of war to prevent. Its purpose to protect civilian populations and prisoners of war from brutality would largely be defeated if the commander of an invading army could with impunity neglect to take reasonable measures for their protection. Hence the law of war presupposes that its violation is to be avoided through the control of the operations of war by commanders who are to some extent responsible for their subordinates.

This is recognized by the Annex to the Fourth Hague Convention of 1907, respecting the laws and customs of war on land. Article 1 lays down as a condition which an armed force must fulfill in order to be accorded the rights of lawful belligerents, that it must be "commanded by a person responsible for his subordinates."

36 Stat. 2295. Similarly Article 19 of the Tenth Hague Convention, relating to bombardment by naval vessels, provides that commanders in chief of the belligerent vessels "must see that the above Articles are properly carried out." 36 Stat. 2389. And Article 26 of the Geneva Red Cross Convention of 1929, 47 Stat. 2074, 2092, for the amelioration of the condition of the wounded and sick in armies in the field, makes it "the duty of the commanders-in-chief of the belligerent armies to provide for the details of execution of the foregoing articles, [of the convention] as well as for unforeseen cases . . ." And, finally, Article 43 of the Annex of the Fourth Hague Convention, 36 Stat. 2306, requires that the commander of a force occupying enemy territory, as was petitioner, "shall take all the measures in his power to restore, and ensure, as far as possible, public order and safety, while respecting, unless absolutely prevented, the laws in force in the country."

These provisions plainly imposed on petitioner, who at the time specified was military governor of the Philippines, as well as commander of the Japanese forces, an affirmative duty to take such measures as were within his power and appropriate in the circumstances to protect prisoners of war and the civilian population. This duty of a commanding officer has heretofore been recognized, and its breach penalized by our own military tribunals.[1] A like principle has been applied so as to impose liability on the United States in international arbitrations. Case of Jeannaud, 3 Moore, International Arbitrations, 3000; Case of The Zafiro, 5 Hackworth, Digest of International Law, 707.

---

[1] Failure of an officer to take measures to prevent murder of an inhabitant of an occupied country committed in his presence. Gen. Orders No. 221, Hq. Div. of the Philippines, August 17, 1901. And in Gen. Orders No. 264, Hq. Div. of the Philippines, September 9, 1901, it was held that an officer could not be found guilty for failure to prevent a murder unless it appeared that the accused had "the power to prevent" it.

We do not make the laws of war but we respect them so far as they do not conflict with the commands of Congress or the Constitution. There is no contention that the present charge, thus read, is without the support of evidence, or that the commission held petitioner responsible for failing to take measures which were beyond his control or inappropriate for a commanding officer to take in the circumstances.[2] We do not here appraise the evidence on which petitioner was convicted. We do not consider what measures, if any, petitioner took to prevent the commission, by the troops under his command, of the plain violations of the law of war detailed in the bill of particulars, or whether such measures as he may have taken were appropriate and sufficient to discharge the duty imposed upon him. These are questions within the peculiar competence of the military officers composing the commission and were for it to decide. *See Smith v. Whitney*, 116 U.S. 167, 178. It is plain that the charge on which petitioner was tried charged him with a breach of his duty to control the operations of the members of his command, by permitting them to commit the specified atrocities. This was enough to require the commission to hear evidence tending to establish the culpable failure of petitioner to perform the duty imposed on him by the law of war and to pass upon its sufficiency to establish guilt.

Obviously charges of violations of the law of war triable before a military tribunal need not be stated with the precision of a common law indictment. *Cf. Collins v. McDonald, supra,* 420. But we conclude that the allegations of the charge, tested by any reasonable standard, adequately allege a violation of the law of war and that the commission had authority to try and decide the issue which it raised. *Cf. Dealy v. United States*, 152 U.S. 539; *Williamson v. United States,* 207 U.S. 425, 447; *Glasser v. United States*, 315 U.S. 60, 66, and cases cited.

It thus appears that the order convening the commission was a lawful order, that the commission was lawfully constituted, that petitioner was charged with violation of the law of war, and that the commission had authority to proceed with the trial in doing so did not violate any military, statutory or constitutional command. We have considered, but find it unnecessary to discuss, other contentions which we find to be without merit. We therefore conclude that the detention of petitioner for trial and his detention upon his conviction, subject to the prescribed review by the military authorities, were lawful, and that the petition for certiorari, and leave to file in this Court petitions for writs of habeas corpus and prohibition should be, and they are.

Denied.

Justice Murphy dissented in *Yamashita* as follows:

The petitioner was accused of having "unlawfully disregarded and failed to discharge his duty as commander to control the operations of the members of his command, permitting them to

---

[2]In its findings the commission took account of the difficulties "faced by the Accused with respect not only to the swift and overpowering advance of American forces, but also to the errors of his predecessors, weaknesses in organization, equipment, supply . . ., training, communication, discipline and morale of his troops," and the "tactical situation, the character, training and capacity of staff officers and subordinate commanders as well as the traits of character . . . of his troops." It nonetheless found that petitioner had not taken such measures to control his troops as were "required by the circumstances." We do not weigh the evidence. We merely hold that the charge sufficiently states a violation against the law of war, and that the commission, upon the facts found, could properly find petitioner guilty of such a violation.

commit brutal atrocities and other high crimes." The bills of particulars further alleged that specific acts of atrocity were committed by "members of the armed forces of Japan under the command of the accused." Nowhere was it alleged that the petitioner personally committed any of the atrocities, or that he ordered their commission, or that he had any knowledge of the commission thereof by members of his command.

The findings of the military commission bear out this absence of any direct personal charge against the petitioner. The commission merely found that atrocities and other high crimes "have been committed by members of the Japanese armed forces under your command . . . that they were not sporadic in nature but in many cases were methodically supervised by Japanese officers and noncommissioned officers; . . . That during the period in question you failed to provide effective control of your troops as was required by the circumstances."

In other words, read against the background of military events in the Philippines subsequent to October 9, 1944, these charges amount to this: "We, the victorious American forces, have done everything possible to destroy and disorganize your lines of communication, your effective control of your personnel, your ability to wage war. In those respects we have succeeded. We have defeated and crushed your forces. And now we charge and condemn you for having been inefficient in maintaining control of your troops during the period when we were so effectively besieging and eliminating your forces and blocking your ability to maintain effective control. Many terrible atrocities were committed by your disorganized troops. Because these atrocities were so widespread we will not bother to charge or prove that you committed, ordered or condoned any of them. We will assume that they must

have resulted from your inefficiency and negligence as a commander. In short, we charge you with the crime of inefficiency in controlling your troops. We will judge the discharge of your duties by the disorganization which we ourselves created in large part. Our standards of judgment are whatever we wish to make them."

Nothing in all history or in international law, at least as far as I am aware, justifies such a charge against a fallen commander of a defeated force. To use the very inefficiency and disorganization created by the victorious forces as the primary basis for condemning officers of the defeated armies bears no resemblance to justice or to military reality.

International law makes no attempt to define the duties of a commander of an army under constant and overwhelming assault; nor does it impose liability under such circumstances for failure to meet the ordinary responsibilities of command. The omission is understandable. Duties, as well as ability to control troops, vary according to the nature and intensity of the particular battle. To find an unlawful deviation from duty under battle conditions requires difficult and speculative calculations. Such calculations become highly untrustworthy when they are made by the victor in relation to the actions of a vanquished commander. Objective and realistic norms of conduct are then extremely unlikely to be used in forming a judgment as to deviations from duty. The probability that vengeance will form the major part of the victor's judgment is an unfortunate but inescapable fact. So great is that probability that international law refuses to recognize such a judgment as a basis for a war crime, however fair the judgment may be in a particular instance. It is this consideration that undermines the charge against the petitioner in this case. The indictment permits, indeed compels, the military commission of a victorious nation to sit in judgment upon the military strategy and actions of the defeated enemy and to use its conclusions to determine the criminal liability of an enemy commander. Life and liberty are made to depend upon the biased will of the victor rather than upon objective standards of conduct.

. . . .

At a time like this when emotions are understandably high it is difficult to adopt a dispassionate attitude toward a case of this nature. Yet now is precisely the time when that attitude is most essential. While peoples in other lands may not share our beliefs as to due process and the dignity of the individual, we are not free to give effect to our emotions in reckless disregard of the rights of others. We live under the Constitution, which is the embodiment of all the high hopes and aspirations of the new world. And it is applicable in both war and peace. We must act accordingly. Indeed, an uncurbed spirit of revenge and retribution, masked in formal legal procedure for purposes of dealing with a fallen enemy commander, can do more lasting harm than all of the atrocities giving rise to that spirit. The people's faith in the fairness and objectiveness of the law can be seriously undercut by that spirit. The fires of nationalism can be further kindled. And the hearts of all mankind can be embittered and filled with hatred, leaving forlorn and impoverished the noble ideal of malice toward none and charity to all. These are the reasons that lead me to dissent in these terms.

A frequent defense in war crimes trials is that the accused was ordered by a superior to commit the offense. For example, in the *Dover Castle* case of World War I, Karl Neumann, the commander of the German submarine that torpedoed the British hospital ship, DOVER CASTLE, raised the defense that he was simply following the orders of the German Admiralty in sinking the vessel. The court at Leipzig held that the "Admiralty Staff was the highest service authority over the accused. He was in duty bound to obey their orders in service matters. So far as he did that, he was free from criminal responsibility. Therefore, he cannot be held responsible for sinking the Hospital Ship DOVER CASTLE according to orders." The next case considers the defense of superior orders raised at a general court-martial by an accused charged with shooting civilians.

United States v. First Lieutenant William L. Calley, Jr., United States Army Court of Military Review
46 C.M.R. 1131
February 16, 1973

Alley, Judge

In much publicized proceedings, appellant was convicted by general court-martial of three specifications of premeditated murder and one of assault with intent to commit murder in violation of Articles 118 and 134, Uniform Code of Military Justice, 10 USC @@ 918 and 934, respectively. He was sentenced to dismissal, forfeiture of all pay and allowances, and confinement at hard labor for life. The convening authority approved dismissal and the forfeitures, but reduced the period of confinement to twenty years. The offenses were committed by First Lieutenant William L. Calley when he was performing as a platoon leader during an airmobile operation in the sub-hamlet of My Lai (4) in Song My village, Quang Ngai Province, Republic of South Vietnam, on 16 March 1968. Although all charges could have been laid as war crimes, they were prosecuted under the UCMJ. *See* paragraph 507b, Field Manual 27-10, The Law of Land Warfare (1956).

. . . .

V—SUFFICIENCY OF THE EVIDENCE

A. The Evidence. On 16 March 1968 Lieutenant Calley was the 1st platoon leader in C Company, 1st Battalion, 20th Infantry, 11th Light Infantry Brigade, as he had been since he arrived in the Republic of Vietnam in December 1967. The 11th Brigade was assigned to the American Division, itself only formally activated in October 1967.

The American Division was assigned a tactical area of operation along the South China Sea Coast from Quang Ngai Province north into Quang Nam Province. That area, approximately 150 kilometers from north to south, was divided among the three constituent brigades, the 11th Brigade receiving the southern-most portion. With the exception of the area in the vicinity of Quang Ngai City, which had been assigned to 2nd Republic of Vietnam Army (ARVN) Division, the 11th Brigade area of operation ran from Duc Pho District north to Binh Son District, and inland for approximately 30 kilometers.

In January 1968, appellant's company; A Company, 3d Battalion, 1st Infantry; and B Company, 4th Battalion, 3d Infantry, were chosen by the brigade commander to compose Task Force Barker.A supporting field artillery battery was organized from the assets of three existing batteries of the brigade's organic field artillery battalion. The Task Force area of operation, designated Muscatine, was located north of the Song

Diem-Diem and east of Highway 1 northward for approximately 12 Kilometers to Binh Son. Its operations were conducted from two fire support bases, Uptight and Dottie (Task Force Barker Head-quarters). (See Appendix A.)

During operations in the southern sector of its area of operation, the units of Task Force Barker drew fire from enemy forces which would withdraw south of the Song Diem-Diem into the area of operations of the 2d ARVN Division. After the Tet offensive in early February 1968 Task Force Barker requested and received authority temporarily to extend its area of operation south of the river into Son My village. Intelligence reports had indicated that the 48th Viet Cong Battalion maintained its base camp in the My Lai (1), or Pinkville, area of Song My. The village reportedly had been controlled by the Viet Cong for twenty years. Prior efforts by friendly forces to enter the area had been sternly resisted. When Task Force Barker made sweeps into Son My later in February, it met only limited success. At the cost of moderate casualties it destroyed some enemy supplies and fortifications, but was unable decisively to engage the main enemy force.

C Company, appellant's unit, had not experienced much combat prior to 16 March 1968. In its three months of overseas duty, two of which were with Task Force Barker, its operations had consisted of uneventful patrolling, attempted ambushes, providing defense for the fire bases, and providing blocking forces for Task Force missions. The casualties it had sustained were mainly from mines and booby traps. While moving into a blocking position on 25 February 1968 the company became ensnared in a mine field, suffering two killed and thirteen wounded. Appellant was not on this operation, for he had just returned from a three day in-country rest and recuperation leave. On 14 March 1968, a popular sergeant in the second platoon was killed and three others were wounded by a booby trap.

The next day, Captain Medina, commander of C Company, was notified that his company would engaged in an upcoming offensive action. He was briefed at Task Force headquarters, then called his officers and men together on the evening of 15 March 1968 for a unit briefing. The content of the briefing (a matter of some dispute as will subsequently be discussed) essentially was that the next morning the unit would engage the 48th VC Battalion, from whom it could expect heavy resistance and by whom it would be outnumbered by more than two to one. C Company was to be inserted by airlift to the west of My Lai (4), sweep through it, and continue toward My Lai (1) or Pinkville (Appendices A and C). There they would be joined in a night defensive position by B Company of the Task Force, which would be conducting a similar operation from south to north into My Lai (1), and by A Company which would be in a blocking position north of the river.

The concept of the operation for C Company was for the 1st and 2nd platoons to sweep rapidly through My Lai (4) and the 3rd platoon to follow. The 3rd platoon would thoroughly search the hamlet and destroy all that could be useful to the enemy. A demolition team of engineers was attached to assist in the destruction of enemy bunkers and facilities.

This was to be the unit's first opportunity to engage decisively the elusive enemy they had been pursuing since their arrival in South Vietnam. The men, as is normal in an untried unit, faced the operation with both anticipation and fear, mindful of the recent casualties taken in less perilous missions.

C Company was transported by helicopter from LZ Dottie about six miles southeast to My Lai (4) in two lifts (Appendix B, Point A). The first lift was completed at approxi-

mately 0730 hours; the second lift at 0747 hours. The insertion was preceded by five minutes of preparatory fires of 105 howitzer high explosive rounds and by gunship fire. The insertion, although within 100 meters of the western edge of My Lai (4), was not opposed by hostile fire. In formation with the first and second platoons on line from north to south, the third platoon in reserve and the mortar platoon remaining with the rear to provide support if needed, C Company laid heavy suppressive fires into the subhamlet as the first and second platoons began the assault.

Despite expectations of heavy resistance based upon specific intelligence briefings, C Company moved through My Lai (4) without receiving any fire. The only unit casualty on 16 March 1968 was one self-inflicted wound. No mines or booby traps were detonated. Lead elements of the company had no occasion to call for mortar fires from the weapons platoon; the forward observer with C Company had no occasion to call for any fires from artillery units in direct support. In My Lai (4), the unit encountered only unarmed, unresisting, frightened old men, women, and children, and not the expected elements of the 48th Viet Cong Battalion. The villagers were found in their homes eating breakfast and beginning their morning chores.

The members of C Company reacted to the unexpected absence of opposition in diverse ways. Some continued the mission as if the enemy was in fact being engaged. Most recognized the difference between actual and expected circumstances, so while continuing with the destruction of foodstuffs, livestock, and buildings, reverted to the unit standing operating procedures on collecting and evacuating Vietnamese. Many soldiers took no action at all, but stood passively by while others destroyed My Lai (4). A few, after witnessing inexplicable acts of violence against defenseless villagers, affirmatively refused to harm them.

No single witness at appellant's trial observed all that transpired at My Lai (4). The testimony of the 92 witnesses was shaded by the lapse of time between 16 March 1968 and the commencement of trial in November 1970. Even in the voluminous record, all that happened is not fully revealed. One reason for vagueness and confusion in testimony offered by both sides is that the operation itself was confused, having been planned on the basis of faulty intelligence and conducted with inexperienced troops without adequate command control.

With this caveat as to the evidence, we come to the events which led to charges against appellant. Twenty out of the twenty-seven persons who were members of Lieutenant Calley's understrength platoon on 16 March 1968 testified at his court-martial.

The first platoon arrived on the first lift about 0730 hours. Its initial task was to provide perimeter defense for the insertion of the remainder of the company. After the company was on the ground and organized for assault, the first platoon moved toward My Lai (4) in formation as follows:[1]

(SP4 Turner (fire team leader)

(PFC Simone (duty not revealed in record)

(PVT E-2 Stanley (ammo bearer & grenadier)

(PFC Bergthold (ass't machine gunner)

(SP4 Maples (machine gunner) 2d Squad

(SSG Bacon (squad leadr)

(PFC Conti (grenadier and mineweeper)

(PFC Doines (rifleman)

(PFC Lloyd (grenadier)

(SP4 R. Wood (fire team leader)

(PFC Kye (rifleman)

(2LT Calley (plt ldr)

(SP4 J. Wood (RTO) Plt Hdg Gp

(SFC Cowan (plt sgt) (SP4 Lee (medic)

(SP4 Sledge (RTO)

(PFC Mauro (duty not revealed in record)

(SP4 Boyce (rifleman)

(SP4 Grzesik (fire team leader)

(PFC Meadlo (rifleman)

(PFC Carter (rifleman/tunnel rat)1st Squad (SSG Mitchell (squad leader)

(PFC Dursi (rifleman)

(SP4 Hall (ass't machine gunner)

(PFC Olsen (machine gunner)

(PFC Haywood (rifleman)

(SGT Lagunoy (fire team leader)

---

[1]This diagram should be viewed with the realization that it only represents a composite from the record which contained inconsistencies as to the position and duty of certain platoon members.

This formation quickly became disorganized in the subhamlet. Thick vegetation made it difficult for the troops to see who was near, and for the squad leaders and Lieutenant Calley to maintain visual contact with their men and with each other. However, the principal reason why the formation broke down and leaders lost control was the discovery of unresisting, unarmed old men, women and children instead of the expected enemy. The platoon had not been specifically instructed what to do in this event. No civilian collection point had been designated; and the first platoon was supposed to move through the village quickly, not to return to the rear with detainees.

Some villagers were shot by some members of the first platoon when it first entered the subhamlet. Some members collected groups of Vietnamese, without knowing what to do with them, and others stopped to kill livestock. The platoon assault formation became a meandering troop. Lieutenant Calley started out behind his platoon on the western edge of the subhamlet, but emerged at a ditch on the eastern edge before several members of his platoon. Sergeant Mitchell similarly lost contact with his squad at one time, leaving most of them to search a small cluster of huts and buildings to the southeast of My Lai (4). Sergeant Bacon testified he never saw his platoon leader or even heard from him as he pushed through the subhamlet. Sergeant Cowan lost contact with Lieutenant Calley soon after they entered the village, did not see him inside the village, and came close to him again only as he exited My Lai (4) on the east.

The Vietnamese who were taken in the first platoon's sweep were herded in two general directions, either toward the southern edge of the hamlet near an intersection of trails or east-early in front of the advancing troops.

In the second squad, Sergeant Bacon detailed men to escort a group of men, women and children villagers down a trail (to his right or south) to where he thought the platoon leader would be. Private First Class Doines, a rifleman in Bacon's squad, took ten to fifteen people along a trail running north-south in the middle of the village and left them with Lieutenant Calley. Specialist Four Wood got some people together and sent them toward the right with a guard. Private First Class Kye found about ten old men, women and children in a hootch. They were whisked away to his right by an American soldier. A key witness, Private First Class Conti, stated he encountered Lieutenant Calley on a trail midway through the village. At Lieutenant Calley's direction he rounded up five or six people and put them with a nearby group of thirty to forty, consisting mostly of women and children. At appellant's order he and Private First Class Meadlo, another critical witness, moved these people down the trail and into rice paddies on the southern side of the subhamlet (Appendix B, Point B). Specialist Four Maples searched hootches, gathered some people, and moved them up front as he continued through My Lai (4).

The first squad's contact with the people of My Lai (4) was more significant. Private First Class Meadlo testified that, upon order from Sergeant Mitchell, he collected thirty to forty people near what he remembered as a clearing in the center of the village. Private First Class Dursi recalled that he moved through the village gathering people in a group. He related coming upon PFC Meadlo, who was guarding a group of Vietnamese near some rice paddies next to a trail on the southern side of the village. PFC Dursi later moved his group of fifteen to a ditch on the eastern side. Private First Class Haywood picked up five or six villagers and was told by someone to take the people to Dursi, whom he saw guarding twenty to thirty others on a trial in the south side of the village. A fire team leader in the first squad, Specialist Four

Grzesik, stated that he found seven or eight unresisting Vietnamese in a hootch immediately upon entering the village. He left these people with another group of twenty-five farther east in the village, in a small clearing. Specialist Four Boyce rounded up about fifteen people, mostly women and children, and passed them on to someone else. The people assembled in the southern portion of the subhamlet were not the only ones met by the first squad. Specialist Four Hall recalled that thirty to forty people were gathered in front of him, herded easterly through the village, and left at a ditch with Lieutenant Calley, Sergeant Mitchell, and others.

After the first platoon's movement through My Lai (4), which took from ninety minutes to two hours to cover only a third of a mile, the majority of the platoon formed a perimeter defense about 50 to 100 meters east of the ditch on the east side of the subhamlet. The rest of C Company more thoroughly searched and destroyed My Lai (4). The first platoon remained in its defensive position for another two hours or so until after the company had taken a lunch break. C Company then continued its mission with less eventful forays into two other subhamlets of Song My village. At one time later in the afternoon C Company was ordered by the brigade commander to return to My Lai (4) to verify reports of civilian casualties; but after an estimate of twenty-eight killed was radioed in by Captain Medina, that order was countermanded by the division commander.

The fate of villagers gathered by appellant's platoon in the southern portion of My Lai (4) and at the ditch on the subhamlet's eastern boundary was alleged in the following charges:[2]

. . . .

As previously described, some of the villagers rooted out of their homes were placed in a group guarded by PFC Paul Meadlo and PFC Dennis Conti. PFC Dursi, who was about fifteen feet from PFC Meadlo watching his own group of Vietnamese, saw Lieutenant Calley come onto the trail and heard him ask Meadlo "if he could take care of that group." A couple of minutes later the appellant returned and, as Dursi remembered, yelled to Meadlo, "why haven't you wasted them yet? PFC Dursi turned and started to move his group down the trail when he heard M-16 fire from his rear.

PFC Conti recounted that Lieutenant Calley told him and Meadlo "To take care of the people," left, and returned:

> "Then he came out and said, 'I thought I told you to take care of them.' Meadlo said, 'We are. We are watching them' and he said 'No, I mean kill them.'"

Conti testified that he saw Lieutenant Calley and Meadlo fire from a distance of ten feet with M-16 rifles on automatic fire into this group of unarmed, unresisting villagers.

Former PFC Meadlo's first appearance as a witness resulted only in his claiming his privilege against self-in-crimination. However, he did return to testify at length under a grant of immunity. By the time of trial, he was a civilian. By the time of his testifying, he was presumably satisfied that he was not facing trial himself before a military commission.

Meadlo testified that he was guarding a group of villagers with Conti when Lieutenant Calley approached him and said, "You know what to do with them, Meadlo." He assumed at the time this meant only to continue guarding them. However, appellant returned in ten or fif-

---

[2]Appellant was originally charged with two other specifications alleging the premeditated murder of seven more persons. These offenses were, however, dismissed upon motion by the Government.

teen minutes and said. "How come they're not dead?" Meadlo replied, "I didn't know we were supposed to kill them," after which Lieutenant Calley directed, "I want them dead." Meadlo remembered that appellant backed away and began firing into the group before he did the same.

Specialist Four Sledge, a radio operator, remembered moving with appellant to the south side of the village, where they found a group of thirty or forty Vietnamese with Meadlo. After Lieutenant Calley asked the group whether they were Viet Cong, which they naturally disclaimed, Sledge heard him tell Meadlo "to waste them." Sledge was walking away when he heard shooting and screaming from behind him. He glanced back and saw a few people start to fall. He did not see appellant firing.

Appellant, testifying in his own behalf, stated that after he got to the eastern edge of the village he received radio messages from the second platoon leader, who asked him to check out some bunkers in the northeast corner of My Lai (4), and from Captain Medina, who asked what he was doing. He told Captain Medina that he had some bunkers and a small portion of the hamlet to the southeast to check out and that he had a lot of enemy personnel with him. As appellant moved over to Sergeant Mitchell's position to the southeast, he came out of the village and encountered Meadlo with a large group of Vietnamese. Lieutenant Calley recalled he said something to the effect, "Did he know what he was supposed to be doing with those people" and, "To get moving, get on the other side of the ditch." About this time he claimed to have stopped Conti from molesting a female. Instead of continuing to the first squad leader, he returned inside the village to insure that Sergeant Bacon was searching the bunkers and placing his men on perimeter defense. Then, he claims to have received another call from Captain Medina telling him to "waste the Vietnamese and get my people out in line, out in the

position they were supposed to be." He yelled to Sergeant Bacon to get moving, and as he passed by Meadlo a second time he told them that if he couldn't move those people to "get rid of them."

There is no doubt that a group of submissive, defenseless Vietnamese, women, children, and old men, being guarded at the trail south of My Lai (4) by PFC Meadlo, were shot down in summary execution either by Meadlo and the appellant or by Meadlo at the order of the appellant. Nor is there doubt that the location of this offense and its occurrence as the first in time of the several charged satisfied the prosecution's responsibility of proof under the specification and Bill of Particulars.

Many of the bodies are depicted in a photograph taken by former Specialist Four Ronald Haeberle near the north-south trail, south of My Lai (4). A great deal of foundation evidence satisfactorily authenticates the photograph as being of the same group of bodies as was the subject of Specification 1 of the Charge and the testimony of Meadlo, Conti, Dursi and Sledge. Although over twenty inert bodies are shown, almost all displaying dreadful wounds, a pathologist witness could point to only one wound on one body which, in his opinion from viewing the photograph, was certain to have been instantly fatal. Most probably his testimony was the reason for findings amending the charged number of decedents to "not less than one."

2. The Ditch. Specification 2 of the Charge alleged the premeditated murder of not less than seventy persons. The court members returned findings of guilty, except the number of victims was reduced to not less than twenty. As outlined by the Bill of Particulars, this offense occurred after the trail incident but before the offenses laid under the Additional Charge.

It is not disputed that during midmorning on 16 March 1968 a large number of unresisting Vietnamese were placed in a ditch on the eastern side of My Lai (4) and summarily executed by American soldiers. We can best begin a recital of the tragic facts and circumstances surrounding this offense by examining the appellant's testimony.

Lieutenant Calley testified that after he passed PFC Meadlo for the second time at the trail, he moved toward Sergeant Mitchell's location in the southeastern part of My Lai (4). He found him near a ditch that ran through that sector. He walked up the ditch until he broke into a clearing. There he discovered some of his men firing upon Vietnamese in another ditch. Lieutenant Calley admitted that he also fired with them and told Meadlo to get his people over the ditch or, if he couldn't move them, to "waste them." He then went north to check out the positions of his men.

Charles Sledge confirmed some of those movements of his platoon leader. However, Sledge remembers important events differently. He heard someone shout that Sergeant Mitchell had some people at a ditch; moved there; saw twenty to thirty Vietnamese women, children, and a few old men; saw Lieutenant Calley and Sergeant Mitchell shove these Vietnamese down into the ditch and fire into them from four or five feet. The victims screamed and fell. A helicopter landed nearby. Lieutenant Calley went to it to talk with the aviator and returned to say to Sledge, "He don't like the way I'm running the show, but I'm the boss here."

Other important witnesses to the mass murder at the ditch were Conti, Hall, Olsen, Dursi, Meadlo, Grzesik and Turner.

After the killings at the trail, Conti went back into the village. Later he exited the east side and heard firing to his front. When he got to its source, Conti found Lieutenant Calley and Sergeant Mitchell firing from six or seven feet into a ditch filled with people who were screaming and trying to crawl up. He described the scene in court:

> "I seen the recoil of the rifles and the muzzle flashes and I looked down, I see a woman try to get up. As she got up I saw Lieutenant Calley fire and hit the side of her head and blow the side of her head off. I left."

Specialist Four Hall collected thirty or forty people, pushed them forward through My Lai (4) to the ditch, left them there, and proceeded to a position in the paddies beyond. He noticed that Sergeant Mitchell, Lieutenant Calley, the platoon's RTO's, and several others stayed behind. Sometime after he got into position Hall heard fully automatic fire behind him coming from the area of the ditch. He saw a helicopter land and appellant converse with its aviator, after which he heard slow, semi-automatic fire from the ditch. Later, when he crossed the ditch on a wooden foot bridge, he saw thirty or forty people in it:

> "They were dead. There was blood coming from them. They were just scattered all over the ground in the ditch, some in piles and some scattered out 20, 25 meters perhaps up the ditch. . . . The were very old people, very young children, and mothers. . . . There was blood all over them."

Olsen did not see Lieutenant Calley fire into the villagers, but did see him by the ditch when about two dozen Vietnamese were in it.

> "They were—the majority were women and children, some babies. I distinctly remember one middle-aged Vietnamese male dressed in white right at my feet as I crossed. None of the bodies were mangled in any way. There was blood. Some appeared to be dead, others followed me with their eyes as I walked across the ditch."

James Dursi, it will be recalled, moved his group away from the trail when appellant yelled to Meadlo there. He moved his people until he came upon the ditch. He stopped. Lieutenant Calley, and then Meadlo, joined him. Dursi heard Lieutenant Calley tell Meadlo, "We have another job to do" and tell Meadlo and him to put the people into the ditch. He and Meadlo complied. The Vietnamese started to cry and yell. Lieutenant Calley said something like, "Start firing," and fired into the group himself. So did Meadlo, but Dursi refused. Asked why, he testified, "I couldn't go through with it. These little defenseless men, women and kids." After the first of the firing ceased, Lieutenant Calley told Dursi to move across the ditch before he (Dursi) got sick. He did move away from the scenes of blood flowing from chest, arm, and head wounds upon the victims. From the perimeter, to the east, he looked back toward the ditch only once and saw the helicopter land.

Meadlo gave the most graphic and damning evidence. He had wandered back into the village alone after the trail incident. Eventually, he met his fire team leader, Specialist Four Grzesik. They took seven or eight Vietnamese to what he labeled a "ravine," where Lieutenant Calley, Sledge, and Dursi and a few other Americans were located with what he estimated as seventy-five to a hundred Vietnamese. Meadlo remembered also that Lieutenant Calley told him, "We got another job to do, Meadlo," and that the appellant started shoving people into the ravine and shooting them. Meadlo, in contrast to Dursi, followed the directions of his leader and himself fired into the people at the bottom of the "ravine." Meadlo then drifted away from the area but he doesn't remember where.

Specialist Four Grzesik found PFC Meadlo, crying and distraught, sitting on a small dike on the eastern edge of the village. He and Meadlo moved through the village, and came to the ditch, in which Grzesik thought were thirty-five to fifty dead bodies. Lieutenant Calley walked past and ordered Grzesik to take his fire team back into the village and help the following platoon in their search. He also remembered that Calley asked him to "finish them off," but he refused.

Specialist Four Turner saw Lieutenant Calley for the first time that day as Turner walked out of the village near the ditch. Meadlo and a few other soldiers were also present. Turner passed within fifteen feet of the area, looked into the ditch and saw a pile of approximately twenty bodies covered with blood. He also saw Lieutenant Calley and Meadlo firing from a distance of five feet into another group of people who were kneeling and squatting in the ditch. Turner recalled he then went north of the ditch about seventy yards, where he joined with Conti at a perimeter position. He remained there for over an hour, watching the ditch. Several more groups of Vietnamese were brought to it, never to get beyond or out of it. In all he thought he observed about ninety or a hundred people brought to the ditch and slaughtered there by Lieutenant Calley and his subordinates.

Other members of the first platoon saw Vietnamese placed into a ditch and appellant and others fire into it. Some members of the third platoon also saw the bloody bodies. Also, the observations of witnesses who were in the supporting helicopters portray a telling, and ghastly, overview of the slaughter at the ditch. Aviators and crew members saw from the air numbers of bodies they variously estimated from about thirty to about one hundred. One aviator, a Lieutenant (then Warrant Officer) Thompson, actually landed near the scene three times. The second time, he spoke with someone, who from the evidence must have been Lieutenant Calley. Thompson succeeded in evacuating a few living Vietnamese despite appellant's deprecations. The evidence from others is certainly persuasive that Lieutenant Calley boasted, "I'm the boss here," after he spoke with an aviator.

. . . .

According to Specialist Four Sledge, five or ten minutes after Lieutenant Calley returned from speaking with a helicopter aviator, he and Calley encountered a forty to fifty year old man dressed in white robes as they moved north up the ditch. Appellant repeatedly questioned the man, "Viet Cong adou?" (Are you Viet Cong), to which the man continually replied, "No vice." Suddenly Lieutenant Calley shot the man in the face at point blank range, blowing half his head away. Immediately after this incident Sledge remembered that:

> "Someone hollered, 'there's a child,' You know, running back toward the village. Lieutenant Calley ran back, the little—I don't know if it was a girl or boy—but it was a little baby, and he grabbed it by the arm and threw it into the ditch and fired."

Sledge observed this from a distance of twenty to thirty feet. He recalled that only one shot was fired at the child from a distance of four or five feet. He did not see whether the round struck.

Lieutenant Calley testified that after talking with the aviator, he moved along the platoon's perimeter checking the position of his troops. He did not recall making any statement to Sledge that, "He [the aviator] don't like the way I'm running the show, but I'm the boss here." But did claim that he told Captain Medina over the radio that "a pilot don't like the way things were being done down here."

As appellant went northerly along the ditch, a man dressed in white was brought to him for interrogation. He admitted butt-stroking the individual with his M-16, bloodying his face, but denies shooting him. Lieutenant Calley also denied the episode concerning a child that Sledge described.

. . . .

B. Legal Responsibility. Although appellant disputes the assault on the child and killing of the man found under the Additional Charge, his theories of defense at trial and on appeal accept as fact his participation in the killings at the trail and ditch. His testimony differs from others' about the details of his participation, the time spent upon the slayings at the ditch, and the number of the dead. These differences pose no substantial factual issues on appeal.

In an argument of extraordinary scope, appellant asks us to hold that the deaths of the My Lai villagers were not legally requitable in that the villagers had no right to continued life cognizable in our law. The two premises for this view are first, that the history of operations around Pinkville discloses villager sympathy and support for the Viet Cong, so extensive and enduring as to constitute all the villagers as belligerents themselves; and second, that appellant's superiors had determined the belligerent status of the villagers before the operation of 16 March—i.e., as belligerents, the villagers were not entitled to the protections of peaceful civilian status under the Geneva Convention Relative to the Protection of Civilian Persons in Time of War, 12 August 1949 [1956], 6 UST 3516, TIAS No. 3365; 75 UNTS 287, or of prisoner of war status because they did not organize under a responsible commander, bear a fixed distinctive sign recognizable at a distance, carry arms openly, and conduct their own operations in accordance with the laws of war, the four minima which must be satisfied by irregular belligerents in order to be regarded as prisoners of war under Article 4, Geneva Convention Relative to the treatment of Prisoners of War, 12 Aug 1949 [1956], 6 UST 3316, TIAS No. 3364; 75 UNTS 135.

This argument is tainted by several fallacies. One is that participation in irregular warfare is done by individuals, although they may organize themselves for the purpose. Slaughtering many for the presumed delicts of a few is not a lawful response to the delicts. We do not know whether the findings specifically included the deaths of infants in arms or children of toddler age, but the fallacy is clear when it is recalled that villagers this young were indiscriminately included in the general carnage. A second fallacy is that the argument is in essence a plea to permit summary execution as a reprisal for irregular villager action favoring the Viet Cong. Reprisal by summary execution of the helpless is forbidden in the laws of land warfare. *See generally* paragraph 497, Field Manual 27-10, The Law of Land Warfare (July 1956). It is not the law that the villagers were either innocent civilians or eligible for prisoner of war status or liable to summary execution. Whether an armed conflict be a local uprising or a global war, summary executions as in My Lai (4) are not justifiable. Articles 3, 32, 33, GC, *supra.*

Though conceding participation in some killings, the defense abstracts appellant's mental state while he was in My Lai to claim that the evidence was insufficient to support the findings under the original charge.

No claim is made that appellant lacked mental responsibility in the sense of the ordinary sanity tests set out in paragraph 120b, Manual, *supra.* Insanity as a defense was expressly disavowed at trial and before us, properly so in light of all the evidence.

Granting his own sanity, appellant contends that he was nevertheless not guilty of murder because he did not entertain the requisite mens rea. His specific claims are:

. . . .

4. His acts were justified because of the orders given to him; or, if the orders and his response do not constitute a complete defense, he is at most guilty of manslaughter.

Of the several bases for his argument that he committed no murder at My Lai because he was void of mens rea, appellant emphasized most of all that he acted in obedience to orders.

Whether appellant was ever ordered to kill unresisting, unarmed villagers was a contested question of fact. The findings of a court-martial being in the nature of a general verdict, we do not know whether the court found that no such orders were given or, alternatively, concluded that the orders were given but were not exculpatory under the standards given to them in instructions.

Responding to a question during direct examination asking why he gave Meadlo the order, "If he couldn't get rid of them to 'waste them'," Lieutenant Calley replied, "Because that was my order. That was the order of the day, sir." The appellant stated he received that order from Captain Medina, "The night before in the company briefings, the platoon leaders' briefing, the following morning before we lifted off, and twice there in the village."

Lieutenant Calley related what he remembered of Captain Medina's remarks to the company at the evening briefing prior to the My Lai (4) operation:

"He [Medina] started off and he listed the men that we had lost, . . . We were down about 50 percent in strength, and that the only way we would survive in South Vietnam would be to—we'd have to unite, start getting together, start fighting together, and become extremely aggressive and we couldn't afford to take anymore casualties, and that it was the people in the area that we had been operating in that had been taking the casualties on us, and that we would have to start treating them as enemy and you would have to start looking at them as enemy, . . . We were going to start at My Lai (4). And we would have to neutralize My Lai (4) completely and not to let anyone get behind us, and then we would move into My Lai (5) and neutralize it and make sure there was no one left alive in My Lai (5) and so on until we got into the Pinkville area, and we would completely neutralize My Lai (5)—I mean My Lai (1) which is Pinkville. He said it was completely essential that at no time that we lose our momentum of attack because the other two companies that had assaulted the time in there before had let the enemy get behind him or he had passed through enemy, allowing him to get behind him and set up behind him, which would disorganize him when he made his final assault on Pinkville. It would disorganize him, they would lose their momentum of attack, start taking casualties, be more worried about their casualties than their mission, and that was their downfall. So it was our job to go through destroying everyone and everything in there, not letting anyone or anything get behind us and move on into Pinkville, sir."

Appellant further recalled Captain Medina saying that "the area had been completely covered by PSYWAR operations; that all civilians had left the area and that there was no civilians in the area and anyone there would be considered enemy," and that the unit had "political clearance to destroy and burn everything in the area."

Lieutenant Calley stated that at a platoon leaders' briefing later in the evening Captain Medina reemphasized "that under no circumstances would we let anyone get behind us, nor would we leave anything standing in these villages."

The next morning at LZ Dottie, according to appellant, he was told by Captain Medina "to hang on to some of the Vietnamese in case we encountered a mine field," and "that everybody in that area would be the enemy and everyone there would be destroyed, all enemies would be destroyed."

Lieutenant Calley testified that during his movement through My Lai (4) he received and made several radio transmissions to Captain Medina. When he reached the eastern part of the village, Captain Medina called to ask what he was doing. Appellant continued:

> "I told him I had some bunkers up here to check out—that I wanted to check, and that I had that small portion of the hamlet to the south-east, and also there was still a lot of enemy personnel I still had with me.—. . . he told me to hurry up and get my people moving and get rid of the people I had there that were detaining me."

Appellant said that after he first encountered PFC Meadlo with a group of people and returned to Sergeant Bacon's location, he received another call from his company commander asking "why I was disobeying his order."

His remembrance of Captain Medina's reply to his explanation of what was slowing him down was the specific order, "to waste the Vietnamese and get my people out in line, out in the position they were supposed to be."

On cross examination Lieutenant Calley indicated some confusion as to when he first saw the Vietnamese who were slowing his progress. He also admitted that he didn't describe these people to Captain Medina, except perhaps as Vietnamese or VC, and that he knew these people were slowing him down because "anytime you are moving Vietnamese people, you will be moving slowly." Lieutenant Calley denied knowing if any of the persons detained by his platoon were women and children, and claimed to have discriminated between sexes only when he stopped Dennis Conti from molesting a female.

Captain Medina, who was called as a witness at the request of the court members, gave a different version of his remarks to the company on the eve of the operation:

"The briefing that I conducted for my company was that C Company had been selected to conduct a combat assault operation onto the village of My Lai (4) beginning with LZ time 0730 hours on the morning of the 16th of March, 1968. I gave them the enemy situation, intelligence reports where the 48th VC Battalion was located in the village of My Lai (4). I told them that the VC Battalion was approximately, numbered approximately 250 to 280 men and that we would be outnumbered approximately two to one, and that we could expect a hell of a good fight and that we probably would be engaged. I told them that even though we were outnumbered that we had a double coverage of gunships that were being provided and that the artillery was being placed onto the village and that this would help make up for the difference in ratio between the enemy forces and our company. I told the people that this would give them a chance to engage the 48th VC Battalion, that the 48th VC Battalion was the one that we had been chasing around the Task Force Barker area of operation, and that we would finally get a chance to engage them in combat, and that we would be able to destroy the 48th VC Battalion. . . . The information that I gave also in the briefing to the company was that the 48th VC Battalion was located at the village of My Lai (4), and that the intelligence reports also indicated that the innocent civilians or noncombatants would be gone to market at 0700 hours in the morning. That this was one

reason why the artillery preparation was being placed onto the village at 0720 hours with the combat assault LZ time 0730 hours. I did not make any reference to the handling of prisoners."

Captain Medina recalled that someone at the company briefing asked, "Do we kill women and children," and that his reply was, "No, you do not kill women and children. You must use common sense. If they have a weapon and are trying to engage you, then you can shoot back, but you must use common sense." He remembered instructing during the briefing:

". . . that Colonel Barker had told me that he had permission from the ARVN's at Quang Ngai to destroy the village of My Lai (4), and I clarified this by saying to destroy the village, by burning the hootches, to kill the livestock, to close the wells and to destroy the food crops."

Captain Medina conceded mentioning to Lieutenant Calley before lift-off "to utilize prisoners to lead the elements through the mine fields." Any congruence between their testimony in regard to communications between them ends here. Although Captain Medina acknowledged that he called the first platoon leader to inform him of the implementation of a contingency plan and so to spread his men out, he denied that Lieutenant Calley ever told him that he had bunkers to check out or that he was having difficulty in handling civilians or that the first platoon had encountered a large number of civilians. Captain Medina further disclaimed that he ever gave an order to the appellant "to move civilians out of the way or get rid of them." He stated he was never informed that the first platoon had gathered women and children and did not know the circumstances under which the inhabitants of My Lai (4) were killed. He came to the pile of bodies at the trail after the killings.

Both appellant and Captain Medina had high stakes in the acceptance of their testimony. Their testimony is not only mutually conflicting, but each conflicts with other witnesses. Of the many witnesses who attended Captain Medina's briefing to C Company on 15 March, no two had precisely the same recollection of his remarks about treatment of noncombatants during the operation, if any were recalled. The only recollection in common is that members of the unit did not expect noncombatant residents of the village to be there the next day. They expected instead to encounter elements of the 48th VC Battalion, their mission being to destroy it. Three defense witnesses interpreted Captain Medina's answer to a question whether women and children were to be considered as enemy as an affirmative directive to kill them. About twenty prosecution and defense witnesses had no recollection of any briefing directive to kill women and children. Whoever are correct, it is important to place Captain Medina's briefing remarks in the context of everyone's anticipation that the insertion of the ground force into My Lai (4) would be resisted by fire from elements of an enemy battalion. Appellant's testimony that during the operation Captain Medina ordered him by radio to kill villagers is not corroborated by the evidence given by third persons. The two radio operators for Captain Medina recalled no orders of that tenor being communicated by him. One had no recollection either way; the other testified positively that no order to kill or waste went over the unit net to Lieutenant Calley. Further, appellant said he ordered the squad leader Sergeant Bacon to search the bunkers which were mentioned in the first purported Medina-Calley radio conversation; and saw and spoke with Sergeant Bacon both before and after the second, telling him at that time where to deploy his squad. Sergeant Bacon, who had previously been called as a defense witness, denied having any contact with or communication from appellant at any of these times.

If the members found that appellant fabricated his claim of obedience to orders, their finding has abundant support in the record. If they found his claim of acting in obedience to orders to be credible, he would nevertheless not automatically be entitled to acquittal. Not every order is exonerating.

The trial judge's instructions under which he submitted the issues raised by evidence of obedience to orders were entirely correct. After fairly summarizing the evidence bearing on the question, he correctly informed the members as a matter of law that any order received by appellant directing him to kill unresisting Vietnamese within his control or within the control of his troops would have been illegal; that summary execution of detainees is forbidden by law. A determination of this sort, being a question of law only, is within the trial judge's province. Article 51(b), UCMJ, 10 USC @ 851(b); paragraph 57b, Manual, *supra*.

The instructions continued:

"The question does not rest there, however. A determination that an order is illegal does not, of itself, assign criminal responsibility to the person following the order for acts done in compliance with it. Soldiers are taught to follow orders, and special attention is given to obedience of orders on the battlefield. Military effectiveness depends upon obedience to orders. On the other hand, the obedience of a soldier is not the obedience of an automaton. A soldier is a reasoning agent, obliged to respond, not as a machine, but as a person. The law takes these factors into account in assessing criminal responsibility for acts done in compliance with illegal orders.

"The acts of a subordinate done in compliance with an unlawful order given him by his superior are excused and impose no criminal liability upon him unless the superior's order is one which a man of ordinary sense and understanding would, under the circumstances, know to be unlawful, or if the order in question is actually known to the accused to be unlawful."

Judge Kennedy amplified these principles by specifying the burden of proof and the logical sequence for consideration of the questions to be resolved. The members were told that if they found beyond reasonable doubt that appellant actually knew the orders under which he asserted he operated were illegal, the giving of the orders would be no defense; that the final aspect of the obedience question was more objective in nature, namely, that if orders to kill unresisting detainees were given, and if appellant acted in response thereto being unaware that the orders were illegal, he must be acquitted unless the members were satisfied beyond reasonable doubt that a man of ordinary sense and understanding would have known the orders to be unlawful.

. . . .

Judge Kennedy's instructions were sound and the members' findings correct. An order of the type appellant says he received is illegal. Its illegality is apparent upon even cursory evaluation by a man of ordinary sense and understanding. A finding that it is not exonerating should not be disturbed. [citations omitted]. Appellant's attempts to distinguish these cases fail. More candidly, he argues that they are all wrongly decided insofar as they import the objective standard of an order's illegality as would have been known by a man of ordinary sense and understanding. The argument is essentially that obedience to orders is a defense which strikes at mens rea; therefore in logic an obedient subordinate should be acquitted so long as he did not personally know of the order's illegality. Precedent aside, we would not agree with the argument. Heed must be given not only to subjective innocence-through-ignorance in the soldier, but to the consequences for his victims. Also, barbarism tends to invite reprisal to the detriment of our own force or disrepute which interferes with the achievement of war aims, even though the barbaric acts were preceded by orders for their commission. Casting the defense of obedience to orders solely in subjective terms of mens rea would operate practically to abrogate those objective restraints which are essential to functioning rules of war. The court members, after being given correct standards, properly rejected any defense of obedience to orders.

We find no impediment to the findings that appellant acted with murderous mens rea, including premeditation. The aggregate of all his contentions against the existence of murderous mens rea is no more absolving than a bare claim that he did not suspect he did any wrong act until after the operation, and indeed is not convinced of it yet. This is no excuse in law.

. . . .

Affirmed.

First Lieutenant Calley was originally sentenced to life imprisonment. The reviewing authority reduced the prison term to twenty years; the sentence was then mitigated to ten years by the Secretary of the Army. First Lieutenant Calley was released on parole prior to serving his entire ten year term. Captain Medina, First Lieutenant Calley's superior, was also tried for the murders at My Lai. At trial, the military judge instructed the jury regarding the culpability of Captain Medina.

After taking or issuing an order, a commander must remain alert and make timely adjustments as required by a changing situation. Furthermore, a commander is also responsible if he has actual knowledge that troops or other persons subject to his control are in the process of committing or are about to commit a war crime and he wrongfully fails to take the necessary and reasonable steps to insure compliance with the law of war. *You will observe that these legal requirements placed upon a commander require actual knowledge plus a wrongful failure to act.* Thus mere presence at the scene without knowledge will not suffice. That is, the commander-subordinate relationship alone will not allow an inference of knowledge. While it is not necessary that a commander actually see an atrocity being committed, *it is essential that he know that his subordinates are in the process of committing atrocities or about to commit atrocities.* [emphasis added].

Captain Medina was acquitted of the charges. Was the instruction to the jury in the *Medina* case in line with *Yamashita*? What are the differences in the two cases? Of the 25 soldiers charged with war crimes or related acts arising out of the My Lai incident, none, except First Lieutenant Calley, were convicted at court-martial. Does this present the same problem raised by the Leipzig trials following World War I?

PROSECUTION OF WAR CRIMES

Article 49 of the *1949 Geneva Convention for the Amelioration of the Conditions of the Wounded and Sick in Armed Forces in the Field* provides:

The High Contracting Parties undertake to enact any legislation necessary to provide effective penal sanctions for persons committing, or ordering to be committed, any of the grave breaches of the present Convention defined in the following Article.

Each High Contracting Party shall be under the obligation to search for persons alleged to have committed, or to have ordered to be committed, such grave breaches, and shall bring such persons, regardless of their nationality, before its own courts. It may also, if it prefers, and in accordance with the provisions of its own legislation, hand such persons over for trial to another High Contracting Party concerned, provided such High Contracting Party has made out a *prima facie case.*

Each High Contracting Party shall take measures necessary for the suppression of all acts contrary to the provisions of the present Convention other than the grave breaches defined in the following Article.

The United States satisfies its obligations described in the above section in several ways. The jurisdiction to try persons suspected of war crimes is addressed in the UCMJ:

Art. 18. Jurisdiction of general courts-martial

General courts-martial also have jurisdiction to try any person who by the law of war is subject to trial by a military tribunal and may adjudge any punishment permitted by the law of war.

Art. 21. Jurisdiction of courts-martial not exclusive.

The provisions of this chapter conferring jurisdiction upon courts-martial do not deprive military commissions, provost courts, or other military tribunals of concurrent with respect to offenders or offenses that by statute or by the law of war may be tried by military commissions, provost courts, or other military tribunals.

Based on the above provisions, forums other than courts-martial still have authority to hear war crimes cases. In what situations would the use of such forums be appropriate/advisable? Consider the following action taken by the United Nations with respect to the former Yugoslavia:

The Security Council,

. . . .

Expressing once again its grave concern at continuing reports of widespread and flagrant violations of international humanitarian law occurring within the territory of the former Yugoslavia, and especially in the Republic of Bosnia and Hercegovina, including reports of mass killings, massive, organized and systemic rape of women, and the continuance of the practice of "ethnic cleansing," including for the acquisition and the holding of territory,

. . . .

Believing, that the establishment of an international tribunal and the prosecution of persons responsible for the above-mentioned violations of international humanitarian law will contribute to ensuring that such violations are halted and effectively redressed,

. . . .

2. Decides hereby to establish an international tribunal for the sole purpose of prosecuting persons responsible for serious violations of international humanitarian law
   in the territory of the former Yugoslavia. . . .

To satisfy its obligations under the Geneva Conventions, the United States military requires training of all of its personnel on the law of war. Also, the Department of Defense requires the prompt reporting and investigation of alleged war crimes, as well as the appropriate disposition of such cases. *See* Department Of Defense Directive 5100.77.

STUDY QUESTIONS

1. What is a war crime? What is the difference between a grave and simple breach of the law of war?

2. What are the sources of war crimes law?

3. Which of the following categories of individuals may be held liable for war crimes?

   a. Individuals who actually commit war crimes.

   b. Individuals who order the commission of war crimes

   c. Superiors who did not know, but reasonably should have known, of the commission of war crimes by forces under their command, and failed to take action to stop them.

   d. All of the above.

   e. (a) and (b) only.

4. Which of the following statements is *FALSE* regarding "grave breaches" of the law of war (*see* Appendix 4)?

   a. They consist of serious violations such as willful killing, torture or inhumane treatment of protected persons.

   b. Signatories to the Geneva Conventions have an affirmative duty to search for and bring to trial persons alleged to have committed grave breaches.

   c. The statute of limitations for prosecuting grave breaches is 5 years from the date of the offense.

   d. U.S. service members who commit grave breaches are subject to prosecution under the UCMJ for the specific offending conduct (murder, rape, destruction of property, etc.)

   e. None of the above; they are all true statements.

5. Upon discovery of war crime activities, the discovering nation has the responsibility to:

   a. Prosecute the war criminal.

   b. Declare the war criminal as an undesirable and deport him.

   c. Turn over the war criminal to another nation for prosecution.

   d. Either (a) or (c).

   e. Either (a) or (c), but only if the prosecution occurs within 5 years, the statute of limitations period for grave breaches of the Geneva Conventions.

6. When, if ever, will the defense that the accused was following orders be successful? Could the defense ever work for killing noncombatants?

7. What other forums besides general courts-martial have jurisdiction to try suspected war criminals? What is the policy of United States regarding prosecution of its own service members for war crimes?

CONSTITUTION OF THE UNITED STATES

We the People of the United States, in Order to form a more perfect Union, establish Justice, insure domestic Tranquility, provide for the common defence, promote the general Welfare, and secure the Blessings of Liberty to ourselves and our Posterity, do ordain and establish this Constitution of the United States of America.

ARTICLE I

Section 1. All legislative Powers herein granted shall be vested in a Congress of the United States, which shall consist of a Senate and a House of Representatives.

Section 2. The House of Representatives shall be composed of Members chosen every second year by the people of the several states, and the Electors in each State shall have the Qualifications requisite for Electors of the most numerous Branch of the State Legislature.

No person shall be a Representative who shall not have attained to the Age of twenty-five Years, and been seven Years a Citizen of the United States, and who shall not, when elected, be an Inhabitant of that State in which he shall be chosen.

Representative and direct Taxes shall be apportioned among the several States which may be included within this Union, according to their respective Numbers, which shall be determined by adding to the whole Number of free Persons, including those bound to Service for a Term of Years, and excluding Indians not taxed, three fifths of all other Persons. The actual Enumeration shall be made within three Years after the first Meeting of the Congress of the United States, and within every subsequent Term of ten Years in such Manner as they shall by Law direct. The Number of Representatives shall not exceed one for every thirty Thousand, but each state shall have at Least one Representative; and until such enumeration shall be made, the state of New Hampshire shall be entitled to choose three, Massachusetts eight, Rhode Island and Providence Plantations one, Connecticut five, New York six, New Jersey four, Pennsylvania eight, Delaware one, Maryland six, Virginia ten, North Carolina five, South Carolina five, and Georgia three.

When vacancies happen in the Representation from any state, the Executive Authority thereof shall issue Writs of Election to fill such Vacancies.

The House of Representatives shall choose the Speaker and other officers; and shall have the sole power of Impeachment.

Section 3. The Senate of the United States shall be composed of two Senators from each State chosen by the Legislature thereof, for six Years and each Senator shall have one Vote.

Immediately after they shall be assembled in Consequence of the first Election, they shall be divided as equally as may be into three Classes. The Seats of the Senators of the first Class shall be vacated at the Expiration of the second Year, of the second Class at the Expiration of the fourth Year, and of the third Class at the Expiration of the sixth Year, so that one third may be chosen every second Year; and if Vacancies happen by Resignation, or otherwise during the Recess of the Legislature of any State, the Executive thereof may make temporary Appointments until the next Meeting of the Legislature, which shall then fill such Vacancies.

No person shall be a Senator who shall not have attained to the Age of thirty Years, and been nine Years a Citizen of the United States, who shall not, when elected, be an Inhabitant of that State for which he shall be chosen.

The Vice-President of the United States shall be President of the Senate, but shall have no Vote unless they be equally divided.

The Senate shall choose their other Officers, and also a President pro tempore, in the Absence of the Vice-President, or when he shall exercise the Office of President of the United States.

The Senate shall have the sole Power to try all Impeachments. When sitting for that Purpose, they shall be on Oath or Affirmation. When the President of the United States is tried, the Chief Justice shall preside: And no Person shall be convicted without the Concurrence of two-thirds of the Members present.

Judgement in Cases of Impeachment shall not extend further than to removal from Office and disqualification to hold and enjoy any Office of honor, Trust or Profit under the United States; but the Party convicted shall nevertheless be liable and subject to Indictment, Trial, Judgment and Punishment, according to Law.

Section 4. The Times, Places and Manner of holding Elections for Senators and Representatives, shall be prescribed in each State by the Legislature thereof: but the Congress may at any time by Law make or alter such Regulations, except as to the Places of choosing Senators.

The Congress shall assemble at least once in every Year, and such Meeting shall be on the first Monday in December, unless they shall by Law appoint a different Day.

Section 5. Each House shall be the Judge of the Elections, Returns and Qualifications of its own Members, and a Majority of each shall constitute a Quorum to do Business; but a smaller Number may adjourn from day to day, and may be authorized to compel the Attendance of absent Members, in such Manner, and under such Penalties as each House may provide.

Each House may determine the Rules of its Proceedings, punish its Members for disorderly Behaviour, and with the Concurrence of two-thirds, expel a Member.

Each House shall keep a Journal of its Proceedings, and from time to time publish the same, excepting such Parts as may in their Judgment require Secrecy; and the Yeas and Nays of the Members either House on any question shall, at the Desire of one fifth of those Present be entered on the Journal.

Neither House, during the Session of Congress shall, without the Consent of the other, adjourn for more than three days, nor to any other Place than that in which the two Houses shall be sitting.

Section 6. The Senators and Representatives shall receive a Compensation for their Services, to be ascertained by

Law, and paid out of the Treasury of the United States. They shall in all Cases, except Treason, Felony and Breach of the Peace, be privileged from Arrest during their Attendance at the Session of their respective Houses, and in going to and returning from the same; and for any Speech or Debate in either House, they shall not be questioned in any other Place.

No Senator or Representative shall, during the Time for which he is elected, be appointed to any Civil Office under the Authority of the United States, which shall have been created, or the Emoluments whereof shall have been increased during such time; and no Person holding any Office under the United States, shall be a Member of either House during his Continuance in Office.

Section 7. All Bills for raising Revenue shall originate in the House of Representatives; but the Senate may propose or concur with Amendments as on other Bills.

Every Bill which shall have passed the House of Representatives and the Senate, shall, before it become a Law, be presented to the President of the United States; if he approve he shall sign it, but if not he shall return it, with his Objections to that House in which it shall have originated, who shall enter the Objections at large on their Journal, and proceed to reconsider it. If after such Reconsideration two-thirds of that House shall agree to pass the Bill, it shall be sent, together with the Objections, to the other House, by which it shall likewise be reconsidered, and if approved by two-thirds of that House, it shall become a Law. But in all such Cases the Votes of Both Houses shall be determined by Yeas and Nays, and the Names of the Persons voting for and against the Bill shall be entered on the Journal of each House respectively. If any Bill shall not be returned by the President within ten Days (Sundays excepted) after it shall have been presented to him, the Same shall be a Law, in like Manner as if he had signed it, unless the Congress by their Adjournment prevent its Return, in which Case it shall not be a Law.

Every Order, Resolution, or Vote to which the Concurrence of the Senate and House of Representatives may be necessary (except on a question of Adjournment) shall be presented to the President of the United States; and before the Same shall take Effect, shall be approved by him, or being disapproved by him, shall be repassed by two thirds of the Senate and House of Representatives, according to the Rules and Limitations prescribed in the Case of a Bill.

Section 8. The Congress shall have Power To lay and collect Taxes, Duties, Imposts and Excises, to pay the Debts and provide for the common Defence and general Welfare of the United States; but all Duties, Imposts and Excises shall be uniform throughout the United States.

To borrow Money on the credit of the United States;

To regulate Commerce with foreign Nations, and among the several States, and with the Indian Tribes;

To establish an uniform rule of Naturalization, and uniform Laws on the subject of Bankruptcies throughout the United States;

To coin Money, regulate the Value thereof, and of foreign coin, and fix the Standard of Weights and Measures;

To provide for the Punishment of counterfeiting the Securities and current Coin of the United States;

To establish Post Offices and post Roads;

To promote the Progress of Science and useful Arts, by securing for limited Times to Authors and Inventors the exclusive Right to their respective Writings and Discoveries;

To constitute Tribunals inferior to the supreme Court;

To define and punish Piracies and Felonies committed on the high Seas, and Offenses against the Law of Nations;

To declare War, grant Letters of Marque and Reprisal, and make Rules concerning Captures on Land and Water;

To raise and support Armies, but no Appropriation of Money to that use shall be for a longer Term than two Years;

To provide and maintain a Navy;

To make Rules for the Government and Regulation of the land and naval Forces;

To provide for calling forth the Militia to execute the Laws of the Union, suppress Insurrections and repel Invasions.;

To provide for organizing, arming, and disciplining, the Militia, and for governing such Part of them as may be employed in the Service of the United States, reserving to the States respectively, the Appointment of the Officers, and the Authority of training the Militia according to the discipline prescribed by Congress;

To exercise exclusive Legislation in all Cases whatsoever, over such District (not exceeding ten Miles square) as may, by Cession of particular States, and the Acceptance of Congress, become the Seat of the Government of the United States, and to exercise like Authority over all Places purchased by the Consent of the Legislature of the States in which the Same shall be, for the Erection of Forts, Magazines, Arsenals, dock-Yards, and other needful Buildings; And

To make all Laws which shall be necessary and proper for carrying into Execution the foregoing Powers, and all other Powers vested by the Constitution in the Government of the United States, or in any Department or Officer thereof.

Section 9. The Migration or Importation of such Persons as any of the States now existing shall think proper to admit, shall not be prohibited by the Congress prior to the Year one thousand eight hundred and eight, but a Tax or duty may be imposed on such Importation, not exceeding ten dollars for each Person.

Privilege of the Writ of Habeas Corpus shall not be suspended, unless when in Cases of Rebellion or Invasion the public Safety require it.

No Bill of Attainder or ex post facto Law shall be passed.

No Capitation, or other direct, Tax shall be laid, unless in Proportion to the Census or Enumeration herein before directed to be taken.

No Tax or Duty shall be laid on Articles exported from any State.

No Preference shall be given by any Regulation of Commerce or Revenue to the Ports of one State over those of another: nor shall Vessels bound to, or from, one State, be obliged to enter, clear, or pay Duties in another.

No Money shall be drawn from the Treasury, but in Consequence of Appropriations made by Law; and a regular Statement and Account of the Receipts and Expenditures of all public Money shall be published from time to time.

No Title of Nobility shall be granted by the United States: And no Person holding any Office of Profit or Trust under them, shall, without the Consent of the Congress, accept of any present, Emolument, Office, or Title, of any kind whatever, from any King, Prince, or foreign State.

Section 10. No State shall enter into any Treaty, Alliance, or Confederation; grant Letters of Marque and Reprisal; coin Money; emit Bills of Credit; make any Thing but gold and silver Coin a Tender in Payment of Debts; pass any Bill of Attainder, ex post facto Law, or Law impairing the Obligation of Contracts, or grant any Title of Nobility.

No State shall, without the Consent of the Congress, lay any Imposts or Duties on Imports or Exports, except what may be absolutely necessary for executing its inspection Laws; and the net Produce of all Duties and Imports, laid by any State on Imports or Exports, shall be for the Use of the Treasury of the United States; all such Laws shall be subject to the Revision and Control of the Congress.

No State shall, without the Consent of Congress, lay any Duty of Tonnage, keep Troops, or Ships of War in time of Peace, enter into any Agreement or Compact with another State, or with a foreign Power, or engage in War, unless actually invaded, or in such imminent Danger as will not admit of delay.

ARTICLE II

Section 1. The executive Power shall be vested in a President of the United States and, together with the Vice President, chosen for the same Term, be elected as follows.

Each State shall appoint, in such Manner as the Legislature thereof may direct, a Number of Electors, equal to the whole Number of Senators and Representatives to which the State may be entitled in the Congress: but no Senator or Representative, or Person holding an Office of Trust or Profit under the United States, shall be appointed an Elector.

The Electors shall meet in their respective States, and vote by Ballot for two Persons, of whom one at least shall not be an Inhabitant of the same State with themselves. And they shall make a List of all the Persons voted for, and of the Number of Votes for each; which List they shall sign and certify, and transmit sealed to the Seat of the Government of the United States, directed to the President of the Senate. The President of the Senate shall, in the Presence of the Senate and House of Representatives, open all the Certificates, and the Votes shall then be counted. The Person having the greatest Number of Votes shall be the President, if such Number be a Majority of the whole Number of Electors appointed; and if there be more than one who have such Majority, and have an equal Number of Electors appointed; and if there be more than one who have such Majority, and have an equal Number of Votes, then the House of Representatives shall immediately choose by Ballot one of them for President; and if no Person have a Majority, then from the five highest on the List the said House shall in like Manner choose the President. But in choosing the President, the Votes shall be taken by States, the Representation from each State having one Vote; a quorum for this Purpose shall consist of a Member or Members from two thirds of the States, and a Majority of all the states shall be necessary to a choice. In every case, after the Choice of the President, the Person having the greatest Number of Votes of the Electors shall be the Vice President. But if there should remain two or more who have equal Votes, the Senate shall choose from them by Ballot the Vice President.

The Congress may determine the Time of the choosing the Electors, and the Day on which they shall give their Votes; which Day shall be the same throughout the United States.

No Person except a natural born Citizen, or a Citizen of the United States, at the time of the Adoption of this Constitution, shall be eligible to the Office of President; neither shall any Person be eligible to that Office who shall not have attained to the Age of thirty five Years, and been fourteen Years a Resident within the United States.

In Case of the Removal of the President from Office, or his Death, Resignation, or Inability to discharge the Powers and Duties of the said Office, the Same shall devolve on the Vice President, and the Congress may by Law provide for the Case of Removal, Death, Resignation or Inability, both of the President and Vice President, declaring what Officer shall then act as President, and such Officer shall act accordingly, until the Disability be removed, or a President be elected.

The President shall, at stated Times, receive for his Services, a Compensation, which shall neither be increased nor diminished during the Period for which he shall have been elected, and he shall not receive within a Period any other Emolument from the United States, or any of them.

Before he enter on the Execution of his Office, he shall take the following Oath or Affirmation: "I do solemnly swear (or affirm) that I will faithfully execute the Office of President of the United States, and will to the best of my Ability, preserve, protect and defend the Constitution of the United States."

Section 2. The President shall be Commander in Chief of the Army and Navy of the United States, and of the Militia of the several States, when called into the actual Service of the United States; he may require the Opinion, in writing of the principal Officer in each of the executive Departments, upon any Subject relating to the Duties of their respective Offices, and he shall have power to grant Reprieves and Pardons for Offenses against the United States, except in Cases of Impeachment.

He shall have Power, by and with the Advice and Consent of the Senate, to make Treaties, provided two thirds of the Senators present concur; and he shall nominate, and by and with the Advice and Consent of the Senate, shall appoint Ambassadors, other public Ministers and Consuls, Judges of the supreme Court, and all other Officers of the United States, whose Appointments are not herein otherwise provided for, and which shall be established by Law. But the Congress may by law vest the Appointment of such inferior Officers, as they think proper, in the President alone, in the Courts of Law, or in the Heads of Departments.

The President shall have Power to fill up all Vacancies that may happen during the Recess of the Senate, by granting Commissions which shall expire at the End of their Session.

Section 3. He shall from time to time give to the Congress Information of the State of the Union, and recommend to their Consideration such Measures as he shall judge necessary and expedient; he may, on extraordinary Occasions, convene both Houses, or either of them, and in Case of Disagreement between them, with Respect to the Time of Adjournment, he may adjourn them to such Time as he shall think proper; he shall receive Ambassadors and other public Ministers; he shall take Care that the Laws be faithfully executed, and shall Commission all the Officers of the United States.

Section 4. The President, Vice President and all civil Officers of the United States, shall be removed from Office on Impeachment for, and Conviction of, Treason, Bribery, or other high Crimes and Misdemeanors.

ARTICLE III

Section 1. The judicial Power of the United States shall be vested in one Supreme Court, and in such inferior courts as the Congress may from time to time ordain and establish. The Judges, both of the Supreme and inferior Courts, shall hold their Offices during good Behavior, and shall, at stated Times, receive for their Services a Compensation which shall not be diminished during their Continuance in Office.

Section 2. The judicial Power shall extend to all Cases, in Law and Equity, arising under this Constitution, the Laws of the United States, and Treaties made, or which shall be made, under their Authority; to all Cases affecting Ambassadors, other public Ministers, and Consuls; to all Cases of admiralty and maritime Jurisdiction; to Controversies to which the United States shall be a Party; to Controversies between two or more States, between a State and Citizens of another State, between Citizens of different States, between Citizens of the same State claiming Lands under Grants of different States, and between a State or the Citizens thereof, and foreign States, Citizens, or Subjects.

In all Cases affecting Ambassadors, other public Ministers and Consuls, and those in which a State shall be a Party, the Supreme Court shall have original Jurisdiction. In all the other Cases before mentioned, the Supreme Court shall have appellate Jurisdiction, both as to Law and Fact, with such Exceptions and under such Regulations as the Congress shall make.

The Trial of all Crimes, except in Cases of Impeachment, shall be by Jury; and such Trial shall be held in the State where the said Crimes shall have been committed; but when not committed within any State the Trial shall be at such Place or Places as the Congress may by Law have directed.

Section 3. Treason against the United States shall consist only in levying War against them, or in adhering to their Enemies, giving them Aid and Comfort. No Person shall be convicted of Treason unless on the Testimony of two Witnesses to the same overt Act, or on Confession in open Court.

The Congress shall have Power to declare the Punishment of Treason, but no Attainder of Treason shall work Corruption of Blood, or Forfeiture except during the Life of the Person attained.

ARTICLE IV

Section 1. Full Faith and Credit shall be given in each State to the public Act, Records, and judicial Proceedings of every other State. And the Congress may, by general Laws, prescribe the Manner in which such Acts, Records, and Proceedings shall be proved, and the Effect thereof.

Section 2. The Citizens of each State shall be entitled to all Privileges and Immunities of Citizens in the several States.

A Person charged in any State with Treason, Felony, or other Crime, who shall flee from Justice, and be found in another State, shall, on Demand of the executive Authority of the State from which he fled, be delivered up, to be removed to the State having Jurisdiction of the Crime.

No Person held to Service or Labor in one State, under the Laws thereof, escaping into another, shall, in Consequence of any

Law or Regulation therein, be discharged from such Service or Labor, but shall be delivered up on Claim of the Party to whom such Service or Labor may be due.

Section 3. New States may be admitted by the Congress into this Union; but no new State shall be formed or erected within the Jurisdiction of any other State, nor any State be formed by the Junction of two or more States, or Parts of States, without the Consent of the Legislatures of the States concerned as well as of the Congress.

The Congress shall have Power to dispose of and make all needful Rules and Regulations respecting the Territory or other Property belonging to the United States; and nothing in this Constitution shall be so construed as to Prejudice any Claims of the United States, or of any particular State.

Section 4. The United States shall guarantee to every State in this Union a Republican Form of Government, and shall protect each of them against Invasion; and on Application of the Legislature, or of the Executive (when the Legislature cannot be convened), against domestic Violence.

ARTICLE V

The Congress, whenever two thirds of both House shall deem it necessary, shall propose Amendments to this Constitution, or, on the Application of the Legislatures of two thirds of the several States, shall call a Convention for proposing Amendments, which, in either Case, shall be valid, to all intents and Purposes, as Part of this Constitution, when ratified by the Legislatures of three fourths of the several States, or by Conventions in three fourths thereof, as the one or the other Mode of Ratification may be proposed by the Congress; Provided that no Amendment which may be made prior to the Year One thousand eight hundred and eight shall in any Manner af-

fect the first and fourth Clauses in the Ninth Section of the first Article; and that no State, without its Consent, shall be deprived of its equal Suffrage in the Senate.

ARTICLE VI

All Debts contracted and Engagements entered into, before the Adoption of this Constitution, shall be as valid against the United States under this Constitution, as under the Confederation.

This Constitution, and the Laws of the United States which shall be made in Pursuance thereof, and all Treaties made, or which shall be made, under the Authority of the United States, shall be the supreme Law of the Land; and the Judges in every State shall be bound thereby, Anything in the Constitution or Laws of any State to the Contrary notwithstanding.

The Senators and Representatives before mentioned, and the Members of the several State Legislatures, and all executive and judicial Officers, both of the United States and of the several States, shall be bound, by Oath or Affirmation, to support this Constitution; but no religious Test shall ever be required as a Qualification to any Office or public Trust under the United States.

ARTICLE VII

The Ratification of the Conventions of nine States shall be sufficient for the Establishment of this Constitution between the States so ratifying the Same.

Articles in Addition to, and Amendment of, the Constitution of the United States of America, Proposed by Congress, and Ratified by the Legislatures of the Several States Pursuant to the Fifth Article of the Original Constitution

AMENDMENT I

Congress shall make no law respecting an establishment of religion, or prohibiting the free exercise thereof; or abridging the freedom of speech, or of the press; or the right of the people peaceably to assemble, and to petition the Government for a redress of grievances.

AMENDMENT II

A well-regulated Militia being necessary to the security of a free State, the right of the people to keep and bear Arms, shall not be infringed.

AMENDMENT III

No Soldier shall, in time of peace, be quartered in any house, without the consent of the Owner; nor in time of war, but in a manner to be prescribed by law.

AMENDMENT IV

The right of the people to be secure in their persons, houses, papers, and effects, against unreasonable searches and seizures, shall not be violated; and no Warrants shall issue, but upon probable cause, supported by Oath or affirmation, and particularly describing the place to be searched and the persons or things to be seized.

AMENDMENT V

No person shall be held to answer for a capital, or otherwise infamous, crime, unless on a presentment or indictment of a Grand Jury, except in cases arising in the land or naval forces, or in the Militia, when in actual service, in time of War, or public danger; nor shall any person be subject, for the same offence, to be twice put in jeopardy of life or limb; nor shall be compelled in any criminal case to be a witness against himself nor be deprived of life, liberty, or property, without due process of law; nor shall private property be taken for public use, without just compensation.

AMENDMENT VI

In all criminal prosecutions, the accused shall enjoy the right to a speedy and public trial, by an impartial jury of the State and district wherein the crime shall have been committed, which district shall have been previously ascertained by law; and to be informed of the nature and cause of the accusation; to be confronted with the witnesses against him; to have compulsory process for obtaining witnesses in his favor; and to have the Assistance of Counsel for his defence.

AMENDMENT VII

In Suits at common law, where the value in controversy shall exceed twenty dollars, the right of trial by jury shall be preserved; and no fact, tried by a jury, shall be otherwise reexamined in any Court of the United States than according to the rules of the common law.

AMENDMENT VIII

Excessive bail shall not be required, nor excessive fines imposed, nor cruel and unusual punishment inflicted.

AMENDMENT IX

The enumeration in the Constitution of certain rights shall not be construed to deny or disparage others retained by the people.

AMENDMENT X

The powers not delegated to the United States by the Constitution, nor prohibited by it to the States, are reserved to the States respectively or to the people.

AMENDMENT XI

The Judicial power of the United States shall not be construed to extend to any suit in law or equity, commenced or prosecuted against one of the United States by Citizens of another State or by Citizens or Subjects of any Foreign State.

AMENDMENT XII

The Electors shall meet in their respective States, and vote by ballot for President and Vice President, one of whom, at least, shall not be an inhabitant of the same State with themselves; they shall name in their ballots the person voted for as President, and in distinct ballots the person voted for as Vice-President; and they shall make distinct lists of all persons voted for as President, and of all persons voted for as Vice-President, and of the number of votes for each, which lists they shall sign, and certify, and transmit, sealed, to the seat of the government of the United States, directed to the President of the Senate; the President of the Senate shall, in the presence of the Senate and the House of Representatives, open all the certificates, and the votes shall then be counted; the person having the greatest number of votes for President shall be the President, if such number be a majority of the whole number of Electors appointed; and if no person have such a majority, then, from the persons having the highest numbers, not exceeding three on the list of those voted for a President, the House of Representatives shall choose immediately, by ballot, the President. But in choosing the President, the votes shall be taken by States, the rep-resentation from each State having one vote; a quorum for this purpose shall consist of a member or members from two-thirds of the States, and a majority of all the States shall be necessary to a choice. And if the House of Representatives shall not choose a President, whenever the right of choice shall devolve upon them, before the fourth day of March next following, the Vice-President shall act as President, as in case of death, or other constitutional disability of the President. The person having the greatest number of votes as Vice-President, shall be the Vice-President, if such number be a majority of the whole number of Electors appointed; and if no person have a majority, then, from the two highest numbers on the list, the Senate shall choose the Vice-President; a quorum for the purpose shall consist of two-thirds of the whole number of Senators; a majority of the whole number shall be necessary to a choice. But no person constitutionally ineligible to the office of President shall be eligible to that of Vice-President of the United States.

AMENDMENT XIII

Section 1. Neither slavery nor involuntary servitude, except as a punishment for crime, whereof the party shall have been duly convicted, shall exist within the United States, or any place subject to their jurisdiction.

Section 2. Congress shall have power to enforce this article by appropriate legislation.

AMENDMENT XIV

Section 1. All persons born or naturalized in the United States, and subject to the jurisdiction thereof, are citizens of the United States and of the State wherein they reside. No State shall make or enforce any law which shall abridge the privileges or immunities of citizens of the United States; nor shall any State deprive any person of life, liberty, or property, without due process of law, nor deny any person within its jurisdiction the equal protection of the laws.

Section 2. Representatives shall be apportioned among the several States according to their respective numbers, counting the whole number of persons in each State, excluding Indians not taxed. But when the right to vote at any election for the choice of electors for President and Vice-President of the United States, Representatives in Congress, the Executive and Judicial officers of a State, or the members of the Legislature thereof, is denied to any of the male inhabitants of such State, being twenty one years of age, and citizens of the United States, or in any way abridged, except for participation in rebellion or other crime, the basis of representation therein shall be reduced in the proportion which the number of such male citizens shall bear to the whole number of male citizens twenty one years of age in such State.

Section 3. No person shall be a Senator or Representative in Congress, or elector of President and Vice President, or hold any office, civil or military, under the United States, or under any State, who, having previously taken an oath, as a Member of Congress, or as an officer of the United States, or as a member of any State legislature, or as an executive or judicial officer of any State, to support the Constitution of the United States, shall have engaged in insurrection or rebellion against the same, or given aid or comfort to the enemies thereof. But Congress may, by a vote of two thirds of each House, remove such disability.

Section 4. The validity of the public debt of the United States, authorized by law, including debts incurred for payment of pensions and bounties for services in suppressing insurrection or rebellion, shall not be questioned. But neither the United States nor any State shall assume or pay any debt or obligation incurred in aid of insurrection or rebellion against the United States, or any claim for the loss or emancipation of any slave; but all such debts, obligations, and claims shall be held illegal and void.

Section 5. The Congress shall have power to enforce, by appropriate legislation, the provisions of this article.

AMENDMENT XV

Section 1. The right of citizens of the United States to vote shall not be denied or abridged by the United States or by any State on account of race, color, or previous condition of servitude.

Section 2. The Congress shall have power to enforce this article by appropriate legislation.

AMENDMENT XVI

The Congress shall have power to lay and collect taxes on incomes, from whatever source derived, without apportionment among the several States and without regard to any census or enumeration.

AMENDMENT XVII

The Senate of the United States shall be composed of two Senators from each State, elected by the people thereof, for six years; and each Senator shall have one vote. The electors in each State shall have the qualifications requisite for electors of the most numerous branch of the State legislatures.

When vacancies happen in the representation of any State in the Senate, the executive authority of such State shall issue writs of election to fill such vacancies: Provided, That the legislature of any State may empower the executive thereof to make temporary appointment until the people fill the vacancies by election as the legislature may direct.

This amendment shall not be so construed as to affect the election or term of any Senator chosen before it becomes valid as part of the Constitution.

AMENDMENT XVIII

Section 1. After one year from the ratification of this article the manufacture, sale or transportation of intoxicating liquors within, the importation thereof into, or the exportation thereof from the United States and all territory subject to the jurisdiction thereof for beverage purposes is hereby prohibited.

Section 2. The Congress and the several States shall have concurrent power to enforce this article by appropriate legislation.

Section 3. This article shall be inoperative unless it shall have been ratified as an amendment to the Constitution by the legislatures of the several States, as provided in the Constitution, within seven years of the date of the submission hereof to the States by Congress.

AMENDMENT XIX

The right of citizens of the United States to vote shall not be denied or abridged by the United States or by State on account of sex.

Congress shall have power to enforce this article by appropriate legislation.

AMENDMENT XX

Section 1. The terms of the President and Vice President shall end at noon on the 20th day of January, and the terms of Senators and Representatives at noon on the 3d day of January, of the years in which such terms would have ended if this article had not ratified; and the terms of their successors shall then begin.

Section 2. The Congress shall assemble at least once in every year, and such meeting shall begin at noon on the 3d day of January, unless they shall by law appoint a different day.

Section 3. If, at the time fixed for the beginning of the term of the President, the President-elect shall have died, the Vice President-elect shall become President. If a President shall not have been chosen before the time fixed for the beginning of his term, or if the President-elect shall have failed to qualify, then the Vice President-elect shall act as President until a President shall have qualified; and the Congress may by law provide for the case wherein neither a President-elect nor a Vice President-elect shall have qualified, declaring who shall then act as President, or the manner in which one who is to act shall be selected, and such person shall act accordingly until a President or Vice President shall have qualified.

Section 4. The Congress may by law provide for the case of the death of any of the persons from whom the House of Representatives may choose a President whenever the right of choice shall have devolved upon them, and for the case of the death of any of the persons from whom the Senate may choose a Vice President whenever the right of choice shall have devolved upon them.

Section 5. Sections 1 and 2 shall take effect on the 15th day of October following the ratification of this article.

Section 6. This article shall be inoperative unless it shall have been ratified as an amendment to the Constitution by three fourths of the several States within seven years from the date of its submission.

AMENDMENT XXI

Section 1. The eighteenth article of amendment to the Constitution of the United States is hereby repealed.

Section 2. The transportation or importation into any State, Territory, or possession of the United States for delivery or use therein of intoxicating liquors, in violation of the laws thereof, is hereby prohibited.

Section 3. This article shall be inoperative unless it shall have been ratified as an amendment to the Constitution by conventions in the several States, as provided in the Constitution, within seven years from the date of the submission hereof to the States by the Congress.

AMENDMENT XXII

Section 1. No person shall be elected to the office of the President more than twice, and no person who has held the office of President, or acted as President, for more than two years of a term to which some other person was elected President shall be elected to the office of the President more than once. But this Article shall not apply to any person holding the office of President when this Article was proposed by the Congress, and shall not prevent any person who may be holding the office of President, or acting as President, during the term within which this Article becomes operative from holding the office of President or acting as President during the remainder of such term.

Section 2. This article shall be inoperative unless it shall have been ratified as an amendment to the Constitution by the legislatures of three-fourths of the several States within seven years from the date of its submission to the States by the Congress.

AMENDMENT XXIII

Section 1. The District constituting the seat of Government of the United States shall appoint in such manner as the Congress may direct:

A number of electors of President and Vice President equal to the whole number of Senators and Representative in Congress to which the District would be entitled if it were a State, but in no event more than the least populous State; they shall be considered, for the purposes of the election of President and Vice President, to be electors appointed by a State; and they shall meet in the District and perform such duties as provided by the twelfth article of amendment.

Section 2. The Congress shall have power to enforce this article by appropriate legislation.

AMENDMENT XXIV

Section 1. The right of citizens of the United States to vote in any primary or other election for President or Vice President, for electors for President or Vice President, or for Senator or Representative in Congress, shall not be denied or abridged by the United States or any State by reason of failure to pay any poll tax or other tax.

Section 2. The Congress shall have power to enforce this article by appropriate legislation.

AMENDMENT XXV

Section 1. In case of the removal of the President from office or of his death or resignation, the Vice President shall become President.

Section 2. Whenever there is a vacancy in the office of the Vice President, the President shall nominate a Vice President who shall take office upon confirmation by a majority vote of both Houses of Congress.

Section 3. Whenever the President transmits to the President pro tempore of the Senate and the Speakers of the House of Representatives his written declaration that he is unable to discharge the powers and duties of his office, and until he transmits to them a written declaration to the contrary, such powers and duties shall be discharged by the Vice President as Acting President.

Section 4. Whenever the Vice President and a majority of either the principal officers of the executive departments or of such other body as Congress may by law provide, transmit to the President pro tempore of the Senate and the Speaker of the House of Representatives their written declaration that the President is unable to discharge the powers and duties of his office, the Vice President shall immediately assume the powers and duties of the office as Acting President.

Thereafter, when the President transmits to the President pro tempore of the Senate and the Speaker of the House of Representatives his written declaration that no inability exists, he shall resume the powers and duties of his office unless the Vice President and a majority of either principal officers of the executive department or of such other body as Congress may by law provide, transmit within four days to the President pro tempore of the Senate and the Speaker of the House of Representatives their written declaration that the President is unable to discharge the powers and duties of his office. Thereupon Congress shall decide the issue, assembling within forty eight hours for that purpose if not in session. If the Congress, within twenty one days after Congress is required to assemble, determines by two thirds vote of both Houses that the President is unable to discharge the powers and duties of his office, the Vice President shall continue to discharge the same as Acting President; otherwise, the President shall resume the powers and duties of his office.

AMENDMENT XXVI

Section 1. The right of citizens of the United States, who are eighteen years of age or older, to vote shall not be denied or abridged by the United States or by any State on account of age.

Section 2. The Congress shall have the power to enforce this article by appropriate legislation.

APPENDIX 2

MANUAL FOR COURTS-MARTIAL (MCM)

MAXIMUM PUNISHMENT CHART

Article	Offense	Discharge	Confinement	Forfeitures
82	Solicitation			
	If solicited offense committed, or attempted, *see* Part IV, ¶ 6.e.			
	If solicited offense not committed:			
	Solicitation to desert[1]	DD, BCD	3 yrs.[1]	Total
	Solicitation to mutiny[1]	DD, BCD	10 yrs.[1]	Total
	Solicitation to commit act of misbehavior before enemy[1]	DD, BCD	10 yrs.[1]	Total
	Solicitation to commit act of sedition[1]	DD, BCD	10 yrs.[1]	Total
83	Fraudulent enlistment, appointment	DD, BCD	2 yrs.	Total
	Fraudulent separation	DD, BCD	5 yrs.	Total
84	Effecting unlawful enlistment, appointment, separation	DD, BCD	5 yrs.	Total
85	Desertion			
	Intent to avoid hazardous duty, shirk important service[1]	DD, BCD	5 yrs.[1]	Total
	Other cases			
	Terminated by apprehension	DD, BCD	3 yrs.[1]	Total
	Otherwise terminated	DD, BCD	2 yrs.[1]	Total
86	Absence without leave, etc.			

Article	*Offense*	*Discharge*	*Confinement*	*Forfeitures*
	Failure to go, going from place of duty	None	1 mo.	2/3 1 mo.
	Absence from unit, organization, etc.			
	Not more than 3 days	None	1 mo.	2/3 1 mo.
	More than 3, not more than 30 days	None	6 mos.	2/3 6 mos.
	More than 30 days	DD, BCD	1 yr.	Total
	More than 30 days and terminated by apprehension	DD, BCD	1 yr., 6 mos.	Total
	Absence from guard or watch	None	3 mos.	2/3 3 mos.
	Absence from guard or watch with intent to abandon	BCD	6 mos.	Total
	Absence with intent to avoid maneuvers, field exercises	BCD	6 mos.	Total
87	Missing movement			
	Through design	DD, BCD	2 yrs.	Total
	Through neglect	BCD	1 yr.	Total
88	Contempt toward officials	Dismissal	1 yr.	Total
89	Disrespect toward superior commissioned officer	BCD	1 yr.	Total
90	Assaulting, willfully disobeying superior commissioned officer			
	Striking, drawing or lifting up any weapon or offering any violence toward superior commissioned officer execution of duty[1]	DD, BCD	10 yrs.[1]	Total
	Willfully disobeying lawful order of superior commissioned officer[1]	DD, BCD	5 yrs.[1]	Total
91	Insubordinate conduct toward warrant, noncommissioned, petty officer			
	Striking or assaulting:			
	Warrant officer	DD, BCD	5 yrs.	Total

Article	Offense	Discharge	Confinement	Forfeitures
	Superior noncommissioned officer	DD, BCD	3 yrs.	Total
	Other noncommissioned or petty officer	DD, BCD	1 yr.	Total
	Willfully disobeying:			
	Warrant officer	DD, BCD	2 yrs.	Total
	Noncommissioned or petty officer	BCD	1 yr.	Total
	Contempt, disrespect toward:			
	Warrant Officer	BCD	9 mos.	Total
	Superior noncommissioned or petty officer	BCD	6 mos.	Total
	Other noncommissioned or petty officer	None	3 mos.	2/3 3 mos.
92	Failure to obey order, regulation			
	Violation, failure to obey general order or regulation[2]	DD, BCD	2 yrs.	Total
	Violation, failure to obey other order[2]	BCD	6 mos.	Total
	Dereliction in performance of duties			
	Through neglect, culpable inefficiency	None	3 mos.	2/3 3 mos.
	Willful	BCD	6 mos.	Total
93	Cruelty, maltreatment of subordinates	DD, BCD	1 yr.	Total
94	Mutiny & sedition	Death, DD, BCD	Life	Total
95	Resisting apprehension, breach of arrest; escape			
	Resisting apprehension	BCD	1 yr.	Total
	Breaking arrest	BCD	6 mos.	Total
	Escape from custody, pretrial confinement, or confinement on bread and water or diminished rations	DD, BCD	1 yr.	Total

Article	Offense	Discharge	Confinement	Forfeitures
	Escape from post-trial confinement	DD, BCD	5 yrs.	Total
96	Releasing prisoner without proper authority	DD, BCD	2 yrs.	Total
	Suffering prisoner to escape through neglect	BCD	1 yr.	Total
	Suffering prisoner to escape through design	DD, BCD	2 yrs.	Total
97	Unlawful detention	DD, BCD	3 yrs.	Total
98	Noncompliance with procedural rules, etc.			
	Unnecessary delay in disposition of case	BCD	6 mos.	Total
	Knowingly, intentionally failing to comply, enforce code	DD, BCD	5 yrs.	Total
99	Misbehavior before enemy	Death, DD, BCD	Life	Total
100	Subordinate compelling surrender	Death, DD, BCD	Life	Total
101	Improper use of countersign	Death, DD, BCD	Life	Total
102	Forcing safeguard	Death, DD, BCD	Life	Total
103	Captured, abandoned property; failure to secure, etc.			
	Of value of $100 or less	BCD	6 mos.	Total
	Of value of more than $100	DD, BCD	5 yrs.	Total
	Looting, pillaging	DD, BCD	Life	Total
104	Aiding the enemy	Death, DD, BCD	Life	Total
105	Misconduct as prisoner	DD, BCD	Life	Total
106	Spying	Mandatory Death, DD, BCD	Not applicable	Total
106a	Espionage			
	Cases listed in Art. 106a(a)(1)(A)-(D)	Death, DD, BCD	Life	Total

Article	Offense	Discharge	Confinement	Forfeitures
	Other cases	DD, BCD	Life	Total
107	False official statements	DD, BCD	5 yrs.	Total
108	Military property; loss, damage, destruction, disposition			
	Selling, otherwise disposing			
	Of value of $100 or less	BCD	1 yr.	Total
	Of value of more than $100	DD, BCD	10 yrs.	Total
	Any firearm, explosive or incendiary device	DD, BCD	10 yrs.	Total
	Damaging, destroying, losing or suffering to be lost, damaged, destroyed, sold or wrongfully disposed:			
	Through neglect, of a value of:			
	$100 or less	None	6 mos.	2/3 6 mos.
	More than $100	BCD	1 yr.	Total
	Willfully, of a value of			
	$100 or less	BCD	1 yr.	Total
	More than $100	DD, BCD	10 yrs.	Total
	Any firearm, explosive, or incendiary device	DD, BCD	10 yrs.	Total
109	Property other than military property of U.S.: loss, damage, destruction, disposition:			
	Wasting, spoiling, destroying, or damaging property of a value of:			
	$100 or less	BCD	1 yr.	Total
	More than $100	DD, BCD	5 yrs.	Total
110	Hazarding a vessel			
	Willfully and wrongfully	Death, DD, BCD, Life	Total	
	Negligently	DD, BCD	2 yrs.	Total
111	Drunken driving			

Article	Offense	Discharge	Confinement	Forfeitures
	Resulting in personal injury	DD, BCD	1 yr., 6 mos.	Total
	Other cases	BCD	6 mos.	Total
112	Drunk on duty	BCD	9 mos.	Total
112a	Wrongful use, possession, etc. of controlled substances[3]			
	Wrongful use, possession, manufacture or introduction of:			
	Amphetamine, cocaine, heroin, lysergic acid diethylamide, marijuana (except possession of less than 30 grams or use), methamphetamine, opium, phencyclidine, secobarbital, and Schedule I, II, and III controlled substances	DD, BCD	5 yrs.	Total
	Marijuana (possession of less than 30 grams or use), phenobarbital and Schedule IV and V controlled substances	DD, BCD	2 yrs.	Total
	Wrongful distribution of, or, with intent to distribute, wrongful possession, manufacture, introduction, or wrongful importation of or exportation of:			
	Amphetamine, cocaine, heroin, lysergic acid diethylamide, marijuana, methamphetamine, opium, phencyclidine, secobarbital, and Schedule I, II, and III controlled substances	DD, BCD	15 yrs.	Total

Article	Offense	Discharge	Confinement	Forfeitures
	Phenobarbital and Schedule IV and V controlled substances	DD, BCD	10 yrs.	Total
113	Misbehavior of sentinel or lookout			
	In time of war	Death, DD, BCD	Life	Total
	In other time:			
	While receiving special pay under 37 U.S.C. 310	DD, BCD	10 yrs.	Total
	Other places	DD, BCD	1 yr.	Total
114	Dueling	DD, BCD	1 yr.	Total
115	Malingering			
	Feigning illness, etc.			
	In time of war or while receiving special pay under 37 U.S.C. 310	DD, BCD	3 yrs.	Total
	Other	DD, BCD	1 yr.	Total
	Intentional self-inflicted injury			
	In time of war or while receiving special pay under 37 U.S.C. 310	DD, BCD	10 yrs.	Total
	Other	DD, BCD	5 yrs.	Total
116	Riot	DD, BCD	10 yrs.	Total
	Breach of peace	None	6 mos.	2/3 6 mos.
117	Provoking speech, gestures	None	6 mos.	2/3 6 mos.
118	Murder			
	Article 118(1) or (4)	Death, mandatory minimum life, DD, BCD	Life	Total
	Article 118(2) or (3)	DD, BCD	Life	Total
119	Manslaughter			
	Voluntary	DD, BCD	10 yrs.	Total

Article	Offense	Discharge	Confinement	Forfeitures
	Involuntary	DD, BCD	3 yrs.	Total
120	Rape	Death, DD, BCD	Life	Total
	Carnal knowledge	DD, BCD	15 yrs.	Total
121	Larceny			
	Of military property of a value of $100 or less	BCD	1 yr.	Total
	Of property other than military property of a value of $100 or less	BCD	6 mos.	Total
	Of military property of a value of more than $100 or of any military motor vehicle, aircraft, vessel, firearm or explosive	DD, BCD	10 yrs.	Total
	Of property other than military property of a value of more than $100 or any motor vehicle, aircraft, vessel, firearm or explosive	DD, BCD	5 yrs.	Total
	Wrongful appropriation			
	Of value of $100 or less	None	3 mos.	2/3 3 mos.
	Of value of more than $100	BCD	6 mos.	Total
	Of vehicle, aircraft, vessel	DD, BCD	2 yrs.	Total
122	Robbery			
	Committed with a firearm	DD, BCD	15 yrs.	Total
	Other cases[1]	DD, BCD	10 yrs.	Total
123	Forgery	DD, BCD	5 yrs.	Total
123a	Checks, etc., insufficient funds, intent to deceive			
	To procure anything of value of:			
	$100 or less	BCD	6 mos.	Total
	More than $100	DD, BCD	5 yrs.	Total
	For payment of past due obligation, and other cases	BCD	6 mos.	Total
124	Maiming	DD, BCD	7 yrs.	Total

Article	Offense	Discharge	Confinement	Forfeitures
125	Sodomy			
	By force and without consent	DD, BCD	20 yrs.	Total
	With child under age of 16 years	DD, BCD	20 yrs.	Total
	Other cases	DD, BCD	5 yrs.	Total
126	Arson			
	Aggravated	DD, BCD	20 yrs.	Total
	Other cases, where property value is:			
	$100 or less	DD, BCD	1 yr.	Total
	More than $100	DD, BCD	5 yrs.	Total
127	Extortion	DD, BCD	3 yrs.	Total
128	Assaults			
	Simple assault	None	3 mos.	2/3 3 mos.
	Assault consummated by battery	BCD	6 mos.	Total
	Assault upon commissioned officer of U.S. or friendly power not in execution of office	DD, BCD	3 yrs.	Total
	Assault upon warrant officer, not in execution of office	DD, BCD	1 yr., 6 mos.	Total
	Assault upon noncommissioned or petty officer not in execution of office	BCD	6 mos.	Total
	Assault upon, in execution of office, person serving as sentinel, lookout, security policeman, military policeman, shore patrol, Master at Arms, or civil law enforcement	DD, BCD	3 yrs.	Total
	Assault consummated by battery upon child under age of 16 years	DD, BCD	2 yrs.	Total

Article	Offense	Discharge	Confinement	Forfeitures
	Assault with dangerous weapon or means likely to produce grievous bodily harm or death:			
	Committed with loaded firearm	DD, BCD	8 yrs.	Total
	Other cases	DD, BCD	3 yrs.	Total
	Assault in which grievous bodily harm is intentionally inflicted:			
	With a loaded firearm	DD, BCD	10 yrs.	Total
	Other cases	DD, BCD	5 yrs.	Total
129	Burglary	DD, BCD	10 yrs.	Total
130	Housebreaking	DD, BCD	5 yrs.	Total
131	Perjury	DD, BCD	5 yrs.	Total
132	Frauds against the United States			
	Offenses under article 132(1) or (2)	DD, BCD	5 yrs.	Total
	Offenses under article 132(3) or (4)			
	$100 or less	BCD	6 mos.	Total
	More than $100	DD, BCD	5 yrs.	Total
133	Conduct unbecoming officer (*see* Part IV, para. 59e)	Dismissal	1 yr. or as prescribed	Total
134	Abusing public animal	None	3 mos.	2/3 3 mos.
	Adultery	DD, BCD	1 yr.	Total
	Assault, indecent	DD, BCD	5 yrs.	Total
	Assault			
	With intent to commit murder or rape	DD, BCD	20 yrs.	Total
	With intent to commit voluntary manslaughter, robbery, sodomy, arson or burglary	DD, BCD	10 yrs.	Total
	With intent to commit housebreaking	DD, BCD	5 yrs.	Total
	Bigamy	DD, BCD	2 yrs.	Total

Article	Offense	Discharge	Confinement	Forfeitures
	Bribery	DD, BCD	5 yrs.	Total
	Graft	DD, BCD	3 yrs.	Total
	Burning with intent to defraud	DD, BCD	10 yrs.	Total
	Check, worthless, making and uttering—by dishonorably failing to maintain funds	BCD	6 mos.	Total
	Cohabitation, wrongful	None	4 mos.	2/3 4 mos.
	Correctional custody, escape from	DD, BCD	1 yr.	Total
	Correctional custody, breach of	BCD	6 mos.	Total
	Debt, dishonorably failing to pay	BCD	6 mos.	Total
	Disloyal statements	DD, BCD	3 yrs.	Total
	Disorderly conduct			
	Under such circumstances as to bring discredit	None	4 mos.	2/3 4 mos.
	Other cases	None	1 mo.	2/3 1 mo.
	Drunkenness			
	Aboard ship or under such circumstances as to bring discredit	None	3 mos.	2/3 3 mos.
	Other cases	None	1 mo.	2/3 1 mo.
	Drunk and disorderly			
	Aboard ship	BCD	6 mos.	Total
	Under such circumstances as to bring discredit	None	6 mos.	2/3 6 mos.
	Other cases	None	3 mos.	2/3 3 mos.
	Drinking liquor with prisoner	None	3 mos.	2/3 3 mos.
	Drunk prisoner	None	3 mos.	2/3 3 mos.
	Drunkenness—incapacitating oneself for performance of duties through prior indulgence in intoxicating liquor or drugs	None	3 mos.	2/3 3 mos.
	False or unauthorized pass offenses			

Article	Offense	Discharge	Confinement	Forfeitures
	Possessing or using with intent to defraud or deceive, or making, altering, counterfeiting, tampering with or selling	DD, BCD	3 yrs.	Total
	All other cases	BCD	6 mos.	Total
	False pretenses, obtaining services under			
	Of a value of $100 or less	BCD	6 mos.	Total
	Of a value of more than $100	DD, BCD	5 yrs.	Total
	False swearing	DD, BCD	3 yrs.	Total
	Firearm, discharging—through negligence	None	3 mos.	2/3 3 mos.
	Firearm, discharging—willfully, under such circumstances as to endanger human life	DD, BCD	1 yr.	Total
	Fleeing scene of accident	BCD	6 mos.	Total
	Fraternization	Dismissal	2 yrs.	Total
	Gambling with subordinates	None	3 mos.	2/3 3 mos.
	Homicide, negligent	BCD	1 yr.	Total
	Impersonation			
	With intent to defraud	DD, BCD	3 yrs.	Total
	All other cases	BCD	6 mos.	Total
	Indecent act, liberties with child	DD, BCD	7 yrs.	Total
	Indecent exposure	BCD	6 mos.	Total
	Indecent language			
	Communicated to child under 16 yrs	DD, BCD	2 yrs.	Total
	Other cases	BCD	6 mos.	Total
	Indecent acts with another	DD, BCD	5 yrs.	Total
	Jumping from vessel into the water	BCD	6 mos.	Total
	Kidnapping	DD, BCD	Life	Total
	Mail, taking, opening, secreting, destroying or stealing	DD, BCD	5 yrs.	Total

Article	Offense	Discharge	Confinement	Forfeitures
	Mails, depositing or causing to be deposited obscene matters in	DD, BCD	5 yrs.	Total
	Misprision of serious offense	DD, BCD	3 yrs.	Total
	Obstructing justice	DD, BCD	5 yrs.	Total
	Wrongful interference with an adverse administrative proceeding	DD, BCD	5 yrs.	Total
	Pandering	DD, BCD	5 yrs.	Total
	Prostitution	DD, BCD	1 yr.	Total
	Parole, violation of	BCD	6 mos.	2/3 6 mos.
	Perjury, subornation of	DD, BCD	5 yrs.	Total
	Public record, altering, concealing, removing, mutilating, obliterating or destroying	DD, BCD	3 yrs.	Total
	Quarantine, breaking	None	6 mos.	2/3 6 mos.
	Restriction, breaking	None	1 mo.	2/3 1 mo.
	Seizure, destruction, removal or disposal of property to prevent	DD, BCD	1 yr.	Total
	Sentinel, lookout			
	Disrespect to	None	3 mos.	2/3 3 mos.
	Loitering or wrongfully sitting on post by			
	In time of war or while receiving special pay	DD, BCD	2 yrs.	Total
	Other cases	BCD	6 mos.	Total
	Soliciting another to commit an offense (*see* Part IV, para. 105e)			
	Stolen property, knowingly receiving, buying, concealing			
	Of a value of $100 or less	BCD	6 mos.	Total
	Of a value of more than $100	DD, BCD	3 yrs.	Total
	Straggling	None	3 mos.	2/3 3 mos.
	Testifying, wrongfully refusing to	DD, BCD	5 yrs.	Total

Article	Offense	Discharge	Confinement	Forfeitures
	Threat, bomb, or hoax	DD, BCD	5 yrs.	Total
	Threat, communicating	DD, BCD	3 yrs.	Total
	Unlawful entry	BCD	6 mos.	Total
	Weapon, concealed, carrying	BCD	1 yr.	Total
	Wearing unauthorized insignia, decoration, badge, ribbon, device or lapel button	BCD	6 mos.	Total

Notes:

1. Suspended in time of war.
2. *See* paragraph 16e(1) & (2) Note, Part IV
3. When any offense under paragraph 37, Part IV, is committed: while the accused is on duty as a sentinel or lookout; on board a vessel or aircraft used by or under the control of the armed forces; in or at a missile launch facility used by or under the control of the armed forces; while receiving special pay under 37 U.S.C. sec. 310; in time of war; or in a confinement facility used by or under the control of the armed forces, the maximum period of confinement authorized for such offense shall be increased by 5 years.

APPENDIX 3

The Commander's Handbook on the Law of Naval Operations

CONTENTS

CHAPTER 2—INTERNATIONAL STATUS AND NAVIGATION OF WARSHIPS AND MILITARY AIRCRAFT

CHAPTER 3—PROTECTION OF PERSONS AND PROPERTY AT SEA

CHAPTER 7—THE LAW OF NEUTRALITY

List of Illustrations in Commander's Handbook

PREFACE

SCOPE

This publication sets out those fundamental principles of international and domestic law that govern U.S. naval operations at sea. Part I, Law of Peacetime Naval Operations, provides an overview and general discussion of the law of the sea, including definitions and descriptions of the jurisdiction and sovereignty exercised by nations over various parts of the world's oceans; the international legal status and navigational rights of warships and military aircraft; protection of persons and property at sea; and the safeguarding of national interests in the maritime environment. Part II, Law of Naval Warfare, sets out those principles of law of special concern to the naval commander during any period in which U.S. naval forces are engaged in armed conflict. Although the primary emphasis of Part II is upon the rules of international law concerned with the conduct of naval warfare, attention is also directed to relevant principles and concepts common to the whole of the law of armed conflict.

PURPOSE

This publication is intended for the use of operational commanders and supporting staff elements at all levels of command. It is designed to provide officers in command and their staffs with an overview of the rules of law governing naval operations in peacetime and during armed conflict. The explanations and descriptions in this publication are intended to enable the naval commander and his staff to comprehend more fully the legal foundations upon which the orders issued to them by higher authority are premised and to understand better the commander's responsibilities under international and domestic law to exe-

cute his mission within that law. This publication sets forth general guidance. It is not a comprehensive treatment of the law nor is it a substitute for the definitive legal guidance provided by judge advocates and others responsible for advising commanders on the law.

Officers in command of operational units are encouraged to utilize this publication as a training aid for assigned personnel.

APPLICABILITY

Part I of this publication is applicable to U.S. naval operations during time of peace. Part II applies to the conduct of U.S. naval forces during armed conflict. It is the policy of the United States to apply the law of armed conflict to all circumstances in which the armed forces of the United States are engaged in combat operations, regardless of whether such hostilities are declared or otherwise designated as "war." Relevant portions of Part II are, therefore, applicable to all hostilities involving U.S. naval forces irrespective of the character, intensity, or duration of the conflict. Part II may also be used for information and guidance in situations in which the U.S. is a nonparticipant in hostilities involving other nations.

RULES OF ENGAGEMENT (ROE)

The Joint Chiefs of Staff and the commanders of the unified and specified commands have the authority to exercise the right of national self-defense and declare forces hostile. Incident to this authority, the commanders of the unified and specified commands may issue directives, *e.g.*, rules of engagement, that delineate the circumstances and limitations under which the forces under their command will initiate and/or continue engagement with other forces encountered. These directives are definitive within the commander's area of responsibility. *This publication provides general information, is not directive, and does not supersede guidance issued by such commanders or higher authority.*

INTERNATIONAL LAW

For purposes of this publication, international law is defined as that body of rules that nations consider binding in their relations with one another. International law derives from the practice of nations in the international arena and from international agreements. International law provides stability in international relations and an expectation that certain acts or omissions will effect predictable consequences. If one nation violates the law, it may expect that others will reciprocate. Consequently, failure to comply with international law ordinarily involves greater political and economic costs than does observance. In short, nations comply with international law because it is in their interest to do so. Like most rules of conduct, international law is in a continual state of development and change.

Practice of Nations. The general and consistent practice among nations with respect to a particular subject, which over time is accepted by them generally as a legal obligation, is known as customary international law. Customary international law is the principal source of international law and is binding upon all nations.

International Agreements. An international agreement is a commitment entered into by two or more nations which reflects their intention to be bound by its terms in their relations with one another. International agreements, whether bilateral trea-

ties, executive agreements, or multilateral conventions, bind only those nations that are a party to them or that may otherwise consent to be bound by them. To the extent that multilateral conventions of broad application codify existing rules of customary law, they may be regarded as evidence of international law binding upon parties and nonparties alike.

U.S. Navy Regulations. U.S. Navy Regulations, 1973, require U.S. naval commanders to observe international law. Article 0605, Observance of International Law, states:

> At all times, a commander shall observe and require his command to observe the principles of international law. Where necessary to fulfillment of this responsibility, a departure from other provisions of Navy Regulations is authorized.

ORDERING DATA

Report any page shortage by speedletter to NAVTACSUPPACT (copy to CNO (OP-953)). Order a new publication or change, as appropriate, by submitting Form DD 1348 to NAVPUBFORMCEN Philadelphia in accordance with Introduction to Navy Stocklist of Publications and Forms, NAVSUP Publication 2002.

RECOMMENDED CHANGES

Recommended changes to this publication may be submitted at any time using the accompanying format for routine changes.

Submit recommendations to:

NAVY JAG (Code 10)
200 Stovall Street
Alexandria, VA 22332-2400

In addition forward two copies of all recommendations to:

Director
Navy Tactical Support Activity
Washington Navy Yard
Washington, D.C. 20374

URGENT CHANGE RECOMMENDATIONS

When items for changes are considered to be urgent (as defined in NWP 0 and including matters of safety), this information shall be sent by priority message (see accompanying sample message format) to NAVY JAG, with information copies to CNO (OP-616B), Naval Safety Center (if appropriate), Navy Tactical Support Activity, and all other commands concerned, clearly explaining the proposed change. Information addressees should comment as appropriate. See NWP 0.

CHANGE SYMBOLS

Revised text is indicated by a black vertical line in either margin of the page, like the one printed next to this paragraph. The change symbol shows where there has been a change. The change might be material added or information restated. A change symbol in the margin by the chapter number and title indicates a new or completely revised chapter.

USE OF ITALICS

Italics are used for emphasis within the text.

Part I

Law of Peacetime Naval Operations

CHAPTER 1

Legal Divisions of the Oceans and Airspace

1.1 INTRODUCTION

The oceans of the world traditionally have been classified under the broad headings of internal waters, territorial seas, and high seas. Airspace has been divided into national and international airspace. In recent years, new concepts have evolved, such as the exclusive economic zone and archipelagic waters, which have dramatically expanded the jurisdictional claims of coastal and island nations over wide expanses of the ocean previously regarded as high seas. The phenomenon of expanding maritime jurisdiction and the rush to extend the territorial sea to 12 nautical miles and beyond were the subject of international negotiation from 1973 through 1982 in the course of the Third United Nations Conference on the Law of the Sea. That conference produced the 1982 United Nations Convention on the Law of the Sea (1982 LOS Convention). Although not signed by the United States and not yet in formal effect, the provisions of the 1982 LOS Convention relating to navigation and overflight codified existing law and practice and are considered by the United States to reflect customary international law.

1.2 RECOGNITION OF COASTAL NATION CLAIMS

In a statement on U.S. oceans policy issued 10 March 1983, the President stated:

"First, the United States is prepared to accept and act in accordance with the balance of interests relating to traditional uses of the oceans—such as navigation and overflight. In this respect, the United States will recognize the rights of other States in the waters off their coasts, as reflected in the [1982 LOS] Convention, so long as the rights and freedoms of the United States and others under international law are recognized by such coastal states.

"Second, the United States will exercise and assert its navigation and overflight rights and freedoms on a worldwide basis in a manner that is consistent with the balance of interests reflected in the Convention. The United States will not, however, acquiesce in unilateral acts of other States designed to restrict the rights and freedoms of the international community in navigation and overflight and other related high seas uses."

The legal classifications ("regimes") of ocean and airspace areas directly affect naval operations by determining the degree of control that a coastal or island nation may exercise over the conduct of foreign merchant ships, warships, and aircraft operating within these areas. The methods for measuring maritime jurisdictional claims, and the extent of coastal or island nation control exercised in those areas, are set forth in the succeeding paragraphs of this chapter. The DOD Maritime Claims

The bow of a Soviet *Mirka* II Class Light frigate is momentarily locked with the port quarter of USS *Caron*. The USS *Caron* was exercising the right of free passage through the Soviet claimed 12 mile territorial waters (12 Feb 88). Photo courtesy of U.S. Naval Institute.

Reference Manual (DOD 2005.1-M) contains a listing of the ocean claims of coastal and island nations.

1.3 MARITIME BASELINES

The territorial sea and all other maritime zones are measured from baselines. In order to calculate the seaward reach of claimed maritime zones, it is first necessary to comprehend how baselines are drawn.

1.3.1 Low-Water Line. Unless other special rules apply, the baseline from which maritime claims of a nation are measured is the low-water line along the coast as marked on that nation's official large-scale charts.

1.3.2 Straight Baselines. Where it would be impractical to utilize the low-water line, as where the coastline is deeply indented or where there is a fringe of islands along the coast in its immediate vicinity, the coastal or island nation may instead employ straight baselines. The general rule is that straight baselines must not depart from the general direction of the coast, and the sea areas they enclose must be closely linked to the land domain. A coastal or island nation which uses straight baselines must either clearly indicate them on its

charts or publish a list of geographical co-
ordinates of the points joining them together. See Figure 1-1. The United States,
with few exceptions, does not employ this
practice and interprets restrictively its use
by others.

1.3.2.1 Unstable Coastlines. Where the
coastline is highly unstable due to natural
conditions, *e.g.*, deltas, straight baselines
may be established connecting appropriate
points on the low-water line. These
straight baselines remain effective, despite
subsequent regression or accretion of the
coastline, until changed by the coastal or
island nation.

1.3.2.2 Low-Tide Elevations. A low-tide
elevation is a naturally formed land area
surrounded by water that remains above
water at low tide but is submerged at high
tide. Straight baselines may generally not
be drawn to or from a low-tide elevation
unless a lighthouse or similar installation,
which is permanently above sea level, has
been erected thereon.

1.3.3 Bays and Gulfs. There is a complex
formula for determining the baseline clos-
ing the mouth of a legal bay or gulf. For
baseline purposes, a "bay" is a well-
marked indentation in the coastline of such
proportion to the width of its mouth as to
contain landlocked waters and constitute
more than a mere curvature of the coast.
The water area of a "bay" must be greater
than that of a semicircle whose diameter is
the length of the line drawn across its
mouth. See Figure 1-2. Where the indentation has more than one mouth due to the
presence of islands, the diameter of the
test semicircle is the sum of the lines
across the various mouths. See Figure 1-3.

The baseline across the mouth of a bay
may not exceed 24 nautical miles in
length. Where the mouth is wider than 24
nautical miles, a baseline of 24 nautical
miles may be drawn within the bay so as to

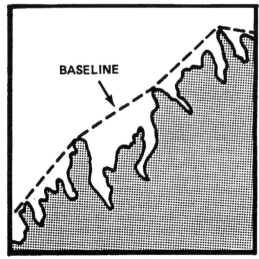

a. DEEPLY INDENTED COASTLINE

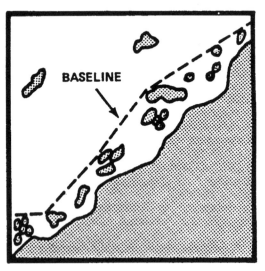

b. FRINGING ISLANDS

Figure 1-1. Straight Baselines

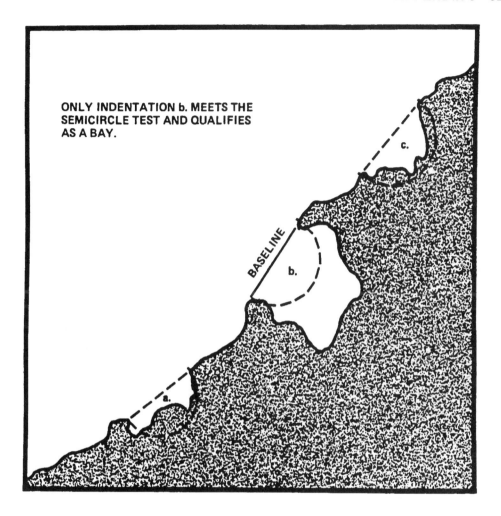

ONLY INDENTATION b. MEETS THE
SEMICIRCLE TEST AND QUALIFIES
AS A BAY.

BASELINE

c.

b.

a.

Figure 1-2. The Semicircle Test

enclose the maximum water area. See Figure 1-4. Where the semicircle test has been met, and a closure line of 24 nautical miles or less may be drawn, the body of water thereby enclosed is a "bay" in the legal sense.

1.3.3.1 Historic Bays. So-called historic bays are not determined by the semicircle and 24-nautical mile closure line rules described above. To meet the international standard for establishing a claim to a historic bay, a nation must demonstrate its open, effective, long term, and continuous exercise of authority over the bay, coupled with acquiescence by foreign nations in the exercise of that authority. The United States has taken the position that an actual showing of acquiescence by foreign nations in such a claim is required, as opposed to a mere absence of opposition.

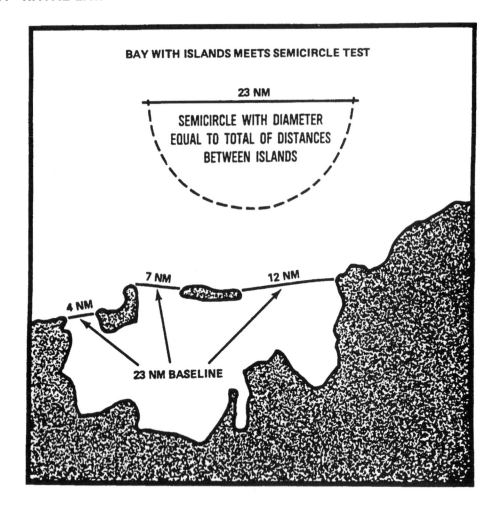

Figure 1-3. Bay With Islands

1.3.4 River Mouths. If a river flows directly into the sea, the baseline is a straight line across the mouth of the river between points on the low-water line of its banks.

1.3.5 Reefs. The low-water line of a reef may be used as the baseline for islands situated on atolls or having fringing reefs.

1.3.6 Harbor Works. The outermost permanent harbor works which form an integral part of the harbor system are regarded as forming part of the coast for baseline purposes. Harbor works are structures, such as jetties, breakwaters, and groins, erected along the coast at inlets or rivers for protective purposes or for enclosing sea areas directly adjacent to the coast to provide anchorage and shelter.

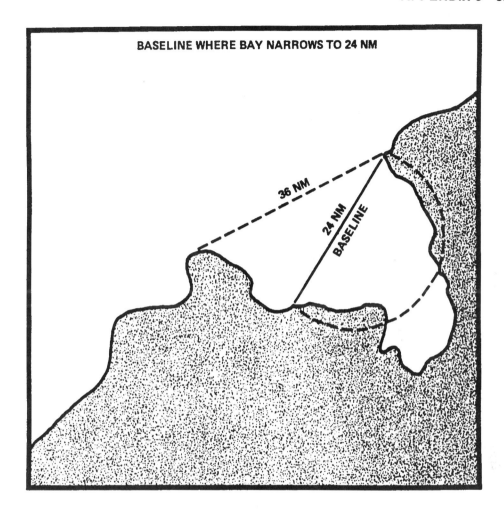

Figure 1-4. Bay With Mouth Exceeding 24 Nautical Miles

1.4 NATIONAL WATERS

For operational purposes, the world's oceans are divided into two parts. The first includes internal waters, territorial seas, and archipelagic waters. These "national waters" are subject to the territorial sovereignty of coastal and island nations, with certain navigational rights reserved to the international community. The second part includes contiguous zones, waters of the exclusive economic zone, and the high

seas. These are "international waters" in which all nations enjoy the high seas freedoms of navigation and overflight. International waters are discussed further in paragraph 1.5.

1.4.1 Internal Waters. Internal waters are *landward* of the baseline from which the territorial sea is measured. Lakes, rivers, some bays, harbors, some canals, and lagoons are examples of internal waters. From the standpoint of international law, internal waters have the same legal character as the land itself. There is no right of innocent passage in internal waters, and, unless in distress, ships and aircraft may not enter or overfly internal waters without the permission of the coastal nation.

1.4.2 Territorial Seas. The territorial sea is a belt of ocean which is measured seaward from the baseline of the coastal or island nations and subject to its sovereignty. The U.S. claims a 12-nautical mile territorial sea and recognizes territorial sea claims of other nations up to a maximum breadth of 12 nautical miles.

1.4.2.1 Islands, Rocks, and Low-Tide Elevations. Each island has its own territorial sea and, like the mainland, has a baseline from which it is calculated. An island is defined as a naturally formed area of land, surrounded by water, which is above water at high tide. Rocks are islands which cannot sustain human habitation or economic life of their own. Provided they remain above water at high tide, they too posses a territorial sea determined in accordance with the principles discussed in the paragraphs on baselines. A low-tide elevation (above water at low tide but submerged at high tide) situated wholly or partly *within* the territorial sea may be used for territorial sea purposes as though it were an island. Where a low-tide elevation is located entirely *beyond* the territorial sea, it has no territorial sea of its own. See Figure 1-5.

1.4.2.2 Artificial Islands and Off-Shore Installations. Artificial islands and offshore installations have no territorial sea of their own.

1.4.2.3 Roadsteads. Roadsteads normally used for the loading, unloading, and anchoring of ships, and which would otherwise be situated wholly or partly beyond the limits of the territorial sea, are included within the territorial sea. Roadsteads included within the territorial sea must be clearly marked on charts by the coastal or island nation.

1.4.3 Archipelagic Waters. An archipelagic nation is a nation that is constituted wholly of one or more groups of islands. Such nations may draw straight archipelagic baselines joining the outermost points of their outermost islands, provided that the ratio of water to land within the baselines is between 1 to 1 and 9 to 1. The waters enclosed within archipelagic baselines are called *archipelagic waters*. (The archipelagic baselines are also the baselines from which the archipelagic nation measures seaward for its territorial sea, contiguous zone, and exclusive economic zone.) The U.S. recognizes the right of an archipelagic nation to establish archipelagic baselines enclosing archipelagic waters, provided that the baselines are drawn in conformity with the 1982 LOS Convention and that the U.S. is accorded navigation and overflight rights and freedoms under international law in the enclosed archipelagic and adjacent waters.

1.4.3.1 Archipelagic Sea Lanes. Archipelagic nations may designate archipelagic sea lanes through their archipelagic waters suitable for continuous and expeditious passage of ships and aircraft. All normal routes used for international navigation and overflight are to be included. If the archipelagic nation does not designate such sea lanes, the right of archipelagic sea lanes passage may nonetheless be exercised by all nations through routes normally used for international navigation and overflight.

1.5 INTERNATIONAL WATERS

International waters include all ocean areas not subject to the territorial sovereignty of any nation. All waters seaward of the territorial sea are international waters in which the high seas freedoms of naviga-

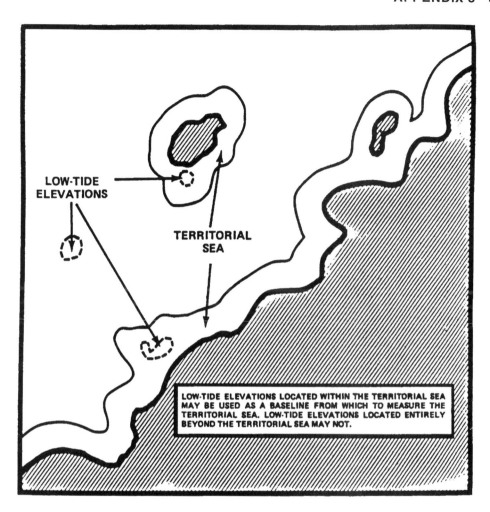

Figure 1-5. Territorial Sea of Islands and Low-Tide Elevations

tion and overflight are preserved to the international community. International waters include contiguous zones, exclusive economic zones, and high seas.

1.5.1 Contiguous Zones. A contiguous zone is an area extending seaward from the territorial sea in which the coastal or island nation may exercise the control necessary to prevent or punish infringement of its customs, fiscal, immigration, and sanitary laws and regulations that occur within

its territory or territorial sea (but not for so-called security purposes—see 1.5.4). The U.S. claims a contiguous zone extending 24 nautical miles from the baselines used to measure the territorial sea. The U.S. will respect, however, contiguous zones up to 24 nautical miles in breadth provided the coastal or island nation recognizes U.S. rights in the zone consistent with the provisions of the 1982 LOS Convention.

1.5.2 Exclusive Economic Zones. Exclusive economic zones (EEZs) are resource-related zones adjacent to the coast and extending beyond the territorial sea. As the name suggests, its central purpose is economic. The U.S. recognizes the sovereign rights of a coastal or island nation to prescribe and enforce its law in the exclusive economic zone, extending up to 200 nautical miles from the baselines used to measure the territorial sea, for purposes of exploration, exploitation, management, and conservation of the natural resources of the waters, seabed, and subsoil of the zone, as well as, for the production of energy from the water current and winds. The coastal or island nation may exercise jurisdiction in the zone over the establishment and use of artificial islands, installations, and structures having economic purposes; over marine scientific research (with reasonable limitations); and over some aspects of marine environmental protection (primarily implementation of international vessel-source pollution control standards). However, in the EEZ all nations enjoy the right to exercise the traditional high seas freedoms of navigation and overflight, of the laying of submarine cables and pipelines, and of all other traditional high seas uses by ships and aircraft which are not resource related. The United States established a 200-nautical mile exclusive economic zone by Presidential Proclamation on 10 March 1983.

1.5.3 High Seas. The high seas include all parts of the ocean seaward of the exclusive economic zone. When a coastal or island nation has not proclaimed an exclusive economic zone, the high seas begin at the seaward edge of the territorial sea.

1.5.4 Security Zones. Some coastal nations have claimed the right to establish military security zones, beyond the territorial sea, of varying breadth in which they purport to regulate the activities of warships and military aircraft of other nations

by such restrictions as prior notification or authorization for entry, limits on the number of foreign ships or aircraft present at any given time, prohibitions on various operational activities, or complete exclusion. International law does not recognize the right of coastal nations to establish zones in peacetime that would restrict the exercise of non-resource-related high seas freedoms beyond the territorial sea. Accordingly, the U.S. does not recognize the peacetime validity of any claimed security or military zone seaward of the territorial sea which purports to restrict or regulate the high seas freedoms of navigation and overflight. (See paragraph 2.3.2.3 for a discussion of temporary suspension of innocent passage in territorial seas.)

1.6 CONTINENTAL SHELVES

The juridical continental shelf of a coastal or island nation consists of the seabed and subsoil of the submarine areas that extend beyond its territorial sea to the outer edge of the continental margin, *or* to a distance of 200 nautical miles from the baseline used to measure the territorial sea where the continental margin does not extend to that distance. The continental shelf may not extend beyond 350 nautical miles from the baseline of the territorial sea *or* 100 nautical miles from the 2,500 meter isobath, whichever is greater. Although the coastal or island nation exercises sovereign rights over the continental shelf for purposes of exploring and exploiting its natural resources, the legal status of the superjacent water is not affected. Moreover, all nations have the right to lay submarine cables and pipelines on the continental shelf.

1.7 SAFETY ZONES

Coastal and island nations may establish safety zones to protect artificial islands, installations, and structures located in their internal waters, archipelagic waters, territorial seas and exclusive economic zones, and on their continental shelves. In the case of artificial islands, installations, and structures located in the exclusive economic zones or on the continental shelf beyond the territorial sea, safety zones may not extend beyond 500 meters from the outer edges of the facility in question, except as authorized by generally accepted international standards.

1.8 AIRSPACE

Under international law, airspace is classified as either *national* airspace (that over the land, internal waters, archipelagic waters, and territorial seas of a nation) or *international* airspace (that over contiguous zones, exclusive economic zones, the high seas, and territory not subject to the sovereignty of any nation). Subject to a right of overflight of international straits (see paragraph 2.5.1.1) and archipelagic sea lanes (see paragraph 2.5.1.2), each nation has complete and exclusive sovereignty over its national airspace. Except as they may have otherwise consented through treaties or other international agreements, the aircraft of all nations are free to operate in international airspace without interference by other nations.

1.9 OUTER SPACE

The upper limit of airspace subject to national jurisdiction has not been authoritatively defined by international law. International practice has established that airspace terminates at some point below the point at which artificial satellites can be placed in orbit without free-falling to earth. Outer space begins at that undefined point. All nations enjoy a freedom of equal access to outer space and none may appropriate it to its national airspace or exclusive use.

CHAPTER 2

International Status and Navigation of Warships and Military Aircraft

2.1 STATUS OF WARSHIPS

2.1.1 Warship Defined. International law defines a warship as a ship belonging to the armed forces of a nation bearing the external markings distinguishing the character and nationality of such ships, under the command of an officer duly commissioned by the government of that nation and whose name appears in the appropriate service list of officers, and manned by a crew which is under regular armed forces discipline. In the U.S. Navy, those ships designated "USS" are "warships" as defined by international law. U.S. Coast Guard vessels designated "USCGC" are also "warships" under international law.

2.1.2 International Status. A warship enjoys sovereign immunity from interference by the authorities of nations other than the flag nation. Police and port authorities may board a warship only with the permission of the commanding officer. A warship cannot be required to consent to an onboard search or inspection nor may it be required to fly the flag of the host nation. Although warships are required to comply with coastal nation traffic control, sewage, health, and quarantine restrictions instituted in conformance with the 1982 LOS Convention, a failure of compliance is subject only to diplomatic complaint or to coastal nation orders to leave its territorial waters immediately. Moreover, warships

are immune from arrest and search, whether in national or international waters, are exempt from foreign taxes and regulation, and exercise exclusive control over all passengers and crew with respect to acts performed aboard.

2.1.2.1 Nuclear Powered Warships. Nuclear powered warships and conventionally powered warships enjoy identical international legal status.

2.1.2.2 Sunken Warships and Military Aircraft. Sunken warships and military aircraft remain the property of the flag nation until title is formally relinquished or abandoned, whether the cause of the sinking was through accident or enemy action (unless the warship or military aircraft was captured before it sank). As a matter of policy, the U.S. Government does not grant permission to salvage sunken U.S. warships or military aircraft that contain the remains of deceased service personnel or explosive material. Requests from foreign countries to have their sunken warships or military aircraft, located in U.S. waters, similarly respected by salvors, are honored.

2.1.2.3 Auxiliaries. Auxiliaries are vessels, other than warships, that are owned by or under the exclusive control of the armed forces. Because they are state owned or operated and used for the time being only on government noncommercial service, auxiliaries enjoy sovereign immunity. This means that, like warships, they are immune from arrest and search, whether in national or international waters. Like warships, they are exempt from foreign taxes and regulation, and exercise exclusive control over all passengers and crew with respect to acts performed on board.

U.S. auxiliaries include all vessels which comprise the Military Sealift Command (MSC) Force. The MSC Force includes: (1) United States Naval Ships (USNS) (i.e., U.S.-owned vessels or those under bareboat charter, and assigned to MSC); (2) the National Defense Reserve Fleet (NDRF) and the Ready Reserve Force (RRF) (when activated and assigned to MSC); (3) privately owned vessels under time charter assigned to the Afloat Pre-positioned Force (APF); and (4) those vessels chartered by MSC for a period of time or for a specific voyage or voyages. The U.S. claims full rights of sovereign immunity for all USNS, APF, NDRF, and RRF vessels. As a matter of policy, however, the U.S. claims only freedom from arrest and taxation for those MSC Force time and voyage charters not included in the APF.

2.2 STATUS OF MILITARY AIRCRAFT

2.2.1 Military Aircraft Defined. International law defines military aircraft to include all aircraft operated by commissioned units of the armed forces of a nation bearing the military markings of that nation, commanded by a member of the armed forces, and manned by a crew subject to regular armed forces discipline.

2.2.2 International Status. Military aircraft are "state aircraft" within the meaning of the Convention on International Civil Aviation of 1944 (the "Chicago Convention") and, like warships, enjoy sovereign immunity from foreign search and inspection. Subject to the right of transit passage and archipelagic sea lanes passage, state aircraft may not fly over or land on the territory (including the territorial sea) of another nation without authorization by special agreement or otherwise. Host nation officials may not board the aircraft without the consent of the aircraft commander. Should the aircraft commander fail to certify compliance with host nation customs, immigration, or quarantine requirements, the aircraft may be directed to leave the territory and national airspace of that nation immediately.

2.2.2.1 Military Contract Aircraft. Civilian owned and operated aircraft, the full capacity of which has been contracted by the Military Airlift Command (MAC) and used in the military service of the United States, qualify as "state aircraft" if they are so designated by the United States. In those circumstances they too enjoy sovereign immunity from foreign search and inspection. As a matter of policy, however, the United States normally does not designate MAC-charter as "state aircraft."

2.3 NAVIGATION IN AND OVERFLIGHT OF NATIONAL WATERS

2.3.1 Internal Waters. As discussed in the preceding chapter, coastal and island nations exercise the same jurisdiction and control over their internal waters and superjacent airspace as they do over their land territory. Because most ports and harbors are located landward of the baseline of the territorial sea, entering a port ordinarily involves navigation in internal waters. Because entering internal waters is legally equivalent to entering the land territory of another nation, that nation's permission is required. To facilitate international maritime commerce, many countries grant foreign merchant vessels standing permission to enter internal waters, in the absence of notice to the contrary. Warships and auxiliaries, and all aircraft, on the other hand, require specific and advance entry permission, unless other bilateral or multilateral arrangements have been concluded.

Exceptions to the rule of nonentry into *internal* waters without coastal nation permission, whether specific or implied, arise when rendered necessary by *force majeure* or by distress, or when straight baselines are established that have the effect of enclosing, as internal waters, areas of the sea previously regarded as territorial waters or high seas. In the latter event, international law provides that the right of innocent passage (see paragraph 2.3.2.1) or that of transit passage in an international strait (see paragraph 2.3.3.1) may be exercised by all nations in those waters.

2.3.2 The Territorial Sea

2.3.2.1 Innocent Passage. International law provides that ships (but not aircraft) of all nations enjoy the right of innocent passage for the purpose of continuous and expeditious traversing of the territorial sea or for proceeding to or from internal waters. Innocent passage includes stopping and anchoring, but only insofar as incidental to ordinary navigation or as rendered necessary by *force majeure* or distress. Passage is *innocent* so long as it is not prejudicial to the peace, good order, or security of the coastal or island nation. Among the military activities considered to be *prejudicial* to peace, good order, and security, and therefore inconsistent with innocent passage, are:

1. Any threat or the use of force against the sovereignty, territorial integrity, or political independence of the coastal or island nation

2. Any exercise or practice with weapons of any kind

3. The launching, landing, or taking on board of aircraft or any military device

4. Intelligence collection activities detrimental to the security of that coastal or island nation

5. The carrying out of research or survey activities.

The coastal or island nation may take affirmative actions in its territorial sea to prevent passage that is not innocent, including, where necessary, the use of force. Foreign ships, including warships, exercising the right of innocent passage are required to comply with the laws and regulations enacted by the coastal or island nation in conformity with established principles of international law and, in particular, with such laws and regulations relating to the safety of navigation. Innocent passage does not include a right of overflight.

2.3.2.2 Permitted Restrictions. For purposes such as resource conservation, environmental protection, and navigational safety, a coastal or island nation may establish certain restrictions upon the right of innocent passage of foreign vessels. Such restrictions upon the right of innocent passage through the territorial sea are not prohibited by international law, provided that they are reasonable and necessary; do not have the practical effect of denying or impairing the right of innocent passage; and do not discriminate in form or in fact against the ships of any nation or those carrying cargoes to, from, or on behalf of any nation. The coastal or island nation may, where navigational safety dictates, require foreign ships exercising the right of innocent passage to utilize designated sea lanes and traffic separation schemes.

2.3.2.3 Temporary Suspension of Innocent Passage. A coastal or island nation may suspend innocent passage temporarily in specified areas of its territorial sea, when it is essential for the protection of its security. Such a suspension must be preceded by published notice to the international community and may not discriminate in form or in fact among foreign ships.

2.3.2.4 Warships and Innocent Passage. All warships, including submarines, enjoy the right of innocent passage on an unimpeded and unannounced basis. Submarines, however, are required to navigate on the surface and to show their flag when passing through foreign territorial seas. If a warship does not comply with coastal or island nation regulations that conform to established principles of international law and disregards a request for compliance which is made to it, the coastal or island nation may require the warship immediately to leave the territorial sea.

2.3.2.5 Assistance Entry. All ship and aircraft commanders have an obligation to assist those in danger of being lost at sea. This long recognized duty of mariners permits assistance entry into the territorial sea by ships or, under certain circumstances, aircraft without permission of the coastal or island nation to engage in *bona fide* efforts to render emergency assistance to those in danger or distress at sea. This right applies only when the location of the danger or distress is reasonably well known. It does not extend to entering the territorial sea or airspace to conduct a search.

2.3.3 International Straits

2.3.3.1 International Straits Overlapped by Territorial Seas. Straits used for international navigation through the territorial sea between one part of the high seas or an exclusive economic zone and another part of the high seas or an exclusive economic zone are subject to the legal regime of *transit passage*. Under international law,

the ships and aircraft of all nations, including warships and military aircraft, enjoy the right of unimpeded transit passage through such straits. Transit passage is defined as the exercise of the freedoms of navigation and overflight solely for the purpose of continuous and expeditious transit in the normal modes of operation utilized by ships and aircraft for such passage. This means that submarines are free to transit international straits submerged, since that is their normal mode of operation, and that surface warships may transit in a manner consistent with sound navigational practices and the security of the force, including formation steaming and the launching and recovery of aircraft. All transiting ships and aircraft must proceed without delay; must refrain from the threat or the use of force against the sovereignty, territorial integrity, or political independence of nations bordering the strait; and must otherwise refrain from any activities other than those incident to their normal modes of continuous and expeditious transit.

Transit passage through international straits cannot be suspended by the coastal or island nation for any purpose during peacetime. This principle of international law also applies to transiting ships (including warships) of nations at peace with the bordering coastal or island nation but involved in armed conflict with another nation.

Coastal or island nations bordering international straits overlapped by territorial seas may designate sea lanes and prescribe traffic separation schemes to promote navigational safety. However, such sea lanes and separation schemes must be approved by the competent international organization in accordance with generally accepted international standards. Ships in transit must respect properly designated sea lanes and traffic separation schemes.

The regime of *innocent passage* (see paragraph 2.3.2.1), rather than transit passage, applies in straits used for international navigation that connect a part of the high seas or an exclusive economic zone with the territorial sea of a coastal or island nation. There may be no suspension of innocent passage through such straits.

2.3.3.2 International Straits Not Completely Overlapped by Territorial Seas. Ships and aircraft transiting through or above straits used for international navigation which are *not* completely overlapped by territorial seas and through which there is a high seas or exclusive economic zone corridor suitable for such navigation, enjoy the high seas freedoms of navigation and overflight while operating in and over such a corridor. Accordingly, so long as they remain beyond the territorial sea, all ships and aircraft of all nations have the unencumbered right to navigate through and over such waters subject only to due regard for the right of others to do so as well.

2.3.4 Archipelagic Waters

2.3.4.1 Archipelagic Sea Lanes Passage. All ships and aircraft, including warships and military aircraft, enjoy the right of archipelagic sea lane passage while transiting through, under, or over the waters of archipelagoes and adjacent territorial seas via designated archipelagic sea lanes. Archipelagic sea lanes include all routes normally used for international navigation and overflight, whether or not designated by the archipelagic nation. Each sea lane is defined by a continuous line from the point of entry into the archipelago to the point of exit. Ships and aircraft engaged in archipelagic sea lanes passage are required to remain within 25 nautical miles to either side of the axis line and must approach no closer to the coastline than 10 percent of the distance between the nearest islands. See Figure 2-1. Archipelagic sea lanes passage is defined under international law as the exercise of the freedom of navigation and overflight for the sole purpose of continuous and expeditious transit through archipelagic waters, in the normal modes of operation, by the ships and aircraft involved. This means that submarines may transit while submerged, and that surface warships may carry out those activities normally undertaken during passage through such waters, including activities necessary to their security, such as formation steaming and the launching and recovery of aircraft. The right of archipelagic sea lanes passage cannot be impeded, or suspended by the archipelagic nation for any reason.

2.3.4.2 Innocent Passage. Outside of archipelagic sea lanes, all surface ships, including warships, enjoy the more limited right of innocent passage throughout archipelagic waters just as they do in the territorial sea. Submarines must remain on the surface and fly their national flag. Any threat or use of force directed against the sovereignty, territorial integrity, or political independence of the archipelagic nation is prohibited. Launching and recovery of aircraft are not allowed, nor may weapons exercises be conducted. The archipelagic nation may promulgate and enforce reasonable restrictions on the right of innocent passage through its archipelagic waters for customs, fiscal, immigration, fishing, pollution, and sanitary purposes. Innocent passage may be suspended temporarily by the archipelagic nation in specified areas of its archipelagic waters when essential for the protection of its security, but it must first promulgate notice of its intentions to do so and must apply the suspension in a nondiscriminatory manner. There is no right of overflight through airspace over archipelagic waters outside of archipelagic sea lanes.

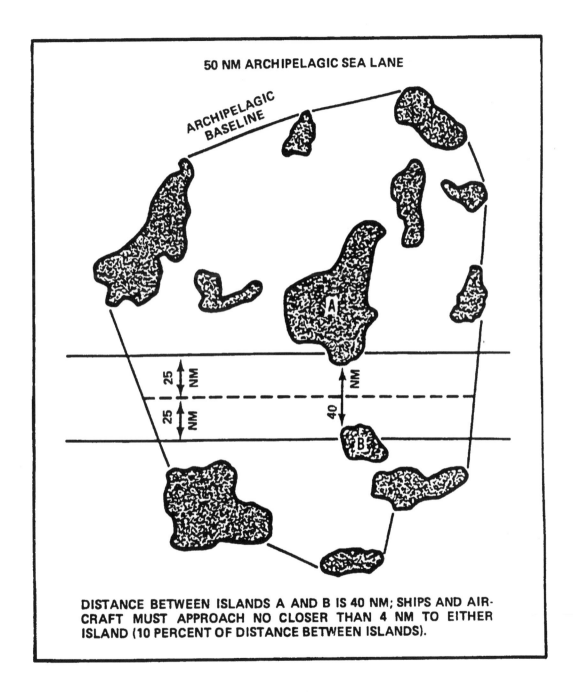

50 NM ARCHIPELAGIC SEA LANE

ARCHIPELAGIC BASELINE

A

B

25 NM

25 NM

40 NM

DISTANCE BETWEEN ISLANDS A AND B IS 40 NM; SHIPS AND AIR-CRAFT MUST APPROACH NO CLOSER THAN 4 NM TO EITHER ISLAND (10 PERCENT OF DISTANCE BETWEEN ISLANDS).

Figure 2-1. Archipelagic Sea Lanes

2.4 NAVIGATION IN AND OVERFLIGHT OF INTERNATIONAL WATERS

2.4.1 The Contiguous Zone. The contiguous zone is comprised of international waters in and over which the ships and aircraft, including warships and military aircraft, of all nations enjoy the high seas freedoms of navigation and overflight as described in paragraph 2.4.3. Although the coastal or island nation may exercise in those waters the control necessary to prevent and punish infringement of its customs, fiscal, immigration, and sanitary laws that may occur within its territory (including its territorial sea), it cannot otherwise interfere with international navigation and overflight in or above the contiguous zone.

2.4.2 The Exclusive Economic Zone. The coastal or island nation's jurisdiction and control over the exclusive economic zone are limited to matters concerning the exploration, exploitation, management, and conservation of the resources of those international waters. The coastal or island nation may also exercise in the zone jurisdiction over the establishment and use of artificial islands, installations, and structures having economic purposes; over marine scientific research (with reasonable limitations); and over some aspects of marine environmental protection. Accordingly, the coastal or island nation cannot unduly restrict or impede the exercise of the freedoms of navigation in and overflight of the exclusive economic zone. Since all ships and aircraft, including warships and military aircraft, enjoy the high seas freedoms of navigation and overflight and other internationally lawful uses of the sea related to those freedoms, in and over those waters, the existence of an exclusive economic zone in an area of naval operations need not, of itself, be of operational concern to the naval commander.

2.4.3 The High Seas. All ships and aircraft, including warships and military aircraft, enjoy complete freedom of movement and operation on and over the high seas. For warships, this includes task force maneuvering, flight operations, military exercises, surveillance, intelligence gathering activities, and ordnance testing and firing. All nations also enjoy the right to lay submarine cables and pipelines on the bed of the high seas as well as on the continental shelf beyond the territorial sea, with coastal or island nation approval for the course of pipelines on the continental shelf. All of these activities must be conducted with due regard for the rights of other nations and for the safe conduct and operation of other ships and aircraft.

2.4.3.1 Closure or Warning Areas. Any nation may declare a temporary closure or warning area on the high seas to advise other nations of the conduct of activities that, although lawful, are hazardous to navigation and/or overflight. The U.S. and other nations routinely declare such areas for missile testing, gunnery exercises, space vehicle recovery operations, and other purposes entailing some danger to lawful uses of the high seas by others. Notice of the establishment of such areas must be promulgated in advance, usually in the form of a Notice to Mariners (NOTMAR) and/or a Notice to Airmen (NOTAM). Ships and aircraft of other nations are not required to remain outside a declared closure or warning area, but are obliged to refrain from interfering with activities therein. Consequently, U.S. ships and aircraft may operate in a closure area declared by a foreign nation, collect intelligence, and observe the activities involved, subject to the requirement of due regard for the rights of the declaring nation to use the high seas for such lawful purposes, as may the ships and aircraft of other nations in a U.S. declared closure area.

2.4.4 Declared Security and Defense Zones. International law does not recognize the right of any nation to restrict the navigation and overflight of foreign warships and military aircraft beyond its territorial sea. Although several coastal nations, including North Korea and Vietnam, have asserted claims that purport to prohibit warships and military aircraft from operating in so-called security zones extending beyond the territorial sea, such claims have no basis in international law in time of peace and are not recognized by the United States.

The Charter of the United Nations and general principles of international law recognize that a nation may exercise measures of individual or collective self-defense against an imminent threat of armed attack or an actual armed attack directed at that nation or at the regional defense organization of which it is a member. Those measures may include the establishment of "defensive sea areas" or "maritime control areas" in which the threatened nation seeks to enforce some degree of control over foreign entry into its territory. Historically, the establishment of such areas extending beyond the territorial sea has been restricted to periods of war or of declared national emergency involving the outbreak of hostilities. International law does not determine the geographic limits of such areas or the degree of control that a coastal or island nation may lawfully exercise over them, beyond laying down the general requirement of reasonableness in relation to the needs of national security and defense.

2.4.5 Polar Regions

2.4.5.1 Arctic Region. The U.S. considers that the waters, icepack, and airspace of the Arctic region beyond the lawfully claimed territorial seas of littoral nations have international status and are open to navigation by the ships and aircraft of all nations. Although several nations, including Canada and the U.S.S.R., have, at times, attempted to claim sovereignty over the Arctic on the basis of discovery, historic use, contiguity (proximity), or the so-called "sector" theory, those claims are not recognized in international law. Accordingly, all ships and aircraft enjoy the freedoms of high seas navigation and overflight on, over, and under the waters and icepack of the Arctic region beyond the lawfully claimed territorial sea.

2.4.5.2 Antarctic Region. A number of nations have asserted conflicting and often overlapping claims to portions of Antarctica. These claims are premised variously on discovery, contiguity, occupation and, in some instances, the "sector" theory. The U.S. does not recognize the validity of the claims of other nations to any portion of the Antarctic area.

2.4.5.2.1 The Antarctic Treaty of 1959. The U.S. is a party to the multinational treaty of 1959 governing Antarctica. Designed to encourage the scientific exploration of the continent and to foster research and experiments in Antarctica without regard to conflicting assertions of territorial sovereignty, the 1959 accord provides that no activity in the area undertaken while the treaty is in force will constitute a basis for asserting, supporting, or denying such claims.

The treaty also provides that Antarctica "shall be used for peaceful purposes only," and that "any measures of a military nature, such as the establishment of military bases and fortifications, the carrying out of military maneuvers, as well as the testing of any type of weapons" shall be prohibited. All stations and installations, and all ships and aircraft at points of discharging or embarking cargo or personnel in Antarctica, are subject to inspection by designated foreign observers. Therefore, classified activities are not conducted by the U.S. in Antarctica, and all classified material is removed from U.S. ships and aircraft prior to visits to the continent. In addition, the treaty prohibits nuclear explosions and disposal of nuclear wastes anywhere south of 600 South Latitude. The treaty does not, however, affect in any way the high seas freedoms of navigation and overflight in the Antarctic region. Antarctica has no territorial sea or territorial airspace.

2.4.6 Nuclear Free Zones. The 1968 Nuclear Weapons Non-Proliferation Treaty, to which the United States is a party, acknowledges the right of groups of nations to conclude regional treaties establishing nuclear free zones. Such treaties or their provisions are binding only on parties to them or to protocols incorporating those provisions. To the extent that the rights and freedoms of other nations, including the high seas freedoms of navigation and overflight, are not infringed upon, such treaties are not inconsistent with international law. The 1967 Treaty for the Prohibition of Nuclear Weapons in Latin America (Treaty of Tlatelolco) is an example of a nuclear free zone arrangement that is fully consistent with international law, as evidenced by U.S. ratification of its two protocols. This in no way affects the exercise by the U.S. of navigational rights and freedoms within waters covered by the Treaty of Tlatelolco.

2.5 AIR NAVIGATION

2.5.1 National Airspace. Under international law, every nation has complete and exclusive sovereignty over its national airspace, that is, the airspace above its territory, its internal waters, its territorial sea, and, in the case of an archipelagic nation, its archipelagic waters. *There is no customary right of innocent passage of aircraft through the airspace over the territorial sea or archipelagic waters analogous to the right of innocent passage enjoyed by surface ships.* Accordingly, un-less party to an international agreement to the contrary, all nations have complete discretion in regulating or prohibiting flights within their national airspace (as opposed to a Flight Information Region—see paragraph 2.5.2.2), with the sole exception of overflight of international straits and archipelagic sea lanes. Aircraft wishing to enter national airspace must identify themselves, seek or confirm permission to land or to transit, and must obey all reasonable orders to land, turn back, or fly a prescribed course and/or altitude. Aircraft in distress are entitled to special consideration and should be allowed entry and emergency landing rights. Concerning the right of assistance entry, see 2.3.2.5.

2.5.1.1 International Straits Which Connect EEZ/High Seas to EEZ/High Seas and are Overlapped by Territorial Seas. All aircraft, including military aircraft, enjoy the right of unimpeded transit passage through the airspace above international straits overlapped by territorial waters. Such transits must be continuous and expeditious, and the aircraft involved must refrain from the threat or the use of force against the sovereignty, territorial integrity, or political independence of the nation or nations bordering the strait. The exercise of the right of overflight by aircraft engaged in the transit passage of international straits cannot be suspended in peacetime for any reason. (See paragraph 2.5.2 for a discussion of permitted activities over international straits not completely overlapped by territorial seas.)

2.5.1.2 Archipelagic Sea Lanes. All aircraft, including military aircraft, enjoy the right of unimpeded passage through the airspace above archipelagic sea lanes. The right of overflight of such sea lanes is essentially identical to that of transit passage through the airspace above international straits overlapped by territorial seas.

2.5.2 International Airspace. International airspace is the airspace over the contiguous zone, the high seas, the exclusive economic zone, and territories not subject to national sovereignty (*e.g.*, Antarctica). All international airspace is open to the aircraft of all nations. Accordingly, aircraft, including military aircraft, are free to operate in international airspace without interference from coastal or island nation authorities. Military aircraft may engage in flight operations, including ordnance testing and firing, surveillance and intelligence gathering, and support of other naval activities. All such activities must be conducted with due regard for the rights of other nations and the safety of other aircraft and of vessels. (Note, however, that the Antarctic Treaty prohibits military maneuvers and weapons testing in Antarctic airspace.) These same principles apply with respect to the overflight of high seas or exclusive economic zone corridors through that part of international straits *not* completely overlapped by territorial seas.

2.5.2.1 Convention on International Civil Aviation. The U.S. is a party to the 1944 Convention on International Civil Aviation (as are most all nations). That multilateral treaty, commonly referred to as the "Chicago Convention," applies to civil aircraft. It does *not* apply to military aircraft or to MAC-charter aircraft designated as "state aircraft" (see paragraph 2.2.2.1), other than to require that they operate with "due regard for the safety of navigation of civil aircraft." The Chicago Convention established the International Civil Aviation Organization (ICAO) to develop international air navigation principles and techniques and to "promote safety of flight in international air navigation."

Various operational situations do not lend themselves to ICAO flight procedures. These include military contingencies, classified missions, politically sensitive missions, or routine aircraft carrier operations. Operations not conducted under ICAO flight procedures are conducted under the "due regard" or "operational" prerogative of military aircraft (For additional information see DOD Dir. 4540.1, and OPNAV-INST 3770.4.)

2.5.2.2 Flight Information Regions. A Flight Information Region (FIR) is a defined area of airspace within which flight information and alerting services are provided. FIRs are established by ICAO for the safety of civil aviation and encompass both national and international airspace. Ordinarily, but only as a matter of policy, U.S. military aircraft on routine point-to-point flights through international airspace follow ICAO flight procedures and utilize FIR services. As mentioned above, exceptions to this policy include military contingency operations, classified or politically sensitive missions, and routine aircraft carrier operations or training activities. When U.S. military aircraft do not follow ICAO flight procedures, they must navigate with "due regard" for civil aviation safety.

2.5.2.3 Air Defense Identification Zones in International Airspace. International law does not prohibit nations from establishing Air Defense Identification Zones (ADIZ) in the international airspace adjacent to their territorial airspace. The legal basis for ADIZ regulations is the right of a nation to establish reasonable conditions of entry into its territory. Accordingly, an aircraft approaching national airspace can be required to identify itself while in international airspace as a condition of entry approval. ADIZ regulations promulgated by the U.S. apply to aircraft bound for U.S. territorial airspace and require the filing of flight plans and periodic position reports. Some nations, however, purport to require all aircraft penetrating an ADIZ to comply with ADIZ procedures, whether or not they intend to enter national airspace. The U.S. does not recognize the right of a coastal or island nation to apply its ADIZ procedures to foreign aircraft in such circumstances. Accordingly, U.S. military aircraft not intending to enter national airspace need not identify themselves or otherwise comply with ADIZ procedures established by other nations, unless the U.S. has specifically agreed to do so.

It should be emphasized that the foregoing contemplates a peacetime or nonhostile environment. In the case of imminent or actual hostilities a nation may find it necessary to take measures in self-defense that will affect overflight in international airspace.

2.6 EXERCISE AND ASSERTION OF NAVIGATION AND OVERFLIGHT RIGHTS AND FREEDOMS

As announced in the President's United States Oceans Policy Statement of 10 March 1983,

"The United States will exercise and assert its navigation and overflight rights and freedoms on a worldwide basis in a manner that is consistent with the balance of interests reflected in the [1982 LOS) Convention. The United States will not, however, acquiesce in unilateral acts of other states designed to restrict the rights and freedoms of the international community in navigation and overflight and other related high seas uses."

When maritime nations appear to acquiesce in excessive maritime claims and fail to exercise their rights actively in the face of constraints on international navigation and overflight, those claims and constraints may, in time, be considered to have been accepted by the international community as reflecting the practice of nations and as binding upon all users of the

seas and superjacent airspace. Consequently, it is incumbent upon maritime nations to protest through diplomatic channels all excessive claims of coastal or island nations, and to exercise their navigation and overflight rights in the face of such claims. The President's Oceans Policy Statement makes clear that the U.S. has accepted this responsibility as a fundamental element of its national policy.

2.7 RULES FOR NAVIGATIONAL SAFETY FOR VESSELS AND AIRCRAFT

2.7.1 International Rules. Most rules for navigational safety governing surface and subsurface vessels, including warships, are contained in the International Regulations for Preventing Collisions at Sea, 1972, known informally as the "International Rules of the Road" or "72 COLREGS." These rules apply to all international waters (i.e., the high seas, exclusive economic zones, and contiguous zones) and, except where a coastal or island nation has established different rules, in that nation's territorial sea, archipelagic waters, and internal waters as well. Article 1120, U.S. Navy Regulations, 1973, directs that all persons in the naval service responsible for the operation of naval ships and craft "shall diligently observe" the 1972 COLREGS.

2.7.2 National Rules. Many nations have adopted special rules for waters subject to their territorial sovereignty (i.e., internal waters, archipelagic waters, and territorial seas.) Violation of these rules by U.S. Navy vessels may subject the U.S. to lawsuit for collision or other damage, provide the basis for diplomatic protest, result in limitation on U.S. access to foreign ports, or provide the basis for other foreign action.

2.7.2.1 U.S. Inland Rules. The U.S. has adopted special Inland Rules applicable to navigation in U.S. waters landward of the demarcation line established by U.S. law for that purpose. (See U.S. Coast Guard publication CG 169, title 33 Code of Federal Regulations part 80, and title 33 U.S. Code sections 2001 to 2073.) The 1972 COLREGS apply seaward of the demarcation line in U.S. national waters, in the U.S. contiguous zone and exclusive economic zone, and on the high seas.

2.7.3 Navigational Rules for Aircraft.

Rules for air navigation in international airspace applicable to civil aircraft may be found in Annex 2 (Rules of the Air) to the Chicago Convention, DOD Flight Information Publication (FLIP) General Planning, and OPNAVINST 3710.7 (series) NATOPS Manual. The same standardized technical principles and policies of ICAO that apply in international and most foreign airspace are also in effect in the continental United States. Consequently, U.S. pilots can fly all major international routes following the same general rules of the air, using the same navigation equipment and communication practices and procedures, and being governed by the same air traffic control services with which they are familiar in the United States.

2.8 U.S.-U.S.S.R. AGREEMENT ON THE PREVENTION OF INCIDENTS ON AND OVER THE HIGH SEAS

In order better to assure the safety of navigation and flight of their respective warships and military aircraft during encounters at sea, the United States and the Soviet Union in 1972 entered into the U.S.-U.S.S.R. Agreement on the Prevention of Incidents On and Over the High Seas. This Navy-to-Navy agreement, popularly referred to as the "Incidents at Sea" or "INCSEA" agreement, has been highly successful in minimizing the potential for harassing actions and navigational one-upmanship between U.S. and Soviet units operating in close proximity at sea. Although the agreement applies to warships and military aircraft operating on and over the "high seas," it is understood to embrace such units operating in all international waters and international airspace, including that of the exclusive economic zone and the contiguous zone.

Principal provisions of the INCSEA agreement include:

1. Ships will observe strictly both the letter and the spirit of the International Rules of the Road.

2. Ships will remain well clear of one another to avoid risk of collision and, when engaged in surveillance activities, will exercise good seamanship so as not to embarrass or endanger ships under surveillance.

3. Ships will utilize special signals for signaling their operations and intentions.

4. Ships of one party will not simulate attacks by aiming guns, missile launchers, torpedo tubes, or other weapons at the ships of the other party, and will not launch any object in the direction of passing ships nor illuminate their navigation bridges.

5. Ships conducting exercises with submerged submarines will show the appropriate signals to warn of submarines in the area.

6. Ships, when approaching ships of the other party, particularly those engaged in replenishment or flight operations, will take appropriate measures not to hinder maneuvers of such ships and will remain well clear.

7. Aircraft will use the greatest caution and prudence in approaching aircraft and ships of the other party, in particular ships engaged in launching and landing aircraft, and will not simulate attacks by the simulated use of weapons or perform acrobatics over ships of the other party nor drop objects near them.

The INCSEA agreement was amended in a 1973 protocol to extend certain provisions of the agreement to include nonmilitary ships. Specifically, U.S. and Soviet military ships and aircraft shall not make simulated attacks by aiming guns, missile launchers, torpedo tubes, and other weapons at nonmilitary ships of the other party nor launch or drop any objects near nonmilitary ships of the other party in such a manner as to be hazardous to these ships or to constitute a hazard to navigation.

The agreement also provides for an annual review meeting between Navy representatives of the two parties to review its implementation.

2.9 MILITARY ACTIVITIES IN OUTER SPACE

2.9.1 Outer Space Defined. As noted in paragraph 2.5.1, each nation has complete and exclusive control over the use of its national airspace. Except when exercising transit passage or archipelagic sea lanes passage overflight in national airspace by foreign aircraft is not authorized without the consent of the territorial sovereign. However, man-made satellites and other objects in earth orbit may overfly foreign territory freely. Although there is no legally defined boundary between the upper limit of national airspace and the lower limit of outer space, international law recognizes freedom of transit by man-made space objects at earth orbiting altitude and beyond.

2.9.2 The Law of Outer Space. International law, including the United Nations Charter, applies to the outer space activities of nations. Outer space is open to exploration and use by all nations. However, it is not subject to national appropriation, and must be used for peaceful purposes. The term "peaceful purposes" does *not* preclude military activity. While acts of aggression in violation of the United Nations Charter are precluded, space-based systems may lawfully be employed to perform essential command, control, communications, intelligence, navigation, environmental, surveillance and warning functions to assist military activities on land, in the air, and on and under the sea. Users of outer space must have due regard for the rights and interests of other space nations to do so as well.

2.9.2.1 General Principles of the Law of Outer Space. International law governing space activities addresses both the nature of the activity and the location in space where the specific rules apply. As set out in paragraph 2.9.1, outer space begins at the undefined upper limit of the earth's airspace and extends to infinity. In general terms, outer space consists of both the earth's moon and other natural celestial bodies, and the expanse between these natural objects.

The rules of international law applicable to outer space include the following:

1. Access to outer space is free and open to all nations.

2. Outer space is free from claims of sovereignty and not otherwise subject to national appropriation.

3. Outer space is to be used for peaceful purposes.

4. Each user of outer space must show due regard for the rights of others.

5. No nuclear or other weapons of mass destruction may be stationed in outer space.

6. Nuclear explosions in outer space are prohibited.

7. Exploration of outer space must avoid contamination of the environment of outer space and of the earth's biosphere.

8. Astronauts must render all possible assistance to other astronauts in distress.

2.9.2.2 Natural Celestial Bodies. Natural celestial bodies include the earth's moon but not the earth. Under international law, military bases, installations and forts may not be erected nor may weapons tests or maneuvers be undertaken on natural celestial bodies. Moreover, all equipment, stations and vehicles located there are open to inspection on a reciprocal basis. There is no corresponding right of physical inspection of manmade objects located in the expanse between celestial bodies. Military personnel may be employed on natural celestial bodies for scientific research and for other activities undertaken for peaceful purposes.

2.9.3 International Agreements on Outer Space Activities. The key legal principles governing outer space activities are contained in four widely ratified multilateral agreements: the 1967 Outer Space Treaty; the 1968 Rescue and Return of Astronauts Agreement; the Liability Treaty of 1972; and the Space Objects Registration Treaty of 1975. A fifth, the 1979 Moon Treaty, has not been widely ratified. The United States is a party to all of these agreements except the Moon Treaty.

2.9.3.1 Related International Agreements. Several other international agreements restrict specific types of activity in

outer space. The U.S.-USSR Anti-Ballistic Missile (ABM) Treaty of 1972 prohibits the development, testing, and deployment of space based ABM systems or components. Also prohibited is any interference with the surveillance satellites both nations use to monitor ABM Treaty compliance.

The 1963 Limited Test Ban Treaty (a multilateral treaty) includes an agreement not to test nuclear weapons or to carry out any other nuclear explosions in outer space.

The 1977 Environmental Modification Convention (also a multilateral treaty) prohibits military or other hostile use of environmental modification techniques in several environments, including outer space.

The 1982 International Telecommunication Convention and the 1979 Radio Regulations govern the use of the radio frequency spectrum by satellites and the location of satellites in the geostationary-satellite orbit.

2.9.4 Rescue and Return of Astronauts. Both the Outer Space Treaty and the Rescue and Return of Astronauts Agreement establish specific requirements for coming to the aid of astronauts. The treaties do not distinguish between civilian and military astronauts.

Astronauts of one nation engaged in outer space activities are to render all possible assistance to astronauts of other nations in the event of accident or distress. If a nation learns that spacecraft personnel are in distress or have made an emergency or unintended landing in its territory, the high seas, or other international area (e.g, Antarctica), it must notify the launching nation and the Secretary-General of the United Nations, take immediate steps to rescue the personnel if within its territory, and, if in a position to do so, extend search and rescue assistance if a high seas or other international area landing is involved. Rescued personnel are to be safely and promptly returned.

Nations also have an obligation to inform the Secretary-General of the United Nations if they discover outer space phenomena which constitute a danger to astronauts.

2.9.5 Return of Outer Space Objects. A party to the Rescue and Return of Astronauts Agreement must also notify the Secretary-General of the United Nations if it learns of an outer space object's return to earth in its territory, on the high seas, or in another international area. If the object is located in sovereign territory and the launching authority requests the territorial sovereign's assistance, the later must take steps to recover and return the object. Similarly, such objects found in international areas shall be held for or returned to the launching authority. Expenses incurred in assisting the launching authority in either case are to be borne by the launching authority. Should a nation discover that such an object is of a "hazardous or deleterious" nature, it is entitled to immediate action by the launching authority to eliminate the danger of harm from its territory.

CHAPTER 3

Protection of Persons and Property at Sea

3.1 INTRODUCTION

The protection of both U.S. and foreign persons and property at sea by U.S. naval forces in peacetime involves international law, domestic U.S. law and policy, and political considerations. Vessels and aircraft on and over the sea, and the persons and cargo embarked in them, are subject to the hazards posed by the ocean itself, by storm, by mechanical failure, and by the actions of others such as pirates, terrorists, and insurgents. In addition, foreign authorities and prevailing political situations may affect a vessel or aircraft and those on board by involving them in refugee rescue efforts, political asylum requests, regulatory enforcement actions, or applications of unjustified use of force against them.

Given the complexity of the legal, political, and diplomatic considerations that may arise in connection with the use of naval forces to protect civilian persons and property at sea, operational plans, operational orders, and, most importantly, the *applicable peacetime rules of engagement* promulgated by the operational chain of command ordinarily require the on-scene commander to report immediately such circumstances to higher authority and, whenever it is practicable under the circumstances to do so, to seek guidance prior to the use of armed force.

3.2 RESCUE, SAFE HARBOR, AND QUARANTINE

Mishap at sea is a common occurrence. The obligation of mariners to provide material aid in cases of distress encountered at sea has long been recognized in custom and tradition. A right to enter and remain in a safe harbor without prejudice, at least in peacetime, when required by the perils of the sea or *force majeure* is universally recognized. At the same time, a coastal nation may lawfully promulgate quarantine regulations and restrictions for the port or area in which a vessel is located.

3.2.1 Assistance to Persons, Ships, and Aircraft in Distress. Both the 1958 Geneva Convention on the High Seas and the 1982 United Nations Convention on the Law of the Sea (1982 LOS Convention) provide that every nation shall require the master of a ship flying its flag, insofar as he can do so without serious danger to his ship, crew, or passengers, to render assistance to any person found at sea in danger of being lost and to proceed with all possible speed to the rescue of persons in distress if informed of their need of assistance, insofar as it can reasonably be expected of him. He is also to be required, after a collision, to render assistance to the other ship, its crew, and its passengers and, where possible, to inform the other ship of the name of his own ship, its port of registry, and the nearest port at which it will call. (See paragraph 2.3.2.5 for a discussion of "Assistance Entry.")

3.2.1.1 Duty of Naval Commanders. Article 0925, U.S. Navy Regulations, 1973, requires that, insofar as he can do so without serious danger to his ship or crew, the commanding officer or senior officer present, as appropriate, shall proceed with all possible speed to the rescue of persons in distress if informed of their need for assistance (insofar as this can reasonably be expected of him); render assistance to any person found at sea in danger of being lost; and, after a collision, render assistance to the other ship, her crew and passengers, and, where possible, inform the other ship of his identity.

3.2.1.2 Duty of Masters. In addition, the U.S. is party to the 1974 London Convention on Safety of Life at Sea, which requires the master of every merchant ship and private vessel not only to speed to the assistance of persons in distress, but to broadcast warning messages with respect to dangerous conditions or hazards encountered at sea.

3.2.2 Safe Harbor. Under international law, no port may be closed to a foreign ship seeking shelter from storm or bad weather or otherwise compelled to enter it in distress, unless another equally safe port is open to the distressed vessel to which it may proceed without additional jeopardy or hazard. The only condition is that the distress must be real and not contrived and based on a well-founded apprehension of loss of the vessel, cargo, or crew. In general, the distressed vessel may enter a port without being subject to local regulations concerning any incapacity, penalty, prohibition, duties, or taxes in force at that port.

3.2.2.1 Innocent Passage. Innocent passage through territorial seas and archipelagic waters includes stopping and anchoring when necessitated by *force majeure* or by distress. Stopping and anchoring in such waters for the purpose of rendering assistance to others in similar danger or distress is also permitted by international law.

3.2.3 Quarantine. Article 0763, U.S. Navy Regulations, 1973, requires that the commanding officer or aircraft commander of a ship or aircraft comply with quarantine regulations and restrictions. While not required under any circumstance to permit inspection of his vessel or aircraft, commanding officers shall afford every other assistance to health officials, U.S. or foreign, and shall give all information required, insofar as permitted by the requirements of military necessity and security.

3.3 ASYLUM

International law recognizes the right of a nation to grant asylum to foreign nationals already present within or seeking admission to its territory. The U.S. defines "asylum" as:

> Protection and sanctuary granted by the United States Government within its territorial jurisdiction or in international waters to a foreign national who applies for such protection because of persecution or fear of persecution on account of race, religion, nationality, membership in a particular social group, or political opinion.

3.3.1 Territories Under the Exclusive Jurisdiction of the United States and International Waters. Any person requesting asylum in international waters or in territories under the exclusive jurisdiction of the United States (including the U.S. territorial sea, the Commonwealth of Puerto Rico, territories under U.S. administration, and U.S. possessions) will be received on board any naval aircraft or vessel or any Navy or Marine Corps activity or station. Persons seeking asylum are to be afforded every reasonable care and protection permitted by the circumstances. Under no circumstances will a person seeking asylum in U.S. territory or in international waters be surrendered to foreign jurisdiction or control, unless at the personal direction of the Secretary of the Navy or higher authority. (See Article 0940, U.S. Navy Regulations, 1973, and SECNAVINST 5710.22 for specific guidance.)

3.3.2 Territories Under Foreign Jurisdiction. Commanders of U.S. warships, military aircraft, and military installations in territories under foreign jurisdiction (including foreign territorial seas, archipelagic waters, internal waters, ports, territories, and possessions) are not authorized to receive on board foreign nationals seeking asylum. Such persons should be referred to the American Embassy or nearest U.S. Consulate in the country, foreign territory, or foreign possession involved, if any, for assistance in coordinating a request for asylum with the host government insofar as practicable. Because warships are extensions of the sovereignty of the flag nation and because of their immunity from the territorial sovereignty of the foreign nation in whose waters they may be located, they have often been looked to as places of asylum. The U.S., however, considers that asylum is generally the prerogative of the government of the territory in which the warship is located.

However, if exceptional circumstances exist involving imminent danger to the life or safety of the person, temporary refuge may be provided. (See paragraph 3.3.4.)

3.3.3 Expulsion or Surrender. Article 33 of the 1951 Convention Relating to the Status of Refugees provides that a refugee may not be expelled or returned in any manner whatsoever to the frontier or territories of a nation where his life or freedom would be threatened on account of his race, religion, nationality, political opinion, or membership in a particular social group, unless he may reasonably be regarded as a danger to the security of the country of asylum or has been convicted of a serious crime and is a danger to the community of that country. This obligation applies only to persons who have entered territories under the exclusive jurisdiction of the United States. It does not apply to temporary refuge granted abroad.

3.3.4 Temporary Refuge. International law and practice have long recognized the humanitarian practice of providing temporary refuge to anyone, regardless of nationality, who may be in imminent physical danger for the duration of that danger. (See Article 0940, U.S. Navy Regulations, 1973, and SECNAVINST 5710.22.)

SECNAVINST 5710.22 defines "temporary refuge" as:

> Protection afforded for humanitarian reasons to a foreign national in a Department of Defense shore installation, facility, or military vessel or aircraft within the territorial jurisdiction of a foreign nation or in international waters, under conditions of urgency in order to secure the life or safety of that person against imminent danger, such as pursuit by a mob.

It is the policy of the United States to grant temporary refuge in a foreign country to nationals of that country, or nationals of a third nation, solely for humanitarian reasons when extreme or exceptional circumstances put in imminent danger the life or safety of a person, such as pursuit by a mob. The officer in command of the ship, aircraft, station, or activity must decide which measures can prudently be taken to provide temporary refuge. The safety of U.S. personnel and security of the unit must be taken into consideration.

3.3.4.1 Termination or Surrender of Temporary Refuge. Although temporary refuge should be terminated when the period of active danger is ended, the decision to terminate protection will not be made by the commander. Once temporary refuge has been granted, protection may be terminated only when directed by the Secretary of the Navy or higher authority. (See Article 0940, U.S. Navy Regulations, 1973, and SECNAVINST 5710.22.)

A request by foreign authorities for return of custody of a person under the protection of temporary refuge will be reported in accordance with SECNAVINST 5710.22 (series). The requesting foreign authorities will then be advised that the matter has been referred to higher authorities.

3.3.5 Inviting Requests for Asylum or Refuge. Personnel of the Department of the Navy shall neither directly nor indirectly invite persons to seek asylum or temporary refuge.

3.3.6 Protection of U.S. Citizens. The limitations on asylum and temporary refuge are not applicable to U.S. citizens. U.S. citizens are entitled to protection from persecution or danger to life or safety in all circumstances. See the peacetime rules of engagement for applicable guidance.

3.4 REPRESSION OF PIRACY

International law has long recognized a general duty of all nations to cooperate in the repression of piracy. This traditional obligation is included in the 1958 Geneva Convention on the High Seas and the 1982 LOS Convention, both of which provide:

> [A]ll States shall cooperate to the fullest possible extent in the repression of piracy on the high seas or in any other place outside the jurisdiction of any state.

3.4.1 U.S. Law. The U.S. Constitution (Article 1, Section 8) provides that:

> The Congress shall have Power . . . to define and punish piracies and felonies committed on the high seas, and offenses against the Law of Nations.

Congress has exercised this power by enacting title 18 U.S. Code section 1651 which provides that:

> Whoever on the high seas, commits the crime of piracy as defined by the law of nations, and is afterwards brought into or found in the United States, shall be imprisoned for life.

U.S. law authorizes the President to employ "public armed vessels" in protecting U.S. merchant ships from piracy and to instruct the commanders of such vessels to seize any pirate ship that has attempted or committed an act of piracy against any U.S. or foreign flag vessel in international waters.

3.4.2 Piracy Defined. Piracy is an international crime consisting of illegal acts of violence, detention, or depredation committed for private ends by the crew or passengers of a private ship or aircraft in or over international waters against another ship or aircraft or persons and property on board. (Depredation is the act of plundering, robbing, or pillaging.)

3.4.2.1 Location. In international law piracy is a crime that can only be committed in or over international waters, including the high seas, exclusive economic zone, the contiguous zone, in international airspace, and in other places at sea beyond the territorial jurisdiction of any nation. The same acts committed in the territorial sea, archipelagic waters, or national airspace of a nation do not constitute piracy in international law but are, instead, crimes within the jurisdiction and sovereignty of the littoral nation.

3.4.2.2 Private Ship or Aircraft. Acts of piracy can only be committed by private ships or private aircraft. A warship or other public vessel or a military or other state aircraft cannot be treated as a pirate unless it is taken over and operated by pirates or unless the crew mutinies and employs it for piratical purposes. By committing an act of piracy, the pirate ship or aircraft, and the pirates themselves, lose the protection of the nation whose flag they are otherwise entitled to fly.

3.4.2.3 Private Purpose. To constitute the crime of piracy, the illegal acts must be committed for private ends. Consequently, an attack upon a merchant ship at sea for the purpose of achieving some criminal end, *e.g.*, robbery, is an act of piracy as that term is currently defined in international law.

3.4.2.4 Mutiny or Passenger Hijacking. If the crew or passengers of a ship or aircraft, including the crew of a warship or military aircraft, mutiny or revolt and convert the ship, aircraft, or cargo to their own use, that act is not piracy. If, however, the ship or aircraft is thereafter used to commit acts of piracy, it becomes a pirate ship or pirate aircraft and those on board voluntarily participating in such acts become pirates.

3.4.3 Use of Naval Forces to Repress Piracy. Only warships, military aircraft, or other ships or aircraft clearly marked and identifiable as being on governmental service and authorized to that effect may seize a pirate ship or aircraft.

3.4.3.1 Seizure of Pirate Vessels and Aircraft. When a pirate vessel or aircraft is encountered in or over U.S. or international waters it may be seized and detained by any U.S. Navy warship or aircraft. The pirate vessel or aircraft, and all persons on board, should be taken, sent, or directed to the nearest U.S. port or airfield and delivered to U.S. law enforcement authorities for disposition according to U.S. law. Alternatively, higher authority may arrange with another nation to accept and try the pirates and dispose of the pirate vessel or aircraft, since every nation has jurisdiction under international law over any act of piracy.

3.4.3.2 Pursuit Into Foreign Territorial Seas, Archipelagic Waters, or Airspace. If a pirate vessel or aircraft fleeing from pursuit by a warship or military aircraft proceeds from international waters or airspace into the territorial sea, archipelagic waters, or superjacent airspace of another country, every effort should be made to obtain the consent of the nation having sovereignty over the territorial sea, archipelagic waters, or superjacent airspace to continue pursuit. The inviolability of the territorial integrity of sovereign nations makes the decision of a warship or military aircraft to continue pursuit into these areas without such consent a serious matter. However, the international nature of the crime of piracy may allow continuation of pursuit, if contact cannot be established in a timely manner with the coastal nation to obtain its consent. In such a case, pursuit must be broken off immediately upon request of the coastal nation, and, in any event, the right to seize the pirate vessel or aircraft and to try the pirates devolves on the nation to which the territorial seas, archipelagic waters, or airspace belong.

Pursuit of a pirate vessel or aircraft through or over international straits overlapped by territorial waters or through or over archipelagic sea lanes may proceed with or without the consent of the coastal nation or nations, provided the pursuit is expeditious and direct and the transit passage rights of others are not unreasonably constrained in the process.

3.5 PROHIBITION OF THE TRANSPORT OF SLAVES

International law strictly prohibits use of the seas for the purpose of transporting slaves. The 1982 LOS Convention requires every nation to prevent and punish the transport of slaves in ships authorized to fly its flag. Commanders should request guidance from higher authority if confronted with this situation.

3.6 SUPPRESSION OF INTERNATIONAL NARCOTICS TRAFFIC

The 1982 LOS Convention provides that all nations shall cooperate in the suppression of the illicit traffic in narcotics drugs and psychotropic substances by ships in international waters. The 1982 Convention also provides that any nation which has reasonable grounds for believing that a ship flying its flag is engaged in such traffic may request the cooperation of other nations in effecting its seizure. Foreign flag vessels are regularly seized by U.S. Coast Guard ships pursuant to such bilateral arrangements. (See paragraph 3.12.4 regarding utilization of U.S. Navy assets in the support of U.S. drug-interdiction efforts.)

3.7 SUPPRESSION OF UNAUTHORIZED BROADCASTING

The 1982 LOS Convention provides that all nations shall cooperate in the suppression of unauthorized broadcasting from international waters. Unauthorized broadcasting involves the transmission of radio or television signals from a ship or off-shore facility intended for receipt by the general public, contrary to international regulation. Commanders should request guidance from higher authority if confronted with this situation.

3.8 WARSHIP'S RIGHT OF APPROACH AND VISIT

As a general principle, vessels in international waters are immune from the jurisdiction of any nation other than the flag nation. However, under international law, a warship may *approach* any vessel in international waters to verify its nationality. Unless the vessel encountered is itself a warship or government vessel of another nation, it may be stopped, boarded, and the ship's documents examined, *provided* there is reasonable ground for suspecting that it is:

1. Engaged in piracy.

2. Engaged in the slave trade.

3. Engaged in unauthorized broadcasting.

4. Without nationality.

5. Though flying a foreign flag, or refusing to show its flag, the vessel is, in reality, of the same nationality as the warship.

Vessels without nationality (also referred to as "stateless vessels") are vessels not entitled to fly the flag of any nation and vessels falsely assuming a nationality. Because these vessels are not entitled to the protection of any nation, they are subject to the jurisdiction of all nations. The procedure for exercising the right of approach and visit is similar to that used in exercising the belligerent right of visit and search described in paragraph 7.6.1. See Article 630.23 of OPNAVINST 3120.32B for further guidance.

3.9 HOT PURSUIT

The hot pursuit of a foreign ship may be undertaken as a law enforcement action when the coastal or island nation has reason to believe that the ship has violated the laws and regulations of that nation. The pursuit must be commenced when the foreign ship or one of its boats is within the internal waters, the archipelagic waters, the territorial sea, or the contiguous zone of the pursuing nation, and may only be continued outside the territorial sea or contiguous zone if the pursuit has not been interrupted. It is not necessary that, at the time when the foreign ship within the territorial sea or the contiguous zone receives the order to stop, the ship giving the order should likewise be within the territorial sea or the contiguous zone. If the foreign ship is within a contiguous zone, the pursuit may only be undertaken if there has been a violation of the rights for the protection of which the zone was established. The right of hot pursuit ceases as soon as the ship pursued enters the territorial sea of its own nation or of a third nation. The right of hot pursuit may be exercised only by warships or military aircraft or other ships or aircraft clearly marked and identifiable as being on government service and authorized to that effect. The right of hot pursuit applies also to violations in the exclusive economic zone or on the continental shelf, including safety zones around continental shelf installations, of the laws and regulations of the coastal or island nation applicable to the exclusive economic zone or the continental shelf, including such safety zones.

3.9.1 Commencement of Hot Pursuit. Hot pursuit is not deemed to have begun unless the pursuing ship is satisfied by such practicable means as are available that the ship pursued, or one of its boats or other crafts working as a team and using the ship pursued as a mother ship, is within the limits of the territorial sea, within the contiguous zone or the exclusive economic zone, or above the continental shelf. Pursuit may be commenced after a visual or auditory signal to stop has been given at a distance which enables it to be seen or heard by the foreign ship.

3.9.2 Hot Pursuit by Aircraft. Where hot pursuit is effected by aircraft:

1. The provisions of paragraphs 3.9 and 3.9.1 apply.

2. The aircraft giving the order to stop must itself actively pursue the ship until a ship or another aircraft of the coastal or island nation, summoned by the aircraft, arrives to take over the pursuit, unless the aircraft itself is able to arrest the ship. The aircraft must do more than merely sight the offender or suspected offender to justify an arrest outside the territorial sea. It must first order the suspected offender to stop. Should the suspected offender fail to comply, pursuit may be commenced alone or in conjunction with other aircraft or ships. Pursuit must continue without interruption.

3.10 RECOVERY OF U.S. GOVERNMENT PROPERTY LOST AT SEA

The property of a sovereign nation lost at sea remains vested in that sovereign until title is formally relinquished or abandoned. Aircraft wreckage, sunken vessels, practice torpedoes, test missiles, and target drones are among the types of U.S. Navy property which may be the subject of recovery operations. Should such U.S. property be recovered at sea by foreign entities, it is U.S. policy to demand its immediate return. Specific guidance for the on-scene commander in such circumstances is contained in the applicable operational order (*e.g.*, CINCPACFLT OPORD 201, CIN-CLANTFLT OPORD 2000).

3.11 PROTECTION OF PRIVATE AND MERCHANT VESSELS AND AIRCRAFT, PRIVATE PROPERTY, AND PERSONS

In addition to the obligation and authority of warships to repress international crimes such as piracy, international law also contemplates the use of force in peacetime in certain circumstances to protect private and merchant vessels, private property, and persons at sea from acts of unlawful violence. The legal doctrines of self-defense and protection of nationals provide the authority for U.S. naval forces to protect both U.S. and foreign flag vessels, aircraft, property, and persons from violent and unlawful acts of others. Consult the JCS Peacetime Rules of Engagement for U.S. Forces or applicable theater CINC ROE for detailed guidance.

3.11.1 Protection of U.S. Flag Vessels, Aircraft, U.S. Citizens, and Property. International law, embodied in the doctrines of self-defense and protection of nationals, provides authority for the use of proportionate force by U.S. warships and military aircraft when necessary for the protection of U.S. flag vessels and aircraft, U.S. citizens (whether embarked in U.S. or foreign vessels), and their property against *unlawful* violence in and over international waters. Peacetime rules of engagement promulgated by the Joint Chiefs of Staff (JCS) to the operational chain of command and incorporated into applicable operational orders, operational plans, and contingency plans provide guidance to the naval commander for the exercise of this inherent authority. Those rules of engagement are carefully constructed to ensure that the protection of U.S. flag vessels and U.S. citizens and their property at sea con-

forms with U.S. and international law and reflects national policy.

3.11.1.1 Foreign Internal Waters, Archipelagic Waters, and Territorial Seas. Unlawful acts of violence directed against U.S. flag vessels and aircraft and U.S. citizens within and over the internal waters, archipelagic waters, or territorial seas of a foreign nation present special considerations. The coastal or island nation is primarily responsible for the protection of all vessels, aircraft and persons lawfully within and over its sovereign territory. However, when that nation is unable or unwilling to do so effectively or when the circumstances are such that immediate action is required to protect human life, international law recognizes the right of another nation to direct its warships and military aircraft to use proportionate force in or over those waters to protect its flag vessels and its citizens. Because the coastal or island nation may lawfully exercise jurisdiction and control over foreign flag vessels, aircraft, and citizens within its internal waters, archipelagic waters, territorial seas, and national airspace, special care must be taken by the warships and military aircraft or other nations not to interfere with the lawful exercise of jurisdiction by that nation in those waters.

3.11.1.2 Foreign Contiguous Zones and Exclusive Economic Zones. The primary responsibility of coastal or island nations for the protection of foreign shipping off their shores ends at the seaward edge of the territorial sea. Beyond that point, each nation bears the primary responsibility for the protection of its own flag vessels and its own citizens and their property. On the other hand, the coastal or island nation may properly exercise jurisdiction over foreign vessels, aircraft, and persons in and over its contiguous zone to enforce its customs, fiscal, immigration, and sanitary laws, and in its exclusive economic zone to enforce its resource-related rules and regulations. When the coastal or island nation is acting lawfully in the valid exercise of such jurisdiction, or is in hot pursuit (see discussion paragraph 3.9) of a foreign vessel or aircraft for violations that have occurred in or over those waters or in its sovereign territory, the flag nation should not interfere. U.S. naval commanders should consult applicable peacetime rules of engagement for specific guidance.

3.11.2 Protection of Foreign Flag Vessels, Aircraft, and Persons. International law, embodied in the concept of collective self-defense, provides authority for the use of proportionate force necessary for the protection of foreign flag vessels and aircraft, and foreign persons from unlawful violence, including terrorist or piratical attacks, at sea. In such instances, consent of the flag nation should be first obtained unless prior arrangements are already in place or the necessity to act immediately to save human life does not permit obtaining such consent. Should the attack or other *unlawful* violence occur within or over the internal waters, archipelagic waters, or territorial sea of a third nation, or within or over its contiguous zone or exclusive economic zone, the considerations of paragraphs 3.11.1.1 and 3.11.1.2 would also apply.

3.12 AID TO DOMESTIC CIVIL LAW ENFORCEMENT OFFICIALS

Except when expressly authorized by the Constitution or act of Congress, the use of U.S. Army or U.S. Air Force personnel or resources as a *posse comitatus*—a force to aid civilian law enforcement authorities in keeping the peace and arresting felons—or otherwise to execute domestic law, is prohibited by the Posse Comitatus Act, title 18 U.S.C. section 1385. As a matter of policy, the Posse Comitatus Act is made equally applicable to the U.S. Navy and U.S. Marine Corps. The prohibitions of the Act are not applicable to the U.S. Coast Guard, even when operating as part of the Department of the Navy. (See SECNAV-INST 5820.7 (series).)

Although the *posse comitatus* concept forbids military authorities from enforcing or being directly involved with the enforcement of civil law, some military activities in aid of civil law enforcement may be authorized under the military purpose doctrine. For example, indirect involvement or assistance to civil law enforcement authorities which is incidental to normal military training or operations is not a violation of the Posse Comitatus Act. Additionally, Congress has specifically authorized the limited use of military facilities, platforms, and equipment to assist Federal authorities in the interdiction at sea of narcotics and other controlled substances.

3.12.1 Providing Information to Law Enforcement Agencies. It is ordinarily permissible to provide Federal, State, or local law enforcement officials with information acquired during the course of military operations that may be relevant to a violation of any law within the jurisdiction of those officials. However, such operations may not be undertaken with the purpose of acquiring such information for law enforcement officials, unless specifically authorized by applicable law or regulation.

3.12.2 Use of Military Equipment and Facilities. Consistent with mission requirements, available equipment (including shipboard or aircraft systems), base facilities, and research facilities may be made available upon request to Federal, State, or local law enforcement authorities subject, to approval of higher authority.

3.12.3 Use of DOD Personnel. The use of U.S. Army or U.S. Air Force personnel for purposes of providing direct assistance to law enforcement authorities is generally prohibited. Absent a waiver from the Secretary of the Navy or other approval authority, that prohibition is applicable to U.S. Navy and U.S. Marine Corps personnel as well.

3.12.4 DOD Mission in Drug Interdiction. The National Defense Authorization Act of 1989 assigned DOD as single lead agency responsible for coordinating all detection and monitoring of aerial and maritime transit of illegal drugs into the United States. It also directed DOD to integrate U.S. command, control, communications and intelligence ($C^3$1) assets dedicated to drug interdiction into an effective communications network.

3.12.5 Use of U.S. Navy Ships In Support of Drug-interdiction Operations. Consistent with Congressional direction, U.S. Navy ships operating in waters designated by the Secretary of Defense (in consultation with the Attorney General) as a drug-interdiction area are required to have embarked a Coast Guard officer who is trained in law enforcement and who has power to arrest, search, and seize property or persons suspected of violations of U.S. law. In consonance with the right of the flag state under international law to exercise jurisdiction over vessels flying its flag, a U.S. Navy ship with an appropriately authorized Coast Guard officer on board may approach and stop, anywhere in international waters or in U.S. national waters, any *U.S.* flag vessel which, on reasonable grounds, is believed to be engaged in

the illicit traffic of narcotics or psychotropic substances. In such circumstances, any resultant search, seizure, or arrest will be accomplished by the embarked Coast Guard officer.

Foreign flag vessels encountered by U.S. Navy ships in the U.S. territorial sea or contiguous zone (see paragraph 1.5.1) under circumstances indicating that the vessel may be engaged in the illicit traffic of narcotics or psychotropic substances may be similarly approached and stopped, and boarded by the embarked Coast Guard officer. In international waters, foreign flag vessels may be boarded and, if warranted, seized for drug-interdiction purposes only under one or more of the following circumstances: with flag state consent, in hot pursuit originating in the U.S. territorial sea or contiguous zone, or if the vessel is the mother ship of one or more craft operating in the U.S. territorial sea or contiguous zone. In addition, a vessel in international waters may be boarded with the consent of the master, but seizure may only occur under one of the foregoing circumstances. Foreign flag nation consent may consist of a bilateral agreement covering all such encounters or may be granted by that nation for the particular occasion. In all drug interdiction cases involving seizure of a foreign flag vessel beyond 12-nautical miles from the U.S. coast, concurrence must be obtained through the Department of State.

CHAPTER 4

Safeguarding of U.S. National Interests in the Maritime Environment

4.1 INTRODUCTION

This final chapter of Part I—Law of Peacetime Naval Operations examines the broad principles of international law that govern the conduct of nations in protecting their interests at sea during time of peace. *As noted in the preface, this publication provides general information, is not directive, and does not supersede guidance issued by the commanders of the unified and specified commands, within the scope of their authority, and in particular any guidance they may issue that delineate the circumstances and limitations under which the forces under their command will initiate and/or continue engagement with other forces encountered.*

Historically, international law governing the use of force between nations has been divided into rules applicable in peacetime and rules applicable in time of war. In recent years, however, the concepts of both "war" and "peace" have become blurred and no longer lend themselves to clear definition. Consequently, it is not always possible, or even useful, to try to draw neat distinctions between the two. Full scale hostilities continue to break out around the world, but few are accompanied by a formal declaration of war. At the same time, the spectrum of armed conflict has widened and become increasingly complex. At one end of that spectrum is total nuclear war; at the other, insurgencies and state-sponsored terrorism. For the purposes of this publication, however, the conduct of armed hostilities involving U.S. forces, irrespective of character, intensity, or duration, is addressed in Part II—Law of Naval Warfare.

4.1.1 Charter of the United Nations. Article 2, paragraph 3 of the Charter of the United Nations provides that:

> All Members shall settle their international disputes by peaceful means in such a manner that international peace and security, and justice, are not endangered.

Article 2, paragraph 4 provides that:

> All Members shall refrain in their international relations from the threat or use of force against the territorial integrity or political independence of any state, or in any other manner inconsistent with the Purposes of the United Nations.

In combination, these two provisions establish the fundamental principle of modern international law that nations will *not* use force or the threat of force to impose their will on other nations or to otherwise resolve their international differences.

Article 39 of the Charter looks to the Security Council to enforce this prohibition by providing:

> The Security Council shall determine the existence of any threat to the peace, breach of the peace, or act of transgression and shall . . . decide what measures shall be taken . . . to maintain or restore international peace and security.

Article 51 of the Charter provides, however, that:

> Nothing in the . . . Charter shall impair the inherent right of individual or collective self-defense if an armed attack occurs against a Member . . . until the Security Council has taken measures necessary to maintain international peace and security. . . .

The following paragraphs discuss some of the measures that nations, acting in conformity with the Charter of the United Nations, may take in pursuing and protecting their national interests at sea during peacetime.

4.2 NONMILITARY MEASURES

4.2.1 Diplomatic. As contemplated by the United Nations Charter, nations generally rely on peaceful means to resolve their differences and to protect their interests. Diplomatic measures include all those political policy actions taken by one nation to influence the behavior of other nations within the framework of international law. They may involve negotiation, conciliation, or mediation, and may be cooperative or coercive (*e.g.*, severing of diplomatic relations). The behavior of an offending nation may be curbed by appeals to world public opinion as in the General Assembly, or, if their misconduct involves a threat to or breach of the peace, by bringing the issue before the Security Council. Ordinarily, however, differences that arise between nations are resolved or accommodated through the normal day-to-day, give-and-take of international diplomacy. The key point is that disputes between the U.S. and other nations arising out of conflicting interests in the maritime environment, or having their origin elsewhere but impacting on U.S. uses of the seas, are normally addressed and resolved through diplomatic channels and do not involve resort to the threat or use of force.

4.2.2 Economic. Nations often utilize economic measures to influence the actions of others. The granting or withholding of "most favored nation" status to another country is an often used measure of economic policy. Similarly, trade agreements, loans, concessionary credit arrangements and other aid, and investment opportunity are among the many economic measures that nations extend, or may withhold, as their national interests dictate. Examples of the coercive use of economic measures to curb or otherwise seek to influence the conduct of other nations include the suspension of U.S. grain sales and the embargo on the transfer of U.S. technology to the offending nation, boycott of oil and other export products from the offending nation, and suspension of "most favored nation" status and the assertion of other economic sanctions.

4.2.3 Judicial. Nations may also seek judicial resolution of their peacetime disputes, both in national courts and before international tribunals. A nation or its citizens may bring a legal action against another nation in its own national courts, provided the court has jurisdiction over the matter in controversy (such as where the action is directed against property of the foreign nation located within the territorial jurisdiction of the court) *and* provided the foreign nation does not interpose a valid claim of sovereign immunity. Similarly, a nation or its citizens may bring a legal action against another nation in the latter's courts, or in the courts of a third nation, provided jurisdiction can be found and sovereign immunity is not interposed.

Nations may also submit their disputes to the International Court of Justice for resolution. Article 92 of the United Nations Charter establishes the International Court of Justice as the principal judicial organ of the United Nations. No nation may bring another nation before the Court unless the latter nation first consents. That consent can be general and given beforehand or can be given in regard to a specific controversy.

In 1946, the U.S. formally accepted compulsory jurisdiction of the Court, in relation to any other nation that had accepted the same obligation, for all disputes involving interpretation of a treaty, a question of international law, or the breach of an international obligation. In doing so, however, the U.S. reserved the right to refuse to accept the jurisdiction of the International Court in any matter that is "essentially within the domestic jurisdiction of the United States as determined by the United States." On 7 October 1985, the United States announced the termination of its acceptance of compulsory jurisdiction effective 7 April 1986. Of the 157 nations that are parties to the International Court of Justice by virtue of their membership in the United Nations, only 45 accept compulsory jurisdiction of the Court. All but six of those 45 nations have reservations similar to that which had been asserted by the U.S.

4.3 MILITARY MEASURES

The mission of all U.S. military forces is to deter aggression and, should deterrence fail, to engage and defeat the aggressor in armed conflict so as to restore international peace and security. In order to deter aggression, U.S. military forces must be both capable and ready, and must be per-

ceived to be so by potential aggressors. Equally important is the perception of other nations that, should the need arise, the U.S. has the will to use its forces in individual or collective self-defense.

4.3.1 Naval Presence. U.S. naval forces constitute a key and unique element of our national military capability. The mobility of forces operating at sea combined with the versatility of naval force composition—from units operating individually to multi-battle-group formations—provide the National Command Authorities with the flexibility to tailor U.S. military presence as circumstances may require.

Naval presence, whether as a showing of the flag during port visits or as forces deployed in response to contingencies or crises, can be modulated to exert the precise influence best suited to U.S. interests. Depending upon the magnitude and immediacy of the problem, naval forces may be positioned near areas of potential discord as a show of force or as a symbolic expression of support and concern. Unlike land-based forces, naval forces may be so employed without political entanglement and without the necessity of seeking littoral nation consent. So long as they remain in international waters and international airspace (i.e., beyond the territorial sea or archipelagic waters), U.S. warships and military aircraft enjoy the full spectrum of the high seas freedoms of navigation and overflight, including the right to conduct naval maneuvers, subject only to the requirement to observe international standards of safety, to recognize the rights of other ships and aircraft that may be encountered, and to issue NOTAMs and NOTMARs as the circumstances may require. Deployment of a carrier battle group into the vicinity of areas of tension and augmentation of U.S. naval forces to deter interference with U.S. commercial shipping in an area of armed conflict provide graphic illustrations of the use of U.S. naval forces in peacetime to deter violations of international law and to protect U.S. flag shipping.

4.3.2 The Right of Self-Defense. The Charter of the United Nations recognizes that all nations enjoy the inherent right of individual and collective self-defense against armed attack. U.S. doctrine on self-defense, set forth in the JCS Peacetime Rules of Engagement for U.S. Forces, provides that the use of force in self-defense against armed attack, or the threat of imminent armed attack, rests upon two elements:

1. Necessity—The requirement that a use of force be in response to a hostile act or hostile intent.

2. Proportionality—The requirement that the use of force be in all circumstances limited in intensity, duration, and scope to that which is reasonably required to counter the attack or threat of attack and to ensure the continued safety of U.S. forces.

Customary international law has long recognized that there are circumstances during time of peace when nations must resort to the use of armed force to protect their national interests against unlawful or otherwise hostile actions by other nations. A number of legal concepts have evolved over the years to sanction the limited use of armed forces in such circumstances (e.g., intervention, embargo, maritime quarantine). To the extent that such concepts have continuing validity under the Charter of the United Nations, they are premised on the broader principle of self-defense.

The concept of maritime quarantine provides a case in point. Maritime quarantine was first invoked by the United States as a means of interdicting the flow of Soviet strategic missiles into Cuba in 1962. That action involved a limited coercive measure on the high seas applicable only to ships carrying offensive weaponry to Cuba and utilized the least possible military force to achieve that purpose. That action, formally ratified by the Organization of American States (OAS), has been widely approved as a legitimate exercise of the inherent right of individual and collective self-defense recognized in Article 51 of the United Nations Charter.

4.3.2.1 Anticipatory Self-Defense. Included within the inherent right of self-defense is the right of a nation (and its armed forces) to protect itself from imminent attack. International law recognizes that it would be contrary to the purposes of the United Nations Charter if a threatened nation were required to absorb an aggressor's initial and potentially crippling first strike before taking those military measures necessary to thwart an imminent attack. Anticipatory self-defense involves the use of armed force where there is a clear necessity that is instant, overwhelming, and leaving no reasonable choice of peaceful means.

4.3.2.2 JCS Peacetime Rules of Engagement (ROE). The JCS Peacetime Rules of Engagement for U.S. Forces are the primary means by which competent military authority in peacetime authorizes commanders to take those actions necessary for the self-defense of the force they command, the self-defense of the nation and its citizens, and the protection of national assets worldwide. Although they do not, and cannot, cover all possible situations that may be encountered by the naval commander at sea, the JCS Peacetime ROE provide definitive guidance for U.S. military commanders for the use of armed force in self-defense commensurate with international law and U.S. national security objectives. A principal tenet of those ROE is the responsibility of the commander to take all necessary and appropriate action for his unit's self-defense. Subject to that overriding responsibility, the full range of options are reserved for the National Command Authorities to determine the response that will be made to hostile acts and demonstrations of hostile intent. As noted in the preceding paragraphs of this chapter, those options may involve nonmilitary as well as military measures.

4.4 INTERCEPTION OF INTRUDING AIRCRAFT

All nations have complete and exclusive sovereignty over their national airspace, i.e., the airspace above their land territory, internal waters, archipelagic waters (if any), and territorial seas. (See paragraph 1.8) With the exception of transit overflight of international straits and archipelagic sea lanes (see paragraphs 2.3.3 and 2.3.4.1) and assistance entry to assist those in danger of being lost at sea (see paragraph 2.3.2.5), authorization must be obtained for any intrusion by a foreign aircraft (military or civil) into national airspace. (See paragraph 2.5) That authorization may be flight specific, as in the case of diplomatic clearance for the visit of a military aircraft, or general, as in the case of commercial air navigation pursuant to the 1944 Convention on International Civil Aviation (the "Chicago Convention").

Customary international law provides that a foreign aircraft entering national airspace without permission due to duress (*e.g.*, air hijacking) or navigational error may be required to comply with orders to turn back or to land. In this connection the Chicago Convention has been amended to provide:

1. That all nations must refrain from the use of weapons against civil aircraft, and, in the case of the interception of intruding civil aircraft, that the lives of persons on board and the safety of the aircraft must not be endangered. (This provision does not, however, detract from the right of self-defense recognized under Article 51 of the United Nations Charter.)

2. That all nations have the right to require intruding aircraft to land at some designated airfield and to resort to appropriate means consistent with international law to require intruding aircraft to desist from activities in violation of the Convention.

3. That all intruding civil aircraft must comply with the orders given to them and that all nations must enact national laws making such compliance by their civil aircraft mandatory.

4. That all nations shall prohibit the deliberate use of their civil aircraft for purposes (such as intelligence collection) inconsistent with the Convention.

The amendment was approved unanimously on 10 May 1984 and will come into force upon ratification by 102 of ICAO's members in respect of those nations which have ratified it. The Convention, by its terms, does not apply to intruding military aircraft. The U.S. takes the position that customary international law establishes similar standards of reasonableness and proportionality with respect to military aircraft that stray into national airspace through navigational error or that are in distress.

PART II
Law of Naval Warfare

CHAPTER 5

Principles and Sources of the Law of Armed Conflict

5.1 WAR AND THE LAW

Article 2 of the United Nations Charter requires all nations to settle their international disputes by peaceful means and to refrain from the threat or use of force against the territorial integrity or political independence of other nations. The United Nations Charter prohibits resort to war except as an enforcement action taken by or on behalf of the United Nations (as in the Korean conflict) or as a measure of individual or collective self-defense. It is important to distinguish between resort to war, or armed conflict, and the conduct of armed conflict. Whether or not resort to armed conflict in a particular circumstance is prohibited by the United Nations Charter (and therefore unlawful), the manner in which that armed conflict is conducted continues to be regulated by the law of armed conflict. (For purposes of this publication, the term "law of armed conflict" is synonymous with "law of war.")

5.2 GENERAL PRINCIPLES OF THE LAW OF ARMED CONFLICT

The law of armed conflict seeks to prevent unnecessary suffering and destruction by controlling and mitigating the harmful effects of hostilities through minimum standards of protection to be accorded to combatants and to noncombatants. To that end, the law of armed conflict provides that:

1. Only that degree and kind of force, not otherwise prohibited by the law of armed conflict, required for the partial or complete submission of the enemy with a minimum expenditure of time, life, and physical resources may be applied.

2. The employment of any kind or degree of force not required for the purpose of the partial or complete submission of the enemy with a minimum expenditure of time, life, and physical resources is prohibited.

3. Dishonorable (treacherous) means, dishonorable expedients, and dishonorable conduct during armed conflict are forbidden.

The law of armed conflict is not intended to impede the waging of hostilities. Its purpose is to ensure that the violence of hostilities is directed toward the enemy's forces and is not used to cause purposeless, unnecessary human misery and physical destruction. In that sense, the law of armed conflict complements and supports the principles of warfare embodied in the military concepts of objective, mass, economy of force, surprise, and security. Together, the law of armed conflict and the principles of warfare underscore the importance of concentrating forces against

562

critical military targets while avoiding the expenditure of personnel and resources against persons, places, and things that are militarily unimportant.

5.3 COMBATANTS AND NONCOMBATANTS

The law of armed conflict is based largely on the distinction to be made between combatants and noncombatants. In accordance with this distinction, the population of a nation engaged in armed conflict is divided into two general classes: armed forces (combatants) and the civilian populace (noncombatants). Each class has specific rights and obligations in time of armed conflict, and no single individual can be simultaneously a combatant and a noncombatant.

The term noncombatant is primarily applied to those individuals who do not form a part of the armed forces and who otherwise refrain from the commission or direct support of hostile acts. In this context, noncombatants and, generally, the civilian population are synonymous. The term noncombatants may, however, also embrace certain categories of persons who, although attached to or accompanying the armed forces, enjoy special protected status, such as medical officers, corpsmen,

Viet Cong suspects captured by U.S. Forces during Operation Rio Grande in the Queng Ngai Privinco, RVN (19 Feb 67). U.S. Forces had serious difficulty distinguishing Viet Cong from noncombatants throughout the Vietnam conflict. Photo by LCPL W.L. Page, USA. Courtesy of U.S. Naval Institute.

chaplains, and civilian war correspondents. The term is also applied to armed forces personnel who are unable to engage in combat because of wounds, sickness, shipwreck, or capture.

Under the law of armed conflict, noncombatants must be safeguarded against injury not incidental to military operations directed against combatant forces and other military objectives. In particular, it is forbidden to make noncombatants the object of attack.

5.4 SOURCES OF THE LAW OF ARMED CONFLICT

As is the case with international law generally, the principal sources of the law of armed conflict are custom, as reflected in the practice of nations, and international agreements.

5.4.1 Customary Law. The customary international law of armed conflict derives from the practice of military and naval forces in the field, at sea, and in the air during hostilities. When such a practice attains a degree of regularity and is accompanied by the general conviction among nations that behavior in conformity with that practice is obligatory, it can be said to have become a rule of customary law binding upon all nations. It is frequently difficult to determine the precise point in time at which a usage or practice of warfare evolves into a customary rule of law. In a period marked by rapid developments in technology, coupled with the broadening of the spectrum of warfare to encompass insurgencies and state-sponsored terrorism, it is not surprising that nations often disagree as to the precise content of an accepted practice of warfare and to its status as a rule of law. This lack of precision in the definition and interpretation of rules of customary law has been a principal motivation behind efforts to codify the law of armed conflict through written agreements (treaties and conventions).

5.4.2 International Agreements. International agreements, whether denominated as treaties or conventions, have played a major role in the development of the law of armed conflict. Whether codifying existing rules of customary law or creating new rules to govern future practice, international agreements are a source of the law of armed conflict. Rules of law established through international agreements are ordinarily binding only upon those nations that have ratified or adhered to them. Moreover, rules established through the treaty process are binding only to the extent required by the terms of the treaty itself as limited by the reservations, if any, that have accompanied its ratification or adherence by individual nations. Conversely, to the extent that such rules codify existing customary law or otherwise come, over time, to represent a general consensus among nations of their obligatory nature, they are binding upon party and nonparty nations alike.

Principal among the international agreements reflecting the development and codification of the law of armed conflict are the Hague Regulations of 1907, the Gas Protocol of 1925, the Geneva Conventions of 1949 for the Protection of War Victims, the 1954 Hague Cultural Property Convention, the Biological Weapons Convention of 1972, and the Conventional Weapons Convention of 1980. Whereas the 1949 Geneva Conventions and the 1977 Protocols. Additional thereto address, for the most part, the protection of victims of war, the Hague Regulations, Geneva Gas Protocol, Hague Cultural Property Convention, Biological Weapons Convention, and the Conventional Weapons Convention are concerned, primarily, with controlling the means and methods of warfare. The most significant of these agreements (for purposes of this publication) are listed chronologically as follows:

1. 1907 Hague Convention Respecting the Laws and Customs of War on Land (Hague IV)

2. 1907 Hague Convention Respecting the Rights and Duties of Neutral Powers and Persons in Case of War on Land (Hague V)

3. 1907 Hague Convention Relative to the Laying of Automatic Submarine Contact Mines (Hague VIII)

4. 1907 Hague Convention Concerning Bombardment by Naval Forces in Time of War (Hague IX)

5. 1907 Hague Convention Relative to Certain Restrictions with Regard to the Exercise of the Right of Capture in Naval War (Hague XI)

6. 1907 Hague Convention Concerning the Rights and Duties of Neutral Powers in Naval War (Hague XIII)*

7. 1925 Protocol for the Prohibition of the Use in War of Asphyxiating, Poisonous, or Other Gases, and of Bacteriological Methods of Warfare*

8. 1936 London Protocol in Regard to the Operations of Submarines or Other War Vessels with Respect to Merchant Vessels (Part IV of the 1930 London Naval Treaty)

9. 1949 Geneva Convention (I) for the Amelioration of the Condition of the Wounded and Sick in Armed Forces in the Field*

10. 1949 Geneva Convention (II) for the Amelioration of the Condition of Wounded, Sick, and Shipwrecked Members of Armed Forces at Sea

11. 1949 Geneva Convention (III) relative to the Treatment of Prisoners of War

12. 1949 Geneva Convention (IV) relative to the Protection of Civilian Persons in Time of War

13. 1954 Hague Cultural Property Convention

14. 1972 Convention on the Prohibition of the Development, Production and Stockpiling of Bacteriological (Biological) and Toxin Weapons and on Their Destruction

15. 1977 Protocol Additional to the Geneva Conventions of 1949 and Relating to the Protection of Victims of International Armed Conflicts (Additional Protocol I)

16. 1977 Protocol Additional to the Geneva Conventions of 1949 and Relating to the Protection of Victims of Non-International Armed Conflicts (Additional Protocol II)

17. 1980 Convention on Prohibitions or Restrictions on the Use of Certain Convention Weapons which may be Deemed to be Excessively Injurious or to have Indiscriminate Effects.

---

*An asterisk indicates that signature or ratification of the United States was subject to one or more reservations or understandings. The United States is a signatory and party to all of the foregoing conventions and protocols, except it has not ratified and, therefore, is not a state party to the numbers 13 and 15 to 17. The United States has decided not to ratify Additional Protocol I.

5.5 RULES OF ENGAGEMENT

U.S. rules of engagement are the means by which the National Command Authorities (NCA) (consisting of the President and the Secretary of Defense, or their duly deputized alternates or successors) and the U.S. military chain of command authorize subordinate commanders to employ military force. Rules of engagement delineate the circumstances and limitations under which U.S. naval, ground, and air forces will initiate and/or continue combat engagement with enemy forces. At the national level, wartime rules of engagement are promulgated by the NCA, through the Joint Chiefs of Staff, to unified and specified commanders to guide them in the employment of their forces toward the achievement of broad national objectives. At the tactical level, wartime rules of engagement are task-oriented and frequently mission-oriented. At all levels, U.S. wartime rules of engagement are influenced by, and are consistent with, the law of armed conflict. The law of armed conflict provides the legal framework within which U.S. rules of engagement during hostilities are formulated. Because rules of engagement also reflect operational, political, and diplomatic factors, they often restrict combat operations far more than do the requirements of international law.

5.5.1 Peacetime and Wartime Rules of Engagement Distinguished. Chapter 4 addresses the JCS Peacetime Rules of Engagement for U.S. Forces and notes that they provide the authority for and limitations on actions taken in self-defense during peacetime and periods short of prolonged armed conflict, for the defense of U.S. forces, the self-defense of the nation and its citizens, and the protection of U.S. national assets worldwide. Wartime rules of engagement, on the other hand, reaffirm the right and the responsibility of the operational commander generally to seek out, engage, and destroy enemy forces consistent with national objectives, strategy, and the law of armed conflict.

CHAPTER 6

Adherence and Enforcement

6.1 ADHERENCE TO THE LAW OF ARMED CONFLICT

Nations adhere to the law of armed conflict not only because they are legally obliged to do so but for the very practical reason that it is in the best interest of belligerents to be governed by consistent and mutually acceptable rules of conduct. The law of armed conflict is effective to the extent that it is obeyed by the belligerents. Occasional violations do not substantially affect the validity of a rule of law, provided routine compliance, observance, and enforcement continue to be the norm. However, repeated violations not responded to by protests, reprisals, or other enforcement actions may, over time, indicate that a particular rule of warfare is no longer regarded by belligerents as valid.

6.1.1 Adherence by the United States. Pursuant to the Constitution of the United States, treaties to which the U.S. is a party constitute a part of the "supreme law of the land" with a force equal to that of laws enacted by the Congress. Moreover, the Supreme Court of the United States has consistently ruled that where there is no treaty and no controlling executive, legislative, or judicial precedent to the contrary, customary international law and the common law are fundamental elements of U.S. national law. The law of armed conflict is, therefore, binding upon the United States, its citizens, and its armed forces. (See DOD Dir. 5100.77.)

6.1.2 Department of the Navy Policy. SECNAVINST 3300.1A states that the De-

partment of the Navy will comply with the law of armed conflict in the conduct of military operations and related activities in armed conflicts. Article 0605, U.S. Navy Regulations, 1973, provides that:

> At all times a commander shall observe, and require his command to observe, the principles of international law. Where necessary to fulfillment of this responsibility, a departure from other provisions of Navy Regulations is authorized.

It is the responsibility of the Chief of Naval Operations and the Commandant of the Marine Corps (see OPNAVINST 3300.52 and MCO 3300.3) to ensure that:

1. The obligations of the United States under the law of armed conflict are observed and enforced by the U.S. Navy and Marine Corps in the conduct of military operations and related activities in armed conflict, regardless of how such conflicts are characterized.

2. Alleged violations of the law of armed conflict, whether committed by or against United States or enemy personnel, are promptly reported, thoroughly investigated, and where appropriate, remedied by corrective action.

3. All service members of the Department of the Navy, commensurate with their duties and responsibilities, receive, through publications, instruc-

tions, training programs and exercises, training and education in the law of armed conflict.

Navy and Marine Corps judge advocates responsible for advising operational commanders are specially trained to provide officers in command with advice and assistance in the law of armed conflict on an independent and expeditious basis. The Chief of Naval Operations and the Commandant of the Marine Corps have directed officers in command of the operating forces to ensure that their judge advocates have appropriate clearances and access to information to enable them to carry out that responsibility (see CNO Washington DC message 111021Z Oct 85 and MCO 3300.3).

6.1.3 Command Responsibility. Officers in command are not only responsible for ensuring that they conduct all combat operations in accordance with the law of armed conflict; they are also responsible for the proper performance of their subordinates. While a commander may delegate some or all of his authority, he cannot delegate responsibility for the conduct of the forces he commands. The fact that a commander did not order, authorize, or knowingly acquiesce in a violation of the law of armed conflict by a subordinate will not relieve him of responsibility for its occurrence, if it is established that he failed to exercise properly his command authority or failed otherwise to take reasonable measures to discover and correct violations that may already have occurred.

6.1.4 Individual Responsibility. All members of the naval service have a duty to comply with the law of armed conflict and, to the utmost of their ability and authority, to prevent violations by others. Members of the naval service, like military members of all nations, must obey readily and strictly all lawful orders issued by a superior. Under both international law and U.S. law, an order to commit an obviously criminal act, such as

the wanton killing of a noncombatant or the torture of a prisoner, is an unlawful order and will not relieve a subordinate of his responsibility to comply with the law of armed conflict. Only if the unlawfulness of an order is not known by the individual, and he could not reasonably be expected under the circumstances to recognize the order as unlawful, will the defense of obedience of an order protect a subordinate from the consequences of violation of the law of armed conflict.

6.2 ENFORCEMENT OF THE LAW OF ARMED CONFLICT

Various means are available to belligerents under international law for inducing the observance of legitimate warfare. In the event of a clearly established violation of the law of armed conflict, the aggrieved nation may:

1. Publicize the facts with a view toward influencing world public opinion against the offending nation

2. Protest to the offending nation and demand that those responsible be punished and/or that compensation be paid

3. Seek the intervention of a neutral party, particularly with respect to the protection of prisoners of war and other of its nationals that have fallen under the control of the offending nation

4. Execute a reprisal action

5. Punish individual offenders either during the conflict or upon cessation of hostilities.

6.2.1 The Protecting Power. Under the Geneva Conventions of 1949, the treatment of prisoners of war, interned civilians, and inhabitants of occupied territory is to be monitored by a neutral nation known as the Protecting Power. Due to the difficulty of finding a nation which the opposing belligerents will regard as truly neutral, international humanitarian organizations, such as the International Committee of the Red Cross, have been authorized by the parties to the conflict to perform at least some of the functions of a Protecting Power.

6.2.2 The International Committee of the Red Cross (ICRC). The ICRC is a nongovernmental, humanitarian organization based in Geneva, Switzerland. The ruling body of the ICRC is composed entirely of Swiss citizens and is staffed mainly by Swiss nationals. (The ICRC is distinct from and should not be confused with the various national Red Cross societies such as the American National Red Cross.) Its principal purpose is to provide protection and assistance to the victims of armed conflict. The Geneva Conventions recognize the special status of the ICRC and have assigned specific tasks for it to perform, including visiting and interviewing prisoners of war, providing relief to the civilian population of occupied territories, searching for information concerning missing persons, and offering its "good offices" to facilitate establishment of hospital and safety zones. Under its governing statute, the ICRC is dedicated to work for the faithful application of the Geneva Conventions, to endeavor to ensure the protection of military and civilian victims of armed conflict, and to serve as a neutral intermediary between belligerents.

6.2.3 Reprisal. A reprisal is an enforcement measure under the law of armed conflict consisting of an act which would otherwise be unlawful but which is justified as a response to the unlawful acts of an enemy. The sole purpose of a reprisal is to induce the enemy to cease its illegal activity and to comply with the law of armed conflict. Reprisals may be taken against enemy armed forces; enemy civilians, other than those in occupied territory; and enemy property.

6.2.3.1 Requirements for Reprisal. To be valid, a reprisal action must conform to the following criteria:

1. Reprisal must be ordered by the highest authority of the belligerent's government.

2. It must respond to illegal acts of warfare committed by an adversary government, its military commanders, or combatants for which the adversary is responsible. Anticipatory reprisal is not authorized.

3. When circumstances permit, reprisal must be preceded by a demand for redress by the enemy of his unlawful acts.

4. Its purpose must be to cause the enemy to cease its unlawful activity. Therefore, acts taken in reprisal should be brought to the attention of the enemy in order to achieve maximum effectiveness. Reprisal must never be taken for revenge.

5. Reprisal must only be used as a last resort when other enforcement measures have failed or would be of no avail.

6. Each reprisal must be proportional to the original violation.

7. A reprisal action must cease as soon as the enemy is induced to desist from its unlawful activities and to comply with the law of armed conflict.

6.2.3.2 Immunity From Reprisal. Reprisals are forbidden to be taken against:

1. Prisoners of war and interned civilians

2. Wounded, sick, and shipwrecked persons

3. Civilians in occupied territory

4. Hospitals and medical facilities, personnel, and equipment, including hospital ships, medical aircraft, and medical vehicles.

6.2.3.3 Authority to Order Reprisals. The National Command Authorities (NCA) alone may authorize the taking of a reprisal action by U.S. forces. Although reprisal is lawful when the foregoing requirements are met, there is always the risk that it will trigger retaliatory escalation (counter-reprisals) by the enemy. The United States has historically been reluctant to resort to reprisal for just this reason.

6.2.4 Reciprocity. Some obligations under the law of armed conflict are reciprocal in that they are binding on the parties only so long as both sides continue to comply with them. A major violation by one side will release the other side from all further duty to abide by that obligation. The concept of reciprocity is not applicable to humanitarian rules of law that protect the victims of armed conflict, that is, those persons protected by the 1949 Geneva Conventions. The decision to consider the United States released from a particular obligation following a major violation by the enemy will ordinarily be made by the NCA.

6.2.5 War Crimes Under International Law. For purposes of this publication, war crimes are defined as those acts which violate the law of armed conflict, that is, the rules established by customary and conventional international law regulating the conduct of warfare and which have been designated as war crimes. Acts constituting war crimes may be committed by the armed forces of a belligerent or by individuals belonging to the civilian population. Belligerents have the obligation under international law to punish their own nationals, whether members of the armed forces or civilians, who commit war crimes. International law also provides that belligerents have the right to punish enemy armed forces personnel and enemy civilians, who fall under their control, for such offenses.

The following acts are representative war crimes:

1. Offenses against prisoners of war, including killing without just cause; torture or inhuman treatment; unhealthy, dangerous, or otherwise prohibited labor; infringement of religious rights; and denial of fair trial for offenses

2. Offenses against civilian inhabitants of occupied territory, including killing without just cause, torture or inhumane treatment, forced labor, deportation, infringement of religious rights, and denial of fair trial for offenses

3. Offenses against the sick and wounded, including killing, wounding, or mistreating enemy forces disabled by sickness or wounds

4. Denial of quarter (i.e., denial of the clemency of not killing a defeated enemy) and offenses against combatants who have laid down their arms and surrendered

5. Offenses against survivors of ships and aircraft lost at sea, including killing, wounding, or mistreating the shipwrecked; and failing to provide for the safety of survivors as military circumstances permit

6. Wanton destruction of cities, towns, and villages or devastation not justified by the requirements of military operations; and bombardment, the sole purpose of which is to attack and terrorize the civilian population

7. Deliberate attack upon medical facilities, hospital ships, medical aircraft, medical vehicles, or medical personnel

8. Plunder and pillage of public or private property

9. Mutilation or other mistreatment of the dead

10. Employing forbidden arms or ammunition

11. Misuse, abuse, or firing on flags of truce or on the Red Cross device, and similar protective emblems, signs, and signals

12. Treacherous request for quarter (i.e., feigning surrender in order to gain a military advantage).

CHAPTER 7

The Law of Neutrality

7.1 INTRODUCTION

The law of neutrality defines the legal relationship between nations engaged in an armed conflict (belligerents) and nations seeking to avoid direct involvement in such hostilities (neutrals). The law of neutrality serves to localize war, to limit the conduct of war on both land and sea, and to lessen the impact of war on international commerce.

Developed at a time when nations customarily issued declarations of war before engaging in hostilities, the law of neutrality contemplated that the transition between war and peace would be clear and unambiguous. With the advent of international efforts to abolish "war," coupled with the proliferation of collective security arrangements and the extension of the spectrum of warfare to include insurgencies and counterinsurgencies, armed conflict is now seldom accompanied by formal declarations of war. Consequently, it has become increasingly difficult to determine with precision the point in time when hostilities have become a "war" and to distinguish belligerent nations from those not participating in the conflict. Notwithstanding these uncertainties, the law of neutrality continues to serve an important role in containing the spread of hostilities, in regulating the conduct of belligerents with respect to nations not participating in the conflict, and in reducing the harmful effects of such hostilities on international commerce.

For purposes of this publication, a belligerent nation is defined as a nation engaged in an international armed conflict, whether or not a formal declaration of war has been issued. Conversely, a neutral nation is defined as a nation that has proclaimed its neutrality or has otherwise assumed neutral status with respect to an ongoing conflict.

7.2 NEUTRAL STATUS

Customary international law contemplates that in the absence of an international commitment to the contrary, all nations have the option to refrain from participation in an armed conflict by declaring or otherwise assuming neutral status. The law of armed conflict reciprocally imposes duties and confers rights upon neutral nations and upon belligerents. The principal right of the neutral nation is that of *inviolability;* its principal duties are those of *abstention* and *impartiality.* Conversely, it is the duty of a belligerent to respect the former and its right to insist upon the latter.

Neutral status, once established, remains in effect unless and until the neutral nation abandons its neutral stance and enters into the conflict or is itself the subject of attack by a belligerent.

7.2.1 Neutrality and the United Nations. The Charter of the United Nations imposes upon its members the obligation to settle international disputes by peaceful means and to refrain from the threat or use of force in their international relations. In the event of a threat to or breach of the peace, the Security Council is empowered to take enforcement action on behalf of all member nations, involving or not involving use of force, in order to maintain or restore international peace. When called upon by the Security Council to do so, member nations are obligated to provide assistance to the United Nations in any action it takes and to refrain from aiding any nation against whom such action is directed. Consequently, member nations may be obliged to support a United Nations action with elements of their armed forces, a result incompatible with the abstention requirement of neutral status. Similarly, a member nation may be called upon to provide assistance to the United Nations in an enforcement action not involving its armed forces and thereby assume a partisan posture inconsistent with the impartiality necessary to a valid assertion of neutrality. Should the Security Council determine not to institute an enforcement action, or is unable to do so due to the imposition of a veto by one or more of its permanent members, each United Nations member remains free to assert neutral status.

7.2.2 Neutrality Under Regional and Collective Self-Defense Arrangements. The obligation in the United Nations Charter for member nations to refrain from the threat or use of force is qualified by the right of individual and collective self-defense, which member nations may exercise until such time as the Security Council has taken measures necessary to restore international peace. This inherent right of self-defense may be implemented individually or through regional and collective security arrangements. The possibility of asserting and maintaining neutral status under such arrangements depends upon the extent to which the parties are obligated to provide assistance in a regional action, or in the case of collective self-defense, to come to the aid of a victim of an armed attack. The practical effect of such treaties is to trans-

form the right of the parties to assist one of their number under attack into a duty to do so. This duty may assume a variety of forms ranging from economic assistance to the commitment of armed forces.

7.3 NEUTRAL TERRITORY

As a general rule of international law, all acts of hostility in neutral territory, including neutral lands, neutral waters, and neutral airspace, are prohibited. A neutral nation has the duty to prevent the use of its territory as a place of sanctuary or a base of operations by belligerent forces of any side. If the neutral nation is unable or unwilling to enforce effectively its right of inviolability, an aggrieved belligerent may resort to acts of hostility in neutral territory against enemy forces, including warships and military aircraft, making unlawful use of that territory. Belligerents are also authorized to act in self-defense when attacked or threatened with attack while in neutral territory or when attacked or threatened from neutral territory.

7.3.1 Neutral Lands. Belligerents are forbidden to move troops or war materials and supplies across neutral land territory. Neutral nations may be required to mobilize sufficient armed forces to ensure fulfillment of their responsibility to prevent belligerent forces from crossing neutral borders. Belligerent troops that enter neutral territory must be disarmed and interned until the end of the armed conflict.

A neutral may authorize passage through its territory of wounded and sick belonging to the armed forces of either side on condition that the vehicles transporting them carry neither combatants nor materials of war. If passage of sick and wounded is permitted, the neutral nation assumes responsibility for providing for their safety and control. Prisoners of war that have escaped their captors and made their way to neutral territory may be either repatriated or left at liberty in the neutral nation, but must not be allowed to take part in belligerent activities while there.

7.3.2 Neutral Ports and Roadsteads. Although neutral nations may, on a nondiscriminatory basis, close their ports and roadsteads to belligerents, they are not obliged to do so. In any event, Hague Convention XIII requires that a 24-hour grace period in which to depart must be provided to belligerent vessels located in neutral ports or roadsteads at the outbreak of armed conflict. Thereafter, belligerent vessels may visit only those neutral ports and roadsteads that the neutral nation may choose to open to them for that purpose. Belligerent vessels, including warships, retain a right of entry in distress whether caused by *force majeure* or damage resulting from enemy action.

7.3.2.1 Limitations on Stay and Departure. In the absence of special provisions to the contrary in the laws or regulations of the neutral nation, belligerent warships are forbidden to remain in a neutral port or roadstead in excess of 24 hours. This restriction does not apply to belligerent vessels devoted exclusively to humanitarian, religious, or nonmilitary scientific purposes. (Vessels engaged in the collection of scientific data of potential military application are not exempt.) Belligerent warships may be permitted by a neutral nation to extend their stay in neutral ports and roadsteads on account of stress of weather or damage involving seaworthiness. It is the duty of the neutral nation to intern a belligerent warship, together with its officers and crew, that will not or cannot depart a neutral port or roadstead where it is not entitled to remain.

Unless the neutral nation has adopted laws or regulations to the contrary, no more than three warships of any one belligerent nation may be present in the same neutral port or roadstead at any one time. When warships of opposing belligerent nations are present in a neutral port or roadstead at the same time, not less than 24 hours must elapse between the departure of the respective enemy vessels. The order of departure is determined by the order of arrival unless an extension of stay has been granted.

7.3.2.2 War Materials, Supplies, Communications, and Repairs. Belligerent warships may not make use of neutral ports or roadsteads to replenish or increase their supplies of war materials or their armaments, or to erect any apparatus for communicating with belligerent forces. Although they may take on food and fuel, the law is unsettled as to the quantities that may be allowed. In practice, it has been left to the neutral nation to determine the conditions for the replenishment and refueling of belligerent warships, subject to the principle of nondiscrimination among belligerents and to the prohibition against the use of neutral territory as a base of operations.

Belligerent warships may carry out such repairs in neutral ports and roadsteads as are absolutely necessary to render them seaworthy. They may not add to or repair weapons systems or enhance any other aspect of their war fighting capability. It is the duty of the neutral nation to decide what repairs are necessary to seaworthiness and to insist that they be accomplished with the least possible delay.

7.3.2.3 Prizes. A prize (i.e., a captured neutral or enemy merchant ship) may only be brought into a neutral port or roadstead because of unseaworthiness, stress of weather, or want of fuel or provisions, and must leave as soon as such circumstances are overcome or cease to prevail. It is the duty of the neutral nation to release a prize, together with its officers and crew, and to intern the offending belligerent's prize master and prize crew, whenever a prize is unlawfully brought into a neutral port or roadstead or, having entered lawfully, fails to depart as soon as the circumstances which justified its entry no longer pertain.

7.3.3 Neutral Internal Waters. Neutral internal waters encompass those waters of a neutral nation that are landward of the baseline from which the territorial sea is measured. The rules governing neutral ports and roadsteads apply as well to neutral internal waters.

7.3.4 Neutral Territorial Seas. Neutral territorial seas, like neutral territory generally, must not be used by belligerent forces either as a sanctuary from their enemies or as a base of operations. Belligerents are obliged to refrain from all acts of hostility in neutral territorial waters except those necessitated by self-defense or undertaken as self-help enforcement actions against enemy forces that are in violation of the neutral status of those waters when the neutral nation cannot or will not enforce their inviolability.

7.3.4.1 Mere Passage. A neutral nation may, on a nondiscriminatory basis, close its territorial waters, except in international straits, to belligerent vessels. When properly notified of its closure, belligerents are obliged to refrain from entering a neutral territorial sea except to transit through international straits or as necessitated by distress. A neutral nation may, however, allow the "mere passage" of belligerent vessels, including warships and prizes, through its territorial waters. To qualify, such passage must be innocent in nature and, in the absence of special laws or regulations of the neutral nation to the contrary, must not exceed 24 hours in duration. While in neutral territorial waters, a belligerent warship must also refrain from adding to or repairing its armaments or replenishing its war materials. Although the general practice has been to close neutral territorial waters to belligerent subma-

rines, a neutral nation may elect to allow mere passage of submarines, either surfaced or submerged. Neutral nations customarily authorize passage through their territorial sea of ships carrying the wounded, sick, and shipwrecked, whether or not those waters are otherwise closed to belligerent vessels.

7.3.4.2 The 12-Nautical Mile Territorial Sea. When the law of neutrality was codified in the Hague Conventions of 1907, the 3-nautical mile territorial sea was the accepted norm, aviation was in its infancy, and the submarine had not yet proven itself as a significant weapons platform. The rules of neutrality applicable to territorial waters were designed primarily to regulate the conduct of surface warships in a narrow band of water off neutral coasts. The 1982 Law of the Sea Convention provides that coastal nations may lawfully extend the breadth of claimed territorial waters to 12 nautical miles. Because of provisions concerning seabed mining (Part XI) the U.S. has not signed the Convention; nonetheless the U.S. is committed to recognizing the rights of nations in the waters off their coasts, as reflected in the Convention. The U.S. claims a 12-nautical mile territorial sea and recognizes the right of all coastal and island nations to do likewise.

In the context of a universally recognized 3-nautical mile territorial sea, the rights and duties of neutrals and belligerents in neutral territorial waters were balanced and equitable. Although extension of the breadth of the territorial sea from 3 to 12 nautical miles removes over 3,000,000 square miles of ocean from the arena in which belligerent forces may conduct offensive combat operations and significantly complicates neutral nation enforcement of the inviolability of its neutral waters, the 12-nautical mile territorial sea is not, in and of itself, incompatible with the law of neutrality. Belligerents continue to be obliged to refrain from acts of hostility in neutral waters and remain forbidden to use the territorial sea of a neutral nation as a place of sanctuary from their enemies or as a base of operations. Should belligerent forces violate the neutrality of those waters and the neutral nation demonstrate an inability or unwillingness to detect and expel the offender, the other belligerent retains the right to undertake such self-help enforcement actions as are necessary to assure compliance by his adversary with the law of neutrality.

7.3.5 Neutral Straits. Customary international law as reflected in the 1982 Law of the Sea Convention provides that belligerent and neutral surface ships, submarines, and aircraft have a right of transit passage through, over, and under all straits used for international navigation. Neutral nations cannot suspend, hamper, or otherwise impede this right of transit passage through international straits. Belligerent forces transiting through international straits overlapped by neutral waters must proceed without delay, must refrain from the threat or use of forces against the neutral nation, and must otherwise refrain from acts of hostility and other activities not incident to their transit. Belligerent forces in transit may, however, take defensive measures consistent with their security, including the launching and recovery of aircraft, screen formation steaming, and acoustic and electronic surveillance. Belligerent forces may not use neutral straits as a place of sanctuary nor a base of operations, and belligerent warships may not exercise the belligerent right of visit and search in those waters. (Note: The Turkish Straits are governed by special rules articulated in the Montreux Convention of 1936, which limit the number and type of warships which may use the Straits, both in times of peace and during armed conflict.)

7.3.6 Neutral Archipelagic Waters. The United States recognizes the right of qualifying island nations to establish archipelagic baselines enclosing archipelagic waters, provided the baselines are drawn in conformity with the 1982 LOS Convention and the U.S. and other nations are accorded their full rights under international law, including the law of armed conflict, in those waters. The balance of neutral and belligerent rights and duties with respect to neutral waters is, however, at its most unsettled in the context of archipelagic waters.

Belligerent forces must refrain from acts of hostility in neutral archipelagic waters and from using them as a sanctuary or a base of operations. Belligerent ships or aircraft, including submarines, surface warships, and military aircraft, retain the right of unimpeded archipelagic sea lanes passage through, over, and under neutral archipelagic sea lanes. Belligerent forces exercising the right of archipelagic sea lanes passage may engage in those activities that are incident to their normal mode of continuous and expeditious passage and are consistent with their security. Visit and search is not authorized in neutral archipelagic waters.

A neutral nation may close its archipelagic waters (other than archipelagic sea lanes whether designated or those routes normally used for international navigation or overflight) to the mere passage of belligerent ships but is not obliged to do so. The neutral archipelagic nation has an affirmative duty to police its archipelagic waters to ensure that the inviolability of its neutral waters is respected. If a neutral nation is unable or unwilling effectively to detect and expel belligerent forces unlawfully present in its archipelagic waters, the opposing belligerent may undertake such self-help enforcement actions as may be necessary to terminate the violation of neutrality. Such self-help enforcement may include surface, subsurface, and air penetration of archipelagic waters and airspace and the use of proportional force as necessary.

7.3.7 Neutral Airspace. Neutral territory extends to the airspace over a neutral nation's lands, internal waters, archipelagic waters (if any), and territorial sea. Belligerent military aircraft are forbidden to enter neutral airspace with the following exceptions:

1. The airspace above neutral international straits and archipelagic sea lanes remains open at all times to belligerent aircraft, including armed military aircraft, engaged in transit or archipelagic sea lanes passage. Such passage must be continuous and expeditious and must be undertaken in the normal mode of flight of the aircraft involved. Belligerent aircraft must refrain from acts of hostility while in transit but may engage in activities that are consistent with their security and the security of accompanying surface and subsurface forces.

2. Unarmed military aircraft may enter neutral airspace under such conditions and circumstances as the neutral nation may wish to impose impartially on the belligerents. Should such unarmed aircraft penetrate neutral airspace without permission, or otherwise fail to abide by the entry conditions imposed upon them by the neutral nation, they may be interned together with their crews.

3. Medical aircraft may overfly neutral territory, may land therein in case of necessity, and may use neutral airfield facilities as ports of call, subject to such restrictions and regulations as the neutral nation may

see fit to apply equally to all belligerents.

4. Belligerent aircraft in evident distress are permitted to enter neutral airspace and to land in neutral territory under such safeguards as the neutral nation may wish to impose. The neutral nation may require such aircraft to land, may intern both aircraft and crew, or may impose nondiscriminatory conditions upon their stay or release.

7.3.7.1 Neutral Duties In Neutral Airspace. Neutral nations have an affirmative duty to prevent violation of neutral airspace by belligerent aircraft, to compel offending aircraft to land, and to intern both aircraft and crew. Should a neutral nation be unable or unwilling to prevent the unlawful entry or use of its airspace by belligerent aircraft, belligerent forces of the other side may undertake such self-help enforcement measures as the circumstances may require.

7.4 NEUTRAL COMMERCE

A principal purpose of the law of neutrality is the regulation of belligerent activities with respect to neutral commerce. For purposes of this publication, neutral commerce comprises all commerce between one neutral nation and another not involving materials of war or armaments destined for a belligerent nation, and all commerce between a neutral nation and a belligerent that does not involve the carriage of contraband or otherwise sustain the belligerent's war-fighting capability. Neutral merchant vessels and nonpublic civil aircraft engaged in legitimate neutral commerce are subject to visit and search, but may not be captured or destroyed by belligerent forces.

The law of neutrality does not prohibit neutral nations from engaging in commerce with belligerent nations; however, a neutral government cannot supply materials of war or armaments to a belligerent without violating its neutral duties of abstention and impartiality and risking loss of its neutral status. Although a neutral may forbid its citizens from carrying on non-neutral commerce with belligerent nations, it is not obliged to do so. In effect, the law establishes a balance of interests that protects neutral commerce from unreasonable interference on the one hand and the right of belligerents to interdict the flow of war materials to the enemy on the other.

7.4.1 Contraband. Contraband consists of goods which are destined for the enemy of a belligerent and which may be susceptible to use in armed conflict. Traditionally, contraband has been divided into two categories: absolute and conditional. Absolute contraband consisted of goods whose character made it obvious that they were destined for use in armed conflict, such as munitions, weapons, uniforms, and the like. Conditional contraband were goods equally susceptible to either peaceful or warlike purposes, such as foodstuffs, construction materials, and fuel. Belligerents often declared contraband lists at the initiation of hostilities to notify neutral nations of the type of goods considered to be absolute or conditional contraband as well as those not considered to be contraband at all, i.e., exempt or "free goods." The precise nature of a belligerent's contraband list varied according to the circumstances of the conflict.

The practice of belligerents in World War II has cast doubt on the relevance, if not the validity, of the traditional distinction between absolute and conditional contraband. Because of the involvement of virtually the entire population in support of the war effort, the belligerents of both sides during the Second World War tended to exercise governmental control over all im-

ports. Consequently, it became increasingly difficult to draw a meaningful distinction between goods destined for an enemy government and its armed forces and goods destined for consumption by the civilian populace. As a result, belligerents considered goods as absolute contraband which in earlier conflicts were considered to be conditional contraband.

7.4.1.1 Enemy Destination. To the extent that the distinction between absolute and conditional contraband has continuing relevance, it is with respect to the rules pertaining to the presumption of ultimate enemy destination. Goods consisting of absolute contraband are liable to capture at any place beyond neutral territory, if their destination is the territory belonging to or occupied by the enemy. It is immaterial whether the carriage of absolute contraband is direct, involves transshipment, or requires overland transport. When absolute contraband is involved, a destination of enemy owned or occupied territory may be presumed when:

1. The neutral vessel is to call at an enemy port before arriving at a neutral port for which the goods are documented.

2. The goods are documented to a neutral port serving as a port of transit to an enemy, even though they are consigned to a neutral.

3. The goods are consigned "to order" or to an unnamed consignee, but are destined for a neutral nation in the vicinity of enemy territory.

These presumptions of enemy destination of absolute contraband render the offending cargo liable to seizure by a belligerent from the time the neutral merchant vessel leaves its home or other neutral territory until it arrives again in neutral territory. Although conditional contraband is also liable to capture if ultimately destined for the use of an enemy government or its armed forces, enemy destination of conditional contraband must be factually established and cannot be presumed.

7.4.1.2 Exemptions to Contraband. Certain goods are exempt from capture as contraband even though destined for enemy territory. Among them are:

1. Exempt or "free goods," i.e., goods not susceptible for use in armed conflict

2. Articles intended exclusively for the treatment of wounded and sick members of the armed forces and for prevention of disease

3. Medical and hospital stores, religious objects, clothing, bedding, essential foodstuffs, and means of shelter for the civilian population in general, and women and children in particular, provided there is not serious reason to believe that such goods will be diverted to other purpose, or that a definite military advantage would accrue to the enemy by their substitution for enemy goods that would thereby become available for military purposes

4. Items destined for prisoners of war, including individual parcels and collective relief shipments containing food, clothing, medical supplies, religious objects, and educational, cultural, and athletic articles

5. Goods otherwise specifically exempted from capture by international convention or by special arrangement between belligerents.

It is customary for neutral nations to provide belligerents of both sides with information regarding the nature, timing, and route of shipments of goods constituting exceptions to contraband and to obtain approval for their safe conduct and entry into belligerent owned or occupied territory.

7.4.2 Certificate of Noncontraband Carriage. A certificate of noncontraband carriage is a document issued by a belligerent consular or other designated official to a neutral vessel (navicert) or neutral aircraft (aircert) certifying that the cargo being carried has been examined, usually at the initial place of departure, and has been found to be free of contraband. The purpose of such a navicert or aircert is to facilitate belligerent control of contraband goods with minimal interference and delay of neutral commerce. The certificate is not a guarantee that the vessel or aircraft will not be subject to visit and search or that cargo will not be seized. (Changed circumstances, such as a change in status of the neutral vessel, between the time of issuance of the certificate and the time of interception at sea may cause it to be invalidated.) Conversely, absence of a navicert or aircert is not, in itself, a valid ground for seizure of cargo. Navicerts and aircerts issued by one belligerent have no effect on the visit and search rights of a belligerent of the opposing side.

7.5 ACQUIRING ENEMY CHARACTER

All vessels operating under an enemy flag, and all aircraft bearing enemy markings, possess enemy character. However, the fact that a merchant ship flies a neutral flag, or that an aircraft bears neutral markings, does not necessarily establish neutral character. Any vessel or aircraft, other than a warship or military aircraft, owned or controlled by a belligerent possesses enemy character, regardless of whether it is operating under a neutral flag or bears neutral markings. Vessels and aircraft acquiring enemy character may be treated by an opposing belligerent as if they are enemy vessels and aircraft. (Paragraphs 8.2.1 and 8.2.2 set forth the actions that may be taken against enemy vessels and aircraft.)

7.5.1 Acquiring the Character of an Enemy Warship or Military Aircraft. Neutral vessels and aircraft, other than warships and military aircraft, acquire enemy character and may be treated by a belligerent as enemy warships and military aircraft when engaged in the following acts:

1. Taking a direct part in the hostilities on the side of the enemy

2. Acting in any capacity as a naval or military auxiliary to the enemy's armed forces.

(Paragraph 8.2.1 describes the actions that may be taken against enemy warships and military aircraft.)

7.5.2 Acquiring the Character of an Enemy Merchant Vessel or Aircraft. Neutral vessels and aircraft, other than warships and military aircraft, acquire enemy character and may be treated by a belligerent as enemy merchant vessels or aircraft when engaged in the following acts:

1. Operating directly under enemy control, orders, charter, employment, or direction

2. Resisting an attempt to establish identity, including visit and search.

(Paragraph 8.2.2 describes the actions that may be taken against enemy merchant ships and civilian aircraft.)

7.6 VISIT AND SEARCH

Visit and search is the means by which a belligerent warship or belligerent military aircraft may determine the true character (enemy or neutral) of merchant ships encountered outside neutral territory, the nature (contraband or exempt "free goods") of their cargo, the manner (innocent or hostile) of their employment, and other facts bearing on their relation to the armed conflict. Warships are not subject to visit and search. The prohibition against visit and search in neutral territory extends to international straits overlapped by neutral territorial seas and archipelagic sea lanes. Neutral vessels engaged in government noncommercial service may not be subjected to visit and search. Neutral merchant vessels under convoy of neutral warships of the same nationality are also exempt from visit and search, although the convoy commander may be required to provide in writing to the commanding officer of an intercepting belligerent warship information as to the character of the vessels and of their cargoes which could otherwise be obtained by visit and search. Should it be determined by the convoy commander that a vessel under his charge possesses enemy character or carries contraband cargo, he is obliged to withdraw his protection of the offending vessel, making it liable to visit and search, and possible capture, by the belligerent warship.

7.6.1 Procedure for Visit and Search. *In the absence of specific rules of engagement or other special instructions* issued by the operational chain of command during a period of armed conflict, the following procedure should be carried out by U.S. Navy warships exercising the belligerent right of visit and search:

1. Visit and search should be exercised with all possible tact and consideration.

2. Before summoning a vessel to lie to, the warship should hoist its national flag. The summons is made by firing

a blank charge, by international flag signal (SN or SQ), or by other recognized means. The summoned vessel, if a neutral merchant ship, is bound to stop, lie to, display her colors, and not resist. (If the summoned vessel is an enemy ship, it is not so bound and may legally resist, even by force, but thereby assumes all risk of resulting damage or destruction.)

3. If the summoned vessel takes flight, she may be pursued and brought to by forcible measures if necessary.

4. When a summoned vessel has been brought to, the warship should send a boat with an officer to conduct the visit and search. If practicable, a second officer should accompany the officer charged with the examination. The officer(s) and boat crew may be armed at the discretion of the commanding officer.

5. If visit and search at sea is deemed hazardous or impracticable, the neutral vessel may be escorted by the summoning of another U.S. Navy warship or by a U.S. military aircraft to the nearest place (outside neutral territory) where the visit and search may be conveniently and safely conducted. The neutral vessel is not obliged to lower her flag (she has not been captured) but must proceed according to the orders of the escorting warship or aircraft.

6. The boarding officer should first examine the ship's papers to ascertain her character, ports of departure and destination, nature of cargo, manner of employment, and other facts deemed pertinent. Papers to be examined will ordinarily include a certificate of national registry, crew list, passenger list, logbook, bill of

health clearances, charter party (if chartered), invoices or manifests of cargo, bills of lading, and, on occasion, a consular declaration or other certificate of noncontraband carriage certifying the innocence of the cargo.

7. Regularity of papers and evidence of innocence of cargo, employment, or destination furnished by them are not necessarily conclusive, and, should doubt exist, the ship's company may be questioned and the ship and cargo searched.

8. Unless military security prohibits, the boarding officer will record the facts concerning the visit and search in the logbook of the visited ship, including the date and position of the interception. The entry should be authenticated by the signature and rank of the boarding officer, but neither the name of the visiting warship nor the identity of her commanding officer should be disclosed.

7.6.2 Visit and Search by Military Aircraft. Although there is a right of visit and search by military aircraft, there is no established international practice as to how that right is to be exercised. Ordinarily, visit and search of a vessel by an aircraft is accomplished by directing and escorting the vessel to the vicinity of a belligerent warship, which will carry out the visit and search, or to a belligerent port. Visit and search of an aircraft by an aircraft may be accomplished by directing the aircraft to proceed under escort to the nearest convenient belligerent landing area.

7.7 BLOCKADE

7.7.1 General. Blockade is a belligerent operation to prevent vessels and/or aircraft of all nations, enemy as well as neutral, from entering or exiting specified ports, airfields, or coastal areas belonging to, occupied by, or under the control of an enemy nation. A belligerent's purpose in establishing a blockade is to deny the enemy the use of enemy and neutral vessels or aircraft to transport personnel and goods to or from enemy territory. Unlike the belligerent right of visit and search, which is designed to interdict the flow of contraband goods into enemy territory and which may be exercised anywhere outside of neutral territory, the belligerent right of blockade is intended to prevent vessels and aircraft from crossing an established and publicized cordon separating the enemy from international waters and/or airspace.

7.7.2 Traditional Rules. In order to be valid under the traditional rules of international law, a blockade must conform to the following criteria.

7.7.2.1 Establishment. A blockade must be established by the government of the belligerent nation. This is usually accomplished by a declaration of the belligerent government or by the commander of the blockading force acting on behalf of his government. The declaration should include, as a minimum, the date the blockade is to begin, its geographic limits, and the grace period granted neutral vessels and aircraft to leave the area to be blockaded.

7.7.2.2 Notification. It is customary for the belligerent nation establishing the blockade to notify all affected nations of its imposition. Because knowledge of the existence of a blockade is an essential element of the offenses of breach and attempted breach of blockade (see 7.7.4), neutral vessels and aircraft are always entitled to notification. The commander of the blockading forces will usually also notify local authorities in the blockaded area. The form of the notification is not material so long as it is effective.

7.7.2.3 Effectiveness. In order to be valid, a blockade must be effective. To be effective, it must be maintained by a surface, air, or subsurface force or other mechanism that is sufficient to render ingress or egress of the blockaded area dangerous. The requirement of effectiveness does not preclude temporary absence of the blockading force, if such absence is due to stress of weather or to some other reason connected with the blockade (e.g., pursuit of a blockade runner). Nor does effectiveness require that every possible avenue of approach to the blockaded area be covered.

7.7.2.4 Impartiality. A blockade must be applied impartially to the vessels and aircraft of all nations. Discrimination by the blockading belligerent in favor of or against the vessels and aircraft of particular nations, including those of its own or those of an Allied nation, renders the blockade legally invalid.

7.7.2.5 Limitations. A blockade must not bar access to or departure from neutral ports and coasts. Neutral nations retain the right to engage in neutral commerce that does not involve trade or communications originating in or destined for the blockaded area.

7.7.3 Special Entry and Exit Authorization. Although neutral warships and military aircraft enjoy no positive right of access to blockaded areas, the belligerent imposing the blockade may authorize their entry and exit. Such special authorization may be made subject to such conditions as the blockading force considers to be necessary and expedient. Neutral vessels and aircraft in evident distress should be authorized entry into a blockaded area, and subsequently authorized to depart, under conditions prescribed by the commander of the blockading force. Similarly, neutral vessels and aircraft engaged in the carriage of qualifying relief supplies for the civilian population and the sick and wounded should be authorized to pass through the blockade cordon.

7.7.4 Breach and Attempted Breach of Blockade. Breach of blockade is the passage of a vessel or aircraft through a blockade without special entry or exit authorization from the blockading belligerent. Knowledge of the existence of the blockade is essential to the offenses of breach of blockade and attempted breach of blockade. Knowledge may be presumed once a blockade has been declared and appropriate notification provided to affected governments. Attempted breach of blockade occurs from the time a vessel or aircraft leaves a port or airfield with the intention of evading the blockade. It is immaterial that the vessel or aircraft is at the time of interception bound for neutral territory, if its ultimate destination is the blockaded area. There is a presumption of attempted breach of blockade where vessels or aircraft are bound for a neutral port or airfield serving as a point of transit to the blockaded area. Capture of such vessels is discussed in paragraph 7.9.

7.7.5 Contemporary Practice. The traditional rules of blockade, as set out above, are for the most part customary in nature, having derived their definitive form through the practice of maritime powers during the nineteenth century. The rules reflect a balance between the right of a belligerent possessing effective command of the sea to close enemy ports and coastlines to international commerce, and the right of neutral nations to carry out neutral commerce with the least possible interference from belligerent forces. The law of blockade is, therefore, premised on a system of controls designed to effect only a limited interference with neutral trade. This was traditionally accomplished by a relatively "close-in" cordon of surface warships stationed in the immediate vicinity of the blockaded area.

The increasing emphasis in modern warfare on seeking to isolate completely the enemy from outside assistance and resources by targeting enemy merchant vessels as well as warships, and on interdicting all neutral commerce with the enemy, is not furthered substantially by blockades established in strict conformity with the traditional rules. In World Wars I and II, belligerents of both sides resorted to methods which, although frequently referred to as measures of blockade, cannot be reconciled with the traditional concept of the close-in blockade. The so-called long-distance blockade of both World Wars departed materially from those traditional rules and were justified instead upon the belligerent right of reprisal against illegal acts of warfare on the part of the enemy. Moreover, recent developments in weapons systems and platforms, particularly nuclear-powered submarines, supersonic aircraft, and cruise missiles, have rendered the in-shore blockade exceedingly difficult, if not impossible, to maintain during anything other than a local or limited armed conflict.

Notwithstanding this clear trend in belligerent practices (during general war) away from the establishment of blockades that conform to the traditional rules, blockade continues to be a useful means to regulate the competing interests of belligerents and neutrals in more limited armed conflict. The experience of the United States during the Vietnam Conflict provides a case in point. The blockade of Haiphong and other North Vietnamese ports, accomplished by the emplacement of mines, was undertaken in conformity with traditional criteria of establishment, notification, effectiveness, limitation, and impartiality.

7.8 BELLIGERENT CONTROL OF THE IMMEDIATE AREA OF NAVAL OPERATIONS

Within the immediate area or vicinity of naval operations, a belligerent may establish special restrictions upon the activities of neutral vessels and aircraft and may prohibit altogether such vessels and air-craft from entering the area. The immedi-ate area or vicinity of naval operations is that area within which hostilities are tak-ing place or belligerent forces are actually operating. A belligerent may not, however, purport to deny access to neutral nations, or to close an international strait to neutral shipping, pursuant to this authority unless another route of similar convenience re-mains open to neutral traffic.

7.8.1 Belligerent Control of Neutral Communications at Sea. The command-ing officer of a belligerent warship may exercise control over the communication of any neutral merchant vessel or civil air-craft whose presence in the immediate area of naval operations might otherwise endan-ger or jeopardize those operations. A neu-tral merchant ship or civil aircraft within that area that fails to conform to a belliger-ent's directions concerning communica-tions may thereby assume enemy character and risk being fired upon or captured. Le-gitimate distress communications should be permitted to the extent that the success of the operation is not prejudiced thereby. Any transmission to an opposing belliger-ent of information concerning military op-erations or military forces is inconsistent with the neutral duties of abstention and impartiality and renders the neutral vessel or aircraft liable to capture or destruction.

7.9 CAPTURE OF NEUTRAL VESSELS AND AIRCRAFT

Neutral merchant vessels and civil aircraft are liable to capture by belligerent war-ships and military aircraft if engaged in any of the following activities:

1. Avoiding an attempt to establish identity

2. Resisting visit and search

3. Carrying contraband

4. Breaking or attempting to break blockade

5. Presenting irregular or fraudulent pa-pers; lacking necessary papers; or de-stroying, defacing, or concealing papers

6. Violating regulations established by a belligerent within the immediate area of naval operations

7. Carrying personnel in the military or public service of the enemy

8. Communicating information in the interest of the enemy.

Captured vessels and aircraft are sent to a port or airfield under belligerent jurisdic-tion as prize for adjudication by a prize court. Ordinarily, a belligerent warship will place a prize master and prize crew on board a captured vessel for this purpose. Should that be impracticable, the prize may be escorted into port by a belligerent warship or military aircraft. In the latter circumstances, the prize must obey the in-structions of its escort or risk forcible measures. (Article 630.23 of OPNAVINST 3120.32B, Standard Organization and Regulations of the U.S. Navy, sets forth the duties and responsibilities of com-manding officers and prize masters con-cerning captured vessels.)

Neutral vessels or aircraft attempting to re-sist proper capture lay themselves open to forcible measures by belligerent warships and military aircraft and assume all risk of resulting damage.

7.9.1 Destruction of Neutral Prizes. Every reasonable effort should be made to avoid destruction of captured neutral ves-sels and aircraft. A capturing officer, therefore, should not order such destruc-tion without being entirely satisfied that the prize can neither be sent into a belligerent port or airfield nor, in his opinion, properly be released. Should it become necessary that the prize be destroyed, the capturing officer must provide for the safety of the passengers and crew. In that event, all documents and papers relating to the prize should be saved. If practicable, the personal effects of passengers should also be safeguarded.

7.9.2 Personnel of Captured Neutral Vessels and Aircraft. The officers and crews of captured neutral merchant vessels and civil aircraft who are nationals of a neutral nation do not become prisoners of war and must be repatriated as soon as circumstances reasonably permit. This rule applies equally to the officers and crews of neutral vessels and aircraft which have assumed the character of enemy merchant vessels or aircraft by operating under enemy control or resisting visit and search. If, however, the neutral vessel or aircraft had taken a direct part in the hostilities on the side of the enemy or had served in any way as a naval or military auxiliary for the enemy, it thereby assumed the character of an enemy warship or military aircraft and, upon capture, its officers and crew may be interned as prisoners of war.

Enemy nationals found on board neutral merchant vessels and civil aircraft as passengers who are actually embodied in the military forces of the enemy, who are en route to serve in the enemy's armed forces, who are employed in the public service of the enemy, or who may be engaged in or suspected of service in the interests of the enemy may be made prisoners of war. All such enemy nationals may be removed from the neutral vessel or aircraft whether or not there is reason for its capture as a neutral prize. Enemy nationals not falling within any of these categories are not subject to capture or detention.

7.10 BELLIGERENT PERSONNEL INTERNED BY A NEUTRAL GOVERNMENT

International law recognizes that neutral territory, being outside the region of war, offers a place of asylum to members of belligerent forces and as a general rule requires the neutral government concerned to prevent the return of such persons to their own forces. The neutral nation must accord equal treatment to the personnel of all the belligerent forces.

With respect to aircrews of belligerent aircraft that land in neutral territory, whether intentionally or inadvertently, the neutral nation should usually intern them.

CHAPTER 8

The Law of Naval Targeting

8.1 PRINCIPLES OF LAWFUL TARGETING

The law of naval targeting is premised upon the three fundamental principles of the law of armed conflict:

1. The right of belligerents to adopt means of injuring the enemy is not unlimited.

2. It is prohibited to launch attacks against the civilian population as such.

3. Distinctions must be made between combatants and noncombatants, to the effect that noncombatants be spared as much as possible.

These legal principles governing targeting generally parallel the military principles of objective, mass, and economy of force. The law requires that only objectives of military importance be attacked but permits the use of sufficient mass to destroy those objectives. At the same time, unnecessary (and wasteful) collateral destruction must be avoided to the extent possible and, consistent with mission accomplishment and the security of the force, unnecessary human suffering prevented. The law of naval targeting, therefore, requires that all reasonable precautions must be taken to ensure that only military objectives are targeted so that civilians and civilian objects are spared as much as possible the ravages of war.

8.1.1 Military Objectives. Only combatants and other military objectives may be attacked. Military objectives are those objects which, by their nature, location, purpose, or use, effectively contribute to the enemy's war-fighting or war-sustaining capability and whose total or partial destruction, capture, or neutralization would constitute a definite military advantage to the attacker under the circumstances at the time of the attack. Military advantage may involve a variety of considerations including the security of the attacking force.

Proper targets for naval attack include such military objectives as enemy warships and military aircraft, naval and military auxiliaries, naval and military bases ashore, warship construction and repair facilities, military depots and warehouses, POL storage areas, docks, port facilities, harbors, bridges, airfields, military vehicles, armor, artillery, ammunition stores, troop concentrations and embarkation points, lines of communication, and other objects used to conduct or support military operations. Proper naval targets also include geographic targets, such as a mountain pass, and buildings and facilities that provide administrative and personnel support for military and naval operations such as barracks, communications and command and control facilities, headquarters buildings, mess halls, and training areas.

Proper economic targets for naval attack include enemy lines of communication used for military purposes, rail yards, bridges, rolling stock, barges, lighters, industrial installations producing war-fighting products, and power generation plants. Economic targets of the enemy that indirectly but effectively support and sustain the enemy's war-fighting capability may also be attacked.

8.1.2 Civilian Objects. Civilian objects may not be made the object of attack. Civilian objects consist of all civilian property and activities other than those used to support or sustain the enemy's war-fighting capability. Attacks on installations such as dikes and dams are prohibited if their breach or destruction would result in the loss of civilian lives disproportionate to the military advantage to be gained. (See also paragraph 8.5.1.7.) Similarly, the intentional destruction of food, crops, livestock, drinking water, and other objects indispensable to the survival of the civilian population, for the specific purpose of denying the civilian population of their use, is prohibited.

8.1.2.1 Incidental Injury and Collateral Damage. It is not unlawful to cause incidental injury or death to civilians, or collateral damage to civilian objects, during an attack upon a legitimate military objective. Incidental injury or collateral damage should not, however, be excessive in light of the military advantage anticipated by the attack. Naval commanders must take all practicable precautions, taking into account military and humanitarian considerations, to keep civilian casualties and damage to the absolute minimum consistent with mission accomplishment and the security of the force. In each instance, the commander must determine whether incidental injuries and collateral damage would be excessive, on the basis of an honest and reasonable estimate of the facts available to him. Similarly, the commander must decide, in light of all the facts known or reasonably available to him, including the need to conserve resources and complete the mission success-

fully, whether to adopt an alternative method of attack, if reasonably available, to reduce civilian casualties and damage.

8.2 SURFACE WARFARE

As a general rule, surface warships may employ their conventional weapons systems to attack, capture, or destroy enemy surface, subsurface, and air targets at sea wherever located beyond neutral territory. (Special circumstances in which enemy warships and military aircraft may be attacked in neutral territory are discussed in Chapter 7 The Law of Neutrality.) The law of armed conflict pertaining to surface warfare is concerned primarily with the protection of noncombatants through rules establishing lawful targets of attack. For that purpose, all enemy vessels and aircraft fall into one of three general classes; i.e., warships and military aircraft, merchant vessels and civilian aircraft, and exempt vessels and aircraft.

8.2.1 Enemy Warships and Military Aircraft. Enemy warships and military aircraft, including naval and military auxiliaries, are subject to attack, destruction, or capture anywhere beyond neutral territory. It is forbidden, however, to refuse quarter to any enemy who has surrendered in good faith. Once an enemy warship has clearly indicated a readiness to surrender by hauling down her flag, by hoisting a white flag, by surfacing (in the case of submarines), by stopping engines and responding to the attacker's signals, or by taking to lifeboats, the attack must be discontinued. Disabled enemy aircraft in air combat are frequently pursued to destruction because of the impossibility of verifying their true status and inability to enforce surrender. Although disabled, the aircraft may or may not have lost its means of combat. Moreover, it still may represent a valuable military asset. Accordingly, surrender in air combat is not generally offered. However, if surrender is offered in good faith so that circumstances do not preclude enforcement, it must be respected. Officers and crews of captured or destroyed enemy warships and military aircraft should be made prisoners of war. (See Chapter 11, Noncombatant Persons.) As far as military exigencies permit, after each engagement all possible measures should be taken without delay to search for and collect the shipwrecked, wounded, and sick and to recover the dead.

Prize procedure is not used for captured enemy warships and naval auxiliaries because their ownership vests immediately in the captor's government by the fact of capture.

8.2.2 Enemy Merchant Vessels and Civilian Aircraft

8.2.2.1 Capture. Enemy merchant vessels and civil aircraft may be captured at sea wherever located beyond neutral territory. Prior exercise of visit and search is not required, provided positive determination of enemy status can be made by other means. When military circumstances preclude sending or taking in such a vessel or aircraft for adjudication as an enemy prize, it may be destroyed after all possible measures are taken to provide for the safety of passengers and crew. Documents and papers relating to the prize should be safeguarded and, if practicable, the personal effects of passengers should be saved. Every case of destruction of a captured enemy prize should be reported promptly to higher command.

Officers and crews of captured enemy merchant ships and civilian aircraft may be made prisoners of war. Other enemy nationals on board such captured ships and aircraft as private passengers are subject to the discipline of the captor. Nationals of a neutral nation on board captured enemy merchant vessels and civilian aircraft are not made prisoners of war unless they have participated in acts of hostility or resistance against the captor.

8.2.2.2 Destruction. Prior to World War II, both customary and conventional international law prohibited the destruction of enemy merchant vessels by surface warships unless the safety of passengers and crew was first assured. This requirement did not apply, however, if the merchant vessel engaged in active resistance to capture or refused to stop when ordered to do so. Specifically, the London Protocol of 1936, to which almost all of the belligerents of World War II expressly acceded, provides in part that:

> In particular, except in the case of persistent refusal to stop on being duly summoned, or of active resistance to visit or search, a warship, whether surface vessel or submarine, may not sink or render incapable of navigation a merchant vessel without having first placed passengers, crew and ship's papers in a place of safety. For this purpose the ship's boats are not regarded as a place of safety unless the safety of the passengers and crew is assured, in the existing sea and weather conditions, by the proximity of land, or the presence of another vessel which is in a position to take them on board.

During World War II, the practice of attacking and sinking enemy merchant vessels by surface warships, submarines, and military aircraft without prior warning and without first providing for the safety of passengers and crew was widespread on both sides. Rationale for these apparent departures from the agreed rules of the 1936 London Protocol varied. Initially, such acts were justified as reprisals against illegal acts of the enemy. As the war progressed, however, merchant vessels were regularly armed and convoyed, participated in intelligence collection, and were otherwise incorporated directly or indirectly into the enemy's war-fighting/war-sustaining effort. Consequently, enemy merchant vessels were widely regarded as legitimate military targets subject to destruction on sight.

Although the rules of the 1936 London Protocol continue to apply to surface warships, they must be interpreted in light of current technology, including satellite communications, over-the-horizon weapons, and antiship missile systems, as well as the customary practice of belligerents that evolved during and following World War II. Accordingly, enemy merchant vessels may be attacked and destroyed by surface warships, either with or without prior warning, in any of the following circumstances:

1. Actively resisting visit and search or capture

2. Refusing to stop upon being summoned to do so

3. Sailing under convoy of enemy warships or enemy military aircraft

4. If armed

5. If incorporated into, or assisting in any way, the intelligence system of the enemy's armed forces

6. If acting in any capacity as a naval or military auxiliary to an enemy's armed forces

7. If integrated into the enemy's war-fighting/war-sustaining effort and compliance with the rules of the 1936 London Protocol would, under the circumstances of the specific encounter, subject the surface warship to imminent danger or would otherwise preclude mission accomplishment.

Rules relating to surrendering and to the search for and collection of the shipwrecked, wounded, and sick and the recovery of the dead, set forth in paragraph 8.2.1, apply also to enemy merchant vessels and civilian aircraft that may become subject to attack and destruction.

8.2.3 Enemy Vessels and Aircraft Exempt From Capture or Destruction. Certain classes of enemy vessels and aircraft are exempt under the law of naval warfare from capture or destruction provided they are innocently employed in their exempt category. These specially protected vessels and aircraft must not take part in the hostilities, must not hamper the movement of combatants, must submit to identification and inspection procedures, and may be ordered out of harm's way. These specifically exempt vessels and aircraft include:

1. Vessels and aircraft designated for and engaged in the exchange of prisoners (cartel vessels).

2. Properly designated and marked hospital ships, medical transports, and known medical aircraft.

3. Vessels charged with religious, nonmilitary scientific, or philanthropic missions. (Vessels engaged in the collection of scientific data of potential military application are not exempt.)

4. Vessels and aircraft guaranteed safe conduct by prior arrangement between the belligerents.

5. Small coastal (not deep-sea) fishing vessels and small boats engaged in local coastal trade. Such vessels and boats are subject to the regulations of a belligerent naval commander operating in the area.

6. Civilian passenger vessels at sea and civil airliners in flight are subject to capture but are exempt from destruction. Although enemy lines of communication are generally legitimate military targets in modern warfare, civilian passenger vessels at sea, and civil airliners in flight, are exempt from destruction unless at the time of the encounter they are being utilized by the enemy for a military purpose (*e.g.*, transporting troops or military cargo) or refuse to respond to the directions of the intercepting warship or military aircraft. Such passenger vessels in port and airliners on the ground are not protected from destruction.

If an exempt enemy vessel or aircraft assists the enemy's military effort in any manner, it may be captured or destroyed. Refusal to provide immediate identification upon demand is ordinarily sufficient legal justification for capture or destruction. All nations have a legal obligation not to take advantage of the harmless character of exempt vessels and aircraft in order to use them for military purposes while preserving their innocent appearance. For example, the utilization by North Vietnam of innocent appearing small coastal fishing boats as logistic craft in support of military operations during the Vietnam Conflict was in violation of this obligation.

8.3 SUBMARINE WARFARE

The law of armed conflict imposes essentially the same rules on submarines as apply to surface warships. Submarines may employ their conventional weapons systems to attack, capture, or destroy enemy surface or subsurface targets wherever located beyond neutral territory. Enemy warships and naval auxiliaries may be attacked and destroyed without warning. Rules applicable to surface warships regarding enemy ships that have surrendered

in good faith, or that have indicated clearly their intention to do so, apply as well to submarines. To the extent that military exigencies permit, submarines are also required to search for and collect the shipwrecked, wounded, and sick following an engagement. If such humanitarian efforts would subject the submarine to undue additional hazard or prevent it from accomplishing its military mission, the location of possible survivors should be passed at the first opportunity to a surface ship, aircraft, or shore facility capable of rendering assistance.

8.3.1 Interdiction of Enemy Merchant Shipping by Submarines. The conventional rules of naval warfare pertaining to submarine operations against enemy merchant shipping constitute one of the least developed areas of the law of armed conflict. Although the submarine's effectiveness as a weapons system is dependent upon its capability to remain submerged (and thereby undetected) and despite its vulnerability when surfaced, the London Protocol of 1936 (paragraph 8.2.2.2) makes no distinction between submarines and surface warships with respect to the interdiction of enemy merchant shipping. The London Protocol specifies that except in the case of persistent refusal to stop when ordered to do so, or in the event of active resistance to capture, a warship "whether surface vessel or submarine" may not destroy an enemy merchant vessel "without having first placed passengers, crew and ship's papers in a place of safety." The impracticality of imposing upon submarines the same targeting constraints as burden surface warships is reflected in the practice of belligerents of both sides during World War II when submarines regularly attacked and destroyed without warning enemy merchant shipping. As in the case of such attacks by surface warships, this practice was justified either as reprisal in response to unlawful acts of the enemy or as a necessary consequence of the arming of merchant vessels, of conveying, and of the general integration of merchant shipping into the enemy's war-fighting/war-sustaining effort.

The United States considers that the London Protocol of 1936, coupled with the customary practice of belligerents during and following World War II, imposes upon submarines the responsibility to provide for the safety of passengers, crew, and ship's papers before destruction of an enemy merchant vessel unless:

1. The enemy merchant vessel refuses to stop when summoned to do so or otherwise resists capture.

2. The enemy merchant vessel is sailing under armed convoy or is itself armed.

3. The enemy merchant vessel is assisting in any way the enemy's military intelligence system or is acting in any capacity as a naval auxiliary to the enemy's armed forces.

4. The enemy has integrated its merchant shipping into its war-fighting/war-sustaining effort and compliance with this rule would, under the circumstances of the specific encounter, subject the submarine to imminent danger or would otherwise preclude mission accomplishment.

8.3.2 Enemy Vessels Exempt From Submarine Interdiction. Rules of naval warfare regarding enemy vessels that are exempt from capture and/or destruction by surface warships apply as well to submarines. (See paragraph 8.2.3.)

8.4 AIR WARFARE AT SEA

Military aircraft may employ conventional weapons to attack and destroy enemy warships and military aircraft, including naval and military auxiliaries, anywhere at sea beyond neutral territory. Enemy merchant vessels and civil aircraft may be attacked and destroyed by military aircraft only under the following circumstances:

1. When refusing to comply with directions from the intercepting aircraft

2. When assisting in any way the enemy's military intelligence system or acting in any capacity as auxiliaries to the enemy's armed forces

3. When sailing under convoy of enemy warships, escorted by enemy military aircraft, or armed

4. When otherwise integrated into the enemy's war-fighting or war-sustaining effort.

To the extent that military exigencies permit, military aircraft are required to search for the shipwrecked, wounded, and sick following an engagement at sea. The location of possible survivors should be passed at the first opportunity to a surface vessel, aircraft, or shore facility capable of rendering assistance.

Historically, instances of surrender of enemy vessels to aircraft are rare. If, however, an enemy has surrendered in good faith, under circumstances that do not preclude enforcement of the surrender, or has clearly indicated an intention to do so, the enemy must not be attacked.

8.4.1 Enemy Vessels and Aircraft Exempt From Aircraft Interdiction. Rules of naval warfare regarding enemy vessels and aircraft that are exempt from capture and/or destruction by surface warships apply as well to military aircraft. (See paragraph 8.2.3.)

8.5 BOMBARDMENT

For purposes of this publication, the term "bombardment" refers to naval and air bombardment of enemy targets on land with conventional weapons, including naval guns, rockets and missiles, and air-delivered ordnance. Bombardment by land forces is not included in this text. Engagement of targets at sea is discussed in paragraphs 8.2 to 8.4.

8.5.1 General Rules.

The United States is a party to Hague Convention No. IX (1907) Respecting Bombardment by Naval Forces in Time of War. That convention establishes the general rules of naval bombardment of land targets. These rules have been further developed by customary practice in World Wars I and II, Vietnam, and the Falklands. Underlying these rules are the broad principles of the law of armed conflict that belligerents are forbidden to make noncombatants the target of direct attack, that superfluous injury and unnecessary suffering are to be avoided, and that wanton destruction of property is prohibited. To give effect to these humanitarian concepts, the following general rules governing bombardment must be observed.

8.5.1.1 Destruction of Civilian Habitation.

The wanton or deliberate destruction of areas of concentrated civilian habitation, including cities, towns, and villages, is prohibited. A military objective within a city, town, or village may, however, be bombarded if required for the submission of the enemy with the minimum expenditure of time, life, and physical resources.

8.5.1.2 Terrorization.

Bombardment for the sole purpose of terrorizing the civilian population is prohibited.

8.5.1.3 Undefended Cities or Agreed Demilitarized Zones.

Belligerents are forbidden to bombard a city or town that is undefended and open to immediate entry by their own or allied forces. A city or town behind enemy lines is, by definition, neither undefended nor open and military targets therein may be destroyed by bombardment. An agreed demilitarized zone is also exempt from bombardment.

8.5.1.4 Medical Facilities.

Medical establishments and units (both mobile and fixed), medical vehicles, and medical equipment and stores may not be deliberately bombarded. Belligerents are required to ensure that such medical facilities are, as far as possible, situated in such a manner that attacks against military targets in the vicinity do not imperil their safety. If medical facilities are used for military purposes inconsistent with their humanitarian mission, and if appropriate warnings that continuation of such use will result in loss of protected status are unheeded, the facilities become subject to attack. The distinctive medical emblem, a red cross or red crescent, should be clearly displayed on medical establishments and units in order to identify them as entitled to protected status. Any object recognized as being a medical facility may not be attacked whether or not marked with a protective symbol.

8.5.1.5 Special Hospital Zones and Neutralized Zones.

When established by agreement among the belligerents, hospital zones and neutralized zones are immune from bombardment in accordance with the terms of the agreement concerned.

8.5.1.6 Religious, Cultural, and Charitable Buildings and Monuments.

Buildings devoted to religion, the arts, or charitable purposes; historic monuments; and other religious, cultural, or charitable facilities should not be bombarded, provided they are not used for military purposes. It is the responsibility of the local inhabitants to ensure that such buildings and monuments are clearly marked with the distinctive emblem of such sites—a rectangle divided diagonally into two triangular halves, the upper portion black and the lower white. (See paragraph 11.10.)

8.5.1.7 Dams and Dikes. Dams, dikes, levees, and other installations, which if breached or destroyed would release flood waters or other forces dangerous to the civilian population, should not be bombarded if the potential for harm to noncombatants would be excessive in relation to the military advantage to be gained by bombardment. Conversely, installations containing such dangerous forces that are used by belligerents to shield or support military activities are not so protected.

8.5.2 Warning Before Bombardment. Where the military situation permits, commanders should make every reasonable effort to warn the civilian population located in close proximity to a military objective targeted for bombardment. Warnings may be general rather than specific lest the bombarding force or the success of its mission be placed in jeopardy.

CHAPTER 9

Conventional Weapons and Weapons Systems

9.1 INTRODUCTION

This chapter addresses legal considerations pertaining to the use of conventional weapons and weapons systems. It is a fundamental tenet of the law of armed conflict that the right of nations engaged in conflict to choose methods or means of warfare is not unlimited. This rule of law is expressed in the concept that the employment of weapons, material, and methods of warfare that are designed to cause superfluous injury or unnecessary suffering is prohibited. A corollary concept is that weapons which by their nature are incapable of being directed specifically against military objects, and therefore that put noncombatants at equivalent risk, are forbidden due to their indiscriminate effect. A few weapons, such as poisoned projectiles, are unlawful, no matter how employed. Others may be rendered unlawful by alteration, such as by coating ammunition with a poison. Still others may be unlawfully employed, such as setting armed contact naval mines adrift so as to endanger innocent as well as enemy shipping. And finally, any weapon may be set to an unlawful purpose when it is directed against noncombatants and other protected persons and property.

Of particular interest to naval officers are law of armed conflict rules pertaining to naval mines, torpedoes, cluster and fragmentation weapons, incendiary weapons, and over-the-horizon and beyond-visual-range weapons systems. Each of these weapons or systems will be assessed in terms of their potential for causing unnecessary suffering and superfluous injury or indiscriminate effect.

9.1.1 Unnecessary Suffering. Antipersonnel weapons are designed to kill or disable enemy combatants and are lawful notwithstanding the death, pain, and suffering they inflict. Weapons that are designed to cause unnecessary suffering or superfluous injury are, however, prohibited because the degree of pain or injury, or the certainty of death, they produce is needlessly or clearly disproportionate to the military advantage to be gained by their use. Poisoned projectiles and dum-dum bullets fall into this category, because there is little military advantage to be gained by ensuring the death of wounded personnel through poisoning or the expanding effect of soft-nosed or unjacketed lead ammunition. Similarly, using materials that are difficult to detect or are undetectable by field x-ray equipment, such as glass or clear plastic, as the injuring mechanism in military ammunition is prohibited, since they unnecessarily inhibit the treatment of wounds. Use of such materials as incidental components in ammunition, *e.g.*, as wadding or packing, is not prohibited.

9.1.2 Indiscriminate Effect. Weapons that are incapable of being controlled so as to be directed against a military target are forbidden as being indiscriminate in their effect. Drifting armed contact mines and long-range unguided missiles (such as the German V-1 and V-2 rockets of World War II) fall into this category. A weapon is not indiscriminate simply because it may cause incidental or collateral civilian casualties, provided such casualties are not foreseeably excessive in light of the military advantage expected to be gained. An artillery round that is capable of being directed with a reasonable degree of accuracy at a military target is not an indiscriminate weapon simply because it may miss its mark or inflict collateral damage. Conversely, uncontrolled balloon-borne bombs, such as those released by the Japanese against the west coast of the United States and Canada in World War II, lack that capability of direction and are, therefore, unlawful.

9.2 NAVAL MINES

Naval mines have been effectively employed for area denial, coastal and harbor defense, antisurface and antisubmarine warfare, and blockade. Naval mines are lawful weapons, but their potential for indiscriminate effects has led to specific regulation of their deployment and employment by the law of armed conflict. The extensive and uncontrolled use of naval mines by both sides in the Russo-Japanese War of 1904–5 inflicted great damage on innocent shipping both during and long after that conflict, and led to Hague Convention No. VIII of 1907 Relative to the Laying of Automatic Submarine Contact Mines. The purpose of the Hague rules was to ensure to the extent practicable the safety of peaceful shipping by requiring that naval mines be so constructed as to become harmless should they break loose from their moorings or otherwise cease to be under the affirmative control of the belligerents that laid them. The Hague rules also require that shipowners be warned of the presence of mines as soon as military exigencies permit.

Although the Hague provisions date from 1907, they remain the only codified rules specifically addressing the emplacement of conventional naval mines. Technological developments have created weapons systems obviously not contemplated by the drafters of these rules. Nonetheless, the general principles of law embodied in the 1907 Convention continue to serve as a guide to lawful employment of naval mines.

9.2.1 Current Technology. Modern naval mines are versatile and variable weapons. They range from relatively unsophisticated and indiscriminate contact mines to highly technical, target-selective devices with state-of-the-art homing guidance capability. Today's mines may be armed and/or detonated by physical contact, acoustic or magnetic signature, or sensitivity to changes in water pressure generated by passing vessels and may be emplaced by air, surface, or subsurface platforms. For purposes of this publication, naval mines are classified as armed or controlled mines. Armed mines are either emplaced with all safety devices withdrawn or are armed following emplacement, so as to detonate when preset parameters (if any) are satisfied. Controlled mines (including mines possessing remote control activation devices) have no destructive capability until affirmatively activated by some form of controlled arming order (whereupon they become armed mines).

9.2.2 Peacetime Mining. Consistent with the safety of its own citizenry, a nation may emplace both armed and controlled mines in its own internal waters at any time with or without notification. A nation may also mine its own archipelagic waters and territorial sea during peacetime when deemed necessary for national security purposes. If armed mines are emplaced in archipelagic waters or the territorial sea, appropriate international notification of the existence and location of such mines is required. Because the right of innocent passage can be suspended only temporarily, armed mines must be removed or rendered harmless as soon as the security threat that prompted their emplacement has terminated. Emplacement of controlled mines in a nation's own archipelagic waters or territorial sea is not subject to such notification or removal requirements.

Naval mines may not be emplaced in the internal, territorial, or archipelagic waters of another nation in peacetime without that nation's consent. Controlled mines, however, may be emplaced in international waters beyond the territorial sea subject only to the requirement that they do not unreasonably interfere with other lawful uses of the oceans. The determination of what constitutes an "unreasonable interference" involves a balancing of a number of factors including the rationale for their emplacement (i.e., the self-defense requirements of the emplacing nation), the extent of the area to be mined, the hazard (if any) to other lawful ocean uses, and the duration of their emplacement. Because controlled mines do not constitute a hazard to navigation, international notice of their emplacement is not required.

Armed mines may not be emplaced in international waters prior to the outbreak of armed conflict, except under the most demanding requirements of individual or collective self-defense. Should armed mines be emplaced in international waters under such circumstances, prior notification of their location must be provided and the anticipated date of their complete removal must be clearly stated. The nation emplacing armed mines in international waters during peacetime also assumes the responsibility to maintain an on-scene presence in the area sufficient to ensure that appropriate warning is provided to ships approaching the danger area. All armed mines must be expeditiously removed or rendered harmless when the imminent danger that prompted their emplacement has passed.

9.2.3 Mining During Armed Conflict.
Naval mines may be lawfully employed by parties to an armed conflict subject to the following restrictions:

1. International notification of the location of emplaced armed mines must be made as soon as military exigencies permit.

2. Mines may not be emplaced by belligerents in neutral waters.

3. Anchored mines must become harmless as soon as they have broken their moorings.

4. Unanchored mines not otherwise affixed or imbedded in the bottom must become harmless within an hour after loss of control over them.

5. The location of minefields must be carefully recorded to ensure accurate notification and to facilitate subsequent removal and/or deactivation.

6. Naval mines may be employed to channelize neutral shipping, but not in a manner to impede the transit passage of international straits or archipelagic sea lanes passage of archipelagic waters by such shipping.

7. Naval mines may not be emplaced off the coasts and ports of the enemy with the sole objective of intercepting commercial shipping, but may otherwise be employed in the strategic blockade of enemy ports, coasts, and waterways.

8. Mining of areas of indefinite extent in international waters is prohibited. Reasonably limited barred areas may be established by naval mines, pro-

vided neutral shipping retains an alternate route around or through such an area with reasonable assurance of safety,

9.3 TORPEDOES

Torpedoes which do not become harmless when they have missed their mark constitute a danger to innocent shipping and are therefore unlawful. All U.S. Navy torpedoes are designed to sink to the bottom and become harmless upon completion of their propulsion run.

9.4 CLUSTER AND FRAGMENTATION WEAPONS

Cluster and fragmentation weapons are projectiles, bombs, missiles, and grenades that are designed to fragment prior to or upon detonation, thereby expanding the radius of their lethality and destructiveness. These weapons are lawful when used against combatants. When used in proximity to noncombatants or civilian objects, their employment should be carefully monitored to ensure that collateral civilian casualties or damage are not excessive in relation to the legitimate military advantage sought.

9.5 DELAYED ACTION DEVICES

Booby traps and other delayed action devices are not unlawful, provided they are not designed or employed to cause unnecessary suffering. Devices that are designed to simulate items likely to attract and injure noncombatants (*e.g.*, toys and trinkets) are prohibited. Attaching booby traps to protected persons or objects, such as the wounded and sick, dead bodies, or medical facilities and supplies, is similarly prohibited.

9.6 INCENDIARY WEAPONS

Incendiary devices, such as tracer ammunition, thermite bombs, flame throwers, napalm, and other incendiary weapons and agents, are lawful weapons. Where incendiary devices are the weapons of choice, they should be employed in a manner that minimizes uncontrolled or indiscriminate effects on the civilian population consistent with mission accomplishment and force security.

9.7 OVER-THE-HORIZON WEAPONS SYSTEMS

Missiles and projectiles dependent upon over-the-horizon or beyond-visual-range guidance systems are lawful, provided they are equipped with sensors, or are employed in conjunction with external sources of targeting data, that are sufficient to ensure effective target discrimination.

CHAPTER 10

Nuclear, Chemical, and Biological Weapons

10.1 INTRODUCTION

Nuclear, chemical, and biological weapons present special law-of-armed-conflict problems due to their potential for indiscriminate effects and unnecessary suffering. This chapter addresses legal considerations pertaining to the development, possession, deployment, and employment of these weapons.

10.2 NUCLEAR WEAPONS

10.2.1 General. There are no rules of customary or conventional international law prohibiting nations from employing nuclear weapons in armed conflict in the absence of such an express prohibition, the use of nuclear weapons against enemy combatants and other military objectives is lawful. Employment of nuclear weapons is, however, subject to the following principles: the right of the parties to a conflict to adopt means of injuring the enemy is not unlimited; it is prohibited to launch attacks against the civilian population as such; and the distinction must be made at all times between persons taking part in the hostilities and members of the civilian population to the effect that the latter be spared as much as possible. The decision to authorize employment of nuclear weapons must emanate from the highest level of government. For the United States, that authority resides solely in the President.

10.2.2 Treaty Obligations. Nuclear weapons are regulated by a number of arms control agreements restricting their development, deployment, and use. Some of these agreements (*e.g.*, the 1963 Nuclear Test Ban Treaty) may not apply during time of war.

10.2.2.1 Seabed Arms Control Treaty. This multilateral convention prohibits the emplacement of nuclear weapons on the seabed and ocean floor beyond a 12-nautical mile coastal zone measured from the baseline of the territorial sea. The prohibition extends to structures, launching installations, and other facilities specifically designed for storing, testing, or using nuclear weapons. This treaty prohibits emplacements of nuclear mines on the seabed and ocean floor or in the subsoil thereof. It does not, however, prohibit the use of nuclear weapons in the water column that are not so affixed to the seabed (*e.g.*, nuclear-armed depth charges and torpedoes).

10.2.2.2 Outer Space Treaty. This multilateral convention prohibits the placement, installation, or stationing of nuclear weapons or other weapons of mass destruction in earth orbit, on the moon or other celestial bodies, or in outer space. Suborbital missile systems are not included in this prohibition.

10.2.2.3 Antarctic Treaty. The Antarctic Treaty is a multilateral convention designed to ensure that Antarctica, defined to include the area south of 60 South Latitude, is used for peaceful purposes only. The treaty prohibits in Antarctica "any measures of a military nature, such as establishment of military bases and fortifications, the carrying out of military maneuvers, as well as the testing of any type of weapons." Nuclear explosions are specifically prohibited. Ships and aircraft at points of discharging personnel or cargo in Antarctica are subject to international inspection. Ships and aircraft operating on and over the high seas within the treaty area are not subject to these prohibitions.

10.2.2.4 Treaty of Tlatelolco. This treaty is an agreement among the Latin American nations not to introduce nuclear weapons into Latin America. The treaty does not, however, prohibit Latin American nations from authorizing nuclear-armed ships and aircraft of nonmember nations to visit their ports and airfields or to transit through their territorial seas or airspace. The treaty is not applicable to the power system of any vessel.

Protocol I to the treaty is an agreement among non-Latin American nations that exercise international responsibility over territory within the treaty area to abide by the denuclearization provisions of the treaty. The Netherlands, the U.K., and the U.S. are parties to Protocol I. U.S. territory within the Latin America treaty area includes Guantanamo Bay in Cuba, the Virgin Islands, and Puerto Rico. Consequently, the U.S. cannot maintain nuclear weapons in those areas. Protocol I nations retain, however, competence to authorize transits and port visits by ships and aircraft of their own or other armed forces in their Protocol I territories, irrespective of armament or cargo.

Protocol II is an agreement among nuclear-armed nations (China, France, the U.S.S.R., the U.K., and the U.S.) to respect the denuclearization aims of the treaty, to not use nuclear weapons against Latin American nations party to the treaty, and to refrain from contributing to a violation of the treaty by the Latin American nations.

10.2.2.5 Nuclear Test Ban Treaty. This multilateral treaty prohibits the testing of nuclear weapons in the atmosphere, in outer space, and underwater. Over 100 nations are parties to the treaty, including the U.S.S.R., the U.K., and the U.S. (France and China are not parties.) Underground testing of nuclear weapons is not included within the ban.

10.2.2.6 Non-Proliferation Treaty. This multilateral treaty obligates nuclear weapons nations to refrain from transferring nuclear weapons or nuclear weapons technology to non-nuclear-weapons nations, and obligates non-nuclear-weapons nations to refrain from accepting such weapons from nuclear-weapons nations or from manufacturing nuclear weapons themselves. The treaty does not apply in time of war.

10.2.2.7 Bilateral Nuclear Arms Control Agreements. The United States and the U.S.S.R. have concluded a number of bilateral agreements designed to restrain the growth of nuclear warheads and launchers and to reduce the risk of miscalculation that could trigger a nuclear exchange. Among these agreements are the Hotline Agreements of 1963 and 1971, the Accidents Measures Agreement of 1971, the 1973 Agreement on Prevention of Nuclear War, the Anti-Ballistic Missile Treaty of 1972 and its Protocol of 1974, the Threshold Test Ban Treaty of 1974, the 1976 Treaty on Peaceful Nuclear Explosions, the SALT Agreements of 1972 and 1977 (SALT I—Interim Agreement has expired; SALT II was never ratified), and the INF Treaty of 1988.

10.3 CHEMICAL WEAPONS

Both customary and conventional international law prohibit the "first use" of lethal chemical weapons in armed conflict.

10.3.1 Treaty Obligations. The United States is a party to the 1925 Geneva Protocol for the Prohibition of the Use in War of Asphyxiating, Poisonous or Other Gases, and of Bacteriological Methods of Warfare ("the 1925 Gas Protocol"). All other NATO nations and all Warsaw Pact nations are also parties. The United States, the U.S.S.R., and most other NATO and Warsaw Pact nations conditioned their adherence to the 1925 Gas Protocol on the understanding that the prohibition against use of chemical weapons ceases to be binding with respect to nations whose armed forces, or the armed forces of their allies, fail to respect that prohibition. This, in effect, restricts the prohibition to the "first use" of such munitions, with parties to the Protocol reserving the right to employ chemical weapons for retaliatory purposes.

The 1925 Gas Protocol does not prohibit the development, production, testing, or stockpiling of chemical weapons, nor does it prevent equipping and training military forces for chemical warfare.

10.3.2 United States Policy Regarding Chemical Weapons. The United States categorizes chemical weapons under the three headings of lethal and incapacitating agents, riot control agents, and herbicidal agents. United States policy with respect to these three categories is summarized in the following paragraphs.

10.3.2.1 Lethal and Incapacitating Agents. The United States considers the prohibition against first use of lethal and incapacitating chemical weapons to be part of customary international law and, therefore, binding on all nations whether or not they are parties to the 1925 Gas Protocol. Lethal chemical agents are those asphyxiating, poisonous, or other gases; analogous liquids; or materials that cause immediate death. Incapacitating agents are those producing symptoms that persist for appreciable periods of time after exposure to the agent has terminated. Because the 1925 Gas Protocol effectively prohibits only first use of such weapons, the United States maintains a lethal and incapacitating chemical weapons capability for deterrence and possible retaliatory purposes only. National Command Authorities (NCA) approval is required for retaliatory use of lethal or incapacitating chemical weapons by U.S. Forces. Retaliatory use of lethal or incapacitating chemical agents must be terminated as soon as the enemy use of such agents that prompted the retaliation has ceased and any tactical advantage gained by the enemy through unlawful first use has been redressed.

10.3.2.2 Riot Control Agents. Riot control agents are those gases, liquids, and analogous substances that are widely used by governments for civil law enforcement purposes. Riot control agents, in all but the most unusual circumstances, cause merely transient effects that disappear within minutes after exposure to the agent has terminated. Tear gas and Mace are examples of riot control agents in widespread use by law enforcement officials. The United States considers that use of riot control agents in wartime is not prohibited by the 1925 Gas Protocol. However, the United States has formally renounced first use of riot control agents in armed conflict except in defensive military modes to save lives. Examples of authorized use of riot control agents in time of armed conflict include:

1. Riot control situations in areas under effective U.S. military control, to include control of rioting prisoners of war

2. Rescue missions involving downed aircrews or escaping prisoners of war

3. Protection of military supply depots, military convoys, and other military activities in rear echelon areas from civil disturbances, terrorist activities, or paramilitary operations.

Use of riot control agents by U.S. forces in armed conflict requires NCA approval.

Employment of riot control agents in peacetime may be authorized by the Secretary of Defense, or in limited circumstances, by the commanders of the unified and specified commands. Examples of authorized use of riot control agents in peacetime include:

1. Civil disturbances and other law enforcement activities in the United States, its territories, and possessions

2. On U.S. bases, posts, embassy grounds, and installations overseas for protection and security purposes, including riot control

3. Offbase overseas for law enforcement purposes when specifically authorized by the host government

4. Humanitarian evacuation operations involving U.S. or foreign nationals.

10.3.2.3 Herbicidal Agents. Herbicidal agents are gases, liquids, and analogous substances that are designed to defoliate trees, bushes, or shrubs, or to kill long grasses and other vegetation that could shield the movement of enemy forces. The United States considers that use of herbicidal agents in wartime is not prohibited by the 1925 Gas Protocol, but has formally renounced the first use of herbicides in time of armed conflict except for control of vegetation within U.S. bases and installations or around their immediate defen-

sive perimeters. Use of herbicidal agents during armed conflict requires NCA approval. Use of herbicidal agents in peacetime may be authorized by the Secretary of Defense or, in limited situations, by the commanders of the unified and specified commands.

10.4 BIOLOGICAL WEAPONS

International law prohibits all biological weapons or methods of warfare whether directed against persons, animals, or plant life. Biological weapons include microbial or other biological agents or toxins whatever their origin (i.e., natural or artificial) or method of production.

10.4.1 Treaty Obligations. The 1925 Gas Protocol prohibits the use in armed conflict of biological weapons. The 1972 Convention on the Prohibition of the Development, Production and Stockpiling of Bacteriological (Biological) and Toxin Weapons and on Their Destruction (the "1972 Biological Weapons Convention") prohibits the production, testing, and stockpiling of biological weapons. The 1972 Biological Weapons Convention obligates nations that are a party thereto not to develop, produce, stockpile, or otherwise acquire biological agents or toxins of types and in quantities that have no justification for prophylactic, protective, or other peaceful means, as well as weapons, equipment, or means of delivery designed to use such agents or toxins in armed conflict. All such materials were to be destroyed by the parties to the Convention by 26 December 1976. The United States, the U.S.S.R., and most other NATO and Warsaw Pact nations are parties to both the 1925 Gas Protocol and the 1972 Biological Weapons Convention.

10.4.2 United States Policy Regarding Biological Weapons. The United States considers the prohibition against the use of biological weapons during armed conflict to be part of customary international law and thereby binding on all nations whether or not they are parties to the 1925 Gas Protocol or the 1972 Biological Weapons Convention. The United States has, therefore, formally renounced the use of biological weapons under any circumstances.

Pursuant to its treaty obligations, the United States has destroyed all its biological and toxin weapons and restricts its research activities to development of defensive capabilities.

CHAPTER 11

Noncombatant Persons

11.1 INTRODUCTION

As discussed in Chapter 5, the law of armed conflict is premised largely on the distinction to be made between combatants and noncombatants. Noncombatants are those individuals who do not form a part of the armed forces and who otherwise refrain from the commission of hostile acts. Noncombatants also include those members of the armed forces who enjoy special protected status, such as medical personnel and chaplains, or who have been rendered incapable of combat by wounds, sickness, shipwreck, or capture. This chapter reviews the categories of noncombatants and outlines the general rules of the law of armed conflict designed to protect them from direct attack.

11.2 PROTECTED STATUS

The law of armed conflict prohibits making noncombatant persons the object of intentional attack and requires that they be safeguarded against injury not incidental to military operations directed against combatant forces and other military objectives. When circumstances permit, advance warning should be given of attacks that might endanger noncombatants in the vicinity. Such warnings are not required, however, if mission accomplishment, including the security of attacking forces, is premised on the element of surprise. On the other hand, a party to an armed conflict that has control over civilians and other noncombatants has an affirmative duty to remove them from the vicinity of targets of likely enemy attack and to otherwise separate military activities and facilities from areas of noncombatant concentration. Deliberate use of noncombatants to shield military objectives from enemy attack is prohibited. The presence of noncombatants within or adjacent to a legitimate target does not, however, preclude its attack.

11.3 THE CIVILIAN POPULATION

The civilian population as such, as well as individual civilians, may not be the object of attack or of threats or acts of intentional terrorization. The civilian population consists of all persons not serving in the armed forces, militia, or paramilitary forces and not otherwise taking a direct part in the hostilities. Women and children are entitled to special respect and protection. Unlike military personnel (other than those in a specially protected status such as medical personnel and the sick and wounded) who are always subject to attack whether on duty or in a leave capacity, civilians are immune from attack unless they are acting in direct support of the enemy's war-fighting or war-sustaining effort. Civilians providing command, administrative, or logistic support to military operations are subject to attack while so engaged. Similarly, civilian employees of naval shipyards, merchant seamen in ships carrying military cargoes, and laborers engaged in the construction of military fortifications, may be attacked while so employed.

Civilians who take a direct part in hostilities by taking up arms or otherwise trying to kill, injure, or capture enemy persons or destroy enemy property lose their immunity and may be attacked. Similarly, civilians serving as lookouts, guards, or intelligence agents for military forces may be attacked.

11.4 THE WOUNDED AND SICK

Members of the armed forces incapable of participating in combat due to injury or illness may not be the subject of attack. Moreover, parties to an armed engagement must, without delay, take all possible measures following the engagement to search for and collect the wounded and sick on the field of battle, protect them from harm, and ensure their care. When circumstances permit, an armistice or cease-fire should be arranged to enable the wounded and sick to be located and removed to safety and medical care. Wounded and sick personnel falling into enemy hands must be treated humanely and cared for without adverse distinction along with the enemy's own casualties. Priority in order of treatment may only be justified by urgent medical considerations. The physical or mental well-being of enemy wounded and sick personnel may not be unjustifiably endangered, nor may they be subjected to any medical procedure not called for by their condition or inconsistent with accepted medical standards.

11.5 MEDICAL PERSONNEL AND CHAPLAINS

Medical personnel, including medical and dental officers, technicians and corpsmen, nurses, and medical service personnel, have special protected status when engaged exclusively in medical duties and may not be attacked. Possession of small arms for self-protection, for the protection of the wounded and sick, and for protection from marauders and others violating the law of armed conflict does not disqualify medical personnel from protected status. Medical personnel may not use such arms against enemy forces acting in conformity with the law of armed conflict. Chaplains engaged in ministering to the armed forces enjoy protected status equivalent to that of medical personnel. Medical personnel and chaplains should display the distinctive emblem of the Red Cross or Red Crescent when engaged in their respective medical and religious activities. Failure to wear the distinctive emblem does not, by itself, justify attacking a medical person or chaplain, recognized as such. Medical personnel and chaplains falling into enemy hands do not become prisoners of war. Unless their retention by the enemy is required to provide for the medical or religious needs of prisoners of war, medical personnel and chaplains must be repatriated at the earliest opportunity.

11.6 THE SHIPWRECKED

Shipwrecked persons, whether military or civilian, may not be attacked. Shipwrecked persons include those in peril at sea or in other waters as a result of either the sinking, grounding, or other damage to a vessel in which they are embarked, or of the downing or distress of an aircraft. It is immaterial whether the peril was the result of enemy action or nonmilitary causes. Following each naval engagement at sea, the belligerents are obligated to take all possible measures, consistent with the security of their forces to search for and rescue the shipwrecked.

Shipwrecked persons do not include combatant personnel engaged in amphibious, underwater, or airborne attacks who are proceeding ashore, unless they are clearly in distress and require assistance. In the latter case they qualify as shipwrecked persons only if they cease all active combat activity and the enemy has an opportunity to recognize their condition of distress. Shipwrecked combatants falling into enemy hands become prisoners of war.

11.7 PARACHUTISTS

Parachutists descending from disabled aircraft may not be attacked while in the air and, unless they land in territory controlled by their own forces or engage in combatant acts while descending, must be provided an opportunity to surrender upon reaching the ground. Airborne troops, special warfare infiltrators, and intelligence agents parachuting into combat areas or behind enemy lines are not so protected and may be attacked in the air as well as on the ground. Such personnel may not be attacked, however, if they clearly indicate their intention to surrender.

11.8 PRISONERS OF WAR

Combatants cease to be subject to attack when they have individually laid down their arms to surrender, when they are no longer capable of resistance, or when the unit in which they are serving or embarked has surrendered or been captured. Combatants that have surrendered or otherwise fallen into enemy hands are entitled to prisoner-of-war status and, as such, must be treated humanely and protected against violence, intimidation, insult, and public curiosity. When prisoners of war are given medical treatment, no distinction among them will be based on any grounds other than medical ones. (See paragraph 11.4 for further discussion of the medical treatment to be accorded captured enemy wounded and sick personnel.) Prisoners of war may be interrogated upon capture but are only required to disclose their name, rank, date of birth, and military serial number. Torture, threats, or other coercive acts are prohibited.

Persons entitled to prisoner-of-war status upon capture include members of the regular armed forces, the militia and volunteer units fighting with the regular armed forces, and civilians accompanying the armed forces. Militia, volunteers, guerrillas, and other partisans not fighting in association with the regular armed forces qualify for prisoner-of-war status upon capture, provided they are commanded by a person responsible for their conduct, are uniformed or bear a fixed distinctive sign recognizable at a distance, carry their arms openly, and conduct their operations in accordance with the law of armed conflict.

Should a question arise regarding a captive's entitlement to prisoner-of-war status, that individual should be accorded prisoner-of-war treatment until a competent tribunal convened by the captor determines the status to which that individual is properly entitled. Individuals captured as spies or as illegal combatants have the right to assert their entitlement to prisoner-of-war status before a judicial tribunal and to have that question adjudicated. Such persons have a right to be fairly tried for violations of the law of armed conflict and may not be summarily executed.

11.8.1 Trial and Punishment. Prisoners of war may not be punished for hostile acts directed against opposing forces prior to capture, unless those acts constituted violations of the law of armed conflict. Prisoners of war prosecuted for war crimes committed prior to or after capture are entitled to be tried by the same courts as try the captor's own forces and are to be accorded the same procedural rights. At a minimum, these rights must include the assistance of lawyer counsel, an interpreter, and a fellow prisoner.

Although prisoners of war may be subjected to disciplinary action for minor offenses committed during captivity, punishment may not exceed 30 days confinement. Prisoners of war may not be subjected to collective punishment nor may reprisal action be taken against them.

11.8.2 Labor. Enlisted prisoners of war may be required to engage in labor having no military character or purpose. Noncommissioned officers may only be required to perform supervisory work. Officers may not be required to work.

11.8.3 Escape. Prisoners of war may not be punished for attempting to escape, unless they cause death or injury to someone in the process. Prisoners of war who make good their escape by rejoining friendly forces or leaving enemy controlled territory, may not be punished if recaptured for offenses committed during their previous escape.

11.8.4 Temporary Detention of Prisoners of War, Civilian Internees, and Other Detained Persons Aboard Naval Vessels. International treaty law expressly prohibits "internment" of prisoners of war other than in premises on land, but does not address temporary stay on board vessels. U.S. policy, however, permits detention of prisoners of war, civilian internees, and detained persons (PW/CI/DET) on naval vessels as follows:

1. PW/CI/DET picked up at sea may be temporarily held on board as operational needs dictate, pending a reasonable opportunity to transfer them to a shore facility or to another vessel for evacuation to a shore facility.

2. PW/CI/DET may be temporarily held on board naval vessels while being transported between land facilities.

3. PW/CI/DET may be temporarily held on board naval vessels if such detention would appreciably improve their safety or health prospects.

Detention on board vessels must be truly temporary, limited to the minimum period necessary to evacuate such persons from the combat zone or to avoid the significant harm such persons would face if detained on land. Use of immobilized vessels for temporary detention of prisoners of war, civilian internees, or detained persons is not authorized without NCA approval.

11.9 INTERNED PERSONS

Enemy civilians falling under the control of a belligerent may be interned if security considerations of the belligerent make it absolutely necessary to do so. Civilians sentenced for offenses committed in occupied territory may also be ordered into internment in lieu of punishment. Enemy civilians may not be interned as hostages. Interned persons may not be removed from the occupied territory in which they reside unless their own security or imperative military reason demands. All interned persons must be treated humanely and may not be subjected to collective punishment nor reprisal action.

11.10 PROTECTIVE SIGNS AND SYMBOLS

11.10.1 The Red Cross and Red Crescent. A red cross on a white field (Figure 11-1a) is the internationally accepted symbol for protected medical and religious persons and activities. Moslem countries utilize a red crescent on a white field for the same purpose (Figure 11-1b). A red lion and sun on a white field, once employed by Iran, is no longer used. Israel employs the Red Star of David, which it reserved the right to use when it ratified

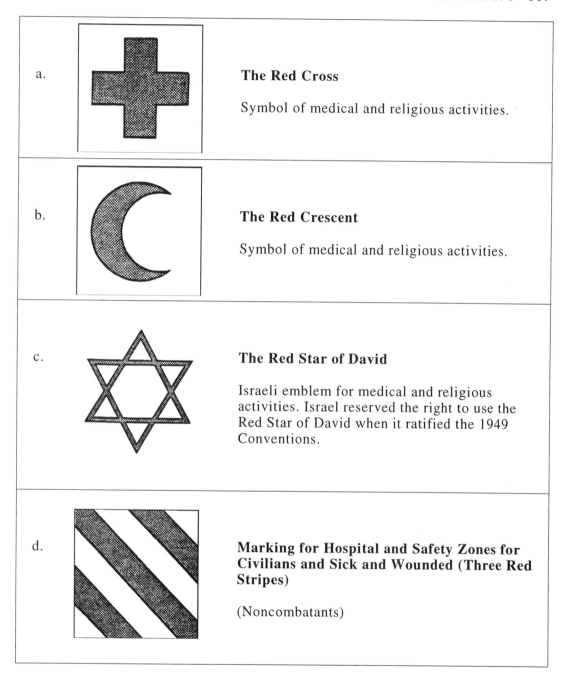

a. **The Red Cross**

Symbol of medical and religious activities.

b. **The Red Crescent**

Symbol of medical and religious activities.

c. **The Red Star of David**

Israeli emblem for medical and religious activities. Israel reserved the right to use the Red Star of David when it ratified the 1949 Conventions.

d. **Marking for Hospital and Safety Zones for Civilians and Sick and Wounded (Three Red Stripes)**

(Noncombatants)

Figure 11-1. Protective Signs and Symbols (Sheet 1 of 3)

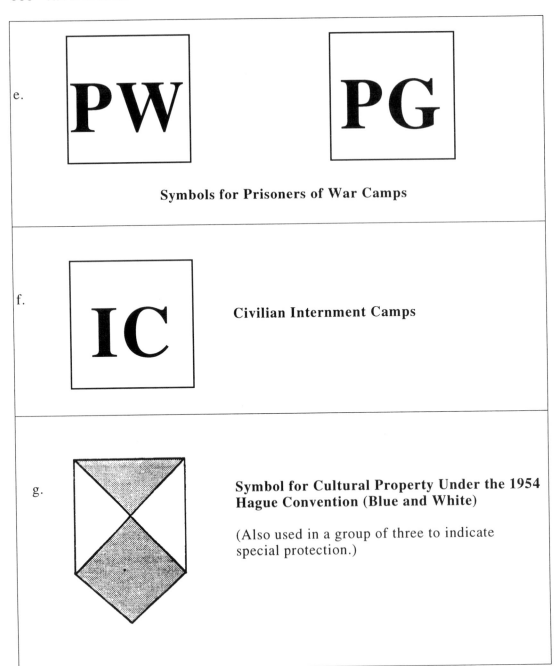

e. Symbols for Prisoners of War Camps

f. Civilian Internment Camps

g. Symbol for Cultural Property Under the 1954 Hague Convention (Blue and White)

(Also used in a group of three to indicate special protection.)

Figure 11-1. Protective Signs and Symbols (Sheet 2 of 3)

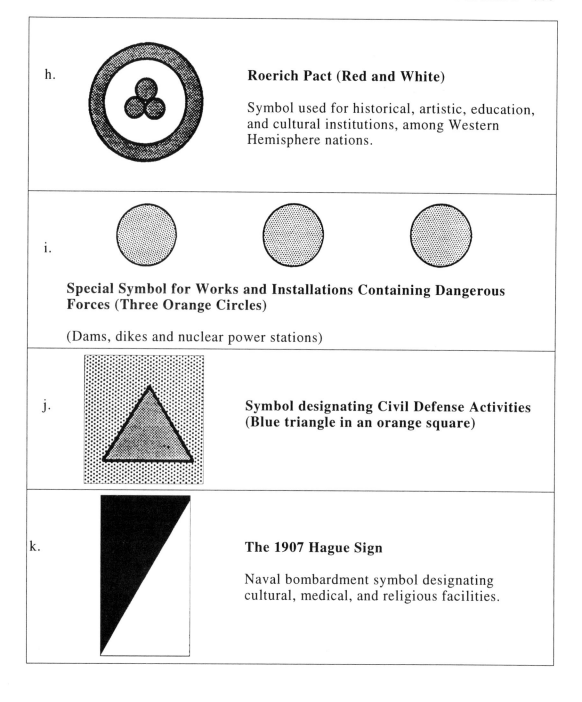

h. **Roerich Pact (Red and White)**

Symbol used for historical, artistic, education, and cultural institutions, among Western Hemisphere nations.

i. **Special Symbol for Works and Installations Containing Dangerous Forces (Three Orange Circles)**

(Dams, dikes and nuclear power stations)

j. **Symbol designating Civil Defense Activities (Blue triangle in an orange square)**

k. **The 1907 Hague Sign**

Naval bombardment symbol designating cultural, medical, and religious facilities.

Figure 11-1. Protective Signs and Symbols (Sheet 3 of 3)

the 1949 Geneva Conventions (Figure 11-1c). The United States has not agreed that it is a protective symbol. Nevertheless, all medical and religious persons or objects recognized as being so marked are to be treated with care and protection.

11.10.2 Other Protective Symbols. Other protective symbols specially recognized by international law include an oblique red band on a white background to designate hospital zones and safe havens for non-combatants (Figure 11-1d). Prisoners-of-war camps are marked by the letters "PV" or "PG" (Figure II-1e); civilian internment camps with the letters "IC" (Figure 11-1f). A royal-blue diamond and royal-blue triangle on a white shield is used to designate cultural buildings, museums, historic monuments, and other cultural objects that are exempt from attack (Figure 11-1g). In the Western Hemisphere, a red circle with triple red spheres in the circle, on a white background (the "Roerich Pact" symbol) is used for that purpose (Figure 11-1h).

Two protective symbols established by the 1977 Protocol I Additional to the Geneva Conventions of 1949, to which the United States is not a party, are described as follows for informational purposes only. Works and installations containing forces potentially dangerous to the civilian population, such as dams, dikes, and nuclear power plants, may be marked by three bright orange circles of equal size on the same axis (Figure 11-1i). Civil defense facilities and personnel may be identified by an equilateral blue triangle on an orange background (Figure 11-1j).

11.10.3 The 1907 Hague Symbol. A protective symbol of special interest to naval officers is the sign established by the 1907 Hague Convention Concerning Bombardment by Naval Forces in Time of War (Hague IX). The 1907 Hague symbol is used to mark sacred edifices, hospitals, historic monuments, cultural buildings, and other structures protected from naval bombardment. The symbol consists of a rectangular panel divided diagonally into two triangles, the upper black, the lower white (Figure 11-1k).

11.10.4 The White Flag. Customary international law recognizes the white flag as symbolizing a request to cease-fire, negotiate, or surrender. Enemy forces displaying a white flag should be permitted an opportunity to surrender or to communicate a request for cease-fire or negotiation.

11.10.5 Permitted Uses. Protective signs and symbols may be used only to identify personnel, objects, and activities entitled to the protected status which they designate. Any other use is forbidden by international law.

11.10.6 Failure to Display. When objects or persons are readily recognizable as being entitled to protected status, the lack of protective signs and symbols does not render an otherwise protected object or person a legitimate target. Failure to utilize internationally agreed protective signs and symbols may, however, subject protected persons and objects to the risk of not being recognized by the enemy as having protected status.

CHAPTER 12

Deception During Armed Conflict

12.1 GENERAL

The law of armed conflict permits deceiving the enemy through stratagems and ruses of war intended to mislead him, to deter him from taking action, or to induce him to act recklessly, provided the ruses do not violate rules of international law applicable to armed conflict.

12.1.1 Permitted Deceptions. Stratagems and ruses of war permitted in armed conflict include such deceptions as camouflage, deceptive lighting, dummy ships and other armament, decoys, simulated forces, feigned attacks and withdrawals, ambushes, false intelligence information, electronic deceptions, and utilization of enemy codes, passwords, and countersigns.

12.1.2 Prohibited Deceptions. The use of unlawful deceptions is called "perfidy." Acts of perfidy are deceptions designed to invite the confidence of the enemy to lead him to believe that he is entitled to, or is obliged to accord, protected status under the law of armed conflict, with the intent to betray that confidence. Feigning surrender in order to lure the enemy into a trap is an act of perfidy.

12.2 MISUSE OF PROTECTIVE SIGNS, SIGNALS, AND SYMBOLS

Misuse of protective signs, signals, and symbols in order to injure, kill, or capture the enemy constitutes an act of perfidy.

Such acts are prohibited because they undermine the effectiveness of protective signs, signals, and symbols and thereby jeopardize the safety of noncombatants and the immunity of protected structures and activities. For example, using an ambulance or medical aircraft marked with a red cross or red crescent to carry armed combatants, weapons, or ammunition with which to attack or elude enemy forces is prohibited. Similarly, use of the white flag to gain a military advantage over the enemy is unlawful.

12.3 NEUTRAL FLAGS, INSIGNIA, AND UNIFORMS

12.3.1 At Sea. Under the customary international law of naval warfare, it is permissible for a belligerent warship to fly false colors and disguise its outward appearance in other ways in order to deceive the enemy into believing the vessel is of neutral nationality or is other than a warship. However, it is unlawful for a warship to go into action without first showing her true colors. Use of neutral flags, insignia, or uniforms during an actual armed engagement at sea is, therefore, forbidden.

12.3.2 In the Air. Use of false or deceptive markings to disguise belligerent military aircraft as being of neutral nationality is prohibited.

12.3.3 On Land. The law of armed conflict applicable to land warfare has no rule of law analogous to that which permits belligerent warships to display neutral colors. Belligerents engaged in armed conflict on land are not permitted to use the flags, insignia, or uniforms of a neutral nation to deceive the enemy.

12.4 THE UNITED NATIONS FLAG AND EMBLEM

The flag of the United Nations and the letters "UN" may not be used in armed conflict for any purpose without the authorization of the United Nations.

12.5 ENEMY FLAGS, INSIGNIA, AND UNIFORMS

12.5.1 At Sea. Naval surface and subsurface forces may fly enemy colors and display enemy markings to deceive the enemy. Warships must, however, display their true colors prior to an actual armed engagement.

12.5.2 In the Air. The use in combat of enemy markings by belligerent military aircraft is forbidden.

12.5.3 On Land. The law of land warfare does not prohibit the use by belligerent land forces of enemy flags, insignia, or uniforms to deceive the enemy either before or following an armed engagement. Combatants risk loss of entitlement to prisoner-of-war status, however, if they are captured while displaying enemy colors or insignia or wearing enemy uniforms in combat.

Similarly, combatants caught behind enemy lines wearing the uniform of their adversaries are not entitled to prisoner-of-war status or protection and, historically, have been subjected to severe punishment. It is permissible, however, for downed aircrews and escaping prisoners of war to use enemy uniforms to evade capture, so long as they do not attack enemy forces, gather military intelligence, or engage in similar military operations while so attired. As a general rule, enemy markings should be removed from captured enemy equipment before it is used in combat.

12.6 FEIGNING DISTRESS

It is unlawful to feign distress through the false use of internationally recognized distress signals such as SOS and MAYDAY. In air warfare, however, it is permissible to feign disablement or other distress as a means to induce the enemy to break off an attack. Consequently, there is no obligation in air warfare to cease attacking a belligerent military aircraft that appears to be disabled. However, if one knows the enemy aircraft is disabled such as to permanently remove it from the conflict (eg., major fire or structural damage) there is an obligation to cease attacking to permit possible evacuation by crew or passengers.

12.7 FALSE CLAIMS OF NONCOMBATANT STATUS

It is a violation of the law of armed conflict to kill, injure, or capture the enemy by false indication of an intent to surrender or by feigning shipwreck, sickness, wounds, or civilian status (but, see paragraph 12.3.1). A surprise attack by a person feigning shipwreck, sickness, or wounds undermines the protected status of those rendered incapable of combat. Similarly, attacking enemy forces while posing as a civilian puts all civilians at hazard. Such acts of perfidy are punishable as war crimes.

12.7.1 Illegal Combatants. Persons who take part in combat operations without distinguishing themselves clearly from the civilian population during battle are illegal combatants and are subject to punishment upon capture. If determined by a competent tribunal of the captor nation to be illegal combatants, such persons may be denied prisoner-of-war status and be tried and punished for falsely claiming noncombatant status during combat. It is the policy of the United States, however, to accord illegal combatants prisoner-of-war status if they were carrying their arms openly at the time of capture.

12.8 SPIES

A spy is someone who, while in territory under enemy control, seeks to obtain information while operating under a false claim of noncombatant or friendly forces status with the intention of passing that information to an opposing belligerent. Members of the armed forces who penetrate enemy-held territory in civilian attire or enemy uniform to collect intelligence are spies. Conversely, personnel conducting recon-naissance missions behind enemy lines while properly uniformed are not spies. Crewmembers of warships and military aircraft engaged in intelligence collection missions in enemy waters or airspace are not spies unless the ship or aircraft displays false civilian, neutral, or enemy markings.

12.8.1 Legal Status. Spying during armed conflict is not a violation of international law. Captured spies are not, however, entitled to prisoner-of-war status. The captor nation may try and punish spies in accordance with its national law. Should a spy succeed in eluding capture and return to friendly territory, liability to punishment terminates. If subsequently captured during some other military operation, the former spy cannot be tried or punished for the earlier act of espionage.

APPENDIX 4

SUMMARY OF THE 1949 GENEVA CONVENTIONS

CONTENTS

CHAPTER ONE

COMMON PROVISIONS OF THE GENEVA CONVENTIONS

I. INTRODUCTION

In the aftermath of World War II, the world's nations recognized that the Geneva Red Cross Convention of 1929, which had been enacted to protect the wounded, sick and prisoners, had numerous shortcomings. In 1949, four new conventions were adopted to protect the victims of war; collectively, these are known as "The Geneva Conventions for the Protection of War Victims". The individual conventions are:

Geneva Convention for the Amelioration of the Condition of the Wounded and Sick in Armed Forces in the Field (abbreviated GWS).

Geneva Convention for the Amelioration of the Condition of the Wounded, Sick and Shipwrecked Members of Armed Forces at Sea (abbreviated GWS SEA).

Geneva Convention Relative to the Treatment of Prisoners of War (abbreviated GPW).

Geneva Convention Relative to the Protection of Civilian Persons in Time of War (abbreviated GC).

These conventions are the most comprehensive code of that segment of Law of Armed Conflict (LOAC) that deals with war victims, and they are among the most widely accepted of all international laws. As of 1987, 170 nations were U.N. members and 163 nations were parties to the Geneva Conventions. Included among these parties are the United States and the former Soviet Union.

The four conventions share a common purpose: the protection of war victims and those who aid war victims. The Geneva Conventions were not intended for the direct regulation of hostilities, although there is unquestionably some indirect effect on the conduct of military operations. "War victims" include civilians who are taking no part in the hostilities and those former combatants who are rendered "hors de combat" ("out of the combat") because of sickness, wounds, shipwreck, or being taken prisoner. The primary focus of the conventions is the protection of these war victims while they are in the hands of the enemy, it being presumed that they do not need the protection of international law while they are under the control of their own government. "Persons who aid war victims" include medical personnel, chaplains, and Red Cross or neutral personnel who use their good offices to assist in the care and treatment of war victims.

II. COMMON PROVISIONS OF THE FOUR GENEVA CONVENTIONS

While dealing with separate subjects, the four conventions share a number of common provisions, the most notable of which are discussed below.

A. Applicability of the Conventions

When does the law set forth in the conventions apply? The simple answer is that it applies in all *international armed conflicts*. Identifying which conflicts fall within this category is not so simple. Obviously, a declared war such as World War II is such a conflict, although it is worthwhile to note that a formal declaration of war is *not* necessary to have an international armed conflict. Also included in this category would be any armed conflict, no matter how small or insignificant, between two (or more) parties to the conventions, or between a party and another nation not a party if the latter announces it will adhere in actual practice to the terms of the conventions. Clearly, a conflict wholly internal in its nature, such as one involving skirmishes with rebel insurgents, is not within the category. But consider what happens when a rebellion ripens into a full scale revolution, with different factions holding territory and claiming independence from the other (and announcing acceptance of the Geneva Conventions). Now the conflict more closely resembles an international armed conflict than it does an internal rebellion. And what about other conflicts such as "Peace-Keeping Operations" (Beirut, the Sinai); "Humanitarian Rescue Operations" (Grenada, the Iran hostage rescue attempt); and "responses" to international terrorism (the capture of the *Achille Lauro* hijackers, the Israeli strikes against P.L.O. targets)? Government officials are quick to claim publicly that these are not "wars", seemingly removing them from the category of "inter-national armed conflicts". But out in the field an "armed conflict" is undeniably underway. Bottom line: always assume that the conventions apply in any action involving foreign (non-American) forces. Unless and until a *specific* renunciation of the application of the Geneva conventions to a particular conflict is announced by the U.S. government, consider that the conventions do apply.

B. Article 3. "Mini-Convention"

What about conflicts *not* of an international character? Do the Geneva Conventions apply? Article 3, in all four conventions, known as the "mini-convention", applies in such conflicts to provide minimal humanitarian protection for the victims of war. This article mandates "humane treatment" for wounded, sick and "non-participants" in the conflict (including members of an armed force who lay down their arms). Article 3 outlaws such acts as murder, torture, hostage taking, and other cruel, humiliating and degrading treatment. While enemy soldiers who are taken prisoner are entitled to humane treatment, it is important to note that, under the "mini-convention", they are not vested with POW status. Therefore, unlike POWs, prisoners captured during a non-international conflict may be tried and punished for their acts of warfare. The "mini-convention" seeks to curb abuses in this area by mandating that sentences may be carried out only after a judgment of guilt by a regularly constituted court (no summary punishments, no sham tribunals) at which the prisoner has been afforded "indispensable judicial guarantees." This vague language (which judicial guarantees are "indispensable" among civilized nations?) leaves room for differences among nations, and you might expect that the rights afforded an accused before a court in Iraq or North Korea would differ markedly from those afforded in U.S. courts. This illustrates something encountered frequently throughout the conventions: provisions are not always specific in their drafting nor perfect in their applicability. Of course, this is to be expected when preparing a document to the satisfaction of a community of sovereign nations. Nevertheless, the conventions do represent a considerable achievement, in that the world's nations have agreed that victims of any war, whether it be international or non-international in character, do have basic rights which ought to be respected.

C. Special Agreements Altering the Conventions

Parties to a conflict may enter into special agreements, but these may only expand upon rights afforded to protected persons by the conventions. Provisions within the conventions will not be overridden, nor will protection thereunder be restricted or renounced, by any agreement between the parties. In addition, individuals may not renounce their rights under *any* circumstances. The absolute nature of the nonrenunciation provision is designed to eliminate instances in which a ruthless captor might torture a prisoner into signing a statement purporting to renounce his or her protection under the conventions.

D. Protecting Powers and Humanitarian Organizations

Neutral nations and humanitarian organizations are interested in adherence to the conventions by warring powers, perhaps for no other reason than the belief that a conflict fought under humane rules stands a better chance of being resolved with a lasting peace than does an inhumane, savage war. The parties to a conflict are obligated to respect the efforts of such nations and organizations as they act in the capacity of a "Protecting Power." "Protecting Powers" are watchdogs; each party to a conflict may designate a Protecting Power to act on its behalf, monitoring compliance with the terms of the conventions and reporting its observations to its sponsor nation. Protecting Powers also lend their "good offices" to attempt resolution of disputes involving the parties to the conflict. Any impartial humanitarian organization may undertake relief efforts for war victims, even while not serving as a Protecting Power. It should be noted that such efforts are subject to the consent of the parties to the conflict. Of course, because these efforts further the spirit of the Geneva conventions, they should usually be welcomed.

E. Obligations to Publish and Enforce the Conventions

Signatories to the Geneva conventions are obligated to publish and enforce the provisions of the conventions. For example, in order to prevent violations, nations must educate their citizens in the principles of the conventions. The course you are now taking is one way in which the U.S. seeks to fulfill this treaty obligation. Also, nations are obliged to take such other actions as may be necessary to suppress all violations of the conventions. Chief among these would be to legislate penalties for offenses and establish courts or other tribunals to enforce such legislation; hopefully, the presence of such statutes and courts would deter misconduct. In the case of "grave breaches," which are the most serious violations of the conventions, the use of the phrase "effective penal sanctions" contemplates harsh penalties such as death, life imprisonment, or imprisonment for a significant period of years. U.S. service members who violate the terms of the conventions are subject to prosecution under the Uniform Code of Military Justice (UCMJ) for the specific offending conduct (murder, rape, larceny, destruction of property, etc.).

"Grave breaches" of the conventions are those involving any of the following acts, if committed against protected persons or property: willful killing, torture or inhumane treatment, including biological experiments; willfully causing great suffering or serious injury to body or health; unlawful deportation or transfer or unlawful confinement of a protected person; compelling a protected person to serve in the forces of a hostile Power; willfully depriving a protected person of the right to a fair trial; taking of hostages; and extensive destruction and appropriation of property not justified by military necessity.

Unfortunately, the existence of penal sanctions and the threat of prosecution do not deter all violations. Offenses sometimes occur, and when they do, there is an obligation to take action against the offenders.

Alleged violations are to be investigated and, if of a continuing nature, halted immediately. Offenders should be tried and punished as warranted by the circumstances. Special obligations exist in the case of grave breaches. All parties to the conventions have an affirmative duty to search for and bring to trial persons alleged to have ordered or committed these heinous offenses. Because grave breaches have no statute of limitations, these obligations may continue, perhaps for years following the end of the conflict, until the offender dies or is brought to trial.

CHAPTER TWO

PROTECTION OF PRISONERS OF WAR

I. INTRODUCTION

Throughout much of history, members of a military force captured by the enemy had no substantial rights. Prisoners were largely at the mercy of their captors; they were mistreated, tortured, enslaved, held for ransom and killed. Even after it became the custom to keep prisoners alive, the lack of any accepted standard of treatment led to abuses. For example, during the American Revolution thousands of American prisoners died due to poor conditions on British prison ships, some of which were located in Baltimore harbor. This experience led the fledgling United States government to have an intense interest in the rights of prisoners of war. One of our first international agreements, a 1785 treaty with the Kingdom of Prussia, contained detailed rules to improve the treatment of POWs. These rules were later incorporated into other treaties.

General Order No. 100, also known as the "Lieber Code," promulgated during the American Civil War by the Union Army, contained 48 articles dealing with prisoners of war. This was the first attempt at codifying the laws, rules and customs which made up the international law on prisoners of war. The humanitarian principles contained in this document provided a significant basis for the treatment of prisoners of war in Hague Convention IV of 1907, in the 1929 Geneva Convention Relative to the Treatment of Prisoners of War, and in the present source treaty for POW rights, the Geneva Convention of 1949 Relative to the Treatment of Prisoners of War (abbreviated GPW).

There are two practical reasons why, as a member of the armed forces, you should be familiar with the rights and obligations of prisoners of war under the GPW.

First, in any combat situation you must be ready to capture and control enemy prisoners until they are sent to permanent POW camps. The GPW provides the basic humanitarian rules for treatment of prisoners. Fear of mistreatment is a significant deterrent to surrender; decent treatment of prisoners may encourage the enemy to surrender.

The second reason is also related to duty, but in a more personal way. If you should ever become a POW, knowing your rights and duties under GPW could help you deal effectively with your captors. Such knowledge could also help you insist on proper treatment for your subordinates in the POW chain of command.

II. PERSONS ENTITLED TO POW STATUS

The protected status of being a POW lasts from the time a person is captured until their final release and repatriation. Article 4 of the GPW defines six categories of per-

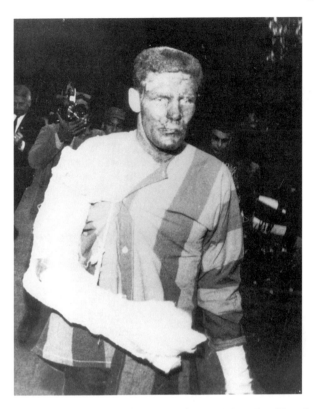

North Vietnam—Lt D.G. Rehman, USN, POW, held by the North Vietnamese. The North Vietnamese consistently violated the Geneva Conventions in mistreatment of U.S. POWs. (Oct 69). Photo courtesy of U.S. Naval Institute.

sons as being entitled to POW treatment upon capture. These are:

A. Members of Armed Forces

This is the most obvious and the principal group protected under GPW. This category also includes any corps or force incorporated into the armed forces during time of war; but, this category does *not* include military chaplains or military medical personnel. Rather than becoming POWs upon capture, they become "retained persons." This special status is discussed in Chapter four.

B. Members of Resistance Movements

During World War II, the Allied Commanders in Europe recognized the French Resistance forces as a component of the Allied forces, and demanded POW treatment for its captured members. The Germans, on the other hand, had treated captured members of the French Resistance as unlawful combatants. GPW seeks to clarify the status of resistance forces in a manner that attempts a balance between a humanitarian concern for the plight of captured belligerents and the legitimate concern of operational commanders for the protection of their regular troops from the attacks of irregular forces. First, you should note that, under GPW, resistance movements are *not* the type of "militia or volunteer corps" which could become incorporated into the regular armed forces during time of war. Second, to obtain the entitlement to POW status upon capture, a resistance movement must meet the following four criteria:

1. The force must have a command structure, with a commander who is responsible for subordinates. This condition is fulfilled if the movement is commanded by a commissioned officer of the armed forces of that nation or by some other person who occupies a similar position of responsibility, as evidenced by documents, badges or other identification. It must be clear that individual soldiers are not operating on their own, but rather are accountable for their actions to a superior.

2. Personnel must wear a fixed, distinctive insignia recognizable at a distance. The wearing of a complete uniform is not necessary to satisfy this requirement. The purpose of the requirement is to make the belligerent forces distinguishable from the general civilian population, and any emblem or insignia that accomplishes this purpose is sufficient.

3. Personnel must carry their arms openly. Again, this will distinguish the members of the resistance force from the general civilian population.

4. The force must conduct its operations in accordance with the LOAC. This condition is satisfied if the resistance movement, as a whole, complies with the LOAC. The fact that an individual member has committed a war crime will not strip the entire group of POW status.

Embodied in the four criteria above is a decided concern with the ability to distinguish true civilians from resistance members. Of course, because the openness

suggested in these criteria would run counter to the secrecy under which many resistance groups operate, it is possible that they would elect not to abide by these requirements. The choice rests with the commander: any member of a resistance group which does not satisfy the four criteria enjoys no legal right under international law to POW status. Therefore, if captured, he or she may be tried and punished as a criminal for assault, murder, property damage or other acts hostile to the enemy.

C. Members of a Regular Armed Force of a Government Not Recognized by the Detaining Power

During World War II, a debate arose about the correct status of General Charles de Gaulle's forces which were under the authority of the French National Liberation Committee. Were they legitimate belligerents, entitled upon capture to POW status? Or were they unlawful combatants, entitled to be tried and punished for their acts of warfare? The Germans did not recognize the FNLC as a legitimate government, and therefore contended that those forces were not operating under the direct authority of a party to the conflict. Eventually, through the intercession of the International Committee of the Red Cross (ICRC), the Germans granted POW status to captured members of these French forces. Consistent with this action, GPW Article 4 now clarifies that such forces are entitled to POW status.

D. Civilian Personnel Who Accompany the Armed Forces

Civilians such as news correspondents, supply contractors, tech reps, and welfare service personnel (such as Bob Hope's USO show) are entitled to POW status if captured. The enemy may choose to afford *better* treatment (i.e., release) to these persons and may indeed do so with news correspondents and welfare service personnel for the favorable propaganda value involved.

E. Civilian Aircraft Crews and Merchant Marine Crews

Whether or not directly supporting the war effort, these crews will be entitled to no worse than POW treatment if captured. Again, they may receive *better* treatment; for example, a civilian aircraft crew may be released and allowed to continue with its flight once the belligerent has determined that the flight is in no way aiding the enemy's war effort.

F. Levee en Masse

This occurs when civilians spontaneously rise up to defend their homeland against the invading force. Undoubtedly, they will not have the organization nor satisfy the "fixed, distinctive sign" requirement necessary to qualify them for POW treatment as a "resistance movement." Nevertheless, they will be entitled to POW status in the event of their capture if they carry their arms openly and generally adhere to the LOAC in their operations. You should note that a *levee en masse* lasts only until the defenders are subdued or their homeland becomes occupied by the invaders. A civilian living in *occupied* territory enjoys no legal right to engage in acts of warfare against the occupying enemy; when captured, such a civilian may be tried and punished for his or her actions.

The determination of who is entitled to POW status is not made by the capturing forces in the field. Rather, in doubtful cases it is made by a tribunal which reviews any relevant evidence which may assist in an accurate resolution of the issue. During the Vietnam war, the U.S. conducted these tribunals on a regular basis; the tribunal consisted of not less than three officers, at least one of whom had to be a judge advocate or a military lawyer familiar with the Geneva Conventions. These tribunals tended to be liberal in granting POW status, even for enemy personnel who did not fit well into any of the six categories found in GPW Article 4. This was done for a political reason rather than for legal reasons: recognizing that U.S. servicemen were being taken prisoner by the enemy, it was hoped that vesting captured enemy personnel with POW status would encourage reciprocal, favorable treatment for captured Americans.

Since the capturing troops are relieved of any responsibility for determining POW status, the task of field personnel is greatly simplified. Any person captured by U.S. troops, even those persons clearly not entitled to POW status, are to be treated humanely. They should be thoroughly searched, secured (blindfolding and handcuffing during transit away from the battle zone is permissible) and removed from the front. Above all, you may not torture or execute any captured persons. All prisoners must be handled with care.

III. PERSONS NOT ENTITLED TO POW STATUS

A. Persons Not in One of the Six Groups

Any person who commits hostile acts and who is *not* included in one of the categories above, is not entitled to POW status. In addition, such persons lack the immunity of a soldier for their hostile acts, and may be tried and punished for murder, assault, or destruction of property, as the case may be. Note that resistance fighters whose units cannot meet the four criteria discussed above fall into this category, as do terrorists.

B. Losing POW Status

Persons normally entitled to POW status may *lose* their right to that status by their actions.

1. Spies

Spies are discussed in NWP 9, paragraph 12.8.

2. Out of Uniform

Traditionally, the wearing of a uniform was considered a prerequisite to POW status if the prisoner was taken on the battlefield. GPW makes no mention of this exclusion, but it seems to have persisted in practice. Soldiers fighting while not wearing their own nation's uniform are traditionally not entitled to POW status and therefore could be tried as common criminals for their violent acts. There are, however, three situations in which a person not wearing a uniform on capture clearly is entitled to POW status.

a. Three exceptions
  (1) Away from the battle zone: A person captured far from the battle zone on leave or liberty could hardly be required to be in uniform.

  (2) Evaders: Evading soldiers are entitled to wear any clothing they desire. An "evading" soldier is one who has been cut off from his unit behind enemy lines, and is merely trying to sneak back to his own forces. If he engages in intelligence gathering or sabotage, however, he becomes a spy and forfeits his POW status.

  (3) Escaping POWs: Escaping POWs are entitled to wear any clothing they desire, and will not forfeit their POW status. Again, they are not entitled to engage in intelligence gathering or sabotage without forfeiting their POW status.

IV. PROTECTION OF POWS

The overall goal and emphasis of GPW is clearly the humane treatment of prisoners.

No power is obliged to (but all warring nations do) hold POWs. The Geneva Conventions are exceedingly clear that if POWs are taken, the international community expects the captor nation to maintain humane standards and bear all of the costs involved.

A. Humane Treatment At All Times

POWs must at all times be humanely treated and are entitled to respect for their persons and their honor. This includes protection from acts of violence, intimidation and public curiosity.

This is absolutely required regardless of the financial costs involved. Also, the killing or mistreatment of POWs is not permitted for any reason, even when their presence retards the captor's movement, diminishes his power of resistance, or endangers his own self-preservation.

This obligation can not be avoided by transferring POWs to another nation. Transferring POWs is permissible, but only if the original capturing state ensures that the receiving state complies fully with GPW. Furthermore, if the receiving state does not comply, then the original capturing state must retake custody of the POWs.

B. Interrogation of POWs

The capturing state is required to report the capture of each individual POW it detains. To facilitate this reporting requirement, every prisoner of war, when questioned on the subject, is bound to give his full name, rank, date of birth, and serial number or equivalent information. It is also for this reason that each nation is required to furnish its forces with personal identification cards. These cards are not to be taken by the capturing state. Indeed, if a POW does not have an ID card, the capturing state must issue one to the POW.

This is the only information a prisoner is required to furnish.

No physical or mental torture, or any other form of coercion may be inflicted on prisoners of war to secure from them information of any kind whatever. Prisoners of war who refuse to answer may not be threatened, insulted, or abused.

C. Personal Effects

All personal effects (except weapons, military equipment and military documents) shall remain in the possession of prisoners of war. Personal effects and articles used for their clothing or feeding shall remain in their possession, even if such effects and articles are part of their regulation military equipment.

Badges of rank and nationality, decorations, and articles of personal or sentimental value may not be taken from prisoners of war. Money and other valuables carried by prisoners of war may not be taken away from them except by order of an officer, and then only for reasons of security. If taken, a receipt must be given to the POW and the items returned upon repatriation.

D. Evacuation of POWs

POWs must be evacuated, as soon as possible after their capture, to camps located far enough from the combat zone for them to be out of danger. They shall not be unnecessarily exposed to danger during evacuation. They must be transported under conditions no worse than the conditions the capturing power uses in transporting its own troops.

V. CONDITIONS OF INTERNMENT

A. POW Camp Location

POW camps may only be located on land, and shall be located in an area that is con-
ducive to the health and hygiene of the POWs. POWs shall not be interned in penitentiaries.

No prisoner of war may at any time be sent to or detained in areas where he or she may be exposed to fire, nor may his or her presence be used to "shield" lawful targets from enemy attack.

Whenever military considerations permit, prisoner of war camps shall be marked with the letters "PW" or "PG" so as to be clearly visible from the air. Only prisoner of war camps shall be marked as such.

B. Parole

Parole is a traditional practice of releasing prisoners in return for their promise not to fight again in the current war; however, no POW can be compelled to accept parole. It was taken quite seriously in the past, to the point that the British actually returned one of their officers who violated his parole to the Germans during World War I. Parole is of obvious benefit to the prisoner, but it can also be a great benefit to the detaining power. The purpose of holding prisoners is to keep them from continuing to fight against you. If you can accomplish that end without the expense and difficulty of maintaining POW camps, so much the better. Partially for that reason, and partially because parole is difficult to enforce and subject to abuse by both sides, United States military personnel generally are not allowed to accept parole.

C. Quarters

Prisoners of war shall be quartered under conditions as favorable as those for the forces of the Detaining Power who are billeted in the same area. These conditions shall make allowance for the habits and customs of the prisoners and *shall in no case* be prejudicial to their health. Separate dormitories shall be provided for female POWs.

Note that prisoner housing standards are tied to those of the captor's troops in the area. If the captor's troops are poorly housed, prisoners may be as well, provided the housing is not so poor as to be unhealthy.

D. Food

The GPW states that food must be "sufficient in quantity, quality, and variety" to keep the prisoners in good health. Further, the detaining power must consider the dietary habits of prisoners. Prisoners must have adequate mess halls and kitchens where they can assist in preparing their own food. The captor must also furnish prisoners with sufficient, safe drinking water. Restricting food as a form of mass punishment is forbidden.

E. Clothing

The detaining power must provide outer clothing, underwear, footwear, and work clothing. It must mend or replace these items regularly. If possible, the detaining power supplies clothing from stocks of uniforms captured from the prisoners' own forces.

F. Health and Medical Care

The Conventions include detailed provisions for meeting the health and medical needs of prisoners. They insure at least a minimum standard of health. For example, camps must include adequate heads, showers, and laundry facilities. The captor "shall be bound to take all sanitary measures necessary to insure the cleanliness and healthfulness of camps and to prevent epidemics." And "Every camp shall have an adequate infirmary." Here, prisoners should receive treatment, preferably by medical personnel from their own captured forces. Sick call occurs regularly; medical inspections, at least monthly. Periodic X-ray examinations for tuberculosis and tests for other infectious and contagious diseases should be made. All needed medical care must be furnished and it is free of charge to the POW.

G. Religious and Recreational Activities

Prisoners may attend services of their faith and otherwise practice their religion. The Conventions require provision for physical exercise. This includes outdoor sports and games. Intellectual and educational activities must be encouraged whenever possible.

H. Mail

As soon as possible after capture, prisoners are to be allowed to inform their families of their whereabouts and health. This is to be done within a week after prisoners reach a POW camp. Usually this message is sent on a standard "capture card." The detaining power also forwards a copy of this card to the Central Prisoner of War Information Agency. This is a clearing house operated by the International Committee of the Red Cross in Geneva. Whenever a prisoner transfers to another camp or hospital, the detaining power must notify this agency. Prisoners have the right to send letters as frequently as the captor's censorship and postal facilities allow. They may also receive letters and relief packages forwarded through neutral agencies.

I. Camp Information

Every POW camp must have copies of the Geneva Conventions, in the prisoners' own language, posted in places where prisoners can read them. All camp notices, regulations, and orders must be in a language prisoners understand.

VI. POW LABOR

GPW does allow the Detaining Power to utilize POW labor, but there are a great number of detailed provisions in GPW concerning POW labor. This resulted because of the abuses on both sides during WWII. For instance, the Nazis used Russian and other POWs as slave labor, often simply working them until they died. On the other had, the Allies used German POWs to remove mines in areas formerly occupied by the Nazis. As you might expect, many were killed in explosions.

General guidelines for POW labor include the following:

- Only POWs who are physically fit may work.

- Commissioned officers may not be compelled to work, but if they volunteer, they may do supervisory work.

- Noncommissioned officers may be required to perform supervisory work.

- Other enlisted personnel may be required to do manual labor.

- POW labor may not be used for military purposes except for work connected with camp administration, installation and maintenance.

- If additional food, clothing, medical care, training, etc., is required in order for the POW to perform his work, this must be furnished by the Detaining Power. Also, the POW must be paid for his labor.

- Working conditions can be no worse for the POWs than that enjoyed by the citizens of the Detaining Power employed in similar work.

- Unless a volunteer, no POW may be tasked to perform labor which is unhealthy or dangerous (such as clearing mines).

VII. PRISONER DISCIPLINE

A. Disciplinary Punishment

Disciplinary punishment is intended to punish infractions of camp rules and minor crimes. The procedure for disciplinary punishment is similar to that for nonjudicial punishment under the UCMJ. A hearing before the POW camp commandant is all that is required prior to implementing the punishment.

The disciplinary punishments applicable to prisoners of war are the following (all have a 30-day maximum):

1. A fine which shall not exceed 50 percent of the advances of pay and working pay which the prisoner of war would otherwise receive.

2. Discontinuance of privileges granted over and above the treatment provided for by the present Convention.

3. Fatigue duties not exceeding two hours daily (cannot be imposed on officers).

4. Confinement

In no case shall disciplinary punishments be inhuman, brutal or dangerous to the health of prisoners of war. The maximum of thirty days provided above may not be exceeded, even if the prisoner of war is answerable for several acts at the same time when he is awarded punishment, whether such acts are related or not.

B. Judicial Punishment

Judicial punishment refers to potentially severe punishment awarded by a court. It is reserved for serious offenses, which could include war crimes. GPW requires that disciplinary punishment should be used whenever possible.

If judicial punishment is used, then the POW can be sentenced only if the trial court and the procedures used in court are the same as those that would be used for a member of the detaining power's own armed forces. However, in no event may a POW be tried unless the court and procedures used guarantee at least the *minimum* generally recognized standards of independence, impartiality and due process. Minimum due process includes the right to assistance of lawyer counsel; to the assistance of an interpreter and a fellow prisoner; to the calling of witnesses; and, if convicted, the right to appeal.

The use of the death penalty is discouraged, though not prohibited. If a death sentence is pronounced, at least six months must elapse before the sentence can be carried out. This allows for maximum diplomatic efforts to take place to prevent execution, if possible. Considerations of reciprocity have often prevented the execution of POWs.

One of the most extensively debated subjects at the 1949 Geneva Conference was whether a POW who is prosecuted for a precapture crime—in particular, offenses against the laws of war—should enjoy the benefits of POW status. It was determined that "Prisoners of war prosecuted under the laws of the Detaining Power for acts committed prior to capture shall retain, even if convicted, the benefits of the present Convention." According to this article, POW status is retained, regardless of the crime of which the prisoner is convicted. The former Soviet Union and many of its former satellite states made a reservation to this provision. They reserved the right to deny POW status to convicted war criminals. While the United States has rejected this reservation as contrary to international law, the existence of this reservation demonstrates the importance many governments attach to allegations of war crimes.

C. Escape

The GPW recognizes that all POWs have the right to attempt escape. While such attempts may be punished, the disciplinary punishment system must be used, thereby limiting the extent of punishment. In addition, *non-violent* acts committed in aid of an escape attempt are subject to the same limitations. Such non-violent offenses include offenses against public property; theft without intention of self-enrichment; making and using false papers; and the wearing of civilian clothing. *Violent* acts committed during an escape or an escape attempt may be dealt with through judicial punishment. The use of weapons against prisoners of war, especially against those who are escaping or attempting to escape, is an extreme measure, which under the GPW can only be used after appropriate warnings and as a last resort.

The escape of a prisoner of war shall be deemed to have succeeded when he or she has done one of the following:

1. joined his or her own armed forces or those of an allied power;

2. left the territory under the control of the Detaining Power and its allies, i.e., reached neutral territory;

3. joined a ship flying the flag of his or her country or of an allied Power.

Prisoners of war who have successfully escaped and who are subsequently recaptured, shall not be liable to any punishment for their previous escape.

CHAPTER THREE

PROTECTION OF CIVILIANS

I. INTRODUCTION AND BACKGROUND

During World Wars I and II, civilians caught in the conflict could look to only one international convention for protection: Hague Convention IV Respecting the Laws and Customs of War on Land. To its credit, that convention sought to establish specific protection for civilians who were under military occupation. The enemy was required to respect family lives, rights and property; pillage and collective punishments were forbidden; and enemy civilians could not be compelled to provide military information or swear allegiance to the occupying power. However, the experiences of two world wars highlighted the limitations of that convention. Those few general provisions pertained only in the case of a formal military occupation. Few articles in the convention could be applied to govern the treatment of civilians in situations other than an occupation, and of those, the terms were unclear, ambiguous, incomplete, and, in some cases, not mandatory. Even in occupied territory, there were no established rules for the trial and punishment of civilians, and no procedures detailed for their internment. Rather than condemning the Hague Convention for these shortcomings, it is well to recall that it was concluded in 1907 when hostilities were confined to the area close to the front, and when widespread guerilla war was not common. Total war, which exposed the civilian population of whole countries to similar dangers as those faced by the Armed Forces, required more com-

prehensive treatment than that provided in Hague IV. From this recognition evolved the Geneva Convention of 1949 Relative to the Protection of Civilian Persons in Time of War (hereafter abbreviated GC), the first international convention devoted exclusively to the codification of the rights of civilians during an armed conflict. GC is the longest of the four Geneva Conventions, with 159 articles. In understanding the substantive provisions of this convention, it is useful to visualize GC as containing three distinct sub-agreements: the first is Article 3; the second is general protection for entire populations (Articles 13-26); and the third is "protected persons" (Articles 27-141).

II. ARTICLE 3: PROTECTION OF CIVILIANS IN A NON-INTERNATIONAL CONFLICT

Recall that this article (the so-called "mini-convention"), discussed in Chapter One of this handout, provides basic humanitarian protection to noncombatants and former combatants who have laid down their arms or otherwise been rendered *hors de combat* due to sickness, wounds, detention or any other cause. The basic rights provided are protection from being used as a hostage, protection from humiliating and degrading treatment, protection from all types of torture and violence (including murder), and protection from summary punishment and executions.

Remember: this article is applicable *only* in conflicts "not of an international character".

III. ARTICLES 13-26: GENERAL PROTECTION OF ENTIRE POPULATIONS AGAINST CERTAIN CONSEQUENCES OF WAR

While this portion of GC applies broadly (to "the whole of the population"), the actual protections provided are very few and, in some cases, are not mandatory.

A. Protect and Respect the Civilian Population

The provisions of GC Articles 13-26 apply to protect the entire populations of the warring opponents from the hardships of war, but the articles do not provide much in the way of specific, binding protection for those populations. Articles 16 and 24 do obligate the parties to "respect and protect" certain civilians: the wounded and sick; the shipwrecked and those otherwise exposed to grave danger; the infirm (usually thought of as invalids and the aged); expectant mothers; and orphaned children (under age 15). The phrase "protect and respect," refers to protection from such outrages as murder, torture, rape, medical or biological experiments, and cruel treatment of a like nature. Children must be cared for ("not left to their own resources") and educated. Also, those under 12 must be given some type of identity card or badge. After World War II, the problem of orphaned and separated children was immense, and no doubt spurred agreement among nations that specific procedures for safeguarding and identifying children be included in GC.

GC expresses concern for the plight of families, but the only *obligation* placed on parties to the convention is limited to *facilitating* personal communication among family members. This obligation serves to help re-unite dispersed family members.

B. Civilian Medical Facilities and Personnel

GC Articles 13-26 also address the issue of respect for civilian medical facilities and personnel. The establishment of hospital and safety zones for the benefit of certain civilians (those being the wounded, sick, aged, children under 15, expectant mothers and mothers of children under 7) is *optional* with a party to the conflict; respect for individual civilian hospitals, however, is *mandatory under all circumstances*. Furthermore, civilian medical personnel, hospital administrators and staff, and medical convoys on land or at sea shall likewise be respected and protected from attack. To facilitate identification of these persons and places, they should prominently display the appropriate emblem (usually a red cross or red crescent on a white background) .

However, civilian hospitals, medical convoys, and medical personnel may be attacked *if* they are being used for military (vice humanitarian) purposes. Note that treating military personnel in a civilian hospital does *not* constitute using the hospital for a military purpose. All wounded and sick, whether civilian or military, are entitled to treatment as a basic humanitarian right. With respect to an attack on a hospital which is being used for military purposes, an attack shall not commence until after the enemy has been warned regarding the misuse of the hospital and then been given a reasonable opportunity to cease the offending military activities. This kind of procedure is fine in situations like that encountered by the U.S. when the North Vietnamese were abusing the protected status of the Boch Mai Hospital: after our protests and warnings were ignored, we bombed the SAM launching sites which had been co-located with the hospital. Of course, this incidentally damaged the hospital in the process. You should note that no protection exists for a hospital from which you are taking live fire. You need not convey any protests or warnings nor wait "a reasonable time limit" for the enemy to cease and desist. Your inherent right of self defense permits you to fire upon the building immediately. It was this situation which existed in Grenada when U.S. troops fired upon the Richmond Hill Institute.

C. Neutralized Zones

Any party to a conflict may propose the establishment, in the regions where fighting is taking place, of neutralized zones intended to shelter from the effects of war both the combatant and non-combatant wounded and sick, plus civilian persons who take no part in hostilities, and who, while they reside in the zones, perform no work of a military character.

When all parties concerned have agreed upon the geographical position, administration, food supply and supervision of the proposed neutralized zone, a written agreement shall be concluded and signed. The agreement shall fix the beginning and the duration of the neutralization of the zone.

D. Siege

GC encourages parties to the conflict to endeavor to conclude local agreements for the removal from besieged or encircled areas, of the wounded, sick, infirm, and aged persons, children and maternity cases, and for the passage of ministers of all religions, medical personnel and medical equipment on their way to such areas.

GC encourages a besieging force to allow the free passage of all consignments of medical and hospital stores and objects necessary for religious worship intended only for civilians, and to allow the free passage of all consignments of essential foodstuffs and clothing intended for children under fifteen, expectant mothers and maternity cases.

The obligation to allow free passage of these consignments is subject to the condition that the besieging force is satisfied that the consignments will not be diverted from their intended, limited destination, and that allowing the consignments will not result in a definite advantage to the military efforts or economy of the enemy.

Note that these provisions do *not* obligate the parties to institute neutralized zones, or to permit the removal of certain persons from besieged areas, or to allow medical and religious supplies, clothing and foodstuffs intended only for civilian use to pass into the hands of the adverse party. These provisions are purely voluntary; they are "urged," not "mandated." As with any voluntary provision, a military commander should carefully evaluate what effect, if any, compliance would have on the accomplishment of the assigned military objective. Consider this: if you were a siege commander, how would permitting wounded, sick, infirmed, children and maternity cases to leave the besieged area affect your objective, the capitulation of the enemy force?

IV. ARTICLES 27-141: PROTECTED PERSONS

To understand GC Articles 27-141 regarding protected persons, it is essential that you first understand who is a "protected person" for purposes of this convention.

A. Persons Entitled to "Protected Persons" Status

The civilians protected by GC Articles 27-141 are those civilians who find themselves in the hands of the enemy or of an occupying power. Also, certain citizens of neutral states are "protected persons" if their state does not have "normal diplomatic relations" with the nation in which that citizen is located. Of course, being members of "the whole of the population," these people would also receive the limited protection of GC Articles 13-26. It is vital to note that an enemy civilian living in his own *unoccupied* territory is *not* a "protected person" under GC. It is presumed that such a civilian will be protected by his own government, and will benefit from its own domestic laws. Thus, there is no need for international law to intervene. International law (in the form of GC) is intended to ensure respect and protection for people who may not benefit from domestic laws: i.e., those civilians who find themselves under enemy control. Also, persons protected under one of the other Geneva Conventions are not considered "protected persons" under GC.

B. Humane Treatment Required At All Times

GC Article 27 provides in part, "Protected persons are entitled, in all circumstances, to respect for their persons, their honor, their family rights, their religious convictions and practices, and their manners and customs. They shall at all times be humanely treated, and shall be protected especially against all acts of violence or threats thereof and against insults and public curiosity."

Succinctly stated, GC Article 27 provides that *in all circumstances*, "protected persons" shall be treated humanely. This means they shall be protected from murder, torture, rape, enforced prostitution, insults, public ridicule, and any form of physical or mental coercion. Protection against these heinous crimes is not the only obligation imposed. The detaining power is obligated also to respect "protected persons," their honor, customs, religion and family rights. It should be obvious that these provisions were intended to address many of the crimes perpetrated against civilians in World War II: the "Rape of Manila," in which thousands of captured civilians were murdered, mutilated, raped and tortured; the use of captured civilians for medical experiments; denying civilians the means to earn a living; uprooting, dispersing or relocating families throughout Europe; and, of course, the Holocaust. A liberal application of the general obligations of respect and humane treatment embodied in the first paragraph of Article 27 likely would obviate the need for further treaty provisions, but experience has shown that, in time of war, "literal" vice "liberal" interpretations are likely. Therefore, many specific protections are stated in the succeeding GC articles, including prohibitions against collective penalties, pillage, hostage taking, and reprisals.

C. Collective Penalties, Pillage and Hostages Prohibited

Collective penalties, supposedly outlawed by Hague IV, were utilized during World War II. GC clearly outlaws them by permitting punishment *only* for offenses personally committed and by requiring a trial before the punishment is administered. Pillage is also proscribed. If "protected persons" and their family rights are to be respected, it seems only natural that their property should be respected and not plundered by the conquering invader. Similarly, a proscription against the use of protected civilians as hostages is consistent with the obligation to respect and to protect against torture, cruelty and collective punishments.

D. Reprisals Prohibited

The GC clearly outlaws acts of revenge taken against protected civilians under the care of the detaining power. The history of warfare is unfortunately dotted with instances in which entire populations of villages, or portions thereof, have been tortured and murdered and had their villages razed as vengeance for acts, whether lawful or criminal, committed against the detaining power. These acts of vengeance against a captive civilian populace are indefensible and unquestionably illegal.

Note: The GC's prohibition against reprisal actions involving *protected* civilians should not be confused with *lawful* reprisals designed to induce the enemy to comply with the LOAC. *See* NWP-9 section 6.2.3.

V. OTHER SECTIONS OF GC

Other protections afforded by the GC include, similar to POWs, that "protected persons" can not be used to shield a legitimate target from attack. It is a law of war violation to attempt to shield a target by surrounding it with protected persons and conversely, the presence of protected persons does not render the target immune from attack.

GC further provides that any party to the conflict into whose hands protected persons may fall, is responsible for the treatment accorded to them by its agents, irrespective of any individual responsibility which may be incurred. You will recall that in 1982 the Israeli occupation forces in Lebanon delegated some security responsibilities to Phalangist Christian Militia (PCM) allied to their cause. In September of that year, the PCM massacred hundreds of Palestinian refugees at the Shatila and Sabra refugee camps, which were located in an area of West Beirut under Israeli occupation. After initial denials, the Israeli government accepted partial responsibility for this brutality. Under the GC, they had no alternative. As the occupying power, Israel had the ultimate responsibility for the proper treatment of "protected persons" under its occupation.

VI. THE COMMON CAVEAT THROUGHOUT GC: THE SECURITY OF THE DETAINING POWER

Throughout GC are provisions which recognize that the detaining or occupying power's ability to maintain control and security must not be compromised. Even Article 27, one of the most powerful articles in the convention with respect to the humane treatment of civilians, states that the Parties to the conflict may "take such measures of control and security in regard to protected persons as may be necessary as a result of the war." Although these frequent caveats to GC provisions clearly authorize detaining or occupying powers some latitude in dealing with protected persons (when necessary for security), they must be read in harmony with the bulk of the convention which mandates respect for protected persons in all circumstances. A protected person who engages in activities hostile to the detaining power continues to be a "protected person"; however, he or she may no longer be entitled to *all* of the rights and privileges that normally accrue to one with that status. Rather, rights and privileges *of that individual* are to be affected (recall the stricture against collective punishments). Note also that the withholding or modification should be limited to only so much as is necessary to maintain security; there is no wholesale forfeiture of all rights, and particularly no forfeiture of the rights associated with a fair trial on the offense charged. Finally, note also that full rights and privileges shall be restored at the earliest possible date. In order to avail oneself of the full protection of GC, the protected person owes a duty to the detaining power to be, in essence, a law abiding and nonhostile person. The protected person who violates this obligation can expect to forfeit some, but not all, of his or her protection under GC.

CHAPTER FOUR

THE WOUNDED, SICK AND SHIPWRECKED CONVENTIONS

I. INTRODUCTION AND BACKGROUND

In June, 1859, 39,000 troops were slain at the battle of Solferino in Northern Italy. Moved by the suffering he witnessed there, Henri Dunant wrote the book *Un Souvenir De Solferino* and, as a result of its publication, an International Congress was held at Geneva in 1863 and 1864 to examine the plight of wounded soldiers in the field. The result was the first Geneva Convention, adopted in 1864, to improve the condition of sick and wounded soldiers. The convention was updated in 1906 and again in 1929; and in 1949, two conventions were enacted which are still in force today. They are the Geneva Convention of 1949 for the Amelioration of the Condition of the Wounded and Sick in Armed Forces in the Field (abbreviated GWS), and the Geneva Convention of 1949 for Amelioration of the Condition of the Wounded, Sick and Shipwrecked Members of Armed Forces at Sea (abbreviated GWS SEA).

Stated generally, these conventions provide protection for armed forces personnel who are rendered *hors de combat* ("out of the combat") owing to sickness, wounds or shipwreck; protection for chaplains and military medical personnel who minister to the needs of those *hors de combat* personnel; and protection for the places where medical care is provided and for medical equipment and supplies. Obviously, GWS deals with situations on land and GWS SEA deals with those peculiar problems of medical care at sea; however, there is a considerable amount of overlap. This chapter will analyze the protection afforded by these conventions.

II. PROTECTION FOR CERTAIN PERSONS

A. The Wounded, Sick and Shipwrecked

Not all wounded, sick and shipwrecked persons are protected by these conventions. For example, wounded or sick civilians are not within the scope of these conventions (recall that they are entitled to certain protection under GC). The persons who are protected by GWS and GWS SEA are the same six categories of people who are entitled to POW status under GPW and who are, in addition, wounded, sick, or shipwrecked. Upon capture by the enemy, they are entitled to POW status.

The definitions accorded the terms "wounded" and "sick" are not technical. A wound is any injury, incurred in battle or otherwise, which requires treatment. Sickness is an illness, vice an injury. "Shipwrecked," on the other hand, is a somewhat technical term. It refers to any person who has suffered the loss of his fighting platform and is now helpless and requires assistance to better his lot. Using the definition offered above, consider the case of personnel who are forced into the

Saudi Arabia—An American air crewman medivacs an Iraqi POW to a rear area field hospital (24 Feb 91). The Geneva Convention requires the humane treatment of all enemy wounded and shipwrecked personnel. Photo courtesy of U.S. Naval Institute.

water from a disabled amphibious landing vehicle. If they continue to advance toward the beach, it cannot be said that they are "helpless" or that they require your assistance to better their lot. They have lost only their means of transport to the beach. Such personnel are not "shipwrecked," and the obligations of respect and protection which are owed to shipwrecked persons are not applicable. Finally, a "shipwrecked" person includes a person from an aircraft downed at sea.

The first duty thrust upon the parties to a conflict under GWS and GWS SEA is to search for and collect the dead, wounded and shipwrecked. In GWS SEA, the duty clearly attaches "after each engagement," and not during the battle itself. On the other hand, under GWS, the duty exists "at all times, and particularly after an engagement." Does this mean there is an obligation under GWS to commit personnel to search and collection operations during the heat of battle? Not at all. If, given the continuing battle, it is impractical or impossible to carry out a search and collection evolution, no violation of GWS has occurred. Even after an engagement, when the obligation surely arises on land or at sea, no violation of the law occurs if it is impossible to discharge this obligation owing to the nature of a unit or its mission. Mere inconvenience, on the other hand, is no excuse for refusing to undertake search and collection efforts after the enemy has disengaged and your unit has the opportunity for reasonably secure movement. Therefore, despite some differing language, the actual obligations under each convention are quite similar. Other measures, such as armistices and local agreements, for the benefit of wounded and sick persons are *not* mandated; they are certainly encouraged, but their implementation is dependent upon the voluntary assent of both sides.

Both GWS and GWS SEA make it clear that protected persons are to be "respected and protected under all circumstances." Once again, that broad, general language has been fleshed out by examples in the paragraphs which follow: no murder, no torture, and no medical experimentation. Also, the detaining power is responsible for providing such medical care as is possible, utilizing available personnel and supplies. Of particular interest is the priority of medical treatment. The GWS and GWS SEA require that all wounded personnel, regardless of nationality, be treated in order of *medical* priority. The common medical procedure which is used to prioritize patients for treatment is called "triage." Roughly stated, this procedure allocates resources first to those who are likely to survive *only* if immediate medical assistance is provided. Next to receive care are those not in need of immediate attention to survive (i.e., lesser wounds), and last in line are those who are unlikely to survive even with medical care (i.e., the mortal wounds). Nationality is *not* an element of the triage process. The practice of treating all Americans first, regardless of the severity of their wounds, would be a violation of these conventions.

B. Obligations Regarding Dead Combatants

GWS and GWS SEA require the parties to a conflict to notify the ICRC's Central Information Bureau (CIB) of the death of individual enemy combatants, and to forward the deceased enemy combatants' personal property to the CIB for return to next-of-kin. The parties are also required to provide dead combatants a dignified funeral, burial, or cremation and, if earthen graves are dug, appropriate markings so the graves may later be located. Compliance with these procedures can eliminate the fear and uncertainty associated with a person being listed as "missing in action" for a lengthy period of time.

C. Medical Personnel and Chaplains

If captured, chaplains and military medical personnel (recall that civilian medical personnel are protected under GC) are not POWs. Rather, they are considered "retained" personnel. This status allows all of the rights and benefits which would accrue to a POW, *plus* whatever additional freedom of the camp is necessary to permit the retained person to minister to the medical and spiritual needs of the POWs. It should be noted that the presence of medical personnel of the same nationality as prisoners does not relieve the detaining power of its obligation to ensure appropriate medical care for wounded and sick POWs.

Captured chaplains or medical personnel should be retained only so long as their humanitarian services are required for the benefit of other prisoners. If their services are not needed, they should be repatriated at the earliest practicable opportunity. This rule is designed to advance the overall objective of humanity permeating the conventions: imprisoning these persons without a need for their services diminishes the amount of assistance available to the wounded, sick and shipwrecked, while allowing chaplains and medical personnel to circulate freely increases the amount of care available.

Only full time medical personnel are given the special status of "retained personnel." Members of the armed forces who are part-time medical personnel, such as those specially trained to be orderlies or stretcher bearers if the need arises, but whose full--time duties are not medical duties, are POWs, not "retained personnel." However, they are to be allowed to continue performing medical duties after capture if they were so employed at the time of capture.

D. Loss of Protected Status

Both GWS and GWS SEA impose the general obligations of respect and protection for protected persons "in all circumstances." These general obligations also include a prohibition against intentionally firing on the wounded, sick and shipwrecked, and chaplains and medical personnel. This is a significant exemption from the general rule of warfare that enemy military personnel are lawful targets whenever and wherever they are found. However, if one of these protected persons engages in acts harmful to the enemy, that person has lost his or her protection.

Persons *hors de combat* (wounded, sick and shipwrecked) who fall into enemy hands sacrifice their usual right to engage in acts of war against the enemy in exchange for the protection of GPW and GWS or GWS SEA, as appropriate. If the protected person engages in acts of war, it should be apparent that the detaining power will be allowed to defend itself with appropriate means, which may include firing upon the transgressor.

Medical personnel likewise may not resist capture or engage in other acts harmful to the enemy (caring for the wounded is not an "act harmful to the enemy," it is a "humanitarian" act). Two consequences may result from medical personnel engaging in "military" (vice "humanitarian") activities. First, the individual risks death or injury

from being fired upon by the enemy. Second, if captured, the individual risks loss of "retained" status and becomes merely a POW because that person was not "exclusively" engaged in medical activities. A third consequence is also possible: the offending individual would risk prosecution for a war crime if they misused a protected symbol, such as the red cross.

III. PROTECTION FOR CERTAIN PLACES

A. Hospitals and Other Medical Units

Military medical facilities, be they hospitals (NRMC Bethesda) or mobile medical units (M*A*S*H 4077), may not be intentionally attacked. To facilitate this immunity and to guard against incidental damage to such facilities, they *should not* be co-located with legitimate targets. This admonition is frequently ignored. Many U.S. military hospitals are located in large military complexes which are themselves valid military objectives. Obviously, if such complexes were attacked, hospitals could expect to be damaged even if the hospital were not intentionally targeted; such "incidental damage" would *not* be a violation of the LOAC.

Military medical facilities are *not* immune from capture. If captured, the humanitarian character of the facility and its personnel should remain unchanged after capture until such time as the capturing power has removed the wounded and sick to another facility.

B. Sickbays on Vessels

Sickbays are treated in much the same way as hospitals and mobile medical units. However, the obligation not to attack the medical area is softened considerably ("shall be . . . spared as far as possible."), in recognition of the necessary co-location of a sickbay aboard a legitimate target.

C. Special Rules: Hospital Ships

Military hospital ships enjoy the same immunity from attack as hospitals and other medical units. However, it is important to note that, unlike other medical facilities, hospital ships *may not be captured*!

Not only may hospitals ships not be captured, but the religious and medical personnel onboard, and the ship's crew, may not be captured. The purpose in this broad protection is to keep hospital ships in circulation for the benefit of *all* the wounded, sick, and shipwrecked. However, this immunity from capture does *not* extend to the actual wounded and sick combatants onboard, who may be taken prisoner by the enemy so long as they are fit to move and so long as the enemy has the facilities available at hand to ensure continued care.

For a ship to receive the protection of being a hospital ship, the enemy must be notified at least 10 days in advance that the ship is being so used, and must be provided a description of the ship including gross tonnage, length, and the number of masts and funnels. In addition, hospital ships must be painted white and marked with several large red crosses or crescents.

Since the enemy is prohibited from destroying or capturing hospital ships, just what rights does the belligerent have over those vessels? Basically, there are two: the right of "visit and search" and the right of "control."

"Visit and search," discussed more fully in NWP 9, involves stopping and boarding a vessel for the purpose of inspecting its true character. If a search of a vessel reveals that it truly is a hospital ship, then the vessel will be permitted to proceed. Of course, if the search reveals that the vessel is engaged in hostile, vice humanitarian activities, such as ferrying troops or ammunition, the vessel will lose its immunity and be subject to capture.

The right of "control" includes the power to order a hospital ship to stand off, to take a certain course and speed, to control certain communications, and even to detain the vessel for a period of up to seven days. For example, a belligerent may wish to employ any of these measures to maintain the secrecy of certain information about ships in company, or formation course and speed, which have been or could be observed by a nearby enemy hospital ship.

There are certain obligations placed upon the nation which operates a hospital ship. Assistance is to be provided to *all* wounded, sick and shipwrecked, regardless of nationality. Recall that only medical reasons will determine the order of medical care to be given. Hospital ships shall not be put to any "military" (vice "humanitarian") purpose. Violation of this provision by a hospital ship risks loss of the protection described earlier.

D. Loss of Protection for Medical Facilities

Hospitals and mobile medical units remain protected so long as they do not commit, outside of their humanitarian activities, acts harmful to the enemy. If acts harmful to the enemy occur, then a hospital or mobile medical unit may be attacked, but only after a warning has been given and the hospital or mobile medical unit fails to heed the warning. This warning requirement does not apply if giving a warning is impractical, such as when taking live fire from an anti-aircraft battery positioned on the hospital roof.

Some people mistakenly believe that by merely possessing weapons, medical personnel forfeit their protected status. The bearing of sidearms by doctors and nurses for self-defense does not change the humanitarian character of a medical facility or of the medical personnel therein. Neither does the posting of armed sentries at a medical facility." The GWS and GWS SEA recognize that individuals may need to defend themselves or their patients from wartime threats other than the threat of capture by the enemy. So long as weapons are not used to resist capture of the medical facility (which would, of course, be an "act harmful to the enemy"), the facility and its personnel remain protected. One caveat: sentries and medical personnel should carry "defensive" weapons only. The use of tanks, artillery, mortars and .50 caliber machine guns in and around a "medical facility" will cause the enemy much suspicion and will dramatically increase the likelihood of an enemy attack. A medical facility will also not lose its protected status due to the presence of arms and ammunition collected from the sick and wounded.

Hospital ships and sickbays of vessels are entitled to all of these same protections. In addition, note that neither the fact that the crews of ships or sickbays are armed for the maintenance of order, for their own defense or the defense of the sick and wounded; nor the presence on board of apparatus exclusively intended to facilitate navigation or communications will deprive them of protection. It is important to note that hospital ships *may not use* secret codes for communicating. The reason for this prohibition is obviously to prevent a hospital ship from being misused as a spy ship.

IV. PROTECTION OF CERTAIN THINGS

A. Medical Supplies

Under the LOAC, captured enemy military property may be put to use by the possessor or it may be destroyed to deny its possible recapture and use by the enemy. However, special rules exist for captured medical supplies. Material from mobile medical units "shall be reserved for the care of wounded and sick." No exceptions are indicated for this rule. A similar, but not identical rule for hospital buildings and hospital supplies requires that they be used for the treatment of wounded and sick after capture. However, this rule does allow their use for other purposes when "urgent military necessity" requires and when other arrangements have been made for the satisfactory care of the wounded and sick. In no case may medical supplies be destroyed in order to deny their use by the enemy.

B. Medical Transports

Medical transports on land shall not be intentionally attacked so long as they are being used for humanitarian purposes, but they may be captured. Captured land transports may be used for non-medical purposes on the condition that any wounded and sick are otherwise first cared for.

Medical transports at sea may be treated similarly to hospital ships. They are subject to visit and search but may not be attacked or captured. However, there is a significant qualifier to obtain this immunity as a medical transport. Notice of the voyage of the medical transport ship must be given to the enemy and the enemy must approve its voyage. These voyages, if they occur at all, likely will occur under the auspices of the ICRC or some neutral nation.

C. Special Rule: Medical Aircraft

Medical aircraft are given very limited protection. They may be fired upon *unless* they are flying at heights, at times, and on routes agreed to *in advance* between the belligerents. Therefore, a helicopter bearing a large red cross usually will *not* be protected when it enters a combat zone to pick up wounded, since it is unlikely that the belligerents have agreed in advance to its appearance. For medical aircraft on agreed upon flights, they shall obey every summons to land. In the event of a landing thus imposed, the aircraft with its occupants may continue its flight after examination, if any. The difference in this special rule for medical aircraft, and the general spirit of respect and protection for medical transports, apparently stems from a deep-rooted mistrust of enemy airborne platforms in the aftermath of World War II, which saw the advent of massive destruction from the skies. In 1949, the world's nations just did not feel comfortable granting an across-the-board immunity to aircraft bearing a medical emblem. *U.S. Rule*: U.S. forces are required to respect and protect the enemy's medical aircraft, even if the craft is not on an agreed upon flight, *if* the aircraft can be recognized as an aircraft being used on a legitimate medical mission. See NWP 9, paragraph 8.2.3.

V. IDENTIFICATION OF PROTECTED PERSONS, PLACES AND THINGS

Under both GWS and GWS SEA, to facilitate identification of medical persons, places and things, a clearly visible red symbol on a white background should be displayed. The only sanctioned symbols are the red cross, the red crescent (used by Islamic countries), and the red lion and sun (the emblem of the Shah of Iran). Iran now uses the red crescent, but has reserved the right to use the lion and sun symbol. Israel uses the red Star of David, which, while not sanctioned, was nevertheless respected in recent Israeli conflicts. These emblems are pictured in NWP 9. The purpose of the emblem is ease of identification. Its display is *not* a prerequisite to protection. If you know that a building is a hospital, it deserves respect even though it does not bear a red cross or crescent.

The conventions prescribe that medical personnel shall display the emblem on an armlet worn on the left arm. Buildings and transports shall bear the emblem in such a manner that it is clearly visible in all directions, including from the air. Hospital ships are to be painted white on all exterior surfaces, and shall display the emblem so it is visible in all directions, including from the air.

The display of the medical emblem is controlled by "competent military authority." Such authority may direct the camouflaging or even the removal of the emblem. While such directives are not violations of the LOAC, the military commander should consider the risks of attack and destruction when these emblems are not used.

APPENDIX 5

HAGUE CONVENTION NO. IV RESPECTING THE LAWS AND CUSTOMS OF WAR ON LAND

18 October 1907

Considering that, while seeking means to preserve peace and prevent armed conflicts between nations, it is likewise necessary to bear in mind the case where an appeal to may be brought about by events which their solicitude could not avert;

Animated by the desire to serve, even in this extreme case, the interests of humanity and the ever progressive needs of civilization;

Thinking it important, with this object, to revise the general laws and customs of war, either with a view to defining them with greater precision or to confining them within such limits as would mitigate their severity as far as possible;

Have deemed it necessary to complete and render more precise in certain particulars the work of the First Peace Conference, which, following on the Brussels Conference of 1874, and inspired by the ideas dictated by a wise and generous forethought, adopted provisions intended to define and govern the usages of war on land.

According to the views of the High Contracting Parties, these provisions, the wording of which has been inspired by the desire to diminish the evils of war, so far as military requirements permit, are intended to serve as a general rule of conduct for the belligerents in their mutual relations and in their relations with the inhabitants.

It has not, however, been found possible at present to concert Regulations covering all the circumstances which arise in practice;

On the other hand, the High Contracting Parties clearly do not intend that unforeseen cases should, in the absence of a written undertaking, be left to the arbitrary judgment of military commanders.

Until a more complete code of the laws of war has been issued, the High Contracting Parties deem it expedient to declare that, in cases not included in the Regulations adopted by them, the inhabitants and the belligerents remain under the protection and the rule of the principles of the law of nations, as they result from the usages established among civilized peoples, from the laws of humanity, and from the dictates of the public conscience.

They declare that it is in this sense especially that Articles 1 and 2 of the Regulations adopted must be understood.

The High Contracting Parties, wishing to conclude a fresh Convention to this effect, have appointed the following as their Plenipotentiaries:

[Here follow the names of the Plenipotentiaries.]

Who, after having deposited their full powers, found in good and due form, have agreed upon the following:

ARTICLE 1.

The Contracting Powers shall issue instructions to their armed land forces which shall be in conformity with the Regulations respecting the Laws and Customs of War on Land, annexed to the present Convention.

ARTICLE 2.

The provisions contained in the Regulations referred to in Article 1, as well as in the present Convention, do not apply except between Contracting Powers, and then only if all the belligerents are parties to the Convention.

ARTICLE 3.

A belligerent party which violates the provisions of the said Regulations shall, if the case demands, be liable to pay compensation. It shall be responsible for all acts committed by persons forming part of its armed forces.

ARTICLE 4.

The present Convention, duly ratified, shall replace as between the Contracting Powers, the Convention of the 29th July, 1899, respecting the Laws and Customs of War on Land.

The Convention of 1899 remains in force as between the Powers which signed it, and which do not also ratify the present Convention.

ARTICLE 5.

The present Convention shall be ratified as soon as possible.

The ratifications shall be deposited at The Hague.

The first deposit of ratifications shall be recorded in a *procès-verbal* signed by the Representatives of the Powers which take part therein and by the Netherlands Minister for Foreign Affairs.

The subsequent deposits of ratifications shall be made by means of a written notification, addressed to the Netherlands Government and accompanied by the instrument of ratification.

A duly certified copy of the *procès-verbal* relative to the first deposit of ratifications, of the notifications mentioned in the preceding paragraph, as well as of the instruments of ratification, shall be immediately sent by the Netherlands Government, through the diplomatic channel, to the Powers invited to the Second Peace Conference, as well as to the other Powers which have adhered to the Convention. In the cases contemplated in the preceding paragraph the said Government shall at the same time inform them of the date on which it received the notification.

ARTICLE 6.

Non-Signatory Powers may adhere to the present Convention.

The Power which desires to adhere notifies in writing its intention to the Netherlands Government, forwarding to it the act of adhesion, which shall be deposited in the archives of the said Government.

This Government shall at once transmit to all the other Powers a duly certified copy of the notification as well as of the act of adhesion, mentioning the date on which it received the notification.

ARTICLE 7.

The present Convention shall come into force, in the case of the Powers which were parties to the first deposit of ratifications, sixty days after the date of the procès-verbal of this deposit, and, in the case of the Powers which ratify subsequently or which adhere, sixty days after the notification of their ratification or of their adhesion has been received by the Netherlands Government.

ARTICLE 8.

In the event of one of the Contracting Powers wishing to denounce the present Convention, the denunciation shall be notified in writing to the Netherlands Government, which shall at once communicate a duly certified copy of the notification to all the other Powers, informing them of the date on which it was received.

The denunciation shall only have effect in regard to the notifying power, and one year after the notification has reached the Netherlands Government.

ARTICLE 9.

A register kept by the Netherlands Ministry for Foreign Affairs shall give the date of the deposit of ratifications made in virtue of Article 5, paragraphs 3 and 4, as well as the date on which the notifications of adhesion (Article 6, paragraph 2) or of denunciation (Article 8, paragraph 1) were received.

Each Contracting Power is entitled to have access to this register and to be supplied with duly certified extracts.

In faith of which the Plenipotentiaries have appended their signatures to the present Convention.

Done at The Hague, the 18th October, 1907, in a single original, which shall remain deposited in the archives of the Netherlands Government, and duly certified copies of which shall be sent, through the diplomatic channel, to the Powers which have been invited to the Second Peace Conference.

ANNEX TO THE CONVENTION. REGULATIONS RESPECTING THE LAWS AND CUSTOMS OF WAR ON LAND

SECTION I. ON BELLIGERENTS.

CHAPTER I. The Qualifications of Belligerents. [*]

ARTICLE 1.

The laws, rights, and duties of war apply not only to armies, but also to militia and volunteer corps fulfilling the following conditions:

1. To be commanded by a person responsible for his subordinates;

2. To have a fixed distinctive emblem recognizable at a distance;

3. To carry arms openly; and

4. To conduct their operations in accordance with the laws and customs of war.

In countries where militia or volunteer corps constitute the army, or form part of it, they are included under the denomination "army."

---

[*]For the most recent provisions relating to prisoners of war, *see* Geneva Convention Relative to the Treatment of Prisoners of War of 12 August 1949.

ARTICLE 2.

The inhabitants of a territory which has not been occupied, who, on the approach of the enemy, spontaneously take up arms to resist the invading troops without having had time to organize themselves in accordance with Article 1, shall be regarded as belligerents if they carry arms openly and if they respect the laws and customs of war.

ARTICLE 3.

The armed forces of the belligerent parties may consist of combatants and noncombatants. In the case of capture by the enemy, both have a right to be treated as prisoners of war.

CHAPTER II. Prisoners of War.

ARTICLE 4.

Prisoners of war are in the power of the hostile Government, but not of the individuals or corps who capture them.

They must be humanely treated.

All their personal belongings, except arms, horses, and military papers, remain their property.

ARTICLE 5.

Prisoners of war may be interned in a town, fortress, camp, or other place, under obligation not to go beyond certain fixed limits; but they can only be placed in confinement as an indispensable measure of safety and only while the circumstances which necessitate the measure continue to exist.

ARTICLE 6.

The State may utilize the labour of prisoners of war according to their rank and aptitude, officers excepted. The tasks shall not be excessive and shall have no connection with the operations of the war.

Prisoners may be authorized to work for the public service, for private persons, or on their own account.

Work done for the State is paid at the rates in force for work of a similar kind done by soldiers of the national army, or, if there are none in force, at a rate according to the work executed.

When the work is for other branches of the public service or for private persons the conditions are settled in agreement with the military authorities.

The wages of the prisoners shall go towards improving their position, and the balance shall be paid them at the time of their release, after deducting the cost of their maintenance.

ARTICLE 7.

The Government into whose hands prisoners of war have fallen is charged with their maintenance.

In the absence of a special agreement between the belligerents, prisoners of war shall be treated as regards food, quarters, and clothing on the same footing as the troops of the Government who captured them.

ARTICLE 8.

Prisoners of war shall be subject to the laws, regulations, and orders in force in the army of the State in whose power they are. Any act of insubordination justifies the adoption towards them of such measures of severity as may be considered necessary.

Escaped prisoners who are retaken before being able to rejoin their own army or before leaving the territory occupied by the army which captured them are liable to disciplinary punishment.

Prisoners who, after succeeding in escaping, are again taken prisoners, are not liable to any punishment on account of the previous flight.

ARTICLE 9.

Every prisoner of war is bound to give, if he is questioned on the subject, his true name and rank, and if he infringes this rule, he is liable to have a curtailment of the advantages accorded to prisoners of his class.

ARTICLE 10.

Prisoners of war may be set at liberty on parole if the laws of their country allow, and, in such cases, they are bound, on their personal honour, scrupulously to fulfil, both towards their own Government and the Government by whom they were made prisoners, the engagements they have contracted.

In such cases their own Government is bound neither to require of nor accept from them any service incompatible with the parole given.

ARTICLE 11.

A prisoner of war can not be compelled to accept his liberty on parole; similarly the hostile Government is not obliged to accede to the request of the prisoner to be set at liberty on parole.

ARTICLE 12.

Prisoners of war liberated on parole and recaptured bearing arms against the Government to whom they had pledged their honour, or against the allies of that Government, forfeit their right to be treated as prisoners of war, and can be brought before the Courts.

ARTICLE 13.

Individuals who follow an army without directly belonging to it, such as newspaper correspondents and reporters, sutlers and contractors, who fall into the enemy's hands and whom the latter thinks fit to detain, are entitled to be treated as prisoners of war, provided they are in possession of a certificate from the military authorities of the army which they were accompanying.

ARTICLE 14.

An information bureau for prisoners of war is instituted on the commencement of hostilities in each of the belligerent States, and, when necessary, in neutral countries which have received belligerents in their territory. The function of this bureau is to reply to all inquiries about the prisoners, to receive from the various services concerned all the information respecting internments and transfers, releases on parole, exchanges, escapes, admissions into hospital, deaths, as well as other information necessary to enable it to make out and keep up to date an individual return for each prisoner of war. The bureau must state in this return the regimental number, name and surname, age, place of origin, rank, unit, wounds, date and place of capture, internment, wounding, and death, as well as any observations of a special character. The individual return shall be sent to the Government of the other belligerent after the conclusion of peace.

It is likewise the function of the information bureau to receive and collect all objects of personal use, valuables, letters, etc., found on the field of battle or left by prisoners who have been released on parole, or exchanged, or who have escaped, or died in hospitals or ambulances, and to forward them to those concerned.

ARTICLE 15.

Relief societies for prisoners of war, which are properly constituted in accordance with the laws of their country and with the object of serving as the channel for charitable effort shall receive from the belligerents, for themselves and their duly accredited agents every facility for the efficient performance of their humane task within the bounds imposed by military necessities and administrative regulations. Agents of these societies may be admitted to the places of internment for the purpose of distributing relief, as also to the halting places of repatriated prisoners, if furnished with a personal permit by the military authorities, and on giving an undertaking in writing to comply with all measures of order and police which the latter may issue.

ARTICLE 16.

Information bureaus enjoy the privilege of free postage. Letters, money orders, and valuables, as well as parcels by post, intended for prisoners of war, or dispatched by them, shall be exempt from all postal duties in the countries of origin and destination, as well as in the countries they pass through.

Presents and relief in kind for prisoners of war shall be admitted free of all import or other duties, as well as of payments for carriage by the State railways.

ARTICLE 17.

Officers taken prisoners shall receive the same rate of pay as officers of corresponding rank in the country where they are detained, the amount to be ultimately refunded by their own Government.

ARTICLE 18.

Prisoners of war shall enjoy complete liberty in the exercise of their religion, including attendance at the services of whatever Church they may belong to, on the sole condition that they comply with the measures of order and police issued by the military authorities.

ARTICLE 19.

The wills of prisoners of war are received or drawn up in the same way as for soldiers of the national army.

The same rules shall be observed regarding death certificates as well as for the burial of prisoners of war, due regard being paid to their grade and rank.

ARTICLE 20.

After the conclusion of peace, the repatriation of prisoners of war shall be carried out as quickly as possible.

CHAPTER III. The Sick and Wounded.

ARTICLE 21.

The obligations of belligerents with regard to the sick and wounded are governed by the Geneva Convention.[*]

SECTION II. HOSTILITIES.

CHAPTER I. Means of Injuring the Enemy, Sieges, and Bombardments.

ARTICLE 22.

The right of belligerents to adopt means of injuring the enemy is not unlimited.

ARTICLE 23.

In addition to the prohibitions provided by special Conventions, it is especially forbidden—

a. To employ poison or poisoned weapons;

---

[*]For the most recent provisions relating to the treatment of sick and wounded, *see* the Geneva Convention for the Amelioration of the Condition of the Wounded and Sick in Armed Forces in the field and the Geneva Convention for Amelioration of the Condition of the Wounded, Sick and Shipwrecked Members of Armed Forces at Sea, 12 August 1949.

b. To kill or wound treacherously individuals belonging to the hostile nation or army.

c. To kill or wound an enemy who, having laid down his arms, or having no longer means of defence, has surrendered at discretion;

d. To declare that no quarter will be given;

e. To employ arms, projectiles, or material calculated to cause unnecessary suffering;

f. To make improper use of a flag of truce, of the national flag, or of the military insignia and uniform of the enemy, as well as the distinctive badges of the Geneva Convention;

g. To destroy or seize the enemy's property, unless such destruction or seizure be imperatively demanded by the necessities of war;

h. To declare abolished, suspended, or inadmissible in a Court of law the rights and actions of the nationals of the hostile party.

A belligerent is likewise forbidden to compel the nationals of the hostile party to take part in the operations of war directed against their own country, even if they were in the belligerent's service before the commencement of the war.

ARTICLE 24.

Ruses of war and the employment of measures necessary for obtaining information about the enemy and the country are considered permissible.

ARTICLE 25.

The attack or bombardment, by whatever means, of towns, villages, dwellings, or buildings which are undefended is prohibited.

ARTICLE 26.

The officer in command of an attacking force must, before commencing a bombardment, except in cases of assault, do all in his power to warn the authorities.

ARTICLE 27.

In sieges and bombardments all necessary measures must be taken to spare, as far as possible, buildings dedicated to religion, art, science, or charitable purposes, historic monuments, hospitals, and places where the sick and wounded are collected, provided they are not being used at the time for military purposes.

It is the duty of the besieged to indicate the presence of such buildings or places by distinctive and visible signs, which shall be notified to the enemy beforehand.

ARTICLE 28.

The pillage of a town or place, even when taken by assault, is prohibited.

CHAPTER II. Spies.

ARTICLE 29.

A person can only be considered a spy when, acting clandestinely or on false pretenses, he obtains or endeavours to obtain information in the zone of operations of a belligerent, with the intention of communicating it to the hostile party.

Thus, soldiers not wearing a disguise who have penetrated into the zone of operations of the hostile army, for the purpose of obtaining information, are not considered spies. Similarly, the following are not considered spies: Soldiers and civilians, carrying out their mission openly, intrusted with the delivery of despatches intended either for their own army or for the enemy's army. To this class belong likewise persons sent in balloons for the purpose of carrying despatches and, generally, of maintaining communications between the different parts of an army or a territory.

ARTICLE 30.

A spy taken in the act shall not be punished without previous trial.

ARTICLE 31.

A spy who, after rejoining the army to which he belongs, is subsequently captured by the enemy, is treated as a prisoner of war, and incurs no responsibility for his previous acts of espionage.

CHAPTER III. Parlementaires.

ARTICLE 32.

A person is regarded as a parlementaire who has been authorized by one of the belligerents to enter into communication with the other, and who advances bearing a white flag. He has a right to inviolability, as well as the trumpeter, bugler or drummer, the flag-bearer and interpreter who may accompany him.

ARTICLE 33.

The commander to whom a parlementaire is sent is not in all cases obliged to receive him.

He may take all the necessary steps to prevent the parlementaire taking advantage of his mission to obtain information.

In case of abuse, he has the right to detain the parlementaire temporarily.

ARTICLE 34.

The parlementaire loses his rights of inviolability if it is proved in a clear and incontestable manner that he has taken advantage of his privileged position to provoke or commit an act of treachery.

CHAPTER IV. Capitulations.

ARTICLE 35.

Capitulations agreed upon between the contracting parties must take into account the rules of military honour.

Once settled, they must be scrupulously observed by both parties.

CHAPTER V. Armistices.

ARTICLE 36.

An armistice suspends military operations by mutual agreement between the belligerent parties. If its duration is not defined, the belligerent parties may resume operations at any time, provided always that the enemy is warned within the time agreed upon, in accordance with the terms of the armistice.

ARTICLE 37.

An armistice may be general or local. The first suspends the military operations of the belligerent States everywhere; the second only between certain fractions of the belligerent armies and within a fixed radius.

ARTICLE 38.

An armistice must be notified officially and in good time to the competent authorities and to the troops. Hostilities are suspended immediately after the notification, or on the date fixed.

ARTICLE 39.

It rests with the contracting parties to settle, in the terms of the armistice, what communications may be held in the theatre of war with the inhabitants and between the inhabitants of one belligerent State and those of the other.

ARTICLE 40.

Any serious violation of the armistice by one of the parties gives the other party the right of denouncing it, and even, in cases of urgency, of recommencing hostilities immediately.

ARTICLE 41.

A violation of the terms of the armistice by private persons acting on their own initiative only entitles the injured party to demand the punishment of the offenders or, if necessary; compensation for the losses sustained.

SECTION III. MILITARY AUTHORITY OVER THE TERRITORY OF THE HOSTILE STATE.

ARTICLE 42.

Territory is considered occupied when it is actually placed under the authority of the hostile army.

The occupation extends only to the territory where such authority has been established and can be exercised.

ARTICLE 43.

The authority of the legitimate power having in fact passed into the hands of the occupant, the latter shall take all the measures in his power to restore, and ensure as far as possible, public order and safety, while respecting, unless absolutely prevented, the laws in force in the country.

ARTICLE 44.

A belligerent is forbidden to force the inhabitants of occupied territory to furnish information about the army of the other belligerent, or about its means of defence.

ARTICLE 45.

It is forbidden to compel the inhabitants of occupied territory to swear allegiance to the hostile Power.

ARTICLE 46.

Faraily honour and rights, the lives of persons, and private property, as well as religious convictions and practice, must be respected.

Private property cannot be confiscated.

ARTICLE 47.

Pillage is formally forbidden.

ARTICLE 48.

If, in the territory occupied, the occupant collects the taxes, dues, and tolls imposed for the benefit of the State, he shall do so, as far as is possible in accordance with the rules of assessment and incidence in force, and shall in consequence be bound to defray the expenses of the administration of the occupied territory to the same extent as the legitimate Government was so bound.

ARTICLE 49.

If, in addition to the taxes mentioned in the above Article, the occupant levies other money contributions in the occupied territory, this shall only be for the needs of the army or of the administration of the territory in question.

ARTICLE 50.

No general penalty, pecuniary or otherwise, shall be inflicted upon the population on account of the acts of individuals for which they cannot be regarded as jointly and severally responsible.

ARTICLE 51.

No contribution shall be collected except under a written order, and on the responsibility of a Commander-in-chief.

The collection of the said contribution shall only be effected as far as possible in accordance with the rules of assessment and incidence of the taxes in force.

For every contribution a receipt shall be given to the contributors.

ARTICLE 52.

Requisitions in kind and services shall not be demanded from municipalities or inhabitants except for the needs of the army of occupation. They shall be in proportion to the resources of the country, and of such a nature as not to involve the population in the obligation of taking part in operations of the war against their country.

Such requisitions and services shall only be demanded on the authority of the commander in the locality occupied.

Contributions in kind shall as far as possible be paid for in cash; if not, a receipt shall be given and the payment of the amount due shall be made as soon as possible.

ARTICLE 53.

An army of occupation can only take possession of cash, funds, and realizable securities which are strictly the property of the State, depôts of arms, means of transport, stores and supplies, and, generally, all movable property belonging to the State which may be used for operations of the war.

All appliances, whether on land, at sea, or in the air, adapted for the transmission of news, or for the transport of persons or things, exclusive of cases governed by naval law, depôts of arms, and, generally, all kinds of ammunition of war, may be seized, even if they belong to private individuals, but must be restored and compensation fixed when peace is made.

ARTICLE 54.

Submarine cables connecting an occupied territory with a neutral territory shall not be seized or destroyed except in the case of absolute necessity. They must likewise be restored and compensation fixed when peace is made.

ARTICLE 55.

The occupying State shall be regarded only as administrator and usufructuary of public buildings, real estate, forests, and agricultural estates belonging to the hostile State, and situated in the occupied country. It must safeguard the capital of these properties, and administer them in accordance with the rules of usufruct.

ARTICLE 56.

The property of municipalities, that of institutions dedicated to religion, charity and education, the arts and sciences, even when State property, shall be treated as private property.

All seizure or destruction of, or wilful damage to, institutions of this character, historic monuments, works of art and science, is forbidden, and should be made the subject of legal proceedings.

APPENDIX 6

STANDING RULES OF ENGAGEMENT FOR U.S. FORCES

1. Purpose and Scope

a.   The purpose of these Standing Rules of Engagement (SROE) is to provide implementation guidance on the inherent right and obligation of self-defense and the application of force for mission accomplishment. The SROE establish fundamental policies and procedures governing the actions to be taken by U.S. force commanders during all military operations, contingencies, or prolonged conflicts. In order to provide uniform training and planning capabilities, this document is authorized for distribution to commanders at all levels to be used as fundamental guidance for training and directing their forces.

b.   Except as augmented by supplemental rules of engagement for specific operations, missions, or projects, the policies and procedures established herein remain in effect until rescinded.

c.   U.S. forces operating with multinational forces:

   (1) U.S. forces assigned to the operational control (OPCON) of a multinational force will follow the ROE of the multinational force unless otherwise directed by the National Command Authorities (NCA). U.S. forces will be assigned and remain OPCON to a multinational force only if the combatant commander and higher authority determine that the ROE for that multinational force are consistent with the policy guidance on unit self-defense and with the rules for individual self-defense contained in this document.

   (2) When U.S. forces, under U.S. OPCON, operate in conjunction with a multinational force, reasonable efforts will be made to effect common ROE. If such ROE cannot be established, U.S. forces will exercise the right and obligation of self-defense contained in this document while seeking guidance from the appropriate combatant command. To avoid mutual interference, the multinational forces will be informed prior to U.S. participation in the operation of the U.S. forces' intentions to operate under these SROE and to exercise unit self-defense.

(3) Participation in multinational operations may be complicated by varying national obligations derived from international agreements; i.e., other members in a coalition may not be signatories to treaties that bind the United States, or they may be bound by treaties to which the United States is not a party. U.S. forces still remain bound by U.S. treaty obligations even if the other members in a coalition are not signatories to a treaty and need not adhere to its terms.

d. Commanders of U.S. forces subject to international agreements governing their presence in foreign countries (e.g., Status of Forces Agreements) are relieved of the inherent authority and obligation to use all necessary means available and to take all appropriate action for unit self-defense.

e. U.S. forces in support of operations not under operational or tactical control of a combatant commander or performing missions under direct control of the NCA, Military Departments, or other U.S. government departments/agencies (i.e., marine security guards, certain special security forces) will operate under use-of-force or ROE promulgated by those departments or agencies.

f. U.S. Coast Guard (USCG) units and units under USCG OPCON conducting law enforcement operations, and USCG personnel using their law enforcement authority, will follow the use-of-force policy issued by the Commandant, USCG. Nothing in the USCG use-of-force policy negates a commander's inherent authority and obligation to use all necessary means available to take all appropriate action for unit self-defense in accordance with these SROE.

g. The guidance in this document does not cover U.S. forces deployed to assist federal and local authorities during times of civil disturbance within the territorial jurisdiction of any state, the District of Columbia, Commonwealths of Puerto Rico and the Northern Marianas, U.S. possessions, and U.S. territories. Forces in these situations will follow use-of-force policy found in DoD Civil Disturbance Plan, "Garden Plot" (Appendix 1 to Annex C of Garden Plot).

h. U.S. forces deployed to assist foreign, federal, and local authorities in disaster assistance missions, such as earthquakes and hurricanes, will follow use-of-force guidelines as set forth in the mission's execute order and subsequent orders.

i. U.S. forces will always comply with the Law of Armed Conflict. However, not all situations involving the use of force are armed conflicts under international law. Those approving operational rules of engagement must determine if the internationally recognized Law of Armed Conflict applies. In those circumstances when armed conflict, under international law, does not exist, Law of Armed Conflict principles may nevertheless be applied as a matter of national policy. If armed conflict occurs, the actions of U.S.

forces will be governed by both the Law of Armed Conflict and rules of engagement.

2. Policy

a. THESE RULES DO NOT LIMIT A COMMANDER'S INHERENT AUTHORITY AND OBLIGATION TO USE ALL NECESSARY MEANS AVAILABLE AND TO TAKE ALL APPROPRIATE ACTION IN SELF-DEFENSE OF THE COMMANDER'S UNIT AND OTHER U.S. FORCES IN THE VICINITY.

b. U.S. national security policy serves to protect the United States, U.S. forces, and in certain circumstances, U.S. citizens and their property, U.S. commercial assets, and other designated non-U.S. forces, foreign nationals, and their property from hostile attack. U.S. national security policy is guided, in part, by the need to maintain a stable international environment compatible with U.S. national security interests. In addition, U.S. national security interests guide out global objectives of deterring armed attack against the United States across the range of military operations, defeating an attack should deterrence fail, and preventing or neutralizing hostile efforts to intimidate or coerce the United States by the threat or use of armed force or terrorist actions. Deterrence requires clear and evident capability and resolve to fight at any level of conflict and, if necessary, to increase deterrent force capabilities and posture deliberately so that any potential aggressor will assess its own risks as unacceptable. U.S. policy, should deterrence fail, provides flexibility to respond to crises with options that:

(1) Are proportional to the provocation.

(2) Are designed to limit the scope and intensity of the conflict.

(3) Will discourage escalation.

(4) Will achieve political and military objectives.

3. Intent

These SROE are intended to:

a. Provide general guidelines on self-defense and are applicable worldwide to all echelons of command.

b. Provide guidance governing the use of force consistent with mission accomplishment.

c. Be used in operations other than war, during transition from peacetime to armed conflict or war, and during armed conflict in the absence of superseding guidance.

4. Combatant Commanders' SROE

a. Combatant commanders may augment these SROE as necessary to reflect changing political and military policies, threats, and missions specific to their AOR. When specific standing rules governing the use of force in a combatant commander's AOR are required that are different from these SROE, they will be submitted to the Chairman of the Joint Chiefs of Staff for NCA approval as necessary and promulgated by the Joint Staff as an Annex to Enclosure C of these SROE.

b. Combatant commanders will distribute these SROE to subordinate commanders and units for compliance. The mechanism for disseminating ROE supplemental measures is set forth in Enclosure B.

5. Definitions

a. **Inherent Right of Self-Defense**. A commander has the authority and obligation to use all necessary means available and to take all appropriate action to defend that commander's unit and other U.S. forces in the vicinity from a hostile act or demonstration of hostile intent. Neither these rules nor the supplemental measures activated to augment these rules, limit this inherent right and obligation. At all times, however, the requirements of necessity and proportionality as amplified in these SROE will be the basis for the judgment of the commander as to what constitutes an appropriate response to a particular hostile act or demonstration of hostile intent.

b. **National Self-Defense**. National self-defense is the act of defending the United States, U.S. forces, and in certain circumstances, U.S. citizens and their property, U.S. commercial assets, and other designated non-U.S. forces, foreign nationals and their property, from a hostile act or hostile intent. Once a force or terrorist unit is declared hostile by appropriate authority exercising the right and obligation of national self-defense (see paragraph 2 of Appendix A to Enclosure A), individual U.S. units do not need to observe a hostile act or determine hostile intent before engaging that force.

NOTE: **Collective Self-Defense**. Collective self-defense, as a subset of national self-defense, is the act of defending other designated non-U.S. forces, personnel and their property from a hostile act or demonstration of hostile intent. Only the NCA may authorize U.S. forces to exercise collective self-defense.

c. **Unit Self Defense**. Unit self-defense is the act of defending a particular unit of U.S. forces, including elements or personnel thereof, and other U.S. forces in the vicinity, against a hostile act of hostile intent. The need to exercise unit self-defense may arise in many situations such as localized low-level conflicts, humanitarian efforts, peace enforcement actions, terrorists response, or prolonged engagements. Individual self-defense is a subset of unit self-defense; see the glossary for a definition of individual self-defense.

d. **Elements of Self-Defense**. The application of armed force in self-defense requires the following two elements:

(1) **Necessity**. A hostile act occurs or a force or terrorist unit exhibits hostile intent.

(2) **Proportionality**. The force used must be reasonable in intensity, duration and magnitude, based on all facts known to the commander at the time, to decisively counter the hostile act or hostile intent and to ensure the continued safety of U.S. forces.

e. **Hostile Act**. A hostile act is an attack or other use of force by a foreign force or terrorist unit (organization or individual) against the United States, U.S. forces, and in certain circumstances, U.S. citizens, their property, U.S. commercial assets, and other designated non-U.S. forces, foreign nationals and their property. It is also force used directly to preclude or impede the mission and/or duties of U.S. forces, including the recovery of U.S. personnel and vital U.S. Government property. When a hostile act is in progress, the right exists to use proportional force, including armed force, in self-defense by all necessary means available to deter or neutralize the potential attacker or, if necessary, to destroy the threat. (See definitions in the Glossary for amplification.)

f. **Hostile Intent**. Hostile intent is the threat of imminent use of force by a foreign force or terrorist unit (organization or individual) against the United States, U.S. forces, and in certain circumstances, U.S. citizens, their property, U.S. commercial assets, or other designated non-U.S. forces, foreign nationals and their property. When hostile intent is present, the right exists to use proportional force, including armed force, in self-defense by all necessary means available to deter or neutralize the potential attacker or, if necessary, to destroy the threat.

g. **Hostile Force**. Any force or terrorist unit (civilian, paramilitary, or military), with or without national designation, that has committed a hostile act, demonstrated hostile intent, or has been declared hostile.

Persian Gulf—A port quarter view of the guided missile frigate USS *Stark* listing to port after being struck by an Iraqi-launched exocet missile (18 May 87). Misunderstanding of the rules of engagement by the *Stark's* crew contributed to the ship's vulnerability to attack. Photo courtesy of U.S. Naval Institute.

6. Declaring Forces Hostile

Once a force is declared hostile by appropriate authority, U.S. units need not observe a hostile act or a demonstration of hostile intent before engaging that force. The responsibility for exercising the right and obligation of national self-defense and declaring a force hostile is a matter of the utmost importance, demanding considerable judgment of command. All available intelligence, the status of international relationships, the requirements of international law, the possible need for a political decision, and the potential consequences for the United States must be carefully weighed. Exercising the right and obligation of national self-defense by competent authority is in addition to and does not supplant the right and obligation to exercise unit self-defense. The authority to declare a force hostile is limited, as amplified in Appendix A to Enclosure A.

7. Authority to Exercise Self-Defense

a. **National Self-Defense**. The authority to exercise national self-defense is outlined in Appendix A to Enclosure A.

b. **Collective Self-Defense**. Only the NCA may authorize the exercise of collective self-defense.

c. **Unit Self-Defense**. A unit commander has the authority and obligation to use all necessary means available and to take all appropriate action to defend the unit, including elements and personnel thereof, or other U.S. forces in the vicinity, against a hostile act or hostile intent. In defending against a hostile act or hostile intent under these SROE, unit commanders should use only that degree of force necessary to decisively counter the hostile act or hostile intent and to ensure the continued safety of U.S. forces.

8. Action in Self-Defense

a. **Means of Self-Defense**. All necessary means available and all appropriate actions may be used in self-defense. The following guidelines apply for unit or national self-defense:

(1) **Attempt to Control Without the Use of Force**. The use of force is normally a measure of last resort. When time and circumstances permit, the potentially hostile force should be warned and given the opportunity to withdraw or cease threatening actions. (See Appendix A to Enclosure A for amplification.)

(2) **Use Proportional Force to Control the Situation**. When the use of force in self-defense is necessary, the nature, duration, and scope of the engagement should not exceed that which is required to decisively counter the hostile act or hostile intent and to ensure the continued safety of U.S. forces or other protected personnel or property.

(3) **Attack to Disable or Destroy**. An attack to disable or destroy a hostile force is authorized when such action is the only prudent means by which a hostile act or hostile intent can be prevented or terminated. When such conditions exist, engagement is authorized only until the hostile force no longer poses an imminent threat.

b. **Immediate Pursuit of Hostile Foreign Forces**. In self-defense, U.S. forces may pursue and engage a hostile force that has committed a hostile act or demonstrated hostile intent and that remains an imminent threat. (See Appendix A to Enclosure A for amplification.)

c. **Defending U.S. Citizens, Property, and Designated Foreign Nationals**

(1) **Within a Foreign Nation's U.S. Recognized Territory or Territorial Airspace**. A foreign nation has the principal responsibility for defending U.S. citizens and property within these areas. (See Appendix A to Enclosure A for amplification.)

(2) **At Sea**. Detailed guidance is contained in Annex A to Appendix B of this Enclosure.

(3) **In International Airspace**. Protecting civil aircraft in international airspace is principally the responsibility of the nation of registry. Guidance for certain cases of actual or suspected hijacking of airborne U.S. or foreign civil aircraft is contained in MCM-102-92, 24 July 1992, "Hijacking of Civil Aircraft."

(4) **Terrorism**. Terrorist attacks are usually undertaken by civilian or paramilitary organizations, or by individuals under circumstances in which a determination of hostile intent may be difficult. The definitions of hostile act and hostile intent set forth above will be used in situations where terrorist attacks are likely. The term "hostile force" includes terrorist units when used in this document. When circumstances and intelligence dictate, supplemental ROE will be issued to meet this special threat.

(5) **Piracy**. Piracy is defined as an illegal act of violence, depredation (i.e., plundering, robbing, or pillaging), or detention in or over international waters committed for private ends by the crew or passengers of a private ship or aircraft against another ship or aircraft or against persons or property on board such ship or aircraft. U.S. warships and aircraft have an obligation to repress piracy on or over international waters directed against any vessel, or aircraft, whether U.S. or foreign flagged. If a pirate vessel or aircraft fleeing from pursuit proceeds into the territorial sea, archipelagic waters, or superjacent airspace of another country every effort should be made to obtain the consent of nation sovereignty to continue pursuit. Where circumstances permit, commanders will seek guidance from higher authority before using armed force to repress an act of piracy.

d. **Operations Within or in the Vicinity of Hostile Fire or Combat Zones Not Involving the United States.**

(1) U.S. forces should not enter, or remain in, a zone in which hostilities (not involving the United States) are imminent or occurring between foreign forces unless directed by proper authority.

(2) If a force commits a hostile act or demonstrates hostile intent against U.S. forces in a hostile fire or combat zone, the commander is obligated to act in unit self-defense in accordance with SROE guidelines.

e. **Right of Assistance Entry.**

(1) Ships, or under certain circumstances aircraft, have the right to enter a foreign territorial sea or archipelagic waters and corresponding airspace without the permission of the coastal or island state to engage in legitimate efforts to render emergency assistance to those in danger or distress from perils of the sea.

(2) Right of assistance extends only to rescues where the location of those in danger is reasonably well known. It does not extend to entering the territorial sea, archipelagic waters, or national airspace to conduct a search.

(3) For ships and aircraft rendering assistance on scene, the right and obligation of self-defense extends to and includes persons, vessels, or aircraft being assisted. The right of self-defense in such circumstances does not include interference with legitimate law enforcement actions of a coastal nation. However, once received on board the assisting ship or aircraft, persons assisted will not be surrendered to foreign authority unless directed by the NCA.

(4) Further guidance for the exercise of the right of assistance entry is contained in the CJCS Instruction 2410.01, 20 July 1993, "Guidance for the Exercise of Right of Assistance Entry."

APPENDIX 7

DESERT SHIELD PEACETIME RULES OF ENGAGEMENT

THESE ARE PEACETIME RULES OF ENGAGEMENT. NOTHING IN THESE RULES LIMITS THE RIGHTS OF INDIVIDUAL SOLDIERS TO DEFEND THEMSELVES OR THE RIGHTS AND RESPONSIBILITIES OF LEADERS TO DEFEND THEIR UNITS.

A. You may not conduct offensive military operations (raids, ambushes, etc.)
B. You may use force in self-defense in response to attacks or threats of imminent attack against U.S. or host nation forces, citizens, property, or commercial assets.
C. You are not permitted to enter the land, sea, or airspace of other countries—besides the host nation.
D. If you inadvertently enter territorial land, sea, or airspace of another country, you may use force in self-defense to withdraw.
E. You may not seize property of others to accomplish your mission in peacetime.
F. Proper contracting processes must be followed to obtain supplies and other items necessary to accomplish the mission.
G. Treat all persons and property with respect and dignity. Remember we are at peace.

REMEMBER

1. WE ARE NOT AT WAR.
2. THESE RULES ARE IN EFFECT UNLESS HOSTILITIES BEGIN.
3. KNOW THE WARTIME ROE AND FOLLOW THEM IF HOSTILITIES BEGIN.

CULTURAL DOs AND DON'Ts

DO:

A. Be friendly and courteous. A handshake accompanied with the phrase Al-Salaama 'Alaykum (Peace be upon you) is the most common form of greeting.
B. If you smoke (most Arab men do), offer to share cigarettes with those present.
C. Sit properly in chairs: upright with feet on the ground.
D. When in doubt, observe locals and imitate their behavior.
E. Avoid contact with Arab women. If introduced, be polite but do not stare or engage in any lengthy conversations.

DON'T:

A. Make critical comparisons of your religion vs. Islam.
B. Ask an Arab not to smoke.
C. Point your finger or use your index finger to beckon people; it is considered demeaning.
D. Use alcohol.
E. Possess or use pornographic or sexually explicit material.

DESERT STORM
RULES OF ENGAGEMENT

ALL ENEMY MILITARY PERSONNEL AND VEHICLES TRANSPORTING THE ENEMY OR THEIR SUPPLIES MAY BE ENGAGED SUBJECT TO THE FOLLOWING RESTRICTIONS:

A. Do not engage anyone who has surrendered, is out of battle due to sickness or wounds, is shipwrecked, or is an aircrew member descending by parachute from a disabled aircraft.
B. Avoid harming civilians unless necessary to save U.S. lives. Do not fire into civilian populated areas or buildings which are not defended or being used for military purposes.
C. Churches, Shrines, Schools, Museums, National Monuments, and any other historical or cultural sites will not be engaged except in self-defense.
D. Hospitals will be given special protection. Do not engage hospitals unless the enemy uses the hospital to commit acts harmful to U.S. forces, and then only after giving a warning and allowing a reasonable time to expire before engaging, if the tactical situation permits.
E. Booby traps may be used to protect friendly positions or to impede the progress of enemy forces. They may not be used on civilian personal property. They will be recovered or destroyed when the military necessity for their use no longer exists.
F. Looting and the taking of war trophies are prohibited.
G. Avoid harming civilian property unless necessary to save U.S. lives. Do not attack traditional civilian objects, such as houses, unless they are being used by the enemy for military purposes and neutralization assists in mission accomplishment.
H. Treat all civilians and their property with respect and dignity. Before using privately owned property, check to see if publicly owned property can substitute. No requisitioning of civilian property, including vehicles, without permission of a company level commander and without giving a receipt. If an ordering officer can contract the property, then do not requisition it.
I. Treat all prisoners humanely and with respect and dignity.
J. ROE Annex to the OPLAN provides more detail. Conflicts between this card and the OPLAN should be resolved in favor of the OPLAN.

REMEMBER

1. FIGHT ONLY COMBATANTS.
2. ATTACK ONLY MILITARY TARGETS.
3. SPARE CIVILIAN PERSONS AND OBJECTS.
4. RESTRICT DESTRUCTION TO WHAT YOUR MISSION REQUIRES.

INDEX